The Message
of
REVELATION

GOD CARES VOLUME TWO

The Message of REVELATION

of

GOD CARES   VOLUME TWO

C. MERVYN MAXWELL, PH.D.

Pacific Press Publishing Association
Boise, Idaho
Montemorelos, Nuevo Leon, Mexico
Oshawa, Ontario, Canada

Target edition:

    Cover design by Howard Larkin
    Charts and general layout by Tim Larson
    Spot drawings by James Converse

Pictorial edition:

    Cover photos as follows: couple on lawn and New York City night skyline, Photofile; family birdwatching, Duane Tank; girl, Joan Walter.
    Charts and general layout by Tim Larson
    Spot drawings by James Converse

Subscription edition:

    Cover design, cover illustration design by Tim Larson
    Cover illustration by Lars Justinen
    Charts and general layout by Tim Larson
    Spot drawings by James Converse

Published jointly by
PACIFIC PRESS PUBLISHING ASSOCIATION
Boise, ID 83707
Oshawa, Ontario, Canada
Montemorelos, Nuevo Leon, Mexico

REVIEW AND HERALD PUBLISHING ASSOCIATION
Washington, D.C. 20039-0555
Hagerstown, MD 21740

ISBN: 0-8163-0611-7

Preface

God Cares

"The Spirit and the Bride say, 'Come.' "

"Let him who hears say, 'Come.' "

"Let him who is thirsty . . . take the water of life without price."

What more generous invitation could we wish for? These cordial words from the closing lines of Revelation reveal anew God's deep desire to do us good and to secure our personal friendship.

In *God Cares*, volume 1, we saw that the book of Daniel reveals God's care in many ways. God gave Daniel the image dream in time to save his life and the lives of the wise men—and to reveal to Nebuchadnezzar and ourselves important developments that were to occur in the future. He preserved Daniel's friends from the fiery furnace. He sent an angel to spend the night with Daniel in the lions' den. He promised that one day He would bring an end to all unfair harassment, inaugurate the final judgment, and entrust this entire world to His own true people. He promised to raise His followers to everlasting life in the time of the end.

Revelation continues the theme of God's protection and care. Trials there would be, tribulations in some ways worse than even Daniel experienced. But like the cumulating waves of an incoming tide, Revelation provides repeated reassurance of God's attention to our needs and His plans for our future. Jesus walks lovingly among the lampstands that represent His imperfect church. He promises to feed us His "hidden manna." He pledges to look after us in earth's final hour of trial. He undertakes to "seal" us, to set us on thrones, and to give us the water of life. "The Spirit and the Bride say, 'Come.' "

Revelation is an open book; it is not described in the Bible as closed. This is in contrast to Daniel, which is described as closed. See Daniel 12:4. It does not mean that all of Revelation is immediately comprehensible, however. The rest of the Bible isn't closed, yet it contains many passages that benefit from painstaking analysis. Even apparently simple Bible passages every time we go back to them seem to yield bright new treasures that were lying beneath the surface.

One key to understanding Revelation is the book of Daniel. Both books present parallel views of prophetic panoramas that sweep from the prophet's time to the end of the world. Both, too, contain animal symbols, the 1260 year-days, several sad predictions of apostasy and persecution, and many happy predictions about victory and joy. Both books deal with the judgment, the sanctuary, and loyalty to God's laws. Both promise a climactic arrival of the Son of man on clouds.

v

Both inspire us to resist unwholesome peer pressure and to develop sound characters. Both reveal God as a very active helper in times of difficulty.

Because of the many links between the two books, we will many times be grateful that we have already studied Daniel.

Many commentators perceive that Jesus, too, gave us an apocalypse, a kind of miniature or condensed Daniel or Revelation. It is His Olivet Discourse, spoken to four of His disciples on the Tuesday night before His crucifixion.

In the Olivet Discourse, Jesus specifically mentions Daniel and one of Daniel's most sentient symbols, "the abomination of desolation." Jesus too spreads before us a prophetic panorama, sweeping from His own day to the end of time. Jesus, like Daniel and Revelation, speaks of apostasy and persecution, followed by the glorious appearance of the Son of man on clouds. He too summons His followers to resist unwholesome peer pressure and to develop sturdy characters.

The Olivet Discourse is richly rewarding when studied for its own sake. It is additionally rewarding when studied as an introduction to Revelation and as a bridge between Daniel and Revelation.

"The secret things belong to the Lord our God; but the things that are revealed belong to us and to our children for ever." Deuteronomy 29:29.

The intriguing symbols and cartoon-like characters used so profusely in Revelation have a strong appeal for children, arousing their curiosity and providing opportunities for parents to explain them.

Some aspects of the Olivet Discourse and Revelation are especially adapted to young people. The famous parable of the ten sleepy girls deals with young folk still in their early teens. Jesus used early teens for one of His major messages about preparing for His second coming.

Even more to the point, perhaps, is the fact that in Revelation, Jesus is twenty-nine times referred to as the Lamb of God. The lamb in Bible times was a reminder of the first Passover night, when the people of Israel made their dramatic escape from Egyptian slavery. That never-to-be-forgotten Passover night was fraught with extreme peril that the eldest child in each family would be destroyed in the final plague suffered by the Egyptians. In fact, the eldest child in the Egyptian families did die that night. But Israelite families sacrificed a lamb, and the father in each family brushed some of its blood on the main doorframe of their house. See Exodus 11, 12.

Applying the blood expressed the family's faith in God and in the coming Messiah Redeemer. It still reminds us that Jesus died to save children. He died to keep families united.

Jesus also *lives* for children and families. For a few tantalizing years almost twenty centuries ago He walked among us, trying in a thousand thoughtful ways to convince us that God cares. Ever since then, He has lived at God's side, serving us in the heavenly sanctuary. See Hebrews 7:25.

When we and our families have learned to have faith in God amid life's daily trials, have lived with Him through earth's final trial, have witnessed Jesus' coming on the clouds, have been caught up to be with Him, have drunk the water of life, and, with our families, have looked into God's dear, friendly face, we'll know beyond all question that indeed God cares.

Contents

GOD CARES

John saw the visions of Revelation on Patmos, a small, horseshoe-shaped island in the Aegean Sea not far from the coast of Asia Minor.

GOD CARES

Matthew 24, 25

Part I, The Olivet Discourse: Jesus Predicts the Future

Introduction

A group of grade-school girls came to our home one year to learn basic cooking methods from my wife. At the end of the course they planned and prepared a meal for their parents. From behind the closed door of my study I heard their excited squeals and gasps as mealtime drew near.

My study door was located close to and just inside the front door. For a bit of mischief, at about the time when the girls expected their parents to arrive, I knocked loudly on the inside of my study door as if I were the first parents arriving. The girls almost exploded. Untying their aprons, running combs through their hair, achieving last-minute changes on the table, they dashed to the front door and flung it wide.

I didn't leave them disappointed long! I opened my study door, and when they saw me laughing, they laughed merrily too. In fact, after their parents did arrive, they laughed about their surprise all through the meal.

The excitement of our young cooks resembles the excitement that all true Christians feel when they think about the second coming of Christ. What joy it is to contemplate the moment when Jesus will return to put a stop to injustice, sickness, and poverty, and to bring in endless ages of prosperity and peace.

Such good news was, of course, the kind of thing Jesus Himself enjoyed talking about; and He did talk about it on different occasions, one of the most notable of which occurred not long before His death. On Tuesday night of Passion Week, the week that led up to His Friday crucifixion, Jesus talked about His glorious return in what is known as the Olivet Discourse.* We have referred to the Olivet Discourse several times before. See *God Cares*, vol. 1, pages 11, 151, and 160 (abbreviated GC 1:11, 151, 160. The pagination matches the revised, full-color edition). Analyzing it now will help us considerably in understanding Revelation.

So very joyous is the prospect of Christ's return, that Jesus knew His followers would become eagerly impatient for His arrival. In such a state of mind they (like our little cooks) could easily fall prey to false signs (like the knock on my study door) and to false teachers, who could entirely

*The Olivet Discourse is recorded principally in Matthew 24 and 25. Parallel records are found in Mark 13 and Luke 21. Luke also has what at first reading seems to be parts of the discourse located in a very different setting. Compare Luke 17:22-37 with Matthew 24:23-28. This lets us know that Jesus must have discussed His second coming on many other occasions and in many different settings.

13

As Jesus began to answer their question, "What will be the sign of Your coming and of the close of the age?" the disciples pressed close to listen.

spoil their preparation. So He began the discourse by warning us against being *deceived*.

And because "hope deferred makes the heart sick" (Proverbs 13:12), Jesus cautioned clearly but tactfully that there would be a *delay*. He would not be coming back right away. He told a story about two supervisors and put into the mouth of one of them the words, **"My master is delayed."** Matthew 24:48. In the famous parable of the talents, He described the master as returning **"after a long time."** Matthew 25:19. In the equally famous parable of the ten sleepy girls He likened Himself to a bridegroom and said plainly, **"As the bridegroom was delayed, they all slumbered and slept."** Matthew 25:5.

Hints of the delay are implied in other verses: **"You will hear of wars and rumors of wars, . . . but the end is not yet."** Matthew 24:6. **"Many will fall away."** Verse 10. **"He who endures to the end will be saved."** Verse 13. **"This gospel of the kingdom will be preached throughout the whole world, as a testimony to all nations; and *then* the end will come."** Verse 14. (Throughout this volume, emphasis in Bible texts is always supplied by the author.)

But if the delay is clear enough, the preparation we need to attend to is made even plainer in several remarks and in four distinct parables. See pages 36-42.

The setting of the Olivet Discourse. The Olivet Discourse was delivered after dark on a Tuesday. It had been a difficult day. For hours Jesus reasoned with crowds in the temple courts. Repeatedly, enemies baited Him with loaded questions. Some of the people seemed to appreciate what He said, but Jesus knew that most, even of them, were looking at Him as a military king, not as the Prince of Peace.

They wanted Him to conquer the Romans. They didn't want Him to conquer their hearts with love. You can read a little of what happened that day in Matthew 22 and 23.

As the afternoon wore on, it became evident that Christ's three and a half years of selfless ministry had changed very few of them. In a couple of days they would yell for His blood, just as their forefathers had demanded the death of the prophets. And their descendants would be just as bad. They too would persecute preachers who tried to help them.

Toward evening Christ's heart was breaking. He knew that without repentance the Jewish people would suffer terrible retribution. Their recalcitrance would at last so infuriate the Romans that the emperor would send armies which in A.D. 70 would erase Jerusalem and its temple from the map. And it would be so unnecessary!

"O Jerusalem, Jerusalem," He sobbed, "killing the prophets and stoning those who are sent to you! How often would I have gathered your children together as a hen gathers her brood under her wings, and *you would not*." Matthew 23:37.

"You would not let me." N.E.B.

"You were unwilling." N.A.S.B.

"Behold!" The anguished sentence came painfully forth: "Your house is forsaken and desolate." Matthew 23:38.

Even Christ's disciples were stunned. The temple of God, the pride of the nation, the house of the Lord, forsaken and desolate!

Ill at ease, the crowd dispersed to prepare the evening meal. Nervously, the disciples called Christ's attention to the exquisite artistry of the famous edifice. See Matthew 24:1. For almost fifty years King Herod and his successors had been rebuilding it at enormous expense. See John 2:20. Its snowy marble glistened in the setting sun. Gold plate flashed and glowed around the main entrance. Some of the temple stones, almost perfectly squared and smoothed, were of nearly incredible dimensions.*

"You see all these?" Jesus asked, almost as if He hadn't heard the disciples. **"Truly, I say to you, there will not be left here one stone upon another, that will not be thrown down."** Matthew 24:2.

The disciples were dumbfounded. How could God permit so great a disaster? Could it be that the end of the world was at hand?

That night Jesus seated Himself on the Mount of Olives. With Him were Peter and his brother Andrew, and James and his brother John, the four former fishermen who had accompanied Him throughout His ministry. See Mark 13:3. Above them in the early darkness rode the moon, nearly full. In its mystic glow the city of Jerusalem loomed a hundred meters, or about three hundred feet, below them across the narrow Kidron Valley. Olive-oil lamps glimmered through countless windows. A spirit as of Christmas or Thanksgiving pervaded the air in anticipation of Passover, due in a couple of days. People from far and near gathered with friends inside the walls or camped outside. Sounds of dogs and donkeys and of families preparing for the night floated up to where the five men sat.

The temple seemed almost close enough to touch. Moonlight heightened its whiteness and size. The disciples contemplated its polished and massive stones. They were deeply troubled by Christ's prediction a few hours earlier that someday not one of these stones would be left upon another. But would that terrible day of disaster also be the glorious day of His return? They didn't understand!

"Tell us," they asked, perplexed, **"when will this be, and what will be the sign of your coming and of the close of the age?"** Matthew 24:3.

You may read Christ's reply in Matthew 24 and 25. His words are printed on the next 3 pages, with headings inserted to help you. After you have read what Jesus said, we'll probe into what He meant.

---

*The well-known Jewish historian, Josephus, who was present at the destruction of Jerusalem, wrote that "the exterior of the building wanted [lacked] nothing that could astound either mind or eye. For, being covered on all sides with massive plates of gold, the sun was no sooner up than it radiated so fiery a flash that persons straining to look at it were compelled to avert their eyes, as from the solar rays. To approaching strangers it appeared from a distance like a snow-clad mountain; for all that was not overlaid with gold was of purest white. From its summit protruded sharp golden spikes to prevent birds from settling upon and polluting the roof. Some of the stones in the building were forty-five cubits in length, five in height, and six in breadth."—*The Jewish War*, 5.222 (Loeb 3:269). A cubit at the time was about half a meter, or around eighteen inches.

MATTHEW 24

INTRODUCTION

1 Jesus left the temple and was going away, when his disciples came to point out to him the buildings of the temple. [2]But he answered them, "You see all these, do you not? Truly, I say to you, there will not be left here one stone upon another, that will not be thrown down."

3 As he sat on the Mount of Olives, the disciples came to him privately, saying, "Tell us, when will this be, and what will be the sign of your coming and of the close of the age?"

GENERAL PROPHETIC SURVEY

Troubles Ahead That Are Not Signs. 4 And Jesus answered them, "Take heed that no one leads you astray. [5]For many will come in my name, saying, 'I am the Christ,' and they will lead many astray. [6]And you will hear of wars and rumors of wars; see that you are not alarmed; for this must take place, but the end is not yet. [7]For nation will rise against nation, and kingdom against kingdom, and there will be famines and earthquakes in various places: [8]all this is but the beginning of the birth-pangs."

Coming Tribulation and Apostasy. 9 "Then they will deliver you up to tribulation, and put you to death; and you will be hated by all nations for my name's sake.[10]And then many will fall away, and betray one another, and hate one another. [11]And many false prophets will arise and lead many astray. [12]And because wickedness is multiplied, most men's love will grow cold.[13] But he who endures to the end will be saved."

Success of the Gospel. 14 "And this gospel of the kingdom will be preached throughout the whole world, as a testimony to all nations; and then the end will come."

THE PRINCIPLE SIGN OF THE FALL OF JERUSALEM

15 "So when you see the desolating sacrilege spoken of by the prophet Daniel, standing in the holy place (let the reader understand) [Luke 21:20—When you see Jerusalem surrounded by armies, then know that its desolation has come near.], [16]then let those who are in Judea flee to the mountains; [17]let him who is on the housetop not go down to take what is in his house; [18]and let him who is in the field not turn back to take his mantle. [19]And alas for those who are with child and for those who give suck in those days! [20]Pray that your flight may not be in winter or on a sabbath."

THE ERA OF GREAT TRIBULATION

21 "For then there will be great tribulation, such as has not been from the beginning of the world until now, no, and never will be. [22]And if those days had not been shortened, no human being would be saved; but for the sake of the elect those days will be shortened. [Luke 21:24 —Jerusalem shall be trodden down by the Gentiles, until the times of the Gentiles are fulfilled.] [23]Then if any one says to you, 'Lo, here is the Christ!' or 'There he is!' do not believe it. [24]For false Christs and false prophets will arise and show great signs and wonders, so as to lead astray, if possible, even the elect. [25]Lo, I have told you beforehand. [26] So, if they say to you, 'Lo, he is in the wilderness,' do not go out; if they say, 'Lo, he is in the inner rooms,' do not believe it. [27]For as the lightning comes from the east and shines as far as the west, so will be the coming of the Son of man. [28]Wherever the body is, there the eagles will be gathered together."

HEAVENLY SIGNS OF THE SECOND COMING

29 "Immediately after the tribulation of those days the sun will be darkened, and the moon will not give its light, and the stars will fall from heaven, and the powers of the heavens will be shaken."

THE ARRIVAL OF THE SON OF MAN

30 "Then will appear the sign of the Son

of man in heaven, and then all the tribes of the earth will mourn, and they will see the Son of man coming on the clouds of heaven with power and great glory; [31]and he will send out his angels with a loud trumpet call, and they will gather his elect from the four winds, from one end of heaven to the other."

CERTAINTY THAT THE SON OF MAN WILL COME SOON AFTER THE SIGNS ARE FULFILLED

32 "From the fig tree learn its lesson: as soon as its branch becomes tender and puts forth its leaves, you know that summer is near. [33]So also, when you see all these things, you know that he is near, at the very gates. [34]Truly, I say to you, this generation will not pass away till all these things take place. [35]Heaven and earth will pass away, but my words will not pass away."

THE EXACT TIME IS UNKNOWN

36 "But of that day and hour no one knows, not even the angels of heaven, nor the Son, but the Father only. [37]As were the days of Noah, so will be the coming of the Son of man. [38]For as in those days before the flood they were eating and drinking, marrying and giving in marriage, until the day when Noah entered the ark, [39]and they did not know until the flood came and swept them all away, so will be the coming of the Son of man. [40]Then two men will be in the field; one is taken and one is left. [41]Two women will be grinding at the mill; one is taken and one is left."

ALERTNESS AND PREPAREDNESS ARE ESSENTIAL

42 "Watch therefore, for you do not know on what day your Lord is coming. [43]But know this, that if the householder had known in what part of the night the thief was coming, he would have watched and would not have let his house be broken into. [44]Therefore you also must be ready; for the

Son of man is coming at an hour you do not expect."

FOUR PARABLES ENCOURAGING PREPARATION

The Two Supervisors. 45 "Who then is the faithful and wise servant, whom his master has set over his household, to give them their food at the proper time? [46]Blessed is that servant whom his master when he comes will find so doing. [47]Truly, I say to you, he will set him over all his possessions. [48]But if that wicked servant says to himself, 'My master is delayed,' [49]and begins to beat his fellow servants, and eats and drinks with the drunken, [50]the master of that servant will come on a day when he does not expect him and at an hour he does not know, [51]and will punish him, and put him with the hypocrites; there men will weep and gnash their teeth."

MATTHEW 25

The Ten Sleepy Girls. 1 "Then the kingdom of heaven shall be compared to ten maidens who took their lamps and went to meet the bridegroom. [2]Five of them were foolish, and five were wise. [3]For when the foolish took their lamps, they took no oil with them; [4]but the wise took flasks of oil with their lamps. [5]As the bridegroom was delayed, they all slumbered and slept. [6]But at midnight there was a cry, 'Behold, the bridegroom! Come out to meet him.' [7]Then all those maidens rose and trimmed their lamps. [8]And the foolish said to the wise, 'Give us some of your oil, for our lamps are going out.' [9]But the wise replied, 'Perhaps there will not be enough for us and for you; go rather to the dealers and buy for yourselves.' [10]And while they went to buy, the bridegroom came, and those who were ready went in with him to the marriage feast; and the door was shut. [11]Afterward the other maidens came also, saying, 'Lord, lord, open to us.' [12]But he replied, 'Truly, I say to you, I do not know you.' [13]Watch therefore, for you know neither the day nor the hour."

17

The Servants and the Talents. 14 "For it will be as when a man going on a journey called his servants and entrusted to them his property; ¹⁵to one he gave five talents, to another two, to another one, to each according to his ability. Then he went away. ¹⁶He who had received the five talents went at once and traded with them; and he made five talents more. ¹⁷So also, he who had the two talents made two talents more. ¹⁸But he who had received the one talent went and dug in the ground and hid his master's money. ¹⁹Now after a long time the master of those servants came and settled accounts with them. ²⁰And he who had received the five talents came forward, bringing five talents more, saying, 'Master, you delivered to me five talents; here I have made five talents more.' ²¹His master said to him, 'Well done, good and faithful servant; you have been faithful over a little, I will set you over much; enter into the joy of your master.' ²²And he also who had the two talents came forward, saying, 'Master, you delivered to me two talents; here I have made two talents more.' ²³His master said to him, 'Well done, good and faithful servant; you have been faithful over a little, I will set you over much; enter into the joy of your master.' ²⁴He also who had received the one talent came forward, saying, 'Master, I knew you to be a hard man, reaping where you did not sow, and gathering where you did not winnow; ²⁵so I was afraid, and I went and hid your talent in the ground. Here you have what is yours.' ²⁶But his master answered him, 'You wicked and slothful servant! You knew that I reap where I have not sowed, and gather where I have not winnowed? ²⁷Then you ought to have invested my money with the bankers, and at my coming I should have received what was my own with interest. ²⁸So take the talent from him, and give it to him who has the ten talents. ²⁹For to every one who has will more be given, and he will have abundance; but from him who has not, even what he has will

be taken away. ³⁰And cast the worthless servant into the outer darkness; there men will weep and gnash their teeth.' "

Separating the Sheep From the Goats. 31 "When the Son of man comes in his glory, and all the angels with him, then he will sit on his glorious throne. ³²Before him will be gathered all the nations, and he will separate them one from another as a shepherd separates the sheep from the goats, ³³and he will place the sheep at his right hand, but the goats at the left. ³⁴Then the King will say to those at his right hand, 'Come, O blessed of my Father, inherit the kingdom prepared for you from the foundation of the world; ³⁵for I was hungry and you gave me food, I was thirsty and you gave me drink, I was a stranger and you welcomed me, ³⁶I was naked and you clothed me, I was sick and you visited me, I was in prison and you came to me.' ³⁷Then the righteous will answer him, 'Lord, when did we see thee hungry and feed thee, or thirsty and give thee drink? ³⁸And when did we see thee a stranger and welcome thee, or naked and clothe thee? ³⁹And when did we see thee sick or in prison and visit thee?' ⁴⁰And the King will answer them, 'Truly, I say to you, as you did it to one of the least of these my brethren, you did it to me.' ⁴¹Then he will say to those at his left hand, 'Depart from me, you cursed, into the eternal fire prepared for the devil and his angels; ⁴²for I was hungry and you gave me no food, I was thirsty and you gave me no drink, ⁴³I was a stranger and you did not welcome me, naked and you did not clothe me, sick and in prison and you did not visit me.' ⁴⁴Then they also will answer, 'Lord, when did we see thee hungry or thirsty or a stranger or naked or sick or in prison, and did not minister to thee?' ⁴⁵Then he will answer them, 'Truly, I say to you, as you did it not to one of the least of these, you did it not to me.' ⁴⁶And they will go away into eternal punishment, but the righteous into eternal life."

The Message of Matthew 24, 25

I. Christ's Caution About "Signs"

How much we depend on signs! Especially on road signs. We search for them—often in vain—at important intersections in unfamiliar cities. We appreciate the prominent signs on major freeways.

I remember a series of signs leading to a particularly bad bend on Salisbury Plain, England, during my childhood. The final sign was oversize and fairly shouted, "YOU HAVE BEEN WARNED."

Just after our son was born I received a traffic ticket for going through a stop sign in Chicago. To be sure, my mind had wandered; but when I returned to see how I could have missed the stop sign, I found a clutter of café and liquor signs hanging from little shops right behind it. I doubt that I would have missed it, even with a new father's fuddle, if it had been like the sign on Salisbury Plain.

"Tell us," pleaded the disciples, **"when will this be, and what will be the *sign* of your coming and of the close of the age?"** Matthew 24:3.

A *dual question*. The disciples' question reveals their confusion. They combined two distinct events. **"When will *this* be?"** they asked, referring to the destruction of the temple, and **"What will be the sign of your *coming* and of the close of the age?"** referring to the end of the world. The end of the temple and the end of the world at the second coming of Christ seemed to the four disciples to be a single event. They supposed that only the end of the world could bring about the destruction of the principal site of the worship of the true God.

Combining the two events into one, they sought a single item of information, **"*When* will this be?"** that is, **"What will be the *sign*"** indicating that it is near?

Commentators feel that in wording His reply, Jesus Himself blended information about both events, the end of the temple and the end of the world. No doubt there was a degree of blending; but the headings provided on pages 16-18 reveal that Christ's statements can be sorted out rather easily. In any case, Jesus provided distinct and different *signs* for the two important events.

Distinct and dependable signs. For the fall of the temple Jesus gave one unmistakable sign: the **"desolating sacrilege . . . standing in the holy place"** (Matthew 24:15), a symbolic prediction which He explained in Luke 21:20 as "Jerusalem surrounded by armies."

For the end of the world, Jesus gave a unique and very short list of signs: The preaching of the gospel in all the world (Matthew 24:14), a cluster of astronomical phenomena (verse 29), and the actual manner of His return—on clouds and visible as lightning (verses 27, 30).

The manner of His return. At first blush, Jesus seems to have evaded the disciples' question. His most emphatic sign of the destruction of Jerusalem was the arrival of the enemy. His most emphatic sign about the end of the world was the manner of His own arrival! But Jesus was deeply in earnest.

As things turned out (and as Jesus knew they would turn out), the arrival of enemy soldiers at Jerusalem in A.D. 66 did prove to be all the sign that the Jerusalem Christians needed. For the soldiers suddenly withdrew from the city, and everyone who wished to escape was able to do so before the Romans returned in force. See pages 27, 28.

As for the signs of His second coming, Jesus was very serious about the *manner* of His return. **"Then will appear the sign of the Son of man in heaven,"** He said, adding, **"all the tribes of the earth will mourn, and they will see the Son of man coming on the clouds of heaven with power and great glory."** Verse 30.

The **"sign of the Son of man"** is His appearance **"on the clouds of heaven."** Just as British royalty drive to state occasions in their well-known golden carriage and United States presidents fly in *Air Force One*, so at supremely significant moments the Son of man travels on supernatural clouds.

The Bible mentions three such cloudy occasions: (1) Christ's ascension from earth to heaven, when "a *cloud* took him out of their [the disciples'] sight." Acts 1:9. (2) The onset of the pre-advent judgment, when the Son of man traveled on *clouds* to the Ancient of Days. See Daniel 7:9-14; Revelation 12 to 14. (3) The second coming, when, Revelation 1:7 says, "He is coming with the *clouds*, and every eye will see him." The visible, on-cloud arrival of Jesus Christ is supremely the **"sign"** of the Son of man.

Cautions and warnings. In asking for a sign of His second coming, the disciples were seeking early-warning data that could tip them off about the timing of God's last-minute countdown. Today, of course, we would like to have the same inside information. So naturally we find ourselves asking, What use is a sign of His coming that is simply the manner of it?

We'll return to this question on page 22. In the meantime, we are impressed that Jesus was not greatly interested in setting up any last-day timetable. Six weeks later, when the disciples asked Him, moments before His ascension, "Will you at this time restore the kingdom to Israel?" He replied, "It is not for you to know times or seasons which the Father has fixed by his own authority." Acts 1:6, 7.

The very first thing Jesus said in the Olivet Discourse in answer to the disciples' request for a sign was this: **"Take heed that no one leads you astray."** Matthew 24:4. Don't be deceived! Don't be misled by false christs and false signs. Don't be conned into assuming that the end of Jerusalem or the end of the world will come sooner than it really will. See verses 5-8. Like the sign on Salisbury Plain, Jesus was stating boldly, "YOU HAVE BEEN WARNED." Don't be confused by any clutter of non-signs.

Signs that aren't signs. It is in the Olivet Discourse that the famous phrase occurs about **"wars and rumors of wars."** Verse 6. For centuries, Bible Christians have quoted this phrase while reflecting on contemporary international events. Over and over they have convinced themselves, for the time being, that Jesus must be coming soon. But Jesus specifically warned that wars and rumors of wars are not necessarily signs of the end. **"The end is not yet,"** He said in respect to them.

"See that you are not alarmed; for this must take place, but *the end is not yet.* **For nation will rise against nation, and kingdom against kingdom, and there will be famines and earthquakes in various places: all this is but the beginning of the birth-pangs."** Verses 6-8.

In any case, the location of the wars, famines, and earthquakes within the Olivet Discourse itself shows that Jesus had in mind events that were to occur during the thirty-nine years that remained prior to the fall of Jerusalem in A.D. 70. Four major *famines* are known even from the short reign of the Roman emperor Claudius (A.D. 41-54). One of them is reported in Acts 11:28. Serious *earthquakes* are known to have occurred around the empire in Crete (in 46 or 47) and in Rome (in 51). Rome fought significant *wars* in Mauretania (41-42), Britain (43-61), and Armenia (early 60s). In Armenia, it happens, Rome suffered a notable setback in A.D. 62, news of which must have falsely encouraged Jewish revolutionaries in Palestine.

Guerrilla and terrorist activity engulfed Palestine during these years. "Galilee," Josephus reports, naming only one area of Palestine, became from end to end "a scene of fire and blood."[1]

Christ's point was that disasters and defeats and wars and famines are not "signs" of the approaching end, either of Jerusalem or of the world. For our sin-drenched planet, sad to say, such sorrows are business as usual.

False christs and false prophets. Jesus warned also about the appearance of false christs and false prophets. See verses 4, 5, 23, 24. Compare Mark 13:6, 21-23.

In the thirty-nine years between the Olivet Discourse (A.D. 31) and the fall of Jerusalem (A.D. 70), numerous false leaders did arise. Josephus[2] says that Palestine was torn by numerous "deceivers and imposters" who preyed on the people's hopes and fears and fomented revolution against Rome "under the pretence of divine inspiration." One of these imposters, a certain Egyptian "false prophet," invited adventuresome Jews to rendezvous at his desert outpost. Thousands responded, believing him to be the messiah who would deliver Jerusalem from Roman control. But the Romans got wind of him and got ready. When the attack took place, almost every Jew who followed this particular false christ lost his life. Only the Egyptian himself and a few of his followers escaped. Some time later, incidentally, a Roman officer mistook the apostle Paul for this same Egyptian. See Acts 21:38.

In the Olivet Discourse, Jesus warned about false christs and false prophets in the section dealing with the second coming as well as in the section dealing with the fall of Jerusalem. See Matthew 24:23, 24. This later portion of the prophecy has also been fulfilled, at least in part. In recent times we have had Jim Jones and the Jonestown massacre. Going back a little, we recall Adolf Hitler, whom millions of educated Westerners devoutly believed at one time would usher in a thousand years of peace. In the nineteenth century, Napoleon led vastly more followers to their deaths than Jim Jones did. And there was Father Divine, who claimed to be God in Philadelphia; and the Shaker leader, Mother Ann Lee, who taught that she was Christ incarnate in a woman. The list goes on. Karl Marx was a false christ too, of sorts.

The manner of Christ's return. We come back now to the manner of Christ's return.

Some informants, Jesus warned, would claim, **"He is in the wilderness,"** or, **"He is in the inner rooms." "Do not believe it!"** He urged. **"Lo, I have told you beforehand."** YOU HAVE BEEN WARNED. Verses 25, 26.

Will Jesus return privately? No, He says, He will not.

Will He return secretly? No, He will not.

How, then, will He come? **"As the lightning comes from the east and shines as far as the west, so will be the coming of the Son of man." "All the tribes of the earth will mourn, and they will see the Son of man coming on the clouds of heaven with power and great glory; and he will send out his angels with a loud trumpet call, and they will gather his elect from the four winds, from one end of heaven to the other."** Verses 27, 30, 31.

It was to preserve His precious followers from disappointment and disaster that Jesus made so much about the manner of His coming. Evidently any teacher who says that Christ will come in any way other than on the clouds of heaven is a false teacher.

Jesus said false prophets would arise and gain great followings. Was He thinking of leaders like Father Divine, Hitler, Karl Marx, Ann Lee, Jim Jones, and Napoleon?

The Holy Spirit impressed Paul to provide a description of the "coming of the Lord" that is similar to Christ's own description of it. "The Lord himself," Paul said, "will descend from heaven with a cry of command, with the archangel's call, and with the sound of the trumpet of God. And the dead in Christ will rise first; then we who are alive, who are left, shall be caught up together with them in the clouds to meet the Lord in the air; and so we shall always be with the Lord." 1 Thessalonians 4:15-17.

Two words in Paul's passage have become famous in Christian circles. One of them is *parousia*, the Greek word translated "coming." *Parousia* was used in ancient times to refer to the state visits of important personages. I had the privilege of reading this word once on a broken piece of pottery, or potsherd, that recorded the arrival of an official at a certain ancient Egyptian community. *Parousia* is used in Matthew 24:3 and in several other places in the New Testament to refer to the return of Jesus.

The other famous word used in some translations of 1 Thessalonians 4:15-17 is *rapture*. It is derived from the Latin word *rapiemur*, which in the Latin Vulgate is used where "caught up" occurs in the Revised Standard Version. To "rapture" means to "catch up" or "carry away." In modern English the word has a pleasant connotation. We talk about being carried away—or raptured—with happy emotions. In ancient times *rapture* was a workaday term for "stealing" something or for "rescuing" somebody.

At His *parousia* (or second coming) Jesus will rapture (or rescue) His own people. And what will the circumstances be? A cry of command, the archangel's call, the piercing blast of a trumpet, our Lord on the clouds.

Any "christ" who comes, or who claims to come, in any other manner than this, is a false christ. And apparently any teacher who says that Christ will come in any other manner is a false teacher.

Christ's warning is urgent. In the Olivet Discourse Jesus made it plain that rejection of false teachers is more important than the possession of timetables.

"I have told you beforehand." Verse 25. Let no one deceive you. YOU HAVE BEEN WARNED.

The other true signs. If the precise manner of His return is a "sign," Jesus also gave a few other signs of His return. In Matthew 24:29, 30, He said, **"The sun will be darkened, and the moon will not give its light, and the stars will fall from heaven, and the powers of the heavens will be shaken; then will appear the sign of the Son of man in heaven."** His words are recorded in Luke 21:25-27 this way, "There will be signs in sun and moon and stars, and upon the earth distress of nations in perplexity at the roaring of the sea and the waves, men fainting with fear and with foreboding of what is coming on the world; for the powers of the heavens will be shaken. And then they will see the Son of man coming in a cloud with power and great glory."

In Matthew 24:33, Jesus said, **"So also, when you see all these things, you know that he is near, at the very gates."** And in Luke 21:28, "When these things begin to take place, look up and raise your heads, because your redemption is drawing near."

Many Christians believe that these signs in sun, moon, and stars have already been fulfilled. So thrilling a possibility deserves our careful attention. The evidence is discussed on pages 193-202.

Also among the "all things" that Jesus said we would see as His second coming approached was one more very impressive and significant sign. "This gospel of the kingdom shall be preached in all the world for a witness unto all nations; and then shall the end come." Matthew 24:14, K.J.V. After we have paid attention to other important matters, we'll discuss this prominent promise on pages 44-46.

II. The Abomination That Makes Desolate

When the disciples asked Jesus, **"Tell us, when will this be?"** they had in mind the destruction of Jerusalem as well as the second coming. We have noted this several times.

In His reply, Jesus referred to the **"desolating sacrilege spoken of by the prophet Daniel."** Matthew 24:15. Because of the wide use made of the King James Version, the **"desolating sacrilege"** is generally known in English as the "abomination of desolation." It will be our goal in the next few pages to study this "abomination" and the "desolation" that it produced. Seeing how fully Christ's prophecies about the fall of Jerusalem were fulfilled around A.D. 70 enhances our confidence in the fulfillment of His prophecies for our day. This is important, for the abomination of desolation has an application to our day as well as to the fall of Jerusalem.

"When you see the desolating sacrilege spoken of by the prophet Daniel, standing in the holy place (let the reader understand), then let those who are in Judea flee to the mountains; let him who is on the housetop not go down to take what is in his house; and let him who is in the field not turn back to take his mantle. And alas for those who are with child and for those who give suck in those days! Pray that your flight may not be in winter or on a sabbath." Matthew 24:15-20.

Prelude to destruction. The fulfillment of this prediction makes for sad reading, but it presents a gripping illustration of the reliability of Bible prophecy.

Let's go back a bit for perspective. The tiny nation of Judea, whose capital was Jerusalem, was incorporated into the Roman Empire when Pompey captured the city in 63 B.C. But whereas most conquered people developed pride in becoming part of the empire, many Jews in Judea and Galilee nourished a spirit of resistance and became noted for their militant opposition to Roman leadership.

The Romans usually, though not always, tried to rule Palestine peacefully. As time passed, however, one bloody incident led to another one still more bloody, until by the mid-60s the number of Palestinian Jews who might lose their lives in a single event is said to have reached 20,000. A climax occurred when the temple priests determined to offer no more sacrifices or prayers on behalf of the Roman emperor. In those days all ethnic groups in the empire offered sacrifices and

24

prayers on behalf of the emperor. Most groups offered sacrifices and prayers *to* the emperor, as though he were a god.

The Jewish decision not to pray for the emperor was considered treason. Punishment was inescapable.[3] Cestius Gallus, governor of the Roman province of Syria, in which Judea was included, marched south from Antioch with the equivalent of two legions of soldiers and numerous auxiliaries. (Auxiliaries resembled our militia. Legions were elite units of about six thousand.) When Cestius Gallus arrived at Jerusalem in October A.D. 66, he met fierce opposition. A guerrilla group attacked him suddenly and killed 515 Romans for a loss of only 22. But the very brilliance of their success caused the guerrillas to fear a severe reprisal, and they retreated uncertainly behind the stout walls of the temple complex.

Moderate Jews encouraged the Romans to take over the temple area at once and to suppress the rebels before they got their second wind. Cestius Gallus did make a move toward the temple. To restore temple prayers on behalf of the emperor was the reason he had come. Inexplicably, however, after an effort lasting less than a week and reaching the verge of success, Cestius Gallus withdrew from the city and headed back to Antioch. His decision was disastrous for his troops. Jewish resistance fighters manned the ridges above the northbound mountain road. With arrows, spears, and rocks, they succeeded in killing almost six thousand of the Romans.

Josephus, the historian, served as a Jewish general for a time during the ensuing war before he joined the Roman side. Looking back several years later, he regarded the governor's unexplained retreat as a turning point. If Cestius Gallus had pressed his attack only a little more decisively, Josephus concluded, Roman peace would have been restored to Jerusalem with little loss to either life or property. Wrote Josephus, "Had he [Cestius Gallus] but persisted for a while with the siege [of the temple complex], he would have forthwith taken the city,"[4] and there would have been no Jewish war and no destruction of the city!

Severely stung by the loss of their soldiers, however, the Romans determined to return. The Emperor Nero summoned from Britain his capable general Vespasian, who laid plans carefully with the help of his son Titus. (Both Vespasian and Titus later became emperors.) Together, father and son launched a campaign in which perhaps a quarter million Palestinian Jews were starved, burned, shot through with arrows, crucified, hacked, or enslaved to death.

Temple and city wiped out. When Titus, with four legions and a large force of auxiliaries, began his siege of Jerusalem in the spring of A.D. 70, Jerusalem was jammed with Jews who had gathered to celebrate Passover.[5]

As the siege progressed, disease, filth, and famine took their grisly toll. Amid mounting panic, three ganglike organizations added to the horror by terrorizing their fellow Jews and competing viciously for control of the dwindling supplies. One starving mother ate her baby.[6]

Titus tried to save the temple. It was an ornament of the empire. In various ways he also attempted to spare the city and its people. But the city leaders re-

25

fused all terms, believing that God would even yet honor them as His people and preserve the temple as His house of worship.

Near the end of August, some of the Romans, infuriated at the seemingly incomprehensible fanaticism of the Jewish resistance, set fire to the gold-plated wood of the temple's walls and ceiling. Modern Jews still memorialize the ensuing conflagration annually on the ninth of the Jewish month Ab. But even after the burning of the temple, the survivors adamantly refused to surrender, and Titus in exasperation turned his troops loose. City and temple disappeared, literally. Except for a small portion of the wall and three towers, "the city was so completely levelled to the ground," says Josephus, "as to leave future visitors to the spot no ground for believing that it had ever been inhabited."[7]

Of the masses of people who had inhabited the city at the beginning of the siege, almost everyone appears to have died; except that at Jerusalem and during the preceding campaign in Galilee and Judea, 97,000 men, women, and children were taken prisoner. Many of the prisoners were sent to the provinces to face wild animals in amphitheaters. Many were compelled to dig the Corinthian canal in Greece. Many others were sent to Egypt to toil there to their death as slaves. Some were offered for sale as slaves to Gentiles living in Judea; they went for "a trifling sum per head, owing to the glut of the market and the dearth of purchasers."[8]

Prophecy fulfilled. The destruction of Jerusalem poignantly fulfilled Christ's prediction of thirty-nine years earlier, **"There will not be left here one stone upon another, that will not be thrown down."** Matthew 24:2. So too were fulfilled His prophecies about famines, earthquakes, rumors of wars, and armies standing round the holy place.

The woman who ate her baby, the slaves who were sold for a pittance, and the captives who were shipped into Egypt fulfilled other prophecies made by Moses some fifteen hundred years earlier in Deuteronomy 28:15, 52, 53, 68, "If you will not obey the voice of the Lord your God or be careful to do all his commandments and his statutes which I command you this day, then . . . they [your enemies] shall besiege you in all your towns, . . . and you shall eat the offspring of your own body, . . . and the Lord will bring you back in ships to Egypt, . . . and there you shall offer yourselves for sale to your enemies as male and female slaves, but no man will buy you."

God cared. The fall of Jerusalem to the Romans reminds us of its fall centuries before to the Babylonians. In GC 1:19-25, we saw how very sadly God "gave up" Jerusalem to King Nebuchadnezzar and how He sent prophet after prophet to prevent the disaster if possible.

God did even more in New Testament times to spare the Jews in Jerusalem their awful disaster at the hands of the Romans. For over thirty years God's own Son walked their roads and streets, pointing them to the way of peace. He taught them to forgive, to return good for evil, and to respect all legally constituted authority. When a Roman soldier, exercising his privileges, compelled a Jew to carry his heavy pack for a mile, Jesus counseled the Jew to carry the pack a second mile as well. See Matthew 5:41.

If all the Jews in Judea and Galilee had accepted Christ's teachings, they wouldn't have engaged in the banditry and sabotage that goaded Romans to retaliate. They wouldn't have refused to pay their taxes. They wouldn't have stopped praying for the emperor—the treasonable act that brought on the war. Neither would they have assumed that God was likely to work miracles for people who long had disobeyed Him unless they repented first. Nor would they have divided into furious factions, but would have generously sustained one another.

But not all Jews rejected Jesus. Thousands accepted Him. See Acts 2:41. They placed confidence not only in His religious instruction but also in His prophecies. They remembered His words, **"When you see the desolating sacrilege spoken of by the prophet Daniel, standing in the holy place"**—that is, "when you see Jerusalem surrounded by armies"—**"then let those who are in Judea *flee to the mountains."*** Matthew 24:15, 16; Luke 21:20.

The astonishing departure of Cestius Gallus in November A.D. 66, when victory was easily within his reach, provided a priceless opportunity for escape. Josephus reports that "many distinguished Jews" at that time "abandoned the city as swimmers desert a sinking ship."[9]

It appears that the Christian Jews left Jerusalem at this time. Moving north, they founded a colony at Pella, southeast of Lake Galilee. The words of Christ translated **"flee to the mountains"** in the Revised Standard Version can appropri-

Christians in Jerusalem saw the withdrawal of the Roman army in A.D. 66 as the sign Christ had promised, and they left the city immediately.

ately be rendered "flee to the hills" or "flee to a country place." Pella is located in the country among rolling hills.

The Christian Jews did as Jesus counseled them because they trusted His prophecy. And not a single Christian Jew, mother, father, or child, is known to have died in the terrible death of Jerusalem.

III. The Abomination and the Christian Church

As we noted on page 24, where the Revised Standard Version in Matthew 24:15 speaks about the **"desolating sacrilege,"** the King James Version—along with several other translations—has the phrase, the "abomination of desolation."

We have seen that Jesus was talking symbolically about the Roman armies that were to surround Jerusalem in the years 66 and 70. Compare Luke 21:20. But what He said deserves further attention. The "abomination of desolation" was to be much more than Roman armies.

Jesus showed that the abomination of desolation had been foretold **"by the prophet Daniel."** This was true; for Daniel—talking a different language, of course, but with exactly the same idea in mind—spoke in Daniel 11:31 about the "abomination that makes desolate." In Daniel 8:13 he called it the "transgression that makes desolate." He predicted that it would cause the "sanctuary and host to be trampled under foot." Speaking of it in still another way in Daniel 9:24-27, Daniel talked about a desolator prince who would appear upon the wing of abominations to destroy the city of Jerusalem and the temple. See GC 1:216-219.

So the prophet Daniel, though he employed different words, had indeed spoken about the abomination of desolation.

Now, in the Old Testament King James Version, the word *abomination* is sometimes used for idol worship. See 2 Kings 23:13; Isaiah 44:19. The word *transgression* obviously refers to something sinful. And a *sacrilege* (Matthew 24:15, R.S.V.) is something irreverent. Thus the "abomination of desolation" and the "transgression of desolation" and the "desolating sacrilege" spoken of by the prophet Daniel and by Jesus were one and the same thing. Essentially, it was a *sinful system of worship that would commit the sacrilege of trampling on and desolating* God's city, God's sanctuary, and His people.

The Roman army that demolished Jerusalem was just such an idol-worshiping, desolating abomination. In place of flags, Roman soldiers carried standards. These were long poles with cross arms near the top from which each legion hung its characteristic symbols. (The "tenth Fretensis" and the "twelfth Fulminata" were among the legions that fought at Jerusalem.[10]) Whereas modern soldiers salute their flags, the Romans at times *worshiped* their standards. The ancient writer Tertullian even asserted that "the camp religion of the Romans is all through a worship of the standards."[11]

After the Roman soldiers destroyed the Jerusalem temple, while the hot smoke was still rising from the ruins and the defeated Jews were still bleeding and cursing and dying on every side, the Romans "carried their standards into the temple

29

Victorious Roman soldiers desecrated the temple by setting up their standards there and sacrificing pigs to them.

court and," says Josephus, "setting them up opposite the eastern gate, [they] there sacrificed to them."[12]

The Roman army that stood in the holy place and destroyed and desolated Jerusalem was intrinsically idolatrous. It was indeed an "abomination" and a "desecration" that produced "desolation."

The abomination was "Rome." Now, in Daniel 8:13 the phrase "transgression that makes desolate" is applied to that chapter's symbolic "little horn." In GC 1:159, 160, 190-192 we saw that some readers of the Bible have supposed that this little horn was Antiochus Epiphanes. We studied about that eccentric little king of Syria (175-164 B.C.), who interrupted the temple sacrifices between 168 and 165 B.C. We found that he really did not fit the numerous specifications of the little horn. And, of course, the fact that in Matthew 24:15 and Luke 21:20 Jesus identified the abomination of desolation with armies whose arrival at Jerusalem was *still future* in A.D. 31 proves beyond a doubt that it was not Antiochus Epiphanes.

What we found the little horn of Daniel 8 really represented was "Rome." Both *pagan* and *Christian* Rome. Both the Roman Empire and the medieval Roman Church.

The prophecies of Daniel 2, 7, and 8 run parallel. See the chart on GC 1:250. Each prophecy starts in Daniel's day and continues through real time to the end of the world. The various symbols for the Babylonian, Persian, and Greek Empires are followed in each chapter by a symbol for Rome: iron in Daniel 2, a monster in Daniel 7, and a little horn in Daniel 8. As we noted in GC 1:122-135, in these prophecies God chose on purpose to overlook the great good accomplished by the Roman Empire and by the Roman Church. He chose in each chapter to emphasize the negative, repressive aspects of Rome in order to teach important lessons.

We are now ready to ask, Did the little horn of Daniel 8—that is, Did the "transgression that makes desolate" of Daniel 8:13—"trample" on God's "sanctuary" and His "host" (or people)? The answer is Yes. In its pagan-empire phase, Rome destroyed the Jerusalem temple, which had been God's principal site of public worship for almost a thousand years. Everyone knows that the Roman Empire also persecuted people who believed in the true God. Rome in its Christian-church phase also persecuted believers. Further, as we saw in GC 1:159-161, 172-178, medieval Christian teaching and behavior seriously obscured the "continual" (Hebrew *tamid*) ministry of Jesus in the heavenly sanctuary. In between Christ and His people, medieval Rome interposed a false priesthood, a false sacrifice, a false head of the church, and a false way of salvation. See GC 1:178. That the medieval church did perform badly has been frankly conceded by prominent Jesuit authors in the years since the second Vatican Council. See GC 1:174, 178.

Viewed from this standpoint, the "abomination of desolation" is seen to be a false system of worship, *Rome* in both pagan and Christian forms. Pagan Rome attacked God's visible sanctuary, the Jerusalem temple, and persecuted true

Christianity. Christian Rome also persecuted, and it opposed the invisible sanctuary where Jesus ministers on our behalf in heaven.

Apostasy and the man of lawlessness. To speak of the medieval Christian church as performing badly is to sound an alarm. How could Christians have behaved that way unless they first had apostatized or left the faith?

This very apostasy was predicted in the Olivet Discourse. Said Jesus, **"Many will fall away."** Matthew 24:10. Some twenty-five years after the discourse, Paul referred to the same tragedy. Said he to the Christian leaders in Ephesus, "I know that after my departure fierce wolves will come in among you, not sparing the flock; and from among your own selves will arise men speaking perverse things, to draw away the disciples [the church members] after them." Acts 20:29, 30.

"Let no one deceive you in any way," said Paul to some new Christians in Thessalonica, who were longing for Christ to come. (His words were a clear echo of one of Christ's warnings in Matthew 24.) "For that day will not come," Paul continued, *"unless the rebellion* [Greek: *apostasia,* apostasy or falling away] *comes first,* and the man of lawlessness ["man of sin," K.J.V.] is revealed, the son of perdition, who opposes and exalts himself against every so-called god or object of worship, so that he takes his seat in the temple of God, proclaiming himself to be God. Do you not remember that when I was still with you I told you this?" 2 Thessalonians 2:3-5.

The "mystery of lawlessness" was already at work, Paul went on, referring to conditions in the middle of the first century. "Only," Paul explained, "he who now restrains it will do so until he is out of the way. And then the lawless one will be revealed, and the Lord Jesus will slay him with the breath of his mouth and destroy him by his appearing and his coming." 2 Thessalonians 2:7, 8.

Paul's point was that the man of lawlessness would not be revealed until some time future to Paul's day, but that once the man of lawlessness arrived, he would continue till the second coming.

It seems unkind, even un-Christian, to suggest that the Roman Church fulfilled this prophecy. But Paul was speaking about an "apostasy," a "rebellion." Apostasies and rebellions happen within the ranks, not outside them. In GC 1:131, 132 we saw that various popes and their admirers indeed made claims to God-status for the papacy, even as recently as the 1890s, claims that have never been repudiated. In GC 1:134-143 we saw how, with the best intentions perhaps, the Roman Church opposed God's law and has not changed its stand.

Leading Christians express concern. At the height of the Middle Ages, educated Christian leaders became deeply concerned about the church's apostasy. At actual risk to their lives they expressed the disturbing conviction that the man of lawlessness, the abomination of desolation, had appeared in their own day. They concluded that the church—or its dogma, or at least its earthly leadership—was the "man of lawlessness" of 2 Thessalonians 2 and the "abomination" of Matthew 24.

Jan Milič (d. 1374) was one of these leaders. Secretary to Emperor Charles IV

31

and archdeacon at the Cathedral of Prague, Milič turned down a promotion and resigned his position in order to gain time for preaching. On a pilgrimage to Rome he addressed a large assembly of clergy and scholars under the title, "Antichrist Has Come!" Imprisoned while in Rome he wrote a tract in which he said, "Where Christ speaks of the 'abomination' in the temple [Matthew 24:15], he invites us to look round and observe how, through the negligence of her pastors, the church lies desolate."[13]

John Wycliffe (d. 1384), the well-known Catholic churchman, English statesman, and Oxford professor, saw the abomination of desolation in the doctrine of transubstantiation, imposed on people as it was by the bishops under threat of excommunication.[14]

Sir John Oldcastle (d. 1417), also called Lord Cobham, deserves to be better known. After Wycliffe's death, Sir John sponsored Oxford students in the study of the Bible and provided means for "Poor Preachers" or "Lollards" to teach the Bible all around the country. Archbishop Arundel of Canterbury got the King of England to rebuke him. Sir John replied that although he would obey the king in harmony with Romans 13, he could not obey an order of the church telling him to stop the preaching of the Bible. He knew by Scripture, he said, that the pope was the "Son of Perdition" (i.e., the man of lawlessness, 2 Thessalonians 2:3) and the "Abomination standing in the holy place." Sir John was imprisoned but managed to escape. Recaptured four years later, he was sentenced to be barbecued, *slowly*, alive. He died singing praise.[15]

In the 1300s Wycliffe sent out his followers with hand-written portions of his new Bible translation to show common people that Christ forgives sin without the intercession of a human priest.

John Huss (d. 1415), a Bohemian like Milič, also identified the pope with the man of sin. "Huss" means "goose" in Bohemian, and he was aware that his goose might well get cooked. It did. On July 6, 1415, the bishops at the ecclesiastical Council of Constance had him burned alive.[16]

Martin Luther (d. 1546) was a monk. His prayers deepened his spiritual concern. He came to see the church of his time as the "abomination . . . of which Jesus speaks in Matthew 24:15" and as the man of lawlessness of 2 Thessalonians 2, who sits "in the temple of God (that means, in the midst of Christendom), showing himself that he is God."[17]

Tragically, the abomination of desolation that Jesus and Daniel spoke about was indeed both pagan and Christian Rome.

IV. Predicted Tribulation—and You

Talking about the tragic deaths of Huss and Oldcastle reminds us that in the Olivet Discourse Jesus predicted that His followers would suffer tribulation. **"Then they will deliver you up to tribulation, and put you to death; and you will be hated by all nations for my name's sake."** Matthew 24:9.

It was not His only reference that evening to tribulation. In verses 21 and 22 He referred to a coming **"great tribulation,"** one unlike any tribulation before it or since, so severe that **"if those days had not been shortened, no human being would be saved."**

Tribulation is translated from a Greek word meaning "trouble, distress, and suffering." In addition to Christ's references to it on the Mount of Olives, the Bible contains several other predictions about periods of notable distress. See the chart on page 35.

The first tribulation in the Olivet Discourse was to begin very soon, within the lifetimes of the disciples. **"They will deliver *you* up to tribulation."** Jesus told them. And it was to continue more or less permanently. When Jesus added, **"You will be hated by all nations for my name's sake,"** He was looking through history to the end of time, as the gospel would spread from one nation to another. Some people out of all the nations would accept the gospel and become His followers. Tragically, He knew that others of all the nations would not only reject Him but would also persecute those who accepted Him.

The other tribulation Jesus spoke of, one unlike any other before it or since (verses 21, 22), was fulfilled during the 1260 year-days of Daniel 7:25 (see GC 1:130, 131) as part of the awful pattern of trial, trouble, and distress that all too often marked the career of Roman Christianity. See the chart.

Yet another tribulation or "time of trouble," also unlike any other before it or since, was foretold in Daniel 12:1, 2. It will take place when the "great prince," Michael, "shall arise." "At that time your people shall be delivered," Gabriel said to Daniel, "every one whose name shall be found written in the book. And many of those who sleep in the dust," he added, "shall awake, some to everlasting life."

This unique tribulation will occur in connection with the resurrection at the second coming. It will occur after the court of judgment described in Daniel 7:9-14 has finished examining the books. It will bring terror only to the wicked. God's people will be delivered from it, "every one" of them.

This terrible trial at the end of time will be unlike any other in that, though relatively brief, it will involve the seven last plagues. The great tribulation of the 1260 year-days, however, was unlike any other in that it lasted for centuries. It affected both believers and unbelievers. At times it carried off as many as a fourth or even a third of the population.

We'll have more to say about the different tribulations when we discuss Revelation 2:10; 3:10 and 6:9-11.

Tribulation and you. In the quiet of that evening on the Mount of Olives, Jesus said to the four disciples seated beside Him, **"They will deliver *you* up to tribulation, and put *you* to death."**

Tribulation is painfully personal. Of those four faithful friends, James and Peter were later imprisoned in Jerusalem by King Herod at the request of Jewish leaders. See Acts 12:1-19. James was beheaded. Peter was rescued by an angel—but years later he was martyred in Rome, evidently crucified upside down. John, another member of the Olivet Four, was dipped into hot oil. See page 53. Surviving miraculously, he was exiled to the island of Patmos, where he saw the visions of Revelation.

But Jesus thought of other sufferers too. He knew that tribulation would not be limited to certain periods or to selected individuals. "In the world you have tribulation," He said. John 16:33. His words constitute a universal axiom like, "In school you have teachers" or "In war you have death." Tribulation is an inevitable aspect of human living. "Man is born to trouble as the sparks fly upward." Job 5:7.

Being a Christian, however, helps a person avoid a good many kinds of trouble and mitigates a good many others. Choosing to live healthfully in order to glorify God (see 1 Corinthians 10:31) helps a Christian avoid many aches and pains. Being courteous helps defuse other people's anger: "A soft answer turns away wrath." Proverbs 15:1. Prayer, too, changes things: "Call upon me in the day of trouble; I will deliver you, and you shall glorify me." Psalm 50:15.

But some trouble is inescapable. "In the world you have tribulation." The Christian Jews who left Jerusalem in harmony with Christ's instruction were gloriously spared the carnage that came to their compatriots, but they were not spared the cost and inconvenience of moving to Pella and starting life over again there. See pages 27, 28. And Christian martyrs obviously suffer very severe tribulation.

But when Jesus said, "In the world you have tribulation," He went on to say, "but be of good cheer, I have overcome the world." John 16:33. Christ is in control, and He will have the last word about our trials!

"They will deliver you up to tribulation," He said in Matthew 24:9. In fact, they

THREE NOTABLE TRIBULATIONS PREDICTED IN THE BIBLE
"In the world you have tribulation; but be of good cheer." John 16:33

Prophecy	Fulfillment

I. PERSECUTION IN THE ROMAN EMPIRE
God's people suffer

"They will deliver you up to *tribulation*, and put you to death." Matthew 24:9.

Christians began to be persecuted by Jews in the year 31, and by Romans, as early as when Nero burned Rome in 64.

"For ten days you will have *tribulation*. Be faithful unto death, and I will give you the crown of life." Revelation 2:10.

A notable wave of Roman persecution during the "Smyrna" period is known as the Diocletian persecution, 303-313. See pages 101, 102, 121 and GC 1:125.

II. THE GREAT TRIBULATION OF THE 1260 YEAR-DAYS (538-1798)
All people suffer

"He [the little horn] shall speak words against the Most High, and shall *wear out the saints* of the Most High, . . . and they shall be given into his hand for a time, two times, and half a time [1260 year-days]." Daniel 7:25.

Repression of deviant views became a well-known characteristic of Roman Christianity during the 1260 year-days. It grew notably more severe after the establishment of the Papal Inquisition in 1232 and again after the Reformation. The worst was over before the sun was notably darkened on May 19, 1780. See Revelation 6 and 7 and GC 1:132, 133.

"When he opened the fifth seal, I saw under the altar the souls of those who had been slain for the word of God. . . . Then they were each given a white robe and told to rest a little longer. . . . When he opened the sixth seal, . . . the sun became black." "After this I looked, and behold, a great multitude . . . clothed in white robes . . . they who have come out of the *great tribulation*." Revelation 6:9-12; 7:9-14.

"There will be *great tribulation, such as has not been from the beginning of the world until now,* no, and never will be. And if those days had not been shortened, no human being would be saved." "Immediately after the *tribulation of those days* the sun will be darkened." Matthew 24:21, 22, 29.

Feudal rivalry, religious hostility, and nationalistic wars spread anguish during this period. At different times the terrible Black Death and the frightful Thirty Years War took perhaps a third of the population. See pages 125, 126.

"I will throw her [Thyatira] on a sickbed, and those who commit adultery with her I will throw into *great tribulation*, unless they repent." Revelation 2:22.

III. THE TIME OF TROUBLE AT THE END
God's people are delivered

"At that time shall arise Michael, the great prince who has charge of your people. And there shall be a *time of trouble, such as never has been since there was a nation till that time;* * but at that time your people shall be delivered, every one whose name shall be found in the book. And many of those who sleep in the dust of the earth shall awake, some to everlasting life." Daniel 12:1, 2.

After the completion of the pre-advent judgment, the seven last plagues and other end-time developments produce unequaled suffering, but God's true people are delivered. See pages 111-113 and GC 1:299, 301.

"Because you have kept my word of patient endurance, I will keep you from the *hour of trial* which is coming on the whole world, to try those who dwell upon the earth. I am coming soon." Revelation 3:10, 11.

*The tribulation of the 1260 year-days was the greatest in history in that it continued for centuries and from time to time produced extremely high percentages of mortality. The tribulation at the end of time will be the greatest in history in that, though very short, it will involve the dreadful seven last plagues. Each is worst in different ways.

will "put [some of you] to death." But *never mind!* "Not a hair of your head will perish." Luke 21:16-18.

Loving paradox! You will be killed, but not a cell in your body will be lost. "Precious in the sight of the Lord is the death of his saints." Psalm 116:15. At the second coming, the Christ who has already overcome the world will raise every one of His sleeping people back to life. See Matthew 24:31; 1 Thessalonians 4: 15-18.

God cares!

He cares about us. He wants us also to care—about other people. "Religion that is pure and undefiled before God and the Father is this: to visit orphans and widows in their affliction [Greek, "tribulation"], and to keep oneself unstained from the world." James 1:27. The mature Christian tends to lose sight of his own problems by helping others with theirs. The Christian knows that everyone— single men and women, divorced people and widows, orphans and parented children, mothers, fathers, the elderly, administrators, and employees—all face trials. The true Christian finds ways to "visit" them "in their affliction."

The true Christian also, after he catches his breath, "rejoices in suffering." How so? By knowing that even during his trials he is precious to God. By knowing also that his personal problems provide an opportunity to demonstrate a patience under provocation that can persuade other people to become Christians too. See Romans 5:3; James 1:2-4. And as for other people's trials, he rejoices in the opportunity they present for him to manifest Christian compassion.

"The things that are revealed belong to us and to our children." Deuteronomy 29:29. Some kind of trouble bothers every family member at least some of the time. Happy is the family that learns how to share trials, and how to rejoice in them too.

V. Parables About Preparation

In the Olivet Discourse Jesus was not concerned about providing a detailed timetable of earth's terminal tribulation. His primary purpose during much of Matthew 24 was to warn us against being deceived by false christs, false prophets, and false signs. See pages 20-22. His emphasis toward the end of Matthew 24 and in Matthew 25 was on our being ready for the second coming whenever it may occur.

Christians are to know when Christ's return is **"near."** Matthew 24:33. Jesus did not, however, specify the **"day and hour"** of His return. On the contrary, He indicated that His actual appearance will come as a surprise even to His most ardent followers.

"Watch therefore, for *you* do not know on what day your Lord is coming." Matthew 24:42.

"You also must be ready; for the Son of man is coming at an hour *you* do not expect." Matthew 24:44.

In the days of Noah, people engaged heedlessly in their daily rounds, **"eating** and drinking," Jesus said, "**marrying and giving in marriage, until the day when Noah entered the ark, and they did not know until the flood came and swept them all away.**" Matthew 24:38, 39.

Eating and getting married are not sins, but *merely* doing such things was not good enough in Noah's day, and it isn't good enough in ours. We must also "**be ready,**" for, like Noah's flood, "**so will be the coming of the Son of man.**" Verse 37. People will be engaged in their ordinary daily tasks, working "**in the field**" or "**grinding at the mill**"; one will be "**taken**" and the other "**left.**" Verses 40, 41.

Noah and his three sons had wives, so we know they were married. They put food on board the ark, so we know they liked to eat. Building the vessel was their daily job. Insofar as they filled life's ordinary rounds, they lived like everyone else. But in addition, they were "**ready.**" They were "**taken**" to safety, and all the other people alive at the time were "**left**" to be destroyed.

It isn't wrong to have a family or hold a job or take a vacation or fill out income-tax forms. But as we perform these basic functions we must continually be ready.

To help us to be ready for His second coming, the Master Storyteller told four famous parables. The first concerned *The Two Supervisors*, one, "**faithful and wise**"; the other, plainly "**wicked.**" The faithful supervisor was fair and honest and made sure that the workers under him got their pay regularly. The wicked supervisor reasoned that since his boss had been delayed so long already, he would probably be delayed a lot longer yet. So he caroused with his pals and abused the other workers. Jesus said that when the owner returned, he would reward the faithful supervisor by promoting him to top management, but he would punish the wicked one by placing him with "**hypocrites**" in a situation where "**men will weep and gnash their teeth.**" Matthew 24:45-51.

The lesson of the story is that readiness for Christ's arrival involves faithfulness in daily duties. One supervisor did his job dependably. The other wasted time and money and then got frustrated with the people where he worked.

Why was the second supervisor shut out of God's kingdom? Evidently because God cares too much about our eternal happiness to let it be marred by despotic little playboys. Which probably also means that He doesn't want to populate heaven with quarrelsome parents and stubborn spouses who waste endless hours at the TV and then fuss horribly with each other because the work isn't done. Part of our preparation for eternity is learning (by God's grace) to use our time wisely and to be pleasant with people.

Ten Sleepy Girls. Christ's second parable about preparation was centered around a wedding. At a typical wedding in Bible times the groom traveled, per-haps by oxcart, to the home of the bride for one phase of the wedding; then he conveyed her to his own home for the wedding feast. Unmarried girls, mostly in their early teens, waited outside the bride's home to welcome the groom and share the joy. For night ceremonies, the girls equipped themselves with olive-oil lamps.

I have observed a similar custom as still practiced today in villages of the Mid-

dle East. The lamps used there today are up to date, but I happen to own a lamp that dates from Bible times. I have found that it burns for as long as six hours on a filling and that walking with it doesn't blow out the flame.

In Christ's story, ten young women gathered outside a bride's home one night to wait for the groom. Assuming that everything would come off as scheduled, five **"foolish"** girls didn't bother to take along an extra little jar of oil. The five **"wise"** girls, however, recognized frankly that their friend the groom might not meet his big appointment on time. They well knew that custom expected them to bring lights to help illuminate the evening's entire outdoor and indoor festivities. So each of these **"wise"** girls carried an extra supply of fuel.

The groom *was* delayed; and while the ten sleepy girls napped, their lights nearly burned out. When they woke up at midnight to hear the groom's oxcart rounding the bend, the wise girls quickly refueled their lamps. The foolish ones, however, begged their friends to share with them. But even the wise girls had only enough oil to keep their own lamps alight during the parade and the feast. While the foolish ones dashed off to arouse the village oil-merchant, the bridegroom arrived. **"Those who were ready"** went in with him to the marriage festivity, and **"the door was shut."** **"Watch therefore,"** Jesus concluded, **"for *you* know neither the day nor the hour."** Matthew 25:1-13.

The point of this story is that in order to be ready for the second coming we must be ready individually. It isn't good enough if only our husband or wife or mother is ready. It isn't good enough just to belong to a church, even if everyone in the church talks a lot about the second coming. All of the sleepy girls believed the bridegroom was coming, and all of them made some sort of preparation. But the only ones who were truly ready were the ones whose individual preparation was adequate.

We may assume that little children will enter the kingdom of heaven on the strength of their parents' faith. Referring to the children of His followers, Jesus said, "Let the children come to me, and do not hinder them; for to such belongs the kingdom of heaven." Matthew 19:14. But as our children grow up, we need to make certain that they grow in Christ and develop their own spirituality. As soon as possible, they should be taught to read the Bible and pray by themselves as well as at family worship. Then by the time they are on their own, they will have their own extra oil for their lamps.

Parable of the Talents. Christ's third story introduced a word into the English language. Today *talent* means the ability to do something special. In Bible times, a talent was originally a weight of about 34 kilograms, or 75 pounds. Later, it was the value of this weight in silver, bronze, or gold. In Christ's day a talent was a huge sum of money, equivalent perhaps to the wages of an ordinary laborer for fifteen years.

In this third parable about preparation, a **"man going on a journey"** entrusted five talents to one of his servants, two talents to another servant, and one talent to a third. Then he went his way. While he was gone, the man with the five talents

39

Symbolizing Christians who believe Christ is coming but do not live close to Him, five virgins were shut out from the wedding feast.

made use of his enormous wealth to double his capital. The man with two talents also doubled his capital. But the man with the single talent groused about how unjust his employer had been to give him so much less than he gave the others. He figured that anything he might earn with the money would go unappreciated by such a boss, and in a burst of ill-humor and self-pity he dug a hole for the talent and buried it.

When the master returned **"after a long time,"** the first two servants gave their reports cheerfully and were warmly commended. **"Well done, good and faithful servant,"** said the master to each one; **"you have been faithful over a little, I will set you over much; enter into the joy of your master."**

The third servant, however, handed his single talent back to the master in very bad grace—and heard himself described in return as a **"wicked and slothful"** person. Like the wicked supervisor in the first story, he too was banished to a place where **"men will weep and gnash their teeth."** Matthew 25:14-30.

The point of this story is similar to the lesson of the first one: While waiting for the Lord to come from heaven, be faithful on the earth! Don't just dream of pie in the sky, but do the job that waits nearby.

But this third parable has its own characteristic significance. The master gave *every* servant a responsibility. There's an implied promise here that any of us can double what God starts us with. There's positive indication, too, that it's not what our talents are but what we do with them that counts. The faithful two-talent man received the same reward as the faithful five-talent man.

God's kingdom will not be peopled by lazy grumblers who give their employers never an ounce of effort more than they get paid for. Picturesquely, Paul exhorts us to labor "not with eyeservice, as men-pleasers, but in singleness of heart, fearing the Lord. Whatever your task" is, he goes on, "work heartily, as serving the Lord and not men, knowing that from the Lord you will receive the inheritance as your reward; you are serving the Lord Christ." Colossians 3:22-24.

Our daily job may be making cars or houses or books or meals, but the way we go about making them is making *us*. There's more character than wood in a well-built house. There's more Christianity than flour in a sweet-smelling loaf of bread, baked with dedication for the health of our family.

If we want our children ready for the Lord's appearing, we'll encourage in them habits of industry. By stages appropriate to their ages, we'll lead them to put away their toys, make their beds, help with the dishes, mow the lawn, and paint the house. They'll probably be slow at first and awfully awkward, but they can be trained to work "heartily, as serving the Lord." As they pull blankets into place each morning, they'll be making more than beds. As they prepare meals on time, they'll be getting more ready than food.

If it isn't the number of talents that makes the difference, the man with one talent would have received the same reward as the men with two and five talents if, like them, he had doubled what he received. No doubt this is so; and every one of us has at least one talent. A person in a wheelchair thinks that we have a talent who are able to walk! A person without eyes thinks we have a talent who can see. Health, time, influence, the power of speech, even a shaky checking account, are all talents in some sense. God wants us to use them all faithfully for Him, in the service of others. I once read of a completely paralyzed Christian who found that his one talent was to pray. And pray he did, for foreign missions. As word about him spread, many thousands of dollars were contributed to mission societies in his name. If you can read this book, you have more talents than he had!

Anything we have is something we can use faithfully for Christ and for the good of others. In the process of so using it, we are preparing ourselves by His grace for His return.

Separating the Sheep From the Goats. Christ's fourth parable about preparation may be the best known of all His parables. In it, the Son of man arrives in His glory attended by all the angels. Seated on His throne, He gathers all people in front of Him and separates them as Middle East villagers still separate the sheep from the goats. In the story the sheep are assigned to His right side, the goats to His left.

"The King will say to those at his right hand, 'Come, O blessed of my Father, inherit the kingdom prepared for you from the foundation of the world; for I was hungry and you gave me food, I was thirsty and you gave me drink, I was a stranger and you welcomed me, I was naked and you clothed me, I was sick and you visited me, I was in prison and you came to me.' "

The righteous people are astonished at His praise and ask *when* they did Him such unheard of kindnesses. The King replies, **" 'Truly, I say to you, as you did it to one of the least of these my brethren, you did it to me.' "**

When parents teach children to put toys away and do family chores, they help them develop character.

Then, as we all know, the King turns to the **"goats"** and orders them to leave Him, because when they saw Him needy and hungry and in prison, they did *not* help Him. Matthew 25:31-46.

The obvious moral of this final story is that our entrance into the kingdom of heaven depends on what kind of neighbors we will make there. And the test is, What kind of neighbors have we been here?

"If any one says, 'I love God,' and hates his brother, he is a liar." 1 John 4:20. This verse was indelibly impressed on my mind when I was a child. My two brothers and I often engaged in what is politely known as sibling rivalry. Mother tried everything she knew to stop us. We were going at each other very unpleasantly one day when—for the hundredth time—she tried again. A little window in the wall of the room faced east. Mother asked, "How would you boys feel if, in the middle of a quarrel, you looked up and saw the cloud approaching with Jesus on it?" She had our attention. Then she quoted from 1 John 4:20, K.J.V., "He that loveth not his brother whom he hath seen, how can he love God whom he hath not seen?"

Mother long ago went to her rest; but each of us brothers, older today than she was then, recalls the moment vividly.

She was right, wasn't she? And so was the Bible! We cannot show our love for God except by showing it to people. Even the tithes we put into the offering at church are not sent by rocket to the throne of God; they are spent on human beings here on earth. We show our love to God by treating His children well, whatever their race, economic status, condition of health, or relative goodness or badness.

Christ's four parables about preparation teach us that the way to be ready for the kingdom of heaven is to be faithful on earth! We should use our talents, many or few, to the best of our ability in serving others. We should treat people of all kinds as if they were Christ. And we should maintain individually a spiritual walk with God.

Especially happy will be whole families who prepare this way together.

Further Interesting Reading

In Arthur S. Maxwell, *The Bible Story*, volume 8:
    "Jesus Unveils the Future," page 155.
    "Radio and Television Foreseen," page 174.
    "Ten Sleepy Girls," page 178.
In *Bible Readings for the Home*:
    "Our Lord's Great Prophecy," page 228.
In Ellen G. White, *The Desire of Ages*:
    "On the Mount of Olives," page 627.
    "The Least of These My Brethren," page 637.

Page numbers for each book refer to the large, fully illustrated edition.

Your Questions Answered

1. Did the Christians have to flee on Sabbath or in the winter? In Matthew 24:20 Jesus advised His followers to pray that their flight from Jerusalem would not have to take place on a Sabbath or in the winter. Their prayers were answered. Cestius Gallus retired from Jerusalem in November, A.D. 66 (see pages 27, 28), a month when the weather is not usually severe in that part of the world. The Christians did not need to flee in winter.

Christ's concern about the Sabbath is instructive. It indicates that He knew the Sabbath would still be in existence in A.D. 66, more than thirty years after His death. Jesus did not do away with the Ten Commandments. Said He in the Sermon on the Mount, "Think not that I have come to abolish the law and the prophets; I have come not to abolish them but to fulfil them. For truly, I say to you, till heaven and earth pass away, not an iota, not a dot, will pass from the law until all is accomplished." Matthew 5:17, 18.

2. What did Jesus mean by "this generation will not pass away"? After giving His short list of second-coming signs, Jesus said, **"Truly, I say to you, this generation will not pass away till all these things take place. Heaven and earth will pass away, but my words will not pass away."** Matthew 24:34, 35.

Jesus intended this statement to be taken seriously. Only three times during His recorded ministry did He refer to the passing away of heaven and earth. On two of these He did so to emphasize, by contrast, the enduring quality of the Ten Commandments. See Question 1, above, and Luke 16:17. The third occasion was here, in Matthew 24, when He did so to emphasize the reliability of His prediction about **"this generation."**

Almost numberless are the interpretations which commentators have attached to the term. They may perhaps be sorted into two basic understandings: (1) that a generation is a period of time, and (2) that a generation is a kind of people.

Generation as a period of time. Under the first understanding, Jesus' words in Matthew 24:34 are taken to mean that the period of time left after the appearance of the signs would be so short that people who saw them would live to see Jesus actually arrive. Similarly, a prediction that He made in Matthew 23:36 about "this generation" and the fall of Jerusalem is interpreted to mean that the period between the prediction and its fulfillment would be short enough that people alive when Jesus spoke would experience the dreadful event.

Generation as a kind of people. Surprising as it may seem, there are several Bible instances in which a generation is a kind of people. The Bible speaks, for example, of "the generation of those who seek him" (Psalm 24:6) and "the generation of the upright" (Psalm 112:2). Each of these generations is a kind of

43

good people. On the other hand, in Luke 16:8 Jesus observed that sinners are more shrewd than saints are in dealing with "their own generation," that is, with their own sinful kind of people. Elsewhere Jesus talked about an "evil and adulterous generation" (Matthew 12:39), a "generation" that wouldn't repent (Matthew 12:41), and a "generation" that refused to listen to Him (Matthew 12:42).

Conclusion. Of these two views, the second seems more probable. On further thought, it also seems more understandable. Only thirty-nine years passed between Christ's prediction in A.D. 31 and the fall of Jerusalem in A.D. 70; nonetheless, granted the shortness of life expectancy in those days, very few responsible adults who heard His prophecy can have lived to see its fulfillment. Even more difficult is locating anybody still alive who observed the astronomical second-coming signs that occurred during the eighteenth and early nineteenth centuries. See Revelation 6 and 7.

It is better to say that in Matthew 23:36 and in Matthew 24:34, 35, Jesus used **"this generation"** to denote the kind of people who resist God and reject His message. It is senseless to hope that the world will get better as time passes, for most people will continue to be rebellious against God until the second coming. The rebellious kind of people will continue till the end. See 2 Timothy 3:1-9; Revelation 16:9.

A specific possibility is that Jesus may have been referring to the Jewish people, of whose race or **"generation"** He was Himself a member. If so, He meant that the Jewish race, largely unchanged in its attitude toward Him, would continue till the end of time in spite of every form of disaster, in spite even of the fall of Jerusalem, medieval pogroms, and the Nazi Holocaust. The continuance of the Jewish people as a distinct race—or **"generation"**—is indeed one of the notable phenomena of human history.

3. Will Jesus come tonight? Gospel singers often ask, "Would your heart be right, if He came tonight?"

Jesus said in Matthew 24:14, **"This gospel of the kingdom will be preached throughout the whole world, as a testimony to all nations; and *then* the end will come."** Before we talk about Christ's coming back tonight, we ought to ask, "By tonight, will the gospel have been preached to all nations?" And before we answer this question, we need to ask what Jesus meant by the term, **"all nations."**

North Americans often think of a nation as something like Canada, the United States, or Mexico, a socio-political entity with international borders and a central government. We may forget that within, say, the United States, there are tribes of Navajo, Pueblo, Modoc, Mohave, Klamath, and other native Americans, and that the dictionary indicates that all of these tribes are nations! In Europe, Yugoslavia is made up of several ethnic groups, each of which considers itself a nation. And so on.

More important, in New Testament times the Greek word for **"nations"** in the manuscripts of Matthew 24:14 is *ethne* (from which our *ethnic* is derived). *Ethne* in Christ's day meant "nations"—but it also meant "peoples," "companies of people," "classes," "castes," and "tribes." Indeed, it often meant simply "foreigners" and in the New Testament is translated more than ninety times by the familiar word *Gentiles*.[18] See, for example, Acts 10:45 and Ephesians 2:11.

To help us intelligently grasp the scope of the Christian's missionary challenge, the Missions Advanced Research and Communication Center (MARC) in southern California has sensibly defined *nations (ethne)* as "peoples"— groups of various sizes sufficiently distinguished from all other peoples by race, language, economics, occupation, or social class as to present distinct and separate challenges to evangelism. In various annual issues of its *Unreached Peoples Directory,*[19] MARC has listed many thousands of such distinct peoples and has shown that a very large number of them are still waiting to hear the gospel of the kingdom of Christ. For example, it speaks of 3000 distinct peoples in India alone, separated from one another by language, caste, religion, or culture. Fewer than 100 of these 3000 peoples have significant numbers of Christians among them.[20]

How can they all be reached? With so many peoples yet unreached, how can we hope that Jesus will come back soon? Mass media and satellites can help, but they aren't likely to carry the gospel quickly to earth's 5390 languages and dialects. In thousands of these languages and dialects there aren't yet any Christians to make a Christian use of the media. Besides, most people would rather "see a sermon than hear one any day."

Among the professed followers of Christ, there should be a new commitment to world evangelism. If Americans, let us say, really wanted Christ to come soon, would they continue to spend six times as much on their pets as they do on missionaries?[21] Would they spend their evenings cheering football and downing beer?

First-world Christians can *give* generously of their means. They can *volunteer* to serve overseas as lay missionaries for several weeks or months, Christian craftsmen and teachers often being more welcome than ministers. Christian families—yours, for instance—can choose a particular area or tribe, find out all about it at the library, and *pray* together for its evangelization.

Meanwhile third-world Christians are reaching successfully into neighboring non-Christian peoples. To me, Billiat Sapa symbolizes the marvelous dedication of such native missionaries. Sapa was a black African and a college graduate. He and his wife agreed to pioneer for Christ in a rice-growing valley in Malawi. When the non-Christian inhabitants refused to let them live in any of their villages, he and his family lived on a platform in a tree. The rainy season swamped the rice paddies. One of the Sapas' children sickened with malaria and died. But the parents didn't turn back. Their other child died, but they didn't turn back. Sapa's wife died, but he still refused to leave. Finally the villagers became convinced that Sapa truly loved them—and that the God he loved, loved them. They let him establish several Christian schools among them.[22]

With more Christians like Billiat Sapa and with a Lord like our Christ, the gospel commission can soon be fulfilled! "Not by might, nor by power, but by my Spirit, says the Lord." Zechariah 4:6. The Holy Spirit, falling at Pentecost on 120 praying, repentant, and obedient Christians, helped them win 3,000 converts in a single day. See Acts 2:1-41. What will happen in our day when thousands of faithful, obedient, repentant Christians worldwide open their hearts fully to receive God's Spirit? See Joel 2:28, 29.

Jesus Christ may not be coming tonight, but we can confidently believe that He's coming soon.

Billiat Sapa dug a grave for his first child. Soon he dug two more graves, but he did not give up till the people let him teach them about God's love.

References

1. Josephus, *The Jewish War*, 3.63. Text and trans. in H. St. J. Thackeray, Ralph Marcus, and Louis H. Feldman, *Josephus: With an English Translation*, 9 vols., Loeb Classical Library (London: William Heinemann, 1956-1965), 2:594, 595.

2. Josephus, *War*, 2.252-265; Loeb 2:420-427.

3. Josephus, *War*, 2.409; Loeb 2:482, 483.

4. Josephus, *War*, 2.539; Loeb 2:531. Compare Josephus, *War*, 2.531, 532; Loeb 2:528, 529.

5. Josephus, *War*, 6.420-427; Loeb 3:496-499. Josephus gives the city's population at the time as 1,200,000. Modern scholars divide his calculations by a factor of three, four, or even ten. See, e.g., Joachim Jeremias, *Jerusalem in the Time of Jesus* (London: SCM Press Ltd., 1969), pp. 77-84.

6. Josephus, *War*, 6.193-213; Loeb 3:434-437.

7. Josephus, *War*, 7.3; Loeb 3:504, 505. Three towers were left standing to illustrate the one-time strength of the city's defenses, and a portion of the west wall was retained to shield the Roman garrison assigned to guard the ruins. The rest of the city and all of the temple were razed.

8. Josephus, *War*, 6.384; Loeb 3:486, 487.

9. Josephus, *War*, 2.556; Loeb 2:536, 537.

10. Josephus, *War*, 7.17, 18; Loeb 3:508-511.

11. Tertullian, *Apology*, 16; ANF 3:31.

12. Josephus, *War*, 6.316; Loeb 3:468, 469.

13. LeRoy Edwin Froom, *The Prophetic Faith of Our Fathers*, 4 vols. (Washington, D.C.: Review and Herald Publishing Assn., 1946-1954), 2:31-39.

14. *Ibid.*, p. 58.

15. *Ibid.*, pp. 87, 88, 91.

16. *Ibid.*, pp. 116-121.

17. *Ibid.*, pp. 277, 278.

18. For one discussion of *panta ta ethne* in Matthew see John P. Meier, "Nations or Gentiles in Matthew 28:19," *The Catholic Biblical Quarterly* 39 (1977):94-102, responding to an article by D. Hare and D. Harrington in the same journal 37 (1975):359-396. Meier prefers "nations" or "peoples" to any translation that might seem to exclude Jews.

19. *Unreached Peoples Directory* (Monrovia, Calif.: Missions Advanced Research and Communication Center, 1974). C. Peter Wagner and Edward R. Dayton, eds., *Unreached Peoples '79* (Elgin, Ill.: David C. Cook Publishing Co., 1978).

20. George Samuel, "Unreached Peoples: An Indian Perspective," in Wagner and Dayton, *Unreached Peoples*, p. 82.

21. Ralph D. Winter, "Penetrating the New Frontiers," in Wagner and Dayton, *Unreached Peoples*, p. 73.

22. S. G. Maxwell, *I Loved Africa* (n.p.: The author, 1975), pp. 150-156.

Part II, Revelation
Who Was John?

A Brief Sketch About His Life and Times

The book of Revelation was written by "God's servant John." See Revelation 1:1.

John was not a common name in New Testament times. There is convincing evidence that the John who wrote Revelation was the well-known disciple of Jesus. See *Your Questions Answered,* pages 63, 64. We met John most recently on the Mount of Olives, listening attentively in the evening moonlight to the Olivet Discourse. See page 15. Nine things about his life and times deserve our attention before we take up his book.

1. *Behold, the Lamb of God!* John saw Jesus for the first time standing in a crowd watching John the Baptist baptize at the River Jordan. John saw John the Baptist stop suddenly in his speech, jab his hand excitedly toward an impressive stranger, and shout like a herald, "Behold, the Lamb of God, who takes away the sin of the world!" John 1:29.[1]

The designation "Lamb of God" deeply impressed itself on John's consciousness. Every day at the temple and especially at Passover, lambs were offered to God in sacrifice for the people's sins. Convinced that Jesus was indeed God's "Lamb," John refers to Him as such twenty-nine times in Revelation.

2. *The disciple Jesus loved.* When he first saw Jesus, John can scarcely have been more than a teenager. Beside John in the crowd was his close friend, Andrew, who was Simon Peter's brother. When John the Baptist pointed out the "Lamb of God," both John and Andrew determined at once to get acquainted with Jesus. See John 1:35-40.

John's contacts with Christ appear to have been sporadic over the next several months. He probably attended the wedding feast in Cana at which Jesus turned water into wine. See John 2:1-11. Most of the time, John and his older brother James, along with Andrew and his brother Peter, spent their time fishing for a living on Lake Galilee. But when Jesus commenced an extensive tour of Galilee and invited the four young friends to quit their fishing and become "fishers of men" (Matthew 4:18-22), they left their nets and followed Him. Life was never to be the same.

Among the twelve disciples whom Jesus chose, three of these four friends, Peter, James, and John formed an inner circle. It was not that Jesus played favorites, but that these three found Him even more significant to their lives than did the other nine. Of these inner three, John in particular came to be known as "the disciple whom Jesus loved." John 20:2; 21: 7, 20.

49

John was a teenager when he heard John the Baptist call Jesus "the Lamb of God." He never forgot the marvelous meaning of that special name.

3. *Nearby at the cross*. John, along with Peter and James, was present in the bedroom when Jesus raised Jairus's little girl to life. See Luke 8:49-56. He was with Christ on the Mount of Transfiguration. See Matthew 17:1-8. He was close to Him as He prayed in Gethsemane. See Matthew 26:36-45. When the mob arrived and the other disciples fled, only Peter and John dared to follow Jesus and enter the courtyard of the palace where He was tried. See John 18:15. When even Peter lost heart and denied that he knew Jesus (see Matthew 26:69-75), John alone stayed by. John was at the cross when Jesus died. See John 19:25-27. On Resurrection Sunday, Peter and John raced each other to the empty tomb; John, sweating no doubt and out of breath, arrived there first. See John 20:1-4.

It was to John, for whom Jesus was so very dear, that God entrusted the "Revelation of Jesus Christ."

4. *"I will come again."* At the Last Supper, John shared the apprehension of the other disciples when they heard Jesus announce, "Where I am going you cannot come." John 13:33. John didn't understand where Jesus was going and couldn't bear to think about it. Nor did he understand the promise that followed, "If I go, . . . I will come again." John 14:3, K.J.V.

Exactly six weeks later, however, John learned at last what Christ's "If I go" really meant. Gathered with the other disciples as Jesus bade His final farewell, John saw Him gradually rise off the ground. He saw His feet reach the level of their waists, then soar slowly past their heads. With arms outstretched to bless and to wave good-bye, Jesus ascended still higher as the disciples strained eyes and necks to follow Him.

Then a cloud surrounded Him, and He was gone.

Almost overcome with foreboding and disconsolation, John and his friends felt hope surge again when two persons in white appeared at their sides and interrupted their anxiety. "Men of Galilee, why do you stand looking into heaven?" they asked. "This Jesus, who was taken up from you into heaven, *will come in the same way* as you saw him go into heaven." Acts 1:11.

Now John understood the words, "If I go, . . . I will come again." He also understood better what Christ had said on Olivet about the "Son of man" "coming [back] on the clouds of heaven." Matthew 24:30.

Is it any wonder that when John saw Jesus again in the first vision of Revelation, he hastened to write, "Behold, he is coming with the clouds, and every eye will see him"? Revelation 1:7. At the end of the book he prayed, "Amen. Come, Lord Jesus." Revelation 22:20.

5. *A place in the kingdom*. John and his brother James were known as Sons of Thunder. See Mark 3:17. They must have been noisy debaters. Angry young haters of Roman injustice, they were attracted to Jesus at first because they thought He was going to overthrow the Roman government. They wanted to fight with Him and then rule with Him.

They persuaded Salome, their mother, to ask Jesus to give them thrones on the right and left of His throne in His new kingdom. See Matthew 20:20, 21. Imagine how their request must have irritated the other disciples! Who did these ambitious stuck-ups think they were?

But Jesus saw love for Him in their selfish request. He didn't scold them.

He asked instead, "Are you able to drink the cup that I am to drink?" Matthew 20:22.

John and James guessed that Jesus was testing their willingness to engage in guerrilla warfare, and they eagerly responded Yes. They didn't understand that Christ's "cup" was one of self-denial. See Matthew 26:39. They didn't realize that Jesus wanted them to serve the needs of other people in a spirit of courageous humility, manly gentleness, and noble patience; that the qualification for Christ's kingdom is not eagerness for combat but willingness to share and serve and suffer and forgive and, if need be, die for the sake of others. See Matthew 25:31-46; 10:38, 39.

6. *Powerful, persecuted worker.* John said he was willing to drink the cup, and Jesus made him so. After Christ's ascent to heaven, John prayed as one of the 120 believers in the upper room until Pentecost, when the Holy Spirit in a special sense filled them all. See Acts 1:12-14; 2:1-4. He testified joyously in the streets of Jerusalem and in the temple courts. He and Peter were arrested and hailed before the authorities. When ordered to stop telling the people about Jesus, he replied with the others, "We cannot but speak of what we have seen and heard." Acts 4:20. The authorities were astonished that "uneducated, common men" could be so bold. They "recognized" that these men "had been with Jesus." Acts 4:13.

James, John's brother, was later arrested and beheaded. See Acts 12:1, 2. But John lived on to serve His master and "drink the cup" over a long and varied career. He lived in Jerusalem for a while, it appears. When Jerusalem was "surrounded by armies"

Men still fish the Lake of Galilee as John and his friends did long ago.

(Luke 21:20, see pages 27, 28), or perhaps at some unknown earlier time, he left the city to work for Christ elsewhere.

In A.D. 70, word arrived that Roman soldiers had returned to Jerusalem, and then that they had demolished the temple. What thoughts broke the heart of this man who once had offered to die in Israel's defense? John saw that Christ's kingdom was indeed "not of this world." John 18:36, K.J.V.

John, the Son of Thunder, became John, the Apostle of Love. He wrote the Gospel of John, and three of his letters also are preserved in the New Testament. The theme of love permeates them all. "Herein is love," he wrote in 1 John 4:10, "not that we loved God, but that he loved us." K.J.V. "A new commandment I give to you," he remembered Jesus saying, "that you love one another; even as I have loved you." John 13:34.

John had oil in his lamp! (See pages 39, 40.) The disciple whom Jesus loved was transformed by the Lord he loved.

7. *Fine family background.* John came from a close-knit, dedicated family. His father Zebedee taught him to work. These three men, Zebedee, James, and John, were hard at their fishnets when Jesus called the boys to follow Him. Salome the mother showed poor judgment when she asked special favors for her sons, but her willingness to go out on a limb for them says a lot about her interest in them. In fact, when the young men chose to follow Jesus, it appears that Salome went with them, joining other women who cooked and mended for Jesus and His followers. Compare Mark 15:40; Matthew 27:56; and Matthew 4:21.

Salome was with John at the cross when Jesus asked John to take care of Mary. Jesus knew He could trust His mother to a man who loved his own mother.

As long as James lived, John and he were almost inseparable companions. Sons of Thunder both of them, they must have engaged in many an angry spat. But they stuck together; and John could say later with authority, "He who does not love his brother whom he has seen, cannot love God whom he has not seen." 1 John 4:20.

8. *Course of the Roman Empire.* As near as we can tell, John was born around A.D. 10, when the great Augustus, the first Roman Emperor, was still in charge of affairs. As the years passed, imperial heralds announced successively the election of the Emperor Tiberius in A.D. 14, of the half-mad Caligula in A.D. 37, of the dull but effective Claudius in A.D. 41, and of the infamous Nero in A.D. 54.

The Emperor Nero, still in his twenties, decapitated Paul. He also set Rome on fire in an attempt to clear an area large enough for his great new palace. The fire got out of control and roared day and night until it damaged ten of Rome's fourteen districts. Hundreds of thousands of people who lost their homes and businesses were out of their minds. To pacify them, Nero arrested a batch of Christians as scapegoats and opened his private grounds for a public entertainment. The Roman historian Tacitus tells us that Nero wrapped some of the Christians in animal hides and fed them to ferocious dogs. Other Christians he crucified. Still others were set on fire to provide light at night—like street lamps.[2]

Nero died in A.D. 68. Before 69 was out, mutinous armies around the empire produced three transient emperors, Galba, Otho, and Vitellius, and a fourth emperor, Vespasian, who did very well for a decade. Prior to becoming emperor, Vespasian launched the Jewish War. When he died in 79, he was succeeded by his son Titus, who had completed the conquest of Jerusalem and was the "darling of the Romans." In 81, two years later, Titus's older brother Domitian came to power.

The Emperor Titus was charming, lucky, and successful. The Emperor Domitian was sullen, a born loser, and awkward. When Roman society refused him the respect that he felt he deserved, he declared himself divine and demanded worship. He styled himself officially as "lord" and "god." Obsequious poets in response described even the fish he ate as "sacred."[3]

Nero's persecution had touched the Christians only in Rome. Domitian's madness reached farther. Christians in many places were required by Domitian to offer incense in worship to his statue. When they refused, Domitian's governors fined, exiled, or in exceptional cases executed them. In his anger, Domitian went so far as to kill his own Christian cousin, the Consul Clemens, and to banish his cousin's Christian wife, Domitilla, to an island.[4]

John, who appears to have been living in Ephesus when Domitian began to persecute, was arrested and banished to the island of Patmos, fifty or sixty miles south of Ephesus in the Aegean Sea. A century later the Christian writer Tertullian remembered hearing that John was first punished in Rome, that he was "plunged, unhurt, into boiling oil, and thence remitted to his island-exile."[5]

John was not the only one who was persecuted. To his readers he described himself as sharing the tribulation "with you." Revelation 1:9.

Domitian's persecution commenced in 95. When the Emperor Nerva followed him to the throne in 96, it is believed that John was released in a general amnesty of Christians and that he returned to Ephesus to finish writing out the Revelation before he died.

9. *John and Daniel.* If in A.D. 27 John was around 17 years old when he heard John the Baptist call Jesus the "Lamb of God," then he was around 85 when he sat alone on Patmos, lost in the past and prepared "in the Spirit" to see the Revelation.

Daniel was approximately 17 when he was led away to Babylon and was in his late 80s when his last vision came. To both prophets were presented vast prophetic panoramas that in successive parallels traced the course of history from their own day to the end of time. Both were given messages rich in symbolism. Both called attention repeatedly to the glorious day when God will take over full management of our planet. Both were shown God's concern to stand beside us every day. Both revealed how very much God cares.

53

The Organization of Revelation

Have you ever read Revelation all the way through? Have you, perhaps, read it through many times?

Either way, the chances are that you have been deeply impressed with the book's vivid pictures and glowing promises, but that you also have come away perplexed at how to fit the pieces all together.

At first glance, and even at the fiftieth glance, Revelation seems to many readers to be the most disorganized book in the Bible. If this is the way the book seems to you, it will come as a surprise to be told that really Revelation is very beautifully organized. In fact, Revelation may be the best organized book of its size in the whole Bible!

Getting acquainted with the basic organization of Revelation will take us only about a dozen pages, and the effort to read them will be eminently worth your while. In less than fifteen minutes together we can perceive easily the intelligent symmetrical pattern that provides order to the apparent confusion. In the process of doing so, we'll gain one of the most helpful possible keys for unlocking the book's meaning. And as a bonus we'll also begin to find the answer to that often repeated question, *"How much of Revelation is still left to be fulfilled?"*

With so many rewards ahead of us, let us give a few moments' thought to the way in which Revelation is organized.

Prophets as poets. You will remember that when studying Daniel 9:24-27 we saw that Old Testament prophets were often poets. (If you *don't* remember reading this, you will find it helpful to review GC 1:210-218.) Old Testament prophets wrote in their own kind of poetry, of course, not in ours. They made use of parallels and contrasts, acrostics, chiasms, and serious puns. Sometimes they made their point by using precise numbers of words. In Daniel 9:24 we observed how three two-word phrases were linked meaningfully to three three-word phrases. We found that awareness of literary structure could definitely aid us in understanding a difficult passage.

It shouldn't be surprising that prophets were poets. Poetry takes more pains to compose than prose and when done right can be more attractive. Prophets, impressed with the importance of their message, worked hard to express it well. Besides, God, who inspired them with their message, helped them communicate it. Don't forget that at Pentecost God gave John the gift of tongues. See Acts 1:12-14; 2:1-4. No wonder he could express himself!

Revelation isn't poetry in the sense that "Mary Had a Little Lamb" and "Three Blind Mice" are poetry. It is poetry in the style of Abraham Lincoln's Gettysburg Address and Martin Luther King's "I Have a Dream." It is literary artistry. It is eloquence with shapeliness. It is inspiration expressed with order and elegance.

Numbers as motifs. Anyone reading Revelation even for the first time notices the recurrence of sevens. There are seven churches, seven angels, seven seals, seven trumpets, seven plagues, and several other sevens as well—including some unnumbered, hidden sevens. You and your family could make your own list. You could start by compiling the more obvious examples; then look for the disguised ones.

Threes, fours, and twelves also play an artistic role in Revelation. The seals and trumpets are divided into groups of three and four. See chapters 6-11. Three *multiplied* by four make up the twelve gates of the New Jerusalem. See chapter 21. Twelve tribes multiplied by 12,000 compose the 144,000 in chapter 7.

As we go along, we'll look at the internal artistry of individual passages and hymns and at the fitness of the book's dramatic symbols. But perhaps the most persuasive evidence of Revelation's literary quality is its overall organization as a chiasm.

Revelation as a chiasm.[6] A chiasm (KIE-asm) is a double list of related items in which the order of the second list is opposite to the order of the first list. You know how couples divide in an old-fashioned square dance or grand march, men and women temporarily taking off in opposite directions. Such entertainment chiasms are still fun. In Bible times, literary chiasms were very popular and were much admired. (You may wish to review our discussion of them in GC 1:213, 255-257, 306.)

If we divide Revelation at the end of chapter 14 into two not-quite-equal *halves*, and if we divide each half into several *divisions*, we find that the divisions from each half can be arranged in pairs which (like the man-woman couples at our square dance or grand march) are related to each other but yet are different, while proceeding in different directions. See the chart on pages 60, 61.

Repeating "I Have a Dream" elevated Martin Luther King's Lincoln Memorial speech into a poem that changed America. Bible writers also used sublime poetry!

PROLOGUE (1:1-8) Introduction	EPILOGUE (22:8-17) Conclusion
Testimony of Jesus. 1:2	I, Jesus, sent this testimony. 22:16
Blessed is he who reads. 1:3	Blessed is he who keeps. 22:7
Behold, He is coming. 1:7	Behold, I am coming soon. 22:12, 20
I am the Alpha and the Omega. 1:8	I am the Alpha and the Omega. 22:13

The easiest way to get acquainted with the Revelation chiasm is to start with the introduction to the book, the prologue, and with the conclusion, or epilogue. Comparing the two, you can easily find several strikingly similar phrases and sentences that occur in each of them.

The similarities are not slavishly precise. For instance, there is a warning in the epilogue that isn't found in the prologue; and Christ's promise to come again is found twice in the epilogue, but in the prologue only once. We are dealing with literary similarities, not mechanical ones. Great writers follow a method but never let their method become more important than their message.

Many commentators have noticed the close relationship that exists between the first division after the introduction and the last division before the conclusion. The first division contains the letters to the seven churches (1:10 to 3:22) and the last division describes New Jerusalem (21:9 to 22:9). Glance over each of them. In the first one, you'll see God's church scattered in seven symbolic cities, severely tempted and persecuted. In the last division, you'll find God's church resettled unitedly in a single city, glorious New Jerusalem. In the first division the church wages war with sin on this present earth. In the final division, it lives in peace and goodness, at home with God on the future new earth. Again, as in the prologue and the epilogue, strikingly similar phrases and sentences occur in the two divisions. Among other similar expressions are references to the tree of life, to an open door (and to gates that never shut), and to New Jerusalem coming down from heaven.

Incidentally, don't be worried because our "divisions" don't line up with the chapters. The chapters in Revelation were not determined by John. They didn't appear in their present form until more than a thousand years after John's death. The chapter arrangement of Revelation, though useful in certain ways, is not inspired. See *Your Questions Answered,* pages 66, 67.

Moving to the next division after the seven churches we come to the seven seals (4:1 to 8:1). Moving backward from the New Jerusalem division we come to the millennium and the events surrounding it (19:11 to 21:8). Look especially at 6:9, 10 in the seven seals.

7 CHURCHES (1:10 to 3:22)	NEW JERUSALEM (21:9 to 22:9)
Christ Counsels His Church, at War, Scattered in Many Cities	*Christ Rewards His Church, at Peace, Gathered Into One City*
Christ walks among seven lamps. 2:1	Christ is the eternal Lamp. 21:23
Tree of life. 2:7	Tree of life. 22:2
Open door. 3:8	Gates never closed 21:25
Christ sits on His Father's throne. 3:21	Throne of God and of the Lamb. 22:1, 3
New Jerusalem comes down from heaven. 3:12	New Jerusalem comes down from heaven. 21:10
I am coming soon. 3:11	I am coming soon. 22:7

There you'll hear the souls of the persecuted martyrs pleading with God to judge their enemies. During the millennium, the martyrs, now resurrected from the dead, are placed on thrones and appointed by God (20:4) to judge their enemies! Both of these divisions begin with a reference to

7 SEALS (4:1 to 8:1)	MILLENNIUM (19:11 to 21:8)
Christ Shields His Afflicted People	*Christ Enthrones His Resurrected People*
Heaven opened. 4:1	Heaven opened. 19:11
Rider on white horse followed by riders on colored horses. 6:2-8	Rider on white horse followed by riders on white horses. 19:11-16
Souls of martyrs, under altar, ask for judgment. 6:9, 10	Souls of martyrs, resurrected, are enthroned as judges. 20:4-6
White robes. 6:11; 7:9-14	White robes 19:14
Kings, generals, etc., ask to be killed. 6:15, 16	Kings, captains, etc., are killed. 19:17-21

heaven's being opened. In both of them, a rider on a white horse is prominent. And in both divisions, kings, military officers, and people of all other classes ask to be killed or are actually killed at the second coming.

Moving still nearer the middle of the book, we find perhaps the most striking case of a chiastic couple. The seven trumpets (8:2 to 11:18) and the seven last plagues (15:1 to 16:21) are in some ways very different. They especially differ in their intensity, the plagues being much worse than the trumpets. But look at them a little closer. You'll find that five of the first six trumpets and five of the first six plagues affect principally the same objects in the same order: earth, sea, rivers, heavenly bodies, and the River Euphrates! The seven trumpets represent severe judgments sent to warn the wicked to change their ways. The seven last plagues represent very severe judgments sent to punish the wicked after they refuse to change their ways.

In the chart on this page, the seven trumpets and the seven last plagues are coupled to boxes labeled "Great Controversy" and "Fall of Babylon." There is a reason for this. Fascinatingly, right after reading about the seven trumpets, we find ourselves reading about a woman dressed in white, a true mother whose children keep God's commandments; and immediately after reading about the seven last plagues we find ourselves reading about a woman dressed in purple, a harlot whose children are also harlots. Both women spend some time in a wilderness. Both women have to deal with a beast that has seven heads and ten horns. In each of these divisions—and nowhere else in Revelation—we hear the mystic cry, "Fallen, fallen is Babylon the great!"

We now need a master chart that puts our individual charts all together. You'll find just such a chart on pages 60, 61, arranged so as to reveal the symmetry or chiastic organization of the whole book. To get the benefit of

7 TRUMPETS (8:2 to 11:18)	GREAT CONTROVERSY (11:19 to 14:20)	7 LAST PLAGUES (15:1 to 16:21)	FALL OF BABYLON (17:1 to 19:10)
Severe Judgments Warn the World		*Very Severe Judgments Punish the World*	
1. Earth. 8:7		1. Earth. 16:2	
2. Sea. 8:8, 9		2. Sea. 16:3	
3. Rivers and fountains. 8:10, 11		3. Rivers and fountains. 16:4	
4. Sun, moon, stars. 8:12		4. Sun. 16:8, 9	
5. Darkness, bottomless pit, locusts. 9:1-11		5. Darkness on throne of the beast. 16:10, 11	
6. River Euphrates 9:13-21		6. River Euphrates. 16:12, 16	
7. Loud voices: The kingdom is Christ's! 11:15-18		7. A loud voice: It is done! 16:17-21	

the chart, read down the left half toward the middle of Revelation. Then read up the right half, toward the end of it. At the same time, send your eyes back and forth across the chart to take in the similarities and contrasts that make the items pairs.

Rewards from our literary analysis. We promised ourselves on page 54 that our study of Revelation's organization would help us "begin" to answer the often repeated question, "How much of Revelation is still unfulfilled?"

How much *is* still future? Well, the chiastic outline shows that virtually all of the second half is still future. Certainly the descent of New Jerusalem to the new earth is future. Certainly the millennium is future. Certainly the seven last plagues are future. Certainly future, also, is the ultimate fall of spiritual Babylon. So the second half of Revelation is virtually all still future.

But what about the first half? When the letters to the seven churches were written, Christians were scattered in many cities. Christians are still scattered today. Many commentators agree that the letters to the seven churches are related to the experience of the church as a whole throughout the Christian era. The great controversy scenes of chapters 12-14 begin with Christ's birth (12:1, 2, 5), continue with the long period of persecution (12:6, 13-16; 13:5-8) that Daniel 7 and 8 predicted, and end with the second coming (14:14-20). Thus the great controversy scenes which close the first half of Revelation cover the history of the Christian church. The seven seals and the seven trumpets parallel the seven churches and the great controversy scenes (just as in Daniel, the visions of chapters 2, 7, 8, and 9 parallel each other. See GC 1:106, 250).

The chiastic structure of Revelation thus divides the prophecies of the book into two major groups, those that deal almost exclusively with last-day events (the second half of the

7 TRUMPETS (8:2 to 11:18)	GREAT CONTROVERSY (11:19 to 14:20)	7 LAST PLAGUES (15:1 to 16:21)	FALL OF BABYLON (17:1 to 19:10)
	Trials of the True Mother & Her Children		*Downfall of the False Mother*
	True mother, dressed in white. 12:1, 2		False mother, dressed in purple. 17:4
	Her children keep the commandments. 12:17		Her children are harlots. 17:5
	Woman in wilderness. 12:14		Woman in wilderness. 17:3
	Beast with 7 heads, 10 horns. 12:3; 13:1		Beast with 7 heads, 10 horns. 17:3
	Fallen is Babylon! 14:8		Fallen is Babylon! 18:2
	Testimony of Jesus. 12:17, K.J.V.		Testimony of Jesus. 19:10

GOD CARES

THE MIRRORLIKE ORGANIZATION

7 CHURCHES
(1:10 to 3:22)

Christ Counsels His Church, at War, Scattered in Many Cities

Christ walks among seven lamps. 2:1

Tree of life. 2:7

Open door. 3:8

Christ sits on His Father's throne. 3:21

New Jerusalem comes down from heaven. 3:12

I am coming soon. 3:11

7 SEALS
(4:1 to 8:1)

Christ Shields His Afflicted People

Heaven opened. 4:1

Rider on white horse followed by riders on colored horses. 6:2-8

Souls of martyrs, under altar, ask for judgment. 6:9, 10

White robes. 6:11; 7:9-14

Kings, generals, etc., ask to be killed. 6:15, 16

7 TRUMPETS
(8:2 to 11:18)

Severe Judgments Warn the World

1. Earth. 8:7

2. Sea. 8:8, 9

3. Rivers and fountains. 8:10, 11

4. Sun, moon, stars. 8:12

5. Darkness, bottomless pit, locusts. 9:1-11

6. River Euphrates 9:13-21

7. Loud voices: The kingdom is Christ's! 11:15-18

GREAT CONTROVERSY
(11:19 to 14:20)

Trials of the True Mother & Her Children

True mother, dressed in white. 12:1, 2

Her children keep the commandments. 12:17

Woman in wilderness. 12:14

Beast with 7 heads, 10 horns. 12:3; 13:1

Fallen is Babylon! 14:8

Testimony of Jesus. 12:17, K.J.V.

Prologue and Epilogue omitted for simplicity

HISTORICAL HALF

The Great Controversy in Progress

Based in general, though not in detail, on the excellent work of Kenneth Strand

Get acquainted with this chart! We will meet it again! As we move through Revelation, various parts will be enlarged and colored to show how each section fits with the rest. See, for example, pages 92 and 148.

book) and those that deal with the experience of God's people during the Christian era (the first half of the book). We may call the first half of the book historical and the second half eschatological. *Eschatological* (es-kat-uh-LOJ-i-kul) comes from a Greek word, *eschaton*, that means "end." It is used quite commonly by laity as well as scholars. It means, "Having to do with the end of the world."

But not all of the historical half of the book has happened yet. Not all of Christian history has happened yet! The seventh seal, the seventh trumpet,

and the final scene in the great controversy division still await their fulfillment. We have already seen that the second half of Revelation is eschatological. We can now say that each division even of the first or historical half of Revelation climaxes in an eschatological development. (In the chart on the next page, arrows indicate the flow of events.)

So, how much of Revelation is still future? Virtually all of the second, eschatological half is as yet unfulfilled. In addition, the final scene in each division of the first, historical half of the

OF THE BOOK OF REVELATION

7 LAST PLAGUES (15:1 to 16:21)	FALL OF BABYLON (17:1 to 19:10)	MILLENNIUM (19:11 to 21:8)	NEW JERUSALEM (21:9 to 22:9)
Very Severe Judgments Punish the World	*Downfall of the False Mother*	*Christ Enthrones His Resurrected People*	*Christ Rewards His Church, at Peace, Gathered Into One City*
1. Earth. 16:2	False mother, dressed in purple. 17:4	Heaven opened. 19:11	Christ is the eternal Lamp. 21:23
2. Sea. 16:3	Her children are harlots. 17:5	Rider on white horse followed by riders on white horses. 19:11-16	Tree of life. 22:2
3. Rivers and fountains. 16:4	Woman in wilderness. 17:3	Souls of martyrs, resurrected, are enthroned as judges. 20:4-6	Gates never closed 21:25
4. Sun. 16:8, 9			Throne of God and of the Lamb. 22:1, 3
5. Darkness on throne of the beast. 16:10, 11	Beast with 7 heads, 10 horns. 17:3	White robes 19:14	New Jerusalem comes down from heaven. 21:10
6. River Euphrates. 16:12, 16	Fallen is Babylon! 18:2	Kings, captains, etc., are killed. 19:17-21	I am coming soon. 22:7
7. A loud voice: It is done! 16:17-21	Testimony of Jesus. 19:10		

← ESCHATOLOGICAL HALF →

The Great Controversy Consummated

book is likewise unfulfilled or as yet partly unfulfilled.

The internal arrangement of the divisions. Before we leave our study of the organization of Revelation for the time being, there is one more basic literary feature that we really must take notice of. Four of the divisions we have been talking about follow an almost identical internal arrangement. Each one begins with a preparatory scene portraying something in the heavenly sanctuary. Each one also has an interruption between items six and seven; that is, between the sixth and the seventh seals, the sixth and the seventh trumpets, the sixth and the seventh scenes in the great controversy, and between the sixth and the seventh plagues there occur parenthetical scenes that we may call "scenes of end-time assignment and assurance."

We mentioned on page 56 that great writers follow a system when they write, but they don't allow their system to become more important than their message. In Revelation, John arranged beautifully the information God showed him in vision, but he provided slots of space (between items six and seven) for pieces of inspired information that didn't readily fit anywhere else. His arrangement for the four divisions we're discussing looks like this:

1. Introductory scene about the heavenly sanctuary.

2. Six of seven items (seals, trumpets, etc.).

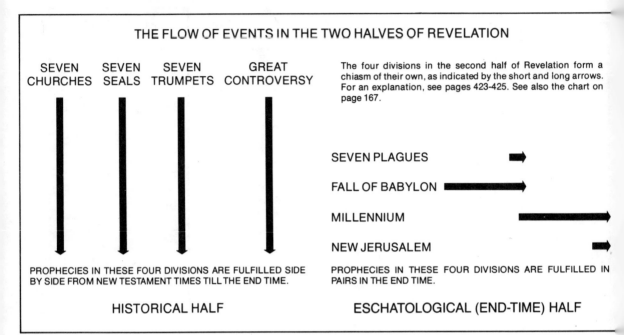

THE FLOW OF EVENTS IN THE TWO HALVES OF REVELATION

SEVEN CHURCHES	SEVEN SEALS	SEVEN TRUMPETS	GREAT CONTROVERSY

The four divisions in the second half of Revelation form a chiasm of their own, as indicated by the short and long arrows. For an explanation, see pages 423-425. See also the chart on page 167.

SEVEN PLAGUES

FALL OF BABYLON

MILLENNIUM

NEW JERUSALEM

PROPHECIES IN THESE FOUR DIVISIONS ARE FULFILLED SIDE BY SIDE FROM NEW TESTAMENT TIMES TILL THE END TIME.

PROPHECIES IN THESE FOUR DIVISIONS ARE FULFILLED IN PAIRS IN THE END TIME.

HISTORICAL HALF

ESCHATOLOGICAL (END-TIME) HALF

Events described in the first half of Revelation span twenty centuries. Events in the second half occur in a brief period near the end.

3. Parenthetical scenes of end-time assignment and assurance.

4. The seventh item (seal, trumpet, etc.).

Dazzling pictures of God's throne, of the saints in glory, and of other impressive concepts occur throughout Revelation, seemingly at random, haphazardly, without apparent relation to what is said immediately before or after. But this simple outline takes care of many such matters. With its help, along with the help of the larger charts we have made, we are able to perceive at once where such appar-

ently random scenes belong. Time and again we're going to feel grateful to the Bible commentators who noticed this arrangement and called it to our attention. It is immensely helpful, as we shall discover from time to time. See especially our discussion of it on pages 164-167.

Revelation is a book of internal artistry inspired by God and composed with loving and intelligent devotion. Even the *form* in which God and God's man John delivered it to us helps confirm our conviction that God cares.

Your Questions Answered

1. Can we be sure that it was John the Apostle who wrote Revelation? Some writers have questioned whether the John who wrote Revelation was the disciple and apostle of Jesus or some other John. They point out (a) that the style of Greek in Revelation is different from the style in the Gospel and letters of John and (b) that the question about the identity of John began to be raised as early as the third century.

In response it can be said, (a) Yes, the Greek in Revelation is different from the Greek in John's Gospel and letters. The Gospel and letters are so grammatically pure that they are widely used as a basis for teaching Greek to seminary students. Revelation, on the other hand, is comparatively colloquial. However, R. H. Charles,[7] a noted scholar, has shown that Revelation is not so much ungrammatical as it is unconventional, with its own inner grammatical consistency. John cites the Old Testament several hundred times. Charles and others have pointed out that in doing so John, instead of using the Septuagint (LXX), the standard Greek translation of his day, preferred to work directly from the original Hebrew or from popular Aramaic translations (called Targums). So John was constantly adapting Greek to the sound of Hebrew and Aramaic. It has also been pointed out by various scholars that certain early accounts such as the second-century Muratorian Canon[8] suggest that when writing his Gospel and letters John had the help of literary assistants who may have helped him polish his Greek, but when he wrote Revelation, he didn't have their assistance.

Balancing the linguistic differences between Revelation and John's Gospel are some striking similarities, the most notable of which is the use of *Lamb* as a designation for Jesus, which occurs twenty-nine times in Revelation but nowhere else in the New Testament except in John 1:29, 36.

Although a question about John's authorship did arise in the third century, the Greek-speaking Christians who lived closest to the time and place where Revelation was written accepted the book enthusiastically as coming from the apostle John.

Justin Martyr lived in Ephesus around A.D. 135. Some years later he attributed Revelation to "a certain man . . . whose name was John, one of the apostles of Christ."[9]

Irenaeus, a church leader in France (Gaul) near the end of the second century, lived as a boy in the Roman province of Asia and knew Polycarp, then an old man who in his youth had been a friend of John.[10] Like Justin, Irenaeus spoke of the author of Revelation as John, "the Lord's disciple." He stated that John saw the "apocalyptic vision" "no very long time since, but almost in our day, towards the end of Domitian's reign."[11]

Clement, who conducted a Christian school in Alexandria, Egypt, about the

63

time Irenaeus labored in France, also indicated that it was the "apostle John" who was on Patmos. He added that after the emperor's death, John returned to Ephesus and then traveled wldely, ordaining ministers and organizing new congregations.[12] Hippolytus, too, a learned church officer who lived near Rome in the first half of the third century, taught that Revelation was written by "blessed John, apostle and disciple of the Lord."[13]

Thus the Christians who lived nearest to Revelation in time and place believed firmly that it came from the hand of the apostle John.

Furthermore, the author of Revelation identified himself simply as "I John, your brother." Revelation 1:9. He knew that he was sufficiently well known that he would not be confused with any other John.

In any case, whoever John was, his message came from God by the Holy Spirit and was a revelation of Jesus Christ. See Revelation 1:1. The John who received this message was inspired.

2. How and when did Revelation get its chapters and verses? The sixty-six books of the Bible were not originally written with the numbered verses that we know today. This is understandable. Most books don't have numbered verses.

But although most modern books do at least have chapters, most ancient books did not have chapters; and neither did the Bible. In ancient times the book of Psalms, of course, was divided up pretty much as we have it today; but the psalms are not chapters. They are individual poems.

The Bible has been studied as no other book, because it has been valued as no other book. Consequently, several different systems have been devised over the centuries to help people find the passages they are looking for.

The verses in the Old Testament as we know them today are the work of a number of different Jewish rabbis, especially of the Masoretic rabbis, or Masoretes, who perfected the art of copying manuscripts. The Masoretic family of Ben Asher standardized the Old Testament versification into 23,100 verses around the year A.D. 900.

Our New Testament versification, a modification of several previous systems, is the work of Robert Stephens. In 1551 Stephens was preparing a concordance to a Greek and Latin printed New Testament, and he needed a precise way to refer readers from his concordance to his New Testament. His son says that he divided up and numbered the verses while traveling on a journey from Paris to Lyons, a circumstance that may explain the strangeness of a few of his verse divisions.

But what about the chapters? The founding of the University of Paris in the 1100s led to a surge of interest in Bible study. Numerous hand-written copies of the Catholic Latin Bible were made and sold to help meet the demand. Further to facilitate Bible study at such a time, Stephen Langton, when he was a professor at the University of Paris, established the chapters that we have today, in the book of Revelation as well as in the rest of the Bible.

Stephen Langton was an Englishman. After leaving Paris he became the Roman Catholic Archbishop of Canterbury who helped compel King John to sign the Magna Carta at Runnymede in 1215. He died in 1228.

Revelation was written about A.D. 95. Thus the chapters in our versions today did not exist until some 1100 years after Revelation was written. The present verses did not appear until more than 1450 years after Revelation was written.[14]

References

1. John the Apostle doesn't actually state that he was present at John the Baptist's preaching, but the inference that he is the unnamed disciple of verses 35-40 is clear. Humility was characteristic of the man. Note how he avoids naming himself in connection with the Last Supper, the trial of Christ, and the resurrection. See John 13:23; 18:15; 20:2-5.

2. Tacitus, *Annals*, 15.44.2-8.

3. Dio Cassius, *Epitome,* 67.14. See Donald McFayden, "The Occasion of the Domitianic Persecution," *The American Journal of Theology* 24 (January, 1920):46-66.

4. *Ibid.*

5. Tertullian, *On Prescription Against Heretics,* 36; ANF 3:260. One wonders how boiling oil can have avoided catching fire, an eventuality Tertullian would have mentioned had it occurred. Perhaps the oil was only heated to a murderous temperature. In any case, we recall that God delivered Daniel's friends from a fiery furnace. See Daniel 3.

6. For many insights expressed in the ensuing discussion about Revelation I am especially indebted to Kenneth A. Strand, *Interpreting the Book of Revelation,* rev. and enl. ed. (Naples, Florida: Ann Arbor Publishers, Inc., 1970, 1972, 1976, 1979). I have departed from Strand only in a number of details.

7. R. H. Charles, *A Critical and Exegetical Commentary on the Revelation of St. John,* 2 vols., The International Critical Commentary (Edinburgh: T. & T. Clark, 1920), 1:cxvii-clix, esp. pp. cxlii-cxliv.

8. The Muratorian Canon is available in various works, such as Daniel J. Theron, *Evidence of Tradition* (Grand Rapids, Mich.: Baker Book House, 1958), pp. 106-113. It claims that John wrote his Gospel with other disciples reviewing it. On pp. 32, 33, Theron gives in addition an anonymous source that says that Papias of Hierapolis "wrote the Gospel correctly, while John dictated it."

9. Justin, *Dialogue With Trypho, a Jew,* 81; ANF 1:240.

10. Irenaeus, *Against Heresies*, 3.3.4; ANF 1:416.

11. Irenaeus, *Against Heresies*, 4.20.11, 5.30.3; ANF 1:491, 558-560.

12. Clement of Alexandria, *Who Is the Rich Man That Shall Be Saved?* 42; ANF 2:603.

13. Hippolytus, *Christ and Antichrist*, 36; ANF 5:211.

14. See, for example, F. F. Bruce, *The Books and the Parchments*, 3d ed., rev. (London: Pickering & Inglis, Ltd., 1963), pp. 120, 121; Ira Maurice Price, rev. by William A. Irwin and Allen P. Wikgren, *The Ancestry of Our English Bible* (New York: Harper & Row, 1956), pp. 184, 185, 203; E. Nestle, "Bible Text," section III, *The New Schaff-Herzog Encyclopedia of Religious Knowledge* (1963 reprint), 2:113-115.

Revelation 1

The Revelation of Jesus Christ

Introduction

The first sentence in the last book of the Bible calls the book **"The Revelation of Jesus Christ."**

It is a "revelation." The book is not a "hiding" or a "mystery," as some people have supposed. The underlying Greek word is *apocalypsis*, from which we get *Apocalypse*, the name given to Revelation in many Bibles. Plainly and simply, the word *apocalypsis* means a "disclosure," an "uncovering," a "revelation."

Many people equate the word *apocalypse* with cataclysm and disaster, a nuclear holocaust, for instance, or World War III. But in the Bible *the* Apocalypse is a revealing of *Jesus Christ*. The book of Revelation provides behind-the-scenes accounts of what Jesus has been doing, is now doing, and will do in the future on behalf of human beings.

How did *apocalypse* get its doomsday connotation? From the fact that Revelation does speak colorfully of human disasters. But it talks of these disasters primarily in order to reveal that in all of them God is at work to comfort and deliver everyone who believes in Him. God cares.

Revelation 1:1 says that *God* gave this revelation of Jesus, and that *Jesus* sent it by His *angel* to His servant *John*. John wrote it out (verse 2) and pronounced a blessing (verse 3) on the person who would **"read"** *the Revelation* **"aloud,"** and on *those who would* **"hear"** *it read and who would* **"keep"** what it says. Verse 10 adds that John was **"in the Spirit"** when the revelation came to him.

The angel was undoubtedly Gabriel, the same great friendly being who gave Daniel the grand prophecies of Daniel 8 and 9 and who came to Mary to announce the birth of Jesus. See Daniel 8:16; 9:21; Luke 1:26.

Mention of the person who reads the revelation aloud reminds us that before the invention of printing, when books were scarce and many people were unable to read, the Scriptures were read aloud extensively at meetings. Jesus read the Bible aloud in Nazareth (see Luke 4:16-20), and the custom prevailed in all Jewish congregations in New Testament times (see Acts 15:21). It still prevails in many Christian churches.

So here is the chain of communication:

From God
to Jesus
by the ministry of an angel
to John
in the Spirit
to the reader
to the obedient listener.

The Trinity and heaven's highest angel of prophecy were concerned to reveal to each of us something of vast importance about our Lord.

67

John was in his eighties when Roman soldiers led him onto Patmos—where he soon saw Jesus as God's Lamb standing by God's throne.

JOHN STEEL, ARTIST, © 1985 PPPA

"To his servant John." When John sat on the Mount of Olives, listening to Jesus give the Olivet Discourse in the evening moonlight (see pages 14, 15, above), he probably was a very young man, as Daniel too had been a very young man when he was led away captive to Babylon. Now, like Daniel at the end of his book, John at the end of the Bible is a very old man and a captive. See page 53.

John addresses his book to **"the seven churches that are in Asia."** He adds, *"Grace* **to you and** *peace* **from him who is and who was and who is to come, and from the seven spirits who are before his throne, and from Jesus Christ."** Verses 4, 5.

In Bible times, Christian letters did not begin with "Dear Jane" or "Dear Sir." Paul, Peter—and John himself—employed the Christian greeting, "Grace and peace." See Romans 1:7; 1 Peter 1:2; 2 John 1:3. "Grace" is God's kindness. "Peace" comes to us when we believe that God, in His kindness, is forgiving us. We also experience peace when we let Him help us forgive our enemies. It is wonderful to be at peace with people whom we have forgiven and with God, who has forgiven us.

Grace and peace are first of all gifts from *God*—and we know that in verse 4 it is God, the eternal Father, who **"is and who was and who is to come."**

"The seven spirits." The phrase in verse 4 **"the seven spirits who are before his throne"** belongs among the frequent references to "seven" that we find in Revelation. We have already noticed that the book is addressed to seven churches (verse 4). Before the chapter is out we will read of seven golden lampstands (verses 12 and 20) and of seven stars (verses 16 and 20). Elsewhere in the book we'll read of a beast with seven heads (13:1), of a dragon with seven crowned heads (12:3), and of seven "mountains" (17:9) that are really seven "kings" (17:10). Major divisions of Revelation deal with the seven churches we have already mentioned (chapters 2, 3), with seven seals (4:1 to 8:1), with seven trumpets (8:2 to 11:18), with seven scenes in the great controversy (11:19 to 14:20), and with the seven last plagues (chapters 15, 16).

With so many sevens in the book, we sense that "seven" represents fullness, completion, and perfection. And as for the **"seven spirits who are before his throne,"** we can conclude that they represent symbolically the completeness and perfection of the Holy Spirit. (Thus all the members of the Trinity not only bring us Revelation but also greet and bless us.) The prophet Isaiah, whose book was not based on the number seven, referred to the Holy Spirit under six of His divine attributes, namely

the spirit of wisdom and understanding,
the spirit of counsel and might,
the spirit of knowledge and the fear [reverence] of the Lord.
Isaiah 11:2

Characteristics of the book. The multiple use of seven is in keeping with the generally *symbolic nature* of the book. Beasts and horns, crowns and women, lampstands and olive trees, locusts swarming from a bottomless pit, and, supremely, the dragon and the Lamb, are only a few of the cartoonlike symbols of this fascinating masterpiece.

In analyzing Revelation, our previous study of the numerous symbols in Daniel will stand us in good stead, for Revelation is *deeply rooted in Daniel*. It is also deeply rooted in the other books of the *Old Testament*. Someone has calculated that of the 404 verses in Revelation, 278 contain material from the Old Testament. A fellow teacher of mine says he has counted 600 words and phrases adapted from the Old Testament. An advanced student says he has found 1000. The links between Revelation and the Old Testament are very important to the understanding of its message.

Revelation is without doubt a book of *predictions*. But there has been misunderstanding here. Some people (futurists) have concluded that it is almost exclusively composed of prophecies still future to our day. On the other hand, other people (preterists) have contended that it gives account only of events contem-

porary to the apostle John. In between are the people (historicists) who believe that John indeed spoke of scenes in his own day, but that he also spoke of events yet future in our day, and that, in addition, he was inspired to foresee the experience of the Christian church throughout all history in between.

This third group (the historicists) must be right—for John's commission was to write **"what *is* [in his own day] and what is to take place *hereafter* [in the future after his day]."** Revelation 1:19. The book cannot have been devoted entirely to the distant future, for the very first verse of the very first chapter says that the Revelation was given in order to show **"what must *soon* take place."** Verse 3 adds, **"The time is near."**

Some things, but by no means all things, in the book were **"near"** and

Christians long ago studied Revelation as avidly as we do today.

"**soon to take place**" in John's day. Some later things would follow the soon things, and other more distant events would follow those later things in their turn. Revelation is not an agglomeration of events exploding in an instant like a classroom of children when the teacher leaves the room. Certainly the events at the *end* of the thousand years of Revelation 20 will occur a thousand years later than events at the beginning of it!

When Revelation 1:1-3 speaks of things that are "**soon**" and "**near,**" it is referring to the beginning of the fulfillment of the predictions found in the book. In John's day these prophecies were straining at the leash, eager to get started on their long journey through history. Daniel, we found, was shown a series of prophecies each of which began in his own day and ran parallel to each other through history. In Revelation also, several lines of prophecy follow a similar parallel course from John's day to the end.

If Revelation is a book of predictions, it is also a book of *great songs*, some sublimely happy, some almost unbelievably sad. Handel drew inspiration for his *Messiah* from Revelation 19:6, K.J.V., for example, "Allelulia: for the Lord God omnipotent reigneth." There's a hint of a hymn even in the very first chapter that we are looking at now.

To him who loves us
  and has freed us from our sins
    by his blood
and made us a kingdom,
  priests to his God and Father,
to him be glory
  and dominion for ever and ever.
  Amen.
        Verses 6, 7

Revelation is also a book of *blessings*. *Blessing* means the same as *beatitude,* and it has been observed that there are seven "blessings" in Revelation, just as there are nine "beatitudes" in the Sermon on the Mount. See Matthew 5:1-12. *There* we read of blessings for the poor and the pure and the persecuted. *Here* we read of blessings promised to everyone who dies in the Lord (14:13), is awake (16:15), who is invited to the marriage supper (19:9), who comes up from the grave in the first resurrection (20:6), who keeps the words of this book (22:7), and who washes his robe (22:14). The *first* of these seven blessings occurs in the chapter we are now discussing: "**Blessed is he who reads aloud the words of the prophecy, and blessed are those who hear, and who keep what is written therein.**" Verse 3.

The first chapter is printed in full on the next two pages. Let us read it with a prayer and begin at once to find the blessing Revelation has in store.

THE REVELATION TO JOHN

THE PREFACE AND JOHN'S GREETINGS

REVELATION 1

The preface and first beatitude. 1 The revelation of Jesus Christ, which God gave him to show to his servants what must soon take place; and he made it known by sending his angel to his servant John, [2]who bore witness to the word of God and to the testimony of Jesus Christ, even to all that he saw. [3]Blessed is he who reads aloud the words of the prophecy, and blessed are those who hear, and who keep what is written therein; for the time is near.

John's greetings and praise. 4 John to the seven churches that are in Asia:

Grace to you and peace from him who is and who was and who is to come, and from the seven spirits who are before his throne, [5]and from Jesus Christ the faithful witness, the first-born of the dead, and the ruler of kings on earth.

To him who loves us and has freed us from our sins by his blood [6]and made us a kingdom, priests to his God and Father, to him be glory and dominion for ever and ever. Amen. [7]Behold, he is coming with the clouds, and every eye will see him, every one who pierced him; and all tribes of the earth will wail on account of him. Even so. Amen.

8 "I am the Alpha and the Omega," says the Lord God, who is and who was and who is to come, the Almighty.

SANCTUARY SCENE INTRODUCES THE LETTERS TO THE SEVEN CHURCHES

John on Patmos sees Jesus among the seven lampstands. 9 I John, your brother,

Obedient to the angel's instructions, John faithfully recorded what he was shown so that we could read and learn how much God cares.

who share with you in Jesus the tribulation and the kingdom and the patient endurance, was on the island called Patmos on account of the word of God and the testimony of Jesus. [10]I was in the Spirit on the Lord's day, and I heard behind me a loud voice like a trumpet [11]saying, "Write what you see in a book and send it to the seven churches, to Ephesus and to Smyrna and to Pergamum and to Thyatira and to Sardis and to Philadelphia and to Laodicea."

12 Then I turned to see the voice that was speaking to me, and on turning I saw seven golden lampstands, [13]and in the midst of the lampstands one like a son of man, clothed with a long robe and with a golden girdle round his breast; [14]his head and his hair were white as white wool, white as snow; his eyes were like a flame of fire, [15]his feet were like burnished bronze, refined as in a furnace, and his voice was like the sound of many waters; [16]in his right hand he held seven stars, from his mouth issued a sharp two-edged sword, and his face was like the sun shining in full strength.

17 When I saw him, I fell at his feet as though dead. But he laid his right hand upon me, saying, "Fear not, I am the first and the last, [18]and the living one; I died, and behold I am alive for evermore, and I have the keys of Death and Hades. [19]Now write what you see, what is and what is to take place hereafter. [20]As for the mystery of the seven stars which you saw in my right hand, and the seven golden lampstands, the seven stars are the angels of the seven churches and the seven lampstands are the seven churches.

The Message of Revelation 1

I. Jesus Has the "Keys of Death"

My mother suffered many years with the creeping paralysis of Parkinson's disease. Toward the end she couldn't feed herself, and my father often visited the convalescent home to attend her. On the evening after the phone call that said she had passed away, I knelt at my bed and read anew God's promises about the resurrection. I was comforted by promises like these:

"The hour is coming when all who are in the tombs will hear his voice and come forth." John 5:28, 29.

"As in Adam all die, so also in Christ shall all be made alive." 1 Corinthians 15:22.

"The Lord himself will descend from heaven . . . and the dead in Christ will rise." 1 Thessalonians 4:16.

"He will wipe away every tear from their eyes, and death shall be no more." Revelation 21:4.

How I wished such promises could be fulfilled right away. How I wish, as I write these lines, that they could be fulfilled now, before any more loved ones pass away.

On the bleak and rocky island of Patmos, John must have been wrapped in similar contemplation. Sixty-five years had passed since the day when Jesus ascended to heaven on a cloud and the angels promised that He would return on a cloud. In the Olivet Discourse, Jesus Himself had promised to return someday. One by one John's friends had fallen in death, some by disease or old age, others by persecution. His parents, Zebedee and Salome, had died. His brother James had been beheaded for Christ's sake. Christ's mother Mary, whom he had cared for after the cross, was evidently not with him anymore. Peter had been crucified for Christ. Paul, like James, had lost his head. All the original Twelve except himself were gone, and he didn't have much longer. How sad that Jesus hadn't come back. Would He *ever* return? Would there ever really be a resurrection?

How much John would give to have another visit with Jesus before he died!

John's first vision begins. All at once, John's reverie was shattered. **"A loud voice like a trumpet"** burst in at him. **"Write what you see in a book and send it to the seven churches,"** it said. Revelation 1:10, 11.

Startled, his old heart pounding, John turned as rapidly as he could to see who was talking. To his amazement, the volcanic terrain of the island seemed aglow. Seven golden lampstands appeared where moments before had been bare rocks. And **"in the midst of the lampstands"** stood **"one like a son of man, clothed with a long robe and with a golden girdle round his breast."** Revelation 1:13. His hair was snowy white, and His face and feet, the parts not covered by His robe, were supernaturally radiant. Here was the Being Daniel beheld in *his* old age. See Daniel 10. Just like Daniel, John too fell to the ground like a dead man.

73

Like Daniel, John too heard the gracious words, **"Fear not."** Looking up, he discerned in spite of all the glory that the speaker was his own dear Lord.

Jesus reintroduced Himself to His faithful old friend. **"I am the first and the last, and the living one,"** He said. **"I died, and behold I am alive for evermore, and I have the keys of Death and Hades."** Revelation 1:17, 18.

So Jesus *was* still alive. Except for the short period between the cross and His resurrection, He had always been alive; and He would always continue to live, for ever and ever.

And He had **"the keys of Death."** Indeed! When Rome, the mightiest empire on earth, had crucified Him and put Him into a cave tomb and posted a one-hundred-man guard, Jesus had raised Himself from the grave and walked right out of the tomb, past the guards, back into life.

I have **"the keys of Death."** If Jesus, when dead, could come back to life and stride out of His own grave, there could be no doubt that He could now visit all other graves and summon their sleeping occupants to life.

And John, there on Patmos, must have remembered again how Jesus called people to life even prior to His own resurrection. Christ's words, **"I am . . . the living one,"** resembled similar words that He had spoken long before, beside the tomb of Lazarus.

The death and resurrection of Lazarus. John himself had recorded the story about Jesus and Lazarus in the eleventh chapter of his Gospel. Lazarus of Bethany had taken sick. His sisters, Mary and Martha, had sent a messenger to inform Jesus of his illness, but they had not presumed to ask Him to come to Bethany to heal him. They knew that Jesus loved Lazarus enough to come without being asked.

But when Jesus got their anxious message, He "stayed two days longer in the place where he was." Verse 6. Only when Jesus in His supernatural way knew that Lazarus had actually died did He start leading His disciples in the direction of Bethany. He explained to them, "Our friend Lazarus has fallen asleep, but I go to awake him out of sleep."

The disciples were surprised. "Lord, if he has fallen asleep," they protested, "he will recover." Sleep would indicate that the fever had subsided and health was on its way.

Jesus spoke so naturally about Lazarus's condition that "they thought that he meant taking rest in sleep." But "Jesus had spoken of his death." Then Jesus told them plainly, "Lazarus is dead." Verses 11-14.

The death of His friend Lazarus held no fear for Jesus. To Him, the death of a believer was only a brief interval between life and life—a period only slightly longer, as eternity goes, than the time between bedtime and morning.

"Lazarus has fallen asleep."

"Lazarus is dead."

"I go to awake him out of sleep."

When Jesus and His entourage arrived in Bethany two days later, Mary and

Martha wept in loving incomprehension. Sobbing, each of them chided Him, "Lord, if you had been here, my brother would not have died." Verses 21, 32. Over and over the words had spilled from their lips during the sleepless hours since Lazarus's death, "If only Jesus had come in time, our brother would still be alive."

I have thought the same words in respect to my mother and my sleeping friends. Doubtless John on Patmos thought the same about the death of his brother James and of his other dear ones. If only Jesus had come back first!

To the sisters of Lazarus Jesus said, "Your brother will rise again."

Martha replied, "I know that he will rise again in the resurrection at the last day." Verses 23, 24.

Jesus said, *"I am the resurrection and the life;* he who believes in me, though he die, yet shall he live, and whoever lives and believes in me shall never die. Do you believe this?" Verses 25, 26. Martha did not understand what Jesus meant, but she knew that she could trust who He was. "Yes, Lord," she answered, "I believe that you are the Christ, the Son of God, he who is coming into the world." Verse 27.

When Jesus said, "Whoever lives and believes in me shall never die," He didn't mean that believers wouldn't die in any sense of the word. After all, Lazarus had believed in Him, and Lazarus had died.

What Jesus meant was that the kind of death a Christian dies is only a sleep in God's sight; for in God's own time the Christian will be awakened to everlasting life. And the promise of everlasting life in Christ is so dependable, so certainly certified, that it is as if our eternal life began here and now and as if death were nothing more than a longer-than-usual rest.

Jesus wept. But though the death of His friends held no horror for Jesus, the record says that at Lazarus's grave, "Jesus wept." Verse 35. It is no denial of our faith to cry when loved ones pass away. We sometimes cry when they merely go off on a trip! It is love that makes us weep for the people we miss, and "love is of God." 1 John 4:7. Christians cry; but in view of the resurrection, they do not grieve "as others do who have no hope." 1 Thessalonians 4:13. Funeral directors confirm the observation that believers and nonbelievers grieve in distinctly different ways.

But Jesus didn't weep for long. Lazarus had been buried in a small cave with a circular stone rolled across its entrance. Jesus was soon to be buried in a similar site. (Being expensive, such tombs were not common; but my university colleagues have recently discovered two in the area east of Jordan,[1] and a few others are known elsewhere.)

Jesus took His stand with the mourners by the entrance to the grave and requested someone to roll the stone aside. By now Lazarus had been dead four days. As the Palestinian sun burst in through the opening, the blanketed corpse on the shelf inside became the focus of everyone's attention. Elderly people gazed at it solemnly, knowing they would be blanketed the same way very soon.

Children stared, joking nervously about how spooky it was. Mary and Martha watched soberly, still wishing Jesus had come sooner.

Then Jesus issued the simple vitalizing instruction: "Lazarus, come out!" On the instant, the corpse in the cave stirred to life. Revived, Lazarus set his feet firmly on the ground, straightened his back, and stepped out to the company of his friends. See John 11:43, 44.

What hugs and tears and laughter followed!

The Capernaum message. Yes, the believer does die, in a certain sense; but in another sense, he also has eternal life here and now. In the Capernaum synagogue, sometime prior to resurrecting Lazarus, Jesus told a congregation, "This is the will of my Father, that every one who sees the Son and believes in him should have eternal life; and I will *raise him up* at the last day." "Truly, truly, I say to you, he who believes *has* eternal life." John 6:40, 47.

He who believes *has* eternal life.

And I will *raise him up* at the last day.

If we believe in Jesus, we have eternal life now as a living, dependable promise. Christ is life; and if we have Christ, we have life. "He who has the Son has life; he who has not the Son of God has not life." 1 John 5:12. But we need to be raised to life at the last day in order to see the promise actually realized. If this were not true, there would be no need for a resurrection.

"Lazarus has fallen asleep."

"Lazarus is dead."

"Lazarus, come out."

Jesus is Resurrection as well as Life. Our life in Him is eternal, not because we never fall asleep but because, in spite of falling asleep and after we fall asleep, we shall be resurrected by Jesus at the second coming on the last day.

"The Lord himself will descend from heaven with a cry of command, with the archangel's call, and with the sound of the trumpet of God. And the dead in Christ will rise." 1 Thessalonians 4:16.

Christ's own resurrection. **"I died,"** said Jesus to John on the island of Patmos, **"and behold I am alive for evermore, and I have the keys of Death and Hades."** Revelation 1:18.

Christ's own death and resurrection are our evidence, our guarantee, that Christ has truly vanquished death. Tourists stand in admiration at the tombs where Abraham Lincoln and Napoleon Bonaparte and Simón Bolívar lie buried; but Christians by the many thousands every year journey to Palestine to marvel at Christ's empty tomb. "He is not here; for he has risen" (Matthew 28:6) is the triumphant cry repeated every Easter sunrise.

Every one of our hopes is vested in the magnificent Easter reality. "If Christ has *not* been raised," Paul reasoned firmly, "your faith is futile and you are still in your sins. Then those also who have fallen asleep in Christ have perished. If for this life only we have hoped in Christ, we are of all men most to be pitied." 1 Corinthians 15:17-19.

76

Paul put all his eggs into this one Easter basket. And he did so confidently. He *knew* Christ had risen! People whom he knew well had actually seen Him. "He appeared to Cephas," Paul recounted, "then to the twelve. Then he appeared to more than five hundred brethren at one time, most of whom [some twenty-five years after the event] are still alive," he said, "though some have fallen asleep. Then he appeared to James, then to all the apostles.

"Last of all," Paul added in a voice of incontestable conviction, *"he appeared also to me."* 1 Corinthians 15:5-8.

On several of the occasions that Paul listed, John had been present to see Jesus; and now it was John's wonderful privilege, on the island of Patmos, in his old age, to see Him once again.

John heard Him say, **"Fear not, I am the first and the last, and the living one; I died, and behold I am alive for evermore, and I have the keys of Death and Hades."**

One day soon Christ will use that key to open the graves of every man and woman, every boy and girl who has fallen asleep "in Him." My mother, I believe, will be among them.

This certainty is a part of the Revelation of Jesus Christ.

Jesus proved He has the keys of death by raising Lazarus to life.

II. Jesus and His Testimony

"I John . . . was on the island called Patmos on account of the word of God and the testimony of Jesus." Revelation 1:9. We want to know what John meant by the **"word of God"** and the **"testimony of Jesus."** We also want to understand whatever else he said in this chapter about Jesus.

"The *faithful witness.***"** Verse 5 says that Jesus is **"the faithful witness."** This means we can trust Him! We may not perhaps be able to trust our automobile salesman or our building contractor or our senator or even our spouse, but we can trust Jesus.

In court, a witness "gives testimony" or "bears witness." Jesus told Pilate, at the trial preceding His crucifixion, that He came into the world in order to "bear witness to the truth." John 18:37. We shall see as we go along in the book of Revelation that Jesus bears a faithful witness (or gives a faithful testimony) by telling us the truth (a) about ourselves and (b) about the frailties, vices, and violence of human nature. He also tells us the truth (c) about Satan and the fierce adversary relationship that he maintains against God. Supremely, Jesus bears witness by telling us the truth (d) about Himself. The book of Revelation is primarily a revelation about Jesus Christ.

"The testimony of Jesus." Jesus gave His witness, or testimony, to John, who received it **"in the Spirit."** Verse 10. We are reminded that one of the gifts of the Spirit is the gift of *prophecy*. See 1 Corinthians 12:10. This leads us to Revelation 19:10, K.J.V., which says that "the testimony of Jesus" is "the spirit of prophecy." We'll say more about this when we come to Revelation 12:17.

The Roman Empire exiled John to Patmos as punishment **"on account of the word of God and the testimony of Jesus."** Revelation 1:9. The Word of God is the Bible, the Sacred Scriptures. See, for example, Hosea 1:1; Joel 1:1; and 2 Timothy 3:15, 16. In John's day the New Testament wasn't finished yet, and the Word of God was mainly the Old Testament. Hundreds of Old Testament phrases used in Revelation show how much John cherished the Old Testament Word of God. He believed its prophecies about Jesus and heeded its commandments against idol worship and other sins. Loyal to the Old Testament, he evidently refused to worship an idol of the Emperor Domitian. Thus John was on Patmos **"on account of the word of God."**

John was there also **"on account of . . . the testimony of Jesus."** We have just seen that the testimony of Jesus is the spirit of prophecy. The Old Testament *prophets* were inspired by the *Spirit* of Christ. See 1 Peter 1:10-12. In the New Testament times also many persons were gifted with the Spirit of prophecy. Matthew, Mark, Luke, Paul, Peter, and John himself were inspired by the Holy Spirit to write out the testimony of Jesus in the Gospels, Acts, and letters of the New Testament. The **"testimony of Jesus"** produced a *living, growing body of literature* that revealed the truth about Jesus.

When John said that he was on Patmos **"on account of . . . the testimony of**

Jesus," he meant that he was there because he believed and taught the truth which the New Testament writers, himself included, were inspired to write about Jesus.

"The first-born of the dead." In verse 5 Jesus is called the **"first-born of the dead."** This doesn't mean that He was the first person ever raised from the dead. Before His own resurrection, Jesus Himself raised to life the daughter of Jairus (Mark 5:21-43), the son of the widow of Nain (Luke 7:11-17), and Lazarus of Bethany (John 11). See pages 74-77.

Without *His* resurrection, however, no one else could have been resurrected. It is only "in Christ" that anyone can be made alive. See 1 Corinthians 15:22.

In Bible times, the first son born into a family received the principal inheritance or birthright. See Genesis 43:33; Deuteronomy 21:17. The privileges of the first-born were so outstanding that the word *first-born* itself came to mean "outstanding," "most important," and "unique." Thus in Job 18:13 even an outstandingly dangerous disease is referred to as a "first-born"!

Jesus is the "firstborn of the dead" because He is supremely the most significant person ever to have died and come back to life.

"Who loves us." How simply verse 5 speaks to our hearts. He **"loves us."** How comforting that, as an exile, John could say this about Jesus. How good that we can know it is true, under any circumstance. How kind of Jesus to let us know! See John 14:23.

The three golden syllables, "I love you," are not only for dreamy sweethearts. We should all use them. They are for everyone in the family. My mother kissed her four sons and said she loved us, almost every bedtime as we were growing up. Not until I visited home when I was around forty and she, no longer well, repeated the affectionate ritual as naturally as when I was six, did I suddenly realize what an exceptional thing she had done all those years.

"Have you hugged your kid lately?"

"And has freed us from our sins by his blood." Verse 5. Love isn't merely saying things. Love is especially doing things. Jesus paid the penalty for our sins by leaving heaven to live a grueling life of service on this earth, taking all kinds of criticism without answering back, and dying in humiliation and intense pain on a cross. "Greater love has no *man* than this, that a man lay down his life for his friends." John 15:13. But "*God* shows his love for us in that while we were yet sinners Christ died for us." Romans 5:8. "If *while we were enemies* we were reconciled to God by the death of his Son, much more, now that we are reconciled, shall we be saved by his life." Romans 5:10.

Our son at fifteen months entered a hospital and teetered on the edge of death for four weeks. My wife and I found comfort in remembering that God, to whom we prayed constantly, loved our boy even more than we did. God's Son died for our child. We had not done that for him.

"And made us a kingdom, priests to his God and Father." Verse 6. When God led the Israelites out of Egypt, He declared them to be "a kingdom of priests."

79

Exodus 19:6. At the close of the seventy weeks of Daniel 9:24-27, God set up a new nation consisting of Christians of all races, including Christian Jews. He called this new "nation" His "royal priesthood." 1 Peter 2:9. See GC 1:231-236.

If you are a Christian, Christ has made you a part of His "royal priesthood." The term is thought provoking. What does it mean?

A few years ago I was memorizing the book of Hebrews. I had reached chapter 5 when it occurred to me to brush up on Revelation, which I had memorized many years earlier. So it happened that as I was driving my car one day I recited to myself, **"Has made us a kingdom, priests to his God."** At almost the same time I found myself repeating Hebrews 5:1, "Every high priest chosen from among men is appointed to act on behalf of men in relation to God."

Because ordinary priests perform many of the same basic functions that high priests perform, I paid special attention to see what functions I, as a royal priest, am privileged by God to perform. I observed that Hebrews 5 says that a high priest is appointed by God to act on behalf of men in relation to God and to offer gifts and sacrifices for his own and other people's sins. I knew that our "gifts" and "sacrifices" include our prayers, offered through faith in Christ's self-sacrifice at the cross. See Hebrews 13:15; James 5:16. I saw that the meaning of our priest-hood is at least this, that we are to pray in Christ's name for forgiveness of our own sins *and* for the forgiveness of other people's sins. We are especially invited to pray for people who are unkind to us. See Matthew 5:44.

I also noticed that God has "appointed" us to be priests. This can only mean that He deeply desires us to act like priests. He wants us to pray for our own forgiveness and for the conversion and prosperity of others—for our spouses, parents and children, our employers and employees, government officials, and business associates. He wants us to pray also for the spread of the gospel among non-Christian people. (To take advantage of my priestly privilege, I list names and needs in a little notebook where they nudge my memory.)

God cares. He wants to help. He has commissioned us to ask Him for things. He has appointed us as priests.

The things that are revealed are for our children as well as for us. See Deuteronomy 29:29. God has appointed Christian children to be priests as surely as He has appointed adults! Boys and girls who love Jesus can pray for others just as much as ordained ministers can. Many a child has had the joy of seeing father or mother led to Christ through his or her prayers.

Jesus has appointed us priests. Let us make the most of it!

"He is coming with the clouds, and every eye will see him." In Revelation 1:7, Christ's promise is repeated from the Olivet Discourse. John had heard it from His lips that moonlit Tuesday evening more than sixty years before. See Matthew 24:30. See pages 22, 23. John had heard it also from the lips of the two "men" who stood beside the disciples as Jesus ascended to heaven on the cloud. See Acts 1:11. Paul, too, inspired by the Spirit of prophecy, bore testimony that Jesus at His coming would appear "in the clouds." 1 Thessalonians 4:17.

But in Revelation 1:7, who are the people who **"pierced him"**? At Christ's trial, Jesus said to the Jewish leader, Caiaphas, "Hereafter you will see the Son of man seated at the right hand of Power, and coming on the clouds of heaven." Matthew 26:64. Caiaphas was the individual most responsible for Christ's death. He was certainly one of those who **"pierced him."** But many other persons were criminally involved, and it appears that they, with Caiaphas, will be raised in a special resurrection in time to see Jesus return, surrounded by the very glory which they attempted to snuff out. Daniel 12:1, 2 helps confirm this understanding. It says that when Michael stands up at the end of time, "many" (not all) of the dead will awaken. Inasmuch as all the righteous will rise at this time (see Revelation 20:6), it is apparent that only some of the unrighteous will do so. (The remainder will wait till the end of the thousand years. See Revelation 20:5.)

Those who **"pierced him"** include all who contributed directly to His crucifixion. But does the term include any others?

In Acts 9:5 Jesus told Saul the Persecutor—the man who later became Paul the Apostle—that in persecuting Christians he was persecuting *Him*. "I am Jesus, whom you are persecuting," Jesus said. This leads us to the somber concept that the principal persecutors of God's people through the centuries may also be included in the number of those who **"pierced him"** and who will arise from the dead in time to witness the second coming.

The God **"who is to come."** Will God the Father accompany Jesus at the second coming? Revelation 1:4 describes Him as the one **"who is and who was and *who is to come*."** As we saw above, in Matthew 26:64 Jesus told Caiaphas that the Son of man will return "seated at the right hand of Power." The word *Power* may well be a name for God. In Revelation 6:16, the unrepentant at the second coming plead with rocks and mountains to fall and hide them from "him who is seated on the throne" *and* from "the wrath of the Lamb." The term, "He who is seated on the throne," is used several times in the book of Revelation to refer to God. See, for example, Revelation 5:6-8. The most probable conclusion is, Yes, God will accompany His Son at the second coming. See also Revelation 7:15; 21:5.

"I am the Alpha and the Omega." The New Testament was written in Greek. Alpha is the first letter of the Greek alphabet and Omega is the last letter. Thus, "Alpha and Omega" is somewhat similar to our "from A to Z."

By calling Himself the Alpha and the Omega in verse 8, God meant that He is the first and the last, the beginning and the ending. He was alive when the universe began, and He will continue to live as long as it exists.

"Omega," incidentally, is really "O-mega" and means "big O" or "long O." The shape of Omega comes from the custom of underlining the long O to distinguish it from the short one, called "omicron."

During the second world war, 1,700,000 Yugoslavian men, women, and children died in the attempt—the successful attempt—to keep their country free. During the actual days of violence, David Fredenthal, an artist reporter, drew a sketch of an elderly peasant sowing grain.[2] Even as soldiers trampled across his

81

plowed fields on their way to a military engagement, this patient farmer calmly went about his springtime duty of sowing his farm by hand, just as he had gone about it since his youth. His unflappable steadfastness in a time of intense crisis has a timelessness about it that in a small way illustrates the never-failing, absolutely dependable, all-of-the-time constancy of our eternal God. Like Jesus, He never changes. He is the "same yesterday and today and for ever." Hebrews 13:8. He is the beginning and the end, the Alpha and the Omega.

III. In the Spirit on the Lord's Day

Because God is the Alpha and the Omega, we know that He is eternal. He is also Lord of the universe. John, however, was mortal like the rest of us, limited to time and place. He tells us that when he saw the Lord he was located on the island of Patmos, and that the time was the Lord's day. **"I was in the Spirit on the Lord's day."** Revelation 1:10.

It was appropriate that he should see the Lord on the Lord's day. The vision took John by surprise, so we know that the choice of the day was not his. The Lord chose to give him the vision of Himself on His own day.

The farmer sowed seed in peace or war; Jesus is dependable in every situation.

But what day is the Lord's day?

Everyone knows that most Christians attach the name to Sunday. The custom of doing so may in fact go back as far as some second-century letters written by Ignatius, a dedicated but eccentric bishop of Antioch. Be that as it may, calling Sunday the Lord's day is so ancient and widespread a custom that "Lord's day" has actually taken the place of "Sunday" in several languages. *Domingo*, the Spanish name for Sunday, and *Dimanche*, the French name, are both derived from *Dominica*, the Latin word for Lord's day. Curiously, around the year 1600 English Puritans began also to attach the name "Sabbath" to the first day of the week. In Britain and America, where Puritan influence has been strong, millions of Christians have come to believe that Sunday is the Sabbath as well as being the Lord's day.

Now if we go to the Bible, we find that, yes, the Lord's day is the same as the Sabbath. But we also find that the Lord's day is not the same as Sunday.

In the Ten Commandments, the Bible says that "the *seventh day* is a *sabbath* to the *Lord* your God." Exodus 20:10. In the New Testament, Jesus says, "The Son of man is *lord* even of the *sabbath*." Mark 2:28. So the Bible presents the Sabbath as the Lord's day. The Lord's day is the seventh-day Sabbath.

But how can we be sure that in the long centuries between Bible times and our own there hasn't been a change?

There has been a change; or at least there has been an attempted change. Just a moment ago we mentioned the possibility that as early as the second century Bishop Ignatius called Sunday the Lord's day. In GC 1:134-143 we studied Daniel's prophecy that the little horn of Daniel 7 would "think" to change God's law. We saw there how the Christian Church enforced the observance of the first day of the week in direct opposition to observance of the seventh day. Jesus, however, told His followers to "think not" that *He* had come to change the law. Said He, "Think not that I have come to abolish the law and the prophets. . . . Truly, I say to you, till heaven and earth pass away, not an iota, not a dot, will pass from the law until all is accomplished." Matthew 5:17, 18. See *Your Questions Answered,* pages 86, 87.

In some parts of the world another change has been attempted. Calendars have begun to be printed showing Monday as the first day of the week and Sunday as the seventh day. The reason—that for many people the work week begins on Monday—seems superficial.

But in spite of the history of the church and in spite of these modern calendars, a person can easily discover which day is the true Sabbath. Mark 15:42 says that Jesus was crucified on the "day of Preparation, that is, the day before the sabbath." Luke 23:56 says that on the Sabbath itself His followers "rested according to the commandment." Matthew 28:1 says that "after the sabbath, toward the dawn of the first day of the week," the women came to anoint His body and found the tomb empty. In summary:

On the day before the Sabbath, Jesus died.

On the Sabbath of the Ten Commandments, His followers rested.

On the day after the Sabbath, He rose from the dead.

Every Christian knows that Jesus rose from the dead on Sunday.

Therefore the Bible Sabbath was—and remains—the day before Sunday, in spite of church history and in spite of those modern calendars that mistakenly locate Sunday as the seventh day of the week.

The Lord's day is for us. If the Bible Sabbath is the "sabbath of the Lord" and the **"Lord's day,"** it is His day. Yet He made it for us! Jesus said that "the sabbath was made for man"—for all men, for humankind. See Mark 2:27.

But why was the Sabbath made for us? What purpose was it to serve? One answer to the question is given in Genesis 2:1-3, the original account of the very first Sabbath. There the Bible says that at the end of creation week God "rested on the seventh day from all his work which he had done. So God blessed the seventh day and hallowed it." The word *hallowed* is the same as *sanctified* and means "set apart for a holy use."

God didn't rest on the first seventh-day Sabbath because He was tired. He rested from creating, because in six days He had completed the creation of the earth. He rested, blessed, and hallowed (or sanctified) the seventh day in order to set the Sabbath aside for a holy purpose.

And what is this holy purpose? Ezekiel 20:12 says, "I gave them my sabbaths, as a sign between me and them, that they might know that *I the Lord sanctify them.*"

The Sabbath was created when God *sanctified* the seventh day. Today it serves as a reminder that God also sanctifies *us*, whenever we let Him! He wants to set *us* aside for a holy, wholesome purpose, to do only good. Through us He wants to make the part of the world where we live a better place. He appoints us to be a kingdom of priests. See pages 79, 80. He calls us to follow Christ's example and live a life of goodness in the service of those nearest us. See John 13: 12-17; 1 Peter 2:21-24.

Because the Sabbath reminds us of the creation of the world, it also reminds us that we cannot make ourselves good any more than we can make ourselves. Only the Creator can "create" in us a "clean heart" and a "right spirit." See Psalm 51:10. "If any one is in Christ, he is a new creation; the old has passed away, behold, the new has come." 2 Corinthians 5:17.

You may not be a Sabbath keeper, yet it is likely that God has already been working in you, cleansing you from sin and recreating you in His likeness. Now as you read these pages, He lets you know from the Bible that the seventh-day Sabbath is His day, the day He has chosen for special, further revelations of Himself and transformations of yourself. He also reminds you that the Sabbath was made "for man," for humanity, for everyone. The Sabbath was made for me. It was made for you.

For this very reason, it was also made for John. That Lord's day on Patmos was John's day. It was one of the very best days in all his wonderful long life.

What glorious blessings came to him because he was **"in the Spirit on the Lord's day,"** even when he was in exile all alone.

What blessings you and I can expect as we too keep the seventh-day Sabbath in the power of the Holy Spirit; this Lord's day that is also ours! Then let us keep it, all of us, together with our loving Lord.

Further Interesting Reading

In Arthur S. Maxwell, *The Bible Story*, vol. 10:
  "The Voice Behind You," page 167.
In *Bible Readings for the Home*:
  The section entitled "Life Only in Christ," beginning on page 365.
In Arthur S. Maxwell, *Your Bible and You:*
  "Shall We Meet Our Loved Ones Again?" page 359.

Page numbers for each book refer to the large, fully illustrated edition.

Your Questions Answered

When did Sunday come to be known as the Lord's day? The name "Sunday" comes from the rituals of sun worship. The Oxford English Dictionary attests the first written occurrence of the word in English about A.D. 700. The day we call Sunday was, by New Testament writers, called "the first day of the week." See, for example, Matthew 28:1; John 20:1; 1 Corinthians 16:2. Second-century Christians appear to have called it "the first day" and sometimes, "the eighth day" (as being the day after the seventh-day Sabbath).[3]

The first unambiguous use of the term "Lord's day" for the first day of the week—in this instance, for Resurrection Sunday—appears in the little book called the Gospel of Peter,[4] composed perhaps around A.D. 175. (Obviously Peter didn't write it!)

An earlier but somewhat ambiguous example of the use of "Lord's day" for Sunday occurs in certain translations of the letters of Ignatius. Ignatius was a rather eccentric bishop of Antioch around A.D. 110. Condemned to die for his faith, he was shipped to Rome to be eaten by animals. On the way he wrote seven letters that have become famous. In his letter to the Christians in Magnesia he spoke—according to a typical translator[5]—of "living . . . for the Lord's day." The translator assumed that Ignatius wanted Christians to focus their life-style on Christ's joyous resurrection.

However, the Greek word for *day* does not occur in what appears to be the earliest Greek text for this passage. The Greek adjective for *Lord's* is present, implying a noun which it modifies. But there is no noun. At some unknown time prior to the eleventh century, a Greek editor supplied a noun, but the noun he chose was not the word for *day*; rather it was the word for *life*. Thus this unknown Greek editor made the passage read, "living . . . for the Lord's life" meaning, perhaps, that a Christian's life-style should harmonize with Christ's life-style.[6]

The difference in meaning is significant. For if Ignatius actually did mean to say that we should live in harmony with the "Lord's *life*," it is wrong to cite this passage as an early use of the expression "Lord's day."

In any event, even if Ignatius did regard Sunday as the Lord's day, his preference should not be considered authoritative by Christians who desire to follow only the Bible.

If it is asked how the name "Lord's day" could be moved from Sabbath to Sunday within the second century, we point to the rapid shift around 1600 of the name "Sabbath" from the seventh day to the first day.[7] Until this occurred, almost all Christians reserved the term "Sabbath" for the seventh day, in harmony with the Bible. Most did not observe Saturday as the Sabbath, but they knew Saturday was the Bible Sabbath even though they attended church on Sunday, their "Lord's day." The fact that around 1600 the English Puritans began all at once to call Sunday the "Sabbath" is analogous to the sudden commencement sometime in the second century of calling Sunday the "Lord's day."

References

1. See S. Douglas Waterhouse, "Areas E and F" [a partial report on the 1971 excavation of Tell Hesban], *Andrews University Seminary Studies* 11 (1973):113-125.

2. Winston S. Churchill and the Editors of *Life, The Second World War,* 2 vols. (New York: Time, Inc., 1959), 2:514, 515.

3. Examples include Barnabas, *Epistle,* 15; ANF 1:147; Justin, *First Apology,* 67; ANF 1:186; *Dialogue,* 24, 41; ANF 1:206, 215; Bardesanes, *Discourse on Fate;* ANF 8:733.

4. The Gospel According to Peter, 9, 12; ANF 10:8.

5. Ignatius, *To the Magnesians,* 9; Loeb Classical Library, Apostolic Fathers, 1:205. Compare the trans. in ANF 1:62, observing that the right hand column represents a spurious interpolated edition which originated more than 200 years after Ignatius's death.

6. For a discussion of the evidence from two somewhat different points of view see Fritz Guy, " 'Lord's Day' in Magnesians," *Andrews University Seminary Studies,* 2 (1964):1-17, and Richard B. Lewis, "Ignatius and the 'Lord's Day,' " *Andrews University Seminary Studies,* 6 (1968):46-59.

7. The new custom was epitomized in Nicolas Bownde, *The Doctrine of the Sabbath, Plainely Layde Forth* (London, 1595) and is discussed in Winston U. Solberg, *Redeem the Time* (Cambridge, Mass.: Harvard University Press, 1977) and in Bryan W. Ball, *The English Connection* (Cambridge, England: James Clarke, 1981).

Revelation 2, 3

Christ Writes to Seven Churches

Introduction

Christ's letters to the seven churches of Asia provide the basis for a delightful experience in family Bible study. For one thing, children old enough to enjoy reading can help prepare a Seven Churches Chart like the one on page 98.

The children can help draw the outline grid. Then, for a few minutes each day they can search with their adults for items to write into the squares. As they gain skill, they will be eager to be first in discovering each new item: the description of Christ, the warning, the special promise, and so on. The whole family can help adapt the Bible wording to make it fit the space available. With the chart pinned to the kitchen bulletin board, everyone can keep track of how the project develops.

Everyone can memorize the promises to the listeners, such as, **"Be faithful unto death, and I will give you the crown of life"** (Revelation 2:10) and, **"If any one . . . opens the door, I will come in to him and eat with him, and he with me"** (Revelation 3:20).

In the process, children can come to understand better how much Jesus loves awkward Christians—Christians who are still learning to be like Jesus.

I have met people who stay away from church because they don't like some of the people they have met there or because they think that church members are hypocrites. Jesus *knows* that Christians are far from perfect (see John 2:25), yet He reveals Himself as a very faithful church attender. He explains that the "seven golden lampstands" of Revelation 1:20 represent the "seven churches"; then He portrays Himself in Revelation 2:1 as a Person who **"walks among the seven golden lampstands."**

A true friend knows our weaknesses and loves us just the same.

At the close of a pastoral visit one evening, I suggested to one of my elderly church members that she invite the woman who shared her apartment to join us for a word of prayer. But my church member declined. "We have agreed," she said, "that she will never come into my side of the apartment, and I will never go into hers."

God doesn't build needless barriers, and He doesn't want us to. He knows that to help people we must come close to them. We must do all we can to maintain communication. "Let us hold fast the confession of our hope," says Hebrews 10:23-25, "not neglecting to meet together, as is the habit of some, but encouraging one another, and all the more as you see the Day [of Christ's return] drawing near."

Jesus walks among the lampstands.

89

Most major visions in Revelation begin with a view of the heavenly sanctuary. Before the message to the seven churches, John saw Jesus among the lampstands.

As a father pities his children,
  so the Lord pities those who fear
   him.
For he knows our frame;
  he remembers that we are dust.
             Psalm 103:13, 14.

The seven "angels." It is surprising to find that John was told to write these seven letters to the angels of the seven churches. Angels are mentioned often in Revelation, and usually they are supernatural beings. It seems foolish for God to ask John to write letters to supernatural, invisible, heavenly angels.

The explanation is that the word *angel* comes from a Greek word, *aggelos*, which really means "messenger." God's heavenly messengers are supernatural beings, to be sure; but the Greek word *aggelos* is translated simply "messenger" or "messengers" in the ordinary, nonsupernatural meaning of the word in Mark 1:2; Luke 7:24; Luke 9:52; and James 2:25. In these verses, the "messengers" (or "angels") are (a) John the Baptist, (b) the disciples of John the Baptist, (c) the disciples of Jesus Christ, and (d) two spies—all very human beings indeed.

The human-being angels, or messengers of the seven churches, are the *ministers* who bring God's *message* to their congregations. Jesus says that He holds these "angel" ministers in His right hand. See Revelation 1:16; 2:1. Encourage everyone in your family to visualize your pastor being held in Jesus' hand. See what this does to their feelings about him.

Identification of the "**seven churches.**" At the time when Jesus asked John to write these seven letters, a Christian congregation had been established in each of the seven

cities named. It is fascinating to read that these cities were so located on interconnecting Roman highways that it was possible to visit each of them in the order in which they are listed. The Roman Imperial Post may have regularly visited them in this order in the course of handling mail. "All the Seven Cities stand on the great circular road that bound together the most populous, wealthy, and influential part of the Province" of Asia, says W. M. Ramsay in his classic work, *The Letters to the Seven Churches of Asia.*[1]

But in a book like Revelation that abounds with symbols, are we to assume that the seven congregations in these seven cities were the only audiences to whom the messages were directed? Or do the seven churches represent, let us say, different conditions of different churches at any and all times? Are the seven messages general admonitions intended for everybody? Do they, perhaps, stand for seven successive phases in the experience of the whole church from John's day to the end of the world? Are the messages in all the letters perhaps intended for everybody? Let us look at these possibilities.

1. *For local congregations.* The seven letters speak of some things that had already happened or that were in process of happening at the time Revelation was written. "**You** [in Ephesus] **have abandoned the love you had at first.**" Revelation 2:4. "**You** [in Pergamum] **have some there who hold the teaching of Balaam.**" Revelation 2:14. "**You** [in Thyatira] **tolerate the woman Jezebel.**" Revelation 2:20. "**You** [in Philadelphia] **have kept my word and have not denied my name.**" Revelation 3:8. "**You** [in Laodicea] **say, I am rich.**" Revelation 3:17.

Obviously, these statements must

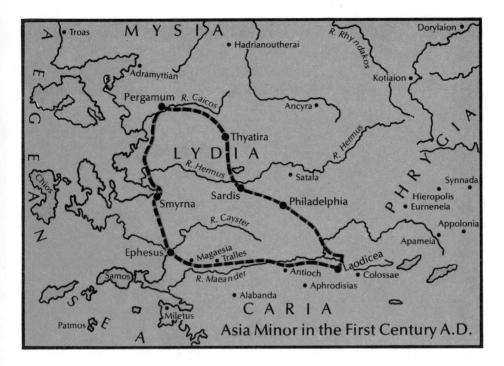

A postal employee traveling Roman roads could deliver letters to the seven cities of Asia in the same order John listed them.

have been true in respect to the local congregations at the time John wrote; otherwise, when the letters arrived, the local Christians would have said, "John surely doesn't know what he's talking about!" So, yes, the letters do deal with conditions in local congregations in John's day.

2. *For everyone*. But they cannot be confined to those local churches. The ending of every letter contains the words, **"He who has an ear, let him hear what the Spirit says to the churches."** The lessons in all the letters apply to everyone everywhere. And so do the promises. Jesus introduces the promises again and again with the phrase, **"He who conquers."** He says, for example, that **"he who conquers"*** will receive of the hidden manna, **"he who conquers"** will walk with Him in white, and **"he who con-**

* "He who conquers" is any person who overcomes or "conquers" a temptation to do wrong.

quers" will sit down with Him in His throne, and so on. The promises were intended for everyone in need of encouragement—for everyone facing pressures today as well as for martyrs facing wild beasts long ago. They are for everyone who **"has an ear,"** that is, for everyone who is willing to listen.

3. *For denominations and movements*. But though the promises are for everyone who is willing to listen, the letters as a whole are addressed to "churches." They are directed primarily to groups. As social beings, we are all organic parts of the organizations we belong to, influencing them and in turn being influenced by them. We are all more or less responsible for the faults of the groups with which we identify and are worthy of their rewards. For this reason, as we observed in Daniel 9, the prophet Daniel confessed the sins of his *group*, sins that he had not committed personally,

91

ORGANIZATION OF REVELATION

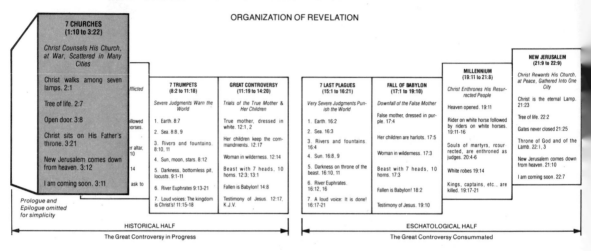

The seven churches are highlighted as we begin studying their letters.

and he asked God to forgive *"us."* See GC 1:200-204.

So, just as the letters applied to seven local churches at one time, and just as they apply to individuals everywhere and at all times, it is evident that they also apply to the various conditions of the church—that is, to the various conditions of congregations, denominations, and movements—at all times.

4. *Symbols of seven phases.* We still need to ask, Do the letters also symbolize seven phases in the experience of the church from John's day to the end of the world? The answer is, Yes, as predictive prophecies, they cover the Christian era. There are several reasons for this conclusion.

a. *Parallels with Daniel.* We have seen that the prophecies of Daniel 2, 7, and 8 parallel each other and run side by side through time from Daniel's day to the end of the world. Daniel and Revelation were both inspired by the same God and reveal many interrelated similarities. It is reasonable to assume that the prophecies in Revelation about the seven seals, the seven trumpets—and the seven churches—like the prophecies in Daniel, also parallel each other and that they run side by side from John's day to the end of the world.

In Christ's day, four great powers, the Roman, Parthian, Kushan, and Han Empires, controlled the vast reaches of civilization between the Atlantic and Pacific Oceans, yet of these four contemporary kingdoms, only Rome was referred to in Daniel 2, 7, and 8. See the map on GC 1:36. Likewise, other contemporary empires existed during the heydays of Babylon, Persia, and Greece, most of which are not even mentioned in the Bible. But the great empires which are the focus of Bible prophecy, Babylon, Persia, Greece, and Rome, controlled one after another the areas in the Middle East and Europe where in their days most of the people lived who read the Word of God and believed in Him. Little would have been achieved if the Bible had given major prophecies about the Kushan or Han Empires, where no

92

Bible believers lived and about which few if any Bible believers were even aware. On GC 1:36 we arrived at the principle that Bible prophecies about nations tend to deal with those parts of the world where the people live who, through their knowledge of the Bible and their faith in God, can benefit from the prophecies the most. We may consider it reasonable to assume that the historical half of Revelation is concerned mostly—though not entirely—with developments in the Middle East and Europe, the areas to which Christianity was largely confined for 1500 long years after the cross. We may also conclude that the letters to the seven churches are concerned chiefly with Christian developments in the same areas.

b. *Self-evident predictions*. Certain elements, especially in the messages to Smyrna and Philadelphia, are predictive. Believers in Smyrna are informed that **"the devil is about to throw some of you into prison"** and that **"for ten days you will have tribulation."** Revelation 2:10. Philadelphia is promised, **"I will make"** false Jews **"bow down before your feet"** and **"I will keep you from the hour of trial which is coming."** Revelation 3:9, 10.

Further, these predictions and some others were going to have their fulfillment at different times and were going to involve different groups. For instance, the devil was going to impose on Smyrna a **"tribulation"** that would last for **"ten days,"** and that would happen so that **"you** [good Christians] **may be tested."** Revelation 2:10. In the letter to Thyatira, however, not the devil but God was going to impose a **"great tribulation"**—one that would strike exclusively at the wicked lovers of **"Jezebel."** See Revelation 2:20-22. Again, the Philadelphia congregation was comforted in connection with the **"hour of trial"** that was going to come on **"the whole world"** (Revelation 3:10), a fearful test that one day will challenge all people, both good and bad. Thus, three different tribulations were predicted, one for true Christians, one for the lovers of Jezebel, and one for the whole world. From these examples alone it is clear that the seven letters contain predictive prophecies dealing with situations future to John's day. See the chart on page 35.

c. *Evidence from fulfillment*. Part of God's way of dealing with us is that some of His prophecies are best understood after they have been fulfilled. At the Last Supper, Jesus announced that one of the disciples would betray Him. The disciples were dumbfounded. "I tell you this now, before it takes place," Jesus explained, "that *when it does take place* you may believe that I am he." John 13:19. At the time, the disciples had no idea that Judas would betray Him. But after Judas had actually done so, the remaining disciples remembered the prophecy, saw how it had been fulfilled, and believed more firmly in the Lord.

Consistently with this principle that some prophecies are best understood after their fulfillment, we look back from our day through nearly 2000 years of Christian experience. We wonder whether events in church history show any correlation with the sequence of events in the seven letters. In doing this we are struck with the rich relationship that, in fact, does exist between the letters and the history of the church. The seven letters, taken in order, march in step with the predominant experience of the Christian church during seven successive eras. Now that it has taken place, we believe!

The churches as dolphins. At a marine park or on TV you have watched dolphins. You have seen the big, good-natured mammals swim vigorously underwater for a while and then leap suddenly up and over the surface, returning again to their underwater play. Sometimes a school of dolphins breaks the surface together, repeatedly, in rhythm. And sometimes a dolphin comes up alone, followed by others, one after another, as in a parade.

Perhaps it will be helpful as we proceed in our study of Revelation 2 and 3 if you will think of the seven churches as seven dolphins! Think of these "dolphins" as movements and trends in the church that have always been present swimming under the water but which, individually, one after another, have surfaced as the most dominant or the most important or the most characteristic Christian movement or trend during a particular era.

But remember: even though the seven churches, viewed as predictive prophecy, foreshadow seven successive eras, the messages they contain are applicable to every individual who is willing to listen to them. May God bless as you read Revelation 2 and 3 on the following pages.

In some ways the seven churches are like dolphins in a marine park.

CHRIST'S LETTERS TO THE SEVEN CHURCHES

REVELATION 2

The first letter: To Ephesus. 1 "To the angel of the church in Ephesus write: 'The words of him who holds the seven stars in his right hand, who walks among the seven golden lampstands.

2 " 'I know your works, your toil and your patient endurance, and how you cannot bear evil men but have tested those who call themselves apostles but are not, and found them to be false; 3I know you are enduring patiently and bearing up for my name's sake, and you have not grown weary. 4But I have this against you, that you have abandoned the love you had at first. 5Remember then from what you have fallen, repent and do the works you did at first. If not, I will come to you and remove your lampstand from its place, unless you repent. 6Yet this you have, you hate the works of the Nicolaitans, which I also hate. 7He who has an ear, let him hear what the Spirit says to the churches. To him who conquers I will grant to eat of the tree of life, which is in the paradise of God.'

The second lette: To Smyrna. 8 "And to the angel of the church in Smyrna write: 'The words of the first and the last, who died and came to life.

9 " 'I know your tribulation and your poverty (but you are rich) and the slander of those who say that they are Jews and are not, but are a synagogue of Satan. 10Do not fear what you are about to suffer. Behold, the devil is about to throw some of you into prison, that you may be tested, and for ten days you will have tribulation. Be faithful unto death, and I will give you the crown of life. 11He who has an ear, let him hear what the Spirit says to the churches. He who conquers shall not be hurt by the second death.'

The third letter: To Pergamum. 12 "And to the angel of the church in Pergamum write: 'The words of him who has the sharp two-edged sword.

13 " 'I know where you dwell, where Satan's throne is; you hold fast my name and you did not deny my faith even in the days of Antipas my witness, my faithful one, who was killed among you, where Satan dwells. 14But I have a few things against you: you have some there who hold the teaching of Balaam, who taught Balak to put a stumbling block before the sons of Israel, that they might eat food sacrificed t idols and practice immorality. 15So you also have some who hold the teaching of the Nicolaitans. 16Repent then. If not, I will come to you soon and war against them with the sword of my mouth. 17He who has an ear, let him hear what the Spirit says to the churches. To him who conquers I will give some of the hidden manna, and I will give him a white stone, with a new name written on the stone which no one knows except him who receives it.'

The fourth letter: To Thyatira. 18 "And to the angel of the church in Thyatira write: 'The words of the Son of God, who has eyes like a flame of fire, and whose feet are like burnished bronze.

19 " 'I know your works, your love and faith and service and patient endurance, and that your latter works exceed the first. 20But I have this against you, that you tolerate the woman Jezebel, who calls herself a prophetess and is teaching and beguiling my servants to practice immorality and to eat food sacrificed to idols. 21I gave her time to repent, but she refuses to repent of her immorality. 22Behold, I will throw her on a sickbed, and those who commit adultery with her I will throw into great tribulation, unless they repent of her doings; 23and I will strike her children dead. And all the churches shall know that I am he who searches mind and heart, and I will give to each of you as your works deserve. 24But to the rest of you in Thyatira, who do not hold this teaching, who have not learned what some call the deep things of Satan, to you I say, I do not lay upon you any other burden; 25only hold fast what you have, until I come. 26He who conquers and who keeps my works until the end, I will give him power over the nations, 27and he shall rule them with a rod of iron, as when earthen pots are

95

broken in pieces, even as I myself have received power from my Father; [28]and I will give him the morning star. [29]He who has an ear, let him hear what the Spirit says to the churches.'

REVELATION 3

The fifth letter: To Sardis. 1 "And to the angel of the church in Sardis write: 'The words of him who has the seven spirits of God and the seven stars.

" 'I know your works; you have the name of being alive, and you are dead. [2]Awake, and strengthen what remains and is on the point of death, for I have not found your works perfect in the sight of my God. [3]Remember then what you received and heard; keep that, and repent. If you will not awake, I will come like a thief, and you will not know at what hour I will come upon you. [4]Yet you have still a few names in Sardis, people who have not soiled their garments; and they shall walk with me in white, for they are worthy. [5]He who conquers shall be clad thus in white garments, and I will not blot his name out of the book of life; I will confess his name before my Father and before his angels. [6]He who has an ear, let him hear what the Spirit says to the churches.'

The sixth letter: To Philadelphia. 7 "And to the angel of the church in Philadelphia write: 'The words of the holy one, the true one, who has the key of David, who opens and no one shall shut, who shuts and no one opens.

8 " 'I know your works. Behold, I have set before you an open door, which no one is able to shut; I know that you have but little power, and yet you have kept my word and have not denied my name. [9]Behold, I will make those of the synagogue of Satan who say that they are Jews and are not, but lie—

behold, I will make them come and bow down before your feet, and learn that I have loved you. [10]Because you have kept my word of patient endurance, I will keep you from the hour of trial which is coming on the whole world, to try those who dwell upon the earth. [11]I am coming soon; hold fast what you have, so that no one may seize your crown. [12]He who conquers, I will make him a pillar in the temple of my God; never shall he go out of it, and I will write on him the name of my God, and the name of the city of my God, the new Jerusalem which comes down from my God out of heaven, and my own new name. [13]He who has an ear, let him hear what the Spirit says to the churches.'

The seventh letter: To Laodicea. 14 "And to the angel of the church in Laodicea write: 'The words of the Amen, the faithful and true witness, the beginning of God's creation.

15 " 'I know your works: you are neither cold nor hot. Would that you were cold or hot! [16]So, because you are lukewarm, and neither cold nor hot, I will spew you out of my mouth. [17]For you say, I am rich, I have prospered, and I need nothing; not knowing that you are wretched, pitiable, poor, blind, and naked. [18]Therefore I counsel you to buy from me gold refined by fire, that you may be rich, and white garments to clothe you and to keep the shame of your nakedness from being seen, and salve to anoint your eyes, that you may see. [19]Those whom I love, I reprove and chasten; so be zealous and repent. [20]Behold, I stand at the door and knock; if any one hears my voice and opens the door, I will come in to him and eat with him, and he with me. [21]He who conquers, I will grant him to sit with me on my throne, as I myself conquered and sat down with my Father on his throne. [22]He who has an ear, let him hear what the Spirit says to the churches.' "

96

The Message of Revelation 2, 3

I. Christ's Care for Smoky Churches

Did you have a kerosene lamp at home when you were a child? Do you have one now? If so, you know how much care such a lamp requires. After almost every use, you have to trim or replace the wick, replenish the oil, and polish the chimney.

In the Old Testament sanctuary, the seven lights on the golden lampstand in the sanctuary had to be cared for by the high priest every day. See Leviticus 24:1-4. Keeping them clean, adjusting and replacing their wicks, and adding olive oil made up part of the high priest's continual or *tamid** responsibility that we talked about in GC 1:161-189.

Revelation 2:1 says that Jesus **"walks among the . . . lampstands."** He is our contemporary High Priest, serving in the heavenly sanctuary. See Hebrews 3:1 and 8:1. He looks after our interests "always." Hebrews 7:25. Symbolically caring for the smoky lamps that represent His church is part of His high-priestly *tamid*.

Of course, Jesus doesn't actually cut wicks and pour olive oil. *How* He cares for His smoky churches and for His all-too-often awkward Christians is illustrated in the seven letters of Revelation 2 and 3. Here He helps His "lamps" to shine with a brighter light by (a) praising their good qualities, (b) rebuking their faults in a straightforward manner and appealing for heartfelt change (repentance), and (c) offering brilliant rewards to anyone whose response is positive.

1. Ephesus, the church that abandoned its first love.
Revelation 2:1-7.

The setting. Ephesus was the principal city in the Roman province of Asia. It was not the capital; Pergamum was. But it had a fine harbor, and its location at the head of an important east-west highway helped it become a strong commercial center. Ephesus enjoyed wide respect also as a pagan religious center. Artemis, a many-breasted goddess of fertility also known as Diana, was worshiped there. See Acts 19:35. Her magnificent temple was known to contemporaries as one of the Seven Wonders of the World.

The Christian church in busy, pagan Ephesus was founded by Aquila and Priscilla, a dedicated lay couple. Apollos, an eloquent evangelist, also helped get it started; and so did the apostle Paul. See Acts 18:18-26. In fact, Paul spent three years in Ephesus. During two of those years he taught the Bible daily in a rented hall during the hot hours, 11:00 a.m. to 4:00 p.m., when city business slowed and the hall was otherwise unused. See Acts 19:8-10; 20:31.

---

*Tamid means "continual." In a very significant way, it is used in the Hebrew manuscripts underlying Daniel 8, where it refers in particular to Christ's *continual* high priestly ministry in our behalf.

GOD CARES CHRIST WRITES TO SEVEN CHURCHES

NAME	EPHESUS	SMYRNA	PERGAMUM	THYATIRA	SARDIS	PHILADELPHIA	LAODICEA
PERIOD	To 100	To 313	To 538	To 1560s	To 1790s	To 1840s	To end
DESCRIPTION OF CHRIST	Holds 7 stars Walks among 7 lampstands	First and Last Died Came to life	Has sharp sword	Son of God Flaming eyes Bronze feet	Holds 7 spirits 7 stars	Holy and True Key of David Opens & shuts	Amen True Witness Beginning of creation
CHRIST KNOWS	works toil endurance	Tribulation Poverty Coming trouble	Dwell where Satan is	Works, Love Faith Service Patience	Works	Works	Works False claims True condition
PRAISE/ COMMEND- ATION	Not weary Test teachers Hate Nicolaitans	You are rich	Hold fast Did not deny	Later works exceed first	A few are worthy	Kept My Word Did not deny Endured	
REBUKE	Abandoned first love		Some Balaamites Nicolait- ans	Tolerates Jezebel Won't repent	Works imperfect Seems alive but dead		Lukewarm Poor Blind Naked
COUNSEL	Repent! Remember! Return to first love, first works	Don't fear! Be faithful to death	Repent!	Repent! Hold fast!	Repent! Remember! Awake! Strengthen!	Hold fast!	Repent! Buy! Open!
WARNING	I will remove lampstand		I will make war	Sickbed Great tribulation Death	I will come as a thief		I will spit out
FALSE JEWS		Slander you				Will worship at your feet	
PROMISE REWARD	Eat from tree of life	Crown of life	Hidden manna White stone New name	Rod, to rule nations Morning Star	White garments Walk with Me Confess name Not blot out	Pillar in temple name of God city of New name	Sup with Sit with on My throne

Some students think they see a chiasm, because, for example, the second and fourth churches have no rebuke and the only references to false Jews. The first and seventh are threatened with destruction. What about other evidence, pro and con? Do you see a chiasm?

98

So many people stopped purchasing silver souvenirs of the goddess Artemis that the local silversmiths staged an anti-Christian riot. See Acts 19:23-41.

Upon visiting the leaders of the Ephesian Christians some time later, Paul warned them that some of their own number would soon start teaching heresy. See Acts 20:29, 30. In a letter he cautioned them, "Let no one deceive you with empty words." "Do not associate with" anyone who tries to do so. Ephesians 5:6, 7.

The commendation. The Ephesian Christians accepted Paul's advice. Thirty years later, in the book of Revelation, Jesus commended them because they had **"tested those who call themselves apostles but are not"** and because they hated **"the works of the Nicolaitans, which,"** Jesus added, **"I also hate."** Jesus commended the Ephesians also for their **"works," "toil,"** and **"patient endurance."** Revelation 2:2, 6.

But who were the Nicolaitans? Irenaeus, a second-century minister who grew up near Ephesus, referred to them in one of his writings. The Nicolaitans claimed to be Christians, he said, but they considered it "a matter of indifference to practise adultery, and to eat things sacrificed to idols."[2] It appears then that the Nicolaitans were Christians who felt that faith in Jesus released them from obedience to some of the Ten Commandments. In 1 John 2:4, John wrote against similar

Christianity got a good start in Ephesus even though the city was the center for worship of the popular goddess Diana.

people who were saying, "I know him [Jesus]," but those same people were breaking the commandments. Anyone who talks this way, John said, is a "liar."

Calling a commandment-flouting Christian a "liar" is strong language. Jesus used strong language when He said He "hated" the teachings of the Nicolaitans. We remember that in the Sermon on the Mount Jesus said, "Not every one who says to me, 'Lord, Lord,' shall enter the kingdom of heaven, but he who does the will of my Father who is in heaven." Matthew 7:21. Such language sobers us, especially when we consider that many people *today* say that faith releases Christians from keeping one or more of the Ten Commandments. Usually these Christians treat lightly the seventh commandment, about adultery, or the fourth, about keeping the seventh-day Sabbath.

The rebuke. We are glad to learn that the Ephesian Christians rejected the misleading ideas of the Nicolaitans. In doing so, they followed Paul's counsel about not associating with deceivers. Apparently, however, they had not done so well in regard to another piece of Paul's advice. In Ephesians 5:2 Paul had urged them to "walk in love, as Christ loved us." But in Revelation 2:4 Jesus had to say, **"I have this against you, that you have abandoned the love you had at first."** The Ephesian Christians had lost the keen edge of their first love for God. They had also lost the warmth of their first affection for one another.

Jesus considered this loss of love as a sin of the first magnitude. **"Remember then from what you have fallen, repent and do the works you did at first,"** He pleaded. **"If not,"** said He, **"I will come to you and remove your lampstand from its place, unless you repent."**

Jesus dealt tactfully but firmly with the awkward Christians in Ephesus. He talked about their good qualities first, then told them plainly about their bad ones. A Christian church, if it wants to be a *Christian* church, a true *light* in the world, has an unavoidable responsibility to live love. "By this all men will know that you are my disciples, if you have love for one another." John 13:35. "Let your light so shine before men, that they may see your good works and give glory to your Father who is in heaven." Matthew 5:16.

Disadvantaged people see the church as a light and glorify God when Christians help them in practical ways. Businessmen see the church as a light and glorify God when Christians pay their accounts on time and register complaints, when they must, only in kind and friendly ways. Non-Christians stand amazed at the power of God when a congregation that is known to be quarrelsome stops being a "smoky church" and loves itself back together again.

The rewards. The joy of restoring a first-love relationship is just the beginning of the rewards available to Ephesian Christians. **"To him who conquers"**—that is, to everyone who overcomes un-love—Jesus says, **"I will grant to eat of the tree of life, which is in the paradise of God."** The tree of life grew originally in the Garden of Eden. See Genesis 2:8, 9. Paradise is now in heaven. See 2 Corinthians 12:2, 3. We all wish we could have had access to the tree of life long ago. Jesus promises that we *can* have access to it, in heaven, soon.

2. Smyrna, the church under persecution.
Revelation 2:8-11.

The setting. The city of Smyrna was located north of Ephesus on a beautiful inlet of the Aegean Sea. Commercially, Smyrna was a rival to Ephesus and in time far outstripped it. We're interested to know that Smyrna boasted the only known three-level market plaza in the ancient world, with stores on two levels above ground and others in the basement. Under the name Izmir, Smyrna still survives, the third largest city in Turkey and the most flourishing of the seven cities named in Revelation 2 and 3.

The church in Smyrna was a persecuted church. It was slandered by false Jews, and it was slated to be tormented by Satan and to receive **"tribulation"** for **"ten days."** Some of its members were to be imprisoned, and some would be put to death.

Within about seventy years after this prophecy was made, Smyrna became the site of a notable series of martyrdoms spread over a period of several literal days. The twelfth and last of the martyrs was grand old Polycarp, who by the time he died had served as principal minister of the Smyrna church for at least forty years. At a very advanced age, Polycarp was arrested in a farm house one Friday night. Immediately he asked the farmer's wife to prepare supper for the soldiers who had come to arrest him. While the soldiers ate, Polycarp stood to one side in

While the crowd shouted for him to be eaten by lions, Polycarp told the Roman governor he could not curse the Christ who had saved him.

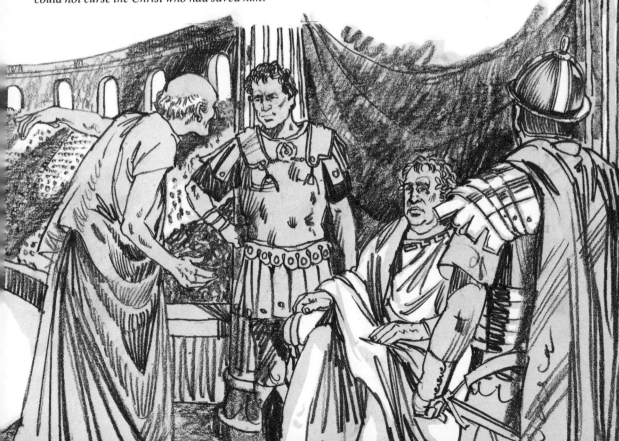

the small cottage and prayed aloud for two hours for every Christian he could think of in the Roman Empire.

At the Smyrna amphitheater next day, Governor Status Quadratus was deeply impressed with Polycarp and tried to save his life. When his efforts proved futile, the governor asked Polycarp to curse Christ. He was certain that so grand a man as Polycarp would be eager to separate himself from Jesus, whom Rome had condemned as a criminal. But Polycarp gave a ringing response:

> Eighty and six years have I served Him,
>   and never has He done me wrong.
> How then can I curse my King,
>   who saved me?

The crowd—including in this instance, members of the Jewish synagogue— screamed for Polycarp to be fed to a lion. But the lions had just gorged themselves on other, non-Christian, victims. A herald explained that anyway it was past the hour in the day's entertainment when using lions was still legal. So the crowd demanded that Polycarp be burned to death. When the governor consented, the Jews, in a most unusual gesture of hostility,* were foremost in gathering firewood, even though it was Sabbath.[3]

The commendation. Jesus knew all about the present and future trials of the Smyrna Christians. He also deeply appreciated the quality of their faith in Him. **"I know your tribulation and your poverty,"** He said, adding quickly, **"but you are rich."** The Smyrna Christians received no rebuke, only commendation and the offer of reward.

The reward. Appropriate to the harassed circumstances of the Smyrna Christians, Jesus introduced Himself to them as the **"first and the last,"** who **"died and came to life."** He than gave them a twofold promise of resurrection. **"Be faithful unto death, and I will give you the crown of life,"** and **"He who conquers shall not be hurt by the second death."**

Jesus is a specialist in resurrection and life! See John 11:25. He resurrected Himself (John 10:17, 18) and has already resurrected a number of other people. See pages 73-75. His amazing promises to Smyrna are perfectly reliable.

But these promises are offered to those who **"conquer,"** who are **"faithful unto death."** They are for Christians who triumph over evil, who would rather die than do wrong. They are for Christians who would rather die than commit adultery or take God's name in vain or break the Sabbath. Christians who would rather die than be dishonest.

Lord Jesus, Keeper of the lamps, help us shine with a pure, clear light.

---

* Various Christian writers in the second and third centuries asserted that the Jews were often active in promoting persecution; however, the *Martyrdom of Polycarp* is the only trustworthy and contemporary account of an actual martyrdom that reports actual participation by Jews. See Herbert Musurillo, ed. and trans., *The Acts of the Christian Martyrs.*

3. Pergamum, the church near Satan's throne.
Revelation 2:12-17.

The setting. The city of Pergamum was located on a high mountain spur, making it an easy site to defend. In the second and third centuries B.C., Pergamum, capital of a kingdom with the same name, was an illustrious cultural center. Its library contained 200,000 scrolls. Many of these scrolls, incidentally, were made of parchment, a highly refined form of leather. Parchment was developed in Pergamum when King Ptolemy V of Egypt cut off the export of papyrus scrolls from his country. Economic sanctions didn't work any better then than they do today. They stimulated the competition to produce a superior product. *Parchment* is a modification of *Pergamum.*

King Attalus III stipulated in his will that at his death Pergamum should be made part of the Roman Empire. In 133 B.C. this was done. As the new capital of the province of Asia, Pergamum could now claim the residence of the Roman governor. As time passed, Pergamum could also boast of temples to several pagan gods, including, ominously, the first known temple (29 B.C.) to the Emperor Augustus. Later, another temple was dedicated to the worship of the Emperor Trajan and, much later, another temple to the Emperor Severus. You remember that compulsory emperor worship resulted in the widespread persecution of John's day and in John's exile to Patmos.

"I know where you dwell," said Jesus to the congregation of Pergamum— **"where Satan's throne is"**!

The commendation. Christ expressed Himself as pleased that, in spite of so wicked an environment, the church in Pergamum had not denied the faith **"even in the days of Antipas my witness, my faithful one, who was killed among you, where Satan dwells."** We would like to know more about Antipas, but nothing more has been discovered. How glad this loyal Christian will be in the resurrection to hear Christ's congratulations: **"Antipas my witness, my faithful one."**

The rebuke. Although Antipas could be commended, other Pergamum Christians could not be. Some of them had accepted the **"teaching of Balaam, who taught Balak to put a stumbling block before the sons of Israel, that they might eat food sacrificed to idols and practice immorality."** Jesus added, **"You also have some who hold the teaching of the Nicolaitans."**

A few pages ago we read that the Ephesian congregation rejected the Nicolaitans; so Pergamum as a whole wasn't doing as well as Ephesus. In our discussion of Ephesus, we learned that the Nicolaitans taught that faith in Christ released them from observing the commandment about adultery and, to a certain extent, released them from the commandment about idolatry. The teachings of Balaam seem to have been similar.

"Balaam" is used here as a metaphor. The historical Balaam was a notorious Old Testament prophet. See Numbers 25:1-9; 31:16. After serving God for many years, Balaam accepted the offer of a bribe from Balak, King of the Moabites, who wanted him to curse the Israelites so they would be unable to defeat the Moabites in battle.

God worked a miracle to keep Balaam from cursing Israel; but Balaam was so determined to get the bribe, that he advised King Balak to invite the Israelites to a pagan festival, supplied with women and wine. Apparently, Balaam reasoned that if he could get the Israelites to sin seriously, God Himself would curse them.

King Balak followed Balaam's insidious advice, and many Israelites succumbed to the temptation. God, of course, did not curse Israel, but He did require the Israelite leaders who had cooperated with Balaam to be hanged. Thousands of Israelite participants also fell prey to disease.

In Revelation 2:16 Jesus wanted the leader (the **"angel"**) of the Pergamum congregation to persuade the Balaam party to **"repent"** and to change their ways. Otherwise, Jesus said solemnly, **"I will come to you soon and war against them with the sword of my mouth."**

The situation in Pergamum was probably more sophisticated than it sounds. We can learn more about it by looking at a similar condition that the apostle Paul had to deal with in the church in Corinth.

Popular banquets sponsored by social clubs and trade guilds were conducted frequently at Corinth (as at Pergamum) in *pagan temples*. The temples were attractive and large and had cooking facilities adequate for sizable crowds. Some of the Christians in Corinth pointed out that an idol really isn't anything and that Christ died to set us free. They convinced themselves that if they wanted to attend temple banquets they would suffer no harm by doing so. They knew that their example might lead weak Christians to fall back into complete paganism; but if so, that would be their own fault, they reasoned. See 1 Corinthians 8:4-13.

In reply, Paul agreed that idols have no personal existence. But, he said, demons do. Participating in a pagan festival, he indicated, was like going to a demon's supper in place of going to the Lord's Supper. And as for your freedom in Christ? Influencing a weak Christian to sin was the same as destroying a person for whom Christ died. See 1 Corinthians 10:14-33; 8:9-13.

Apparently, what troubled Jesus in the church at Pergamum was this same perverted kind of Christianity that claims that in Christ we are all free to do our own thing, even when doing so is contrary to the commandments, and that any bad influence our behavior may have on others is their fault, not ours.

But today, as in Pergamum, there are still Christians who stay away from questionable places of entertainment rather than risk influencing weaker Christians to get hooked on bad habits. There are big brothers and sisters who choose their reading and their TV programs carefully to avoid influencing their younger brothers and sisters to read or see things that would hurt them. Such Christians are not Nicolaitans!

The reward. **"To him who conquers I will give some of the hidden manna, and I will give him a white stone, with a new name written on the stone which no one knows except him who receives it."** Revelation 2:17.

In many non-Western cultures, a person's name is chosen to fit his character or personality or some event in his life. Sometimes the name is altered after several years as the person's character or career changes.

In the Bible, Jesus changed the name of Simon to Simon Peter in order to signify that his personality was like a stone or rock. See Mark 3:16; Matthew 16:18. Peter means "stone."

Christ's name, Jesus, means "a person who saves." See Matthew 1:21.

In the Old Testament, Jacob meant "supplanter" in a bad sense, a person who takes someone else's place by deceit. Jacob was "tricky Jake." But he changed. After his successful night of wrestling with the Angel of God at Peniel, his name was altered to "Israel." "Your name shall no more be called Jacob, but Israel," said the Angel, "for you have striven with God and with men, and have prevailed." Genesis 32:28. No longer a trickster, Jacob was no longer to be known as Jacob but as Prevailer, Overcomer, Conqueror, because this is what he had become. He was now Israel, a prevailer, an overcomer, a conqueror.

Are we not all tricky Jakes, more or less? Like the Balaamites and the Nicolaitans, we are great at finding plausible reasons why it's all right for *us* to do wrong.

Some Christians in Corinth were sure that attending banquets in pagan temples was not wrong and tried to seduce other Christians into going with them.

But as we *take hold of God in faith*, through Bible study and prayer, we can be changed until each of us too can become a prevailer, an overcomer, a conqueror—an Israel. Then God gives us, too, a new name.

He also promises to give us **"some of the hidden manna."** In the Old Testament, a mysterious but nutritious food called manna appeared on the desert floor each morning while the Israelites were traveling from Egypt to the Promised Land. In John 6:31-35 Jesus told His followers that, in a spiritual sense, He Himself is the manna, the true Bread from heaven. If we, *unlike* the Nicolaitans and the Balaamites, refuse to engage in questionable activities and entertainments, we will find that we have time enough to "gather manna" every day; that is, to "feed" on Christ through studying His Word.

4. Thyatira, the church that tolerated Jezebel.
Revelation 2:18-29.

The setting. The city of Thyatira was not a seaport like Ephesus and Smyrna. Standing on only a gentle rise, it was not defended by mountainous slopes like Pergamum. But its location on a main highway where two valleys meet provided it with ample trade. Madder roots that grew nearby provided its craftsmen and merchants with a bright red dye known in ancient times as purple. Lydia, the businesswoman who accepted Christ in the city of Philippi, sold bright red fabrics and dyestuffs—"purple goods"—that she obtained from Thyatira. See Acts 16:11-15.

The commendation. Christ complimented the Christians in Thyatira for their **"works"** and for their **"love and faith and service and patient endurance."** He noted in fact that their good works grew even better as time progressed. **"Your latter works exceed the first."** Revelation 2:19.

The rebuke. But in spite of their numerous charities and commendable virtues, the Thyatira Christians needed more help from the heavenly Lamp Trimmer than any of the others except the Laodiceans. Whereas the Ephesians had rejected the Nicolaitans and whereas only some of the Pergamese had accepted the Balaamites, the church as a whole in Thyatira actually tolerated Jezebel, a woman who claimed to be a **"prophetess"** and who taught the church members to **"practice immorality and to eat food sacrificed to idols."** Verse 20.

Like Balaam, the real Jezebel was an infamous person in the Old Testament. She married King Ahab and thus became queen of Israel, queen that is, of the northern Israelite nation of the day. See GC 1:19-21. Daughter of the pagan king of Tyre, Jezebel brought pagan priests with her to Israel and soon converted most of the Israelites to the immoral worship of Baal. Many Israelites who refused to give up the worship of God she martyred. See 1 Kings 16 to 21.

We recognize that in Thyatira the Jezebel problem—immorality and eating food sacrificed to idols—was the same compromise with pagan culture that was advocated by the Nicolaitans and the Balaamites. The degree of compromise, however, was devastatingly worse. Jezebel had ripened her rebellion. Granted time for repentance, she had stubbornly refused to change her ways.

As a result, she was to suffer from a dread disease, presumably brought on by her own excesses. **"Behold, I will throw her on a sickbed."** Unless they repented, her followers were to endure **"great tribulation."**

In the days of the Old Testament Jezebel, 7000 Israelites courageously refused to go along with the contemporary compromise with pagan culture. See 1 Kings 19:18. We are cheered to learn that in Thyatira also there was a group who did not **"hold this teaching** [of **Jezebel],"** who had not learned **"what some call the deep things of Satan."** Christ encouraged them: **"Hold fast what you have, until I come."**

The pre-advent judgment. Immediately following His words about punishment, Jesus said, **"All the churches shall know that I am he who** *searches mind and heart,* **and I will give to each of you as your works deserve."**

In the Old Testament, even the prophet Elijah was unaware that those 7000 faithful believers we mentioned a moment ago were standing firm. He thought he was the only one doing so. But God knew about all 7000 of them. God is constantly observing our conduct. He has His friendly eyes on every individual who is faithful to Him.

When Jesus said that **"all the churches"** would know that He **"searches mind and heart"** and that He would one day **"give to each of you as your works deserve,"** He was talking about judgment. He was talking about His personal role as the Judge of all Christians and of all Christian churches.

A misunderstanding of Christ's words in John 5:24 has unfortunately given the impression that true Christians should forget about the final judgment as applying to themselves. "He who hears my word and believes him who sent me, has eternal life; he does not come into judgment," says Jesus in John 5:24, as translated in the Revised Standard Version. Some other modern versions also give His words a similar sense.

But 2 Corinthians 5:10 says that "we must all appear before the judgment seat of Christ, so that each one may receive good or evil, according to what he has done in the body." And Christ's statement here in Revelation 2:23 is unmistakable: *"All the churches* **shall know that I am he who searches mind and heart, and I will give to** *each of you* **as your works deserve."**

Instead of saying that true Christians won't come into judgment, the King James Version correctly translates John 5:24 as saying that they won't "come into *condemnation,"* a translation that is fully supported by the underlying Greek words. Plainly, this is the real meaning of the passage, the translation that is consistent with the rest of the Bible and with Christ's words to Thyatira.

On GC 1:242, we looked at the first phase of God's final judgment. This first phase is sometimes called the "investigative judgment"; and, because it occurs just prior to Christ's second coming (or second advent), it is also known as the "pre-advent judgment." We found that it concerns all members of "Israel," all

those persons who at any time have professed faith in the true God. One purpose of this first phase of the final judgment is to *reveal* to the universe who have and who have not remained faithful to their initial commitment. Another purpose is to *vindicate* the faithful believers who have been treated harshly by unfaithful fellow believers. We'll have more to say about this judgment on the next two pages, and also when we get to Revelation 14.

The reward. To all who refuse at any cost to compromise with worldly culture, Jesus promises to grant power, friendship, and glory that transcend everything worldly. **"He who conquers and who keeps my works until the end, I will give him power over the nations, and he shall rule them with a rod of iron, . . . even as I myself have received power from my Father; and I will give him the morning star."**

In ancient times, a **"rod of iron"** was a metal cane used by shepherds. See Psalm 23:4. Its function was not aggression but defense of the shepherd's flock. The destruction of all evildoers will eternally safeguard the innocent. Jeers, threats, and obscenities will never torment them again.

The **"morning star"** that Jesus promises to give is Himself! See Revelation 22:16. Though He is King of kings and Lord of lords (Revelation 19:16), He offers Himself to us as our royal Companion—and even as our divine Servant. See Luke 12:37; 22:27. How wonderful of Him! How persuasively He induces us to resist peer pressure and the loss of ordinary friends when we are tempted to compromise!

5. Sardis, the stagnant church.
Revelation 3:1-6.

The setting. Sardis considered itself impregnable. Somewhat like Pergamum, it was located high on a mountain spur. The main part of the town was perched 300 meters, or close to 1000 feet, above the valley floor at the top of almost perpendicular cliffs. In ancient times the proverbially wealthy monarch, King Croesus of Lydia, chose Sardis as his capital and felt that his enormous treasure was safe there. Coins were first minted in Sardis.

No army could surmount the city's protective precipices; but Cyrus the Great in 547 B.C. took Sardis and its treasure away from Croesus; and Antiochus the Great in 218 B.C. conquered the city again. In each case a hardy volunteer scaled the wall-like escarpments and opened the city gates from the inside—while the population, feeling perfectly safe, was sound asleep.

The rebuke. The Christians of Sardis in John's day felt safe enough to go to sleep. **"If you will not awake,"** Jesus said to them, **"I will come upon you." "You have the name of being alive, and you are dead."**

We have all been disappointed at finding that something we depended on is no longer what it used to be. A restaurant, perhaps, or a department store, a brand of tools, a football team, a popular teacher—when we try them again after the lapse of a few years we find they simply haven't been keeping up. They're resting on

109

Above thousand-foot cliffs citizens of Sardis relaxed, sure their city was impregnable–till an enemy scaled the cliffs and opened the gate from inside.

their earlier reputation and are slipping badly. We wish they were as good as we remember them.

The Sardis congregation was leaning on its laurels. Its charter members had been famous for their spirituality. The evangelists who had won them to Christ had brought them excellent preaching. Now it was time for the church to get back to what it used to be. **"You have the name of being alive, and you are dead." "Remember . . . what you received and heard; keep that, and repent." "Awake, and strengthen what remains."**

The situation in Sardis was serious, but it was not hopeless. Christ's concern for everyone then as now was as warm and attentive as if each individual were the only person for whom He gave His life. So even in this self-satisfied "smoky" congregation, Jesus knew **"a few names"** of people who had not **"soiled their garments."**

The reward. As a matter of fact, it wasn't too late for any member of the church. **"He who conquers,"** Jesus encouraged all the members, **"shall be clad . . . in white garments, and I will not blot his name out of the book of life; I will confess his name before my Father and before his angels."**

"He who conquers" in the context of the Sardis letter means, "Whoever gets over being sleepy and wakes up." So Jesus was saying, "If you will wake up and get back to the religious vitality you once had, I will not blot your name out of the book of life but will confess your name before my Father and the angels."

When Jesus said that if a person woke up He would *not* blot his name out but would instead confess it in front of God and the angels, He made it evident that if a Sardis Christian *didn't* wake up, He would then have to erase his name. And when Christ referred to a book of life and to confessing names before God and the angels, we realize He was talking about the same pre-advent investigative judgment we were discussing a few pages ago in connection with Thyatira. It is the judgment of Daniel 7:

> As I looked, thrones were placed
>   and one that was ancient of days took his seat; . . .
> the court sat in judgment,
>   and the books were opened.
>   Daniel 7:9, 10.

Here is additional evidence that all Christians, as well as all other people, are equally subject to the final judgment.

We have reason to believe that in the judgment, Nicolaitan and Balaamite Christians will not be granted eternal life. Jezebelites won't be, either. And neither will merely sleepy Christians.

Jesus *died* to make it possible for every one of us to live forever. He wasn't playing games then, and He isn't now. He is serious and honest with us, and He has a right to expect us to be serious and honest with Him.

6. Philadelphia, church of the open door.
Revelation 3:7-13.

The setting. Not many miles southeast of Sardis lay Philadelphia, located, like Thyatira, on a broad hill between two fertile valleys. One of the valleys offered a natural gateway—an **"open door"**—through the mountains eastward, contributing considerably to Philadelphia's commercial success and cultural influence. Like the other cities on our list, Philadelphia was shaken by earthquakes from time to time. The Philadelphians apparently became particularly nervous after one of these earthquakes, living in the surrounding fields in huts and booths during the long period of aftershocks.[4]

Philadelphia means "brotherly love." This attractive name was given to the city by King Attalus II of Pergamum in memory of his older brother, King Eumenes II. Under the name of Alasehir, the "reddish city," a reasonably prosperous town of 20,000 exists today on the same site.

The commendation. Jesus commended the Philadelphian Christians and chose to overlook their faults. As with the Smyrna Christians, He sent them no rebuke. Instead He referred to their having only a **"little power,"** excusing rather than blaming them. Just before He went to the cross, He stated that we are all powerless. "Apart from me," He said on that occasion, "you can do nothing." John 15:5. **"You have kept my word,"** He said to the Philadelphian Christians with appreciation, **"and have not denied my name."**

The reward. Jesus lavished promises on the Philadelphian Christians. The **"synagogue of Satan,"** He said, would bow at their feet and learn that Christ loved them. By the synagogue of Satan He may have been referring to renegade Jews or, quite likely, to persons who claimed falsely to be Christians. See GC 1:231-236. He promised that Philadelphians who conquered would become pillars in God's temple and would never need to go out. The stability and security of eternal life with God is here contrasted with the nervousness of the people of Philadelphia after the earthquake.

Jesus also promised that conquerors would receive **"the name of my God, and the name of the city of my God, . . . and my own new name."** We have already learned the significance of a person's name as an indication of character. See pages 104-106. When Jesus promises to give us God's name, He means that, if we will cooperate with Him, He will help us develop characters of sterling quality like His own. What a promise it is!

Promising us **"the name of the city of my God"** means that we can become citizens of New Jerusalem, the capital of God's universal kingdom. See Hebrews 11:14-16; Philippians 3:20. It reminds us of the promise in Daniel 7:27, "The kingdom and the dominion and the greatness of the kingdoms under the whole heaven shall be given to the people of the saints of the Most High."

Protection in tribulation. What comfort there is in reading that Christ promised to **"keep"** the Philadelphia Christians **"from the hour of trial which is coming on**

the whole world, to try those who dwell upon the earth." The reference is to the tribulation spoken of in Daniel 12:1, "a time of trouble, such as never has been since there was a nation till that time." From *this* tribulation, Daniel 12:1 says, "your people shall be delivered." In Revelation 3:10, likewise, Jesus promised to **"keep"** the Philadelphians **"from the hour of trial."***

The supreme final hour of trial will come at the end of the world, when Michael shall arise (Daniel 12:1) after the books have been examined in the pre-advent judgment (Daniel 7:9-14) and just before the resurrection (Daniel 12:2) at the second coming.

Now, Smyrna had been faced with a ten-day tribulation, a tribulation during which it would be necessary to be **"faithful unto death."** It was to be a tribulation of persecution directed against true Christians, in which some of the faithful believers would be put to death. Thyatira also had been warned about a tribulation, but its tribulation was to be an era of punishment in which those who suffered would be the evil followers of Jezebel. See the chart on page 35.

So the letters to the seven churches talk about three different eras of tribulation: (1) The persecution of Smyrna, in which some saints would die; (2) the punishment of Thyatira, in which the followers of Jezebel would suffer; and (3) the final hour of trial, in which the whole world will be tested but from which God's people will be delivered. See pages 33-36. We must keep these distinct tribulations in mind when we ask (on pages 120-132) if the seven churches symbolize seven eras in church history.

Before we do that, however, let us ask what we need to do in order to be preserved in the coming tribulation. We are interested—and we remember that the promises are for anyone **"who has an ear,"** that is, for anyone who wants to listen.

Jesus replies, *"Because you have kept my word of patient endurance,* **I will keep you from the hour of trial which is coming."** In the Greek language in which Revelation was first written, the Greek term underlying *word* can signify "message," "instruction," or "command." The New International Version gives, "Since you have kept my *command* to endure patiently, I will also keep you." The point is that (a) Christ instructs us to face patiently the trials of everyday life, and (b) He promises that if we hold onto Him now, by His help overcoming our ordinary day-by-day temptations, He will most certainly hold on to us when the big crisis comes.

We started our discussion of Philadelphia by calling it the church of the open door. Christ introduced Himself to it as the one **"who has the key of David, who opens and no one shall shut, who shuts and no one opens."** The picture is taken from Isaiah 22:22, where, on a very local level, the words were used about a government official called Eliakim who held office for only a short period. By contrast, Jesus is the true and eternal Key-Holder, the possessor of transcendent authority.

---

*The promise to "keep" the Philadelphian Christians from the hour of trial does not mean that Christ will take them out of the world before the trial begins. It should be compared with His prayer in John 17:15, "I do not pray that thou shouldst take them out of the world, but that thou shouldst keep them from the evil one."

Jesus added in Revelation 3:8, **"I have set before you** [the Philadelphian Christians] **an open door, which no one is able to shut."** We'll discuss the concept on pages 133-139.

7. Laodicea, the insipid church.
Revelation 3:14-22.

The setting. Laodicea, the seventh and final city on Christ's correspondence list, was a business person's paradise. It was enormously wealthy and was proud of the fact. When an earthquake laid the city low around A.D. 60, Laodicea did not, like other towns, accept disaster relief from Rome. Instead, it rebuilt itself at its own expense.

Much of Laodicea's wealth came from commercial and banking interests. Significantly, an expensive black wool, soft and glossy, was marketed there and processed into prized garments and rugs. Laodicea was also famous for a medical school and for an eye ointment made from local ingredients. It was a resort town too. Hot springs bubbled out of the hills a few miles to the south. By the time the hot water reached the city via an aqueduct, it had become lukewarm, sickening to drink but just right to bathe in.

The rebuke. The congregation of Christians in Laodicea appears to have shared the city's sense of proud self-adequacy, but without justification. Jesus sent them a particularly stinging rebuke and no commendation at all. **"You say, I am rich, I**

The ruins of Laodicea's aqueduct remind us God doesn't like lukewarmness.

113

have prospered, and I need nothing," said Jesus to them, **"not knowing that you are wretched, pitiable, poor, blind, and naked."** He added, **"You are neither cold nor hot"**; you are **"lukewarm."**

Christ's way of introducing Himself to the Laodicean Christians was especially appropriate. He called Himself, **"the faithful and true witness."** He chose this title because He was talking to people who were self-deceived. He wanted them to trust His unpleasant diagnosis.

He also introduced Himself as the **"Amen,"** a Hebrew term meaning, "in truth." It was another way of reminding the self-deceived Laodiceans that He could undeceive them.

But when He called Himself **"the beginning of God's creation,"** He had something quite different in mind. He implied that if they would admit the truth of what He told them, He could turn them completely around. He could re-create them! (For a further discussion of **"the beginning of God's creation,"** see *Your Questions Answered,* pages 141, 142.)

Jesus went on to phrase His prescription for their illness in terms that the local Laodiceans could readily relate to. He pictured Himself as a heavenly merchant offering the very products they desperately needed but which they supposed they didn't need. **"I counsel you to buy from me gold refined by fire, that you may be rich, and white garments to clothe you and to keep the shame of your nakedness from being seen, and salve to anoint your eyes, that you may see."**

To people who thought they were rich, He presented Himself as the source of true riches. To people who thought they had the remedy for all sorts of eye trouble, He offered the only effective eye ointment. To people who thought they made some of the finest garments in the world, He offered the white, not black, robes of His own righteousness.

The **"white garments"** are identified in Revelation 19:7, 8, where we read about the "fine linen" of the Lamb's bride, defined as the "righteous deeds of the saints." And where do their righteous deeds come from? From Christ, for the "Lord is our righteousness." See Jeremiah 23:6. Only as Christ atones for our sinfulness, changes our motives, encourages and helps us, can we be good or do anything good.

As for the eye medicine, it is the Holy Spirit, is it not, that bothers our consciences after we've done wrong and helps us to *see* our faults. See John 16:8-10. We may think of the salve for the eyes as a symbol of the Holy Spirit.

The most valuable things in life are *faith* and *love*. We may think of them as the **"gold."** But is God's grace for sale? Can faith, love, righteousness, and the Holy Spirit be purchased?

"Ho, every one who thirsts," says God in Isaiah 55:1. "Come, buy wine and milk *without money and without price*." But in Luke 14:33 Jesus says, "Whoever of you does not renounce *all that he has* cannot be my disciple."

Christ's greatest gifts are free, but they cost everything. No coins or checks or credit cards can buy them—only the whole of our hearts.

The reward. Even the rewards promised to Laodicea imply a rebuke. **"I stand at the door and knock,"** says Jesus, implying that His presence is not at present within the Laodicean heart. But, **"if any one . . . opens the door, I will come in."**

The lavish garments, gold, and eye salve that Jesus offers are free, but they aren't sent through the mail. They are delivered personally by Jesus, Himself; and He will not force them on us. He will not enter and place them in our houses while we sleep. We must wake up and get up. We must admit that really we do not have anything to wear. We must exert ourselves to open the door, accept His white raiment, and invite Him in.

It is good to want to be a Christian; but evidently wanting to be one isn't enough. Many people will be lost while hoping and desiring to be saved. We must decide to be Christians. We must *choose* to live faith when we feel like grumbling; to live love when we feel like being bitter; to do good when we feel like doing nothing or being mean. And we must choose to do so in the only way possible, through a vital personal relationship with Jesus Christ. We must open the door and let Him in. If we want ours to be a Christian family, we must exert ourselves to bring Christ into it.

The Laodiceans were **"lukewarm,"** like the water in their aqueduct. Not very bad. Not very good. Not hostile to Christ. Not vitally committed. Not absolutely stingy. Not enthusiastically generous. Not opposed to helping people. Not doing very much for them.

Neither cold nor hot. **"Would that you were cold or hot!"** sighed Jesus. We understand why He would want us to be hot, for then we would be eager to do good, flushed with first love, full of praise and joy. But why would He want us to be cold? Because then we would be uncomfortable enough to sense that something was wrong.

"Because you are lukewarm, and neither cold nor hot, I will spew you out of my mouth."

Tough words. But not last words. **"Those whom I love, I reprove and chasten; so be zealous and repent."** Christ rebukes us to rebuild us. **"He who conquers, I will grant him to sit with me on my throne, as I myself conquered and sat down with my Father on his throne."**

Laodiceanism is the worst of the deadly diseases afflicting the churches. Lukewarmness. The blahs. Being insipid. Yet even it can be overcome. If we let Christ come fully into our lives now, He will take us into His life for eternity. He can make even smoky Laodiceans "shine . . . like the stars for ever." See Daniel 12:3.

II. Encouragement for Personal Development

Marriages are not all the same.

One of the shortest marriages I know of ended when an ambulance and a paddy wagon arrived at a wedding reception. The ambulance took the bride and her

115

attendants to a hospital. The paddy wagon took the groom and his men to the local jail.

Not very many marriages are so short! Even in divorce-prone America, well over half of first marriages still persist "till death do us part." But not all lifelong marriages are happy. Some actually flourish on spite! When asked if she ever thought of terminating her marriage, one warrior wife responded, "By divorce? Never! By murder? Every day!"[5]

With so many marriages running so long, it is sad that many of them merely persist without being genuinely successful.

Marriages and divorces happen to people. Really happy married people show personal characteristics that make up what we call "maturity." In the words of a widely used textbook, happy married people tend to be "emotionally stable, considerate of others, yielding, companionable, self-confident, and emotionally dependent."[6]

The Bible presents Jesus Christ as possessing ideal human characteristics. What a marvelous husband Jesus would have made! Manly, courageous, and self-confident, He was considerate and companionable enough to enjoy children, to forgive His personal enemies, to attract throngs of disadvantaged people, and to put His great wisdom into stories that the uneducated could understand. He had integrity enough to live out His lofty principles and to practice what He preached. And He stood up boldly to the "establishment" of His day, even single-handedly driving a crowd of protected swindlers out of the temple courts.

Most of us admire Jesus and would like to be like Him—if only it didn't seem so hard. At the moment of temptation, we too often forget our good resolutions. To help us do better and to mature our personalities, Christ's letters to the seven churches can be looked on as a series of inducements encouraging us.

In the seven letters, Jesus expresses His appreciation for the good qualities in His followers, the characteristics that resemble His own. In our families, we should express appreciation for the good qualities we see in one another. Jesus refers gratefully to **"toil"** (hard work), **"patience,"** **"faith"** (or faithfulness), **"service"** (serving others), and **"love."**

Encouraging Promises. We can find encouragement also in the tremendous promises that He offers to the people who "conquer," or overcome, the particular temptations of their time and place. The temptations referred to in the seven letters still confront us, even though in different shapes. For example, in three of the churches, Ephesus, Pergamum, and Thyatira, the strong temptation was one of compromising with aspects of contemporary culture that really were incompatible with Christianity but which many people did not think were incompatible.

Youthful Christians, new converts, and pillar-of-the-faith church members who had grown tired were easy targets for friends who pointed to the desirable or enjoyable in what the Bible forbade. It was especially hard for those young, weak, or weary Christians to resist persuasion when the persuaders were fellow Christians—Nicolaitans, Balaamites, and "Jezebel."

It is hard for Christians today to resist friends who persuade them that this and that sinful aspect of modern culture really isn't bad after all. Historian William Warren Sweet pointed out years ago that when America divided over slavery, American denominations split on the same issue. When the Civil War began, American Christians put on both blue and gray and killed each other. When America went isolationist in the 1920s, Christian support of overseas missionaries languished.[7] When (in the 1840s) millions of American Christians hotly defended slavery, when (in the 1860s) they went out to kill slaveholders, and when (in the 1920s) they reneged on their foreign-mission pledges and spent the money to erect big churches in America, they persuaded themselves that they were doing God's will. But in each case they were following the popular public trend of the hour. Like the Nicolaitans and Balaamites, they were eagerly succumbing to temptation rather than resisting their contemporary culture and really seeking out God's will.

Evangelical Christians have rejoiced when college students have shown a rising interest in religion, as they did in America in the mid-1920s, early 1950s, and late 1960s, and as they appear to be doing in the mid-1980s. Dean R. Hoge, sociologist at Catholic University, has studied such trends in religious commitment and has found that they float up and down in remarkable parallel with the interest of college students in such other concerns as "fear of communism" and "conformity to college social norms." Like most grownups, many students are good—or bad—depending largely on what their peers are.[8]

If all of this isn't surprising, here is something that may be. Eunice Kennedy Shriver, executive vice-president of the Joseph P. Kennedy Foundation, which takes a particular interest in teenage pregnancy, said once that "our young people want support and do have a sense of values." (Her conclusions resemble those of many youth workers I know.) She complained that "society itself may be encouraging teen-age sex, and then hypocritically condemning its results." On the basis of her twenty-five years of experience with teenage girls, she said she had "discovered that they would rather be given standards than contraceptives." To illustrate her point, she told of attending a particular class of teenage girls and observing the response as the teacher suggested a series of likely topics, none of which aroused their interest. But when the teacher asked, "Would you like to discuss how to say No to your boy friend without losing his love?" all hands shot up.[9]

Mrs. Shriver's point was that many young people would like to be good. Many of them would resist peer pressure if they knew how to and if they received adequate encouragement. Beneath their facade of rebelliousness, many youth "do have a sense of values" and "want support."

Bible promises can provide this support, if they are incorporated deeply into a young person's life.

> How can a young man keep his way pure?
> By guarding it according to thy word. . . .

I have laid up thy word in my heart,
that I might not sin against thee.
Psalm 119:9-11.

Some of the grandest promises of God's Word are offered us in the letters to the seven churches. **"Be faithful** [to God] **unto death, and I will give you the crown of life."** Revelation 2:10. **"To him who conquers** [i.e., who overcomes temptation] **I will grant to eat of the tree of life."** Revelation 2:7. **"He who conquers and who keeps my works until the end, I will give him power over the nations."** Revelation 2:26. **"He who conquers shall be clad . . . in white garments."** Revelation 3:5. **"If any one hears my voice and opens the door, I will come in to him and eat with him, and he with me."** Revelation 3:20.

It is too late to offer such promises for the first time to a youthful couple breathing heavily on the back seat of a car. They need to know them before they set out on their date. Christian business people need to know them before they are tempted to cheat on their income taxes, and before they spend on a cocktail party several hundred dollars that they might have contributed to an inner-city charity.

Personalize the promises! Visualize the joys of Christ's presence with us now and of spending eternity with Him later. Life on this earth is short at best. Marred though it may be, it is pretty sweet. I like to live. So do you. Christ's resurrection means everything to us, because it means He is alive and

A boy who sees his father pay an honest income tax isn't likely to cheat on his own taxes later.

that we can live happily forever. If we and the members of our families build into our conscious and subconscious minds the reality of the resurrection and of the promises of life given us in the letters to the seven churches, we can develop an almost instinctive basis for wanting to do the right thing when provoked or seduced. The Holy Spirit will remind us of the promises in all their force when we need help. Thus our characters will grow and mature.

Thoughtful warnings. Along with the promises that promote personal maturity, the letters to the seven churches alert us to our dangerous tendency to become overconfident. The Christians in Sardis and Laodicea were so sure they were OK that they lapsed into an aimless, dreamy state. The Ephesians abandoned their first love. Frankly, over-confidence is one of the risks inherent in Christianity. We know so much about God's love, about His forgiveness and His willingness to accept us the way we are (and we do need to know these wonderful things), that we can easily fool ourselves into thinking that He is content to have us *stay* the way we are.

Have relatives ever stopped by your place on their way home from vacation, with all their kids, their huge dog, and a mountain of dirty clothes? You invited them to stay overnight and they stayed for a week? They emptied your refrigerator, tore your couch, stained your carpet, and left at long last in a huff?

Well, you welcomed them, didn't you? You accepted them, just as they were. But did you want them to stay the way they were?

We cannot possibly pay God for the meals He serves us or for the white garments and gold that He sells. He doesn't want us to pay for them. He doesn't want us even to offer to pay for them. But He does want us to develop as men and women of character, serving other people intelligently for His sake, telling them about His goodness, and providing an example that they can look to for inspiration. He wants our families to become an inspiration to the whole neighborhood.

The members of our families wish that each of us would change and "grow up" on a number of points—and we know it.

Calls for repentance. Because we haven't reached the ideal yet, another recurring theme in the seven letters is the call to *repent*. Repentance means "undergoing a change of mind." God wants us to think differently today from the way we thought yesterday, especially in regard to the kind of people we are. He wants us to admit that we don't love as well as we ought to, that we compromise when we should stand firm, that we are stubborn and irritable when we should be understanding, and that we think altogether too highly of ourselves. Repentance involves admitting the truth about ourselves and making an appropriate response.

One appropriate response is a courageous determination by God's grace to be different. Another appropriate response is apologizing to people we have hurt.

I've had to apologize to my boy a lot of times for blowing my stack at him; to my wife, too, for not being exactly gracious. I'm glad to say that apologizing hasn't hurt our relationships. In fact, it seems to have helped.

Think back to Watergate. Can you remember the moment when you first real-

119

ized that the American President wasn't being honest? Can you recall how you felt? Can you conceive this imaginary scenario?

Announcer: Ladies and Gentlemen, the President of the United States.
The President: My fellow Americans, I have made a mistake. When I did it, I thought I was right; but now I realize I was wrong. I apologize to each of you. Although I don't deserve your confidence, I ask you all to help me repair the damage I have done.

Some people would have called it hypocrisy and weakness. But I think the majority of ordinary citizens would have said, "That was hard! Good for him." I think the credibility gap would have narrowed and confidence in government would have been enhanced.

Most of us are afraid to repent and apologize because we think that if we admit to having done something wrong, people will believe we really did it. Why don't we have sense enough to recognize that they've known it all along?

Have you heard of the man who by mistake put salt instead of sugar on his strawberries? He hated salty strawberries, but rather than let his wife think he had made a mistake, he kept on salting his strawberries for a decade or more.

Our faults are so evident that people wonder why we are blind to them.

That's what Jesus said about the Laodiceans: they were blind, and didn't realize it.

And naked. And poor. And insipid.

To help us wake up and become persons of rich, attractive personalities, mature men and women, successful husbands and wives, Jesus Christ offers us everything we need, the gold of loving faithfulness, the white robe of His goodness, the eye salve of Spirit-led integrity, fellowship with Himself, life after death, and a place on His throne forever.

What encouragement for character development!

III. The Seven Churches as Prophecy

Sir Isaac Newton[10] and a number of other brilliant expositors of Daniel and Revelation have suggested that the seven churches of Revelation prefigured seven eras in the future history of the church. This understanding of the letters as predictive prophecy is *in addition to* their usefulness as spiritual messages directed to the first churches that received them and to all other churches and Christians at all times.

We looked at this predictive possibility on pages 92, 93. To the considerations given there others are added under *Your Questions Answered,* on pages 142, 143. In view of the persuasive evidence pointing in this direction, it seems worthwhile to spend a few moments looking again at the letters to the seven churches to see whether they do match up with seven phases in the experience of the church between Christ's ascension and His second coming.

120

1. *Ephesus, 31-100.**

Ephesus was rebuked for having abandoned its early love. At the same time, it was praised for its perseverance and good works and, in particular, it was praised for having tested and repudiated false teachers. Its zeal was tarnished, but its beliefs were bright. Everyone will agree that the description very acceptably matches the church during the age of the New Testament down to roughly A.D. 100. The purity of the New Testament church represents an ideal to which numerous reform movements since have sought to return.

2. *Smyrna, 100-313.*

Nothing is said in the seven letters about the doctrines of the Smyrna Christians. We are directed instead to their loyalty under persecution. Again, everyone will agree that the description reliably fits the experience of the church during the second and third centuries, that is, between 100 and the close of the Diocletian persecution in 313. See GC 1:125. Some important doctrinal aberrations did develop in the church during this period, but more noteworthy in Christ's evaluation was His follower's constancy under fire.

The remark in the Smyrna letter about persons who **"say that they are Jews and are not"** (Revelation 2:9), may perhaps be a literal reference to those Jewish people who, in their excitement, assisted in the burning of Polycarp. In the symbolic understanding of Smyrna as a period of church history, however, false **"Jews"** may perhaps be understood as false Christians. See GC 1:231-236. Such an understanding fits the large number of Gnostic Christians (see GC 1:123, 126), whose ingenious reinterpretations of the Bible gave the Bible Christians of the period a vast amount of concern.

3. *Pergamum, 313-538.*   4. *Thyatira, 538-1565.*

In painful contrast to the first two churches, the second two, Pergamum and Thyatira, deserved severe rebukes for their erroneous doctrines. Pergamum needed to repent, as a whole church, because it permitted Nicolaitans and Balaamites. Even worse, Thyatira tolerated Jezebel.

Few people acquainted with the facts will deny that Christianity underwent a serious declension with the so-called Christianization of the Roman Empire and with the advance of the Middle Ages.

When the seven churches are viewed as we are viewing them now, as *symbols*, the sins of the Nicolaitans, Balaamites, and Jezebel are also taken symbolically. The Old Testament prophets used "adultery" to describe the wickedness of God's people when entering into *religious* and *political alliance* with the pagan nations of their day. See, for example, Ezekiel 16 and 23. The ancient Israelites adulterated God's truth and purity with the philosophy, immorality, and coercive techniques of the nations around them. In the process, they gave up their faith in

*The dates given for the seven church eras are in most cases only approximate. Eras in human thought and experience usually do not begin and end neatly at specific moments!

121

God, lost sight of their potential as His people, and grievously abased themselves. The terms **"Nicolaitans," "Balaamites,"** and **"Jezebel"** are symbolic of the *deepening progress* of Christian apostasy. In the Old Testament, Jezebel epitomized the most degrading adulteration of God's people with the harmful culture of their neighbors.

Now, we have noticed that in the book of Daniel, the prophecies about the two little horns of Daniel 7 and 8 are primarily concerned with the bad side of the Roman Church. It is a pleasure in the seven letters to see the emphasis Christ chooses to place on the good aspects that were mixed with the bad.

In spite of the presence of Nicolaitans and Balaamites in the church of Pergamum, Jesus could say, **"You hold fast my name and you did not deny my faith."** One excellent feature of this period—one among many good features that might be mentioned—was the close attention given to the understanding of the person of Jesus Christ. The great Council of Nicaea (A.D. 325) concluded after much study and deliberation that Jesus is truly God. The Council of Constantinople (381) concluded that He is also truly man. The Council of Ephesus (431) concluded that His Godhood and manhood are combined in a single unified Person; and the Council of Chalcedon (451), that He nonetheless continues to possess two distinct divine and human natures. Each decision was made in response to the challenge of individuals who had taken an opposite position. These grand affirmations arrived at during the Pergamum period are in harmony with the Bible and are still cherished by millions of Catholics and Protestants around the world.

For the Thyatira period, Christ spoke not only about Jezebel and her followers but also about the church's **"works, . . . love and faith and service and patient endurance."** He could say that with the passing of time their good works grew even better: **"Your latter works exceed the first."** Revelation 2:19. He could also speak of **"the rest of you in Thyatira, who do not hold"** to the teachings of Jezebel and **"who have not learned what some call the deep things of Satan."** Verse 24.

Here we are happily reminded that during the Thyatira period (roughly 538 to 1565), the Roman Church deserved high praise for its hospitals, orphanages, schools, and missions. Even Martin Luther, who in his later years was not widely known for complimenting Catholics, spoke warmly of the "splendidly built" hospitals in Italy, with their "very diligent" attendants, "very clean" beds, and "learned" physicians.[11]

Jesus refers to **"the *rest* of you in Thyatira, who do not *hold*"** to the teachings of Jezebel and **"who have *not* learned what some call the deep things of Satan."** He seems to be thinking of such earnest Christians as Jan Milič of Prague; John Wycliffe and his followers, the Lollards; and John Huss and his numerous Hussites. See pages 31-33. We think also of Peter Waldo and the Waldenses, and, perhaps, St. Francis of Assisi and the early Franciscans.

Marvelous as were the good works of the medieval church and brave as were many of its members, something went seriously awry. There is wide agreement that the church descended to a very low ebb during the Middle Ages, when all

122

Europe was nominally Christian. The unhappy story has been surveyed before (see pages 29-33 and GC 1:122-135) and does not need repeating here. Paul's prophecy that there was to be a "falling away" (2 Thessalonians 2:3, K.J.V.) was all too tragically fulfilled.

Basic to the "falling away" was the willingness of the medieval church to substitute the human for the divine. Scripture, the cross, and Christ's priesthood were never denied. Far from it; they were referred to often with reverence. But in day-to-day practice, heavenly truths came to be obscured by churchly traditions. Good works, either one's own or those of chosen saints, came to be valued as being at least as essential as having faith in Jesus.

The result of this turning away from the divine to the human was most unfortunate for the morals of the church and its leadership. Around 1500, just prior to the Reformation, the famous Catholic intellectual, Erasmus, said that in his day the easiest way to offend a layman was to call him a priest or a monk. Looking back to the same era, Cambridge historian Owen Chadwick says that "everyone that mattered in the Western Church was crying out for reformation."[12]

"I gave her time to repent," said Jesus prophetically about **"Jezebel,"** but **"she refuses to repent."** Revelation 2:21. Impetus toward reform came repeatedly—in the tenth century and later from the monastery of Cluny, in the thirteenth century from Francis of Assisi, in the fourteenth and fifteenth from general councils, and

Herbs for the doctor. During the Middle Ages, Catholics provided almost the only hospitals. Jesus praised them. He said, "I know your works."

in the sixteenth from Martin Luther and others. Everyone knows how God blessed the world through Martin Luther, even in his early days when he was still a Catholic professor in a Catholic university and the administrator of several monasteries. While studying the Catholic version of the Bible he read to his delight, "A man is justified by faith apart from works of law." Romans 3:28.

Of course, he read it in Latin, which the Douay Bible would later translate, " . . . by faith, without the works of the law."

Luther found the same blessed message in Ephesians 2:8, 9, "By grace you have been saved through faith; and this is not your own doing, it is the gift of God—not because of works, lest any man should boast."

The great discovery of the Reformation was that salvation isn't earned; it's accepted. And it's free.

The story has been told a thousand times about the elderly American Quaker who outbid all competitors to purchase a particularly stalwart—and indomitable—black slave. Repeatedly as the bidding progressed, he heard the black man express his indignation at slavery by declaring emphatically, "I won't work. I won't work."

The Quaker took the slave home and explained several times that he had bought him only to set him free. When the truth at last came clear, the black man knelt at the Quaker's feet and pledged with tears, "Master, I'll work for you all of my life. I'll serve you as long as I live."

Here is the simple gospel—and the effect of it. Jesus paid the price, the whole price, to set us free. When we see ourselves as real sinners and when we see Christ as our personal Saviour, hanging on the cross to set us free, we long to kneel at His feet in gratitude and consecrate ourselves to Him forever.

Luther's discovery changed the course of history. The Reformation is still seen as a watershed.

Here was Thyatira's grandest opportunity to date. **"I gave her time to repent."** But sadly the words follow, **"She refuses to repent."**

The official reaction to Luther is well known. The pope called him a "wild boar" in 1520 and excommunicated him in 1521. Later, the celebrated Council of Trent (1545-1563) insisted[13] that after baptism justification is no longer by faith alone but requires priestly pardon, penance, and a period in purgatory. See GC 1:177, 178.

The Council of Trent is often referred to as one of the principal features of the Catholic Counter-Reformation. In response to Luther's challenge it did effect a number of reforms, but these were largely of an administrative nature. Priests, for example, were required to be better educated and to observe higher moral standards, bishops were ordered to live within their dioceses rather than in palaces elsewhere, and so on. The Council of Trent also codified Catholic theology into an official system for the first time. In doing this, unfortunately, it elected to stand solidly with the Middle Ages. Vigorous debates were held at the council, for on several important points a number of Catholic leaders urgently desired to

124

see changes made in line with the Protestant Reformation. But the debates were continued until traditional views won out. Shortly after the council's close, Pope Pius V declared St. Thomas Aquinas to be a doctor (that is, a principal teacher) of the church. Aquinas was the greatest theologian of the later Middle Ages.

The close of the Council of Trent in 1563 seems an appropriate place to end the Thyatira period. But in history, trends and movements do not ordinarily begin and end on specific dates. Nor has the Christian church ever been homogeneous. Look at the differences among the seven literal churches during the symbolic Ephesus period! So if we think of Thyatira as a dolphin (see page 94) that dominated the Christian scene for a particular period, we are bound to think of it also as swimming not far beneath the surface as we enter the later periods.

Williston Walker, whose textbook has been widely used in colleges and seminaries for nearly a century, says that about this time (the 1560s) a new spirit stirred those parts of Europe that continued to be Catholic. This new spirit was "[1] intense in its opposition to Protestantism, [2] mediaeval in its theology, but [3] ready to fight or to suffer for its faith."[14]

To fight for one's faith is intrinsically different from suffering for one's faith. The new Catholics were, if anything, too willing to fight. So also were the Protestants, as we shall see in our discussion of Sardis.

Jesus had indicated that if **"Jezebel"** refused to repent, He would have to allow events to run their natural course. **"Behold,"** He said, **"I will throw her [Jezebel] on a sickbed, and those who commit adultery with her I will throw into great tribulation, unless they repent of her doings; and I will strike her children dead."** Revelation 2:22, 23.

This **"great tribulation"** is not the time of trouble at the end of the age from which all true Christians will be delivered (Revelation 3:10); nor is it the tribulation experienced by Smyrna, when the saints suffered (Revelation 2:10). It appears rather to be the same "great tribulation" foretold in the Olivet Discourse, a crisis so severe that it would seem to threaten the existence of humanity. See pages 33-36.

As Europe successively rejected its various opportunities for reform, as never before, not even during the century of the Roman Empire's collapse, "Western people walked through the valley of the shadow of death. The greatest famine of the Middle Ages struck in the second decade of the fourteenth century, and an estimated two-fifths of the overall population of Europe died when bubonic plague, or the Black Death, following the trade routes, erupted in midcentury. The Hundred Years' War between England and France not only spanned the fourteenth and fifteenth centuries, but also introduced the weaponry of modern warfare, in the form of gunpowder and heavy artillery, during its later stages. Great agrarian and urban revolts by the poor rent the social fabric in both town and countryside."[15]

The Black Death was a form of bubonic plague that caused dark patches under the skin. Most of its victims died in a few days, many in a few hours. In some

125

communities it left no one alive to bury the dead. It remained endemic for three hundred years. Was this Thyatira's sickbed?

Along with the continued presence of the plague, in Europe in the 1600s religious hostilities cumulated between Catholics in the south and Lutherans in the north. The populace staggered sullenly into the Thirty Years' War of 1618-1648. When at the end of that horrendous conflict common sense revived at last, the survivors found that central Europe had been plowed from end to end by soldiers and lawless brigands, bands of wild orphans were wandering everywhere, countless women had been ravished, and both industry and agriculture were paralyzed. Estimates of casualties have been set as high as ten million deaths out of an initial population of only eighteen million in Germany alone![16]

If the Catholic south of Europe had adopted justification by faith and its related Reformation principles, and if the Protestant north had remembered them, the frightful Thirty Years' War would not have occurred.

5. Sardis, 1565-1740.

Viewed as a prophetic symbol, Sardis aptly reflects the stagnant, self-satisfied condition of Protestantism for two centuries (from about 1565 to around 1740) following the initial brilliance of the Reformation. Relying on its Reformation reputation, Sardis had the **"name"** of life but was largely **"dead."** Revelation 3:1.

The Lutheran Reformation gave Christianity a new start. For a while, millions

So many people died of the Black Death that their bodies were carted away in wagons.

reveled in a clearer view of our gracious God than they had ever known before. The Bible became prominent. Education was markedly improved, for the Reformers desired everyone to be able to read the Bible and understand it for himself. Large sums, formerly spent to pay priests to say endless masses for the dead, were now spent to relieve the poor. Monks left their monasteries to get jobs out in the world. Priests, monks, and nuns were encouraged to marry. Countless fathers led out daily in family worship.

But the sweetness soured. By a tragic turn of events, it came to seem more important to express justification by faith in precisely correct terminology than to experience it in one's life. Says Lutheran historian Lars Qualben, "The Gospel was treated as doctrine rather than as a power of God unto salvation, and Christianity was presented as a religion of right thinking without a corresponding emphasis on the right condition of the heart." The Bible became a kind of arsenal of theological weapons. Debates produced "quarrelsome theologians and a parched Protestantism."[17] So unpleasant did these debates become that Philipp Melanchthon, Luther's closest ally, rejoiced as his death approached in 1560 that soon he would escape the "rage of the theologians."[18]

In 1577, a rigid peace was achieved among the Lutherans with the Formula of Concord and, in 1580, with the Book of Concord, signed by representatives of eighty-six small Lutheran state-churches and by about 8000 Lutheran pastors and teachers. The followers of Luther now had their definitive dogmatic creed just as, through the Council of Trent, the Roman Catholics had theirs. Lutheranism became a "Sardis" atop its mountain spur, protected by precipices seemingly unassailable and, sad to say, strangely cold, formal, and stagnant.

In Britain, the Church of England also lost much of its original fervor and took lofty refuge behind its creed, the Thirty-Nine Articles.

The followers of John Calvin, the second greatest leader of the Reformation, demonstrated outstanding creativity over a longer period. They were known as Reformed Christians in central Europe, Huguenots in France, and Puritans in England. In time, the Puritans became known as Presbyterians and Congregationalists and, still later in the United States, as Baptists, as well.

In spite of the heroic initial contributions of each Protestant movement, Protestant Europe in the 1700s became vastly different from what the Reformers had envisaged. Intellectuals denied the resurrection and the second coming and became rationalists, leading to the dark period known strangely as the Enlightenment or Aufklärung. Ordinary people were expected only to attend church and believe what they were taught. England drifted to the verge of godlessness. There, in the early 1700s, "popular amusements were coarse, illiteracy wide-spread, law savage in its enforcement, jails sinks of disease and iniquity. Drunkenness was more wide-spread than at any other period in English history."[19]

If only the Protestants in Sardis had remembered the glorious things they had **"received and heard"** (Revelation 3:3) when the Reformation began, how differently things would have turned out!

But what about the **"few names"** in Sardis who had not **"soiled their garments,"** the people who were wide awake and **"worthy"**? Verse 4.

The Lutherans had a good many of them. Paul Gerhardt (1607-1676) wrote deeply spiritual hymns still loved by many denominations, including "O Sacred Head Now Wounded." George Fredrick Handel (1685-1759) composed the *Messiah*. Johann Sebastian Bach (1685-1750) enriched the worship of the entire Western church. Johannes Bengel (1687-1752) produced an outstanding commentary on the New Testament.

We don't want to omit George Fox (1624-1691), the warmly religious founder of the Quakers. Or John Bunyan (1628-1688), the Baptist who helped multitudes in all denominations with his *Pilgrim's Progress* and his *Grace Abounding to the Chief of Sinners*. Or Dorothy Traske (died around 1640), who suffered sixteen years in prison because she loved Christ's seventh-day Sabbath. See GC 1:139.

Philipp Jacob Spener (1635-1705) made a grand contribution. He got Christians to meet in small groups for devotional Bible study and prayer. His "Pietism" had profound effects. Partly under the influence of Spener's Pietism, Count Nikolaus von Zinzendorf (1700-1760) sponsored a group of Moravian Brethren who settled in a village called Herrnhut on his large private estate. These Moravians, who maintained ties with the Lutherans, developed a deeply spiritual relationship to God and to each other. Honoring Christ's command to send the gospel everywhere before His second coming, they sent out members of their movement as missionaries to the hardest possible places—to the Arctic and to South Africa, for instance, when such places seemed truly to be at the ends of the earth.

Twenty-six Moravians went as missionaries to Georgia shortly after that American colony was founded. During a storm on the Atlantic, they remained amazingly calm and peaceful. The same storm thoroughly frightened John Wesley, who was also on board. Wesley, the future founder of Methodism, was then a pious young minister of the Church of England going out as a missionary to America. He became very curious to know what it was the Moravians had that he didn't have.

Later, on land, A. G. Spangenberg, a prominent Moravian leader, talked personally with young John. "Do you know Christ?" he asked.

"I know He is the Saviour of the world," Wesley replied.

"True," acknowledged Spangenberg, "but do you know He has saved *you*?"

Wesley returned from America to England two or three years later, determined to know more about the Moravians' Jesus. While praying for light, on May 24, 1738, he attended an Anglican meeting in a chapel on Aldersgate Street in London. He heard someone read aloud from Luther's preface to his *Commentary on Romans*. This means that he heard about justification by faith from the pen of the Reformer who had learned so much about that subject.

"About a quarter before nine," wrote Wesley later in words that seem immortal, "while he [Luther] was describing the change which God works in the heart through faith in Christ, I felt my heart strangely warmed. I felt I did trust in

128

Christ, Christ alone, for salvation; and an assurance was given me, that He had taken away my sins, even mine, and saved me from the law of sin and death."

In this enlightened moment, Wesley **"remembered"** what Christians had **"received and heard"** in the wonderful new days of the Reformation. But the *result* of his discovery of Jesus as His own personal Saviour belongs in the Philadelphia era of the church.

6. *Philadelphia 1750-1844.*

The Philadelphia era may be thought of as running approximately between the middle of the 1700s and the middle of the 1800s. Jesus spoke only good of the Philadelphia church. **"You have kept my word and have not denied my name,"** He said. **"You have kept my word of patient endurance."** The name, Philadelphia, connotes brotherly love.

Philadelphia was a beautiful church and foreshadowed a beautiful era in the church's ongoing experience. (We'll discuss its open door in our next section.)

After John Wesley's heart was "strangely warmed," something very appealing happened to his ministry, and people in large numbers were attracted to his messages. Mostly, but by no means altogether, these were the less-fortunate people of those bad old days—the coarse, the illiterate, and the drunk—that we spoke of on page 127. Ministers who had churches large enough to hold such crowds disdained

In western Britain John Wesley preached outdoors to crowds of coal miners at sunrise.

them, so Wesley took to the fields. He preached outdoors, on weekdays, at sunrise, before the men went to work. He encouraged his listeners and their families to attend regular Church of England services, but he organized them into societies like the Pietist prayer groups.

George Whitefield, a close friend of John Wesley's, held vast audiences spellbound with his messages too. And John's brother, Charles Wesley, wrote hundreds of hymns. "Jesus, Lover of My Soul" and "Hark! The Herald Angels Sing" are two of the most famous of them.

A change came over England so profound it has a name, the evangelical awakening. It led to the formation of the Methodist Church which today numbers many millions worldwide. George Whitefield's preaching contributed largely to the Great Awakening in New England (1740), which revived the Congregational and Presbyterian churches there and led to the formation of the Baptist church, which like the Methodist has a vast worldwide membership.

While the evangelical awakening continued in England, another awakening occurred later in the century in America and yet another, even greater, in the early 1800s. In fact, the early part of the nineteenth century was a prodigious time for evangelism in the cities, towns, and forests of the new United States. A surge of piety pulsed also in Catholic France, as Christian people there reacted against the popular atheism of the French Revolution.

The era of revivals stirred a magnificent missionary undertaking. British Christians, for example, resolved to make the most of the rising British Empire to teach Christ's salvation where British guns spoke imperialism.

It is said that in 1785 there existed only twenty Protestant mission stations in the world, half of them operated by the small group of Moravians. Then William Carey, a shoemaker and lay Baptist pastor, heard God's call. Before Carey left England and sailed to India in 1793, he helped organize the Baptist Missionary Society, which proceeded to raise money and to select other individuals to send as missionaries. Three years later, the interdenominational London Missionary Society (L.M.S.) was organized, and after another two years, a third missionary society in Holland; then one in Berlin, and in 1810 the American Board of Commissioners for Foreign Missions (A.B.C.F.M.) in America, and so on, until there were dozens of Protestant missionary societies. In 1804 the British and Foreign Bible Society came into being to help provide inexpensive Bibles and Bible portions in the new languages the missionaries needed. It was followed by numerous other Bible societies in Europe and America.

Overseas missions by no means exhausted the energies of the awakened "Philadelphians." "Religion is a commodity of which the more we exported the more we had remaining," observed an American Christian in the early 1800s.[20]

A new interest was taken in children. Robert Raikes in Britain launched the Sunday School movement, which affected for good millions of children in Europe and America. George Müller began an orphange in 1832 that grew until it cared for 2000 homeless waifs at a time; and it was only one of many orphanages. William Wilberforce got slavery outlawed in the British Empire in 1833; other Christians worked for its abolition in America. Hundreds of church-related colleges took birth. Many, many Christian societies and associations came into existence to improve people's happiness. And most of the grand projects were interdenominational and were staffed and supported largely by laity. It was an era of interchurch cooperation and of remarkable enthusiasm and self-sacrifice. It was coupled with a devotional belief in Jesus Christ as everyone's personal Saviour. It is appropriate to call it Philadelphia.

And still we have said nothing about the tremendous new interest in Bible prophecy that exploded in many denominations during this exciting era. God had promised Daniel that in the "time of the end," at the close of the 1260 year-days, his book would be opened. See Daniel 12:4. We'll reserve our discussion about this development till we come to Revelation 11 and 14.

7. Laodicea, 1844-.

But now we face a disappointment. After the Philadelphia era comes Laodicea. The beauty of brotherly love is replaced by lukewarmness and conceit. During the Philadelphia period Jesus stated, **"I am coming soon."** Revelation 3:11. Jesus *is* coming soon; but in spite of His promise, His church turns away.

Nothing is said here directly, one way or the other, about Laodicea's doctrinal beliefs. The problem Christ chooses to call attention to is even more basic, one of deep-seated attitude. The Laodicean church is half-hearted and content. It is half-hearted about its good works and content with a religious experience that seems to be spiritual but is virtually Christless.

We have learned already that at any given time some Christians and some whole congregations may reflect any one of the seven churches. As predictive symbols, the seven churches represent only the *dominant* experience of Christ's church in each era.

Long after the mid-nineteenth century (when Philadelphia closed), Christianity as a whole seemed to continue virile and vital and even in some aspects to advance. The missionary enterprise expanded. New denominations arose full of zeal. Immense sums were donated to charity. Actually, however, deep changes had begun to set in, changes that we'll understand better when we discuss Revelation 12 to 14.

It may be enough now to call attention to such things as the startling fissure that split the Methodists and Baptists of America in 1844, with one half of each denomination bitterly determined to preserve slavery as a God-blessed institution! More subtle and more permanently pervasive was the alacrity with which Protestants hurried to adapt themselves to Darwinian evolution. New ideas about the inevitability of human progress, based on evolution, combined with strange new ideas about the second coming of Christ began to turn the attention of millions of Christians from their need of Jesus as a personal Saviour. Along with these developments arose a surprising hostility to the seventh-day Sabbath.

And, of course, creeping materialism eroded Christian values.

When a person has life insurance, a boat, three cars, and two homes, it is easy to think that he doesn't need a personal relationship with God as well. Said Jesus, "You cannot serve God and mammon" (Matthew 6:24); that is, "You cannot serve both God and money." T.E.V. But most of us try to serve both of them— and end up being neither good worldlings nor good Christians.

On May 2, 1980, *Christianity Today*, the principal mouthpiece of Evangelical Christians in America, published the results of a poll showing that 94 percent of all Americans believe in God, 79 percent claim to have been converted, and 45 percent believe that salvation is granted through faith in Christ. The magazine concluded that "clearly, the country's religious pulse is strong."

Tragically, *Christianity Today* also pointed out that one third of the Catholics polled said they never read the Bible, that only 24 percent of the Protestants claimed to attend church every week, and that 42 percent even of the Evangelicals could not name more than four of the Ten Commandments.

So 94 percent of Americans claim to believe in God—yet they spend six times more on their pets than they give to foreign missions. See page 45.

Fifteen million children under five years of age die in the third world every year. The United Nations tells us that 90 percent of them (that is, that more than *thirteen million* boys and girls every year) could be saved if only their families had access to clean water. The cost of cleaning up third-world water supplies has been estimated at three to four billion dollars a year for ten years. Such a price tag sounds expensive, and it is. But it is only a fraction of what the almost-Christian United States spends annually on alcoholic beverages.

"Clearly, the country's religious pulse is strong," said the magazine. Well, yes, but it could be far stronger.

And if America is far short of Christ's ideal, the condition of the church in Europe and other Western nations is still less favorable.

That the church of the last days would be lax and lukewarm was foreshadowed not only in the seven letters, but also in Christ's anguished inquiry, "When the Son of man comes, will he find faith on earth?" Luke 18:8. It was revealed also in His parable of the ten sleepy girls, five of whom foolishly failed to supply enough oil for their lamps. (See pages 37-39.) As a group, the ten girls were half-and-half, like Laodicea. In a similar vein, Paul spoke of Christians "in the last days" as "holding the form of religion but denying the power of it." 2 Timothy 3:1, 5.

Our survey of church history has justified our anticipation. Viewed as predictive symbols, the seven churches do match up with seven great eras. How patient Christ has been through the years! What care the divine Lamptrimmer has shown for His smoky churches and awkward Christians.

How sobering, however, to realize that, with Christ's second coming drawing very close, we are today living in Laodicea.

Thank God that Jesus represents Himself as standing and knocking outside *our* door.

IV. Two Open Doors

To the Philadelphian church Jesus said, **"I have set before you an open door, which no one is able to shut."** Revelation 3:8.

To the Laodiceans He said, **"I stand at the door and knock; if any one . . . opens the door, I will come in."** Revelation 3:20.

Two doors—one in heaven, already open; the other one on earth, needing to be opened.

One, a door that none of us can close; the other, a door that only we can open.

The first, a door that Christ has opened so that we may go through it; the second, a door that we are to open so Christ may go through it.

Christ's open door. Because Paul often spoke of an opportunity for missionary service as being like an open door (see 1 Corinthians 16:9; 2 Corinthians 2:12), some commentators have supposed that the open door in the letter to the Philadelphians is also a door of missionary opportunity. Doors of missionary opportunity, unfortunately, have a way of being closed by all sorts of people, whereas the door in Revelation 3:8 is one that **"no one is able to shut."**

For an identification of this open door, it is better to look within the book of Revelation. And the first verse of Revelation 4 says, "Lo, *in heaven* an open door."

In His Sermon on the Mount, Jesus said, "Ask, and it will be given you; . . . knock, and it will be opened to you." Matthew 7:7. By inviting us in this passage to "knock," He was encouraging us to pray, and His advice still stands. But in Revelation He lets us know that the door to heaven is already open. All we need to do is walk through it, by faith.

There is no need to make an appointment. There's no waiting in line. And no receptionist says, "I'm sorry, but my boss is too busy."

There is no mediator between God and men except the man Christ Jesus (see 1 Timothy 2:5); and Jesus says, **"I have set before you an open door."**

When King Henry IV tried to apologize to Pope Gregory VII in January 1077, high in the north Italian Alps, the Pontiff, who claimed to be Christ's representative, kept the monarch waiting in the snow for three days. He did finally allow the king to enter, but, according to the Pope's own correspondence,[21] only with great reluctance. It was by such an attitude that Christ's *tamid*, His "continual" ministry in the heavenly sanctuary, was obscured. See GC 1:130, 131, 161-172.

Many doors in public buildings are marked, "Keep this door closed." Jesus says that the door to His heavenly sanctuary is open—"Please come in."

Inasmuch then as "we have a great high priest who has passed through the heavens, Jesus, the Son of God, let us . . . with confidence draw near to the throne of grace, that we may receive mercy and find grace to help in time of need." Hebrews 4:14-16.

We all have troubles, children as well as adults. Jesus wants every one of us, when trials and temptations occur, to accustom ourselves to thinking that be-

133

tween us and our heavenly Father there is nothing at all, nothing except a big door, opened as wide as the sky.

He doesn't mean that when we run through this open door to see Him He will always give us what we ask. He's too wise and loving to do that. He means that He really cares and that He will do for us even better than we ask. As we just read, He will certainly give us "mercy" and "grace to help in time of need."

Is our door open? Heaven's door is wide open. But what about ours? **"Behold,"** says Jesus, **"I stand at the door and knock; if any one hears my voice and opens the door, I will come in to him and eat with him, and he with me."** Revelation 3:20.

In person, of course, Jesus is resident with the Father in the heavenly sanctuary. We read this too a moment ago in Hebrews 4:14-16. But on earth the Holy Spirit is so truly and fully Christ's representative that Jesus speaks of the Spirit almost as if the Spirit were Himself. See, for example, John 14:16-18. So we too will speak, as the Bible does, of Jesus at the door, at our door.

Jesus has the **"key of David."** Revelation 3:7. He has authority to open any door. Why then doesn't He open our door and walk in on His own?

Because He has no desire to compel us. He values our freedom of choice. In fact, He came to make us free. "If the Son makes you free, you will be free indeed." John 8:36. His life, death, and continual ministry in our behalf in heaven (see Hebrews 7:25) show how deeply He values our freedom.

Because He wants us to be free—free from sin and truly free to choose our own life-styles—He simply would not consider barging uninvited into our privacy. So let us look through the window and observe Him standing there, at our door.

He has traveled a very long way.

James and Ellen White, young people who helped found the Seventh-day Adventist Church, once became concerned over the spiritual state of some of their friends who lived about 240 kilometers (about 150 miles) away from them. Their only transportation—in the early winter of 1856—was by open sleigh. Deep snow and bitter winds reduced their speed to 40 kilometers (25 miles) a day.

The bridgeless Mississippi posed a threat. Not yet frozen hard, it was too nearly frozen for a ferry. As the horses' hooves splashed into the floating icy slush and the Mississippi waters swirled up over the sleigh's wooden floor, James and Ellen saw local farmers gather on the river banks to watch them drown.

James and Ellen *really* wanted to reach their friends and persuade them to reopen their hearts to Christ. I'm glad to report that their gallant effort and lengthy journey were not in vain. The people opened their hearts.

Jesus has traveled much farther and harder to reach our hearts. He has come by the route of the cross. And He has knocked lovingly on every door along the way.

You can see Him out there now. He is carrying presents: white garments, eye salve, gold. And concerned though He is with the salvation of the whole world, He nonetheless has as much time for each one of us as we have for Him. **"If any one . . . opens . . . , I will come in to him and eat with him, and he with me."**

135

Creator and Redeemer, Jesus is also the Divine Salesman knocking at our door, offering righteousness "without money and without price."

The Saviour is waiting to enter your heart,
　　Why don't you let Him come in?
There's nothing in this world to keep you apart,
　　What is your answer to Him?

Time after time He has waited before,
　　And now He is waiting again
To see if you're willing to open the door;
　　O how He wants to come in![22]

Kings and queens with Him. Christ's ultimate purpose in knocking on our doors is not merely to visit with us for a while here and now but, as the next verse reveals, it is to help us "conquer" so we can reign with Him forever. The Christian life is a happy one, but it is also a battle against temptation and sin. **"He who conquers,"** says Jesus, that is, he who defeats sin and comes off conqueror, **"I will grant him to sit with me on my throne, as I myself conquered and sat down with my Father on his throne."** Revelation 3:21.

The purpose of all the promises in the seven letters to the churches is to encourage us to be conquerors in life's battle against temptation and sin. The tree of life is promised in Christ's Ephesian letter to him **"who conquers"**; that is, it is promised to the person who overcomes the temptation to be spiritually cold and, instead, returns to his or her first love. Exemption from the second death is promised in the Smyrna letter to him **"who conquers,"** that is, to the person who bravely overcomes all temptations to doubt or bitterness and instead maintains a cheerful Christian faith even when persecuted. The iron rod and the morning star are promised in the Thyatira letter to him **"who conquers,"** that is, to the person who consistently resists the sensuous temptations of Jezebel. And so on.

Christ conquered. **"I myself conquered and sat down with my Father on his throne."** Now He comes to help us conquer.

"I can do all things in him who strengthens me," writes Paul triumphantly from his prison. Philippians 4:13. And on another occasion: "If any one is in Christ, he is a new creation; the old has passed away, behold, the new has come." 2 Corinthians 5:17.

"Christ *in you*, the hope of glory." Colossians 1:27.

Conquerors. Revelation 2 and 3. New creations. 2 Corinthians 5. A bride "without spot or wrinkle." Ephesians 5. "The people of the saints of the Most High." Daniel 7. They are all different pictures of Christ's glorious goal, a vast assemblage of genuine Christians, men and women, boys and girls, who are fit to live together happily in His wonderful new earth for eternity. People who in this life on this present earth know by experience the power of *"Christ in you,"* a power that neither earth nor death nor hell can master. This is why He wants to come in. This is why He wants us to open our door.

Many Christians are content to be ordinary. They're Christians and they're glad to be such. And when they find themselves not much different from other people, they give the matter little thought. Yet Jesus wants us to be more than merely ordinary.

Sometimes I try to get youthful Christians to think of Christ as standing at the doors of various rooms *inside* their hearts. They have invited Christ into the "house" of their lives. They intend to be Christians; but too often they leave Jesus alone in the front parlor while they sneak off to their favorite sin room deep inside their minds.

When we're young, some of us have, let us say, a green room. The walls, furniture, and carpet are green. There we settle down to stroke the green doll of our jealousies. "What makes Lisa think she's so good?" we grumble. "If her folks weren't rich, no one would pay attention to her. I'm a lot smarter than she is." Or whatever.

Suddenly we're startled by a knock. Jesus is at the door of our green room, asking to be allowed in.

Or we have a purple room where we rehearse angry phrases we would like to say to people who have been unkind to us—phrases which, of course, "we would never think of saying."

We have gray rooms, where we take pity on ourselves. (It feels so good to feel bad.) And ambition rooms, entertainment rooms, friendship rooms, music rooms, sex rooms, and more.

Older Christians too seem to have such rooms.

Into all our inner rooms Christ seeks entrance. He is the grand Redecorator. He would like to help us choose different colors. He would like to suggest different thoughts for us to think. He would like to show us how to overcome bitterness and selfishness deep inside the workings of our minds. He would like to help us make close friends out of our enemies, direct our ambitions to the happiness of other people, and stand as kings and queens over our bad habits.

When my wife and I step outside in the spring, the grackles that nest in our yard scold and fret. They eat their fill at our feeding station, but they see no relation between our generosity and our presence. They fear that if we get too close, we'll harm them or their nestlings. "Birds lack faith," said Luther once. "They fly away when I enter the orchard, though I mean them no ill. Even so do we lack faith in God."[23]

Are we perhaps afraid of letting Christ come all the way in, even though we know He is our Friend? Or are we eager to trust Him and entrust our all to Him?

How serious are we about wanting to be fully His and about wanting our families to be fully His?

The Ephesian Christians were serious enough for a while, but they fell away from their first enthusiasm. The Pergamum Christians tolerated the Nicolaitan heresy, urging that it didn't matter what they did as long as they "believed in Jesus." In Thyatira, many Christians wanted to be Christian, while they openly flirted with Jezebel. In the process, they allowed her earthly priesthood to come

137

between themselves and their heavenly High Priest. They chose to believe that their own efforts and donations could help buy eternal life. They willingly neglected the Bible. They ignored God's Sabbath. They wove pagan Greek philosophy and imperial Roman oppressiveness into their daily life-style. And when the Reformation came, too many of them continued to favor familiar traditions above rediscovered Bible truths. The Sardis Christians looked alive, but they were nearly dead. They claimed to be reformed, but they made no heartfelt commitment. The Laodicean Christians didn't care.

How much do we care? "Sanctify them in the truth; thy word is truth." John 17:17. Do we really desire an intelligent, personal, conquering relationship with the loving God of the Bible? Do we, more than anything else, want God's *Bible truth* to transform and energize our lives?

The Indomitable Snowman. It appears that Kim Bin Lim wanted such a thing. According to an American Bible Society bulletin, Kim Bin Lim and his family, who lived in Korea about eighty kilometers (fifty miles) from Seoul, were Christians who had no Bible to help maintain their faith. Their nearest church was in a village on the other side of a mountain.

One day news arrived that a Bible Society representative planned to visit the village church on the other side of the mountain. Because the farmers in the area had very little cash, the society would let them buy their Scriptures with farm produce: a Bible for so much grain, a New Testament for a chicken, a Gospel portion for an egg or two, and so on.

On the appointed day, the little village church was crowded. Hens, beans, grain, and people competed for the small space inside. Outside a blizzard ravaged the mountains.

Soon grain and beans, chickens and eggs were being traded for the Word, and happy owners were murmuring quietly to themselves as they read.

The door swung open. A fierce blast swirled in, followed by a plodding little snowman. For a moment there was silence. Then a clatter of voices. Someone pushed the door shut while others brushed the snow from the clothes of the strange figure.

Under the snow they found a boy of twelve. On his shoulders were two fat bags of beans. His face, though icy cold, sparkled with excitement.

The boy walked stiffly to the front. The Bible Society representative asked his name.

"I am Kim Bin Lim," the lad replied. "I live on the other side of the mountain, eighteen kilometers from here. I have come to buy a Bible because I heard you were selling them in exchange for grain or beans. May I have one?"

It took a while for his story to sink in. Eighteen kilometers, eleven miles, over a high mountain pass, along a snow-covered track, in a raging blizzard. And he was twelve.

"You are welcome, Kim Bin Lim," replied the distributor. "But why didn't your father come?"

138

"He couldn't leave the farm. We have a few animals which he has to tend in this kind of weather; and my mother isn't well."

"But how did you find the way?"

"I got lost several times, and I nearly fell over a precipice because the path was slippery and narrow. I was afraid I would not get here in time, so I hurried all the way. May I have a Bible?"

Of course he could have a Bible. They gave him one and kept him there until the blizzard stopped. Then he set out for home very happily carrying the Book he had risked so much to obtain.[24]

I think Kim Bin Lim wanted Jesus to come into his heart. I think his "door" was open.

Kim wanted Jesus so much he braved a blizzard to buy a Bible.

Further Interesting Reading

In Arthur S. Maxwell, *The Bible Story*, volume 10:
   "Conquerors for Christ," page 171.
   "Someone at the Door," page 176.
In *Bible Readings for the Home:*
   "A Prophetic History of the Church," page 217.
In Ellen G. White, *The Triumph of God's Love:*
   "The First Christians—Loyal and True," page 21.
   "Rejecting God's Word," page 29.

Page numbers for each book refer to the large, fully illustrated edition.

Your Questions Answered

1. In what sense is Jesus the "beginning of God's creation" (Revelation 3:14)? The issue at stake here is the whole Christian concept of offering worship to Jesus as to God. As translated in the King James and Revised Standard versions, the phrase can be interpreted to mean that Jesus is merely a created being, the first created being God ever made. If this is really the meaning of the passage, Jesus should not be worshiped as God.

A full understanding of the passage must begin with an analysis of the underlying Greek. *Beginning* is translated from *arch ̄e* (ar-KAY or ar-KEE), a word that shows up in *arch*bishop (a *principal* bishop) and *arch*enemy (a *principal* enemy). It also shows up in mon*arch* (a lone *ruler*, such as a king or queen). To people who spoke Greek, *arch ̄e* did often carry the meaning of our English word *beginning*, but as these examples illustrate, this was not always the case by any means.

Gerhard Kittel's *Theological Dictionary of the New Testament*, translated by G. W. Bromiley, says that *arch ̄e* "always signifies 'primacy,' whether in time . . . or in rank." For primacy in time it gives the meaning "beginning," the first one in order of time; for primacy in rank it gives "power," "dominion," and "office," connoting the first one in order of authority. Walter Bauer's *A Greek-English Lexicon of the New Testament*, translated by W. F. Arndt and F. W. Gingrich, in addition to "beginning" gives "first cause" and "origin," that is, first in the sense of where things come from. H. S. Jones's revision of H. G. Liddell and R. Scott's standard *Greek-English Lexicon* similarly gives "first place," "first principle," and "origin," along with several other meanings.

So in Revelation 3:14, the passage we are discussing, the underlying Greek, taken alone, can be held to mean that Jesus is, in some sense, the first of God's created beings, but it can also support the entirely different conclusion that Jesus is the "origin" or "first cause" of God's creation.

Now, Jesus is in some sense a created being. In view of His incarnation, the Bible calls Him even now in His glorified state a "man." 1 Timothy 2:5. But if it is Christ's incarnate creatureliness that Revelation 3:14 is talking about, the reference cannot be to His being the earliest of all created beings. Incontestably, Jesus did not become a man until millions of other men and women had been born.

Other New Testament passages lead us to a still loftier view. John 1:1-3 takes note of Christ's existence with God "*in* the beginning [*arch ̄e*]" and then goes on to say that "*all things* were made through him, and without him was not anything made." Jesus is presented here not as a created being, but as the agent by whom all created things were made. He appears with His Father as co-Creator of all things.

The book of Colossians is of special interest in this connection because, like

141

the letter to the Laodiceans we are now discussing, it too was intended to be read by the congregation in Laodicea. See Colossians 4:16. One of the best-known passages in this book, Colossians 1:15-20, calls Jesus the "first-born of all creation" and goes on to say in language even stronger and more specific than John 1:1-3 that "all things . . . , visible and invisible, whether thrones or dominions or principalities or authorities—all things were created through him and for him. He is before all things." If in His essential being Jesus was *before* all things, and if *all* things were created through and for Him, then He Himself cannot appropriately be regarded as merely a created being.

In Revelation 22:13 Jesus calls Himself the Alpha and the Omega, employing the very term the Father uses to describe Himself in Revelation 1:8. Only the infinite Deity can rightly claim this all-encompassing ascription.

In view of these considerations and others, several modern versions differ significantly from the Revised Standard and King James versions in their treatment of Revelation 3:14. Instead of calling Jesus "the beginning of God's creation,"

The N.E.B. has, "the prime source of all God's creation."

The N.I.V. has, "the ruler of God's creation."

The T.E.V. has, "the origin of all that God has created." Margin, "or ruler."

The Jerusalem Bible, "the ultimate source of God's creation."

Monsignor Knox, "the source from which God's creation began."

The N.A.S.B., "the Beginning of the creation of God." Margin, "i.e., origin or source."

Any translation that portrays Christ as above creation, either as its source or at least as its ruler, fairly reflects the meaning of the underlying Greek. Nothing in Revelation 3:14 can be rightly used to minimize Christ's position as an object of true worship. The same Laodicean message goes on to say that He sits with God on God's throne! See verse 21.

2. What further evidence is there that the seven letters prefigure seven eras of church history? On page 120 we promised to look at some further considerations in support of the view that the letters to the seven churches are symbolic of seven eras in the course of church history. We have already considered three:

a. The statue vision of Daniel 2 is the key to both Daniel and Revelation. It clearly covers the course of secular history from the prophet's day to the end of the world. It prepares us convincingly to see that the other main visions in Daniel, in chapters 7, 8, and 11, also commence in the prophet's day and run—side by side—to the end of the world. Revelation is constructed solidly on the foundation of Daniel. Thus Daniel 2 prepares us to see that at least the main visions of the first, historical, half of Revelation—the seven seals, the seven trumpets, the great controversy scenes, *and* the seven churches—also run side by side from the prophet's day to the end of the world.

b. The seven letters contain distinctly predictive elements, such as **"You *will* have tribulation"** (Revelation 2:10, written to the Smyrna church) and **"I *will* keep you from the hour of trial which *is coming*"** (Revelation 3:10, to the Philadelphians).

c. In John 13:19 Jesus said, "I tell you this now, before it takes place, that when it does take place you may believe that I am he." Applying Christ's own principle of interpretation, on pages 120-132 we looked backward from our present day and found that the seven letters do correlate closely with the events of church history.

To these considerations we may add the following, among others:

d. In the Olivet Discourse, Jesus, like Daniel, scanned the entire course of church history from His own day to the second coming. If Daniel and Jesus did that, it is reasonable to conclude that John did also.

e. The Smyrna Christians were warned that they would suffer tribulation for **"ten days."** Revelation 2:10. At the time Polycarp was martyred, around A.D. 155 or 156 (or according to some historians, 166), they did undergo a persecution lasting several literal days. See pages 101, 102. But they suffered again under the Emperor Decius in A.D. 250, and they also underwent the terrible *ten years* of persecution, 303-313, under the Emperor Diocletian and his successors. Many centuries later, in 1402, 1424, and 1922, they were massacred by

Jesus Christ designed the atom, created our world, and formed the universe.

the thousands with a butchery that far exceeded even the misery of the Diocletian persecution. If the **"ten days"** were supposed to be understood only literally, we would be left wondering why Jesus forewarned the Christians of Smyrna only in respect to one of the least of their persecutions. But if Smyrna represents an early era of the church as a whole, and if the **"ten days"** represent ten years within that era, then the message in the letter makes sense.

f. As a matter of fact, all of the seven literal churches suffered under the Diocletian persecution, 303-313. If the seven letters had been intended exclusively for their seven local addressees, we would wonder why all seven congregations were not alike alerted to the Diocletian persecution which they were all to experience. On the other hand, if the letters to the seven churches represent seven successive periods of time, it is logical that the Diocletian persecution, which was to strike all Christians during one of those periods, should have been foretold only in respect of the Smyrna church, which symbolized that period.

g. The second-coming promise in Revelation 1:7 is unconditional, "He is coming with the clouds, and every eye will see him." Other promises—or rather warnings—of a coming of Christ occur in the letters to Ephesus (2:5), Pergamum (2:16), and Sardis (3:3), but all of these are conditional. They indicate what Christ would come and do *if* the congregations wouldn't repent. By contrast, the loyal believers in Thyatira were encouraged to **"hold fast"** **"until I come"** (2:25); and, to encourage the Christians in Philadelphia to **"hold fast,"** Christ made to them the outright promise, **"I am coming soon"** (3:11). These unconditional promises refer to the second coming at the end of the world. At the same time, the calls to **"hold fast"** presuppose a certain amount of delay. It is noteworthy that the only reference to Christ's coming *soon* is made in the letter to the sixth church, almost at the end of time.

Taken together, the considerations reviewed here encourage us to view the letters to the seven churches as symbolic, like so many other features of Daniel and Revelation. They persuade us to see them, like the prophecies of Daniel and the Olivet Discourse of Jesus Christ, as covering the sweep of history from the prophet's time till the end of the world.

References

1. W. M. Ramsay, *The Letters to the Seven Churches of Asia*, reprint of the 1904 ed. (Grand Rapids, Mich.: Baker Book House, 1979), p. 183. (Many comments about the seven churches in this section are based on this work.)

2. Irenaeus, *Against Heresies*, 1.26; ANF 1:352.

3. *The Martyrdom of Polycarp*, in *The Apostolic Fathers*; LCC 2:312-345.

4. Ramsay, *Seven Churches*, pp. 396, 397.

5. Adapted from Diane E. Papalia and Sally Wendkos Olds, *Human Development* (New York: McGraw-Hill Book Company, 1978), p. 346.

6. See *Ibid.*, p. 344.

7. William Warren Sweet, *The Story of Religion in America*, rev. and enl. ed. (New York: Harper & Brothers, 1950), pp. 6, 7.

8. Dean R. Hoge, "National Contextual Factors Influencing Church Trends," in Dean R. Hoge and David A. Roozen, eds., *Understanding Church Growth and Decline: 1950-1978* (New York: The Pilgrim Press, 1979), pp. 96, 97.

9. Eunice Kennedy Shriver, "There *Is* a Moral Dimension," *The Reader's Digest*, November 1977, pp. 153, 154.

10. Sir Isaac Newton, *Observations Upon the Prophecies of Daniel, and the Apocalypse of St. John* (London: 1733), pp. 285-293. But he ends the seven churches—and the seven seals—around A.D. 400.

11. Martin Luther, *Table Talk*, Theodore G. Tappert, Jaroslav Pelikan, and Helmut T. Lehmann, eds., *Luther's Works*, American ed., 55 vols. (Philadelphia: Fortress Press, 1955 -), 54:296.

12. Owen Chadwick, *The Reformation*, The Pelican History of the Church, vol. 3 (Grand Rapids, Mich.: Wm. B. Eerdmans Publishing Co., 1964), pp. 21, 11.

13. See H. J. Schroeder, O.P., trans., *Canons and Decrees of the Council of Trent* (St. Louis: B. Herder Book Co., 1941), pp. 29-46.

14. Williston Walker, *A History of the Christian Church*, rev. ed. (New York: Charles Scribner's Sons, 1959), p. 379.

15. Steven Ozment, *The Age of Reform 1250-1550: An Intellectual and Religious History of Late Medieval and Reformation Europe* (New Haven: Yale University Press, 1980), p. 8.

16. Walker, *History*, p. 396. A lower but still heartbreaking estimate puts the deaths at 8 million out of 18 million. See James Hastings Nichols, *History of Christianity 1650-1950* (New York: The Ronald Press Company, 1956), p. 42.

17. Lars P. Qualben, *A History of the Christian Church*, rev. and enl. ed. (New York: Thomas Nelson and Sons, 1958), p. 357.

18. Walker, *History*, p. 390.

19. *Ibid.*, p. 454.

20. Sydney E. Ahlstrom, *A Religious History of the American People* (New Haven, Conn.: Yale University Press, 1972), p. 424.

21. Oliver J. Thatcher and Edgar Holmes McNeal, eds., *A Source Book for Mediaeval History* (New York: Charles Scribner's Sons, 1905, 1933), pp. 158, 159.

22. Ralph Carmichael. Copyright 1958 by Sacred Songs, a division of Word, Inc. Used by permission.

23. In Roland H. Bainton, *Here I Stand: A Life of Martin Luther* (New York: Abingdon-Cokesbury Press, 1950), p. 295.

24. Adapted from "The Strange Case of the Indomitable Snowman," *American Bible Society Record*, August-September, 1978, pp. 20-22.

Revelation 4, 5

God Reveals His Throne

Introduction

The four horsemen of the Apocalypse. A lion that is a lamb. A mysterious angel sealing the servants of God. Souls under an altar crying out, "How long?" A voice from heaven commanding four angels to hold the four winds.

The four chapters that extend from the first verse of Revelation 4 to the first verse of Revelation 8 portray Christ's concern for His church as it faces ever-increasing distress. When we analyzed the organization of the book on pages 54-62, we titled this division of Revelation, "Christ Shields His Afflicted People." The division contains the seven seals and two scenes of last-day assignment and assurance. It is introduced by an extraordinary view of the heavenly sanctuary. See the outlines in the boxes on the next two pages.

Although the sanctuary scene serves basically to introduce us to the seven seals, it has great importance on its own account and occupies two entire chapters, Revelation 4 and 5. In view of its significance, we are going to take time to discuss it separately, leaving Revelation 6:1 to 8:1 and its seven seals until later.

The existence of the heavenly sanctuary and Christ's presence there beside His Father are taught in the book of Hebrews. See especially Hebrews 8:1, 2 and our discussion in GC 1:164-172. As we proceed with our study of Revelation, we'll notice that in the early chapters John's attention centers first on the holy place of the heavenly sanctuary in connection with the seven churches, the seven seals, and the seven trumpets. Later, in connection with the seven scenes in the great controversy, his attention is called to the most holy place. See pages 162-166.

Revelation 4 begins with the words, **"After this I looked, and lo, in heaven an open door! And the first voice, which I had heard speaking to me like a trumpet, said, 'Come up hither, and I will show you what must take place after this.' At once I was in the Spirit, and lo, a throne stood in heaven, with one seated on the throne!"** Verses 1, 2.

The **"first voice"** that John **"had heard speaking"** to him **"like a trumpet"** was the voice of Jesus. He had heard it speaking to him when he was "in the Spirit on the Lord's day" on the "island called Patmos." See Revelation 1:9, 10.

That was some time previous. Now, on this new occasion, he hears Christ's voice again and finds himself once more in the Spirit. We have no indication that this new experience came to him on a Lord's day. The place may no longer have been the island of Patmos. But John was enfolded in the Spirit. We can trust what he reports.

147

As Revelation's visions progressed, John saw that Jesus in heaven is surrounded by such glory as he had never imagined.

GOD REVEALS HIS THRONE
ORGANIZATION OF REVELATION

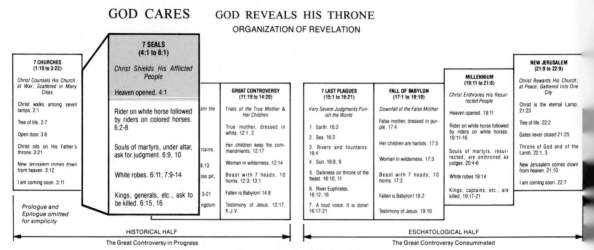

Only part of the seven-seals panel is highlighted because the present chapter studies only the introduction to the seals.

Jesus said, **"Come up hither, and I will show you what must take place after this."** Christ was about to unveil to John—and through him, to us—His foreknowledge of the suffering that His people were to endure through the coming centuries. He also wanted to show John and us something of His activity in protecting and planning for us, even when we feel that we are quite deserted. Before revealing this, Jesus first invited John to stand at an open door in heaven and observe God's throne room in action.

What a sight John saw. It left him with no reason to doubt that Someone is in command of this universe. Someone is in charge.

Revelation 4 and 5 are easy to read and in general seem self-explaining. Chapter 4 focuses on God, seated on His throne, surrounded by intelligent beings who deeply admire Him. These beings include the **"four living creatures,"** the **"twenty-four elders,"** and **"myriads of myriads"** of angels. A myriad is ten thousand. **"Myriads of myriads"** (Revelation 5:11) is literally "hundreds of millions" or, more

loosely, "millions and millions." While John watched, enraptured, the elders and the living creatures rendered a magnificent anthem in God's honor.

As we move into chapter 5, we observe God graciously directing our attention away from Himself to Jesus Christ. He produces a mysterious scroll sealed with seven seals that no one but Christ can open. As Jesus steps up to receive the scroll and open the seals, the living creatures and twenty-four elders sing again, a different song, till heaven's arches ring. Their music is too moving, too exciting, for the onlooking angels merely to enjoy. They want to join in as well. Indeed, it seems to John that everyone and everything in all the universe wants to sing.

And sing they do, with a **"loud voice"**—no doubt with a very loud voice. And a very glorious one. **"To him who sits upon the throne and to the Lamb,"** they sing, **"be blessing and honor and glory and might for ever and ever!"** Verse 13.

Handel used their words, as given in

SEVEN SEALS: Christ Shields His Afflicted People. 4:1 to 8:1

1. *Introductory sanctuary scene: God seated on His throne; the Lamb declared worthy to open the seals. 4:1 to 5:14*

2. First six seals. 6:1-17.

3. Scenes of end-time assignment and assurance. 7:1-17
   a. Assignment: To seal God's servants (on earth)
   b. Assurance: 144,000 and the great multitude (in heaven)

4. Consummation: Seventh seal, silence in heaven. 8:1

Item 1 is discussed in the present chapter. Items 2-4 are discussed in the following chapter, beginning on page 174.

---

the King James Version, for his *Messiah*. He may have used their heavenly melodies too. He tells us that while he wrote *Messiah*, a task that took him only 23 wonderful days, he often felt that he, like John, could hear the angels sing.

The angels' song is finished. Tremendous silence follows. The universe is stunned with glory and beauty.

Then the four living creatures, deeply stirred, do what Christian worshipers still do after an impressive musical rendition. They say, **"Amen!"**

We too say, **"Amen."** It is good and right that the Lamb and He who sits upon the throne should be praised. We too want to praise them.

It's time for us to read chapters 4 and 5—but, please, wait a minute! This book you are reading, *God Cares*, is intended to help us see how Daniel and Revelation can help our families. Please pause a minute and ask yourself, "What is *family* praise?"

Douglas Cooper, an Alaskan pilot, has charmingly expressed one kind of family praise in his delightful little book *Living God's Joy*. "Praise," he says, "is much deeper than just thanking someone. After a meal I can thank my wife for fixing dinner and take up the newspaper again. That is expressing thanks. Or I can grab her when she is not looking, squeeze her tight, and say, 'Honey, that was a delicious meal! *You* are an absolutely wonderful cook! Let me help you clean up the dishes.' That is praise!"[1]

Praise, he explains, stresses the fine inherent qualities within a person. It is gratefulness not simply for what the person has done but for what the person *is*.

Thank you for allowing the interruption. *Now* you can read chapters 4 and 5.

SANCTUARY SCENE INTRODUCES THE SEALS

REVELATION 4

John sees God's Throne. 1 After this I looked, and lo, in heaven an open door! And the first voice, which I had heard speaking to me like a trumpet, said, "Come up hither, and I will show you what must take place after this." ²At once I was in the Spirit, and lo, a throne stood in heaven, with one seated on the throne! ³And he who sat there appeared like jasper and carnelian, and round the throne was a rainbow that looked like an emerald. ⁴Round the throne were twenty-four thrones, and seated on the thrones were twenty-four elders, clad in white garments, with golden crowns upon their heads. ⁵From the throne issue flashes of lightning, and voices and peals of thunder, and before the throne burn seven torches of fire, which are the seven spirits of God; ⁶and before the throne there is as it were a sea of glass, like crystal.

Heavenly beings sing praises to God. And round the throne, on each side of the throne, are four living creatures, full of eyes in front and behind: ⁷the first living creature like a lion, the second living creature like an ox, the third living creature with the face of a man, and the fourth living creature like a flying eagle. ⁸And the four living creatures, each of them with six wings, are full of eyes all round and within, and day and night they never cease to sing,

"Holy, holy, holy, is the Lord God
    Almighty,
who was and is and is to come!"

⁹And whenever the living creatures give glory and honor and thanks to him who is seated on the throne, who lives for ever and ever, ¹⁰the twenty-four elders fall down before him who is seated on the throne and worship him who lives for ever and ever; they cast their crowns before the throne, singing,

¹¹ "Worthy art thou, our Lord and
    God,
to receive glory and honor and
    power,

for thou didst create all things,
and by thy will they existed and were
    created."

REVELATION 5

John sees the Lamb take the seven-sealed scroll. 1 And I saw in the right hand of him who was seated on the throne a scroll written within and on the back, sealed with seven seals; ²and I saw a strong angel proclaiming with a loud voice, "Who is worthy to open the scroll and break its seals?" ³And no one in heaven or on earth or under the earth was able to open the scroll or to look into it, ⁴and I wept much that no one was found worthy to open the scroll or to look into it. ⁵Then one of the elders said to me, "Weep not; lo, the Lion of the tribe of Judah, the Root of David, has conquered, so that he can open the scroll and its seven seals."

6 And between the throne and the four living creatures and among the elders, I saw a Lamb standing, as though it had been slain, with seven horns and with seven eyes, which are the seven spirits of God sent out into all the earth; ⁷and he went and took the scroll from the right hand of him who was seated on the throne.

Heavenly beings sing praises to the Lamb. 8 And when he had taken the scroll, the four living creatures and the twenty-four elders fell down before the Lamb, each holding a harp, and with golden bowls full of incense, which are the prayers of the saints; ⁹and they sang a new song, saying,

"Worthy art thou to take the scroll
    and to open its seals,
for thou wast slain and by thy blood
    didst ransom men for God
from every tribe and tongue and
    people and nation,
¹⁰and hast made them a kingdom and
    priests to our God,
and they shall reign on earth."

¹¹Then I looked, and I heard around the throne and the living creatures and the elders the voice of many angels, numbering myriads of myriads and thousands of thou-

sands, [12]saying with a loud voice, "Worthy is the Lamb who was slain, to receive power and wealth and wisdom and might and honor and glory and blessing!"

The entire universe praises God and the Lamb. 13 And I heard every creature in heaven and on earth and under the earth and in the sea, and all therein, saying, "To him who sits upon the throne and to the Lamb be blessing and honor and glory and might for ever and ever!" [14]And the four living creatures said, "Amen!" and the elders fell down and worshiped.

The Message of Revelation 4, 5

I. Someone Is in Charge

No one can read Revelation 4 without getting the message that however confused things appear to us on our sad and troubled planet, there really is "Someone upstairs" who is in charge.

We got the same message when we read Daniel. "The Most High rules the kingdom of men." Daniel 4:25. "There is a God in heaven." Daniel 2:28.

In the vision of the wild animals and the judgment, Daniel saw a throne on which the Ancient of Days took His seat. See Daniel 7:9, 10. Now it was John's turn to see it: **"Lo, in heaven an open door,"** and inside the open door, **"lo, a throne stood in heaven, with one seated on the throne!"** Revelation 4:1, 2. It was good of God to open the door and to ask John (Revelation 1:11) to tell us what he saw. He did it for our encouragement as well as for John's.

Others who have seen God's throne. Besides Daniel and John, God has also let others see His throne. The Old Testament prophets Isaiah, Micaiah, and Ezekiel saw it; so did Stephen and Paul in the New Testament. In vision, Isaiah wrote, "I saw the Lord sitting upon a throne, high and lifted up." Alongside the throne Isaiah saw six-winged seraphs singing, "Holy, holy, holy is the Lord of hosts." The sight made him repent deeply of his sins. See Isaiah 6:1-5.

To Isaiah, God's throne was a very holy place.

To the prophet Ezekiel, God's throne was a very dynamic place. He came away from his vision of it impressed with burning coals and torches and supernatural wheels and living creatures soaring and a rainbow glowing and "the appearance of the likeness of the glory of the Lord." See Ezekiel 1.

To Stephen, one of the seven early assistants to the apostles, God's throne seemed a very friendly place. Stephen was allowed to see it just before he gave up his life as the first Christian martyr. Delighted to see Jesus and greatly encouraged, he cried out to his persecutors, "I see the heavens opened, and the Son of man standing at the right hand of God." Acts 7:56. This is how John also saw it; God on His throne with Jesus at His side in a time of trial for the church.

The sea of glass. In front of God's throne John saw a **"sea of glass."** Revelation 4:6. Perhaps it was made of what we call glass, or perhaps of some other material that reflected like glass. John had often watched sunsets that seemed to turn the Mediterranean into a sea of glass blazing with fire.

The sea of glass in heaven no doubt still reflects the **"jasper and carnelian"** brilliance of Him who sits on the throne and the glowing brightness of the rainbow and the strobelike flashes of angels as they come and go. I hope to stand on that sea someday. I hope you will stand there too. God has offered us the opportunity. See Revelation 7:9; 15:2.

The twenty-four elders. On the sea of glass and very near the throne, John saw **"twenty-four elders"** seated on **"twenty-four thrones."** The number twenty-four recalls the twenty-four courses into which the priests were organized by King David in Old Testament times. See 1 Chronicles 24, especially verse 18. Like priests, the heavenly elders were represented to John as holding censers and as offering incense when people pray. See Revelation 5:8.

The King James Version quotes the twenty-four elders as saying, "Thou . . . hast redeemed *us* to God by thy blood out of every . . . nation; and hast made *us* . . . priests." This translation has led to the attractive assumption that the elders are human beings chosen from those persons whom God raised from the dead when He resurrected Jesus. Many faithful persons *were* raised on resurrection Sunday and, apparently, Jesus did take them to heaven. See Matthew 27:51-53; Ephesians 4:8.

Biblical scholars are agreed, however, that the twenty-four elders really said that Christ redeemed **"men"** (not "us") and that Christ made **"them"** (not "us") priests to God. The Greek manuscripts of Revelation overwhelmingly support the scholars, and so do the modern translations.

But even if the twenty-four elders are not necessarily human, they are nonetheless our friends. They assist us in prayer. John saw them symbolically offering incense as we pray. We should be grateful for every one of them.

The four living creatures. On the four sides of the throne, within the circle formed by the elders, John saw **"four living creatures"** unlike any beings he had seen before.

He had read about them before, however. They were the same beings Isaiah had reported seeing near the throne, who sang, "Holy, holy, holy." Isaiah called them seraphs (or *seraphim,* which is the Hebrew plural of *seraph*). He remembered each of them as having six wings. See Isaiah 6.

Ezekiel saw them too in his visions of the throne. In writing about them in Ezekiel 1, he, like John, called them living creatures, but in Ezekiel 10 he called them cherubs (or *cherubim*, which is the Hebrew plural of *cherub*). To Ezekiel each one seemed to have four wings and four heads, the heads of a man, a lion, an ox, and an eagle. See Ezekiel 1:6, 10. Each was close to the throne and was associated with a wheel that seemed full of eyes. Wherever God wanted to go, the four cherubs went, straight as an arrow and at lightning speed.

When John saw the seraphs or cherubs or living creatures, he, like Isaiah, thought they had six wings. Unlike Ezekiel, he thought that each had only one face; but the four faces he saw were the same that Ezekiel saw, the faces of a man, a lion, an ox, and an eagle. John noticed no wheels full of eyes; to him, the living creatures themselves seemed **"full of eyes."**

In any case, the shapes of the living creatures were probably symbolic. (In this same vision Jesus was represented as both a lion and a lamb, symbolizing simultaneously His power and His gentleness.) The human face presumably symbolized the intelligence of the living creatures; the lion's face, their strength; the ox's, their willingness to be of service; and the eagle's, their swiftness and perceptiveness.

153

Like Isaiah, John heard the living creatures sing, **"Holy, holy, holy."** In fact, John says that **"day and night they never cease to sing, 'Holy, holy, holy, is the Lord God Almighty, who was and is and is to come!'** " Revelation 4:8. With their numerous eyes and supernatural vision, the living creatures continually notice glorious things all over God's universe, and they praise Him for them—for every glorious thing they see, one after another.

Anyone who has sung in a quartet knows what a pleasure it can be. What a privilege it must be to belong to the Living Creature Quartet! What an honor to live at the ultimate heart of things, right up close to God, observing His goodness night and day. Of course they want to sing!

John evidently didn't mean that they sing exactly the same words over and over! In just the two chapters we are looking at now they sing other words and also say, **"Amen."** In chapter 6 we'll find that they took an active part in helping John understand the seven seals. And so on. But praising God is a joy for them. They see so much beauty and benevolence in the universe to sing about.

Satan was once a "living creature." We are intrigued to learn from Ezekiel 28 that once upon a time one of the original guardian cherubs, or living creatures, had to be removed from his position and driven from God's throne in disgrace. Undoubtedly this privileged person was Lucifer the Lightbearer. See Isaiah 14:12, K.J.V. He served as a cherub back in the good old days before he turned himself into Satan. The New International Version gives us a better translation of Ezekiel's account than does the Revised Standard:

> You were anointed as a guardian cherub,
>   for so I ordained you.
> You were on the holy mount of God;
>   you walked among the fiery stones.
> You were blameless in your ways
>   from the day you were created
>   till wickedness was found in you. . . .
>
> Your heart became proud
>   on account of your beauty,
> and you corrupted your wisdom
>   because of your splendor.
> So I threw you to the earth.
>   Ezekiel 28:14-17, N.I.V.
>   See also GC 1:269, 270, 274.

It is hard to imagine why so privileged a being would squander away heaven's wonderful happiness. But we have been offered the privilege of enjoying heaven's wonderful happiness someday. Let us be sure we don't squander it.

He who sits on the throne. John was interested in the twenty-four elders and the four living creatures. So are we. But he noticed that the principal object of their thought, as of his own, was the Person seated on the throne. He was the Maker of the universe. He was the ultimate Center. He was God.

And He was in charge. A dozen times or more (in chapters 4, 5, 6, 7, 20, 21) John defined God as He **"who is seated on the throne."** On *the* throne. On the one throne that really matters.

Standing behind John and gazing intently over his shoulder, we know that we are not peering into the White House or the Kremlin or Buckingham Palace! On television we've watched Mission Control direct spaceships to the moon and guide space shuttles back to earth. But Cosmic Control (as we may term God's throne room) guides the galaxies, hundreds of billions of them, each of them an island universe.

The myriads of angels. John thought he heard thunder as God and the living creatures spoke. Compare Revelation 4:5; 6:1. He saw lightning as angels flashed away to fill God's loving requests. Compare Hebrews 1:7. But where does God send the angels? And while we're asking that question, here's another: With so much going on around God all the time, how can our timid, whispered prayers get through to Him? How can even our anguished, shouted prayers get through?

The glorious answer is that during the ongoing sin emergency, all of heaven's resources are concentrated on our needs. The activity around Him doesn't distract God from us; it is directed by God to us and for us.

God has placed everything in the universe at our service. "God causes all things to work together for good to those who love" Him. Romans 8:28, N.A.S.B. He has even placed Himself and His Son at our service. "He who did not spare his own Son but gave him up for us all, will he not also give us all things?" Romans 8:32. And He has placed the angels at our service. "Are they not all ministering spirits sent forth to serve, for the sake of those who are to obtain salvation?" Hebrews 1:14.

The beings around God's throne find their greatest delight in observing God's love for us—and in observing our willing response to His love. "There is joy before the angels of God over one sinner who repents," said Jesus in Luke 15:10. The thought that caused the heavenly rapture in Revelation 5:9, 10 was that Christ was **"slain"** for **"men,"** for human beings, that He had **"ransomed"** them, so that they—you and I—can one day **"reign on earth."** How unselfish of the universe to be so interested in us!

The ministry of angels. We would all feel better if we gave more thought more often to what the angels do on our behalf. All through the Bible angels are represented as being interested in our affairs. Jacob, for example, saw angels ascending and descending between earth and heaven (Genesis 28:12). Angels brought food to Elijah (1 Kings 19:5), destroyed an entire army (2 Kings 19:35), and saved Daniel from hungry lions (Daniel 6:22). An angel promised a baby boy to Zechariah (Luke 1:13). Angels sang when Jesus was born (Luke 2:13), encouraged Him on the mount of temptation (Matthew 4:11), and rolled away the stone from His

155

tomb (Matthew 28:2). They opened prison doors for Peter (Acts 5:19) and stood by Paul during a storm at sea (Acts 27:23). They also encouraged non-Christians in Bible times to ask about the gospel (Acts 10:1-7).

Angels still accompany us. "The angel of the Lord encamps around those who fear him, and delivers them." Psalm 34:7.

I confess that I often forget about my angel. How much I lose! But sometimes, when I'm driving, for instance, I think of him as riding beside me. I even talk to him—just to make his presence seem more real. Once or twice, when setting out on a trip *apparently* alone, I have opened the door on the passenger side as if to let him in.

Don't forget that angels are assigned to care for girls and boys. Jesus, who was well acquainted with such heavenly matters, said once, "See that you do not despise one of these little ones; for I tell you that in heaven their angels always behold the face of my Father who is in heaven." Matthew 18:10. Tell your children that their angels have direct access to God's throne, that they can fly through the open door whenever they need to.

God has assigned angels to give special protection to children.

Cosmic Control thunders as God assigns His angels to help us. Lightning flashes as they speed away to meet our needs. It flashes again as they return to God to tell Him our prayers and convey our gratitude.

The rainbow of promise. Above the throne John saw a **"rainbow,"** one in which green or **"emerald"** wavelengths predominated. The Bible says that early in this earth's history, when Noah thanked God for delivering his family from the great Flood, God alerted him to a rainbow shining in the sky. God explained that it was the sign of His covenant never again to send a worldwide flood. See Genesis 9.

A covenant is a promise. See GC 1:170, 171. The rainbow above the throne reminds us that our heavenly Father makes promises to us and keeps them. He is never too busy to honor the commitments He has made to us through His hundreds of Bible promises.

The Lamb. Revelation 4 speaks primarily about God, about **"him who is seated on the throne."** In Revelation 5 the center of attention shifts to the Lamb, the Lamb who is also the **"Lion of the tribe of Judah"** and the **"Root of David."**

Jesus was a member of the Judah tribe. Hebrews 7:14. The lion was an ancient symbol for Judah. See Genesis 49:9. The expression **"Root of David"** is better understood as "Shoot of David," that is, as referring to a descendant, rather than to an ancestor, of King David. It's an ancient idiom. For example, in 1 Maccabees 1:10, Antiochus Epiphanes is called a "sinful root," that is, a sinful *descendant*, of his father, Antiochus III the Great. On earth Jesus was often referred to as the Son of David. Hence, in Revelation 5 He is the Root of David.

But how can a lion be a lamb? Almost anything can happen in dreams and divine visions! But as for Christ's being a lamb, do you remember the first time John set eyes on Jesus? It was by the river Jordan, while John the Baptist was preaching. Suddenly the Baptist stopped and pointed to Jesus, who had just arrived, and said, "Behold, the Lamb of God, who takes away the sin of the world!" John 1:29. See page 49.

Jesus wasn't literally a lamb by the river Jordan. In heaven He is neither literally a lamb nor literally a lion. But to those who seek His mercy with repentance and confession, He is still the Lamb who takes away our sin. And to those who persistently refuse Him, He will one day appear as a lion. In the time of the sixth seal, the rejectors of His mercy will call on rocks and mountains to fall and hide them from the "wrath of the Lamb." Revelation 6:16.

We want to know why only the Lamb could open the seven-sealed scroll. And we want to know more about the scroll itself. We'll be better prepared to understand these important matters after we've looked at the seven seals in Revelation 6:1 to 8:1.

In the meantime, let us join the heavenly choirs in ascribing praise to Him who sits on the throne. He created us. He commissions angels constantly to assist us. He keeps His promises to us. He sent His Son, the Lamb, on a very expensive errand to redeem us. Soon He will welcome us and our families to the sea of glass, where we can personally hear the hymns and see His face.

II. The God Who Comes

When the four living creatures sing, **"Holy, holy, holy, is the Lord God Almighty,"** they go on to describe God as the One who **"was and is and *is to come*."** Revelation 4:8.

Some commentators have assumed that the term **"who . . . is to come"** ought to be translated, "who is to be," as if the whole phrase ought to read, "Who was, and is, and *is to be*." They understand the expression to mean simply that God is eternal; He has always existed, He does so now, and He always will.

Without a doubt, God is eternal. Verse 9, in fact, speaks of Him as the One who **"lives for ever and ever."** But in the phrase we are talking about, His eternalness is implied in the term **"who is."** The Greek term translated **"who is"** is equivalent to the name God chose for Himself at the burning bush when He introduced Himself to Moses as "I AM." See Exodus 3:14.

The Greek language has words for saying "who is *to be*," just as English does. But in Revelation 4:8, the verse that we're discussing, the living creatures don't use them. Instead, they use Greek words that mean **"who . . . is to come,"** or, translated more simply, "the one who comes."

Professor Marvin Vincent has made this point clear in his widely used *Word Studies in the New Testament*. Quoting the King James Version, he says,

> *Which is to come (ho erchomenos)*. . . . This is not equivalent to *who shall be*; i.e., the author is not intending to describe the abstract existence of God as covering the future no less than the past and the present. If this had been his meaning, he would have written *ho esomenos, which shall be*. . . . The name does not emphasize so much God's abstract existence, as it does His permanent covenant relation to His people.[2]

Something similar occurs twice in Revelation 1. Verse 4 says, "Grace to you and peace from him who is and who was and who *is to come*." Verse 8 has, " 'I am the Alpha and the Omega,' says the Lord God, who is and who was and who *is to come*, the Almighty."

Thus three times (in Revelation 1:4, 8, and 4:8) Revelation speaks of God as the coming One, the One who comes. It will do us good to think of Him this way.

Mothers know the difference between the child who comes in, say, from the sandbox as soon as she's called, and the child who has to be dragged in. The Bible says that when we need Him, *God comes*.

In fact, God doesn't even wait for us to call. Knowing that we're in trouble, He comes looking for us. He takes the initiative in our salvation. "In this is love, not that we loved God but that he loved us and sent his Son to be the expiation for our sins." 1 John 4:10.

The "coming God" in the Old Testament. When God was preparing to deliver the Ten Commandments on Mount Sinai, He said to Moses, "Lo, I am coming to you in a thick cloud." Exodus 19:9. He wanted it known that when His people especially needed instruction about right and wrong, He actually came to Mount Sinai to teach them.

When He asked the Israelites to erect worship centers wherever they traveled, He promised, "In every place . . . I will come to you and bless you." Exodus 20:24. Many ancient religions believed that their gods were restricted to certain local areas, or to single nations. But God wanted people to know that wherever we seek His fellowship in prayer, He comes and blesses us.

The prophet Hosea indicated that God comes with healing grace whenever we confess our sins and need assurance of forgiveness. "It is the time to seek the Lord," he said, "that he may come and rain salvation upon you." Hosea 10:12. And again,

> He will come to us as the showers,
> as the spring rains that water the
> earth.
>
> Hosea 6:3.

God at the second coming? Some Christians who believe ardently in the second coming of Christ have not supposed that God the Father will come with His Son. We touched this question briefly on page 81. The evidence seems to be that, Yes, He will come with Jesus. In Revelation 6:16, at the climax of the sixth seal, the wicked wail to the rocks and mountains, "Fall on us and hide us from the face of him who is seated on the throne, and from the wrath of the Lamb." We have learned that the One "who is seated on the throne" is God the Father. See page 154.

Psalm 50:3-6 anticipates the end of the world, when God will come in flame and whirlwind to rescue His people from all their enemies:

> Our God comes, he does not keep silence,
> before him is a devouring fire,
> round about him a mighty tempest.
> He calls to the heavens above
> and to the earth, that he may judge his people:
> "Gather to me my faithful ones,
> who made a covenant with me by sacrifice!"
> The heavens declare his righteousness,
> for God himself is judge!

Perhaps these passages help us comprehend the temporary "silence in heaven" that will occur at the opening of the seventh seal. "When the Lamb opened the seventh seal, there was silence in heaven for about half an hour." Revelation 8:1. If Jesus is in the "air" (1 Thessalonians 4:17) just above the earth at this time, if "all the angels" are at the earth "with him" (see Matthew 25:31), and if the Father is in the cloud accompanying Him, who is left in heaven? Momentarily, the singing there will have ceased, and heaven's throne room will be hushed.

Jesus and the Holy Spirit as coming ones. When an army officer asked Jesus to heal his paralyzed servant, Jesus responded quickly, "I will come and heal him." Matthew 8:7. When a religious official asked Him to heal his dying twelve-year-old daughter, Jesus set out for her home at once. See Luke 8:40-56. His words and behavior were symbolic. The Bible presents Jesus, too, as a coming one.

Jewish people who had long looked for the Messiah to come asked Him, "Are you he who is to come?" Matthew 11:3. A Samaritan woman asked if He was the coming Messiah, and He acknowledged that He was. See John 4:26. On one occasion He said of Himself, "The Son of man came to seek and to save the lost." Luke 19:10. On another occasion He said, "I came that they may have life." John 10:10. "He came unto his own." John 1:11, K.J.V.

Like the Father, Jesus too was a coming one. And, of course, He still is. In reference to the second coming He said at the Last Supper, "I will come again." John 14:3.

It is good to know that Jesus came and that He's coming back. But what about the meantime? Does He come when we need Him now?

At the Last Supper, after promising the second coming, Jesus talked about the meantime. Said He, "I will not leave you desolate; I will come to you." John 14:18. Then He mentioned His Father and added, "*We* will come." Verse 23.

It's a beautiful thought; but with Jesus and His Father up in heaven, where John saw them, how can it be true?

Jesus explained: "I will pray the Father, and he will give you another Counselor, to be with you for ever, even the Spirit of truth." John 14:16, 17. "The Counselor, the Holy Spirit, whom the Father will send in my name, he will teach you all things." Verse 26. Jesus meant that He and the Father would send the Holy Spirit as Their representative, and that in this way, prior to the literal second coming, He and God would keep on coming to us.

When the Holy Spirit comes to us, He does the kinds of things that the Bible says God and Jesus do for us. The Holy Spirit teaches us and leads us into truth. See John 14:26. He convicts us of sin and of our need for righteousness. John 16:8. He also intercedes for us. Romans 8:26.

Jesus called the Holy Spirit the Counselor (John 14:26) or the Comforter (K.J.V.). Actually, in John 14:16, Jesus called Him *another* Counselor, meaning another Counselor in addition to Himself. The underlying Greek word is *parakletos*, "paraklete," meaning "a person who is called to someone's aid." In 1 John 2:1, Jesus is called our Advocate, a person called on to help someone who is facing a courtroom trial. The underlying Greek word is again *parakletos,* "paraklete." Jesus is our Paraklete, the special Person whom we are invited to call on for help whenever we need it. The Holy Spirit is *another* Paraklete (John 14:16), whom we can also call on for help.

While Jesus and the Father minister on our behalf in the heavenly sanctuary, the Holy Spirit serves among us here on earth. He dwells among us. In some mysterious way He even dwells in us. See 1 Corinthians 6:19.

The Holy Spirit, the third member of the divine Godhead, is a God who comes; a God who comes to stay. The author of *The Desire of Ages* has expressed it this way:

> At all times and in all places,
> in all sorrows and in all afflictions,
>   when the outlook seems dark
>   and the future perplexing,
>   and we feel helpless and alone,
> the Comforter will be sent
> in answer to the prayer of faith.
>
> Circumstances may separate us
>   from every earthly friend;
>   but no circumstance, no distance,
> can separate us from the heavenly Comforter.
>
> Wherever we are,
>   wherever we may go,
> He is always at our right hand
>   to support,
>   sustain,
>   uphold, and
>   cheer.[3]

Many Christians find that in order to remember that God is eager to be with us everywhere and always, it helps if we pause frequently in regular places to recharge our memory batteries. We need to pause regularly to talk to Him and reflect on His promises.

Do you have a regular time and place for prayer? Your bedside will do or the living room or the dinette. Said God in Exodus 20:24, "In every place" where you worship Me, "I will come to you and bless you."

But don't rush in and out of your special meeting place so fast that you don't recognize His presence there. Don't hurry off with your fears and doubts unchanged. Pause a moment until you know again that He's with you, helping and guiding you.

"The things that are revealed belong to us and to our children." Deuteronomy 29:29. God comes to children too. The promise of the Holy Spirit, Peter said, is "to you and to your children." Acts 2:39. The words of John 14:18, N.I.V., are especially adaptable for children when they feel neglected and lonely: "I will not leave you as orphans; I will come to you."

161

It is one of the dominant themes in the message of Revelation to you and every member of your family that God is not remote from our daily needs. Even in the chapter that describes Him seated on His throne in heaven's Cosmic Control, He is introduced to us by the living creatures as the God who comes.

God cares.

III. The Sanctuary Is a Friendly Place

One of the most endearing things about Jesus is His priesthood. We are deeply impressed, we are sometimes overwhelmed, by the love He showed in coming to earth and dying for us long ago. But there is more, much more, to His ministry on our behalf than His living and dying for us long ago. All of the time during all of the centuries since the cross Jesus has been serving as our High Priest at the throne of God. "He always lives to make intercession" for us. Hebrews 7:25.

Christ's heavenly priesthood is a major teaching of the New Testament. When the early Jewish Christians wondered why Jesus hadn't come back already and asked whether perhaps they should return to their familiar Jewish priests and sacrifices at the Jerusalem temple, the book of Hebrews was written. Evidence was piled on evidence to prove the reality of Christ's heavenly ministry and His utter superiority to any earthly priest. "The point in what we are saying is this," summed up Hebrews 8:1, 2: "we have such a high priest, one who is seated at the right hand of the throne of the Majesty in heaven, a minister in the sanctuary and the true tent which is set up not by man but by the Lord."

When John himself, on Patmos, wondered why Jesus hadn't already come back again, Jesus appeared to him as a priest in the heavenly sanctuary, robed in white, walking among the lampstands beside the Father's throne. To every Christian who asks today, "Where is Jesus and what is He doing during the delay before the second coming?" the answer comes from the New Testament, especially from Hebrews and Revelation, that He is doing things *for us*, that He is serving as our High Priest in the presence of God.

Professor Fritz Guy, one of my seminary colleagues, has expressed the matter this way:

> We do not say that Christ *was* our High Priest; we say that He *is* our High Priest. He not only did something to save us nineteen and a half centuries ago; He is active for us now, today, at this very moment. The process of reconciliation, of forgiveness, of healing, of restoring broken relationships and shattered lives—all this goes on, because "He always lives to make intercession" for "those who draw near to God through Him" (Hebrews 7:25).[4]

In Bible times, Christ's heavenly ministry was *illustrated* by the priests who served in the tent-sanctuary that God instructed Moses to construct. See Exodus 25 to 30, Hebrews 8, 9, and GC 1:164-170. It was only a model sanctuary, mind you. In fact, it was only a small portable tent, a "tabernacle." In time it was replaced by the magnificent Jerusalem temple, based on the same plan. The temple in heaven is vastly larger and indescribably more glorious than either the tent or the Jerusalem temple. It is good to keep this in mind. Yet sometimes the Bible calls the heavenly sanctuary a temple, like the one in Jerusalem. Sometimes the Bible calls it a tent, "the true tent" (Hebrews 8:2), in honor of the original portable model.

In the outer court of that small model sanctuary, lambs were sacrificed every day on the *altar of burnt offering*. The altar represented the cross. The daily death of lambs taught that only through Christ's death for us on the cross are we able to receive our daily life.

Inside the sanctuary, the first room was called the holy place. The *table of the bread of the Presence* (the "table of shewbread," Numbers 4:7, K.J.V.) was located there. It represented God's heavenly throne, and the bread on it represented our living Saviour. Jesus said, "I am the bread of life." John 6:35, 48. The *seven-branched lampstand*, also located in the holy place, symbolized, among other things, the light that the Holy Spirit shines into our lives from Jesus, the

The great temple or sanctuary of God in heaven was symbolized in Old Testament times by a tent or "tabernacle" sanctuary.

Light of the world. The incense rising from the little *golden altar* signified Chist's continual prayers on our behalf.

The second, or inner, room of the sanctuary was called the most holy place. It held a gold-plated wooden chest containing the Ten Commandments and was sometimes referred to as the *ark of the covenant*. The ark too represented God's throne. The presence of the Ten Commandments inside the ark taught that God's government isn't arbitrary. It is based on law, law that has been written out, a law of love that shows us how to love one another and how to express our love for God. The high priest entered the most holy place once a year, on the Day of Atonement that was also the yearly day of judgment. See GC 1:181-188. The yearly judgment taught that our actions are important to God. We are responsible beings, and God respects our decisions and evaluates them.

Jesus died for us on the cross (the altar of burnt offering). Jesus Himself is the Bread of Life (on the table of the bread of the Presence). Jesus is the Light of the world (shining from the seven-branched lampstand). See John 9:5. Jesus is the High Priest, who symbolically offers incense with our prayers (at the golden altar). Jesus is also our High Priest on the Day of Atonement/Day of Judgment. For everyone who truly repents, Jesus stands beside God's inner throne (the ark of the covenant that contains the Ten Commandments we have broken) and secures our forgiveness.

Thank God! Right now, at this very moment, we have in the heavenly sanctuary a High Priest who lives to make intercession for us.

Revelation and the sanctuary. Because Revelation is a book that reveals Jesus, and because Jesus is now in the heavenly sanctuary, we are not surprised that the heavenly sanctuary (or temple) is mentioned in Revelation repeatedly. In fact, it is referred to fourteen times—and specifically located *in heaven*. It is called "the temple *in heaven*" (14:17), "God's temple *in heaven*" (11:19), "the temple of the tent of witness *in heaven*" (15:5). God's throne, which is located inside the heavenly temple, is referred to forty times. God is characteristically identified as the One "who sits on the throne."

The heavenly sanctuary is a central pivot of the message of Revelation. Five of the major divisions of the book are introduced with scenes that center on it. The introductory sanctuary scenes in the first three divisions are related to the holy place. The sanctuary vision in the fourth division is related to the most holy place; and in the fifth division, to the temple as a whole.

These five sanctuary scenes are landmarks, guiding us to the meaning of Revelation. Please examine the chart on the next page.

1. *The seven churches.* Before John heard Jesus deliver His letters to the seven churches, he first saw Him represented as walking among the *lampstands* of the holy place. Jesus identified the lampstands this time as representing His church, which is supposed to reflect to the world His light. ("You are the light of the world," He said once to His loyal followers. Matthew 5:14.) The point was clear. Christ is with His church, serving as its pastor and priest, tending it, encouraging

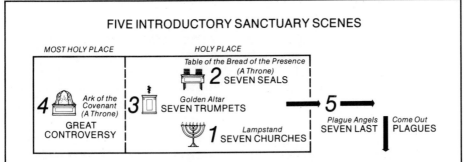

FIVE INTRODUCTORY SANCTUARY SCENES

God's temple, the heavenly sanctuary, is vast and glorious. We cannot see it, but we can learn important things about it from the little earthly sanctuary that Moses built. See Exodus 25 to 30; Hebrews 8, 9; GC 1:164-170.

Five of the divisions of Revelation are introduced by scenes related to the heavenly sanctuary. The diagram gives a floor plan of the earthly sanctuary integrated with these divisions. The model furniture only *symbolizes* heavenly things, of course.

HISTORICAL HALF OF REVELATION, CHAPTERS 1 to 14

Scenes in the Holy Place

1. SEVEN CHURCHES. Jesus, dressed as a priest, walks among the *lampstands* that here represent the churches which transmit Christ's light to the world. Jesus sends letters to the churches.
2. SEVEN SEALS. Jesus, the slain and resurrected Lamb, opens the seven seals of a scroll while standing beside the *table throne*. His message is that though suffering is coming, He is able to shield His people and seal them.
3. SEVEN TRUMPETS. At the *golden altar* an angel who represents Jesus offers incense representing His intercession, then throws fire onto the earth, symbolic of scourges sent in love to teach, restrain, and punish.

A Scene in the Most Holy Place

4. GREAT CONTROVERSY. The *ark of the covenant* is revealed, containing the Ten Commandments. Messages emphasize the commandments, the last judgment, and the final condemnation of those who break the commandments.

ESCHATOLOGICAL HALF OF REVELATION, CHAPTERS 15 to 22

A Scene Outside the Temple

5. SEVEN LAST PLAGUES. The sanctuary opens to release the seven plague angels, then closes up, signifying the end of human probation.

and purifying it, helping it to burn brightly with His own pure and loving light. See page 97.

2. *The seven seals*. John watched Jesus open the seven seals. He heard warnings about troubles ahead; he heard promises too, that Jesus would shield and seal His people. First, though, he saw Jesus like a slain Lamb standing in God's presence at the *throne* (the "table of the bread of the Presence") in the holy place. Again the point was clear. Christ understands our sufferings and is more than a match for them. After He Himself was tortured to death, He came back to life. If difficult trials shorten our lives, He will one day bring us back to life. See pages 214-220.

3. *The seven trumpets*. Just before John saw God's scourges falling on the earth in connection with the seven trumpets, he saw an angel who represented Jesus offering incense at the *golden altar* and then throwing fire onto the earth. Christ hears our prayers. In answer to our prayers He sometimes sends fiery trials to restrain our enemies and to punish people who do wrong. See pages 228-233.

4. *The great-controversy scenes*. The final division of the first, historical, half of Revelation outlines the great controversy between Christ and Satan. In doing so, it emphasizes the commandments of God and announces the final judgment. Appropriately, the sanctuary scene which commences this division shows the inner area of the heavenly temple "opened" (Revelation 11:19) so that "the ark of his covenant was seen within his temple." Viewing earth's final judgment, John saw God's throne in heaven's most holy place, just as the high priest saw it on the annual Day of Atonement/Day of Judgment in the model tent sanctuary.

5. *The seven last plagues*. John's fifth scene of the heavenly sanctuary occurs in the end-time, or eschatological, half of Revelation. The sanctuary is opened only long enough to release the angels who hold the seven last plagues. Then it closes up. God's glory fills it, and no one is able to enter it. For the wicked who have refused to repent, mercy at last has ended. The seven last plagues begin to fall.

Appropriately, the remaining divisions of Revelation are not introduced with sanctuary scenes. At the time these divisions will be fulfilled, the sanctuary will cease to be in service. It is no surprise, then, that in Revelation 21:22 John says that there won't be a structural temple in New Jerusalem.

When the city comes down from heaven to earth, the saints will already have been redeemed. They will be able to look directly into God's great kindly face. God will still have a throne, of course, but there will be no need any more for the sanctuary as we know it.

Right now, however, we still need the heavenly sanctuary. Thank God it's still there and that inside it is a living, loving High Priest.

How good it is to know that the One who sits on the throne loves us just as much as Jesus does—and that circled around Him in Cosmic Control are four living creatures, the twenty-four elders, and uncounted angels, every one of whom has our best interests at heart. The heavenly sanctuary is a friendly place.

166

LOCATIONS OF INTRODUCTORY SANCTUARY SCENES

SEVEN CHURCHES	SEVEN SEALS	SEVEN TRUMPETS	GREAT CONTROVERSY

Scenes using symbols from the heavenly sanctuary (or temple) introduce each division in the first half of Revelation and the first division in the second half. Each sanctuary scene is related to the message of the division it introduces. See also page 424.

IN THE HOLY PLACE ———— IN THE MOST HOLY PLACE

LAMP STANDS	"TABLE" THRONE	INCENSE ALTAR	ARK OF THE COVENANT

SANCTUARY MINISTRY ENDS

SEVEN PLAGUES

FALL OF BABYLON

MILLENNIUM

NEW JERUSALEM

THESE FOUR DIVISIONS ARE FULFILLED SIDE BY SIDE FROM NEW TESTAMENT TIMES TILL THE END TIME. MOST EVENTS OCCUR WHILE CHRIST CONTINUES HIS PRIESTLY MINISTRY IN THE HEAVENLY SANCTUARY AND SO ARE MIXED WITH MERCY.

THESE FOUR DIVISIONS ARE FULFILLED IN THE END TIME. CHRIST'S PRIESTLY MINISTRY TERMINATES, THE SANCTUARY CLOSES UP, AND JUDGMENTS FALL WITHOUT MERCY. ETERNAL JOYS FOLLOW AT ONCE.

HISTORICAL HALF

ESCHATOLOGICAL (END-TIME) HALF

Further Interesting Reading

In Arthur S. Maxwell, *The Bible Story*, volume 10:
"The Throne of God," page 180.
In Ellen G. White, *The Triumph of God's Love:*
"The Mystery of the Temple of God," page 353.
"Jesus Christ Our Advocate," page 367.

Page numbers for each book refer to the large, fully illustrated edition.

Your Questions Answered

1. Is the heavenly sanctuary an actual structure? John's account of God's throne in the heavenly sanctuary is brilliant and vivid; nonetheless, some Bible commentators have taught that the heavenly sanctuary is not an actual structure. They point to Revelation 21:22, which says that the New Jerusalem temple is "the Lord God the Almighty and the Lamb." They have also observed that a first-century Jewish writer, Philo, spoke of heavenly things in such a way as to deny their reality except in the realm of thought. They have assumed that the New Testament writers of Hebrews and Revelation were strongly influenced by Philo's kind of thinking. They have claimed that when Hebrews and Revelation talk about a heavenly sanctuary, they have in mind merely a conceptual reality that exists, like Philo's, only in the realm of thought.

Popular as the argument from Philo has been for some time among certain prominent scholars and their students, in recent years Ronald Williamson[5] and D. McNichol[6] have met their learned arguments with other arguments equally learned and have shown that the book of Hebrews for sure is *not* influenced by Philo's thoughts. Williamson speaks at the conclusion of his masterly work of the "striking and fundamental" differences between Philo and Hebrews and states, "On such fundamental subjects as time, history, eschatology, the nature of the physical world, etc., the thoughts of Philo and the Writer of Hebrews are poles apart."[7]

One wonders what motivated the other scholars in the first place to describe Hebrews as only an echo of Philo!

As for Revelation 21:22, which says that the New Jerusalem temple is "the Lord God the Almighty and the Lamb," we should notice that it occurs at the end of Revelation, after John has seen the heavenly temple and its furnishings several times. See, for example, Revelation 4:1-5; 8:3; 11:1, 19; 15:5, 8. The divine temple, or heavenly sanctuary, is needed during the sin emergency. But evidently it will no longer be needed in its present form when the sin emergency has been adequately dealt with. After a manner of speaking, we might say that God will engage in a sublime kind of celestial urban redevelopment, eliminating the present heavenly temple and using its space for some other purpose. We know that we are to have a new heaven and a new earth in place of the old ones that we now have. See Revelation 21:1. Evidently we are also to have something new in place of the heavenly sanctuary that now exists.

Several lines of evidence encourage us to believe that the sanctuary now in use is an actual structure.

1. Hebrews 8:2 speaks emphatically of the "true tent which is set up not by man but by the Lord." This true tent or heavenly sanctuary is the location where Jesus ministers, and *Jesus is a human being*. He is not a vaporous spirit. After His resurrection, He invited His disciples to feel Him. "Handle me, and

His scarred hands assure us that our divine High Priest is still also human.

see," He said to them, "for a spirit has not flesh and bones as you see that I have." Luke 24:39. A human being with an actual body needs an actual structure to work in.

2. God is the Creator. He is the only Creator, the only Person who has ever brought anything new into existence. He is the only Person who has truly *made* anything. (All that the rest of us can do is to change the shape of what He has made!) God made our earth. He made the stars. He made the island universes. He made New Jerusalem, "the city . . . , whose builder and maker is God." Hebrews 11:10. It would not have been difficult for Him to create an actual heavenly sanctuary. It would be like Him to have done so.

3. The inauguration of the final judgment is described in Daniel 7:9-14 in *literal* language. Thrones are set up, books of some sort are opened, the Son of man arrives. The scene presupposes an actual location.

4. The sanctuary must be very large and very glorious. In Daniel 7:9-14, the Son of man travels there on the "clouds of heaven." Clouds are always "of" something—clouds of dust, clouds of locusts, clouds of water droplets, for example. In this case the clouds are most likely composed of loyal angels. In addition, "ten thousand times ten thousand" other angels surround God's throne. Compare Revelation 5:11. The heavenly sanctuary cannot be small.

5. Nonetheless, certain references to the heavenly sanctuary do seem to refer to a small structure closely resembling the earthly tabernacle in size and

169

shape. In Exodus 25:40, Moses was instructed to construct his tabernacle and its furnishings according to the *"pattern* for them, which is being shown you on the mountain." In the Greek Septuagint (LXX) translation of Exodus 25:40, and in Hebrews 8:5, which quotes it, the word used for "pattern" is *tupos*, type. Since the days of Lefèvre d'Étaples (c. 1450-1537)[8] some commentators have seen in this language a possible reference to a model sanctuary—a "type" of the true functional sanctuary—which is also located in heaven. The language allows the possibility that God created such an architect's model in heaven for Moses to study when constructing his own tabernacle. Such a model would have found secondary usefulness in helping intelligent beings from other parts of the universe to become acquainted with the earthly tabernacle and its function and message. A recent writer who has commended this possibility is Richard Davidson in his doctoral dissertation, "Typology in Scripture."[9]

But whether or not we are right in speaking of a small architect's model in heaven, the existence of an actual temple structure, vast and glorious, seems highly reasonable in view of John's many visions of it, the literal language of Daniel 7, the clear statements in Hebrews 8 and 9, the unique capacity of God to create things, and the actuality of Christ's human body.

William Johnsson, in another recent study of these matters,[10] has shown that the book of Hebrews encourages faith in *"real* deity, *real* humanity, a *real* priest, a *real* covenant, a *real* sacrifice, *real* purification, *real* access [to God], and, in keeping with these, a *real* heavenly sanctuary." We can rest assured that Revelation also presents a *real*, actual heavenly sanctuary.

2. Do Revelation 4 and 5 and Daniel 7:9-14 both describe the judgment? When Revelation 4 and 5 is compared with the judgment scene of Daniel 7:9-14, several similarities become apparent at once. Each account begins with references to God's throne, additional thrones, and vast numbers of attendants; each one talks about books (or at least one book); and each describes a subsequent appearance of Jesus Christ. Because of such clear similarities, many commentators have assumed that the two scenes are virtually identical. And because Daniel 7:9-14 is explicitly a judgment scene, they have held that Revelation 4 and 5 is also a judgment scene—the same judgment scene.

There are significant differences, however, between the two accounts which show upon analysis that the two scenes are really not the same.

The Differences. Daniel 7:9-14 begins with the setting up of thrones in some new place in heaven and with God's taking His seat on one of them. Revelation 4 and 5, however, begins with God already seated on His throne.

Daniel 7:9-14 presents a very dramatic arrival of the Son of man on the clouds of heaven. In Revelation 4 and 5, on the other hand, John simply becomes aware all of a sudden that the Lamb is *present*.

In Daniel 7:9-14 the books are already open *before* the Son of man makes

His appearance. In striking contrast, a focal emphasis of Revelation 4 and 5 is that the little scroll is closed—it is thoroughly closed; it is sealed with seven seals—until the Lamb undertakes to open it. The remaining portion of the seven-seals division (Revelation 6:1 to 8:1) continues to describe the Lamb's activity as He continues to break open the seals.

Whoever it may have been who opened the books of Daniel 7, we are not informed. We are simply told that they were opened. But in Revelation 4 and 5, the point is *emphasized* that no created being in the entire universe could break the seals of the scroll; only the Lamb could break them.

Daniel 7:9-14 is unquestionably a judgment scene. Daniel 7:10, 22, and 26 expressly indicate that it is. By contrast, Revelation 4 and 5 is not labeled a judgment scene.

We conclude that Daniel 7:9-14 and Revelation 4 and 5 describe not the same but two different events.

God's throne, movable or immovable? If the differences are so obvious, how can intelligent commentators have merged the scenes together? The words of one commentator represent the presupposition of many: "The dwelling place of God in the sanctuary *is* the holy of holies" (emphasis supplied).[11] In other words, many commentators have incorrectly assumed that in the heavenly sanctuary God has only one throne room and that it corresponds to the inner apartment, often called the most holy place, of the Old Testament earthly sanctuary.* They have concluded—needlessly—that because Revelation 4 and 5 shows God on His throne in heaven, it must be a portrayal of the heavenly most holy place.

The assumption that God's celestial throne is located only in the heavenly most holy place overlooks the fact that in Old Testament times God's presence was not always confined to the most holy place but was sometimes represented in the holy place. See, for example, Exodus 33:9 and Ezekiel 9:3. It also overlooks the symbolic purpose of the table of the bread of the Presence (the table of shewbread, K.J.V.).

Hebrews 8:1, 2, written in the first century A.D., unequivocally portrays Jesus as High Priest already seated on the Father's throne in the heavenly sanctuary. Revelation 4 and 5, also written in the first century, likewise locates the Lamb at the throne of God.

By contrast, Daniel 7:9-14 foretells an occasion after the close of the 1260 year-days (that is, sometime after 1798), when thrones would be set up in a new location, the Father would move to these thrones and take His seat upon one

---

*In Leviticus 16, the principal Bible chapter dealing with the area usually known as the most holy place, this inner area is designated simply "the holy place." Several different names are used for the two apartments. In Numbers 18:10, Moses calls the first apartment a "most holy place." Hence, we need not make too much of the name "*most* holy place" when asking for the location of God's throne. *Any* place God is, is holy, even a burning bush in a desert. See Exodus 3:2-5.

of them, and numerous other living beings would join Him there. After books were opened and the judgment was set, the Son of man would move to the new location in order to resume His position close to His Father.

The simple and logical conclusion to be drawn is that at His ascension in A.D. 31 Jesus went at once to the side of the Father, seated on heaven's celestial equivalent of the table of the bread of the Presence (the table of shewbread) in the heavenly sanctuary's vast and glorious "holy place." In *that* location, John saw Him break open the seven seals. Subsequently, after the close of the 1260 year-days, or more specifically in 1844 at the close of the 2300 year-days, thrones were set up in another sacred arena of the vast and glorious heavenly sanctuary. To alert the universe to the dramatic news that the final judgment was at last ready to begin, the Father moved in state to this new location, the four living creatures and the twenty-four elders moved to their new thrones, the open books were set in place, and when everything was prepared, the Son of man also moved. It is only this new place, this *second* sacred arena of heaven's vast and glorious sanctuary, that is equivalent to the most holy place in the Old Testament tabernacle.

Uriah Smith's view of God's movable throne. Uriah Smith is one popular but scholarly nineteenth-century commentator who perceived the mobility of God's throne and the true location of the throne in Revelation 4 and 5:

> That God immovably fixed himself to that position between the cherubim on the ark, and did not meet nor commune with his people from any other place . . . is contrary to the record; for at times he met with both Moses and the children of Israel at the door of the tabernacle. Exodus 29:42, 43; 33:9, 10. And again, was God dwelling between the cherubim of the ark when the sons of Eli rashly took it out to battle, and it fell into the hands of the Philistines? . . .
>
> Even though God did meet and commune with his servants from between the cherubim of the ark here below, so much so that it is spoken of as his dwelling place, . . . [it] would not inevitably follow [that it must also be so in heaven]; for in his intercourse with men this might be the best mode of procedure, but not necessarily so in Heaven. . . .
>
> It appears from Ezekiel's vision of God and his throne, in Ezekiel, chapters 1 and 10, that the throne of God itself is a living throne, supported by the most exalted order of cherubim. . . .
>
> That God's throne in Heaven is immovably fixed to one place . . . cannot be shown; for in Ezekiel's vision above referred to it is represented as full of awful life and unapproachable majesty, and moving whithersoever the Spirit was to go. And as in the earthly tabernacle, so here, it sometimes stood at the door of the Lord's house. Ezekiel 10:18, 19. . . .
>
> We have seen from Ezekiel's sublime description that God's throne is in itself a throne of life and motion. The Creator of the universe, the

172

Upholder and Ruler of all this vast realm, is not immovably confined to any one locality. And yet he dwells between the cherubim, because his throne itself is upheld by those wonderful beings. We now have evidence to show that when Christ commenced his ministry above, on the throne of his Father, that throne was in the first apartment of the heavenly sanctuary. . . .

The scene [of Revelation 4 and 5] opens with the commencement of Christ's ministry, and at that time the throne of God was in the first apartment of the sanctuary.[12]

Conclusion. Inasmuch, then, as the events, the description, the emphases, and the locations of the two scenes are all different, we may conclude that Revelation 4 and 5 and Daniel 7:9-14 describe not the same but different scenes. Only Daniel 7:9-14 portrays the judgment.

References

1. Douglas Cooper, *Living God's Joy* (Mountain View, Calif.: Pacific Press Publishing Association, 1979), p. 54.

2. Marvin R. Vincent, *Word Studies in the New Testament*, 4 vols., reprint (Grand Rapids, Mich.: Wm. B. Eerdmans Publishing Co., 1946, 1957), 2:412, 413.

3. Ellen G. White, *The Desire of Ages* (Mountain View, Calif.: Pacific Press Publishing Association, 1898, 1940), pp. 669, 670.

4. Fritz Guy, "Confidence in Salvation: The Meaning of the Sanctuary," *Spectrum,* 11, no. 2 (1980):47. Emphasis supplied. Orthography slightly altered.

5. Ronald Williamson, "Philo and the Epistle to the Hebrews," in K. H. Rengstorf, et al., eds., *Arbeiten zur Literatur und Geschichte des Hellenistischen Judentums* (Leiden: E. J. Brill, 1970).

6. D. McNichol, "The Relationship of the Image of the Highest Angel to the High Priest Concept in Hebrews" (Ph.D. dissertation, Vanderbilt University, 1974), in William G. Johnsson, "The Heavenly Cultus in the Book of Hebrews—Figurative or Real?" in Arnold V. Wallenkampf and W. Richard Lesher, eds., *The Sanctuary and the Atonement* (Washington, D.C.: General Conference of Seventh-day Adventists, 1981), p. 370.

7. Williamson, "Philo and Hebrews," pp. 576, 577. See also pp. 578-580.

8. Henry Alford, *The New Testament for English Readers*, 4 vols. (Grand Rapids, Mich.: Baker Book House, 1983 reprint), 4:1517.

9. Richard M. Davidson, *Typology in Scripture: A Study of Hermeneutical* ΤΥΠΟΣ *Structures,* Andrews University Seminary Doctoral Dissertation Series, vol. 2 (Berrien Springs, Mich.: Andrews University Press, 1981), pp. 342, 343, 358-360.

10. Johnsson, "Heavenly Cultus," p. 374.

11. Mario Veloso, "The Doctrine of the Sanctuary and the Atonement as Reflected in the Book of Revelation" (an otherwise very helpful study), Wallenkampf and Lesher, eds., *Sanctuary and Atonement*, p. 399.

12. Uriah Smith, *The Sanctuary and the Twenty-three Hundred Days of Daniel VIII, 14* (Battle Creek, Mich.: Steam Press of the Seventh-day Adventist Publishing Association, 1877), pp. 231-234.

Revelation 6:1 to 8:1

Christ Shields His Afflicted People

Introduction

In spite of his advanced years, the apostle John was as eager as a child to see what was inside the seven-sealed scroll.

Jesus had promised to show him

"what must take place after this." Revelation 4:1. Undoubtedly John knew that the prophet Ezekiel had once been handed a scroll that was written on both sides, similar to the one that Jesus had just now taken from God's hand. Ezekiel's scroll was full of "lamentation and mourning and

woe." See Ezekiel 2:8-10. Was the world's future, John must have wondered, to be marked by continual lamentation, mourning, and woe?

Yes, evidently it was. But that wasn't the main thing Jesus wanted John—and us—to know. Rather, He wanted to tell us that in all our afflictions He would offer Himself as our protector and shield.

Many times in the Bible, God is called a shield. During a period of military tension, God Himself encouraged Abraham to remember that "I am your shield." Genesis 15:1. Frequently under enemy fire, David encouraged

himself with the same promise. "The Lord is my strength and my shield." Psalm 28:7. "Thou art my hiding place and my shield." Psalm 119:114.

Affliction, oppression, and distress come to all of us. But in the seven-seals division of Revelation, Jesus lets us know that through the power of the gospel He can shield us from many of the ravages of ordinary disasters (Revelation 6:1-8); at death He can shield us from fear by guaranteeing our resurrection (6:9-11; 7:9-17); and even from the worst distress of the end-time crisis, He can shield us with the **"seal of the living God"** (7:1-3).

175

As Jesus opened the first four seals, out galloped four horsemen known to history as "the Four Horsemen of the Apocalypse."

ORGANIZATION OF REVELATION

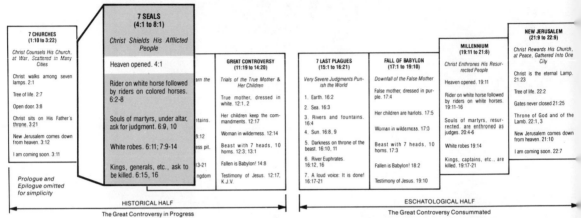

The chart shows we are about to discover the secrets of the seven seals.

The opening of the seven seals was *introduced* by the dramatic throne-room scene that we looked at in our previous chapter. It is *interrupted* between the sixth and seventh seals with scenes of end-time assignment and assurance. The assignment is made to a group of angels to keep on **"holding back"** the **"four winds"** until the **"servants of our God"** have been sealed **"upon their foreheads."** Revelation 7:1-3. There is a serious, sacred pun here. (Closely related words are used in the underlying Greek.) While Jesus opens the seven *seals* of the scroll, an angel *seals* God's people on their foreheads.

In these scenes of assignment and assurance John sees 144,000 people and then, in addition, a huge crowd of others. Happy and rejoicing, they stand at the throne of God, alongside the Lamb and the living creatures and the angels. In spite of wars, epidemics, famines, and persecution, Christ will have brought His people through to victory and everlasting joy.

This is good news; and it applies to us. For through the **"blood of the Lamb"** (7:14) we and our families can expect to be there with that happy multitude one of these days. We can be grateful that the Lamb opened the seals to let us know this. We can be glad that He will shield us all along the way between now and then.

SEVEN SEALS: Christ Shields His Afflicted People. 4:1 to 8:1

1. *Intro. sanctuary scene: God on His throne, the Lamb worthy to open seals. 4:1 to 5:14*

2. First six seals. 6:1-17

3. Scenes of last-day assignment and assurance. 7:1-17
   a. Assignment: To seal God's servants (on earth)
   b. Assurance: 144,000 and the great multitude (in heaven)

4. Consummation: Seventh seal, silence in heaven. 8:1

THE LAMB OPENS THE FIRST SIX SEALS

REVELATION 6

The first seal opened: The white horse and its rider. 1 Now I saw when the Lamb opened one of the seven seals, and I heard one of the four living creatures say, as with a voice of thunder, "Come!" ²And I saw, and behold, a white horse, and its rider had a bow; and a crown was given to him, and he went out conquering and to conquer.

The second seal opened: The red horse and its rider. 3 When he opened the second seal, I heard the second living creature say, "Come!" ⁴And out came another horse, bright red; its rider was permitted to take peace from the earth, so that men should slay one another; and he was given a great sword.

The third seal opened: The black horse and its rider. 5 When he opened the third seal, I heard the third living creature say, "Come!" And I saw, and behold, a black horse, and its rider had a balance in his hand; ⁶and I heard what seemed to be a voice in the midst of the four living creatures saying, "A quart of wheat for a denarius, and three quarts of barley for a denarius; but do not harm oil and wine!"

The fourth seal opened: The pale horse and its rider. 7 When he opened the fourth seal, I heard the voice of the fourth living creature say, "Come!" ⁸And I saw, and behold, a pale horse, and its rider's name was Death, and Hades followed him;

Summary statement about the three colored horses and their riders. and they were given power over a fourth of the earth, to kill with sword and with famine and with pestilence and by wild beasts of the earth.

The fifth seal opened: The souls under the altar. 9 When he opened the fifth seal, I saw under the altar the souls of those who had been slain for the word of God and for the witness they had borne; ¹⁰they cried out with a loud voice, "O Sovereign Lord, holy and true, how long before thou wilt judge and avenge our blood on those who dwell upon the earth?" ¹¹Then they were each given a white robe and told to rest a little longer, until the number of their fellow servants and their brethren should be complete, who were to be killed as they themselves had been.

The sixth seal opened: End-time signs lead up to the second coming. 12 When he opened the sixth seal, I looked, and behold, there was a great earthquake; and the sun became black as sackcloth, the full moon became like blood, ¹³and the stars of the sky fell to the earth as the fig tree sheds its winter fruit when shaken by a gale; ¹⁴the sky vanished like a scroll that is rolled up, and every mountain and island was removed from its place. ¹⁵Then the kings of the earth and the great men and the generals and the rich and the strong, and every one, slave and free, hid in the caves and among the rocks of the mountains, ¹⁶calling to the mountains and rocks, "Fall on us and hide us from the face of him who is seated on the throne, and from the wrath of the Lamb; ¹⁷for the great day of their wrath has come, and who can stand before it?"

PARENTHETICAL SCENES OF END-TIME ASSIGNMENT AND ASSURANCE

The 144,000 and the Great Multitude

REVELATION 7

Sealing of the 144,000 selected out of "Israel." 1 After this I saw four angels standing at the four corners of the earth, holding back the four winds of the earth, that no wind might blow on earth or sea or against any tree. ²Then I saw another angel ascend from the rising of the sun, with the seal of the living God, and he called with a loud voice to the four angels who had been given power to harm earth and sea, ³saying, "Do not harm the earth or the sea or the trees, till we have sealed the servants of our God upon their foreheads." ⁴And I heard the number of the sealed, a hundred and forty-four thousand sealed, out of every tribe of the sons of Israel, ⁵twelve thousand

177

sealed out of the tribe of Judah, twelve thousand of the tribe of Reuben, twelve thousand of the tribe of Gad, [6]twelve thousand of the tribe of Asher, twelve thousand of the tribe of Naphtali, twelve thousand of the tribe of Manasseh, [7]twelve thousand of the tribe of Simeon, twelve thousand of the tribe of Levi, twelve thousand of the tribe of Issachar, [8]twelve thousand of the tribe of Zebulun, twelve thousand of the tribe of Joseph, twelve thousand sealed out of the tribe of Benjamin.

Rejoicing of the great multitude gathered from every nation. 9 After this I looked, and behold, a great multitude which no man could number, from every nation, from all tribes and peoples and tongues, standing before the throne and before the Lamb, clothed in white robes, with palm branches in their hands, [10]and crying out with a loud voice, "Salvation belongs to our God who sits upon the throne, and to the Lamb!" [11]And all the angels stood round the throne and round the elders and the four living creatures, and they fell on their faces before the throne and worshiped God, [12]saying, "Amen! Blessing and glory and wisdom and thanksgiving and honor and power and might be to our God for ever and ever! Amen."

13 Then one of the elders addressed me, saying, "Who are these, clothed in white robes, and whence have they come?" [14]I said to him, "Sir, you know." And he said to me, "These are they who have come out of the great tribulation; they have washed their robes and made them white in the blood of the Lamb.
[15]Therefore are they before the throne of God,
and serve him day and night within his temple;
and he who sits upon the throne will shelter them with his presence.
[16]They shall hunger no more, neither thirst any more;
the sun shall not strike them, nor any scorching heat.
[17]For the Lamb in the midst of the throne will be their shepherd,
and he will guide them to springs of living water;
and God will wipe away every tear from their eyes."

THE LAMB OPENS THE SEVENTH SEAL

REVELATION 8

The seventh seal opened: A brief silence in heaven. 1 When the Lamb opened the seventh seal, there was silence in heaven for about half an hour.

The Message of Revelation 6:1 to 8:1

I. One of the Riders Had a White Horse

Almost everyone has heard about the "four horsemen of the Apocalypse." Most people think that they represent epidemics, famines, and war.

And so they do; but not all of them. Not the one who rides on a white horse. He's different.

By the way, is your family getting involved with the seven seals? Little children are familiar with TV cartoons, especially animal cartoons. And, if anything, they are all too familiar with violence and sudden death. Tell them about the four horsemen, and especially about the rider on the white horse who makes all the difference.

The four horsemen and their steeds. One at a time, Jesus broke each of the first four seals. As He did so, one of the four living creatures near God's throne said in a voice like thunder, **"Come!"**

The participation of the living creatures impresses us. They are concerned about our welfare.

In response to their invitation, four riders, the four horsemen of the Apocalypse, came galloping into view, one at a time. Each was riding a different colored horse.

As Jesus broke the first seal, a **"white"** horse appeared. **"Its rider had a bow; and a crown was given to him, and he went out conquering and to conquer."** Revelation 6:2. When Jesus broke the second seal, the horse that appeared was **"bright red."** **"Its rider was permitted to take peace from the earth, so that men should slay one another; and he was given a great sword."** Verses 3, 4.

The horse of the third seal was **"black."** **"Its rider had a balance in his hand; and I heard what seemed to be a voice in the midst of the four living creatures saying, 'A quart of wheat for a denarius, and three quarts of barley for a denarius; but do not harm oil and wine!' "** Verses 5-7.

The fourth horse was **"pale."** The New English Bible says it was "sickly pale." The New American Standard Bible has "ashen." Its rider's name was **"Death,"** and **"Hades"** followed him.

All together, these three fearsome horsemen were given **"power over a fourth of the earth, to kill with sword and with famine and with pestilence and by wild beasts of the earth."** Verses 7, 8.

Horses of similar colors are found in two series in Zechariah. In Zechariah 1 there are two red horses but no black horse. Zechariah 6 has at least eight horses, arranged in a different order, red, black, white, and dappled gray, all of them harnessed to chariots. Their job is to "patrol the earth." They have no riders. They are evidently not the same as the four horses in Revelation.

179

In Revelation, the rider on the bright red horse is given a **"sword"** and is permitted to **"take peace from the earth"** and to provoke people to **"slay one another."** Plainly, he is a symbol of violence and war.

The man on the black horse, who measures out food at a fixed price, represents scarcity and famine. **"Wheat," "barley," "oil,"** and **"wine"** were staple foods in ancient times. Barley, being easier to raise than wheat and not as desirable, was sold at a lower price and was especially important for the poor in some areas. Oil was essential for baking. Wine seemed more healthful than water from old cisterns and polluted streams. Price ceilings were often established by law, especially in times of scarcity. Bakers who charged too much at such times were in danger of severe punishment.[1]

The Bible identifies the fourth rider as **"Death."** The grave, **"Hades,"** accompanied him like some underworld Tonto, constantly available.

Summarizing, John tells us that the riders on the red, black, and pale horses were horribly equipped for their deadly careers with **"sword," "famine," "pestilence,"** and **"wild beasts."**

At first glance, there is not very much that is really new here. Tragically, wars and famines and epidemics have long been recognized as classic scourges of mankind.

In His Olivet Discourse, Jesus said that "wars and rumors of wars," "famines," and "earthquakes in various places" were not special signs limited to the end of the world. Matthew 24:6, 7. They were to be expected as normal calamities throughout history. (See pages 20, 21. For a helpful comparison with the Olivet Discourse, see the chart on the next page.)

How to beat the three evil riders. But evidently wars and shortages and epidemics didn't need to be normal, or at least not for everyone. Away back in Leviticus 26, soon after Israel left Egypt, God promised the Israelites through Moses that if they remained loyal to His teachings and if they kept His commandments, God would see to it that they remained prosperous, healthy, and at peace. That is, God would shield them from the ravages of the three evil horsemen. Look closely at His promise.

> You shall keep my sabbaths and reverence my sanctuary:
> I am the Lord.
>
> If you walk in my statutes and observe my commandments and do them,
> then I will give you your rains in their season. . . .
>
> You shall eat your bread to the full. . . .
>
> I will give peace. . . .
>
> You shall chase your enemies. . . .

PARALLELS BETWEEN THE OLIVET DISCOURSE AND THE SEVEN SEALS

We chose to begin this second volume of *God Cares* by analyzing Christ's Olivet Discourse before coming to Revelation itself. The Olivet Discourse is a vital link between Daniel and Revelation and sheds much light on both of them.

When the outline of the discourse is placed in parallel with the outline of the seven seals, the relationship between the discourse and Revelation becomes quite apparent.

THE OLIVET DISCOURSE	THE SEVEN SEALS
(Matthew 24, 25)	*(Revelation 4:1 to 8:1)*
General Prophetic Survey	*Four Horsemen of the Apocalypse*
This gospel will be preached. 24:14.	Seal 1. A rider on a white horse proclaims Christianity 6:1, 2.
Wars and rumors of wars: famines and earthquakes. The end not yet. 24:6-8.	Seals 2, 3, 4. Riders on red, black, and pale horses inflict war, famine, and epidemics. 6:3-8.
Period of Tribulation	*Period of Tribulation*
There will be great tribulation. 24:21.	Seal 5. Souls under the altar protest persecution. 6:9-11.
Signs and the End	*Signs and the End*
Signs in sun, moon, stars immediately follow the tribulation. 24:29.	Seal 6. Great earthquake; signs in sun, moon, stars. 6:12, 13.
The Son of man returns. 24:30.	Sky rolls back. The Lamb arrives. 6:14-17.
Angels gather the elect. 24:31.	Seal 7. Half an hour silence in heaven (while heavenly beings accompany Christ to earth to gather the elect). 8:1.

I will walk among you, and will be your God,
and you shall be my people.
                              Leviticus 26:2-12.

But, if, on the other hand, Israel disregarded God's commandments and chose a life-style like that of unbelievers, Moses said they would suffer the same distresses as unbelievers. In other words, God would have no basis for shielding them from the evil horsemen. Diseases would worsen into epidemics, scarcity would harden into famine, and defeat would escalate to total devastation. See Leviticus 26:14-33.

The rider on the white horse. And so we come back to the rider on the white horse. Who is this mystery horseman, and what is the significance of the color **"white"**?

George Eldon Ladd has pointed out that

> in the Revelation, white is always a symbol of Christ, or of something associated with Christ, or of spiritual victory. Thus the exalted Christ has white hair white as wool (1:14); the faithful will receive a white stone with a new name written on it (2:17); they are to wear white garments (3:4, 5, 18); the twenty-four elders are clad in white (4:4); the martyrs are given white robes (6:11) as is the great numberless throng (7:9, 13); the son of man is seen on a white cloud (14:14); he returns on a white horse accompanied by the armies of heaven who are clad in white and ride white horses (19:11, 14); in the final judgment, God is seen seated on a white throne (20:11).[2]

So white is the color of Christ and His righteousness.

Then is the first rider Jesus Christ? In Revelation 19, as Ladd observes above, Jesus unmistakably does appear riding on a white horse. He is expressly introduced as King of kings and Lord of lords and as the Word of God. See Revelation 19:11-16. In John 1:1-3 "Word of God" is a name for Jesus. In Revelation 19, Jesus has a weapon and He "makes war," so very similar to the white horse rider of the first seal.

We want to know what the Bible is telling us. On second reading, it doesn't seem likely, after all, that this rider of the first seal really is Jesus. Jesus is the *Lamb* who *opens* the seal; He is not likely to be symbolized by the horseman of the seal. In any case, the other riders are not actual persons. **"Death"** and **"Hades"** certainly aren't persons.

Still, the close similarity with the rider in Revelation 19 must be intentional. Inasmuch as the three other riders in the seals represent *concepts*—warfare, scarcity, and death—this one must also represent a concept, the concept that Jesus Christ stands for. This concept is, of course, true Bible religion or, more specifically, *true Christianity*. The white horse rider is related to the other riders some-

182

what as day is related to night. Offering inner peace and the bread of life, true Christianity is the *opposite* of warfare, scarcity, and death.

Before His ascension, Jesus commissioned His followers to go into all the world and to preach the gospel, the message of true Christianity. See Matthew 28:18-20. He promised to go with them, but not literally, of course, for He would be in heaven. He would accompany them in the person of His representative, the Holy Spirit. See pages 160-162.

Out went Christianity from Jerusalem to Judea, to Samaria, and on toward the end of the earth, conquering and to conquer. See Acts 1:8. Paul could claim that in his lifetime the whole world as he knew it had heard the gospel. See Colossians 1:6, 23. Opponents said that Christians had turned the world upside down. See Acts 17:6.

Tragically, in course of time the world turned the church upside down. Pagan Rome adopted some of the doctrines, customs, and the name of the Christians. But Christians adopted the authoritarianism, the political intrigue, much of the philosophy, and even the name of pagan Rome. See GC1: 127-133.

There *were* changes. Christian Rome did not crucify people as pagan Rome had done. No, Christian Rome burned them alive.

Pagan Rome tortured criminals for stealing. Christian Rome tortured Christians for reading the Bible their own way.

Did the church conquer the world, or did the world conquer the church?

To prepare people in advance for the preaching of the gospel, it appears that God had purposely overruled in political affairs to establish the Roman peace, the *Pax Romana*. Travel and communication in the Roman world were in some ways easier in early Christian times than they have ever been since. "The countries of the Roman Empire were never before and never afterwards more free from the shadow of war than in the first two centuries A.D."[3]

In such an environment, the gospel spread rapidly, unimpeded by political barriers. Many persons in the empire accepted it.

If only the church had remained pure and the empire had been wholly influenced by it! Suppose love not hate, generosity not greed, and trust not treachery had held full sway! "God shows no partiality." Acts 10:34. "God has no favourites." N.E.B. He would have treated the Roman Empire and the Roman Church as well as He had promised to treat the Jews in Leviticus 26 (see above). Prosperity, health, and peace would have remained and improved. He would have kept the three evil horsemen at bay.

We saw in our discussion about the fall of Jerusalem that if the Jews had accepted Christ's counsel about how to treat the Romans and how to treat one another, Jerusalem need never have been destroyed. See pages 26-28.

But Christ on the Mount of Olives knew that it would not be so for the Jews. In opening the seven seals, He showed that He also knew it would not be so for the Roman West. And it wasn't. When true Christian love was largely laid aside, unity and peace broke down. Barbarian peoples divided the empire and fought

Pope Julius II led armed soldiers on military excursions to enforce his kind of Christianity. Some Protestant leaders did the same for theirs.

over the pieces. They adopted the corrupted concept of Christianity held by their Roman victims and went on fighting.

In the Middle Ages, England and France, supposedly Christian nations, fought the Hundred Years' War (1337-1453). Central Europe, supposedly Christian, separated into a thousand jealous little states. Bubonic plague, the Black Death, struck in the 1340s and recurred repeatedly for centuries, killing millions that the wars didn't get. In the Christian West, the three evil horsemen found plenty to keep them busy.

Most perplexing, the church itself became a principal cause of warfare, famine, and desolation. Protestant versus Catholic fought the devastating Thirty Years' War (1618-1648) we referred to on page 126. The church drove the Huguenots out of France, depriving the nation of an invaluable resource. Political and economic demands of bishops and priests led directly, as everyone knows, to the stark terror of the French Revolution.

World War I was fought principally by self-styled Christian nations—Lutheran Germany, Anglican Britain, Protestant America, Orthodox Russia, and largely Catholic France. Millions perished. Hundreds of thousands were killed or wounded on the single battlefield of Verdun. At the end of the war, millions more died of famine and epidemic in the Soviet Union. The three evil horsemen were kept busy indeed—while the rider on the white horse, whom almost everyone said he admired, rode by largely ignored.

Indeed, the markedly brutal contribution made to earth's disasters by nominally Christian entities has led some thoughtful commentators to identify the four horsemen of the Apocalypse with the Christian church! The New Testament church, with all its winsome purity, these commentators identify with the rider on the white horse. The moral decline of the medieval church they associate with the riders on the red, black, and pale horses. They may have a point.*

Be that as it may, the rider on the white horse is still riding! In fact, he is today conquering more hearts in more places around the world than ever before, in fulfillment of Matthew 24:14. His finest days of conquest are still ahead. "This gospel of the kingdom will be preached throughout the whole world as a testimony to all nations; and then the end will come." As you read about him in your Bible, perhaps you can see him, even now, approaching your home.

If you *can* see him coming, do welcome him in. Although the three evil horsemen have had their historical fulfillment in large-scale disasters, there is a sense in which we experience them daily. Incessant quarreling, economic setbacks, and premature disease pose serious family threats. But true Christianity, true Bible religion, can shield our homes from them.

Christian love can shield us from family infighting. "A soft answer turns away wrath." Proverbs 15:1. Speaking kindly in a gentle voice, as Jesus would if He were at our house, can work wonders to reduce tension and restore affection.

True Christianity can help fend off family economic crises. In the Sermon on the Mount, Jesus emphasized that our heavenly Father knows that we need food, clothing, and shelter. So He counseled us about budget priorities. Put God first! "Seek first his kingdom and his righteousness, and all these things [food, clothing, and shelter] shall be yours," He said. Matthew 6:33.

The prophet Malachi was specific. Put God "to the test," he urged! Pay "full tithes"—a tenth of your net income; then see for yourself whether or not God will "open the windows of heaven for you and pour down for you an overflowing blessing." Malachi 3:10. God sits on the throne at Cosmic Control, in charge of the universe. You can count on Him. In consideration of your weakness, He probably won't make you rich; but He will surely see to it that you don't go without. Millions of prosperous tithers testify that the experiment works. God keeps His financial promises.

True Christianity, true Bible religion, can improve your family's health. "Whether you eat or drink, or whatever you do, do all to the glory of God." 1 Corinthians 10:31. Several surveys in recent years have revealed the superior health of groups who seek to regulate their life habits for the "glory of God."

---

* Identification of the four horsemen with the first four symbolic churches, Ephesus, Smyrna, Pergamum, and Thyatira, has also been attempted. But Smyrna, the second church, instead of using a sword to kill people like the second horseman, was itself the object of severe persecution. Rather than comparing the seven seals with the seven churches, it is better to compare them with the sequence of events outlined by Jesus in the Olivet Discourse. See the chart on page 181.

Seventh-day Adventists, for example, have measurably fewer diseases and tend to live several years longer than the general population.[4]

God cares. He cares about our health, about our financial problems, about the quality of love in our homes. He has a thousand ways to help.

The three evil horsemen who have caused so much trouble in the world threaten our families. One of the messages of the book of Revelation is that the rider on the white horse—true Christianity—can make all the difference.

II. Does God Really Care?

We believe that true Christianity can shield us from many of life's serious trials. Just the same, earnest believers in God often seem to suffer as much as everyone else.

Last fall one of my students and his wife skidded on an icy road while driving home for Thanksgiving. Regaining control, they paused on the shoulder to pray earnestly for safety. Yet only a few miles later, an oncoming car crossed the double line, smashed into their subcompact, and killed the young wife.

Three weeks ago a darling four-year-old in our church was crushed in a car accident. About the same time, the fiancé of one of our college coeds died in a plane crash, a couple of months before their wedding.

We have read of Christian tribespeople massacred in East Africa, of missionary nuns raped and murdered in Central America, of Evangelical Baptists imprisoned in Asia. You perhaps are a faithful believer, and yet your own life, it may be, has been shattered by disease or divorce or death or some bitter disappointment.

At times even the stoutest of us is tempted to question whether the rider on the white horse does make a difference, whether God really cares. Habakkuk was an inspired prophet, yet even he cried out,

> How long, O Lord, must I call for help,
>   but you do not listen?
> Or cry out to you, "Violence!"
>   but you do not save? . . .
> Why do you tolerate wrong?
> Habakkuk 1:2, 3, N.I.V.

In a moment of tragic disappointment, good King David sobbed, "My God, my God, why have you forsaken me?" Psalm 22:1, N.I.V.

C. S. Lewis, the widely read Christian professor at Cambridge University, felt a similar dereliction after his wife died of cancer. To his anguished mind heaven seemed silent and empty, its door double-bolted. Dejected, he analyzed his thoughts:

> Meanwhile, where is God? This is one of the most disquieting symptoms. When you are happy, so happy that you have no sense of needing Him, so

happy that you are tempted to feel His claims upon you as an interruption, if you remember . . . and turn to Him with gratitude and praise, you will be—or so it feels—welcomed with open arms. But go to Him when your need is desperate, when all other help is vain, and what do you find? A door slammed in your face, and a sound of bolting and double bolting on the inside. After that, silence. You may as well turn away. The longer you wait, the more emphatic the silence will become. There are no lights in the windows.[5]

Human suffering and the seven seals. If God is in charge (see page 152), why doesn't He do something? If He really cares, why doesn't He answer our prayers?

It is especially appropriate to ask such sober questions in the setting of the seven seals. The introductory sanctuary scene shows God on His throne. The first seal shows Christianity galloping over the earth, bringing joy and reassurance and shielding believers from the horsemen of war, famine, and pestilence. But the fifth seal shows the **"souls"** of martyrs languishing under an **"altar"** crying out in anguish, **"O Sovereign Lord, holy and true, how long before thou wilt judge and avenge our blood on those who dwell upon the earth?"** Revelation 6: 9, 10.

There is a distinct, worlds-apart difference between the throne scene of Revelation 4 and 5, where God rules and angels sing, and the altar scene in chapter 6, where souls demand, **"How long?"**

The souls under the altar represent faithful martyrs, sacrificed as if on an altar **"for the word of God and for the witness they had borne."** Verse 9. If God was in charge, if He cared, why didn't He answer *their* prayers? Surely they deserved it.

The fact is, of course, that God did care. He didn't tell His precious martyrs the reason for the delay or precisely when their prayers would be answered, but this doesn't mean He didn't love them. "It is not for you to know times or seasons which the Father has fixed by his own authority," said Jesus once to His own disciples. Acts 1:7.

Nonetheless, God did something very wonderful for His martyrs. He invited them to **"rest a little longer"**—to *rest,* leaving their cases entirely in His hands—**"until the number of their fellow servants and their brethren should be complete, who were to be killed as they themselves had been."** And God saw to it that each treasured victim received a **"white robe."** Revelation 6:11.

Jesus taught in one of His parables (Matthew 22:1-14) that all that God requires of us for admission to His heavenly banquet is possession of the wedding garment, His own white robe. Receiving the white robe is akin to receiving the rider on the white horse. The garment represents His own purity and righteousness, which we accept and make our own through faith.

When the martyrs received the white robe, they also got everything else that matters, life and health and joy with God and His people in His kingdom forever.

187

Comfort for the 1260 year-days. The seven seals, like the letters to the seven churches, occur in the first half of Revelation; they belong to the historical half of the book that stretches from the time of Christ to the second coming. See pages 61-63. The persecution under the fifth seal parallels the "great tribulation" that fell on "Thyatira" (Revelation 2:22) and the "war" that the little horn made with the "saints" (Daniel 7:24, 25). See pages 125, 126 and GC 1:122-133.

The martyrs prayed for judgment. **"How long before thou wilt *judge* and avenge our blood?"** they asked. Their request places the fifth seal prior to the final judgment. On GC 1:237-247 we found that the first phase of the final judgment was to commence in 1844, at the close of the 2300 year-days of Daniel 8:14. The martyrs didn't know when the judgment would begin and, as we just noticed, God didn't choose to tell them.

Centuries earlier, in the vision of Daniel 8, the prophet Daniel had heard the time of the judgment announced. First he had heard someone ask the same question that the martyrs (and Habakkuk) asked, "How long?" But the answer Daniel heard was given in the symbolic language of the 2300 days, and Daniel was told to leave his book closed—not fully understood—until the time of the end arrived. See Daniel 12:4. This helps explain why, when the martyrs raised the question again, they didn't discover the answer.

We have seen on GC 1:130 that the 1260 year-days ran from 538 to 1798. Thus they terminated a short time before the judgment began in 1844. More than once we have also discussed the tribulation of the 1260 year-days in connection with the prophecies that deal with it. See pages 33, 35, 125, 126 and GC 1:132, 133. One thing we haven't yet asked is what effect persecution had on a martyr's relatives. W. E. H. Lecky, a widely read historian and former member of the British Academy, gives us something of an idea of how his family members must have felt.

"It is appalling," Lecky says, "to reflect what the mother, the wife, the sister, the daughter of the heretic must have suffered. . . . She saw the body of him who was dearer to her than life, dislocated and writhing and quivering with pain; she watched the slow fire creeping from limb to limb till it had swathed him in a sheet of agony, and when at last . . . the tortured body was at rest, she was told that all this was acceptable to the God she served, and was but a faint image of the sufferings He would inflict through eternity upon the dead."[6]

How often must the relatives of the martyrs have cried out, **"How long?"** "Why have You forsaken me?" How often must *they* have felt, with C. S. Lewis, that heaven was deserted and its doors double-bolted!

Lecky observes in the same passage that "the Spanish heretic was led to the flames in a dress covered with representations of devils and of frightful tortures to remind the spectators to the very last of the doom that awaited him." Lecky might have referred also to the tall conical cap that was similarly decorated to match the gown. The authorities asserted, sincerely no doubt, that the martyrs would burn eternally in hell unless they abandoned their unusual convictions.

They hoped the fearsome clothing would frighten their victims into last-minute repentance.

The true martyrs didn't falter. They looked away from the devil gown to God's gown. What a blessing to have Heaven's white robes to change into! And we all hope that the martyrs' relatives kept their eyes on the white robe too. Many of them no doubt did, and were greatly comforted.

In the scenes of end-time assignment and assurance near the close of the seven seals, God showed John His faithful martyrs standing around His throne—as they will be one day soon—**"clothed in white robes**[there are those glorious garments], **with palm branches in their hands** [like the happy people at Christ's triumphal entry on Palm Sunday (see John 12:13)]," singing their hearts out for joy. Revelation 7:9.

As John gazed on them all in prophetic vision, one of the twenty-four elders assured him that they will have the privilege of serving God **"day and night** [just like the living creatures]" and also that **"they shall hunger no more, neither thirst any more," "for the Lamb in the midst of the throne will be their shepherd, and he will guide them to springs of living water; and God will wipe away every tear from their eyes."** Revelation 7:13-17.

Their enemies attempted to destroy them, but Jesus *shielded* them from final

A martyr's agony was severe but brief. His family suffered far longer.

destruction. He gave them white robes, allowed them to rest awhile in death, and guaranteed them everlasting life.*

The 144,000 sealed. In addition to the martyrs, another significant group was selected for special reference. This was the 144,000, who are to live not during the 1260 year-days but during the decades of the end time. Before the four winds of final trial will be permitted to release their unprecedented forces of destruction, an angel is especially commissioned to "seal" every one of the 144,000 with the **"seal of the living God."** See Revelation 7:1-3.

The **"seal of the living God"** here appears to be the same as the "Father's name" in Revelation 14:1. Both the "seal" of God and His "name" are placed on people's foreheads. God's "name" is a term often used to represent His character. The meaning seems to be that Christ seals His end-time people by developing in each of them a beautiful reproduction of His own lovely character. We'll say more about the seal when we come to chapters 12 to 14.

So Christ clothed the martyrs with His righteousness in order to shield them from eternal death. He promised to develop His righteous character in the 144,000 in order to seal them from the terrors of the four winds. The sixth and seventh seals remind us also of Christ's standing promise to come back to earth a second time.

Phenomenal signs and the second coming. As the Lamb opened the sixth seal, following the persecution of the 1260 years, **"behold,"** says John, **"there was a great earthquake; and the sun became black as sackcloth, the full moon became like blood, and the stars of the sky fell to the earth as the fig tree sheds its winter fruit** [its "unripe figs," N.A.S.B.] **when shaken by a gale; the sky vanished like a scroll that is rolled up, and every mountain and island was removed from its place."** Revelation 6:12-14. We'll discuss these phenomenal signs in the next section. For now we'll just observe that many Bible students believe that the first ones have already been fulfilled and that we are living today between the falling of the stars and the rolling back of the skies.

Not yet have the heavens vanished as a scroll or all the islands and mountains danced out of their places; but when they will have, **"the kings of the earth and the great men and the generals and the rich and the strong, and every one, slave and free,"** says John, looking on the event prophetically as though it had already happened, **"hid in the caves and among the rocks of the mountains, calling to the mountains and rocks, 'Fall on us and hide us from the face of him who is seated on the throne, and from the wrath of the Lamb; for the great day of their wrath has come, and who can stand before it?' "** Verses 15-17.

What a contrast there is between the crowds under the rocks and the souls under the altar! What a difference between the cry of the wicked to the mountains and rocks to accomplish their destruction, and the prayer of the martyrs to the Lord, the Rock of their salvation. See Psalm 95:1.

---

*For the important question whether the souls under the altar are even now still alive, see *Your Questions Answered,* pages 214-220.

What a contrast there is between the fear of those who desire to hide from the Lord, and the joy of those who welcome His return. See Isaiah 25:9. What a difference between being terrified by the Lamb's wrath and being robed in His righteousness.

Those who want to hide from the Lamb want to hide also from **"him who is seated on the throne."** God the Father accompanies His Son. All the holy angels come as well. See Matthew 25:31. This explains why, under the seventh seal, there is for a short time **"silence in heaven."** Revelation 8:1. No one is left up there to make a song.

Help sufficient for our trials. For true Christians, the second coming is "our blessed hope." Titus 2:13. Paul confidently referred to it when he wanted to comfort Christians whose loved ones had recently passed away. See 1 Thessalonians 4:13-18. The answer we seem to get to our prayers now is not God's final answer. The second coming is.

But when we're ill or lonely or mistreated or sad, the second coming can seem a long way off. We shouldn't let it seem so far away. We should train our minds to visualize its joys habitually. We should accustom ourselves to thinking what the second coming will mean to ourselves and to specific individuals whom we know. When I do this, I am always refreshed. This is why the Lamb opened the sixth seal and told us about it.

But when both God and the second coming seem a long way off and God Himself doesn't seem to care, we ought to reappraise what we can sensibly expect God to do when we pray. Too often, I think, we misinterpret what the Bible teaches about prayer. We focus too narrowly on Christ's statement that "whatever you ask in prayer, you will receive, if you have faith." Matthew 21:22. We should seek to understand His words in the context of other things the Bible teaches.

Didn't Jesus also say, "In the world you have tribulation"? John 16:33.

Didn't Jesus allow Lazarus to die?

Didn't He allow John the Baptist to die, beheaded, while in prison?

Didn't He portray His faithful martyrs as souls under an altar?

On one occasion Jesus said, "Whatever you ask *in my name,* I will do it." John 14:13. Here He added a condition that we must meet. "In my name" means, in my *character.* Professor Goodspeed's translation tries to reveal this implication. "I will grant anything you ask me for *as my followers.*" That is, I will grant you what you ask for if you follow My way of acting and thinking, and if you follow My way of praying.

When Jesus in Gethsemane prayed three times to be excused from being crucified, He added, "Nevertheless, not as I will, but as thou wilt." Matthew 26:39. Phillips has put His words into more ordinary English, "Yet it must not be what I want, but what you want." To pray in Christ's name, in His character as His true followers, means always to submit our desires to God's love and wisdom, to let God do what He knows is best, even if the answer for now turns out to be No.

191

Christ's deepest desire, even in Gethsemane, was to help others and glorify God. How different were His motives from some of our self-centered ones. Explaining why some of our prayers aren't answered, James 4:3 says, "You ask and do not receive, because you ask wrongly, to spend it on your passions."

So we should yield our desires to God's decision, and we should always pray unselfishly. But can we be selfish when we pray for someone else, or when we pray for health so we can be of service to others?

Our prayers may seem unselfish and yet at the same time be self-willed.

Can we not believe that God loves our loved ones even more than we do? Can we not trust Him to do better for us in the long run than we even know how to ask? Or do we want God to do less for us than His very best?

The souls under the altar prayed for vengeance and vindication. God offered them something far better, the white robes of His righteousness and eternal life.

The apostle Paul was ill for years. He longed to be healed of his mysterious malady so he could be of greater service to others. But when he prayed for healing, God answered instead with grace. "My grace is sufficient for you," He said, "for my power is made perfect in weakness." Paul learned that God's choice for him was best after all, that he was actually a better man, a better minister, when he was ill. To his surprise, he discovered that he prayed more, depended more on God, trusted Him more truly. And so he said, "I will all the more gladly boast of my weaknesses, that the power of Christ may rest upon me. For the sake of Christ, then, I am content with weaknesses, insults, hardships, persecutions, and calamities; for *when I am weak, then I am strong.*" 2 Corinthians 12:9, 10.

"In the world you have tribulation; but be of good cheer." John 16:33.

Heaven's door only *seems* to be double-bolted. Says God, "I have set before you an open door." Revelation 3:8. He really does hear our prayers. He answers them too, in ways that are best for us.

The prophet Habakkuk, whom we read about on page 186, eventually learned to lay aside his doubts. He even picked up a musical instrument and began to sing. Instead of complaining, "How long, O Lord, must I call for help?" he chose to say, in the farming language of his day,

> Though the fig tree do not blossom,
>   nor fruit be on the vines,
> the produce of the olive fail
>   and the fields yield no food, . . .
> yet I will rejoice in the Lord,
>   I will joy in the God of my salvation.
> Habakkuk 3:17, 18.

Sometime in the 1530s, during a persecution of the 1260 year-days, Anthony Parsons, a priest, became a Protestant. Angrily, the Bishop of Salisbury sentenced him and a number of other Protestants to be burned publicly at the stake.

While they were being tied up early in the morning soon afterward, Parsons asked someone for a drink. When he got it, he boldly proposed a kind of toast, using figurative language. "Be merry, my brethren," he said, exhorting the others, "and lift up your hearts to God. For after this sharp *breakfast* I trust we shall have a good *dinner* in the Kingdom of Christ, our Lord and Redeemer."

Parsons reached down and drew the combustible materials, that were soon to be set on fire, close to himself and spoke out to the spectators. "I am a Christian soldier prepared for battle," he said. "I look for no mercy but through the merits of Christ. He is my only Saviour. In Him do I trust for salvation."[7]

Anthony Parsons chose to have faith in God, in the white robe, and in the future joys around the throne. In spite of the painful death he was about to suffer, he chose to believe that God really cares.

III. Signs of the End Time

We have promised ourselves more than once that we would look at Revelation's list of end-time signs. As we do so now, let us remember that in the Olivet Discourse Jesus didn't seem eager to give the disciples very many signs.

The disciples wanted a sign so they could know when Jerusalem would fall and Christ would return. See Matthew 24:3. In His answer, Jesus helpfully showed that the fall of Jerusalem would not be the same as the end of the world. But instead of providing many signs, Jesus dwelt on the importance of *preparing* for the second coming through personal religion, service to others, and character development. See pages 19, 20, 36-42.

But Jesus did give the disciples a few signs. For the fall of Jerusalem He gave one sign, the "abomination of desolation"—Roman armies (Luke 21:20)—surrounding the Jerusalem temple. See Matthew 24:15, K.J.V. In connection with His second coming, He spoke about the gospel going to all the world. And He mentioned especially the supreme "sign of the Son of man," His personal appearance on the clouds, as visible as the lightning. Verses 30 and 27.

But in the course of the Olivet Discourse, Jesus also talked about the "great tribulation" of the 1260 year-days and added that "*immediately after* the tribulation of those days" and prior to His reappearance "the sun will be darkened, and the moon will not give its light, and the stars will fall from heaven, and the powers of the heavens will be shaken." Matthew 24:29.

This list of signal phenomena is strikingly similar to John's list recorded in Revelation 6:12-14, except that John's list is longer and more detailed. The similarity is not surprising, inasmuch as Jesus was the source of both lists. **"When he**[Jesus Christ, the Lamb] **opened the sixth seal,"** John says, **"I looked, and behold, there was a great earthquake; and the sun became black as sackcloth, the full moon became like blood, and the stars of the sky fell to the earth as the fig tree sheds its winter fruit when shaken by a gale; the sky vanished like a scroll that is rolled up, and every mountain and island was removed from its place."**

In comparing the two lists, many Bible students have become convinced that

193

Christ's Olivet list has already been remarkably fulfilled and that the longer list He gave John under the sixth seal has already been fulfilled in part. The sky hasn't yet rolled back nor has the final earthquake taken place. But the other predictions, they say, have been fulfilled in the Lisbon earthquake of November 1, 1755, the dark day (accompanied by a peculiarly red moon) of May 19, 1780, and the magnificent display of Leonid meteors in the early morning of November 13, 1833.

The suggested events are well worth looking into.

The Lisbon earthquake. The Lisbon earthquake of November 1, 1755, was no mere dish-rattler. It is still listed in almanacs and encyclopedias as one of the major earthquakes of world history.

Lisbon, the capital of Portugal, is a commercial port on the Tagus River. Rich and religious in the 1750s, it boasted wealthy merchants and more than forty large churches. The Inquisition had a headquarters there.

November 1, 1755, All Saints Day and a Saturday, dawned bright and clear. But at 9:30 a.m. the ground roared and trembled, tearing fearsome fissures in the fabric of public edifices. After a pause, homes, churches, government buildings, and palaces swayed for two eternal minutes like reeds in the wind. Masonry crumbled, marble beams and pillars tore like tissue, roofs and walls crashed to the ground. After another pause, another attack. Then a suffocating, all encompassing cloud that turned morning into night as the dust thrown up by the falling masonry settled back down.

When the obscurity cleared, people were seen crawling out of the wreckage, bleeding, an arm or a leg useless. Children ran around screaming for their parents. Parents searched and shouted for their children. Injured dogs and horses struggled. Priests, some of them badly hurt, spoke comfort and held up crucifixes.

Cries could be heard from beneath the ruins. They would be heard for several days. Flames flickered, the onset of a week's holocaust. Tidal waves, surging up the Tagus River, engulfed crowds who thought the open waterfront safer than the city streets.

Some old accounts, even one by the famed geologist Sir Charles Lyell, reported that fire mysteriously leaped out of cracks in the ground. Surprisingly, a recent study gives scientific support to the possibility.[8]

How many victims died? Early reports spoke of 100,000. Modern almanacs and encyclopedias may give 60,000. Lately the toll has been lowered to 15,000 or 10,000.

Casualty counts in several other earthquakes have been far higher; the Lisbon earthquake, nonetheless, was impressive. It could even be called the Lisbon-Fes earthquake, for when Lisbon suffered, the North African city of Fes, 400 miles away, and its sister city, Meknes were leveled, with heavy loss of life. The ground shook noticeably in other North African cities as well and in Europe as far off as Strasbourg, 1100 miles distant. Rivers and lakes were disturbed all the

Its date and extent mark the Lisbon disaster as the earthquake Christ predicted.

way to Scandinavia, 1500-2000 miles distant. About 6:00 p.m. a tidal wave struck the island of Barbados in the Caribbean, some 4000 miles away.

For a comparison on North American terrain, imagine the 1906 earthquake destroying not only San Francisco but also Los Angeles as well, nearly 400 miles to the south. Imagine the earthquake also shaking Seattle, Salt Lake City, Denver, and Albuquerque, and disturbing the Great Lakes and even the Hudson River.

For much of this survey we've been following *The Lisbon Earthquake,* an excellent study written in honor of the 1955 bicentennial by Sir Thomas Kendrick, then director of the British Museum.[9] Kendrick says that although not the greatest disaster of its kind, "the earthquake of 1 November 1755 was nevertheless a colossal seismic disturbance that was felt over so large an area that it caused general alarm and astonishment and a great output of scientific speculation."[10]

Kendrick shows that the quake also produced a considerable output of theological and philosophical speculation, much of it centering on the disaster's relationship to God, the age-old "theodicy" question about God and the presence of evil. Kendrick's chapter "Optimism Attacked" cites the wrestlings of such renowned philosophers as Kant, Rousseau, and Voltaire. Voltaire's highly influential *Candide* included scenes set in the Lisbon disaster and did much to stimulate skepticism. With the assistance of Voltaire and others, the earthquake helped to

195

bring the "end of optimism." Thereafter, says Kendrick, "pessimism became a more familiar and understandable mood."[11]

More and more people began to say, "If God isn't looking out for us, we'd better look out for ourselves." It was a mood that burgeoned until it expressed itself a generation later in the gross violence of the French Revolution, an earthquake of a different sort that certainly helped change the course of history.

The Dark Day of May 19, 1780. The dark day of May 19, 1780, followed hard on the heels of a tough New England winter.[12] Patches of snow still stubbornly spotted the countryside. America's Declaration of Independence was not yet four years old. The Revolutionary War had drawn many husbands and sons from their farms. Inflation was rampant and the future uncertain.

On May 12 the skies over New England became noticeably overcast and the air hazy. The sun was sometimes dim enough to look at with the naked eye. A farmer planting corn on the seventeenth couldn't make out the end of his field. On the eighteenth a thick gloom settled on the lowlands. The sun disappeared half an hour early. The calm was portentous. When the full moon came up, it was coppery red and stayed that way.

Sunrise on Friday the nineteenth was visible in most of New England, but like the moon the night before, the sun remained red as it climbed. A large black cloud loomed ominous in the southwest. A fresh wind from the same direction spread the cloud steadily to the northeast. It continued to Boston, to Portland, Maine, and beyond, and affected 25,000 square miles.

Trees and grass exchanged their springtime green for yellowish brown and vanished in the gloom. Cattle returned lowing to their barns. Cocks crowed and sought their roosts. People flocked into the streets to share their fears—and rushed to their churches to find meaning.

The Connecticut legislature adjourned at eleven o'clock because the members couldn't see one another's faces. At the Connecticut council, however, a motion to adjourn was defeated when Colonel Davenport remarked that either the day of judgment was at hand or it was not. If it wasn't, he said, there was no cause for alarm. If it was, he would like to be found at his duty. Would someone light the candles?

Candles were lit in the council chambers. They were lit in many other places too, for the darkness became so dense, even at noon, that newspapers and almanacs couldn't be read and women couldn't see to cook.

The 25,000 square miles we mentioned a moment ago in western New York, northern New Jersey, and southern New England, were not darkened all at once or all at the same time. The center of the darkness kept moving, so that its intensity was felt typically in a place for two or three hours. At varying times in the afternoon it lifted considerably, only to return rather generally before night. In many places, the moon, still nearly full, was not seen until hours after it was expected. The strange darkness in some localities actually seemed to shroud and impede candlelight.

196

Contemporaries attributed the phenomenon both to natural causes and to God. A smoky smell in the air, a sooty scum on still water, a belt of ash washed up along the shore, all attested the action of fire. Numerous forest fires were known to be raging in northern Vermont, northern New Hampshire, and in Canada, some set by settlers to clear the land.

Calm weather for several days had kept the smoke from dissipating. Then layers of wind, transporting the accumulated smoke from the north, and ocean clouds from the east, produced a double-decker obscurity that completely eclipsed the sun.

But why then? And why there? There have been other exceptionally gloomy days, even in North America, before and since. But none, in North America at least, has been as dark, or has remained as dark for so long.[13] Many readers of this book can remember the strange darkness of September 24-30, 1950, when smoke from a vast Alberta forest fire spread deep gloom from the Great Lakes to the East Coast, and the Cleveland Indians took the Detroit Tigers 2-1 under lights in the afternoon. But, as on the other occasions, the darkness of September 1950 failed to reach the intensity of May 19, 1780, except locally perhaps for a few minutes. Nor apparently did it cause the same sober reflection.

In the Olivet Discourse Jesus said, "Immediately after the tribulation of those

The Connecticut Council needed candles at 11 a.m. on May 19, 1780.

days [the 1260 year-days] the sun will be darkened, and the moon will not give its light." Matthew 24:29. Catholic persecution virtually ceased in Europe in the middle of the eighteenth century. The last "heretic" to be martyred in France, a Reformed pastor, died in 1762. Pope Clement XIV personally outlawed the Jesuits (the Society of Jesus) in 1773.

So the timing of the May 19, 1780, event was right. And people reflected on it, for the place was right. New England was a center of Bible study, noticeably so even in comparison with the other newly independent American states.

The Leonid star shower of November 13, 1833. The same observation about time and place applies to the brilliant display of shooting stars seen on the long-remembered morning of November 13, 1833.[14]

This amazing stellar performance began to attract attention along the eastern seaboard of North America about nine the previous evening, as the frequency of meteors increased well above normal. By two in the morning the display was bright enough to awaken people. The peak came about four, and only with difficulty did the dawn finally put it out. On the Great Plains, American Indians recorded the event on their calendars and named the ensuing season the "Plenty-Stars" or "Storm of Stars" winter. In sparsely settled California, a military company saw the sky "completely thickened" with meteors. Their army horses tried repeatedly to stampede.

Normally in one hour a careful observer, scanning a clear, dark sky, may see about ten meteors brightly scar the heavens. Subjective estimates at the height of the 1833 star shower ran to 60,000 or more an hour. Some people spoke of a "snowstorm" of stars. Significantly, the meteors seemed to proceed from a central point. Many of them left a glowing trail, or train. As the thousands of trains lingered momentarily, all radiating outward from the common center, they appeared like the ribs of a gigantic umbrella.

Most of the meteors appeared to be star-sized; a few seemed as large as the moon. A good many burst into shiny fragments. They burst *silently*, as the vast, shimmering, celestial spectacle sailed entrancingly overhead in the frosty chill of the early morning.

The 1833 star shower was significant for astronomy as well as for prophecy. It gave birth to the modern study of star showers. Denison Olmstead, professor of science and mathematics at Yale, prepared a careful report for the January 1834 issue of *The American Journal of Science and the Arts*. In it he noted that the meteors radiated outward from a point (the "radiant") in the sickle of the constellation Leo. He also made the pregnant observation that this central point proceeded westward along with the constellation as the night advanced. The display was named "Leonid" after the constellation Leo, and a search was launched for other historic Leonid showers. H. A. Newton, also of Yale, discovered records of occasional displays dating back to A.D. 902.

Calculations were carried out and a theory was developed. According to the theory, a certain comet, later labeled Temple-Tuttle, swings around the sun on a

Many Christians saw the stupendous star shower of 1833 as a sign of Christ's return.

far-flung elliptical orbit that carries it through Earth's orbit and out beyond Uranus, some 2 billion miles, or 3 billion kilometers, from the sun. The comet itself is slowly coming apart. All along its orbital path, many miles apart, particles of it called meteoroids are strung out individually; and right behind the comet, a great number of these particles cluster together.

Our earth passes through the comet's orbit each year in November. As it does, our gravity intercepts some of the straggling particles and attracts them into our atmosphere for their moment of incandescent glory. Thus, every year in mid-November larger numbers of meteors than usual seem to fall from the constellation Leo.

They do not actually come from Leo. They seem to do so, because faraway Leo shines directly behind them. They do not really radiate like the ribs of an umbrella. They fall parallel to one another, but perspective plays optical tricks.

Every thirty-third and thirty-fourth year our earth may, if we are lucky, plow head on at over 150,000 miles an hour into the main swarm just to the comet's rear. If it does, our gravity attracts vast numbers of the meteoroids into our atmosphere, and we enjoy a celestial celebration like the one of November 13, 1833.

Good showers were anticipated for November 1866 and 1867, and observers in

199

different parts of the world were gratified. But the learned forecasts of astronomers to the contrary notwithstanding, no special shower greeted eager eyes in 1899. Or in 1933. The theory was restudied and hopes were set on 1966.

I stepped outdoors in my bathrobe in the small hours of November 17, 1966, and was deeply disappointed to find the sky overcast in Lincoln, Nebraska, where I was living. I didn't bother to waken my wife. Most of eastern North America was also overcast, disappointing millions of other would-be stargazers. But after all, the cloud cover made very little difference; astronomers who flew above the overcast encountered only a dismal performance.

But about 5:00 a.m., when the sun had already risen in the east and Leo twinkled high above the horizon of Arizona, the skies of the American Southwest told a very different story. For one enchanted hour before the dawn, a snatch of 1833 returned. While observers exulted, precision instruments recorded a rate of up to 100,000 meteors an hour.

But let's go back for a moment. If astronomers were edified on November 13, 1833, not a few ordinary people were terrified. Some lay on the earth imploring the Lord to have mercy. Many others, alarmed that judgment day might find them thieves, returned what they had stolen, giving rise to the appropriate appellation, "The Night of Restitution."

But many ordinary people, filled with awe, were also inspired with joy in the hope of the second coming. Frederick Douglass, the future journalist and diplomat, was still a slave in 1833. To him the star shower was a "sublime scene," a "gorgeous spectacle," a "harbinger of the coming of the Son of Man." He had read in the Bible that the stars would fall, and here they were now falling. "I was suffering very much in my mind," he wrote in his autobiography. "I was looking away to heaven for the rest denied me on earth." "I was prepared to hail Him as my friend and deliverer."[15]

Another serious but joyful observer was Henry Dana Ward, a Harvard graduate and the rector of the Anglican church of St. Jude in New York City. Ward jumped up from a deep sleep when he heard someone shouting. He took one look out the window, awakened his wife, and hurriedly pulled on his clothes. Soon he was out on the street, and as the shower continued, he walked with a couple of friends to a local park for a fuller view.

"We felt in our hearts," he wrote almost immediately to the *New York Journal of Commerce*[16] "that it was a sign of the last days. For, truly, 'the stars of heaven fell *unto the earth,* even as a fig tree casteth her untimely figs, when she is shaken by a mighty wind.'—Revelation 6:13. This language of the prophet has always been received as metaphorical," he said. "Yesterday it was literally fulfilled. . . .

"How did they fall?" he asked—and answered, "The falling stars did not come, as if from several trees shaken, but from one: those which appeared in the east fell toward the East; those which appeared in the north fell toward the North; those which appeared in the west fell toward the West, and those which appeared

200

in the south (for I went out of my residence into the Park,) fell toward the South; and they fell, not as the *ripe* fruit falls. Far from it. But they *flew*, they WERE CAST, like the *unripe* fruit, which at first refuses to leave the branch; and, when it does break its hold, flies swiftly, *straight off*, descending."

Ward assumed that "natural causes" undoubtedly produced the phenomenon; but he saw it as nonetheless a fulfillment of the prophecy made 1800 years before.

Significance of these events. Before leaving these events, the Lisbon earthquake of 1755, the dark day of 1780, and the Leonid star shower of 1833, let us take another overview of them. How well do they qualify as the fulfillment of Christ's prediction in the Olivet Discourse and John's prediction made under the sixth seal?

1. *Their magnitude.* Each event was notable in its own right. The Lisbon earthquake shook an unusually large portion of the earth's surface. It also shook up people's thinking, helping to end an era of optimism and open an era of gloom. The dark day of May 19, 1780, has not been equalled, at least in North America, in the 200 years that have since come and gone. The Leonid shower of November 13, 1833, launched a new branch of astronomy, and it, too, has not been matched since, in spite of scientific expectations that it would be. The 1966 shower, though at least equally brilliant, was much shorter and was visible over a much smaller area. Our three events were noteworthy.

2. *Their location.* Our events occurred in Europe and North America primarily, where people were studying the Bible and pondering the prophecies. They happened where people were prepared to perceive their importance, where communication could take place. A dark day over the Sahara or in New Guinea would have said little about the second coming of Christ to cannibal headhunters or Muslim nomads.

Events don't need to be universal to deliver a global message. A few square miles at Hiroshima and Nagasaki were sufficient to announce the atomic age. A stable in Bethlehem ushered in the Christian era.

Only a few hundred people saw Jesus after His resurrection (see 1 Corinthians 15:3-8), but these told others. Thomas said he wouldn't be convinced unless he himself saw Christ. Jesus obliged him, and Thomas believed. "My Lord and my God," he cried. But Jesus said, "Blessed are those who have not seen and yet believe." John 20:28, 29. Not one of us living today was there when He rose from the dead, but some people were there to pass the word along, and that was enough.

Some years ago a newsmagazine told of a train that tooted its horn regularly and rapidly as it approached a crowded station. The waiting passengers paid little if any attention. A few railroad personnel, however, recognized the sound as a signal—a "sign"—that the train's brakes had failed. At once, they ordered everyone off the platform and out of the waiting rooms. The train plowed into the platform and ground to a halt. Equipment was damaged, but no one was hurt—because a few people understood the "sign" and interpreted it to others. Because

201

our phenomena occurred where they did, some people understood them likewise and passed the meaning on. That was enough.

3. *Their timing.* Jesus said that the sun and moon would be darkened and the stars would fall "immediately after the tribulation of those days." And so it came about. Our events came at the right time.

Nonetheless, Jesus also said, "Then will appear the sign of the Son of man in heaven, . . . and they will see the Son of man coming on the clouds of heaven . . . ; and he will send out his angels . . . , and they will gather his elect from the four winds." Matthew 24:30, 31. These events have not happened yet.

So what shall we say about timing? Well, within a few years of the 1833 star shower Jesus fulfilled one of the most notable of all Bible prophecies. In 1844, at the close of the 2300 year-days of Daniel 8:14, He traveled as Son of man on the clouds of heaven to the Ancient of Days (see Daniel 7:9-14) to inaugurate the final judgment. See GC 1:237-243. Ever since, He has been holding the four winds in check while actively sealing His 144,000 precious end-time people. See Revelation 7:1-8. Through the symbolic angels of Revelation 14 He has been notably expanding the proclamation of the gospel toward His goal of reaching every nation, tribe, tongue, and people.

When everyone living at that time has had a chance to accept or reject the gospel, the plagues must fall on the finally impenitent. God delays that somber development, "not wishing that any should perish, but that all should reach repentance." 2 Peter 3:9. But when the gospel has been preached throughout the whole world, "then the end will come." Matthew 24:14. See pages 44-46.

The events we have been discussing on the earth and in the sun, moon, and stars have done double duty as signs. They have witnessed to the coming of the Son of man to the judgment as well as to the general nearness of His coming as Son of man at the second advent.

Will the signs be repeated, as some have suggested, immediately prior to Christ's return? They may be. See *Your Questions Answered,* page 214. In the excitement of Christ's actual arrival, our solar system may perform some amazing and startling tricks. But the series of signs that were to take place "immediately after the tribulation of those days" has evidently been fulfilled.

In terms of the sixth seal, we stand today between the star shower of Revelation 6:13 and the momentous time in verse 14 when the heavens will roll back like a scroll, the mountains and islands will move out of their places, and sinners will ask the rocks to hide them from the Lamb.

The information communicated to us through the events we have discussed may be regarded as part of the "sealing" process. To be forewarned is to be forearmed. Knowing that we are indeed living in the end time and that the judgment is already in process helps us evaluate our priorities. It energizes our will to live close to the Lord and be ready for His appearing.

The Lamb seals and shields us, not only with His blood and His name, but also by opening the seven seals and revealing to us the course of history and prophecy.

IV. Why Only the Lamb Could Open the Seals

Before we leave the seven-seals division of Revelation, we really ought to ask ourselves the basic question: Why was the Lamb the only one who could break the seven seals and open them? When John first saw the seven-sealed scroll in God's hand, you remember, he "wept much," because no one anywhere was found "worthy" to break the seals. See Revelation 5:1-4.

However, one of the twenty-four elders comforted him. The "Lion" of Judah could break them, he said, because He had "conquered." All at once, a Lamb "with seven horns and with seven eyes" stepped up and took the scroll out of God's hand. Verse 6. As He did so, a song of praise burst out on the air:

> Worthy art thou to take the scroll
>   and to open its seals,
> for thou wast slain and by thy blood
>   didst ransom men for God
> from every tribe and tongue and
>   people and nation,
> and hast made them a kingdom and
>   priests to our God,
> and they shall reign on earth.
>
> Verses 9 and 10.

So *there* are the reasons, or many of them anyway, why only the Lamb could open the seals. They need a little analyzing, however—and additional reasons may also be implied elsewhere in the book. As we have been studying the seals, you and your family or study group have developed your own insights into this question. Share them with one another. For your discussion, here are seven reasons as I understand them.

1. *The Lamb is our Mediator.* The first verse of Revelation shows that the entire message of the book was a revelation "which *God gave [to] him* [Jesus Christ] to show to his servants what must soon take place." When the Lamb, Jesus Christ, took the scroll from the Father and opened its seals in order to show us the future, He was acting out the language of this verse. Actually, Christ is the channel or "mediator between God and men" (1 Timothy 2:5) for *every* blessing that comes to us from God.

2. *The Lamb sees the future.* The Lamb's "seven eyes" (Revelation 5:6) represent fullness of perception, insight, and foresight. Like His Father, Jesus is "the Alpha and the Omega," the beginning and the end. Revelation 22:13; 1:8; compare Isaiah 44:6-8. He sees the future as clearly as He sees the present and the past. Jesus knew "from the first," for example, which of His disciples would betray Him. John 6:64. Only Deity can reliably predict the future. When King Nebuchadnezzar asked Daniel to explain the prophetic statue vision, Daniel re-

plied that "no wise men, enchanters, magicians, or astrologers" could explain the future, but "there is a God in heaven" who was letting the king know "what will be in the latter days." Daniel 2:27, 28. See GC 1:35.

3. *The Lamb has "seven horns."* The Lamb's seven horns (Revelation 5:6), as most commentators agree, symbolize fullness of His authority. "All authority in heaven and on earth has been given to me," He told His disciples just before He went back to heaven. Matthew 28:18. "You will see the Son of man [at the second coming] seated at the right hand of Power," He told the high priest at the time of His trial. Matthew 26:64.

The sixth seal that the Lamb opened described the second coming. Revelation 6:16, 17. The Lamb was trying to tell us something. Our daily troubles with the three evil horsemen and our painful trials with our personal persecutors are not the end of the world. Even our death isn't the end of the world. The second coming is—when Jesus the Lamb will step with "all authority" into human affairs and take command. At the second coming, the Lamb will use His authority to make right all the wrongs that we have suffered.

4. *The Lamb has suffered.* When Jesus stepped up to take the scroll, He looked like a Lamb "as though it had been slain." Revelation 5:6. The language comes from Isaiah 53: "Like a lamb that is led to the slaughter." "A man of sorrows, and acquainted with grief." "He was despised." Jesus knows by experience what it's like to have anguished prayer go unanswered; to feel (with C. S. Lewis) that heaven's door is double-bolted; to cry out (with King David), "My God, why hast thou forsaken me?" Matthew 27:46. Compare Psalm 22:1 and see pages 186, 187. For a while, Jesus was even a "soul under the altar."

"Because he himself has suffered and been tempted, he is able to help those who are tempted." Hebrews 2:18. Much of the prophetic information revealed by the broken seals was extremely bad. Evil horsemen would horribly harass humanity. Loyal believers would be martyred. The innocent would suffer with the guilty and often more than the guilty. Prayers for justice and the second coming would be long deferred.

God foresaw this bad news. It was thoughtful of Him to have Jesus break it to us. By experience, the Lamb understands such things, and it should encourage us to know that He does.

Christ the Lamb suffered and died *for us.* When we are tempted to think that God doesn't really care, shouldn't we remember this?

How much do we love Him in return? In Old Testament times, Satan told God that Job worshiped Him only because He prospered him. If his prosperity were taken away, Satan sneered, Job would curse God like anyone else. Job's friends apparently agreed with Satan. But God understood Job. He knew that Job would continue to be faithful whatever happened. So He gave Satan permission to bankrupt him; and Satan wiped out his assets in a single day. See Job 1:6-19.

True to God's confidence in him, Job said only, "The Lord gave, and the Lord has taken away; blessed be the name of the Lord." Job 1:21.

205

Dying as the Lamb of God, Jesus suffered the anguish guilty sinners will experience on the day of judgment–but He died in triumph.

In due course, God rewarded Job with greater prosperity than ever before, but that isn't the point. The point is that Job loved and trusted God no matter what happened to him. Job's example, the "patience of Job," has been an inspiration to distressed people ever since.

Jesus suffered for us. He also offered us white robes and eternal life. If after doing all this for us, He (let us say) chooses *not* to help us find a billfold that we've lost through carelessness, shall we give Him up? Shall we give Him up if, much more seriously, He lets us suffer pain for twenty endless years so that He can use us, like Job, to illustrate faith and patience to our neighbors? What is twenty years of pain compared with eternal life?

"Many waters cannot quench [true] love," says a Bible proverb. Song of Solomon 8:7.

Death itself couldn't quench Christ's love for us. He wants us to remember this when the three evil horsemen ride by, when our prayers aren't answered, and when our private persecutors kick us under an altar.

5. *The Lamb has "conquered."* During the years that He spent on earth, Jesus was the victim of libel, bribery, mob justice, and police brutality. He was laughed at, misinterpreted, tortured, and killed. And yet the elder who introduced Him to John as a slain Lamb said that He "conquered"! Revelation 5:5. Jesus conquered all bitterness. He overcame all temptation to "get back at" people. In the letters to the seven churches, He himself said that He had conquered, and He gave His victory as the reason He was seated on God's throne. See Revelation 3:21. He invited us also to conquer and to sit with Him on His throne.

Peter says that by acting the way He did when He was mistreated, Jesus left us "an example." "When he was reviled, he did not revile in return; when he suffered, he did not threaten." But what was the secret of His self-control? "He trusted to him who judges justly," explains 1 Peter 2:23. He believed that God cares.

Uncouth soldiers cleared their throats and spat in Christ's face while His hands were tied. They pulled out tufts of His beard. They beat Him till He was a mass of wounds. But Jesus remained calm. Centuries earlier, the prophet Isaiah, like Peter, had perceived the secret of His success. He foresaw that Christ would remain confident that in the long run God would take care of His rights, so He wouldn't need to fight for them Himself. "Surely my right is with the Lord," He kept reminding Himself. "He who vindicates me is near." Isaiah 49:4; 50:6-8.

The most important enemies Jesus overcame were of course the devil, "who has the power of death," and death itself. Hebrews 2:14. Tortured and killed, Jesus came back to life and brought others back to life. He is "the resurrection and the life." John 11:25. He holds the "keys of death." Revelation 1:18.

Because Jesus conquered sin, death, and Satan, He is the very one to tell us about the evil horsemen and the souls under the altar. Trusting God to look after our rights, we too can conquer difficulties, bitterness, the devil, and death.

6. *The Lamb was "slain,"* sang the elders and the living creatures. He re-

The night before leaving Egypt, anxious Israelite families watched fathers sacrifice lambs and spread the blood on the doorframes of their homes.

deemed and ransomed men for God. He gathered them "from every tribe and tongue and people and nation" and formed them into a "kingdom and priests to our God, and they shall reign on earth." Revelation 5:9, 10. Slaves and captives and kidnap victims are ransomed or redeemed when someone pays their ransom fee. Jesus ransomed or redeemed us when He died to pay our ransom fee on Calvary. The concept of taking ransomed slaves and organizing them into a kingdom of priests leads us to the most basic reason why only the Lamb could open the seals.

7. *Jesus is our Passover Lamb.* In the Old Testament ceremonies, lambs representing Jesus were offered every day at the temple, along with many other sacrifice animals. But the most special occasion when lambs were employed was the annual Passover. The Passover lamb was the principal lamb. Jesus died to ransom us on Passover day. See GC 1:167, 257, 258. Paul wrote in 1 Corinthians 5:7 that "Christ, our paschal lamb, has been sacrificed."

The King James Version translates the passage, "Christ our passover is sacrificed for us." "Christ, our Passover lamb, has been sacrificed," says the New International Version. (The word *paschal* means "Passover.")

Christ is our Passover Lamb. It is important for us to remember this. When we read "Lamb" in Revelation we should think, "Passover Lamb."

In Bible times, just as today, Passover was celebrated every year in honor of the wonderful, never-to-be-forgotten night when the Israelites escaped after long decades of Egyptian slavery. Passover also recalled the era when their nation was born. Gathering the triumphant escapees together several weeks later at the foot of Mount Sinai, the Lord said to them through Moses, "You shall be to me a kingdom of priests and a holy nation." Exodus 19:6.

Priests by definition have the privilege of enjoying personal access to God. To be a kingdom of priests is a very high honor.

But before the honor, came the escape from Egypt. And one price of the escape was the Passover lamb. See below.

Today Christ is helping not just Israelites but individuals from "every tribe and tongue and people and nation" escape from their private Egypts of sin-slavery and the fear of death. His white-horse rider is galloping around the world spreading the invitation. Everyone who responds is made a member of the new "chosen race," Christ's polyethnic "royal priesthood" and "holy nation." 1 Peter 2:9; see GC 1:231-236. John saw these happy people surrounding God's throne in the scenes of last-day assignment and assurance down near the end time of the seven seals. The price of their new status was the death of the Passover Lamb.

The Passover Lamb and your family. In order to understand Passover better, we need to know that it was not only a national celebration but a family festival as well. The ceremony involved the members of the family and was carried out mostly at home.

By the time of the original Passover night, God had for some weeks been trying unsuccessfully to persuade the Egyptian government to release His people peacefully. Neither kind words nor a series of terrible plagues had seemed to help. A few days before the tenth and most severe plague was due, God directed Moses to publish the information that the final punishment would be so severe it would cause the cruel Egyptian government at last to let His people go. In the tenth plague, God would visit the wicked land of Egypt and slay the eldest child in every home.

Graciously, before imparting this frightening information, God told the Israelites through Moses what they could do to protect their own families. God would spare the eldest child in every family, He said, if the family killed a lamb in the afternoon. The lamb itself was to be roasted and eaten after sunset, and some of its blood was by all means to be painted on the sides and top of the main doorframe of the house. At night the family was to stay indoors together. At midnight God would see the lamb's blood on the doorframe and *pass over* their home. In such a home the eldest child would be safe. (The word *Passover* comes from "pass over.") See Exodus 12.

The Israelite families resolved to follow God's advice. Typically the father in each family took control. Slave families that could barely afford a lamb felt the price was not too high to save their child.

As midnight approached, nervous children and mothers in many homes must have asked repeatedly, "Father, are you sure you have applied the lamb's blood? Are you sure you applied enough for God to see it easily in the dark?"

As midnight came and passed, loud wails arose from Egyptian homes where the blood had not been applied. But hugs of joy and tears of relief filled every Israelite home that had applied it.

Actually, there was a death in *every* home—either the death of the eldest child or the death of the Passover lamb. The original Passover lamb was killed to save children. It died to keep families united.

Let us never forget this. Of all the symbols of Himself that Jesus might have chosen in Revelation, He chose the Passover lamb. The designation occurs twenty-nine times. Every time we read it, let us remember that it recalls His love for children as well as for adults, His concern for whole families as well as for His big new royal nation and kingdom of priests.

Christian children are not infrequently abused by unbelieving teachers and peers. Sometimes, when they stand up for what is right, they're so embarrassed they think they would like to die. They feel like souls under the altar. But Christ's white robe, His seal, His second coming, the joy around the throne—and His death on the cross—are for children as much as for everyone else.

Long ago, fathers applied the lamb's blood. In fatherless Israelite families, mothers, uncles, or grandfathers did it. Adults today can apply the blood by daily praying over their children, asking God for Christ's sake to bless and guide and forgive them, and by inviting the rider on the white horse, the message of true Christianity, to visit their homes every day.

Without Jesus Christ there would be no happy throng around the throne, no white robes, no white-horse rider, no Christianity! Jesus Christ is our Mediator. Jesus Christ, the seven-eyed, seven-horned Passover Lamb, ransomed us by His death and gathers us into His royal nation destined splendidly for everlasting life. He shields us from the worst of this life and seals us for the best of the next one. Who but He could be worthy to open the seven seals?

"Worthy, worthy is the Lamb!"

Further Interesting Reading

In Arthur S. Maxwell, *The Bible Story,* volume 10:
In *Bible Readings for the Home:*

Page numbers for each book refer to the large, fully illustrated edition.

Your Questions Answered

1. What were sealed scrolls like in Bible times? Some scrolls in Bible times were made of a kind of leather called parchment, but most were made of papyrus. Papyrus was a coarse paper made in Egypt from thin slices of the papyrus reed. (Our word *paper* comes from *papyrus*.) Two layers of the slices were arranged crosswise in the size and shape of a page; then they were moistened, pounded till they adhered, and dried. See page 103. A single sheet was enough for a simple letter. For longer documents, various numbers of pages were stuck together in strips that sometimes extended about ten meters, or thirty-three feet. Rolled up, they formed a scroll.

Serious documents of various kinds were often sealed in order to keep unauthorized persons from opening and reading them. In the case of a scroll, a string was tied around it, a lump of moist clay was placed over the string, and an engraved stamp or seal was pressed into the clay. Both the engraved stamp and the stamped clay were known as seals. *Seal* has a similar double meaning in English today. After the clay dried, it could not be removed without breaking. Often wax was used in the same way, instead of clay. An interesting story about the sealing of a contract is told in Jeremiah 32.

Private individuals as well as government officials and business establishments used seals, which were engraved with the owner's name and sometimes also with portrayals of pagan gods and strange animals. Each seal was distinctively the owner's and served as a signature.

Documents such as deeds, divorce decrees, contracts, covenants, and wills might receive several seals. Nehemiah 10 tells of a covenant that carried more than eighty seals.

2. What was written on the Lamb's seven-sealed scroll? Revelation 5:1 says that the Lamb's seven-sealed scroll, like Ezekiel's, was written on both sides—which was unusual—but it says nothing further about the scroll's actual contents. Though the Lamb was qualified to break the seals and open the book, the Bible nowhere says He actually opened it. We learn only what happened as He broke the seals.

This silence as to the content of the scroll has led to speculation. A number of scholars have noted that under Roman law in the time when Revelation was written a person's will required the seals of seven witnesses. One of the seven witnesses, incidentally, was known traditionally as the balance man, as if his job were to weigh out the value of the estate on an old-fashioned balance.[17] After the person's death, the seven witnesses assembled in the presence of a legal officer. The officer required each witness to identify his own seal and break it, so the will could be read.

Something like such a document-opening picture comes to mind on reading Revelation 7. At the breaking of each of the first four seals, one of the four living creatures issues an order to **"Come!"** In response, a rider on horseback steps into view, suggesting not only the response of a witness called to identify his seal but also, perhaps, the engraved animals sometimes used on seals (see the previous question). One of the riders holds a balance in his hand, recalling the traditional balance man. Some commentators have suggested that the seven-sealed scroll in Revelation is in fact the New Covenant, God's will or testament for His people.

Undoubtedly the vision does make use of familiar customs to help communicate heavenly truth; however, so much in this visionary scene is different from known customs that we cannot use those customs to identify the scroll as a will or testament.[18] Other documents, too, had seven (or more) seals, so the number of seals alone cannot identify the Lamb's scroll as a will or testament. Quite unlike a normal will-opening, the riders appear only *after* each seal is broken. They do not, like legal witnesses, break their own seals; the Lamb breaks them all. And when the final three seals are opened, *no* rider appears. Indeed, at the breaking of the seventh seal, nothing at all happens. **"There was silence in heaven."** Revelation 8:1.

Moreover, the best Roman practice wouldn't have been to use a scroll for a will in the first place. For wills, Romans preferred the traditional hinged pair of

In ancient times, seals ensured the integrity of important documents. This seven-sealed scroll records the sale of an important slave in 335 B.C.

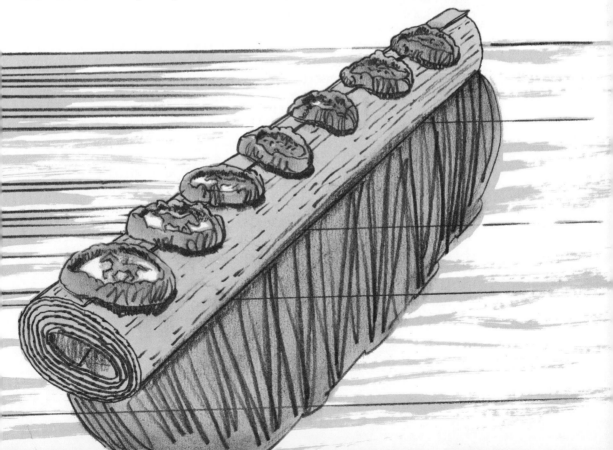

wooden tablets coated with wax. Writing was done with a pencillike stylus pressed into the wax. When the will was finished, the tablets were folded together like a book and sealed with seals.[19]

Recognizing the problems involved in identifying the Lamb's scroll with a will or convenant, some commentators have suggested that it is the Lamb's book of life containing the names of all the saved. Compare Revelation 13:8. But the Bible doesn't say that this is what it is.

In fact, the Bible doesn't specifically identify the actual contents of the book, and we shouldn't speculate! The Bible tells us only what happened as each seal was broken. We are on surest ground when we limit ourselves to this.

3. Are we to take the 144,000 literally or symbolically? Revelation abounds with so many symbols that it is always good to ask ourselves whether any item in the book may rather be symbolic than literal. Of course, when dealing with the details of unfulfilled prophecy, modesty and caution should prevail; such matters may not turn out as we expect.

Nonetheless, if the number 144,000 is taken literally, we must admit that many difficulties seem to confront us. The 144,000 sealed persons are said to come **"out of every tribe of the sons of Israel,"** 12,000 coming from each tribe, Judah, Reuben, Gad, Asher, Naphtali, Manasseh, Simeon, Levi, Issachar, Zebulun, Joseph, and Benjamin. We are accustomed to thinking of God as extending His grace to everyone freely and accepting all who choose to respond. Knowing this, and knowing human nature, we are amazed that precisely 12,000, no more and no less, would respond from each of the twelve tribes. Nothing like this has happened before.

Ever since the Jews returned from Babylon in the sixth century B.C., some 2500 years ago, no serious attempt—often no attempt at all—has been made to prevent intermarriage among the tribes, except perhaps for an attempt to do so within the priestly tribe of Levi. Already by the time of Jesus the twelve tribes were largely amalgamated, and it has been suggested that in a genetic sense almost every Jew was a "son of David." It is extremely difficult to conceive that there exist today 12,000 pure-blooded representatives of each of the twelve tribes listed in Revelation 7.

For that matter, the list of the tribes presented in Revelation 7 poses its own problems if taken literally. It is unlike the tribal lists found elsewhere in the Bible. It is even unlike the tribal list in Ezekiel 48 which, like the one in Revelation 7, is eschatological. Compare the lists on the next page.

The prophecy in Ezekiel 48 foretells the final salvation of Israel and the eschatological division of the land of Palestine. If both it and Revelation 7 really talk about the eschatological salvation of *literal* Israel, we would expect them to be the same.

John's list in Revelation differs from the others in omitting Dan and Ephraim. It can be argued that Ephraim is included indirectly on the basis that Joseph is

THE TWELVE TRIBES OF ISRAEL		
As listed in three different Bible passages		
Genesis 49	*Ezekiel 48*	*Revelation 7*
Reuben	Dan	Judah
Simeon	Asher	Reuben
Levi	Naphtali	Gad
Judah	Manasseh	Asher
Zebulun	Ephraim	Naphtali
Issachar	Reuben	Manasseh
Dan	Judah	Simeon
Gad	Benjamin	Levi
Asher	Simeon	Issachar
Naphtali	Issachar	Zebulun
Joseph	Zebulun	Joseph
Benjamin	Gad	Benjamin

mentioned and Ephraim was a son of Joseph; but on this basis we would have to say that Manasseh is included twice, for Manasseh was also a son of Joseph.

No satisfactory explanation of this irregular list of names has been offered, unless it be this: John intends to say that the twelve tribes of Israel are not really literal Israel, but the true, spiritual Israel—the church. Some interpreters have tried to avoid the greatest difficulty—that of the omission of Dan (which is the first tribe mentioned in the eschatological people of Ezekiel 48)—by suggesting that the Antichrist was expected to arise from the tribe of Dan. This tribe is therefore considered to be apostate and excluded from the people of God and their inheritance of the land. This view can be traced back as far as Irenaeus. It founders, however, on the fact that Dan is included in the salvation of the eschatological people in Ezekiel 48.[20]

The difficulty vanishes if the 144,000 are indeed perceived not as a revival of literal Israel (which they cannot be, the list of tribes being so different) but rather as a symbol of Christ's spiritual Israel, His true church. On the whole basic question of the fulfillment of Old Testament prophecies to literal Israel in the last days, see GC 1:231-236.

To many commentators, the number 12,000 assigned to each tribe, and the number 144,000 based on the square of 12, represent completion, a promise that God's people in the last days will include *all* the people who call on Him by faith and that together they will make up Christ's complete church, symmetrical, glorious, beautiful, not having "spot or wrinkle or any such thing." See Ephesians 5:25-27; compare Revelation 14:5.

4. Will the "signs" of Matthew 24:29 be repeated? The possibility that another dark day, blood-red moon, and shooting-star shower will take place immediately prior to Christ's actual return is not denied in the Bible. Jesus didn't say how many times these events might occur, and neither did John, when presenting his similar list under the sixth seal. Since 1833 there already has been another notable star shower. Since 1755 there have been many serious earthquakes. There have been several other dark days.

It may be significant that the prophet Joel gives two lists of signs, similar to those of Jesus and John but in some ways different from theirs and even different from each other. In both of Joel's lists, as in the others', the sun is spoken of as being darkened. But only one of Joel's lists talks about a blood-red moon, and this list also speaks of "blood and fire and columns of smoke." Joel 2:30. Joel's other list says that the moon, like the sun, will be "darkened," and adds that the stars too will "withdraw their shining." Joel 3:15. The stars on November 13, 1833, didn't withdraw their shining!

Joel's lists are not tied to the "tribulation of those days." Perhaps both of his entire lists remain to be fulfilled, on some vast cosmic scale, as God in mercy seeks to call earth's attention to Christ's near return.

Or perhaps the lists John and Jesus gave are simply different formulations of the same information Joel presented.

In the Olivet Discourse, Christ was not keen on multiplying last-day signs. The evidence already before us is arresting. The Lisbon earthquake of 1755, the dark day of May 19, 1780, and the Leonid star shower of November 1833 were each noteworthy events. As a series they came in the right order and at the proper time. They occurred where people lived who could take appropriate notice of them. They stimulated wide reflection. They played a distinct part in alerting those who had "ears to hear" to the commencement of the final judgment and the arrival of the end time. "Blessed are those who have not seen and yet believe." John 20:29.

5. Are the "souls" under the "altar" actually alive? A good many readers have assumed that the martyred souls of Revelation 6:9-11 are alive and in heaven. The souls **"cried out"** and received **"white robes,"** which seems to prove that they're alive—even though they have been **"slain"** and are underneath an **"altar."**

It will help us in discussing this interesting and important question if we recognize to begin with that we all use words that don't mean the same things that they used to. *Nice,* believe it or not, once meant "foolish"! A *nephew* was once a grandchild. At some time in the past, *quick* meant "alive."

Cemetery is a case in point. Today it means a place to bury the dead. But the ancient Greek word it comes from, *coimaterion,* meant a place in which to sleep. A cemetery is thus a dormitory! To see for yourself, check your favorite dictionary.

Soul is another word with an interesting history. Today most people use the word *soul* to describe an entity separate from the body, something immortal that goes on living when we die. They believe that the Bible uses the word this way. But, strange as it may sound, the Bible really doesn't say the soul is immortal. It says that God alone has immortality. See 1 Timothy 6:16; compare 1:17. As for the soul, the Bible speaks of it as something we mortals *are* rather than as something that we have.

Our English Bibles are translations. In the Greek manuscripts of the New Testament, *soul* is represented by the word *psyche.* In the Hebrew manuscripts of the Old Testament, the word for soul is *nephesh.*

Nephesh is very common. It occurs 755 times in the Old Testament. The classic statement about the origin of the soul (that is, the origin of the *nephesh*) is found in the creation account. Genesis 2:7, as translated in the King James Version, says, "The Lord God formed man of the dust of the ground, and breathed into his nostrils the breath of life; and man became a living soul." *Soul* here translates *nephesh.*

Early Christians met in catacombs—underground rock quarries near Rome. They buried their dead in the walls and longed for the resurrection.

Notice that Adam didn't get a living soul; he became one. The living man, Adam, was a living soul.* Notice the two ingredients that made up this living soul. Our heavenly Father took (1) "dust of the ground" and added to it (2) "breath of life."

In the phrase, "breath of life," the Hebrew word for breath is *ruach* (ROO-ahkh), a word that also means "wind." It is often translated in the Bible as "breath" and sometimes as "spirit." The English word *spirit* comes from an old Latin word, *spiritus,* that also means breath or wind. Think of our word *respiration,* which means breathing.

Both Adam and his wife were made "in the image of God." Genesis 1:27. This honor set them a great distance above the animals. But in the creation account, each animal, like Adam, is also called a "living *nephesh,*" translated "living creature" in Genesis 2:19, but identical with "living soul." Animals, like people, are made of the same two ingredients, (1) earth and (2) breath of life. See Genesis 1:24, 30. Your family's pet dog or cat or guinea pig is a living soul. Horses, too, are living souls. So are the animals at the zoo.

Now what happens when a person dies? According to the Bible, at death the two ingredients, (1) dust of the ground and (2) breath of life separate from each other for the time being. Temporarily, the dust and the breath go back to where they came from.

> The dust returns to the earth as it was,
> and the spirit *(ruach,* the breath) returns to God who gave it.
> Ecclesiastes 12:7.

The Jerusalem Bible translates Ecclesiastes 12:7, somewhat awkwardly, this way, "The dust returns to the earth as it once came from it, and the breath to God who gave it." Today's English Version has, "Our bodies will return to the dust of the earth, and the breath of life will go back to God, who gave it to us."

So what happens to the soul (the *nephesh*) at death? Well, what happens to the children's swingset when you move from one city to another? When you first erect a swingset, you combine two basic ingredients, (1) a pile of pipes, rods, and ropes, and (2) a plastic bagful of nuts and bolts. When you have to move, you take the swingset apart—and once more you find yourself with (1) a pile of pipes, rods, and ropes, and (2) a plastic bagful of nuts and bolts. So, what happens to the swingset? It ceases to exist as a swingset, and doesn't exist as one again until you reassemble it in your new backyard.

And yet, after a certain manner of speaking, you can talk in the meantime about "the swingset in the cardboard box."

*Kittel's scholarly *Theological Dictionary of the New Testament* 9:619, 620 says, "*Nephesh* is the usual term for man's total nature, for what he is and not just what he has. . . . The *nephesh* . . . has no existence apart from the body."

216

The souls under the altar. We still want to know about the souls under the altar. Revelation 6:10 says that they cry out with a loud voice, **"O Sovereign Lord, holy and true, how long before thou wilt judge and avenge our blood on those who dwell upon the earth?"** The souls are spoken of as being **"under the altar"** because, like sacrificial animals, they have been sacrificed. They are martyrs. They have been **"slain"** for the word of God and for the witness they have borne. And yet they pray out loud. Are they alive or dead?

The difficulty isn't in the Bible. The passage in front of us says clearly enough that the souls have been **"slain"** and that their **"blood"** needs to be avenged. The trouble lies in our custom of thinking that the soul is immortal.

But the Bible doesn't call the soul immortal. As we have just seen, it says that only God has immortality. See 1 Timothy 6:16; compare 1:17.

When God created the first man and the first woman, His deep desire was that they should live forever. He didn't make human beings to die! He is the Author of life, and He made us to live. In order for never-ending life to be readily available, God provided Adam and Eve with the fruit of the tree of life. See Genesis 2:9, 16, 17. But they sinned. And God, knowing the sufferings that their sin would produce, shortened their lives by depriving them from eating the tree of life anymore. See Genesis 3:24.

With the tree of life available, human beings could have been immortal. Without it, we all must die. The soul is not immortal. The soul is what we are, and we are all mortal. When we die, our souls die. And when that happens, all our thoughts and plans and hopes come to an end for the time being.

> Sheol [the grave] cannot thank thee,
>   death cannot praise thee;
> those who go down to the pit cannot hope
>   for thy faithfulness.
> The living, the living, he thanks thee,
>   as I do this day;
> the father makes known to the children
>   thy faithfulness.
>   Isaiah 38:18, 19.

> Put no faith in princes,
>   in any man, who has no power to save.
>   He breathes his last breath,
>   he returns to the dust;
> and in that same hour all his thinking ends.
>   Psalm 146:3, 4, N.E.B.

If, according to verses like these, the souls under the altar cannot even think any more, how can they pray out loud? The answer is that they cry for vengeance *in the same way that Abel's blood cried for vengeance* after his brother Cain murdered him. Said God to Cain, "The voice of your brother's blood is *crying to me* from the ground." Genesis 4:10.

It's as simple as that. It's as simple as one of our rather ordinary ways of speaking. "A serious crime," we say, "*demands* serious punishment."

The martyrs themselves are not demanding vengeance. In their hour of supreme suffering they probably died forgiving their persecutors just as Jesus and Stephen did. See Luke 23:34; Acts 7:60. It is the monstrous inhumanity of their murder which demands punishment, that "cries out to God" for vengeance. The very fact that someone forced these souls to be "under the altar" demands redress.

Christ's word for death. If it has been your sorrow recently to lay a loved one to rest, it may come as an uncomfortable shock to hear that the soul is not immortal. Your loss has seemed easier to bear as you have perceived your loved one living like the angels, beholding Jesus, enjoying heaven, and watching over you. You feel you cannot give up such beautiful thoughts.

It may help you to think about Mary. On Resurrection Sunday Mary Magdalene came to weep at Jesus' tomb. She thought it would help a bit if she could cry beside His grave. She hadn't heard yet about His resurrection. When she found the stone rolled away and Jesus not inside the tomb, she was unconsolable.

When after a while Jesus stepped up to her quietly, she couldn't believe her eyes and thought He was the groundskeeper. "They have taken away my Lord," she sobbed, "and I do not know where they have laid him."

Then Jesus called her by name, and she recognized His voice. He was alive! See John 20:11-18.

Jesus is still alive, even though for the time being your loved one may not be. Let Jesus talk to you about your grief. Let Him comfort you. You know He cares! Go back and reread the other things we have discussed about Jesus as our Life-giver on pages 73-77. There is more on the same theme in our discussion of Revelation 20.

Although our souls perish for a while when we die, death is not the end. God remembers all about us. (He still sees the "swingset in the cardboard box.") And our resurrection day is coming very soon.

What we need is a word to describe this temporary interruption in our activity. Jesus long ago supplied this word. Said He of Lazarus, "Our friend Lazarus has fallen *asleep.*" "Lazarus is dead." John 11:11, 14. See pages 74-76.

People wondered why Jesus didn't mourn for Jairus's dear little daughter. He had a beautiful explanation. "She is not dead," He said, "but *sleeping.*" And He proved it, by going into her bedroom (where she most certainly lay dead) and waking her up. After that, nobody mourned for her! See Luke 8:49-56.

Annie Smith died of tuberculosis at age twenty-seven. They called it con-

Blinded by tears, Mary did not realize Jesus was alive, talking to her.

sumption in her day, and it was a terrible youth-killer. In 1853, a few years before her own passing, she composed a poem for loved ones who were mourning the loss of a mutual friend, Robert Harmon, who himself had just died of consumption, also at age twenty-seven.

> He sleeps in Jesus—peaceful rest—
>   No mortal strife invades his breast;
> No pain, nor sin, nor woe, nor care
>   Can reach the silent slumberer there.
>
> He sleeps in Jesus—cease thy grief;
>   Let this afford thee sweet relief,
> That, freed from death's triumphant reign,
>   In heaven he will live again.

In ancient times, non-Christian people used words like *sepulcher, tomb,* and *grave* to name their burial places. Bible writers used the same words, adopting them from the common culture. But in view of what Jesus taught about death, Christians developed their own word for burial places. By the early 200s, if not even sooner, Christians called their burial places "cemeter-

219

ies," dormitories, places to sleep in. The early Christians believed that their loved ones who had died were only asleep, temporarily. They took Christ's authority for it.

It is our wonderful privilege as Christians to do the same.

References

1. See, e.g., A. H. M. Jones, *The Later Roman Empire 284-602* (Norman, Okla.: University of Oklahoma Press, 1964), vol. 1, pp. 445-449, 735.

2. George Eldon Ladd, *A Commentary on the Revelation of John* (Grand Rapids, Mich.: Wm. B. Eerdmans Publishing Co., 1972), pp. 97, 98.

3. M. Cary, *A History of Rome Down to the Reign of Constantine,* 2d ed. (London: Macmillan and Co., 1954), p. 663, citing Edward Gibbon. Cf. p. 698.

4. See, e.g., GC 1:28, 29. A recent report showing fewer carcinomas among Seventh-day Adventists is found in Committee on Diet, Nutrition, and Cancer, Assembly of Life Sciences, National Research Council, *Diet, Nutrition, and Cancer* (Washington, D.C.: National Academy Press, 1982), ch. 16, p. 10. There have been others.

5. C. S. Lewis, *A Grief Observed* (New York: Bantam Books, Inc., 1961, 1976), pp. 4, 5.

6. W. E. H. Lecky, *History of the Rise and Influence of the Spirit of Rationalism in Europe,* authorized ed., 2 vols. in 1 (London: Longmans, Green and Co., 1910), 2:36.

7. J. Byron Forbush, ed., *Foxe's Book of Martyrs* (Philadelphia: John C. Winston Company, 1926), chapter on persecutions in Great Britain and Ireland prior to the reign of Queen Mary I, adapted.

8. Thomas Gold and Steven Soter, "The Deep-Earth-Gas Hypothesis," *Scientific American,* June 1980, pp. 154-161. After examining many earthquake accounts, this article suggests that the escape of methane and/or other gases from the earth's mantle may explain ocean bubblings, killed fish, reports of fire issuing from cracks, and even tsunamis better than any other proposed explanations of such earthquake phenomena.

9. T. D. Kendrick, *The Lisbon Earthquake* (Philadelphia: J. B. Lippincott Co., n.d.).

10. *Ibid.*, pp. 46, 47.

11. *Ibid.*, preface and p. 209.

12. The information about the dark day, including a few paraphrasings, is taken from various sources but mainly from Deryl Herbert Leggitt, "An Investigation Into the Dark Day of May 19, 1780: Its Causes, Extent, and Duration" (M.A. thesis, Seventh-day Adventist Theological Seminary, 1951).

13. Leggitt, "Dark Day," pp. 60, 105.

14. The information about the 1833 star shower is based on various sources including *Encyclopaedia Britannica,* 15th ed., 1979, art. "Meteors," by P. M. Millman; "November Showers," *Time,* November 18, 1966, pp. 118, 119; "Stars Fell on Arizona," *Time,* November 25, 1966, pp. 71, 72; and LeRoy Edwin Froom, *The Prophetic Faith of Our Fathers,* 4 vols. (Washington, D.C.: Review and Herald Publishing Assn., 1946-1954), 4:289-300.

15. Frederick Douglass, *Life and Times of Frederick Douglass* (New York: Pathfinder Press, 1941), in Froom, *Prophetic Faith,* 4:298.

16. Ward's letter was published in the November 16, 1833, issue of *The New York Journal of Commerce* (misdated November 14), and part of it was repeated in the issue for November 27. See Froom, *Prophetic Faith,* 4:298, 299.

17. See, e.g., James Muirhead, *Historical Introduction to the Private Law of Rome,* 3d. ed.

London: A. & C. Black, 1916), pp. 262, 263; John Crook, *Law and Life of Rome* (Ithaca, N.Y.: Cornell University Press, 1967), p. 128; and R. W. Leage, *Roman Private Law*, ed. C. H. Ziegler (London: Macmillan and Co., 1946), pp. 204, 205. There seems to be some doubt whether the balance man, the *familiae emptor*, was counted as a witness.

18. Gottfried Fitzer, *"Sphragis, Sphragizo, Katasphragizo,"* Gerhard Kittel and Gerhard Friedrich, *Theological Dictionary of the New Testament*, trans. and ed., Geoffrey W. Bromily, 9 vols. (Grand Rapids, Mich.: Wm. B. Eerdmans Publishing Company, 1964-1974), 7:950. But although Fitzer notes similarities between the scroll and a legal will, he stops well short of identifying the scroll with a will, noting that the Revelation metaphor is not worked out consistently and listing several points in which the Revelation scenario is distinctly different from what one would expect in relation to a legal Roman will. A footnote attributes to E. Lohmeyer, "The choice of the no. seven is not based on Roman law; the number is a religious symbol."

19. For the use of tablets for wills, see, e.g., Allan Watson, *The Law of the Ancient Romans* (Dallas: Southern Methodist University Press, 1970), pp. 84, 85; Muirhead, *Private Law of Rome*, pp. 154, 155; Leage, *Roman Private Law*, pp. 201, 202.

20. Ladd, *Revelation*, p. 115.

Revelation 8:2 to 9:21

Trumpets Warn of Judgment

Introduction

Locusts streaming from a bottomless pit.

An eagle that shouts.

Horses by the hundred million.

A burning mountain that plunges boiling and hissing into the sea.

We arrive now at the seven trumpets. But not at the seven trumpets alone—for first of all, as we have come to expect, we're going to find an introductory scene located in the heavenly sanctuary. And between the sixth and seventh trumpets we'll find scenes of end-time assignment and assurance.

You remember we found a similar arrangement of sanctuary scenes and end-time scenes when we studied the seven seals.

The seven trumpets and the seven seals. We can, in fact, make several comparisons between the seven trumpets and the seven seals in addition to this matter of their sanctuary and end-time scenes. For example, both the trumpets and the seals are arranged in groups of four and three. The first four *seals* form a group, the four horsemen of the Apocalypse. See Revelation 6:1-8. The last three *trumpets* likewise form a group, the three fearful **"woes."** See chapters 8:13 to 9:21;

SEVEN TRUMPETS: Severe Judgments Warn the World. 8:2 to 11:18

1. Introductory sanctuary scene: Angel at altar offers incense, casts fire. 8:2-5.

2. First six trumpets. 8:7 to 9:21.

3. Scenes of end-time assignment and assurance. 10:1 to 11:14.
   a. Assignment: John is told to eat the little scroll.
      An angel instructs John to prophesy again (on earth).
      John is told to "measure the temple" (in heaven).
   b. Assurance: The angel (on earth) affirms the end of time.
      Two witnesses are caught up (to heaven).
      The mystery of God will be fulfilled.

4. Consummation: Seventh trumpet, Christ reigns, judgment has come! 11:15-18.

Items 1 and 2 are discussed in the present chapter. Items 3 and 4 are discussed in the following chapter, beginning on page 269.

Rampaging Moslem cavalry, fiercely spreading Islam, posed such a serious threat to Christianity it is discussed at length in Revelation.

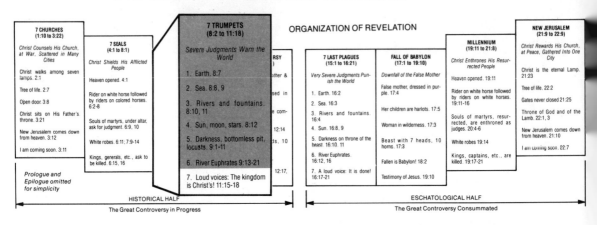

Notice where the seven trumpets fit into the whole Revelation chiasm.

11:14-18. Besides, four angels hold four winds between the sixth and seventh *seals;* and four angels are seen bound near the River Euphrates under the sixth *trumpet.* See chapters 7:1-3; 9:14, 15.

There are interesting contrasts too. The four angels who hold the four winds in the seven *seals* are told to keep on holding them in order to *delay* judgment. See Revelation 7:3. But the four bound angels in the sixth *trumpet* are released in order to *inflict* judgment. Chapter 9:14, 15. Under the seventh seal there is "silence in heaven." Chapter 8:1. Under the seventh trumpet, Christ's coronation is acclaimed by "loud voices." Chapter 11:15.

The trumpets as warning judgments. There are also many interesting comparisons to be made between the seven trumpets and the seven last plagues, so many, in fact, that some readers have suggested that the trumpets are the same as the plagues. See *Your Questions Answered,* p. 262. The *differences* between the trumpets and the plagues, however, lead us to call the seven trumpets "warning judgments." People who learn the lessons

the trumpets are designed to teach won't have to suffer the catastrophic judgments of the seven last plagues.

But the seven trumpets are bad enough in their own right. They constitute *severe* judgment warnings. In many places in the Bible God talks to us quietly, but not here. In the trumpets He fairly shouts at us, "Watch where your're going! Look out!"

On a very much smaller and far more intimate scale, there are rare occasions in every family when our love for one another leads us to shout out a needed warning. And sometimes love has to punish as well as shout. There is a vast degree of difference between gently paddling the tender bottom of a mischievous three-year-old and issuing a divine decision to leave to the cruelty of its enemies an entire society that for hundreds of years has harassed its neighbors and opposed the truth. Nonetheless, the warning judgments of the seven trumpets may be perceived as an expression of love. Their purpose was to persuade **"the rest of mankind"** to "repent"—but tragically, they **"did not repent."** Revelation 9:20.

224

The trumpet judgments are initiated by an act of one of the angels who ministers in the heavenly sanctuary. On page 162 we called the heavenly sanctuary "a friendly place." And it *is* a loving, friendly place. On pages 155, 157 we called it Cosmic Control, because the sanctuary is the place where God on His throne conducts the affairs of the entire universe.

While conducting the affairs of the entire universe, God observes each sparrow that falls. He knows the number of hairs on our heads. See Matthew 10:29, 30. The angels too take a keen personal interest in us, being "sent forth to serve" God's children everywhere. Hebrews 1:14.

In Daniel 4:13-18 we read about an angel "watcher" who demanded the humiliation of King Nebuchadnezzar when his pride and ambition made him excessively oppressive to his subjects. God's rich personal interest in us as our heavenly Father makes Him deeply concerned when we, as the "brothers and sisters" in His very large family, don't treat each other as we should.

There is a truly impressive grandeur about the scope of the seven trumpets. Like the seven letters and the seven seals, the seven trumpets are located in the historic half of the Revelation chiasm. Like those others, the trumpets deal with the sweep of Christian history. But whereas the seven letters deal almost exclusively with the Christian church and the seven seals deal mainly with Western Christianized civilization, the seven trumpets are concerned with all three of the great world religions that worship the God of the Bible. The trumpets reveal God's concern for Judaism and Islam, as well as for Christianity; and in dealing with Christianity, they focus, in turn, on the great Eastern Orthodox Church as well as on the Western church. The seventh trumpet involves all mankind. Surveying the trumpets is a breathtaking experience.

To facilitate our discussion of the four Revelation chapters containing the seven seals (chapter 4:1 to 8:1), we devoted two chapters to them. We're going to do the same with the four Revelation chapters (8:2 to 11:18) that contain the seven trumpets. This means that we're going to leave the scenes of end-time assignment and assurance and the seventh trumpet (which are found in 10:1 to 11:18) until our next chapter.

REVELATION 8

2 Then I saw the seven angels who stand before God, and seven trumpets were given to them. ³And another angel came and stood at the altar with a golden censer; and he was given much incense to mingle with the prayers of all the saints upon the golden altar before the throne; ⁴and the smoke of the incense rose with the prayers of the saints from the hand of the angel before God. ⁵Then the angel took the censer and filled it with fire from the altar and threw it on the earth; and there were peals of thunder, voices, flashes of lightning, and an earthquake.

6 Now the seven angels who had the seven trumpets made ready to blow them.

The First Four Trumpets

The first trumpet: Fire burns a third of the earth. 7 The first angel blew his trumpet, and there followed hail and fire, mixed with blood, which fell on the earth; and a third of the earth was burnt up, and a third of the trees were burnt up, and all green grass was burnt up.

The second trumpet: A mountain falls into a third of the sea. 8 The second angel blew his trumpet, and something like a great mountain, burning with fire, was thrown into the sea; ⁹and a third of the sea became blood, a third of the living creatures in the sea died, and a third of the ships were destroyed.

The third trumpet: A star poisons a third of the rivers. 10 The third angel blew his trumpet, and a great star fell from heaven, blazing like a torch, and it fell on a third of the rivers and on the fountains of water. ¹¹The name of the star is Wormwood. A third of the waters became wormwood, and many men died of the water, because it was made bitter.

The fourth trumpet: A third of the heavenly bodies dimmed. 12 The fourth angel blew his trumpet, and a third of the sun was struck, and a third of the moon, and a third of the stars, so that a third of their light was dark-ened; a third of the day was kept from shining, and likewise a third of the night.

The Fifth and Sixth Trumpets
(The First Two Woes)

13 Then I looked, and I heard an eagle crying with a loud voice, as it flew in midheaven, "Woe, woe, woe to those who dwell on the earth, at the blasts of the other trumpets which the three angels are about to blow!"

REVELATION 9

The fifth trumpet: Locusts torture for five months. 1 And the fifth angel blew his trumpet, and I saw a star fallen from heaven to earth, and he was given the key of the shaft of the bottomless pit; ²he opened the shaft of the bottomless pit, and from the shaft rose smoke like the smoke of a great furnace, and the sun and the air were darkened with the smoke from the shaft. ³Then from the smoke came locusts on the earth, and they were given power like the power of scorpions of the earth; ⁴they were told not to harm the grass of the earth or any green growth or any tree, but only those of mankind who have not the seal of God upon their foreheads; ⁵they were allowed to torture them for five months, but not to kill them, and their torture was like the torture of a scorpion, when it stings a man. ⁶And in those days men will seek death and will not find it; they will long to die, and death will fly from them.

7 In appearance the locusts were like horses arrayed for battle; on their heads were what looked like crowns of gold; their faces were like human faces, ⁸their hair like women's hair, and their teeth like lions' teeth; ⁹they had scales like iron breastplates, and the noise of their wings was like the noise of many chariots with horses rushing into battle. ¹⁰They have tails like scorpions, and stings, and their power of hurting men for five months lies in their tails. ¹¹They have as king over them the angel of the bottomless pit; his name in Hebrew is

Abaddon, and in Greek he is called Apollyon.

12 The first woe has passed; behold, two woes are still to come.

The sixth trumpet: 200,000,000 horsemen kill a third of mankind. 13 Then the sixth angel blew his trumpet, and I heard a voice from the four horns of the golden altar before God, ¹⁴saying to the sixth angel who had the trumpet, "Release the four angels who are bound at the great river Euphrates." ¹⁵So the four angels were released, who had been held ready for the hour, the day, the month, and the year, to kill a third of mankind. ¹⁶The number of the troops of cavalry was twice ten thousand times ten thousand; I heard their number. ¹⁷And this was how I saw the horses in my vision: the riders wore breastplates the color of fire and of sapphire and of sulphur, and the heads of the horses were like lions' heads, and fire and smoke and sulphur issued from their mouths. ¹⁸By these three plagues a third of mankind was killed, by the fire and smoke and sulphur issuing from their mouths. ¹⁹For the power of the horses is in their mouths and in their tails; their tails are like serpents, with heads, and by means of them they wound.

20 The rest of mankind, who were not killed by these plagues, did not repent of the works of their hands nor give up worshiping demons and idols of gold and silver and bronze and stone and wood, which cannot either see or hear or walk; ²¹nor did they repent of their murders or their sorceries or their immorality or their thefts.

The Message of Revelation 8:2 to 9:21

I. Sometimes Love Has to Shout—and Punish

"Jimmie! Get out of the street! Right now!"

Quiet reminders aren't enough when a child chases a ball into heavy traffic. Ordinary tones of voice won't do, either, when a toddler is about to overturn a boiling kettle. Every parent knows this. Sometimes love has to shout.

God prefers to talk to us quietly. Jesus made this clear. Most of the time when Jesus was on earth He went about telling stories and helping people. But when He found the temple courts cluttered with cutthroat merchants and pious swindlers, He shook a small whip in the air and shouted, "Take these things away." See John 2:13-17. The people departed in panic.

Every autumn in Bible times God had His priests *blow trumpets* to warn the people to get ready for the upcoming Day of Atonement, which was also the annual day of judgment. See GC 1:178-186. In Revelation 8 to 11, God warns us of our need to repent and change our ways by having seven of His angels blow seven trumpets.

Introductory sanctuary scene. But before the angels blow their seven trumpet warnings, Revelation 8:2-5 presents an introductory sanctuary scene.

We have come to expect these introductory sanctuary scenes! Just before reading the letters to the seven churches, we found Jesus in His sanctuary dressed as a High Priest, walking among the lampstands. Prior to the opening of the seven seals, we saw Jesus symbolized as a Passover lamb, standing at the throne of God. This time an angel offers incense at the golden altar. (A lampstand, a table, and a golden altar stood in the first room, or holy place, of the symbolic Old Testament sanctuary. See the chart on page 167.)

"Another angel," says John, **"came and stood at the altar with a golden censer; and he was given much incense to mingle with the prayers of all the saints upon the golden altar before the throne; and the smoke of the incense rose with the prayers of the saints from the hand of the angel before God. Then the angel took the censer and filled it with fire from the altar and threw it on the earth; and there were peals of thunder, voices, flashes of lightning, and an earthquake."** Revelation 8:3-5.

Instead of finding an angel, we might have expected to see Jesus standing at the golden altar offering incense with our prayers. Some readers have in fact assumed that this angel really is Jesus; and in GC 1:272-275 we learned that in the Bible Jesus sometimes *is* referred to as an angel. See, for example, Exodus 3:1-6; Genesis 48:16. Of course, Jesus isn't an ordinary angel. He isn't what we usually think of as an angel at all. He's God! The word *angel* means "messenger," and Jesus is the ultimate bearer of God's messages.

But the angel at the altar in the passage we're looking at now seems not to be

Jesus. Rather, he seems to be the angel of altar and fire who is mentioned again in Revelation 14:18.

In Revelation 5:8 we noticed happily that the four living creatures and the twenty-four elders, who occupy seats encircling God's throne, hold "golden bowls full of incense" representing the prayers of the saints. In the present chapter we learn that an important angel also offers incense as we pray. We are encouraged as we contemplate the compassionate concern for our welfare shown by these magnificent heavenly beings.

The angel **"was *given* much incense."** No doubt the incense was given to him by Jesus Christ, our High Priest. Priests offered sweet-smelling incense at the little golden altar in the Old Testament sanctuary. Maybe in heaven Jesus has the angel also offer literal incense. In any case the incense is symbolic of Jesus Himself. It represents His sweetness and kindness, and especially His sacrificial death on the cross. It stands for everything that constitutes His goodness—His "merits," to use a theological term—that convinces the universe that it's all right for God to answer our prayers. The incense, whatever it is, is not offered to persuade God to love us. God already loves us. See John 16:27. It is because God loves us that He sent Jesus to live and die for us. See John 3:16 and GC 1:117.

The Bible doesn't explain everything we'd like to have explained. But it does inform us that heaven is personally interested in our prayers. John saw an angel at heaven's golden altar offering incense as we pray.

But John tells us that he saw the angel do something else as well. **"The angel took the censer and filled it with fire from the altar and threw it on the earth; and there were peals of thunder, voices, flashes of lightning, and an earthquake."** Revelation 8:5.

What took place when that fire reached the earth is revealed under the first trumpet. **"A third of the earth was burnt up, and a third of the trees were burnt up, and all green grass was burnt up."** Verse 7.

How can we explain such a sudden change of mood? If the golden altar is associated with our earnest prayers, is it also a source of our suffering? Does God both love us and hurt us? Does our High Priest, who "always lives to make intercession" for us (Hebrews 7:25), sometimes punish us?

Evidently, yes. Sometimes love does have to shout—and punish. When we looked at the letters to the seven churches, we heard Christ tell stubborn sinners in the Pergamum church that if they wouldn't repent, He would "war against them" with the "sword" of his mouth. Revelation 2:16. We heard Him say to the self-satisfied, lukewarm Laodiceans, "Those whom I love, I reprove and chasten; so be zealous and repent." Revelation 3:19.

The New International Version renders that last verse, "Those whom I love I *rebuke and discipline.* So be earnest, and repent." Today's English Version has, "*I rebuke and punish* all whom I love. Be in earnest, then, and turn from your sins." Sometimes love does have to shout—and punish.

Some reasons why love punishes. Punishment is ordinarily applied to make us

229

suffer the due deserts of our misbehavior. But there are other basic reasons why love punishes and shouts at us. (1) Love often punishes *us* (as we have just seen) in order to persuade us to repent and change our ways. (2) Love often punishes our *enemies* to protect us from their unkindness.

When Billy roughly shoves little Tod away from the cooky jar, Mother or Father firmly removes Billy from the cooky jar and gives him a brief lecture on acceptable manners. Why so? In order (1) to help Billy be sorry and stop being mean, and (2) to protect the legitimate interests of little Tod.

By the way, we ought to remove Billy firmly—with ourselves firmly under control. And if Billy is a repeater and milder measures have failed and he needs a physical touch of what counselors call "negative reinforcement," before spanking him we can talk the situation over with him. We can affirm our faith in Billy and help him work out better ways to handle his ambitions. We can even pray briefly with him, asking God to forgive and help him. And if we're too upset at the time to talk this way, we can say, "Billy, you must be punished for what you have done, but I'm too upset to discuss it now. This afternoon we'll have a talk."

I know parents who actually do treat their children this way.

Over a century ago, one successful mother, whose writings some people regard as inspired, wrote down this practical advice:

> Scolding and fretting never help. Instead, they stir up the worst feelings of the human heart. When your children do wrong and are filled with rebellion, and you are tempted to speak and act harshly, wait before you correct them. Give them an opportunity to think, and allow your temper to cool.

> Your children may have done something that demands punishment; but if you deal with them in the spirit of Christ, their arms will be thrown about your neck; they will humble themselves before the Lord and will acknowledge their wrong.

> Before correcting them, go by yourself, and ask the Lord to soften and subdue the hearts of your children and to give you wisdom in dealing with them.

> You should correct your children in love.[1]

This is the way God corrects and punishes us. In love. God doesn't get angry the way we often do. It is inconceivable that He loses His temper. He is amazingly patient. He is "a God ready to forgive, gracious and merciful, *slow to anger* and abounding in steadfast love." Nehemiah 9:17.

Let's remember how patient God is! Next time we want Him to work a miracle to remove or restrain someone who is unfair with us, let's remind ourselves that God is as patient with the other person as He is with us.

How does God punish? As to *how* God punishes, we found when we examined Belshazzar's feast in GC 1:86-89, that one of His ways is to *remove some of His protection from us* and let our own behavior reap its *natural harvest*. We quoted from Romans 1:18, 26-28, "The wrath of God is revealed from heaven against all ungodliness and wickedness of men who by their wickedness suppress the truth." "God *gave them up* to dishonorable passions. . . . God *gave them up* to a base mind and to improper conduct."

We will not know until we see His face and hear His voice how many times or in how many ways God has daily protected us from ourselves. But this protection is often misinterpreted. "Because sentence against an evil deed is not executed speedily, the heart of the sons of men is fully set to do evil." Ecclesiastes 8:11. Mostly God speaks quietly to us; He prefers not to shout. But if we stubbornly refuse to change our ways, at a certain point when He knows it's best He removes some of His special protection. He punishes us by allowing us to punish ourselves.

Another way God punishes is by removing His protection from us and allowing our enemies to punish us.

When God lets our enemies punish us, the Bible often speaks of Him as actually calling on our enemies to do it. Secular historians, looking on without believing in God, assume in such circumstances that only human factors are at work.

A classic example of God's using enemies to punish people is found in Isaiah 10:5, 6. God informs the Israelites that He is commissioning the unbelievably cruel nation of Assyria to come and oppress them. "Ah, Assyria," He says, "the rod of my anger. . . . I command him, to take spoil and seize plunder."

But we must notice that this isn't all God says about Assyria. In verse 12 He goes on to say, "When the Lord has finished all his work on Mount Zion and on Jerusalem," that is, when He sees that Assyria has sufficiently punished the Israelites, "he will punish the arrogant boasting of the king of Assyria and his haughty pride."

In actuality, it would be a sin for Assyria to conquer and oppress the Israelites. The Assyrians were probably the most bloodthirsty and oppressive of all the major ancient peoples. So in due course God would have to punish the Assyrians too. And how would He do it? By removing His protection from the Assyrians and allowing the Babylonians to conquer them. See GC 1:12, 20, 60.

So God punishes (1) by removing some of His protection and letting us punish ourselves, and (2) by removing some of His protection and letting other sinners punish us. He has other ways. His ultimate punishment will be (3) to send an overwhelming fire from heaven that will consume our entire planet. "Earth and sky" will flee away. See Revelation 20:9-11. In *this* fire all the incorrigibly wicked people will be consumed. This will be God's final means of delivering His true people from their oppressors. And sometime prior to this final punishment, God will (4) pour out the judgments known as the seven last plagues.

Whom do the trumpets punish? We'll look carefully at the seven last plagues and the final fire when we come to them in due course. For now, we want to know just whom the seven trumpets were designed to punish.

In answer, there seems to be a Bible principle that punishments characterist-

231

cally *begin with the people of God*. For example, God's people of Israel were punished by Assyria before Assyria itself was punished, as we noted a moment ago. God's people of Judah were punished by Babylon before Babylon suffered defeat.

"Begin at my sanctuary," God commanded His judgment angels in Ezekiel 9:6. "Jerusalem and the cities of Judah" were the *first* of a long list of communities to receive the cup of God's wrath in Jeremiah 25:17-26. "The time has come for judgment to begin with the household of God," said Peter in the New Testament. 1 Peter 4:17. "God's own people are the first to be judged," is the way Today's English Version has it.

And why not? "To whom much is given, of him will much be required." Luke 12:48. The more we know about God's truth and kindness, the better persons we ought to be—and the more reprehensible we are if we aren't better.

So we'll look for the *first* trumpet to represent a judgment on the people of God. We'll look for the other trumpet judgments to involve either God's people or their enemies.

Many interpretations of the seven trumpets have been offered. One of the most helpful has been suggested by Professor Edwin R. Thiele. Biblical scholars, Protestant, Catholic, and Jewish, acclaim Professor Thiele's masterful analysis of the chronology of Old Testament history in his *The Mysterious Numbers of the Hebrew Kings.*[2] In another work of his, *Outline Studies in Revelation,* Professor Thiele makes another wise proposal:

> [1] The first trumpet symbolizes the Divine judgments that came upon *Jerusalem and the Jewish nation* when it set itself against Christ and His followers; [2] the second symbolizes judgments upon the *western Roman world;* [3] the third fell upon the professed *church of Christ* when it allowed itself to become defiled and sent forth streams of death rather than life; [4] the fourth was the ensuing *darkness of the middle ages;* [5] the fifth constituted the *Mohammedan scourges* that swept over the Middle East and into Europe; [6] the sixth consisted of the scourges that continued under *Turkish control* of large sections of Asia, Africa, and Europe; and [7] the seventh constitutes the *final terrifying outbreaks of human passion and hate* that characterize the final period of earth's history prior to the second coming of Christ.[3]

The trumpets as warning judgments. We have said that the seven trumpets are "severe judgments" that "warn the world." See pages 58, 223. Inasmuch as the seven trumpets, though severe, are not the seven last plagues, they have served to warn the world of those seven far more severe judgments which are yet to come. The judgments that have punished specific communities in the past shout to us today to change our ways—not merely so we can avoid overwhelming pain but also, of course, so we can become fit to live in the sunshine of God's presence for eternity. On a serious and cosmic scale, they shout to all of us, "Jimmie—and Janie—get out of the street! Right now!"

We'll study each of the trumpets in detail beginning on page 237. In the meantime, we need to address ourselves to a very basic question, Is the language of the trumpets literal or impressionistic?

II. Literal or Impressionistic?

A few pages ago you read the first six trumpets of Revelation. As you finished them, your mind was awhir with locusts that had lions' teeth. It was ablur with horses galloping out of the river Euphrates. You read of things awash with blood, aglow with fire, and darkening the sun.

How should such things be understood? Are those word pictures literal, or are they impressionistic?

Help from the Old Testament. We have more than once observed that Revelation makes frequent use of the Old Testament, borrowing phrases and ideas perhaps a thousand times. John had Old Testament language on his mind when he wrote Revelation! Reviewing Old Testament passages has helped us understand difficult passages before. Doing so now can help us again.

The Old Testament book of Joel is immediately helpful. Joel is only three chapters long, but its language is colorful and dramatic, in many ways resembling the language of Revelation. Joel 1:4-7 and 2:2-11 speak about locusts with lions' teeth that act like herds of horses, much the same as Revelation does.

Joel's locusts seemed horselike and lion-toothed because they occurred as a devastating migratory swarm. Their numberless mandibles consumed almost everything edible, the food crop for a large population and even the bark of full-grown trees. See Joel 1:7. Leaving the open country, Joel's locusts, like a disciplined army, scaled city walls and climbed through open windows. See Joel 2:7-9. (Imagine their coming indoors, hopping about on your floors and furniture, landing on your face, and crawling on your clothes. You couldn't take a step without crushing several and stirring up a flight of them.)

When Joel's whole swarm took to the air, its millions of invertebrate bodies and chitinous wings formed a cloud that darkened much of the sky. When it landed, the earth itself seemed to shake:

> The earth quakes before them,
>   the heavens tremble.
> The sun and the moon are darkened,
>   and the stars withdraw their shining.
>   Joel 2:10.

Being a prophet, Joel used his locust swarm as a reason for religious revival. He urged fathers, mothers, children, whole families, to join with their ministers in heartfelt repentance:

Blow the trumpet in Zion;
   sanctify a fast;
call a solemn assembly;
   gather the people.
Sanctify the congregation;
   assemble the elders;
gather the children,
   even nursing infants. . . .
Let the priests, the ministers of
   the Lord, weep.

Joel 2:15-17.

God promised that if the people would sincerely respond, He would fully restore their prosperity. "I will restore to you the years which the swarming locust has eaten." Joel 2:25.

But what if the people wouldn't repent? Joel's prophetic eye scanned the future until he saw the end time, our time. He saw real soldiers gathering like a swarm of locusts. He also saw God's heavenly warriors arriving at the battlefield. He saw earth's final military engagement—and the final judgment—taking place in the valley of Jehoshaphat, his name for Armageddon. Being an inspired prophet, Joel perceived in the locust swarm of his day a warning sent by God to lead the people

Ancient prophets taught that disasters, like trumpets, call for repentance.

to repent and change their ways. Armageddon would one day follow as an ultimate judgment if the people refused to respond.

Keep in mind that Joel said, "Blow the trumpet," when he wanted the people to come together and repent. Joel linked trumpets and locusts to heartfelt national and family repentance. Revelation also links trumpets to repentance. See Revelation 9:20, 21.

But before returning to Revelation, let us spend a few more moments in the Old Testament, first with Isaiah and then with David.

The prophet Isaiah, foreseeing an imminent invasion of enemies into the territory of unrepentant Judah (this was around 700 B.C.), predicted that "in that day the Lord will whistle for the *fly* which is at the sources of the streams of Egypt, and for the *bee* which is in the land of Assyria. And they will all come and settle . . . on all the thornbushes, and on all the pastures" in the land of Judah. Isaiah 7:18, 19.

Isaiah didn't have in mind that literal bees and flies would settle on literal thornbushes and pastures. He used impressionistic language to describe invading swarms of Egyptian and Assyrian soldiers, administrators, and tax collectors. His use of flies as a symbol for the Egyptians was especially apt in view of the unhappy abundance of flies in Egypt then and now.

A few chapters later (Isaiah 10:16-19), Isaiah likened Assyria to a forest being consumed by a raging *fire*.

In the Old Testament, David also used impressionistic language—spectacular poetic imagery—to describe his military experiences. In Psalm 18:7-14 one of his many battles appears described as if it had been a *thunderstorm*. Thunderclaps shake the mountains. Black clouds lower the heavens to treetop level. Lightning flashes and burns like fireballs; and God imperiously routs all of David's enemies.

> Then the earth reeled and rocked;
> the foundations also of the mountains trembled. . . .
> Smoke went up from his [God's] nostrils,
> and devouring fire from his mouth;
> glowing coals flamed forth from him.
>
> The Lord also thundered in the heavens,
> and the Most High uttered his voice. . . .
> And he sent out his arrows,
> and scattered them [David's enemies];
> he flashed forth lightnings,
> and routed them.
> Psalm 18:7, 8, 13, 14.

While we're still in the Psalms, let us look a moment at Psalm 11:4-6. Here David spoke of God as being *"in his holy temple."* Then he added, "On the

235

wicked he will *rain coals of fire* and brimstone." The Jerusalem Bible shows that David was describing a customary action of God. God, it says, from His holy temple "rains [as a customary act of His] coals of fire and brimstone on the wicked." Today's English Version and Moffatt's translation also convey this customary sense. God "sends down" flaming coals. He "showers down" coals of fire.

From heaven the Lord rained down literal fire on the homosexual cities of Sodom and Gomorrah in the days of Abraham. See Genesis 19:24. He set fire to unjust, idolatrous Jerusalem in the days of Daniel, Jeremiah, and Ezekiel. See Jeremiah 17:27; Lamentations 2:4; Ezekiel 15:6-8. He once used Israel as "fire" to burn up the dry "stubble" of wicked Edom. See Obadiah 18. Evidently in our own day and from time to time on many different days God has sent and does still send "fire" of various sorts to burn and punish the wicked.

Back to Revelation. Surely we are better prepared now to look at Revelation's seven trumpets! As we turn to them again we at once recognize word pictures of thunderstorms, forest fires, and insect swarms that Joel, David, and Isaiah once used.

In the first trumpet we recognize the fire that David said God from time to time rains down from His sanctuary in heaven onto the earth. In the introductory scene (Revelation 8:2-5), the angel of the golden altar filled his censer with fire and **"threw it on the earth."** Verse 5. As the first trumpet was blown, **"hail and *fire*, mixed with blood . . . fell on the earth."** Verse 7.

We conclude that the language of the seven trumpets is largely impressionistic.

Being largely impressionistic, it is not usually to be taken literally; nonetheless, it bears a relationship to reality. The Bible doesn't use tempests and insect swarms to prefigure prosperity and peace! The seven trumpets of Revelation represent scourges, wars, and judgments.

Trumpets are associated with warfare and judgment in many places in the Bible. In ancient times trumpets called soldiers to war and communicated messages during battles. See Jeremiah 4:19; 1 Corinthians 14:8. Trumpets were blown ten days before the annual day of judgment. In Revelation's seventh trumpet, warfare and judgment are expressly combined. "The nations *raged*"; "the time for the dead to be *judged*" has arrived. Revelation 11:18.

But let us keep in mind that Joel said, "Blow the trumpet," when he wanted people to repent because of the swarm of locusts. As we continue our study of Revelation's seven trumpets, we are going to remind ourselves that they too convey a call to repentance. The seventh trumpet speaks of the final judgment when repentance will forever be too late; but the first six trumpets announce less ultimate—though nonetheless serious—judgments, sent to persuade people to repent while there is still time for them to do so.

Blow the trumpet in Zion;
    sanctify a fast;

call a solemn assembly;
    gather the people.
Sanctify the congregation;
    assemble the elders;
gather the children,
    even nursing infants. . . .
Let the priests, the ministers of
    the Lord, weep.
                    Joel 2:15-17.

III. The First Four Trumpets

The first trumpet. **"The first angel blew his trumpet, and there followed hail and fire, mixed with blood, which fell on the earth; and a third of the earth was burnt up, and a third of the trees were burnt up, and all green grass was burnt up."** Revelation 8:7.

As we have seen, **"hail"** and **"fire"** come from poetic descriptions of battles as thunderstorms. Hail, fire, and **"blood"** taken together characterize warfare. Destruction of roughly a **"third"** of the available greenery indicates significant military activity but certainly not global annihilation.

We have established the important Bible principle (1) that judgment falls first on apostate people of God. "God's own people are the first to be judged." 1 Peter 4:17, T.E.V. "Begin at my sanctuary." Ezekiel 9:6. See pages 231, 232. We have also noticed another principle, (2) that the seven churches and the seven seals cover the span of Christian history and that the first church and the first seal saw fulfillment during the first century—while John, who wrote Revelation, was still alive. So for the fulfillment of the first trumpet we look during the lifetime of the apostle John for an outstanding military disaster affecting people who claimed to believe in God.

Unquestionably, the disaster we are looking for was the epochal destruction of the Jewish nation and the fall of its capital city Jerusalem in A.D. 70.

In our previous section we found as a third principle (3) that the impressionistic language of the trumpets can be understood by comparing it with the language of other parts of the Bible. Applying this principle confirms our understanding of the first trumpet. In the Old Testament, green *grass* represents a people flourishing in righteousness (see Isaiah 44:3, 4), and *trees* too stand for the people of God (see Psalms 1:3; 52:8; 92:12). The prophet Jeremiah called the Jewish nation an olive tree and said that the Babylonians would come (they came around 587 B.C.) and burn its branches like a forest fire. See Jeremiah 11:16, 17. Jesus epitomized the Jewish nation of His day as a fig tree that didn't bear fruit. In a parable (Luke 13:6-9) He pictured Heaven as patiently giving the fig tree yet another chance. Just before His crucifixion, Jesus finished the parable. Passing a fruitless fig tree growing beside the road, He stepped over to it and said, "May no fruit ever come from you again." The tree at once withered away. See Matthew 21:18, 19.

237

There is no need to retell the terrible story of the fall of Jerusalem. On pages 24-26 we watched as in A.D. 70 the Roman armies starved, crucified, shot with arrows, or hacked to death hundreds of thousands of Jews. Jerusalem disappeared. In the words of Josephus, the Jewish historian who was present at the scene, the Romans left "future visitors to the spot no ground for believing that it [Jerusalem] had ever been inhabited."[4]

The Jewish nation had persistently rejected God's prophets. Finally they demanded the death of the Son of God, who had come to save us all. So God reluctantly left them to the result of their own choices. "Your house is left unto you desolate," Jesus said tearfully in Matthew 23:38, K.J.V. Jerusalem fell to its enemies because it first fell away from God. The decision that Jerusalem should be left to its fate fell like fire from heaven, but the fiery destruction was accomplished by the city's pagan enemies, the Romans. See our discussion on pages 230, 231.

Happily, many people learned a lesson from this "trumpet warning." Many individual Jews became staunch Christians. In the writings of early Christian leaders, the fall of Jerusalem was cited as evidence that God's true people need to be more deeply spiritual than were the Jews who worshiped God but rejected His Son.[5]

Before going on to the second trumpet, we can infer from the first one a fourth principle for understanding the trumpets: (4) that a **"third"** of something represents some specific entity, such as a nation and its capital city (as Judea and Jerusalem), or, perhaps, a religion and its principal center of worship (as Judaism and the Jerusalem temple). From our earlier analysis on GC 1:36 we can also add (5) that the entities which are selected for mention in Bible prophecy tend to be ones which involve sizable numbers of God's people, apparently because they have access to the Scriptures and opportunity to perceive the fulfillment of their prophecies.

The second trumpet. **"The second angel blew his trumpet, and something like a great mountain, burning with fire, was thrown into the sea; and a third of the sea became blood, a third of the living creatures in the sea died, and a third of the ships were destroyed."** Revelation 8:8, 9.

In Revelation 17:1, 15, *waters* symbolize "peoples and multitudes and nations and tongues." In the Old Testament, the Babylonian Empire, made up of numerous peoples and tongues (or languages), is called a "destroying *mountain*." See Jeremiah 51:24, 25. Christ's future kingdom, including its numerous happy and loyal "nations" and "peoples," is also called a "mountain" in Daniel 2:35, 44, 45.

Thus, the **"sea"** of the second trumpet is a sea of humanity. The **"living creatures in the sea"** and their **"ships"** are people and their material possessions. The fiery **"mountain"** that plunges into the sea, destroying the sea-dwellers and their ships, is invading tribes on the rampage, a complex of hostile peoples barging into some section of the sea of humanity like a bowling ball carroming into a set of ninepins.

238

Such an invasion occurred during the final century of the western Roman Empire, between 378 and 476, as the "ten kings" of Daniel 7:24 barged through the Roman boundaries. See GC 1:129. For example, at Adrianople (now Edirne, on the western border of Turkey) the invading Visigoths in 378 wiped out an entire Roman army, including the Roman Emperor Valens. In 410 they ravaged Rome itself, the first time anyone had done so in 800 years. Consternation flashed through the empire.

Imagine a Third World army today invading Washington and setting fire to the Pentagon and the White House.

In 455, the Vandals—to mention another invading tribe—ransacked Rome for a second time. They *vandalized* the city for two weeks, systematically and persistently. They looted everything of value they could lift. They carried off to Carthage (in North Africa) the solid-gold seven-branched lampstand, the very one that in A.D. 70 Titus had carried off to Rome from the temple in Jerusalem.[6]

Gaiseric, leader of the Vandals, was a human predator. From his naval base in North Africa he regularly sailed away to devastate and depopulate any Roman

In A.D. 455 the Vandals stole from Rome the golden lampstand which the Romans had once stolen from Jerusalem.

coastland that struck his fancy.* "Where shall we go this time?" his navigator asked him. "Against those with whom God is angry," Gaiseric is said to have replied.[7]

Gaiseric was more right than he may have realized. Not that God was responsible for his crimes; of course He wasn't. God merely removed some of His protection from the Roman Empire and allowed its enemies to wreak what they sinfully wanted to.

Like Assyria and Babylon long before (see pages 230, 231), Rome too had punished God's people. Like Assyria and Babylon, Rome, in turn, had to be punished. Once Romans had stolen the golden lampstand from the Jews; now the Vandals stole it from the Romans. The Roman Empire, unlike Assyria and Babylon, had meanwhile adopted Christianity; but Rome's claim to Christianity made its crimes the more reprehensible.

Emperor Valens (364-378) chose to favor Arian Christians and to persecute Trinitarian Christians. Emperor Theodosius (379-395) favored Trinitarian Christians and persecuted both heathens and Arian Christians. He also revoked an order to repair a Jewish synagogue which Christians had burned down when his minister, Bishop Ambrose, refused to give him communion until he did so.[8]

Individual examples of Roman crimes are too numerous to mention. For example, the Christian Emperor Arcadius ordered the aged and self-sacrificing archbishop, John Chrysostom, to march with a unit of the Roman army until he died.[9] The Christian Emperor Zeno banished a political enemy to mountainous Cappadocia in midwinter under orders that he and his wife and children be left in the cold without food. They died, wrapped for warmth in one another's arms.[10]

Long immoral, corrupt, and oppressive, the Roman Empire by now had become Christian—and immoral, corrupt, and oppressive. C. D. Gordon is only one historian who has observed that "standards of public conduct certainly had not improved with the Christianizing of the empire."[11]

It is noteworthy that the century of disasters (378-476) we have been talking about befell Rome after she adopted Christianity. The Roman Empire had become in a sense an *apostate people of God,* ripe for experiencing the judgment of God inflicted by her enemies.

The third trumpet. **"The third angel blew his trumpet, and a great star fell from heaven, blazing like a torch, and it fell on a third of the rivers and on the fountains of water. The name of the star is Wormwood. A third of the waters became wormwood, and many men died of the water, because it was made bitter."** Revelation 8:10, 11.

Wormwood is a bitter plant that makes a poisonous juice. The Wormwood **"star"** of the third trumpet, like the fire of the first trumpet, **"fell from heaven."** Angels are called stars in Job 38:7. The **"Wormwood"** angel is a bitter and poisonous angel. In Luke 10:18 Jesus spoke of *Satan* as falling from heaven. Revelation 12:7-9 indicates that Jesus, there called Michael, thrust Satan out of heaven. We can

---

* Incidentally, Gaiseric twice defeated Roman navies sent against him. One fleet had 1100 ships. On these occasions, the burning mountain literally plunged ships and sea-dwellers into the sea.

believe that the Wormwood star of the third trumpet is Satan, fallen from heaven.

"Fountains," more commonly called springs, have always been precious as sources of drinking water. Revelation 21:6 offers spiritually thirsty people an opportunity to drink of the *"fountain* of the water of life." In Isaiah 12:3, Proverbs 13:14, and John 7:37, salvation, true wisdom, and Christ Himself are likened to springs, wells, and water. In Jeremiah 2:13 God rebukes His people for forsaking *Him,* "the *fountain* of living waters," and hewing out for themselves "broken cisterns, that can hold no water."

Now, Satan promulgates his errors through human teachers. Fountains of waters, in contrast to the heavenly bodies of the next trumpet, are found on earth. We conclude that the third trumpet foreshadowed a polluting of Christian truth in God's church on earth by poisonous Satanic errors taught by Christian teachers.

Once again God left His people to the results of their own choices. Hosea 4:17: "Ephraim is joined to idols, *let him alone."* Matthew 23:38, K.J.V.: "Your house is left unto you desolate." The western medieval church succumbed to the seductions of Satan, the fallen Wormwood angel, step by step conforming to the patterns of secular and pagan culture. God allowed it to do so. In the process, the church lost much of its power to transform people. Instead, it often abetted them in their crimes. The sweet, sparkling fountain of life became muddied and bitter.

The fourth trumpet. **"The fourth angel blew his trumpet, and a third of the sun was struck, and a third of the moon, and a third of the stars, so that a third of their light was darkened; a third of the day was kept from shining, and likewise a third of the night."** Revelation 8:12.

Just as Jesus is the ultimate fountain of life (see above), He is also the *"sun* of righteousness" (Malachi 4:2), the source of all true light. Twice John heard Jesus say, "I am the *light* of the world." John 8:12; 9:5. On one of these occasions, Jesus added, "He who follows me will not walk in *darkness."*

The first two trumpets make a pair. In the first, the Roman Empire devastates the Jewish nation; in the second, invading tribes devastate the Roman Empire. The third and fourth trumpets also make a pair. In the third, error pollutes Christ's church on earth. In the fourth, error obscures Christ's work in heaven.

The fourth trumpet parallels the letter to Thyatira, the fourth church of Revelation 2. It also parallels the little horns of Daniel 7 and 8. See pages 106-109 and GC 1:122-135, 159-161, 172-179. It leads us to look for an obscuring of the truth about God and about Christ's priestly ministry (His *tamid*) in the heavenly sanctuary. Not a removal of the whole truth about God and our High Priest, however! Only a **"third"** of the light would fail to shine.

The several centuries following the fall of Rome are appropriately known as the Dark Ages. For a couple of centuries or so the only center for serious learning in all of Europe was located in Ireland. Then around 800, King Charlemagne stimulated research at Aachen (now on the Belgian border in West Germany). Only a degree of civilization and a form of Christianity remained.

Daniel 7:25 had foreseen that the little horn (the medieval Christian church) would "speak words against the Most High," "wear out the saints of the Most High," and "think to change the times and the law." The prophecy added, "They shall be given into his hand for a time, two times, and half a time."

The fulfillment of this sobering passage we discussed in GC 1:122-135. Church officials encouraged, even demanded, persecution and torture in spite of the Golden Rule and the Ten Commandments. Also in spite of the Ten Commandments they demanded Sunday observance and forbade Sabbath observance. In 1054 the Roman Church angrily excommunicated the Greek Orthodox Church and all its millions of members because, among other matters, the Greek Orthodox Christians insisted on observing the seventh-day Sabbath.[12] Yet by the 1500s the same Roman Church had caused a scandal by imposing on the peasants of Europe more than *150* nonbiblical holy days of its own.[13] Roughly half of all the days in the year were declared holy and work on them forbidden. No wonder the economy was seriously impoverished and religion widely despised. God's law and Christ's priestly ministry in the heavenly sanctuary (His *tamid*, or continual intercession) were surely obscured by an all-too-earthly system of laws and priests and sacrifices.

The medieval church maintained schools and hospitals. It made copies of the Bible. It enlisted numerous priests and nuns of exemplary character. But it unquestionably misinterpreted Scripture and misrepresented Christ. Under its administration, the **"Light"** of heaven was **"dimmed."** The fourth trumpet was fulfilled.

We have described the seven trumpets as "warning judgments." Their judgments come in time to persuade us to repent, in contrast to the seven last plagues, which will come too late for true repentance. The trumpets shout at us to become real and sincere Christians, heartily obedient to God's will and genuinely kind and generous to our neighbors. Over the centuries, some people have taken heed. Large numbers of Jews learned a lesson from their nation's troubles and became Christians. During the Dark Ages, various reform groups arose, such as the Cistercians, Waldenses, and Franciscans. In the sixteenth century appeared still other reform groups, Lutherans, Calvinists, and others, these based more surely on the Bible.

Last night my son asked me to get him up at a certain time in the morning. He has an alarm clock, but it no longer awakens him. He has slept through it too many times.

Can any of us afford to sleep through the trumpets?

IV. The Fifth and Sixth Trumpets: Islam in Bible Prophecy

As John pondered the meaning of the first four trumpets, the scene on his prophetic screen changed once again. A cry of alarm made him scan the heaving heavens. Overhead an eagle soared. *"Woe, woe, woe,"* it screamed, **"to those who dwell on the earth, at the blasts of the other trumpets which the three angels are about to blow!"** Revelation 8:13.

The first four trumpets had been frightful enough; but if the next three trumpets were three "woes," what fearsome horrors lay ahead, John must have wondered.

He didn't have long to wait. Suddenly, as the fifth angel trumpeted, John noticed a **"star"** that had earlier fallen from heaven. Watching, he saw the fallen star—a fallen angel, really—receive the **"key of the shaft of the bottomless pit."** As the fallen angel made use of the key, thick clouds billowed from the bottomless pit **"like the smoke of a great furnace,"** and the **"sun"** and the **"air"** grew dark.

Peering anxiously into the fearsome murk, John was startled by a swarm of flying locusts. Not ordinary insects, these locusts seemed to have **"human faces"** and to be wearing **"crowns of gold"** above their **"women's hair."** They came on aggressively, **"like horses arrayed for battle."**

Ordinary locusts don't sting; but these locusts seemed to have **"tails like scorpions."** (Scorpions sting with their tails, very painfully but not often fatally.) They were told to **"torture"** people, with the notable exception of people who had the **"seal of God."** Ordinary locusts die quickly without food; but even though these locusts, like Joel's, had **"lions' teeth,"** they were apparently forbidden to eat anything for **"five months."**

Quite unlocustlike, these astonishing insects had a **"king"** in charge of them. Their king was the **"angel of the bottomless pit."** His name was **"Abaddon"** in Hebrew, **"Apollyon"** in Greek, and in English meant "Destroyer." Revelation 9: 1-11.

John's vision didn't cease. A sixth trumpet, the second **"woe,"** followed right after the fifth trumpet (the first **"woe"** that we have just been talking about).

As John listened, a **"voice"** from the **"golden altar"** in the heavenly sanctuary ordered the **"release"** of the **"four angels who are bound at the great river Euphrates."** The voice presumably came from the same angel of fire and altar we were introduced to in the sanctuary vision. The four angels he spoke about had been **"held ready for the hour, the day, the month, and the year, to kill a third of mankind."**

Suddenly the four angels were exchanged on John's visionary screen for an almost incomprehensibly immense army of 200,000,000 riders on horseback. Their number was twice as large as the number of the angels gathered around the throne in Revelation 5:11. As their seemingly endless array advanced menacingly into view, John observed that the riders seemed to be wearing red, blue, and yellow breastplates, **"The color of fire and of sapphire and of sulphur."** They were a murderous multitude, massacring **"a third of mankind"** with the **"fire and smoke and sulphur"** that seemed to pour out of their horses' mouths.

Suggested interpretations. Whatever can we make of these frightful word pictures? Some interpreters (called *preterists*) have assumed that everything predicted in the trumpets is now in the *past.* They say that in writing about the fifth and sixth trumpets John was predicting an upcoming invasion of the Roman Empire by the massive armies of the Parthian Empire, Rome's often-hostile neighbor to the east. The Romans in John's day feared such an invasion, we are told, much as Americans and Soviets fear an invasion by each other's forces today. But no Parthian invasion of the Roman Empire actually did take place.

In harmony with the renowned Jesuit commentator, Francisco Ribera (1537-1591), some other interpreters *(futurists)* assign these two trumpets (along with all the other trumpets), to a time still *future* to our day. Many futurists see in the locusts a flight of demons not long before the second coming of Christ, swarming out of hell like bats out of the Carlsbad Caverns.

But many Christian expositors, including Martin Luther, the great Reformer; Joseph Mede, the Cambridge University professor who helped revive premillennialism (see pages 515-520); and Sir Isaac Newton, the famous scientist, have seen in the fifth and sixth trumpets the *rise and progress of Islam.*[14] In view of the tremendous military, cultural, religious, and economic impact Islam has had on Christianity and Christian nations for thirteen hundred years since its rise in the 600s, this third interpretation deserves our serious attention.

A closer look. But let us look at the fifth and sixth trumpets a little closer. First let's look at the notable *similarities* between them. In both trumpets large numbers of *creatures* (horselike locusts and locustlike horses), each with specialized *tails* (scorpionlike and serpentlike), are linked to specific *time* slots (five months, and an hour, day, month, and year), and emerge out of specific *locations* (the bottomless pit, and beyond the Euphrates).

Besides these similarities, there are of course some *differences*. The tails, times, and places are not identical. Most conspicuously, the horselike locusts of the fifth trumpet are allowed only to *torture* people, whereas the horseback riders of the sixth trumpet are commanded to *kill* "a third of mankind." And only the horseback riders have the "three plagues," the fire, smoke, and sulphur, to do the killing with.

We have come to see that in trumpet imagery, a **"third"** of something represents a specific entity in each case: (1) The Jewish nation and its capital, Jerusalem (or Judaism and its Jerusalem temple), (2) western Roman Empire and its capital city, Rome, (3) western Christianity as headed up by the Roman Church, (4) and the kingdom of God, centered in the heavenly sanctuary. Under the fifth and sixth trumpets, the **"third of mankind"** may be understood to represent (5) the Greek Orthodox eastern Roman Empire and its religious and political capital, Constantinople.

The Byzantine Empire. The eastern Roman Empire is often referred to as the Byzantine Empire. The name comes from Byzantium, the village that in 330 became Constantinople (now Istanbul), the capital city. The Byzantine Empire was even more closely linked to the Eastern Orthodox Church than the western Empire was to the Roman Catholic Church. The Byzantine Empire lasted almost 1000 years longer than the western Empire did, which was a very long time indeed. It came to its end when an *Islamic* army finally defeated and entered Constantinople in 1453.

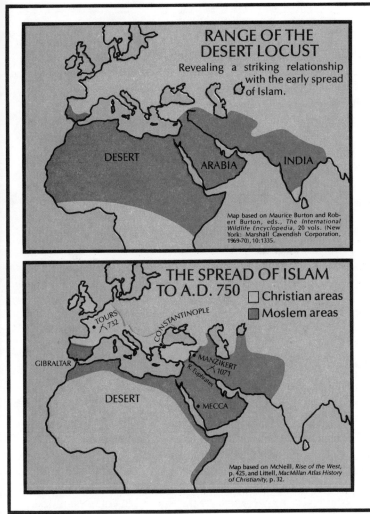

RANGE OF THE DESERT LOCUST
Revealing a striking relationship with the early spread of Islam.

DESERT

ARABIA

INDIA

Map based on Maurice Burton and Robert Burton, eds., *The International Wildlife Encyclopedia*, 20 vols. (New York: Marshall Cavendish Corporation, 1969-70), 10:1335.

THE SPREAD OF ISLAM TO A.D. 750
☐ Christian areas
◼ Moslem areas

TOURS ✗ 732

CONSTANTINOPLE

GIBRALTAR

MANZIKERT ✗ 1071

R. Euphrates

DESERT

• MECCA

Map based on McNeill, *Rise of the West*, p. 425, and Littell, *MacMillan Atlas History of Christianity*, p. 32.

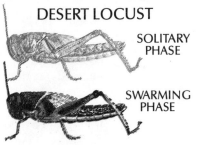

DESERT LOCUST
SOLITARY PHASE

SWARMING PHASE

Frontispiece, Sir Boris Uvarov, *Grasshoppers and Locusts: A Handbook of General Acridology.* 2 vols. Cambridge: The University Press, 1966. vol, 1, frontispiece. © 1966.

Readers of Revelation have long puzzled over the locusts of the fifth trumpet. They don't eat grass, they sting like scorpions, and they are shaped like horses with men's faces and women's hair. What are they? These two maps—as the text explains— suggest a satisfying solution for this intriguing problem.

NOTE: The Battle of Manzikert is shown for convenience, even though it applies to the later, Turkish stage of Islamic conquest.

This brings us back to our study of Islam. But inasmuch as we are dealing with Islam under the Bible figure of locusts, it will help if we pause a moment to get acquainted with these fascinating and ravenous little animals.

The desert locust. Biologists tell us that the principal locust in Bible times—as also today—is known as *Schistocerca gregaria*, the desert locust.[15] They say that in unfavorable years, when water and food are hard to come by, relatively few desert locust eggs hatch, and those that do produce green individuals that hop around by themselves.

But in favorable years, desert locusts breed in large numbers and adopt their swarming behavior. They also change their coloration and become smartly spotted and striped with black and bright yellow or orange.

After gobbling up the local food supply, the young locusts, who have no wings as yet, set off like a marching army. They eat up almost everything green they find and march on relentlessly, over walls, through ditches, and even across small bodies of water. As they grow, they develop wings, and the wind carries them hundreds, even thousand of miles. Wherever they touch down they consume all the crops, leaving behind famine and suffering.

On reaching maturity, the locust females lay several hundred eggs each, in froth-capped tubes in the ground. Their next generation may number hundreds of millions and cover several square miles. Repeating the lifecycle, a locust plague can continue as long as favorable conditions last. A modern plague lasted from 1950 to 1962. (Happily, national and international locust-control centers have been established, and there is hope that in the future such plagues can be prevented.)

The range of the desert locust is notable for our purposes. It spreads over some sixty different countries—all over northern Africa, up into Spain in the west, northward into Asia Minor (Turkey) in the east, and eastward through Iran into Pakistan and India. As we shall see in a moment, its northern range is roughly comparable to the *spread of Islam* in the Middle Ages.

In the *fifth* trumpet we have a swarm of flying locusts. John mentions the noise made by their wings. In the *sixth* trumpet, we seem to have a subsequent generation of the same locusts, but in their youthful state. They don't have wings. Their faces and tall knees give the appearance of mounted cavalry. They travel like an ancient army. Their colors are gaudy. Their number has greatly increased. John says he saw 200,000,000 of them. Their destructiveness has also increased. The earlier ones could only torture, but these can kill.

The language is impressionistic. Some items cannot possibly apply to literal locusts, such as the crowns and hair and human faces, the lions' teeth, and the smoke that comes out of their mouths. The fifth and sixth trumpets represent a two-phase invasion by fierce armies.

As we mentioned a moment ago, great Christian expositors like Martin Luther, Joseph Mede, and Sir Isaac Newton were among the first Bible commentators to perceive in these locust scenes representations of the vast Moslem armies that have repeatedly fought against Christians during the long centuries since Mohammed's birth. We could have added the names of other great expositors who have held similar views, such as Heinrich Bullinger, the well-known Swiss Reformer; Thomas Goodwin, outstanding early Congregationalist and vice-chancellor of Oxford University; Thomas Newton, the Anglican bishop whose commentary on Revelation went through eighteen editions; and Cotton Mather, described as "the most distinguished clergyman of his day, and one of the most remarkable men of his age."[16]

Everyone is interested in the part Islam is playing in our world today. As a matter of fact, Islam has frequently played a decisive role in world affairs during the past *thirteen hundred years*. Islam certainly deserves a place in Bible prophecy.

Now, more often than not, what Moslems have done in politics and warfare has been rooted in what they believe. A glance at Islamic beliefs will help us understand better their role in Bible prophecy.

What Moslems believe. Islam, the religion of the followers of Mohammed, originated around A.D. 612, when Mohammed began to believe that God was giving him visions. Mohammed at the time was a merchant living in Mecca, an Arabian city.

Mohammed's fundamental conviction was that there is only one God, the God whom he called Allah, the Arabic form of one of the names for God in the Hebrew Bible. He identified Allah as the same God whom Abraham, the Jews, and Jesus worshiped. He told his followers to give up their idols and their worship of many gods (polytheism). He also told them that God had had many prophets, including Noah, Abraham, and Jesus, but that he, Mohammed, was Allah's final and most important prophet. Five times a day from the tall minarets beside the mosques that stand in every Islamic community today, the cry is still given as Mohammed required it to be, calling the faithful to prayer, "There is no God but Allah, and Mohammed is His prophet." I have heard it many times. The first daily call, given about an hour before sunrise, sounds striking indeed.

Mohammed laid down numerous rules for his followers. After his death, these rules were collected into a book called the Koran or *Qur'an*, the Islamic Bible. *Koran* means a book of readings to be recited by memory. *Islam* means "fully surrendered" to the will of Allah as taught in the Koran. A Moslem is a person who is thus surrendered.

The Koran contains many prophecies about the end time. On the last day—which is spoken of as likely to come very soon—the Koran says that God will raise the dead and summon everyone to final judgment. At the judgment, Allah will consign the wicked to hell, to drink blood and boiling water and burn in agony for ever. But Allah will be very compassionate to the righteous. He will invite them all into heaven, to dine at sumptuous banquets with gazelle-eyed virgins.

The Koran speaks unquestionably in favor of holy war, or jihad. It says that although all believers will find pleasure in heaven, those believers who risk their lives in holy war will find far richer pleasures. Allah, says the Koran, "has promised all a good reward; but far richer is the recompense of those who fight for Him."[18] "Allah loves those who fight for His cause." "He will lodge you in pleasant mansions in the gardens of Eden. That is the supreme triumph."[19]

Mohammed definitely required holy war. It conquered new territory and provided vast new riches to plunder. But we would be wrong to assume that he forced Jews and Christians to choose between "Allah and the sword." Mohammed admired Jews and Christians as worshipers like himself of Allah, the true God of Abraham and Jesus. Because they believed in the Old Testament, he respected them as "People of the Book."[20] Modern Arab hostility to the Jews stems from Nazi anti-Semitism and Israeli militarism and stands in strong contrast to Islamic tradition.[21]

Without doubt, large numbers of Jews and Christians were killed during the

247

course of the many holy wars; but they were killed as common enemies, not merely because of their beliefs. Once peace was restored, they were allowed to continue on in their beliefs. To be sure, they were second-class citizens, forbidden, for example, to ride horses or own weapons and required to pay extra taxes and sometimes required to wear a distinctive badge. Unmistakably, they were denied the right to make converts. Moslems on their part were denied the right to change their religion. To this day, the Koran specifically requires Moslems to execute any of their own people who are converted to Christianity. "If they desert you [and become Jews or Christians], seize them and put them to death," it says.[22]

Over the course of time, in countries that the Moslems conquered, large numbers of Christians—but by no means all Christians in every country—became Moslems for one reason or another. And because the Christians who remained were effectively prevented from making converts, the churches that survived became increasingly ritualistic and sterile. In Islamic countries, Christianity was not necessarily destroyed, but it was largely paralyzed.

Islamic expansion. Islam is a missionary religion, intent on winning converts. Mohammed's first converts were his first wife, Khadija, his close friend, Abu Bakr, and his cousin, Ali, who married Mohammed's daughter, Fatima. Islam began as a family religion. But by Mohammed's death, almost everyone in Arabia was a follower. The Arab tribes, usually at war with one another, became united over the prospect of holy war. There was wealth to be gained by fighting unitedly in the name of the prophet against the Zoroastrians of Iran and against the Christians of the Roman Empire (by now called the Byzantine Empire).

After Mohammed's death, Abu Bakr became his first successor or "caliph." He rallied the Arabs and commenced an aggressive agenda of military expansion.

In the name of Mohammed and Allah, the united Arab armies by the year 651 controlled Syria, Iraq, Mesopotamia, Iran, and Egypt. Imagine the headlines and TV special reports if a Middle East nation today were suddenly to change its religion and then carry out a similar series of successful conquests!

And the Middle East was only the beginning of the conquests. The Moslems soon extended their control east to the borders of India and west across North Africa to the Atlantic Ocean. In 711 seven thousand Moslems crossed from North Africa to Spain. The name "Gibraltar" means the "Mount [*Jabal* in Arabic] of Tariq." It memorializes Tariq, the Moslem general who led the invasion.[23]

Southern Spain fell. France was next. The goal seemed to be the conquest of all of Europe. But in 732 the Moslem tide was turned back by Charles Martel the Hammerer, a Christian general. Christian and Moslem armies faced each other in open fields between the towns of Poitiers and Tours. The Christian horsemen had the advantage of the newly invented stirrup, which gave them a stability and force when fighting that the Moslem horsemen didn't possess.[24] But the Moslems were doughty and experienced warriors. So evenly were the armies matched that for seven days neither side dared shoot the first arrow.

At last the invading Moslems struck. Before dark, thousands of men on both

The victory of Christians over Moslems at the Battle of Tours in 732 has affected Western life-style to the present day.

sides lay dead and dying on the grass. But even the crack Moslem horsemen were unable to defeat the solidly united and better equipped Christians. At sunup next morning, the Christians found to their great relief that during the night the Moslems had abandoned their tents and fled back toward Spain. Outside of southern Spain, Europe continued nominally Christian.[25]

But it was a close call. Without this victory on the fields near Tours, all of Europe might today be Islamic.

The Battle of Tours and your family. It is not fanciful to suggest that without this victory on the fields near Tours, even you and your family might today be Islamic. We have seen that wherever the early Moslem armies were successful, Christianity was greatly reduced in strength or wiped out. The so-called Arab nations of the Middle East and northern Africa were Christian nations until the Moslems arrived. Everyone knows that they aren't Christian nations today.

If the Islamic armies had not been stopped at the Battle of Tours, Christianity might have survived in Europe, but most likely France and Germany and Italy and Britain and Belguim and Holland and Spain would be dotted everywhere with Moslem mosques and minarets; and everyone there, like everyone in Morocco and Algeria and Turkey and Saudi Arabia and Iran, would awaken in the morning to the Moslem call to prayer sounding out from all the minarets, "There is no God but Allah, and Mohammed is His prophet."

And inasmuch as North America was colonized from Europe, even the United

States and Canada and Mexico might today be Islamic nations. And if so, Americans and Canadians and Mexicans would awaken to the Moslem call to prayer; and your children would be growing up in an essentially Islamic culture. Even your family might well be Islamic.

But it was not so to be. We may believe that God in His providence gave special strength to the armies of Charles Martel the Hammerer in 732. God cares! You and your family can thank Him at your family worship for the victory won by the brave Christian men who fought and died at the pivotal Battle of Tours.

The Moslems attack eastern Europe. Western Europe remained nominally Christian. Eastern Europe did too, though at a heavy price. Constantinople, the capital of the Byzantine Empire, stood at the head of eastern Europe. As such, it found itself compelled to endure repeated Moslem attacks. Between 674 and 677 and in 717 and 718, the Moslems launched really massive amphibious assaults on Constantinople. Their second attempt is said to have involved 1800 ships![26]

The Christians counterattacked with a terrifying secret weapon known as Greek fire. Burning with intense heat, Greek fire could be floated among the Moslem ships on little barges or attached to arrows and shot from bows and catapults or blown out of tubes. Its complete formula still remains a secret.[27] It burned even more ferociously on water than on land. It wrought terrible havoc among the attacking Moslems.

Determined Moslem forces made further vigorous attacks on Constantinople under Aaron the Righteous (Caliph Harun al-Rashid, 786-809). But by 821-823 the Moslems, who had once brought 1800 ships against Constantinople, were reduced to merely assisting a *Christian* rebel in *his* ineffective attempt to take the city.[28] In eastern as in western Europe, the Moslems were turned back.

Small groups of Mohammed's followers then and later carried Islam to points as far east as Indonesia and even on to China. But if you will look at the maps on page 245, you will notice that the main progress of Islam in its first burst of expansion coincided remarkably with the northern range of the desert locust!

Islam and the fifth trumpet. The locusts of the fifth trumpet flew out of dark **"smoke"** that arose from the **"bottomless pit."** The darkness we may believe represents here, as under the fourth trumpet, erroneous teachings that veiled or denied the truth about God and about Jesus Christ. We think of the Koran.

"Bottomless pit" is translated from *abussos* ("abyss"), a Greek word meaning "unmeasurable" or "boundless." *Abussos* is a name for the "ocean" in the Greek translation of Genesis 1:2 and for the "grave" in Psalm 71:20. The ocean's depth was "unmeasurable" in ancient times, and the grave's appetite for dead bodies was "boundless" then and remains so. In Revelation *abussos* is impressionistic. The utter deadness of the grave aptly symbolizes the vast deserts of Arabia, the home of Mohammed, great sweeps of which are still totally uninhabitable.

The **"star"** which had previously **"fallen"** from heaven—the **"king"** called **"Abaddon,"** **"Apollyon,"** and "Destroyer"—is obviously Satan, working through Islamic teachers and caliphs. (Remember again that Revelation calls attention to

250

the worst side of human societies.) The **"crowns"** on the locusts can be viewed as turbans. The **"women's hair"** can be seen as the long hair that Arabs are said to have worn in those days. The horselike appearance of the locusts we can associate with the real horses that the Arabs used so masterfully in very large numbers. The locust **"wings,"** like the leopard wings in Daniel 7, represent the rapidity of the early Arab conquests. In an era without trucks, steamships, or radios, the Islamic forces mastered hostile territory from the Middle East to the Atlantic in one direction and to the borders of India in the other (with an outpost in faraway China) in less than a hundred years. And in most of the areas they reached, they settled in permanently.

Our symbolic locusts were forbidden to eat anything **"green"** or to hurt persons who had the **"seal of God."** We saw on page 237 that **"green grass"** stands for people of God. We have already observed that Islam granted Jews and Christians a good many liberties as "People of the Book." Notably, Sabbath-keeping Christians survived in Armenia and Ethiopia. See GC 1:137, 141. The **"locusts"** were permitted to **"torture"** for **"five months."** When we examine the sixth trumpet, we'll find power being granted to **"kill a third of mankind."** As we suggested on page 244, this **"third of mankind"** appears to be the Byzantine Empire and its religion, and Constantinople, the eastern capital of Christianity. **"Five"** prophetic **"months"** at thirty days to the month represent, at the outside, 150 years. See Revelation 11:2, 3.

From the first fierce but futile Moslem attack on Constantinople, in 674, to the last futile Moslem attack, in 823, there elapsed a period *only one year short of 150 years!*

The Turks muscle in. After failing for virtually 150 years in their repeated attempts to conquer Constantinople, the Islamic peoples gave up trying. They fought with one another and divided into several separate nations. Left alone, the Byzantine Empire had its own ups and downs.

Around the year 1000 news arrived that should have startled both sides. The Seljuk Turks were on their way!

For some time hordes of Turkish tribes had been moving west across the vast prairies of southern Russia. Breaking away from the others, the Seljuk Turks headed their horses south, invaded Iran, and *adopted the Moslem religion.* At once the Seljuk Turks became the most dynamic and energetic of all the Islamic peoples. Quarrelsome, aggressive, and numerous, they soon divided into factions around popular leaders (the **"four angels,"** perhaps) and forced their way toward the headwaters of the **"river Euphrates."*** Their goal was Asia Minor, the heartland of the Byzantine Empire. But they were largely held in check (**"bound"** at the **"river Euphrates"**) by the Byzantine guards stationed in the Pontic and Taurus Mountains.

---

*This metaphorical mention of the river Euphrates gives us a general geographic reference. The same river is cited metaphorically in Isaiah 8:7 as a reference to the empire which lay along its banks in Isaiah's day.

251

At this critical moment, the Byzantine emperor died, leaving as his successor only a boy. The empress quickly married a general, Romanus by name, who in the best ancient tradition led his forces personally against the Seljuk Turks, only to be decisively beaten in 1071 at the epochal Battle of Manzikert (now Malazgirt), near the headwaters of the Euphrates River. The Byzantine army was killed off and Romanus was taken prisoner. When after a while Romanus was allowed to return home, his son had him blinded and treated so cruelly that he soon died.[29]

Meanwhile, having destroyed the main Byzantine army at Manzikert, the Turks dashed through the unguarded passes in the Taurus and Pontic Mountains and quickly took control of most of Asia Minor. They even gave to Asia Minor the name Turkey by which we know it today. As they swarmed through the mountain passes, many of them skillfully mounted on horses, and spread everywhere, greedily consuming the resources of the countryside, they surely appeared like an army of 200,000,000 horsemen.

The Turks "kill" the Byzantine Empire. Leadership of the Seljuk Turks in time fell to Othman and to his successors, the "Ottomans." In due course the Ottoman Turks developed the Ottoman Empire, which is important to our story.

Revelation 9:15 indicates that the locustlike swarm of Turkish Moslems was to **"kill a third of mankind,"** an entity which we have identified as the Byzantine Empire and its capital city Constantinople. And according to the prophecy, the Moslems would conquer the empire by using **"fire and smoke and sulphur,"** that would seem to come out of their horses' mouths. Revelation 9:17-19.

The smoke coming out of the horses' mouths—and the snakelike tails that could kill, and the huge number 200,000,000—are of course figures of speech, like the horses themselves; but they are figures related to what they stand for. The Ottoman Turks did use numerous skillful horsemen, and they were able to conquer Constantinople once they incorporated the use of gunpowder weapons.

One of the principal ingredients in gunpowder (along with carbon and saltpeter) is **"sulphur."** Gunpowder burns with great quantities of **"smoke,"** which is one reason it hasn't been used much since the end of the first world war. Gunpowder is used to shoot projectiles out of long tubes, which may be what was represented to John as the horses' deadly **"tails."**

Early gunpowder weapons used by the Ottomans, and by the European powers as well, included some personal firearms, especially the clumsy arquebus. They also included hand grenades, mortars, and cannon. The largest cannon, made at first of bronze, were so heavy for oxen to drag around that the Ottoman Turks sometimes carried chunks of bronze on their military wagons and melted the metal and cast it into cannon right at the site of use. These early cannon weren't accurate enough to fire at soldiers on a battlefield, but they were highly effective against the brick and stone walls that still defended castles and principal cities. A battery of, say, a dozen such weapons, firing a dozen shots each in a day, could soon break a hole through the stoutest masonry walls.

Constantinople had stout masonry walls. By firing their massive bronze can-

253

Belching "fire and smoke and sulphur," Islam's huge guns hurled such heavy stones that Orthodox Constantinople's thick walls crumbled in 1453.

non, the Ottoman Turks finally conquered the city on May 29, 1453, and thereby **"killed"** at last the long-lived Byzantine Empire.

The man who led the Turks to victory at Constantinople, Mohammed (Mehmet) II, was only twenty-three at the time. People called him Mohammed the Conqueror. He died before he was fifty, but not before he had established the powerful and wealthy Ottoman Empire that we mentioned a moment ago.

The Ottoman Empire helps the Reformation. While memory of the epochal fall of Constantinople was still fresh, the Ottoman Turks—amazing as it may seem—played a vital role in the success of the Protestant Reformation! Mohammed the Conqueror's most illustrious successor was Suleiman the Magnificent, whose reign (1520-1566) over the Ottoman Empire coincided closely with the reign (1519-1556) of Charles V, the emperor of Germany when the Reformation began.

Charles V was a devout Roman Catholic as well as a devoted and intelligent administrator. He was deeply disturbed by the Reformation that Martin Luther began in 1517. He became even more disturbed as he watched its rapid progress over northern Europe. He recognized that the Catholic church needed some sort of reformation, but he wanted to improve mainly the priests' behavior, not so much what they taught.

The territory which Charles V ruled included Spain, parts of eastern Europe, and Spain's vast new colonies in North and South America. It also included what in those days was called the Holy Roman Empire but which today we call Holland, Switzerland, most of Germany, and parts of Italy. He deserved to be called Emperor!

Well, inasmuch as Charles V sat at the head of so very much power and wealth, why did he *not* stamp out Protestantism, seeing he wanted to so badly?

Partly because of the Ottoman Turks and the fall of Constantinople.

The King of France (named Francis I), some of the German princes, and even the pope himself were fearful of Charles V and thought that he had too much power. Neither Francis, nor any of the German princes, nor the pope was strong enough alone to withstand Charles V; but each of them was strong enough to withstand him with the support of Suleiman the Magnificent, the head of the Ottoman Empire.

Thus it came about that Moslem armies and navies and financial subsidies frequently came to the aid of Christians in their battles against Charles V.

Thus it came about, also, that during the years when Protestantism was beginning to make its way, Charles V couldn't fight against it because he was too busy fighting Catholic France and the Catholic pope. (In 1527 his troops sacked Rome and put the pope in prison!)

In 1529, the very year that the word *Protestant* was first used to describe the new religious movement, Charles V thought for a moment that circumstances were right for an attack on the "heretics." But just then—at the personal request of the Catholic king of France—Suleiman the Magnificent sent an Islamic army to attack the Catholic city of Vienna.[30] Charles V couldn't possibly fight both Protestants and Moslems at the same time. In fact, he had to have the help of the Protestants if he was going to beat back the Moslems. Once more he overlooked religious differences.

"Ottoman pressure on the Habsburgs [that is, on Charles V and his relatives] . . . was an important factor in the consolidation of the forces of the Reformation and in their final recognition," observes a typical modern scholar. "In the sixteenth and seventeenth centuries support and encouragement for Protestants and Calvinists were . . . one of the fundamental principles of Ottoman policy."[31] "There would have been no Protestantism had there been no Turk," says another researcher.[32]

Not until 1547, the year after Luther died, was Charles V finally in a position to fight the Lutheran princes. At long last, at the head of a Spanish Catholic army he invaded the territory of his own German Lutheran princes—and beat them! But his victory completely failed to stamp out Protestantism, for by now it was deeply entrenched in the hearts and minds of the people.

In the words of historian Thomas M. Lindsay,[33] "The German tongue had displaced mediaeval Latin in public worship, and the worshippers could take part in the services with full understanding of the solemn acts in which they were engaged. A German Bible lay on every pulpit, and the people had their copies in the pews. Translations of the Psalms and German evangelical hymns were sung, and sermons in German were preached." "Provisions had [also] been made for the education of children."

Charles V abdicated his imperial throne in frustration, deeply disappointed at his failure to stamp out the Protestants. He retired to "San Gerónimo de Yuste," a small but lavish villa built right next to a monastery in Spain. One of his last acts was to charge his son Philip to "take care that the heretics" in Spain "were repressed . . . without regard to any plea in their favor." He died holding the same exquisite crucifix that his auburn-haired wife Isabella had held when she died. "I'm coming, Jesus," he whispered.[34] We cannot question his sincerity.

The heyday of the Ottoman Empire continued only from around the fall of Constantinople until around 1600. By 1699 "the Ottoman empire, which had terrified Christendom for over three hundred years, ceased to be an aggressive power."[35] In the providence of God, its supremacy had peaked at the precise moment when its influence was needed to preserve the existence of Protestantism.

An hour, and a day, and a month, and a year. One of the more challenging symbols in the sixth trumpet is its reference (in the King James Version) to "an hour, and a day, and a month, and a year." The ancient King James Version expects us to *add* the periods of time together. From our study of Daniel we are well aware that a symbolic day in long-time Bible prophecy represents an actual year. In Revelation 11:2, 3 a month stands for 30 days. On this basis, a year of twelve thirty-day months represents 360 years. When we add 1 year plus 30 years plus 360 years, we get 391 years.

The Revised Standard Version, however, and quite a few other modern versions as well, translate the passage, **"the hour , the day, the month, and the year,"** making it refer to a specific point of time rather than to an extended period of time. But there are good reasons to prefer the King James Version translation. See *Your Questions Answered,* pages 262, 263.

Assuming then that the expression refers to 391 years, we ask, What particular beginning and ending dates did God have in mind?

We mentioned above that the Battle of Manzikert in 1071, which allowed the Turks to leave the Euphrates Valley and overrun the heartland of the Christian Byzantine empire, was a major event. From that event until the Turks finally "killed" the Byzantine Empire in 1453 was a period of 382 years. This may be close enough to 391 years to satisfy some minds, but not close enough to satisfy others. More striking is the fact that from 1453, the death of the Byzantine Empire, until 1844, the close of the most significant long-time prophecy in the Bible, was precisely 391 years.

In 1453 the Ottoman Empire was a powerful and dangerous threat to Christian Europe. By 1844, however, the once invincible empire had fallen so low that it would not have survived unless Christian nations had come to its aid! Actually, a series of significant events clusters around both 1453 and 1844. For more on this subject, see *Your Questions Answered,* pages 263-265.

The trumpets and your family. "The things that are revealed belong to us and to our children." Deuteronomy 29:29. We have noticed in passing (on page 230) that the trumpets remind us of certain aspects of family discipline. Our attention has also been called to the Moslem defeat at the Battle of Tours (pages 248-250) and to the Ottoman contribution to the Reformation (pages 254, 255), developments which have had a striking influence on the religious complexion of the communities where we and our families live.

But it seems there's something deeper. Most of those people in the first six trumpets we've been talking about, the people who deceived, excommunicated, and, when opportunity offered, ransacked, burned, murdered, and massacred one another, believed in God. In fact, even though they gave Him different names—Allah, Jehovah (Yahweh), and Lord—these Moslems, Jews, and Christians worshiped the same God. They were members of the three great world religions that worship the God of the Bible.

They were religious people—in certain ways. The Jews were very loyal to their temple and their ritual. The Moslems knelt in prayer five times a day. The Christians in Constantinople when the city fell jammed the great cathedral of St. Sophia, believing God would certainly protect them there.

In their early years, these kings and queens, priests, soldiers, and ordinary folk whose lives wove the tapestry of the tragic story we've been following were girls and boys, growing up in homes that believed in God. Don't you wonder what their parents taught them about God and about how He wants His children to live?

In September 1982, 800 people—parents, grandparents, young people, and ba-

256

bies—were massacred in a Beirut refugee camp. Bulldozers smashed houses with people still inside. Little girls got bullet holes in their heads. A baby's face was left protruding through a mound of rubble. The people who died were Moslems. The people who killed them were Christians. The guards who stood by while the victims screamed were Jewish.[36]

Everyone at the massacre believed in God. What had their parents taught them to believe about Him and about the way He wants His followers to live?

We have seen, especially when looking at Revelation 4 and 5, how happy a place heaven is, how great an interest heavenly beings take in our welfare, and how glad they are that Jesus died to redeem us. Some heavenly beings, including the angel of fire and altar at the beginning of the seven trumpets, offer incense when we pray.

But heavenly beings don't want cheaters and schemers and fighters to mar the peace of heaven. Of course they don't! For their sakes as well as ours, Jesus bids us be true and honest and to love even our enemies. In the Sermon on the Mount He warned that only those who actually live like this "shall enter the kingdom of heaven." See Matthew 7:21.

Are we doing all we can to help the members of our families become loving, honest, thoughtful, and generous—true and genuine Christians, who in their inmost lives follow all the aspects of God's will?

The members of our families have free wills. They may refuse to become true Christians, in spite of all we do for them. But let's not assume they'll become true Christians without our doing something special for them. James Dobson, the well-known radio family counselor, says wisely in his *Straight Talk to Men and Their Wives,* "The greatest delusion is to suppose that our children will be devout Christians simply because their parents have been [devout Christians]."[37]

Urging parents to travail in prayer for their children, Dobson adds that for years one of the things he and his wife did for their two children was to *fast* and pray for them once a week. Their special fast-day prayer went something like this: O Lord, "keep the circle of our little family unbroken when we stand before you on the Day of Judgment. Compensate for our mistakes and failures as parents, and counteract the influences of an evil world that would undermine the faith of our children. And especially, Lord, we ask for your involvement when our son and daughter stand at the crossroads, deciding whether or not to walk the Christian path. They will be beyond our care at that moment, and we humbly ask you to *be there.* Send a significant friend or leader to help them choose the right direction. They were yours before they were born, and now we give them back to you in faith, knowing that you love them even more than we do. Toward that end, we dedicate this day of fasting and prayer."[38]

When we pray like this, the four living creatures, the twenty-four elders, and the angel at the golden altar offer up their fragrant incense. Jesus, the Lamb who died so that families could live, intercedes. And all heaven stands at attention, ready to make our prayers come true.

257

SUMMARY OF TRUMPET TERMINOLOGY

The First Four Trumpets

The First Trumpet. 8:7.

Hail and fire mixed with blood: The Roman war against Judea.

One third of the earth and trees and all green grass: The people of God, still in the Old Testament sense of the Jewish nation and their capital city Jerusalem, destroyed by the Romans in A. D. 70. "Begin at my sanctuary." Ezekiel 9:6.

The Second Trumpet. 8:8, 9.

A great fiery mountain: The warlike tribes which invaded the Roman Empire.

A third of the sea, sea creatures, and ships: The western Roman Empire, its inhabitants, and its capital city Rome, defeated by the invading tribes in 476.

The Third Trumpet. 8:10, 11.

"Wormwood," the blazing fallen star: Satan, and the Christian teachers who served his purposes.

A third of the rivers and fountains: The true religion of Jesus and the truth about Him, entrusted to the Christian Church of the Middle Ages, especially as centered in the Church of Rome and polluted by "wormwood" error.

The Fourth Trumpet. 8:12.

A third of the light and of the heavenly bodies: The priestly ministry of Jesus—the Sun of Righteousness, the Light of the world—centered in the heavenly sanctuary and obscured by a new churchly priesthood.

The Three Woes

The Fifth and Sixth Trumpets. 9:1-19.

A fallen star: Satan, and the Islamic leaders who served his purposes.

A bottomless pit: Arabia viewed as a vast, mostly uninhabitable wasteland, a place of death.

Flying horselike locusts: Islamic armies in their early, Arabic phase of conquest.

Grass and green trees: People of God whom the Moslems allowed to go on living.

People with God's seal on their foreheads: Sincere Christians whom the Moslems allowed to go on living.

Five months' torture: Approximately 150 years, probably the years between the beginning (674) and end (823) of the early series of Islamic attacks on Constantinople.

"Destroyer," the locust king: Mohammed, viewed intentionally from his bad side.

The four angels: Islamic leaders, or, perhaps, "demon princes" (see GC 1: 270, 274).

The Euphrates: General geographic term for Mesopotamia, the area immediately east and southeast of Asia Minor.

The 200,000,000 horsemen: The later Islamic armies, dominated by Turks and especially by the Ottoman Turks.

Fire, smoke, and sulphur: The use of gunpowder weapons by the Ottoman Turks.

A third of mankind: The eastern Roman or Byzantine Empire, or the Eastern Orthodox Church, and its capital city, Constantinople, which fell to the Ottoman Turks in 1453.

An hour, and a day, and a month, and a year (K.J.V.): A period of 391 years separating (1) a series of events clustering around the fall of Constantinople in 1453 from (2) another, opposite series clustering around 1844, the close of the 2300 year-days.

The Seventh Trumpet. 11:15-18.

The language of this trumpet, which applies to the end time, is all literal. It announces a phase of the final judgment.

259

LESSONS TAUGHT BY THE SEVEN TRUMPETS

Basic lesson: Heaven is not pleased with nations, empires, and churches that worship God if at the same time they grossly misrepresent Him by misleading and mistreating people. After protecting such societies for extended periods, God removes His protection and allows their errors to confuse them and their enemies to conquer them. The seven last plagues will constitute an ultimate punishment on all corrupt human societies. But we can learn a lesson from the seven trumpets. God wants us not only to worship Him but also to be genuine, generous, loving, and law-abiding (see also Revelation 2, 3). If we repent and become true Christians of this sort, He will seal us (Revelation 7) and also preserve us from the seven last plagues (Revelation 16).

First and second trumpets: The destruction of Jerusalem in A. D. 70 taught that because the Jewish nation (God's Old Testament people) had rejected God's way of life, God reluctantly left the nation to the mercy of the Romans. Contemplating this rejection, thousands of Jews and millions of Gentiles determined to become members of God's new people, the Christian church.

The decline of the western Roman Empire and its fall in 476, long after it had been nominally Christianized, taught that belonging to the Christian religion without genuinely practicing Christianity is little different from being a nominal Jew. Reluctantly, God at last left the Christianized western Roman Empire to the mercy of the invading tribes.

Third and fourth trumpets: The invading tribes soon made up the bulk of the western Roman Church—the church that chose to oppose Sabbath observance, enforce Sunday observance, venerate images, wage repeated military conflicts, silence "heretics," and interpose its own system of priests, sacrifices, penances, and politics between the people and Christ's heavenly priesthood (His *tamid* ministry, see GC 1:172-179). God permitted this, because God respects free will. He does not compel the church to obey Him or to teach only the truth. They "perish, because they refused to love the truth and so be saved." 2 Thessalonians 2:10.

Fifth and sixth trumpets: The eastern Roman or Byzantine Empire was closely allied to the Eastern Orthodox Church. Unlike the western church, the Eastern Orthodox Church chose to observe both Sabbath and Sunday, and it did not venerate images; however, it did venerate elaborate pictures known as "icons," and it, too, silenced "heretics" and interposed its priesthood between the people and Christ's heavenly priesthood. Like the western Roman Church, it also became heavily involved in political scandals, often encouraging the empire to engage in injustice and in military aggression. God permitted eastern Rome to be attacked by Islamic armies.

Looking on, many individuals advanced into a purer Christianity during the Reformation; but whether Catholic, Orthodox, or Protestant, the Christian nations, sad to say, continued in many ways to be just about as aggressive, unjust, and corrupt as other nations. They **"did not repent of the works of their hands nor give up worshiping demons and idols of gold and silver and bronze and stone and wood. . . ; nor did they repent of their murders or their sorceries or their immorality or their thefts."** Revelation 9:20, 21. The Moslem empires, after filling their roles in prophecy, suffered punishment like the Jewish and Christian entities. The lesson is plain that no one is better than another unless the worship of God is combined with genuine and generous relationships with people.

Seventh trumpet: In spite of all the evidence from the history of the first six trumpets, the nations continued—and still continue—in their wrongdoing. Whereas God has thus far reluctantly punished individual nations and churches (by finally leaving them to their errors and their enemies), under the seventh trumpet He will judge and punish human society worldwide. "The nations raged, but thy wrath came, and the time for the dead to be judged, . . . and for destroying the destroyers of the earth." Revelation 11:18.

Further Interesting Reading

In *Bible Readings for the Home:*
    "Child Training," page 515.
    "Teaching the Children," page 519.
In Arthur S. Maxwell, *Your Bible and You:*
    "Seven Secrets of Child Training," page 239.

Page numbers for each book refer to the large, fully illustrated edition.

Your Questions Answered

1. Are the trumpets the same as the seven last plagues? On page 58 and in our organizational chart we have noticed some of the similarities between the seven trumpets and the seven last plagues. Influenced by these similarities, some readers have suggested that the trumpets and the plagues are the same.

However, in spite of the striking similarities, the trumpets and the plagues really cannot be the same. At least four overriding differences distinguish them:

1. The size of the areas affected. Most of the trumpets affect a symbolic "third" of the areas they touch. See Revelation 8:7-12. No such restriction is imposed on the plagues.

2. The time involved. In the trumpet chapters we encounter the relatively long periods of "five months," "forty-two months," and others. Revelation 9:5, 15; 11:2, 11. By contrast, the seven plagues fall in "a single day" or even in "one hour." Revelation 18:8, 10.

3. Relationship to the sanctuary. The sanctuary scene that introduces the trumpets portrays intercessory ministry as still in progress. An angel is offering incense. See Revelation 8:2-5. On the other hand, in the scene that introduces the plagues, the sanctuary is closed, so that "no one could enter" it. Revelation 15:5-8.

4. Location in the chiasm. Our organizational chart shows that the trumpets appear in the first or historical half of the Revelation chiasm, while the plagues appear in the end-time or eschatological half.

We conclude that the plagues are still future to our day. They will fall during a very short period immediately following the close of human probation when repentance is no longer possible, and immediately prior to the second coming. The trumpets, on the other hand, have been sounding since the days of the apostle John. They represent warnings sent in love to lead us to repent of our sins while we still have time to do so. If we who are living in the end time respond appropriately to the trumpet warnings, we will be spared the dire punishment of the seven last plagues.

See also our discussion of Revelation 15 and 16.

2. What is the "hour, and a day, and a month, and a year"? We observed on pages 255, 256 that in the sixth trumpet the King James Version expects us to *add* together "an hour, and a day, and a month, and a year," making 391 years. But doing this leaves us with two questions: Is the King James Version correct? and, How shall we understand the **"hour"**?

Let us look at the **"hour"** first. Because an hour is the twenty-fourth part of a day, some readers have suggested that the hour here represents a twenty-fourth part of a year, or 15 days, leading to a total of 391 years and 15 days.

There is, however, another attractive interpretation. In Revelation 14:6, 7 an angel uses the term "hour" in the phrase "the hour of his judgment," referring to the final judgment. Revelation 20 shows that the final judgment will last for at least 1000 years. So—because the 391 years are related to one of the trumpet *judgments*—some commentators suggest that the "hour" in our passage represents another "hour of judgment," this one lasting 391 years.

As for which translation is correct, the Revised Standard Version renders the passage, **"for the hour, the day, the month, and the year,"** a rendition that seems intended to make the phrase refer to a specific point of time rather than to an extended period of judgment. A number of other recent translations do something similar. Today's English Version goes so far as to say, "for this very hour of this very day of this very month and year."

What about the underlying Greek? The Greek for this passage has only the plain and simple statement, "for the hour, and day, and month, and year," in which only *hour* is preceded by *the*. Thus, in the underlying Greek there is no hint of *"this very* hour" or *"this very* day," or *"this very* month." The earliest English translations were more faithful to John's original statement than the modern ones are. In 1525 Tyndale had, "for an houre, for a daye, for a moneth, and for a yeare." And the King James of 1611 was closest of all with "for an houre, and a day, and a moneth, and a yeere."

Commentators who prefer to think of an "hour" of judgment extending 391 years call attention (1) to this use of the article *the* (in the Greek) only with "hour," setting the "hour" apart from all the other terms. Thus, they say, the "hour" can indeed mean an "hour of judgment," even though the day, month, and year retain their more ordinary meanings. These commentators also remind us (2) that in New Testament times it was a common practice in Greek to use *and* in an explanatory or epexegetical manner.[39] See, for example, 1 Corinthians 15:38, "God gives it a body as he has chosen, *and* [or rather, *that is to say*] to each kind of seed its own body."

In the light of these considerations we can helpfully translate the phrase this way, "for the hour: *and* [or rather, *that is to say*] for a day, and a month, and a year." So now, interpreting the "hour" as an hour of judgment, we get this: "For the hour of judgment; that is to say, for a period of judgment extending over a day and a month and a year, symbolic of 391 years."

3. What happened to mark the 391 years? Assuming then that the expression refers to 391 years, what particular beginning and ending dates did God have in mind when he gave John the vision of the sixth trumpet?

We pointed out on page 256 that from 1453, the death of the Byzantine Empire, until 1844, the close of the most significant long-time prophecy in the Bible, was precisely 391 years. We also noted that a series of salient events clustered around 1453 and 1844—and that whereas around 1453 the Ottoman Turks were a powerful threat to Christian nations, by the mid-1840s the once

Mohammed (Mehmet) II the Conquerer (1451-1481) ruled the Ottoman Empire as the 391 years began. Suleiman the Magnificent (1520-1566) opposed Charles V. Mahmud II (1808-1839) and Abdulmecid I (1839-1861) ruled as the 391 years ended.

mighty Ottoman Empire had become so weak it could not have survived without Christian assistance.[40]

In 1451 (near the beginning of the 391 years) a sultan named Mohammed II the Conqueror began a reign, based on the armed power of the Janissaries. (The Janissaries were a body of several thousand, many of whom, as boys, had been handed over like a tax to the Ottomans by their Christian parents. The Ottomans brought up the Janissaries strictly in the Islamic religion, trained them expertly as soldiers and government officials, and forbade them to marry.[41]

For a long time the expertise, loyalty, and military prowess of the Janissaries made them the core of each sultan's authority.) In 1451 Mohammed II launched a hundred-year process of creating a new Islamic law code called the *kanun-names.* In 1826 (near the other end of the 391 years) another sultan named Mahmud II massacred the Janissaries; and in November 1839 (391 years after the Janissaries came to powers, his successor, Abdulmecid I, under pressure from the Christian powers, issued the Noble Edict of the Rose Chamber, announcing the creation of a new series of Moslem laws called the *tanzimat* to take the place of the old law code, *kanun-names.* Among its other provisions, the *tanzimat* "guaranteed certain fundamental rights to all Ottoman subjects without distinction

264

of religion." These provisions guaranteed to Christians not only the right to practice their religion, which the Moslems had nominally permitted all along, but also an equalization of political opportunity and taxation, which the Moslems had long vigorously denied. Codes of law define a society. Basic changes in a society's laws flag basic changes in the society's fabric. So here was an epochal victory for the Christian nations and a bitter pill for the Moslems, for "the changes that the [Christian] powers most insistently urged upon the Ottoman government concerned the status of its [the Empire's] Christian subjects."[42]

In January 1449 (to turn now to other events marking the beginning and ending of the 391 years) Constantine XI was crowned Byzantine Emperor only after he first asked for and received the approval of the Ottoman sultan. When a king has to get the approval of an enemy king before he can sit on his own throne, it is quite obvious who is ahead. As famed historian Edward Gibbon observed, "The gracious approbation of the Turkish sultan announced his [own] supremacy, and the approaching downfall of the Eastern empire."[43] In 1449 the Turks were on top.

By contrast the Ottoman sultan 391 years later found himself by no means on top. Rather, he was defeated by Mohammed Ali (Mehemet Ali), the pasha or governor of Egypt, who had captured the sultan's fleet and conquered Syria, long a part of the Ottoman Empire. In fact, the sultan was quite helpless—until for political reasons (not for love!) Christian nations came to his rescue. On July 15, 1840, representatives of Britain, Austria, Prussia, and Russia (all Christian nations in those days) signed the Treaty of London, ordering Mehemet Ali of Egypt to return the sultan's fleet and get out of Syria. When Mehemet Ali swore by Allah that he would do nothing of the sort, British gunboats in September pounded Beirut (then a Syrian city) to rubble, literally, in a few hours. Egypt responded by getting out of Syria and giving the sultan back his boats. Meanwhile, the London Morning Herald observed that "the sultan has been reduced to the rank of a puppet."[44]

The Ottoman Empire limped along as the "sick man of Europe" until the end of the first world war. Neither its existence nor its atrocities terminated in every sense in the 1840s, any more than they had begun their existence in every sense in the 1450s. But its period of dominance over specified Christian affairs, its power to **"kill"** a particular **"third of mankind,"** can be significantly identified with the 391 years we have spoken of here.

References

1. Ellen G. White, *Child Guidance* (Nashville, Tenn.: Southern Publishing Association, 1954), pp. 244, 245, 246.

2. Edwin R. Thiele, *The Mysterious Numbers of the Hebrew Kings: A Reconstruction of the Chronology of the Kingdoms of Israel and Judah,* rev. ed. (Grand Rapids, Mich.: Wm. B. Eerdmans Publishing Company, 1965).

3. Edwin R. Thiele, *Outline Studies in Revelation* (Angwin, Calif.: The author, n. d.), p. 162.

4. Josephus, *War*, 7.3; Loeb 3:504, 505. See also note 7 on page 47, and discussion on pages 24-26.

5. See, for example, Barnabas, *Epistle*, 16; ANF 1:147; Justin, *First Apology*, 47-49; ANF 1:178, 179; John Chrysostom, *Discourses Against Judaizing Christians*, 5; The Fathers of the Church 68:97-145.

6. Edward Gibbon, *The Decline and Fall of the Roman Empire*, chap. 36.

7. Procopius, *History of the Wars*, 3.5.23-25; Loeb 2:53-55.

8. Ambrose, *Letters* 40, 41; NPNF, 2d ser., 10:440-450.

9. Chrysostomus Bauer, O.S.B., *John Chrysostom and His Time*, trans. M. Gonzaga, 2 vols. (vol. 1, Westminster, Md.: The Newman Press, 1959; vol. 2, London: Sands & Co. Publishers, 1960), 2:415-428.

10. Procopius, *Wars*, 3.7.23-25; Loeb 2:71.

11. C. D. Gordon, *The Age of Attila: Fifth-Century Byzantium and the Barbarians* (Ann Arbor: The University of Michigan Press, 1960), p. ix.

12. R. L. Odom, "The Sabbath in the Great Schism of A.D. 1054," *Andrews University Seminary Studies* 1 (1963):74-80.

13. Winton U. Solberg, *Redeem the Time* (Cambridge, Mass.: Harvard University Press, 1977), p. 45.

14. See Le Roy Edwin Froom, *The Prophetic Faith of Our Fathers*, 4 vols. (Washington, D.C.: Review and Herald Publishing Association, 1946-1954), 2:273-275, 542, 547, 548, 666.

15. See Sir Boris Uvarov, *Grasshoppers and Locusts: A Handbook of General Acridology* (Cambridge, England: Cambridge University Press, 1966).

16. See Froom, *Prophetic Faith* 2:343, 573, 574, 686; 3:147-149.

17. The source of classic Moslem beliefs is the Koran, which is available in convenient translations in the Penguin Classics and in Everyman's Library. See especially chapters *(suras)* on "Women," "The Table," "Battle Array," "Counsel," "Iron," "That Which Is Coming," "Paradise Joys," etc.

18. The Koran, Penguin ed., p. 367.

19. *Ibid.*, pp. 104, 105.

20. *Ibid.*, pp. 196, 107, 108. Compare William H. McNeill, *The Rise of the West* (Chicago: University of Chicago Press, 1963), pp. 424, 499, 512-514. "Jewish or Christian subjects, . . . as 'People of the Book' were allowed to retain their own religion, customs, and institutions as long as they paid tribute." In fact, Jews often preferred Moslem to Catholic (or "Frank") rule as providing greater freedom.

21. Bernard Lewis, *Islam in History: Ideas, Men and Events in the Middle East* (LaSalle, Ill.: Open Court Publishing Co., 1973), pp. 138-157.

22. The Koran, Penguin ed., p. 366.

23. Laura Veccia Vaglieri, "The Patriarchal and Umayyad Caliphates," in *The Cambridge History of Islam*, ed. P. M. Holt, Ann K. S. Lambton, and Bernard Lewis, 2 vols. (Cambridge, England: Cambridge University Press, 1970), 1:86.

24. McNeill, *Rise of the West*, pp. 443, 444.

25. Vaglieri, "Caliphates," pp. 95, 96.

26. *Ibid.*, pp. 93, 94.

27. See, e.g., *The World Book Encyclopedia* (1973), art. "Greek Fire."

28. C. W. Previté-Orton, *The Shorter Cambridge Medieval History*, 2 vols. (Cambridge, England: Cambridge University Press, 1953), 1:252.

29. Previté-Orton, *Shorter Medieval History*, 1:278-281.

30. Halil Inalcik, "The Heyday and Decline of the Ottoman Empire," in *History of Islam*, ed. Holt et al, 1:325.

31. *Ibid.*, p. 329.

32. Kenneth Oster, *Islam Reconsidered,* An Exposition-University Book (Hicksville, N. Y.: Exposition Press, 1979), p. 72.

33. Thomas M. Lindsay, *A History of the Reformation,* 2 vols., 2d ed. (Edinburgh: T. & T. Clark, 1907), 1:387.

34. Royall Tyler, *The Emperor Charles the Fifth* (Fair Lawn, N. J.: Essential Books, 1956), pp. 268-285; William Stirling, *The Cloister Life of the Emperor Charles the Fifth,* 2d London ed. (Boston: Crosby, Nichols & Company, 1853), pp. 238, 246, 247.

35. Uriel Heyd, "The Later Ottoman Empire in Rumelia and Anatolia," in *History of Islam,* ed. Holt et al, 1:354.

36. See William G. Johnsson, "Killing for God's Sake," *Liberty,* May-June 1983, pp. 2-5. God does require murderers to be executed (Genesis 9:6; Romans 13:4, 5), but some observations in the article are very sound.

37. James C. Dobson, *Straight Talk to Men and Their Wives* (Waco, Tex.: Word Books, Publisher, 1980), p. 49.

38. *Ibid.,* pp. 52, 53.

39. See, e.g., F. Blass and A. Debrunner, *A Greek Grammar of the New Testament and Other Early Christian Literature,* trans. Robert W. Funk (Chicago: The University of Chicago Press, 1961), section 442(9).

40. This answer is based on various sources including Robert Darnell, letter to the author, March 22, 1982; Gibbon, *Decline and Fall,* chs. 67, 68; Heyd, "The Later Ottoman Empire," pp. 354-369; James Westfall Thompson and Edgar Nathaniel Johnson, *An Introduction to Medieval Europe, 300-1500* (New York: W. W. Norton & Company, 1937), pp. 942-948; Previté-Orton, *Shorter Medieval History,* 2:1010, 1011; and news reports and comments in *Signs of the Times,* August 1, 1840, to February 1, 1841.

41. Thompson and Johnson, *Medieval Europe,* pp. 943, 944.

42. Heyd, "The Later Ottoman Empire," p. 365.

43. Gibbon, *Decline and Fall,* ch. 67.

44. Quoted in *Signs of the Times,* January 1, 1841, p. 152.

Revelation 10:1 to 11:18

An Angel Announces the End Time

Introduction

We're all familiar with the football game that goes terribly wrong for our favorite team until the last few minutes of the fourth quarter. Just when we're about to turn off the TV in despair, our men come alive. They pass and receive, run, block, and kick like the heroes we knew they were. The crowd goes mad. The scoreboard runs wild. And when the final whistle blows, our side is ahead after all.

The book of Revelation isn't exactly like this; but it contains so many judgments and warnings about judgments that it almost gives the impression at times that gloom, destruction, and violence are the exclusive lot of everyone who lives on planet Earth, even of God's loyal and obedient people. But God cares enough to interrupt the program every now and then with the encouraging message that His eyes are always on His team and He will see that they win gloriously in the end.

Such moments of reassurance occur in several of Revelation's major divisions. Some writers call these moments "parentheses" and "interludes." We've been calling them "scenes of end-time assignment and assurance."

We found momentary scenes of this sort between the sixth and seventh seals. They showed that God is in full control of the "four winds" while His "servants" are being "sealed" and that an uncountable multitude of His people will soon throng the heavenly throne. We're going to find other such scenes later on. Right now we're looking at a group of them that occurs in Revelation 10:1 to 11:14, between the sixth and seventh trumpets.

In the first scene of this group, a scene which occupies all of chapter 10, a magnificent angel stands on sea and land holding an open book or **"scroll."** He raises his right hand and swears that **"there should be no more delay"**—or, better, that "there should be *time* no longer," as the King James Version has it. (See *Your Questions Answered*, pages 304, 305.) Here is the first *assurance:* Prophetic time is at an end. The end time has begun!

John is told to take the little scroll from the angel's hand and eat it. Here is the first *assignment*. The prophet Ezekiel in vision once ate a scroll. See Ezekiel 2:8 to 3:3. The prophet Jeremiah spoke about eating God's Word and finding it a delight. See Jeremiah 15:16. But John is warned that although the angel's scroll will taste sweet when he eats it, it will shortly afterward give him a sour stomach. Obediently he steps up, eats the scroll, and finds that it does indeed

269

As the Bible's long-time prophecies closed, an angel raised his hand and swore "that there should be time no longer." Earth's end was near!

taste sweet and then feel bitter. A second *assignment* follows, **"You must again prophesy."**

In chapter 11, John is handed a kind of yardstick and given a third *assignment,* namely, to **"measure"** God's **"temple,"** its **"altar,"** and the people who **"worship there."** He is told not to measure the **"court outside the temple"** but to **"leave that out."** An explanation is offered: **"It is given over to the nations, and they will trample over the holy city for forty-two months."** Revelation 11:2.

Meanwhile, says God, **"I will grant my two witnesses power to prophesy for one thousand two hundred and sixty days, clothed in sackcloth."** Revelation 11:3. The forty-two months of the nations and the 1260 days of the two witnesses are the same period. (Forty-two months times thirty days in a month equals 1260 days.) The two witnesses preach in the holy city while the "nations" trample on it. The sackcloth represents sorrow and a call to repentance. See Jeremiah 4:8; Esther 4:1; Job 16:15.

John hears the witnesses identified. They are **"olive trees"** and **"lampstands"** and **"prophets."** They breathe **"fire"** onto their enemies and generate **"every plague."** But a marauding **"beast,"** emerging from the **"bottomless pit,"** murders them. We're going to see how this was fulfilled in the astonishing and world-changing events of the French Revolution. The monster leaves their bodies unburied on a city street. A fiendish celebration ensues. But **"three and a half days"** later their bodies begin to stir. They come back to life. A heavenly voice calls out, **"Come up hither!"** As people everywhere look on, God publicly raptures them, and a cloud carries them away. Christianity's best days so far have occurred since the French Revolution.

The experience of the two witnesses provides *assurance* that God's message is safe at all times. The worst its enemies can inflict is but a prelude to its greater glory.

The seventh trumpet follows. It is called **"the third *woe*"** because in it the nations that have been trampling on the holy city reach a pinnacle of anger. **"The nations raged."** Is this a forecast of the final world war and of Armaged-

As we begin the seven trumpets, compare them with the seven plagues.

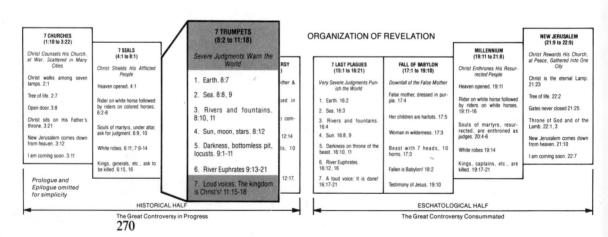

7 CHURCHES (1:10 to 3:22)	7 SEALS (4:1 to 8:1)	7 TRUMPETS (8:2 to 11:18)		ORGANIZATION OF REVELATION	7 LAST PLAGUES (15:1 to 16:21)	FALL OF BABYLON (17:1 to 19:10)	MILLENNIUM (19:11 to 21:8)	NEW JERUSALEM (21:9 to 22:9)
Christ Counsels His Church, at War, Scattered in Many Cities	*Christ Shields His Afflicted People*	*Severe Judgments Warn the World*			*Very Severe Judgments Punish the World*	*Downfall of the False Mother*	*Christ Enthrones His Resurrected People*	*Christ Rewards His Church, at Peace, Gathered Into One City*
Christ walks among seven lamps. 2:1	Heaven opened. 4:1	1. Earth. 8:7				False mother, dressed in purple. 17:4	Heaven opened. 19:11	Christ is the eternal Lamp. 21:23
Tree of life. 2:7	Rider on white horse followed by riders on colored horses. 6:2-8	2. Sea. 8:8, 9			1. Earth. 16:2	Her children are harlots. 17:5	Rider on white horse followed by riders on white horses. 19:11-16	Tree of life. 22:2
Open door. 3:8		3. Rivers and fountains. 8:10, 11			2. Sea. 16:3	Woman in wilderness. 17:3		Gates never closed 21:25
Christ sits on His Father's throne. 3:21	Souls of martyrs, under altar, ask for judgment. 6:9, 10	4. Sun, moon, stars. 8:12			3. Rivers and fountains. 16:4	Beast with 7 heads, 10 horns. 17:3	Souls of martyrs, resurrected, are enthroned as judges. 20:4-6	Throne of God and of the Lamb. 22:1, 3
New Jerusalem comes down from heaven. 3:12	White robes. 6:11; 7:9-14	5. Darkness, bottomless pit, locusts. 9:1-11			4. Sun. 16:8, 9	Fallen is Babylon! 18:2	White robes 19:14	New Jerusalem comes down from heaven. 21:10
I am coming soon. 3:11	Kings, generals, etc., ask to be killed. 6:15, 16	6. River Euphrates 9:13-21			5. Darkness on throne of the beast. 16:10, 11		Kings, captains, etc., are killed. 19:17-21	I am coming soon. 22:7
Prologue and Epilogue omitted for simplicity		7. Loud voices: The kingdom is Christ's! 11:15-18			6. River Euphrates. 16:12, 16	Testimony of Jesus. 19:10		
					7. A loud voice: It is done! 16:17-21			

HISTORICAL HALF — The Great Controversy in Progress

ESCHATOLOGICAL HALF — The Great Controversy Consummated

SEVEN TRUMPETS: Severe Judgments Warn the World. 8:2 to 11:18.

1. Introductory sanctuary scene: Angel at altar offers incense, casts fire. 8:2-5.

2. First six trumpets. 8:7 to 9:21.

3. Scenes of end-time assignment and assurance. 10:1 to 11:14.
   a. Assignment: John is told to eat the little scroll.
      An angel says, "Prophesy again (on earth)."
      John is told to "measure the temple" (in heaven).

   b. Assurance: The angel (on earth) affirms the end of time.
      Two witnesses are caught up (to heaven).
      The mystery of God will be fulfilled.

4. Consummation: Seventh trumpet, Christ reigns, judgment has come! 11:15-18.

Items 3 and 4 are discussed in the present chapter. Items 1 and 2 were discussed in the previous chapter.

don? God's wrath also matures: **"Thy wrath came."** Is this a reference to the seven last plagues? See Revelation 16. And the **"destroyers of the earth"** are themselves at last destroyed. Revelation 11:14-18.

But the period of the seventh and final trumpet isn't marked only by woe. The angel with the little scroll tells John that in the days of the seventh trumpet, **"the mystery of God, as he announced to his servants the prophets, should be fulfilled."** Revelation 10:7. Here is further *assurance* that the gospel will prevail over every opposition; in fact, that its best time will be the terrible end time. And we are living in the end time now.

In the *very* end of time, God's servants will be rewarded, every one of them, **"prophets and saints,"** **"both small and great."** Revelation 11:18.

"Prophets and saints," **"both small and great."** God cares! A promise like this includes the never-heard-of as well as the very-well-known. The timid as well as the prominent. Boys and girls as well as corporate executives. Every individual will be rewarded who elects loyally to stick it out with God's great "football team"—recruiters as well as pass receivers, custodians and cheerleaders as well as centers and quarterbacks.

And it won't be very long now, for the final quarter is already underway.

REVELATION 10:1 TO 11:18

SCENES OF END-TIME ASSIGNMENT AND ASSURANCE

REVELATION 10

Assurance that the end time has arrived and God's mystery will be fulfilled. 1 Then I saw another mighty angel coming down from heaven, wrapped in a cloud, with a rainbow over his head, and his face was like the sun, and his legs like pillars of fire. [2]He had a little scroll open in his hand. And he set his right foot on the sea, and his left foot on the land, [3]and called out with a loud voice, like a lion roaring; when he called out, the seven thunders sounded. [4]And when the seven thunders had sounded, I was about to write, but I heard a voice from heaven saying, "Seal up what the seven thunders have said, and do not write it down." [5]And the angel whom I saw standing on sea and land lifted up his right hand to heaven [6]and swore by him who lives for ever and ever, who created heaven and what is in it, the earth and what is in it, and the sea and what is in it, that there should be no more delay, [7]but that in the days of the trumpet call to be sounded by the seventh angel, the mystery of God, as he announced to his servants the prophets, should be fulfilled.

Assignment to eat the scroll and to prophesy again. 8 Then the voice which I had heard from heaven spoke to me again, saying, "Go, take the scroll which is open in the hand of the angel who is standing on the sea and on the land." [9]So I went to the angel and told him to give me the little scroll; and he said to me, "Take it and eat it; it will be bitter to your stomach, but sweet as honey in your mouth." [10]And I took the little scroll from the hand of the angel and ate it; it was sweet as honey in my mouth, but when I had eaten it my stomach was made bitter. [11]And I was told, "You must again prophesy about many peoples and nations and tongues and kings."

272

REVELATION 11

Assignment to measure the temple. 1 Then I was given a measuring rod like a staff, and I was told: "Rise and measure the temple of God and the altar and those who worship there, [2]but do not measure the court outside the temple; leave that out, for it is given over to the nations, and they will trample over the holy city for forty-two months.

Assurance that God's two witnesses will triumph. 3 And I will grant my two witnesses power to prophesy for one thousand two hundred and sixty days, clothed in sackcloth."

4 These are the two olive trees and the two lampstands which stand before the Lord of the earth. [5]And if any one would harm them, fire pours from their mouth and consumes their foes; if any one would harm them, thus he is doomed to be killed. [6]They have power to shut the sky, that no rain may fall during the days of their prophesying, and they have power over the waters to turn them into blood, and to smite the earth with every plague, as often as they desire. [7]And when they have finished their testimony, the beast that ascends from the bottomless pit will make war upon them and conquer them and kill them, [8]and their dead bodies will lie in the street of the great city which is allegorically called Sodom and Egypt, where their Lord was crucified. [9]For three days and a half men from the peoples and tribes and tongues and nations gaze at their dead bodies and refuse to let them be placed in a tomb, [10]and those who dwell on the earth will rejoice over them and make merry and exchange presents, because these two prophets had been a torment to those who dwell on the earth. [11]But after the three and a half days a breath of life from God entered them, and they stood up on their feet, and great fear fell on those who saw them. [12]Then they heard a loud voice from heaven saying to them, "Come up hither!" And in the sight of their foes they went up to heaven in a cloud. [13]And at that hour there was a great earthquake, and a tenth of the city

fell; seven thousand people were killed in the earthquake, and the rest were terrified and gave glory to the God of heaven.

The Seventh Trumpet
(The Third Woe)

The Seventh trumpet: Loud voices speak in heaven. 14 The second woe has passed; behold, the third woe is soon to come.

15 Then the seventh angel blew his trumpet, and there were loud voices in heaven, saying, "The kingdom of the world has become the kingdom of our Lord and of his Christ, and he shall reign for ever and ever." 16And the twenty-four elders who sit on their thrones before God fell on their faces and worshiped God, 17saying,

> "We give thanks to thee, Lord God Almighty, who art and who wast, that thou hast taken thy great power and begun to reign.
> 18The nations raged, but thy wrath came,
> and the time for the dead to be judged,
> for rewarding thy servants, the prophets and saints,
> and those who fear thy name, both small and great,
> and for destroying the destroyers of the earth."

273

The Message of Revelation 10:1 to 11:18

I. The End Time Has Begun

What a contrast there is between Revelation chapters 9 and 10! To our great relief, locusts and sulphur and horses' tails suddenly give way to a colossal but friendly angel who dominates our prophetic screen with supernatural glory.

With his feet planted firmly on both **"sea"** and **"land,"** with a **"little scroll"** held **"open"** in one hand, and with his other hand raised reverently to swear an oath, this majestic being reminds us immediately of someone we read about in Daniel's final vision. See Daniel 12:5-9. The person whom Daniel saw stood "above the waters of the *stream*" while an honor guard flanked him on the stream's *banks*. (Here is a parallel reference to water and land.) He raised his hands to swear an oath "by him who lives for ever." John's angel too swore **"by him who lives for ever and ever"**—**"who created heaven and what is in it, the earth and what is in it, and the sea and what is in it."** Revelation 10:6.

Daniel's "man" swore his oath just after Daniel was told to "shut up the words, and seal the book, until the time of the end." When someone asked, "How long shall it be till the end of these wonders?" the man swore an oath that "it would be for a time, two times, and half a time." And when Daniel gasped at such a prospect, the man replied, "Go your way, Daniel, for the words are shut up and sealed until the time of the end."

John's angel also had a scroll, an *open* one; and he, too, swore an oath about time. He swore that **"there should be no more delay"** (or rather, that "there should be time no longer," K.J.V.) **"but that in the days of the trumpet call to be sounded by the seventh angel, the mystery of God, as he announced to his servants the prophets, should be fulfilled."**

Quite plainly, Daniel and John saw the same person. When we studied Daniel 12, we found that the person Daniel saw was Michael, who really is Jesus, the Son of God. See GC 1:272-274, 301, 302. Now we notice that John's angel had a face **"like the sun, and his legs like pillars of fire"**—just as Jesus does in Revelation 1:13-16. His voice (in 10:3) is **"like a lion roaring"**; Christ's voice (in 1:15) is like the roar of rushing waters. The **"rainbow over his head"** recalls the rainbow around God's throne (in 4:3). So we conclude that the "man" whom Daniel saw and the **"angel"** whom John saw were indeed Jesus—who appears elsewhere in their books as the Son of man, as a lion, as a rider on a white horse, as our High Priest, as the Lamb, and also, in Daniel 12:1 and in Revelation 12:7, as Michael the Archangel.

In Revelation, the Angel's oath appears to be based on the language of the Sabbath commandment, "Remember the sabbath day, to keep it holy. . . . For in six days the Lord *made heaven and earth, the sea, and all that is in them,* and rested the seventh day." Exodus 20:8-11. When Revelation deals with the end time, it often uses language that calls attention to the Sabbath.

So here again, as in the book of Daniel, we hear the Son of God swearing by the living God; and He bases His oath on the Ten Commandments. His concern must be of utmost urgency. What He is concerned about is an open scroll, the time of the end, and the completion of God's mystery. We need to know what these things mean.

What is the little scroll? The document that is *open* in John's vision is the same document that was *sealed* in Daniel's vision. Its "words" were in some sense "shut up" in Daniel's day, but not for all days; they were shut up only "*until* the time of the end." After "a time, two times, and half a time"—that is, after three and a half symbolic years or 1260 symbolic days—"many shall run to and fro," Daniel was promised, "and knowledge shall increase." Daniel 12:4-7. John's vision expressed what Daniel's vision implied, namely, that an era would arrive, near the end of time, at the end of the 1260 years, when Daniel's book would be opened.

The **"little scroll"** is the book of Daniel. Its being opened in the last days means

The "man" of Daniel 12 is identical with the "angel" of Revelation 10.

that prophecies heretofore not understood were about to be understood. The magnificence of the Angel and the solemnity of His oath impress us with the seriousness God attaches to Daniel's prophecies and to the time when they were to be understood.

The little scroll opened. We need to remember that not everything in the book of Daniel was sealed. The head of gold was identified at once as symbolizing Nebuchadnezzar and his kingdom of Babylon. "You are the head of gold," Daniel told the king. "After you shall arise another kingdom." Daniel 2:38, 39. In chapter 8 the second and third prophetic animals were quickly identified as Media-Persia and Greece. See verses 20, 21.

The one aspect of the visions that baffled even Daniel himself was the long-time prophecies. After seeing a ram and a goat and hearing about the 2300 days (or 2300 *"evenings and mornings"*) in chapter 8, he heard someone explain what the animals meant; but he also heard someone say, "The vision of *the evenings and the mornings* which has been told is true; but *seal up* the vision, for it pertains to *many days* hence." "I was appalled by the vision," Daniel commented, "and did *not understand* it." Daniel 8:26, 27.

It is a matter of record that Daniel's long-time prophecies have come to be better and better understood as time has gone along. The seventy symbolic weeks of Daniel 9:24-27 foretold events during Christ's first appearance on the earth. They were rather clearly understood by the time of Julius Africanus, a Christian historian who lived around A.D. 200. He correctly saw the seventy weeks as 490 years running "from Artaxerxes . . . up to the time of Christ."[1] And perhaps the "three wise men" at least partially understood the seventy weeks 200 years earlier, when they followed the Christmas star to Bethlehem.

But if the seventy weeks were fairly well understood some 700—or maybe 500—years after Daniel's death, the 1260 *days* were not seen to be 1260 *years* until around A.D. 1200, some 1700 years after Daniel's death. Joachim of Flora was a brilliant and loyal monk in southern Italy who loved his Catholic Church enough to call it "Babylon" and to pray for its reformation. His writings did move the Catholic Church powerfully toward reform. Joachim concluded that the 1260 days represent approximately 1260 years, a period which he called the "age of the Son." He suggested that they began when Christ lived on earth, that they ran through the history of the Catholic Church, and that they would end at the beginning of what he called the "age of the Holy Spirit," an era which he hoped would arrive shortly after his own time.[2]

The great Reformer, Martin Luther, who was born some 2000 years after Daniel, also, like Joachim of Flora, applied the 1260 year-days to the history of the medieval church. He suggested they may have begun in the reign of the Eastern Roman Emperor Phocas (602-610), who called the pope "head of all the Holy Churches."[3]

Later commentators agreed with Luther in general. Some used his beginning era, the pontificate of Phocas. Some experimented with other events more or less close to it. In the American colonies, John Cotton (1639), known as the Patriarch of New England, suggested the period 395-1655. Increase Mather (1708), sometime president of Harvard, offered 456-1716. Jonathan Edwards (1739), sometime president of Princeton, recommended 606-1866.[4]

Assuming that the 1260 days would end at the second coming of Christ and hoping that Jesus would come back very soon, most commentators tended to start the 1260 days with some significant event in early church history that fitted an ending date not very far future to their own times, when they hoped Jesus would return.

A dramatic shift took place with the arrival of the epochal French Revolution (1789-1799) and the exiling of Pope Pius VI by the French in 1798. Commentators suddenly perceived that the end of the 1260 year-days was not the second coming of Christ and was no longer future. It was now! It had already occurred. The 1260 days had come to an end.

George Bell, Edward King, William Cunninghame, Charles Maitland, Alexander Keith, Edward Bickersteth, Edward Irving, George Croly, Matthew Habershon, Joseph Wolff, and many other commentators now came to understand correctly that the 1260 days began early in the reign of the Roman Emperor Justinian (in the 530s) and ended in the era of the French Revolution (in the 1790s). Many chose the dates 538 and 1798.[5] (We're going to say more about the tremendous significance of the French Revolution in the next section.)

With the arrival of the French Revolution, the "time, two times, and half a time" of Daniel 12:7 had run out. Now Daniel's 1260 days were understood. Knowledge had increased. The "wise" were able to understand. See Daniel 12:10. A prophecy that Daniel himself hadn't understood was now being explained. The little scroll was open. The end time had begun.

In the meanwhile, as the commentators we have named and others were earnestly reexamining the 1260 days, fervent attention was also being paid to the 2300 days (or 2300 "evenings and mornings") of Daniel 8:14. The 2300 *days* had been seen as 2300 *years* as early as the time of Benjamin ben Moses Nahawendi, a prominent rabbi in the ninth century, and by a good many other important rabbis in succeeding centuries.[6] Arnold of Villanova, a Christian theologian and physician, had also seen the 2300 days as years in the thirteenth century.[7] But no clear beginning date had been established; hence no ending date could be agreed on.

But in 1769 Johann Petri, a studious minister of the Reformed Church in Germany, came to realize that—of course—the prophecy of the seventy weeks in Daniel 9 was given to help us "understand" the 2300 days of Daniel 8. See GC 1:205-226. Petri knew that the seventy weeks started with the decree of Artaxerxes in the 450s B.C. If the 2300 days also started in the 450s B.C., Petri reasoned, would they not end in the 1840s?[8]

In 1787, Hans Wood of Ireland arrived at a conclusion roughly the same as Petri, though apparently without knowing about Petri's work.[9] In 1810, John

Aquila Brown, an influential Scottish writer, recommended 457 B.C. to A.D. 1843, revised later to end in 1844.[10]

Professor Ernest R. Sandeen, a well-known specialist in this area, has perceptively observed in a recent study that the fulfillment of the 1260 days in the French Revolution became a key to the confident new study of the 2300 days. "Encouraged by the fulfillment of the 1,260 days in Daniel 7, prophetic scholars became convinced that the next great event would be the fulfillment of the 2,300 days, [the end of] which they dated to 1843-1847."[11] The fulfillment of the 1260 days as 1260 years confirmed the understanding of the 2300 days as 2300 years and thus became a key to the further understanding of the *sanctuary* prophecy of Daniel 8:14: "For [or rather, *until*] two thousand and three hundred evenings and mornings; then the *sanctuary* shall be restored to its rightful state."

The sweetness and the bitterness. Complete understanding of Daniel's time prophecies didn't arrive all at once, even after the 1260 years terminated and the end time had begun. In the same way that some Christians had hoped Jesus would return at the end of the 1260 days, so now many hoped He would return at the end of the 2300 days. Close study led them to narrow the date for the end of the period—and for the second coming—to a day in October 1844. How their hearts beat with anticipation and joy as the longed-for day drew near. "Yours in the blessed hope," many of them signed their letters. "This was the happiest year of my life," recalled an active teenager. "My heart was full of glad expectation."[12]

But oh, how their hearts were broken when the glad expectations failed to materialize, the blessed hope didn't happen, and Jesus didn't return! We'll have more to tell of this deeply moving story when we come to Revelation 14.

The experience of these believers was remarkably foreshadowed in John's vision of the Angel with the open scroll. Like John in vision long before, but now in real life, the believers had **"eaten"** the little opened scroll. They had fairly devoured the wonderful new understanding of Daniel's long-time prophecies. Doing so had brought them unspeakable happiness. Most certainly the taste was **"sweet as honey."** But when Jesus didn't come, they felt a bitter and unspeakable sorrow.

"Measure the temple." We remind ourselves again that the chapters of Revelation were not marked out in the original document. See pages 64, 65. Revelation 10 continues without a break into Revelation 11, which is one reason we are discussing the two chapters together. After John was assigned (1) to get the little scroll and eat it, he was next informed (2) that he must **"again prophesy."** And after that he was required (3) to **"measure the temple of God and the altar and those who worship there."** The assignment to **"again prophesy"** indicated that the disappointment of October 1844 was not the collapse and end of everything! Life, and the need to study, teach, and preach, would go on. The beginning of the end time is not the same as the very end of time.

The command to **"measure,"** that is, to examine and evaluate, the **"temple"** or sanctuary was just what the disappointed believers needed in 1844. Daniel 8:14

says that at the end of the 2300 days, "then the sanctuary shall be restored to its rightful state." The solution to their confusion and disappointment lay in paying closer attention to the meaning and ministry of the heavenly sanctuary. It is a historical fact that the disappointed believers did immediately restudy the significance of the sanctuary. As they did so, they perceived the real value of Daniel and Revelation for the end time.

By means of this new study, they were prepared to take the **"mystery of God"** to **"people and nations and tongues and kings."** But more on this, too, in our discussion of Revelation 14.

How long is the end time? Perhaps you are puzzled to hear that the end time and the very end of time are not exactly the same, and that the end time began almost two centuries ago, at the close of the 1260 days in 1798.

We should notice first of all that John's Angel did not announce the end of *all* time. He stated emphatically that the long-promised fulfillment of the mystery of God (the final preaching of the gospel to all the world) was yet to be accomplished in the **"days"** of the trumpet call of the seventh angel. Revelation 10:7. And Revelation 20 shows that the "thousand years" of the great millennium were still future! No, the angel didn't anounce the end of all time. Nor did he announce the end of *probationary* time, the time when God's grace is still available and the gospel is still being preached. John himself, symbolizing the people of God after their bitter disappointment, was assigned to **"again prophesy"** as a missionary to **"peoples and nations and tongues and kings."**

John's Angel didn't announce the end of all time or the end of probationary time. He announced the end of the time that had been the subject of His earlier oath in Daniel 12. He announced the end of the 1260 days and of the 2300 days. He announced the end of *prophetic* time.

It's as simple as that.

It is also as impressive as that. If the scroll to be closed until the "time of the end" (Daniel 12:4) is now opened—and it is opened—then we are living today in the time of the end, in the end time.

Or does it seem altogether too strange that the end time could run on almost 200 years? The 1260 days ended in 1798; the 2300 days ended in 1844. We are living now in the late 1980s.

If 1798 and 1844 sound like a long time ago, we need to develop a sense of perspective. (We can hide a mountain range with a fingertip if we hold the fingertip too close to our eye. Looking backward, especially when we're young, even last year can seem like the Dark Ages.)

So let's put ourselves for a moment at the gate of the Garden of Eden in Genesis 3. Doing this will take us back at least 6000 years. With our first human parents standing beside us, freshly loaded with remorse over their very first sin, let us peer down through the long centuries of Bible history. First of all, let's see if we can pick out the cross. From Eden to the cross, according to Bible chronology, is about 4000 years. We'll need binoculars for sure! To find the cross,

279

Viewed as Adam and Eve might have seen it–past the Flood, the cross, and the three angels of Revelation 14–the end time is short indeed.

we'll have to stretch our eyes past Noah's Flood, past the Exodus, past the reign of David, and on down hundreds of years beyond the time of Daniel.

Having located the cross, we'll now need to find 1798 and 1844. To do so, we must strain our eyes almost another 2000 years, past the fall of Rome, past the discovery of America, and even beyond the Declaration of Independence.

Viewed this way, in the 6000-year arena of the great controversy between Christ and Satan, the interval between 1798 and our own day is short indeed. Relatively speaking, the end time is not very long.

We are living in it now.

II. Reject the Reformation, Reap the Revolution

When we said on page 277 that the 1260 year-days ended during the French Revolution, we promised ourselves that we'd look further into that famous world-changing event in our following section.

Professor William H. McNeill, in his highly acclaimed masterwork, *The Rise of the West,* speaks of a great "Western Explosion" that carried European concepts and technology all around the world. In general harmony with numerous other scholars, McNeill dates this Western explosion as commencing in 1789, the year when the French Revolution began.[13]

At the outbreak of the French Revolution in 1789 [observes McNeill], the geographical boundaries of Western civilization could still be defined with reasonable precision. By . . . 1917, this was no longer the case. Western history had merged into world history.[14]

McNeill analyzes the Western explosion under three major subheads, "Territorial Expansion," "Industrialism," and "Democratic Revolution." All three aspects have a direct bearing on the prophecies that we're looking at.

The success of the British Empire in the 1800s was only part of a giant process that thrust European culture and civilization over very large areas of Africa and Asia and greatly expanded its influence over North and South America. In addition, the Industrial Revolution, which began in Britain in the second half of the 1700s, provided Western technology—such as steam engines for factories, steam trains, steam boats, power printing presses, the telegraph, and advanced weaponry—for the rest of the world. Western territorial expansion, combined with the new industrialism, made possible the grand distribution of Christianity that led Kenneth Scott Latourette to call the 1800s the "Great Century" of Christianity, a century of "abounding vitality and unprecedented expansion."[15]

Thus, Western industrialism and Western expansion strikingly fulfilled prophecies about the close of the 1260 years. Daniel 12:4 predicted that at the end of those years "knowledge shall increase" and "many shall run to and fro"; and John heard a voice at the end of those years calling for the proclamation of the gospel to "many peoples, and nations, and tongues, and kings." Revelation 10:11, K.J.V.

An "earthquake" revolution. At the end of the 1260 years John also saw that **"the beast that ascends from the bottomless pit"** would **"make war upon"** God's **"two witnesses"**—His **" two olive trees and the two lampstands which stand before the Lord of the earth"**—and would **"conquer them and kill them"** and leave their **"dead bodies"** in the **"street of the great city which is allegorically called Sodom and Egypt."** **"For three days and a half"** **"those who dwell on the earth"** would **"rejoice over them and make merry and exchange presents."** But after the three and a half days, the two witnesses would return to life and go up to heaven. **"At that hour,"** John saw, **"there was a great earthquake, and a tenth of the city fell; seven thousand people were killed in the earthquake, and the rest were terrified and gave glory to the God of heaven."** Revelation 11:3-13.

This brings us to the third aspect of Professor McNeill's Western Explosion, the "Democratic Revolution," and more particularly, to the French Revolution.

The French Revolution deserves a place in prophecy! It has had a most significant influence on the world in which we and our families live today. More than any other single factor, it changed world history by inducing the spirit of modern nationalism and by producing modern universal conscription, leading, in turn, to the immense armies and drastically murderous wars that characterize our times.[16]

281

The French Revolution brought France the beginnings of democracy, equality of its citizens before the law, and a long-delayed end to "divine right" royal dictatorship. And it was by no means an isolated event. At roughly the time it was going on (1789-1801) there were other revolutions in Holland, Ireland, Belgium, Switzerland, Italy—and, of course, in America. (Before our word *democrat* became popular in the American Colonies, it was born in Holland and brought up in France and Italy.) During those same years, agitation for revolution appeared in Germany, Hungary, Poland, and Greece. "All of these agitations, upheavals, intrigues, and conspiracies," says Professor R. R. Palmer of Princeton University, a renowned specialist in the period, "were part of one great movement."[17]

Professor Palmer adds a most appropriate observation a few pages later. He says that a contemporary historian described this revolutionary era as an *earthquake*.[18] John too had spoken of an **"earthquake"** in Revelation 11:13. The choice of word was appropriate!

The notorious French Revolution. In this whole revolutionary era, the French Revolution was outstanding for its hatred of Christianity and for its violence. During its bloody Reign of Terror, day after day for months dozens of men and women, sometimes daily fifty or sixty men and women—shopkeepers and craftsmen and day laborers as well as nobles, royalty, and politicians—were decapitated by a falling-knife device recommended by Dr. J. I. Guillotine and named after him.[19]

No one was safe during the Terror, rich or poor. Everyone had a different idea about how far the Revolution ought to go, and anyone could be accused of disloyalty. There was no legal defense, sometimes scarcely a mock trial.[20] Eventually even Maximilien Robespierre, the Terror's principal promotor, became one of its last terrified victims.

There was much more horror. When a Paris mob attacked the palace to take away the king, 1000 people were trampled to death or shot, including the 600 Swiss Guards who, at the king's request, had already laid down their arms. In the "September Massacres," mobs broke into the Paris prisons and butchered more than half the inmates. Guillotines were erected in many cities; and when they seemed too slow, people accused of counterrevolutionary activity were herded into trembling huddles of a hundred or more at a time and destroyed with shrapnel fired from a cannon. The disposal of bodies became a problem; so in one locality, 2000 men, women, and children were forced onto boats and sunk in the River Loire.

If, perchance, the figures seem unimpressive, familiarity with violence has dulled the mind. Remember, too, that France had less than half the population then that it has now.*

War took the most lives. Popular interest in democratic government led to the first truly national army in any Western country. Austria and Prussia declared war

---

* Assuming a French population of about 54,200,000 today but of only around 20,000,000 during the Revolution.

Death by guillotine. France suffered terribly for rejecting the Reformation.

on France to put a stop to the Revolution. The Frenchman's cry, "Our nation is in danger," led to the *levée en masse,* the first general conscription in modern history. At once it raised an enthusiastic and enormous (for those days) citizen's army of 300,000. In a democracy everyone was equal and the nation was his own; and so, the reasoning went, everyone should serve.

After using their army to drive back the invaders, the French used it to impose their Revolution on everyone alike. "We cannot rest until all Europe is ablaze," cried Jacques-Pierre Brissot, one of the Revolutionary leaders. Soon France was at war with almost every part of Europe. She remained at war for twenty-three years. How much violence was there? How many deaths?

Napoleon was France's leader for most of these war years. Outside of France, understandably, Napoleon was also Europe's most hated individual. After imposing his will for years on the countries that he conquered, he turned against his ally Russia. He set out for Moscow in 1812 with 510,000 men, the largest army Europe had ever yet seen. But reduced by disease and defeat, fewer than half his men arrived at their destination. Those who did found Moscow deserted, and the wooden city soon caught fire. Retreating wearily across barren wastes as winter came on, deprived of food and shelter, harrassed by the Cossacks, losing 25,000

283

men at a single bridge-crossing under fire, Napoleon watched his once immense force melt away to almost nothing. Then he jumped into his carriage, rushed home to France, and conscripted yet another army—only to have it killed off piecemeal in other campaigns at five, ten, or twenty thousand men a day.[21]

How much violence was there? How many deaths?

By contrast, the earlier American Revolution, bad as it was, was fought and decided with almost unbelievably small forces. When George Washington defeated Lord Cornwallis at the crucial battle of Yorktown, his army consisted of fewer than 17,000 men! Cornwallis had only about 8,000.[22]

"Until the French Revolution all European wars had been fought with mercenary and professional armies, paid for by the government," a historian reminds us. It often had made little difference to the people whether this or that king ruled them, and they rarely felt any responsibility to help him fight his wars. But in the French Revolution the people identified themselves with their own government. The first general conscription, the *levée en masse,* "was the first modern example of conscription of the manpower of any European nation. . . . So, was born the idea of a national war, and, with the *levée en masse,* the means were made available for waging it. . . . Europe would never be the same again."[23]

No, Europe would never be the same again; and neither would anywhere else. In the second world war, America put 16,000,000 men and women into uniform. In the same conflict, Soviet casualties alone reached 20,000,000.

Certainly the French Revolution has left an impact on us and our families. No wonder it has a place in Bible prophecy.

In addition to conscription, huge national armies, and staggering casualties, another continuing legacy of the French Revolution is Communism. Karl Marx in defining Communism, and Lenin and Trotsky in preparing for the violent Bolshevik Revolution of 1917, carefully analyzed the course of the French Revolution.[24] In the process they learned all too well a related lesson taught by the Frenchman Jean Jacques Rousseau. This was the doctrine that a minority who know what's best for the people should impose themselves on the majority for their own good. Today only 5 percent of all Soviet citizens are members of the ruling Communist party. Says Professor Palmer, "The Communist movement would never have taken form as it did except for the prior occurrence of the French Revolution."[25]

"We are in no position as yet," writes the respected British historian, V. H. H. Green, "to measure the full impact of the French Revolution on the course of world history. It was one of those decisive events which opened a sluice-gate, and in the streams it released we are still swimming, sometimes finding it difficult to keep our head above the waters."[26]

The revolution and de-Christianization. Professor Green's words are all too fitting. Indeed, we live with yet another serious sequel to the French Revolution, anti-Christian atheism. Today, roughly one fourth of the human race is ruled by atheistic (Marxist) governments.

This brings us back to the **"two witnesses"** and their apparent murder by the

284

"beast" from the "bottomless pit"; for the anti-Christian stance of the French Revolution was intense and has indeed left a legacy.

We are assuming that in Revelation 11 the "tenth of the city" is France and the "two witnesses" are the Old and New Testaments, or the Bible. See *Your Questions Answered,* pages 299-302.

The anti-Christian stance of the French Revolution was a long time developing. Under the direction of Pope Innocent III in the 1200s, France attacked the progressive but "heretical" Albigenses and committed genocide on them. See GC 1:132. During the Protestant Reformation in the 1500s, an estimated 400,000 French Catholics quickly adopted the Bible-centered doctrines taught by the French Reformer of Geneva, John Calvin. How different the country's history might have been if it had granted the Huguenots (as the French Protestants were known) full religious freedom! For a while, the "two witnesses" preached joyously in France; but not for long. The French kings, encouraged by their bishops and by many of their nobles, fought no fewer than eight civil wars against the Protestant Huguenots.

On August 18, 1572, during a peace between two Huguenot wars, the king's sister actually married a leading Huguenot at a high-society wedding, and the king officially promised that the Huguenots would be free. Most regrettably, the mother of the bride, Catherine de Medici (who of course was also the mother of the king), became infuriated. Angrily she arranged for what quickly came to be known as the Massacre of Saint Bartholomew. The signal was the tolling of a bell at two o'clock in the morning on the eve of St. Bartholomew's day, less than a week after the wedding. According to a conservative modern estimate, within a short time "not improbably 8000 in Paris, and several times that number in the whole of France,"[27] were systematically hunted down and butchered. It is well known that when a messenger hurriedly got the news to Rome, a French cardinal handsomely rewarded him. Pope Gregory XIII commissioned frescoes to be painted and ordered a medal designed to celebrate the event. Rome rocked with the ringing of bells, the singing of praise anthems *(Te Deums)* by church choirs, and a magnificent procession.[28]

When, in the course of a couple of decades, a Huguenot nobleman, Henry of Navarre, happened to come next in line for the hereditary throne of France, Pope Sixtus V declared him ineligible. But Henry of Navarre got to be King Henry IV nevertheless—and soon made himself a Catholic to please the majority of his people. ("Paris is well worth a mass," he is reported to have said.[29]) But King Henry in 1598 issued the famous Edict of Nantes, which he made legally irrevocable, granting the Huguenots many freedoms, though excluding them entirely from Paris, Lyon, and some other major cities. Where they were allowed to do so, the Huguenots excelled in crafts, education, agriculture, and business, and became virtually France's middle class. Their numbers increased toward 2,000,000, a tenth of the population.

But over the years, their freedoms were step by step withdrawn. Churches were torn down, ministers expelled, colleges closed, and cruelest of all in some ways, rough boorish soldiers called dragoons were sent to live inside Huguenot homes. The dragoons were authorized by the state and encouraged by local priests to force the Huguenots back to the state church by any means of annoyance, obscenity, theft, vandalism, intimidation, or torture short of actual rape and murder.

In October 1685, King Louis XIV formally revoked the "irrevocable" Edict of Nantes, in the same act making all the Huguenots outlaws but forbidding them to leave the country. Some 500,000 (no one knows the exact number) abandoned their homes and possessions rather than abandon their faith. "Persons brought up in every luxury, pregnant women, old men, invalids, and children," some disguised as pilgrims, sportsmen, and peasants, traveling unfamiliar trails by night, passing the day in forests and caves, hiding in wagons and ships under bales of hay or heaps of coal or in empty barrels, contrived somehow to reach freedom abroad. These were the fortunate ones. Those who couldn't get away or who were caught, suffered indescribably. The infamous revocation of the Edict of Nantes reduced the Huguenots "to a persecuted, martyr church, to be proscribed till the eve of the French Revolution, and drove thousands of their numbers into exile, to the lasting gain of England, Holland, Prussia, and America"[30]—and to the everlasting loss of France.

Rejecting the Protestants, France also to a large extent rejected the light of the Bible, God's **"two witnesses"** and **"lampstands."** Turning their backs on God's true light, many French people in the 1700s accepted instead the contemporary wave of philosophy known as the "Enlightenment."

The Enlightenment. The 1700s were an age that could encompass all of human knowledge in twenty-eight encyclopedia volumes (with a seven-volume appendix). People were intoxicated with the discovery that the universe operates in harmony with natural laws. In such an age, God seemed increasingly unimportant. Deism became popular, portraying God as a super clocksmith who made the universe like a watch, wound it up, and left it running on its own. Human reason appeared increasingly respectable, inasmuch as it was able to figure all of this out. Christian doctrine was despised, with its miracles of the virgin birth, the resurrection, and personal answers to prayer.

The Enlightenment spread thinly over Europe and North America, but it flourished exuberantly in Paris. There men and women of all classes, though nominally Christian, found it fashionable to join a club or *salon* and discuss the latest writings of contemporary intellectuals, called *philosophes*.

Among the most prominent of the Enlightenment *philosophes* were Jean Jacques Rousseau and Francois Voltaire, both French. Rousseau taught some quite contradictory things, including the doctrines that all people ought to be free, and (as we mentioned a moment ago) that a minority who think they know what is best, ought to impose their will on the majority for their own good.[31]

We have already seen on page 195 how Voltaire used the Lisbon Earthquake of

Persecuted Huguenot leaders set up headquarters in the French desert. A tunnel still leads from a kitchen cupboard to safety in the hills.

November 1, 1755, to reason that God doesn't care about us and so we'd better look out for ourselves. This was one of the arguments that paved the way for the French Revolution. Voltaire was a Deist. His god created the world but was incapable of loving anyone or of having any personal relationship with us. Voltaire repeatedly rejected the inspiration of the Bible and felt that human reason was far superior to Christianity. He especially rejected the Old Testament, claiming that it reduces humans to brutes.[32]

It is significant that during the French Revolution, an American citizen was voted in as a member of the French National Assembly! He was Thomas Paine, the eccentric American patriot, who agreed strongly with Voltaire on many subjects. In *The Age of Reason,* written while he was in Paris, Paine stated angrily, "I sincerely detest" the Old Testament.[33]

De-Christianization carried out. Before the Revolution began, almost all of France's bishops had been members of the nobility, closely leagued with the other nobles and with the king. This being the case, the bishops refrained from rebuking the king and nobles for their oppressive rule or their extravagant luxuries. So it is not surprising that when the French people threw out their old monarchy, their old nobility, and their old oppressive tax system, they also threw out their old religion.

In the first spasms of hatred against the only form of religion they had been allowed to know, the French Revolutionaries proposed a wholly new calendar, one that commenced not with the birth of Jesus but with the first year of their own Revolution.

The old calendar was burdened with some 200 holy days (out of 365 days in the year), drastically reducing the capacity of the poor to earn their daily bread. In the new calendar, all holy days were abolished. Even Sunday was sent to the trash heap, along with any lingering memory it conveyed of the Bible Sabbath. How different had been the case in England, where during the Reformation the people had quickly won the right to read the Bible for themselves. There, when most of the church-made holy days were discarded, Sunday—on the mistaken assumption that it was the Sabbath—had been invested with a sacred, restful quality almost equal to that of the true Sabbath.

In France, however, under the new anti-Christian calendar, the week was made ten days long, and only every tenth day or "Decade day" was left as a holiday, dedicated to celebrating the Republic and its new pagan religion. The months were renamed after the seasons and were called, in French of course, Snowy, Rainy, Windy, Foggy, Harvest, Hot, and so on.

The first celebration of the Revolutionary religion harmonized with the new emphasis on nature. On August 10, 1793, a large image representing Goddess Nature was set up in a prominent place. As the people of Paris crowded in front of it, water squirted from its breasts into an ornamental pool. An actor solemnly addressed it with a blasphemous prayer, "Sovereign of Nations, savage or civilized! Oh, Nature, this great people is worthy of Thee."[34]

The Revolution didn't exactly abolish Christianity; in fact, it proclaimed freedom of worship for all religions. But at the same time, it forbade the enthusiastic street processions characteristic of Catholicism at the time; and it persuaded the bishop of Paris and his associates to abdicate their vocations, or renounce their ministry. Hearing of this, the forty-eight sections of Paris went wild with delight.

The people in one section of Paris sparked a celebration by lighting a bonfire and burning confessionals and other religious books used in the churches. Other sections of Paris spread word that they were renouncing Christianity. The busts of "martyred" Revolutionaries and of Liberty and Equality replaced the familiar images of saints in the Catholic churches, while ancient Gothic arches echoed to the alleluias of the Revolutionary religion.[35] Soon all churches in Paris were officially closed—in spite of the proclamation about freedom of worship. People flaunted shirts made from choirboy surplices. Reports told of naked dancers in the churches and out among the gravestones. Second-hand shops displayed priestly gowns and altar cloths next to pantaloons and lavatory seats.[36]

This violent process of de-Christianization was by no means confined to Paris. In fact, other cities commenced it before Paris did.[37] In some places the churches were ravaged by mobs; in others, offensive symbols were removed and pipe organs dismantled by masons and carpenters hired by local authorities. Out went crucifixes, images, expensive communion plates and chalices. Out too went lavish coats of arms from the burial crypts of the nobility. A very large quanity of gold and silver taken from the churches was sent to Paris, where much of it was used to pay for the new national army. As shipments of religious treasure arrived at the capital, "the rabble," says a famous French historian, "indulging their taste for the burlesque, caricatured in the most ludicrous manner the ceremonies of religion, and took as much delight in profaning as they had formerly done in celebrating them."[38]

How sadly and foolishly were the words of Revelation 11:10 fulfilled, **"And those who dwell on the earth will rejoice over"** the two witnesses, **"and make merry."**

On the second Decade day in Foggy month (November 10 in the Christian calendar), a young woman was chosen instead of a statue to represent Goddess Reason. Draped in white with a mantle of blue, her flowing hair crowned with the red cap of the Revolution, she was worshiped in France's most prestigious cathedral, where for centuries prayers had ascended to "Our Lady" ("Notre Dame"), the Mother of Jesus. Cheers echoed and reechoed from Gothic walls as an orator, on behalf of everyone present, obsequiously embraced the woman. Outside of Paris, in many of France's numerous cities and villages, Goddess Reason took the form of selected local women.

In the important and ancient city of Lyon, when the mayor died, his bust and ashes were carried in procession to an outdoor altar. In the procession plodded a donkey, with a crucifix and a Gospel tied to its tail. After the ceremony, the donkey was given a drink from a communion chalice. The crucifix and the Gospel were untied and thrown on a fire.[39]

Says M. A. Thiers, a French statesman of the following century, "It is impossible to view with any other feeling than that of disgust these scenes, possessing neither reflection or sincerity, exhibited by a nation that had changed its worship, without comprehending either the previous, or the present, form of adoration."[40]

At the very time when the people of France were making a god out of human reason and in its name overthrowing the only form of Christianity they had been permitted to know, people who used their reasoning powers to object to what was going on were thrown into prison at a wholesale rate. In Paris, with a population under 700,000,[41] there were thought to be 100,000 arrests; and the guillotine was flowing red.[42]

Worship of a Supreme Being. The *philosophes,* you remember, though they praised nature and human reason, still believed a god created the universe (and left it to run on its own). Thus Robespierre, the principal creator of the reign of terror, insisted after a while that the new Republic shouldn't worship merely human reason but should proclaim belief in a Supreme Being and in the immortality of the soul. He presented a grand speech in favor of *this* new Revolutionary religion. His arguments favoring the worship of a Supreme Being were not religious but political. Such worship, he said, was appropriate "to man in a state of society." To prove the immortality of the soul he appealed to ancient Greeks and Romans, Socrates, Cicero, Brutus, and Leonidas. "Priests are to morality," Robespierre went on, "what quacks are to medicine." "I know nothing," he said, "that so nearly resembles atheism as the religions which they [the priests] have

289

invented. By grossly misrepresenting the Supreme Being, they have annihilated him as far as lay in their power. . . . The priests have created a God after their own image; they have made him jealous, capricious, greedy, cruel, and implacable."[43]

On the second Decade day of Grassy (June 8, 1794), Robespierre clothed himself as the prophet, or priest, or, as his enemies said, the pope, of his new Revolutionary religion. The day chosen was the Sunday on which Catholics had planned to honor Pentecost. A vast crowd followed him in procession.

We are not discussing a Reformation from Catholic tradition to the Protestant understanding of the Bible. We are watching the convulsions of a nominally Christian society as it discarded, almost vomited, the only form of Christianity it had been permitted to know, and erected in its place a form of paganism.

"For the *first time in European history* since the days of the [Roman] Emperor Julian the Apostate *a state deliberately embarked on a policy of de-Christianization."*[44]

France had another "first" to its credit in addition to being the first Christian nation in Europe deliberately to oppose Christianity. Among the tribes that invaded and took over the western Roman Empire, the Franks in 496 were the first people permanently to accept Catholic Christianity. France came to be honored as "the eldest daughter of the church," and Moslems often called all Catholics "Franks." It was such a nation that was the first in modern Europe to turn officially against the religion of Jesus.

A bad lesson learned too well. Over the centuries, the established church had taught the French to fine, execute, and exile their "heretics." In the present crisis, the church found it had taught the lesson only too well. The people of France, now regarding the churchmen themselves as in error, treated them as for centuries they had been taught. During the Revolution they executed at least 2000 priests and possibly as many as 5000. On one ghoulish day, in one pathetic location, they shot 83 of them.

For centuries, a favorite punishment for heretics, as for many other persons deemed undesirable, was consignment to the frightful slave galleys, to row until they rotted at the handles of the great oars. The enraged people of France, in their hatred of the only kind of Christianity they had been permitted to know, sent 850 priests to slavery in the galleys.

The church had taught the king to send Huguenots into exile. Now some 30,000 or 40,000 priests went into exile, fleeing France to save their lives. Some went to Spain, some to the Papal States in central Italy, and others to safety in Protestant England. And on February 15, 1798, French soldiers entered the Sistine Chapel in Rome and actually forced the pope into exile, where he died! (More on this astonishing development in our study of Revelation 13.)

Under circumstances such as these, 20,000 priests who chose to stay in France "abdicated their vocation," resigning the priesthood according to the example of the Bishop of Paris.[45]

290

French revolutionaries shackled priests to galley oars.

So who was worse? Exceedingly reluctant as we are to admit it, perhaps it was just as well that those 20,000 did renounce their priesthood. The evidence seems to be that Robespierre's bitter accusation was closer to the truth than we wish it were. "The priests have created a God after their own image," he said; "they have made him jealous, capricious, greedy, cruel, and implacable." "I know nothing that so nearly resembles atheism as the religions which they have invented. By grossly misrepresenting the Supreme Being, they have annihilated him as far as lay in their power."

Solemn, solemn words. We're constrained to admit they are all too true when applied to the Judaic priests in Christ's day who worshiped God but crucified God's Son and persecuted the early Christians. And as we looked at Christian and Moslem worshipers of God in our study of the seven trumpets, we were often unable to perceive much practical improvement.

In the name of the God of the Bible, Christian priests of France burned people they didn't agree with, tortured or exiled them, and sent some of them to the galleys. In the name of the Supreme Being (or the Goddess Reason), French revolutionaries guillotined people they didn't agree with, shot or exiled them, and sent some of them to the galleys.

Was there really any difference?

Poor unhappy France! Philip Schaff, dean of American church historians in the

291

1800s, stated to the American Society of Church History over a century ago, "France rejected the Reformation—and reaped the Revolution."[46]

We can agree with Professor Schaff if by "Reformation" he meant both a new set of doctrines *and* a new way of life. How we behave is as important as what we believe. "If you love me, you will keep my commandments," Jesus said, and, "A new commandment I give to you, that you love one another; even as I have loved you." John 14:15; 13:34.

Reformation to *this* kind of Bible Christianity could evidently have prevented the French Revolution.

People who with God's help practice this kind of Christianity in their daily lives say it prevents a lot of problems in their families too.

III. Life That's Unconquerable!

An esteemed acquaintance of mine was taken to the hospital with terminal leukemia. He was in his fifties and had scarcely sensed that he was ill. Now he was given only weeks to live.

My friend and his wife were active Christians. In many lesser crises they had found real workaday courage in reading Bible passages. Three days after he left home (the date was now July 6), she leafed prayerfully through her Bible, which was a copy of the New International Version. Psalm 108 leaped from the page.

She jumped into the car and was soon at her husband's side. But a happy surprise awaited her. She found that on the margin of Psalm 108 he had just written "July 6" in *his* Bible!

They had not been reading the Psalms together. The Holy Spirit had led them both to the same passage on the same day. They wept in wonder as she read aloud:

> My heart is steadfast, O God;
>   I will sing and make music with all my soul.
>
> With God we will gain the victory,
>   and he will trample down our enemies.
> Psalm 108:1, 13, N.I.V.

At the funeral, when she told how God had sustained both of them, and in the difficult weeks of readjustment that followed, it was obvious that her heart was truly "steadfast." She enjoyed a real, practical victory over her deep sense of loss.

The joyful assurance of victory over our enemies is found not only in Psalm 108 but in many other Bible passages as well. We found it in Daniel 3 and 6, where God rescued Daniel from lions and walked with Daniel's friends in a furnace. It applies to all of life's trials and tribulations, including the future great tribulation. "In the world you have tribulation; but be of good cheer, I have overcome the world," says Jesus in John 16:33. Victory over our enemies is a basic Christian privilege. It applies to July 6 in any year, and to every other day besides.

For Christians, to whom Christ is the "resurrection and the life" (John 11:25) and the One who owns the key to the grave (see Revelation 1:18), victory is assured even over our "last enemy," death (see 1 Corinthians 15:26). Such unconquerable vitality is a part of the nature of God. It is a quality He has vouchsafed to us who believe in Him and take Him at His word. It is something He has also bestowed on His Word itself, so that in a real sense the Bible, too, can say,

> With God I will gain the victory,
> and he will trample down my enemies.

The Bible's great new era. Assurance that God's Word does enjoy life unconquerable is the message of Revelation 11:1-13. First, John foresaw the symbolic death for **"three days and a half"** of God's **"two witnesses"**—the Old and New Testaments that together make up the Bible. (See *Your Questions Answered*, pages 299-302.) This was a prophecy of the brief but brutal suppression of the Bible during the era of the French Revolution, some highlights of which we looked at in the previous section.

Right after seeing this, John saw a dramatic change in the Bible's fortunes. **"A breath of life from God entered them** [the two witnesses]," he tells us, **"and they stood up on their feet, and great fear fell on those who saw them. Then they heard a loud voice from heaven saying to them, 'Come up hither!' And in the sight of their foes they went up to heaven in a cloud."** Verses 11, 12.

Hardly had the French Revolution passed its peak and the grisly gore of the guillotine begun to recede from center stage, than Christianity entered its most brilliant era to date!

To be sure, seeds of this new era had been germinating all through the difficult 1700s. In England various strains of "evangelical revival" had been nurtured by Benjamin Ingham, George Whitefield, the Countess of Huntington, and especially Charles and John Wesley, sowers of Methodism. In the American Colonies, George Whitefield had nurtured the Great Awakening of 1740, which in turn had sprouted the vigorous Baptist movement and other good things. In the mid-1700s Methodism was disseminated from Great Britain to North America.[47]

Also during the difficult 1700s, various groups sensed the need of inexpensive Scriptures for the poor and so started small Bible societies here and there. And a few highly motivated missionaries were commissioned by the Moravians, by the Society for the Propagation of the Gospel (S.P.G.), and by a few other missionary societies.

But near the close of the 1700s, as the 1260 years came to an end, these germinating seeds of revivalism, Bible distribution, and missionary commissioning burst onto the world's landscape spectacularly, like weeds crowding up after rain—or like children dashing out of school, or like the sun on a cloudy morning,

293

suddenly appearing high in the sky. Taking advantage of the industrial revolution and the "Western expansion" foreseen in Bible prophecy, Christianity spread by leaps and bounds.

We glanced at this sudden burgeoning of the gospel on pages 129-131 and don't need to repeat here what we said there. We can add that the Methodists under the Wesleys in Britain had scarcely passed 70,000 by John Wesley's death in 1791.[48] But by 1860 in the United States alone they numbered around 2,000,000![49] Other evangelical denominations also experienced amazing growth.

Foreign missions entered a new era through the founding of numerous missionary societies and the dedication of numerous individuals. "Let me burn out for God," cried Henry Martyn, twenty-five-year-old Cambridge graduate as he arrived in India as a missionary in 1806.[50] Within six years he did just that; and a similar spirit animated and energized thousands of others. Judson of Burma, Carey of India, Morrison of China, Moffat and David Livingstone of Africa became household terms as Christian families back home wondered at the marvelous devotion of such giant servants of the Lord, and Christian boys and girls promised God in their prayers that they would follow them at any cost.

And follow them they did, replacing "witch doctors" with hundreds of hospitals, showing people how to fertilize their fields and rotate their crops, conducting thousands of schools so people could read the Bible and better manage their affairs. Reducing hundreds of tribal tongues to writing for the first time, they translated the Bible into them. And all too often their personal possessions molded in the damp, their mission cemeteries filled up with loved ones and colleagues, and their own bodies shook with malarial chills or ached with typhus or blackwater fever.

They gave their all—and by no means in vain. "For the first time in its history, Christianity [in the 1800s] made actual its inherent genius and became worldwide," observes Kenneth Scott Latourette, Sterling Professor of Missions at Yale University. "In this it surpassed the achievement of every other religion." He concedes that "mankind was far from conforming fully to Christian standards." In most lands "professed Christians" after a century of church growth "were still but a small fraction of the population." Yet Latourette can say that by the early 1900s, "nearly every culture felt to a greater or less extent the influence of Christianity."[51]

And, of course, Christianity is living still. Slashed back and long stunted in the formerly Christian lands of the Soviet Union, it is today observed even there by a marvelous 40 percent of the population![52] Slashed back and stunted during the 1950s and 1960s in long-pagan China, Christianity is now cherished even *there* (according to glowing reports from Chinese believers) by some 10,000,000 Chinese. This number is the same as the number who held to Christianity only nominally before the vigorous onslaughts began around 1950. And whispered reports hint that the miraculous growth of Christians in China has really reached two or three times 10,000,000.[53]

Billions can read the Scriptures translated into their own languages thanks to dedicated missionaries assisted by articulate nationals.

This magnificent flowering of gospel progress has coincided with a lush flourishing of Bible distribution. The Bible societies we know today began to emerge around 1800, when Joseph Hughes, a Baptist, became burdened to provide inexpensive Bibles for the people of Wales; "and if for Wales," he asked himself, *"why not for the world?"* In 1804, only a few years after the peak of the French Revolution, Hughes and others founded the great British and Foreign Bible Society. Its first wagon load of Scriptures was welcomed in Wales "like the ark of the covenant; and the people with shouts of joy dragged it into the city."[54]

This was the beginning. Very soon the British and Foreign Bible Society was publishing hundreds of thousands of Bibles and of Bible portions in dozens of languages every year. By 1904, after a century of service, its annual production exceeded five million copies. Even more helpfully, the British and Foreign Bible Society stimulated the founding of other permanently effective Bible societies, notably the American Bible Society in 1816, which, by the early 1900s was annually distributing over two million copies.

In the early 1980s, the United Bible Societies (all the major societies reporting together) distributed in a single year 11,211,617 whole Bibles, 12,174,328 New Testaments, and enough gospels, books, and portions to bring the grand total to 497,715,345. The whole Bible was available in 283 languages, the New Testament alone in an additional 572 languages, and at least one Bible book in yet another 930 languages, making some part of the Bible available in 1785 forms of human speech!

295

Since its inception in 1816, the American Bible Society alone had by 1983 distributed 105,955,562 Bibles and 3,790,330,919 (that's more than three and three quarter *billion*) New Testaments and portions.[55]

Though killed and left unburied (see Revelation 11:7, 9), God's **"two witnesses"** most assuredly came back to life—and as it were **"went up to heaven"** in sight of the onlooking world. Truly they triumphed over their enemies; and today they flourish vigorously, in spite of the French Revolution with its deadly legacy of anti-Christian atheism, which today dominates the governments that rule a fourth of the human race, and the rampant nationalism and universal militarism which have produced the most devastating wars in human experience.

Unconquerable life of the Bible. Yes, God sees to it that His Bible is a "living and abiding word." 1 Peter 1:23. He invests it with His own life unconquerable.

Human beings admittedly seem more alive than printed books; but people die, while God's Word still lives.

> Surely the people is grass.
> The grass withers, the flower fades;
>   but the word of our God will stand for ever.
>   Isaiah 40:7, 8.

Tom Paine once said, "I sincerely detest" the Old Testament. See page 287. Tom Paine is dead, but the Bible he detested lives on. The skeptic Voltaire arched high his intellectual eyebrows at the grand Bible miracles of the virgin birth and the resurrection of Christ. Voltaire is dead; but Christians still rejoice on Christmas Day and Easter. Inflamed ordinary people hurled Bibles onto bonfires, tied a Gospel to a donkey's tail, closed all the churches in Paris, and butchered their ministers. These violent people too are dead; but the Bible lives.

"The words that I have spoken to you are spirit and life," said our Jesus. John 6:63.

The words of the Bible not only have life; they are able to give life. Paradoxically, when planted in our hearts like seeds, they make *us* germinate into new kinds of people. "You have been born anew," said the apostle Peter to the people who had accepted his Bible messages. "You have been born anew, not of perishable seed but of imperishable, through the living and abiding word of God." 1 Peter 1:23.

The people of our world are polarizing, taking sides. "Evil men and imposters will go on from bad to worse, deceivers and deceived," warned the apostle Paul with prophetic insight in 2 Timothy 3:13. But as God's living Word grips human hearts, other people around the world are growing on from glory to glory, like the rising brightness of the summer sun. "And we all," promises Paul in 2 Corinthians 3:18, "with unveiled face, beholding the glory of the Lord, are being changed into his likeness from one degree of glory to another; for this comes from the Lord who is the Spirit."

"Speaking the truth in love, we are to grow up in every way into him who is the head, into Christ" "until we all attain to the unity of the faith and of the knowledge of the Son of God, to mature manhood, to the measure of the stature of the fulness of Christ." Ephesians 4:15, 13.

The seventh trumpet and the **"mystery of God."** In this connection we want to notice again that the Angel with the little scroll swore a solemn oath not only about the end of the long-term Bible prophecies but also that **"in the days of the trumpet call to be sounded by the seventh angel, the *mystery of God,* as he announced to his servants the prophets, should be fulfilled."** Revelation 10:7. We're leaving out for now what the seventh trumpet says about the time **"for the dead to be *judged*."** Revelation 11:18. We'll take this up when we come to the message of the first angel of Revelation 14, "The hour of his judgment has come."

But what is the **"mystery of God"**? In the New Testament, a "mystery" is a wonderful truth or a wonderful divine plan that we would never have known about if God hadn't told us about it. "Unto you," said Jesus to His disciples, "it is given to *know* the mysteries of the kingdom of God." Luke 8:10, K.J.V. Paul refers to "the mystery which . . . now is *made manifest* to his saints." Colossians 1:26, K.J.V. And Peter, like John, speaks of the interest of the Old Testament prophets in the grace that was later to be *revealed* through Jesus Christ. See 1 Peter 1:10-12.

The greatest mystery of all is the "mystery of our religion":

He [Christ] was manifested in the flesh,
vindicated in the Spirit,
    seen by angels,
preached among the nations,
believed on in the world,
    taken up in glory.
                    1 Timothy 3:16.

Another great mystery is the comforting but impelling, transforming, and altogether beautiful relationship Christians can enjoy with their Lord and Saviour, "this mystery, which is *Christ in you,* the hope of glory." Colossians 1:27.

Paul speaks of the "mystery of the gospel." Significantly, he says that it brings about "the obedience of faith." Ephesians 6:19; Romans 16:25, 26.

Elsewhere, Paul speaks of God's "plan for the *fulness of time,* to unite all things in him, things in heaven and things on earth." Ephesians 1:9, 10. Here, like the Angel with the scroll, Paul places the final fulfillment of the mystery of God in the end time, the "fulness of time," the time we're living in now.

In one of the most exciting statements in all of his writings, Paul says that it is a part of God's mystery "that *through the church* the manifold wisdom of God *might now be made known* to the principalities and powers in the heavenly places." Ephesians 3:10.

We have become accustomed to the gracious, friendly interest that heavenly beings take in helping us. But here we are introduced to the breathtaking realization that in God's great plan we can teach the angels something! As heavenly beings observe the unfolding of the mystery of God in our lives, in our families, in our work and worship, they learn something about what God can do for sinners.

The heavenly beings see ordinary people, through faith in the promises of the living Word, making God's unconquerable life their own.

These people are conquering with Christ in spite of the ever sharpening polarization against God spurred on by the legacy of the French Revolution—anti-Christian atheism and secular materialism, fanatic divisive nationalism, and increasingly oppressive militarism.

We're playing in the fourth and final quarter! Every wholly dedicated and well-informed member of God's team is bound to win. The secret of success is choosing to make the Bible, the living Bible, God's resurrected, restored, and elevated **"two witnesses,"** the manager, referee, and coach at the center of our lives.

Such a choice explains the mystery of the intrepid courage of the missionaries we mentioned a moment ago. Doubtless it helps explain the faithfulness of many earnest Christians living under atheistic governments.

It surely explains the triumphant peace experienced by my esteemed friend and his wife when faced with his terminal leukemia and the imminent breakup of their family. They knew that God cared so deeply about their affairs that through His Word He was giving them life unconquerable. This is why even in a hospital room they could open their Bibles to Psalm 108 (N.I.V.) and read together,

> My heart is steadfast, O God;
> I will sing and make music with all my soul.

> With God we will gain the victory,
> and he will trample down our enemies.

Further Interesting Reading

In *Bible Readings for the Home:*
"Power in the Word of God," page 29.
"The Life-giving Word," page 32.
In Arthur S. Maxwell, *Your Bible and You:*
"What the Bible Can Do for You," page 56.
"Glorious Saviour," page 111.
In Ellen G. White, *The Triumph of God's Love:*
"Terror and Retribution in France," page 223.

Page numbers for each book refer to the large, fully illustrated edition.

Your Questions Answered

1. Who are the "two witnesses" and how do they send "plagues"? Immediately after John was assigned to measure the temple, its altar, and the worshipers, he was instructed, **"Do not measure the court outside the temple; leave that out, for it is given over to the nations, and they will trample over the holy city for forty-two months."** (For the **"nations"** in the **"outer court"** see Question 3.) God added, **"I will grant my two witnesses power to prophesy for one thousand two hundred and sixty days, clothed in sackcloth."** Revelation 11:2, 3.

If we have retained any uncertainty that the little scroll of chapter 10 was indeed the book of Daniel, such uncertainty must by these verses be entirely removed. The scroll is open and John's attention is called at once to the time prophecies of Daniel 7 and 8.

Daniel 7 contains the 1260-day prophecy about a system that would blaspheme, persecute, and attempt to change God's law. Daniel 8 contains the parallel 2300-day prophecy about a system that "trampled" on the "sanctuary" and "host."

John was told that God's **"two witnesses"** would **"prophesy"** during the 1260 days **"clothed in sackcloth."** The people of Nineveh put sackcloth on when Jonah urged them to repent. See Jonah 3:6-9. Daniel clothed himself in sackcloth when he was most earnest in his prayers. See Daniel 9:3. Evidently the two witnesses were to preach earnestly for repentance. Their message wouldn't be popular. People who heard it would be in a **"torment"** over it. See Revelation 11:10. They would resist and oppose it throughout the 1260 days, but at all times God stood ready to intervene. In vision, John watched the two witnesses and saw that **"if any one would harm them, fire pours from their mouth and consumes their foes."** He saw, too, that they had power to keep the **"rain"** away, to turn **"waters"** into **"blood,"** and **"to smite the earth with every plague, as often as they desire."** Revelation 11:5, 6.

Who are these two mysterious witnesses? We have assumed that they are the Old and New Testaments, comprising together the whole Bible.

In verse 4 John refers to them as **"two olives trees"** and **"two lampstands."** The language, like so much of Revelation, is borrowed and *adapted* from the Old Testament. The prophet Zechariah spoke of "two olive trees" standing at the "right" and the "left" of a certain "lampstand." Zechariah 4:2, 3. But Zechariah had only *one* lampstand (defined in 4:6 as representing the Holy Spirit), and his olive trees were evidently Joshua and Zerubbabel, the secular and spiritual leaders of Israel at the time. Neither Joshua nor Zerubbabel is known to have prevented rain or sent a plague. We cannot very well equate John's two witnesses with Zechariah's olive trees.

On the other hand, we know that the Old Testament prophet Elijah (whom the Old Testament nowhere calls an olive tree) did **"shut"** heaven, stopping

299

the **"rain"** and bringing about a famine, which lasted for three and a half years (I Kings 17: Luke 4:25), corresponding perhaps to the **"three and a half days"** in Revelation 11:11. Subsequently, Elijah twice summoned heavenly **"fire"** to consume military units commissioned to execute him. See 2 Kings 1. We know too that Moses (whom, again, the Old Testament nowhere calls an olive tree) was instrumental in turning the "water" of the river Nile to **"blood"** and in bringing one **"plague"** after another on Egypt. See Exodus 7-12. We know further that Elijah and Moses appeared together, with Jesus, on the Mount of Transfiguration. See Matthew 17:1-8. So some Bible readers have supposed that the two witnesses are Moses and Elijah, literally restored to life in the end time for a literal 1260 days.

But we are dealing with symbols and perhaps in some instances only with impressions. Symbols and impressionistic language point away to something other than themselves. The 1260 days point to 1260 years. In a book like Revelation, the last thing we should expect the two witnesses to represent is two literal prophets!

So who are the two witnesses? A witness is a person who bears a witness, someone who makes a testimony or testifies about something. The words *witness, bear witness,* and *testify* are closely related in meaning. When they occur in the New Testament, they are translated from Greek words related to *martureo,* from which comes our word *martyr.* A martyr is a person who in life and death testifies to or bears witness to his faith in God.

In John 5:39, Jesus said of (1) the *Old Testament scriptures,* "It is they that bear witness to me." And during the Olivet Discourse He said, (2) "This *gospel* of the kingdom will be preached throughout the whole world, as a *testimony* [or *witness*] to all nations." Matthew 24:14.

The Old Testament contains the witness of the prophets. The New Testament contains the witness of the early preachers of the gospel. When Jesus said that the Old Testament scriptures bore witness of Him, the New Testament hadn't been written yet. By the time John was recording Revelation 11, however, the New Testament was nearly complete. Thus by John's time, New Testament scriptures as well as Old Testament scriptures were ready to bear witness to Christ during the upcoming 1260 years. See also our discussion on pages 78, 79.

John says that the two witnesses were **"olive trees"** and **"lampstands."** In ancient times olive oil was the primary fuel for lamps. "Thy *word is a lamp* to my feet and a light to my path," says Psalm 119:105, using the olive-oil lamp as a symbol of the Bible. "The unfolding of *thy words* gives *light*; it imparts understanding," says Psalm 119:130. The two witnesses whom John saw were called olive trees and lampstands because the Old and New Testaments are our main sources of spiritual light.

Viewed like this, Moses and Elijah—yes, and all the other Old Testament prophets—are included in the first of the two witnesses. Included in the second witness are the writers of the New Testament. We conclude that the **"two witnesses"** are the Old and New Testaments or, taken together, are what we today call the Bible.

How, then, can we say that the Old and New Testaments have had power to send plagues? An answer is found in Revelation 22:18, which warns that "if any one adds [to the prophecies of the book of Revelation], God will add to him the *plagues* described in this book."

The meaning, simply, is that if we distort or oppose God's messages of love in the book of Revelation, sent to the world by the Lamb who died that we might live, we forfeit the special protection which obedience and faith are intended to provide. As a result of our disrespect for the Word of God, plagues may fall on us as surely as on the most obstinate heathen, whoever that unfortunate person may happen to be. We have seen in our study of Revelation 8 and 9 how the judgments of the seven trumpets have indeed fallen on both Jewish, Christian, and Moslem people when they disregarded the true meaning of the Word.

During the 1260 years, communities of people who disparaged Bible light and distorted Bible truth sometimes suffered seriously. We observed when studying "Thyatira," how western Europe was "cast into a bed of sickness," experiencing recurrent dreadful epidemics of the Plague, or Black Death. And speaking of famine: Taking the seventy-eight years between 970 and 1048 as an

Famines, like other disasters, will afflict the world till Jesus comes.   UPI

example, we learn that an incredible and tragic forty-eight of those years were famine years.[56] Imagine the human suffering.

Slighting the gracious white-horse rider offered in the Bible, the Christian world had no choice but to be confronted by the three terrifying horsemen of war, famine, and epidemic. See pages 179-186. Societies which ignored the early trumpets underwent the "woes" of the later ones. In this sense, the two witnesses (or the Bible) sent out their plagues.

2. What is the "great city"? Revelation 11:7, 8 says, **"And when they** [the two witnesses] **have finished their testimony,"** that is, when they have finished prophesying clothed in sackcloth during the 1260 years, **"the beast that ascends from the bottomless pit will make war upon them and conquer them and kill them, and their dead bodies will lie in the street of the great city which is allegorically called Sodom and Egypt, where their Lord was crucified."**

We must identify the **"great city."** Some readers equate it with the **"holy city"** of verse 2 and conclude that it is the literal city of Jerusalem, where Jesus was literally crucified. Revelation 21:2, however, identifies the **"holy city"** with New Jerusalem, not with the old city of Jerusalem. Says John, "I saw the *holy city,* new Jerusalem, coming down out of heaven from God, prepared as a bride adorned for her husband."

Many things in Revelation come in pairs of opposites. For instance, there are two insignia, the "seal of God" and the "mark of the beast." There are two resurrections, the first for the "blessed and holy," the second for everyone else. There are two mothers, one pure clothed in white, the other a harlot draped in red. Among still other pairs, there are two cities, the holy city and the great city.

As we have just seen, the holy city is New Jerusalem. The other city, the great city, is Babylon. "Alas! alas! thou *great city,* thou mighty city, Babylon!" Revelation 18:10. See also 18:2, 16, etc.

We all know that a literal city of Babylon flourished back in Daniel's day. By John's time it was a ghost town, and it has never been an inhabited city since. Thus the "Babylon" of Revelation cannot be a literal city. It is a symbol of the vast community of people who, *like* Babylon of old, were to blaspheme God and persecute the true saints.

There is a literal New Jerusalem, just as once there was a literal Babylon. Unlike literal Babylon, New Jerusalem exists at this very hour in heaven. According to Revelation 21:1-4, it will one day exist literally on the earth. But like Babylon, New Jerusalem also symbolizes something. It is called the Lamb's "bride," who has "made herself ready" and is "clothed" with the "righteous deeds of the saints." Revelation 19:7, 8. Like Babylon, it is a symbol of a vast community, but not of the wicked! New Jerusalem is the community of the righteous, the true church, the "host" of Daniel 8:13, 14, which is "trampled" on by the citizens of the great city, Babylon.

But the great city is described in Revelation 11:8 as the place **"where their Lord was crucified."** As we mentioned a moment ago, this is what has led some readers to assume that it is old literal Jerusalem. But the same place is **"allegorically called Sodom and Egypt."** *Sodom* stood for vice and luxury. See Genesis 19:4-8 and Ezekiel 16:49, 50, 56-58. It fittingly represented the exorbitant luxury and vice of European nobility and royalty and the orgy of immorality associated with the French Revolution. (Paris was wide open, and at least one eighth of all marriageable women may be estimated to have practiced prostitution.) The pharaoh of *Egypt* in Moses' time enslaved the Israelites and scoffed, "I do not know the Lord, and moreover I will not let Israel go." Exodus 5:2. Egypt symbolized the bold skepticism of the *philosophes* and the blatant de-Christianization of the Revolution.

Hebrews 6:4, 5 settles the matter! It shows that Jesus has been crucified *wherever His people have apostatized seriously from Bible truth.* "It is impossible to restore again to repentance those who have once been enlightened, who have tasted the heavenly gift, and have become partakers of the Holy Spirit, and have tasted the goodness of the word of God and the powers of the age to come, if they then *commit apostasy,* since they *crucify the Son of God* on their own account and hold him up to contempt."

The holy city was trampled on during the entire 1260 days. The two witnesses during the same time prophesied in sadness and sackcloth. But at the end of the period the French Revolution uniquely fulfilled this reference to crucifying Jesus.

The epicenter of the **"earthquake"** was located in a **"tenth part"** of the city and was observed at the close of the 1260 years, in the 1790s.

France was the oldest Christian nation in western Europe. It was this oldest of western Christian nations that so passionately apostatized and which so grotesquely overthrew its Christianity during the French Revolution. In this undeniably biblical sense, France cruelly crucified Christ.

But inasmuch as the earthquake occurred in only a **"tenth"** of the great city, we perceive that the great city as a whole is much larger than France. The great city is the whole community, that is, it is western European Christendom. This point may come clearer as we look at the answer to the next question.

3. Who are the "nations" in the "court outside"? Revelation 11:2 speaks of the **"nations"** who occupy the **"court outside the temple."** First off we ought to know that the word translated **"nations"** is the same word translated over ninety times in the New Testament as "Gentiles." (See our discussion of Matthew 24:14 on pages 44-46.) The venerable King James Version and such modern ones as the New English Bible and the New International Version do, in fact, use the word *Gentiles* in translating this present passage.

The translation "Gentiles" helps immediately when we learn that in New Testament times the great temple in Jerusalem included inner courts, where

303

only Jews could worship, and a large *outer court,* for devout *Gentiles* who desired to worship God. (The low wall separating the Gentile court from the Jewish courts is referred to symbolically in Ephesians 2:14.)

Now, in Revelation 11 the Gentiles who come to worship in the outer court **"trample"** for 1260 years on the **"holy city,"** which we have come to see, above, represents the community of righteous people. At once we are reminded of the little horn of Daniel 7, which was to persecute the saints during the same period, and of the little horn of Daniel 8, which "trampled" on the "host." These little horns, as we found in GC 1:122-135, 158-161, principally represent the bad side of Christianity during the Middle Ages and later. Inasmuch as the "Gentiles" (or **"nations"**) in Revelation 11 are in the outer court, we know they are worshipers of God. This encourages our interpretation that they represent a kind of Christian.

The Gentiles, or nations, then, are the same as the citizens of the great city, who crucify Christ by apostatizing from genuine worship. Thus we find symbolized the opposition of the great city against the holy city. We also find a distinction between the true worshipers who are in the inner court, and the others who worship in the outer court. John is told to **"measure"** the inner worshipers, along with the temple itself and its altar. But he is told to **"leave out"** the other worshipers. The underlying Greek word actually suggests a stronger translation, "throw out," or "discard." A judgment is involved, separating true Christians from people who merely profess to be Christians. We'll have more to say about this judgment when we discuss the first angel's message in Revelation 14:6, 7.

In the meantime we conclude that the **"nations"** or "Gentiles" of Revelation 11:2 are Christians who do not live up to their profession and who harass other Christians who do.

4. Did the Angel say, "No more time" or "No more delay"? The earliest English translation of the New Testament (Wycliffe, 1382) in my copy of *The English Hexapla*[57] has in Revelation 10:6, "tyme schal no more be." Tyndale's translation (1525) in the same compilation has, "there shulde be no lenger tyme." Other early Protestant and Catholic versions are similar. The Authorized or King James Version (1611) has "there should be time no longer."

But in the nineteenth century, private translators like Alexander Campbell (1826) and George R. Noyes (1869) used the word *delay* instead of *time,* and the (English) Revised Version (1881) honored *delay* by placing it in the margin. The American Standard Version (1901) placed *delay* right into the text. And this is where it has remained for most translators since then, though some have used *waiting,* which conveys about the same idea.[58]

The key Greek word involved is *chronos.* It is familiar to us in such words as *chronology* and *chronometer.* Chronology is the study of time itself and also of events with respect to the time when they occurred. A chronometer measures time with unusual precision. *Chronos* is translated "time" in some thirty places in the New Testament, as in Matthew 2:7, "what *time* the star appeared," and Luke 1:57, "the *time* came for Elizabeth to be delivered." *Chronos* is rendered "delay" only once, in the passage that we're looking at.

The great lexicon of ancient Greek edited by Liddell and Scott provides numerous examples of *chronos* as meaning "time" in ancient Greek writings. It provides almost no space at all to the possible interpretive meaning "delay" in ancient documents. The great lexicon of patristic Greek edited by G. W. H. Lampe provides numerous examples of *chronos* as meaning "time" in the writings of early Christians, but it provides no examples at all of its use meaning "delay."

The Greek clause in question is *hoti chronos ouketi estai,* which translated in the most literal fashion reads, "that time no longer will be." New Testament Greek, like modern English, had an *unambiguous* way of speaking about experiencing a delay. To do so, it used the related but clearly distinct verb *chronizo,* as in Matthew 24:48, "My master *is delayed."* This word is *not* used in Revelation 10:6.

The plainest meaning of *chronos* in Revelation 10:6 is simply "time." The translation **"no more delay"** obscures the direct linkage that exists between Revelation 10 and the book of Daniel. In Daniel 12 the "man" swore that the book would be closed until the *time* of the end, that is, until the time when the 1260 days and the 2300 days would come to an end. In Revelation 10 the "angel" holds the book open and swears that *time*—that is, prophetic time— has come to an end.

We conclude that what the Angel said is best translated directly from the underlying Greek and should be rendered, "There shall be no more time," meaning that the prophetic time of the 1260 days and 2300 days was coming to an end.

References

1. Julius Africanus, *Chronography,* fragment 16; ANF 6:134, 135. See also LeRoy Edwin Froom, *The Prophetic Faith of Our Fathers*, 4 vols. (Washington, D.C.: Review and Herald Publishing Association, 1946-1954), 1:279-281. Though nearly right, Africanus mistakenly commenced the period with Artaxerxes' memo in Nehemiah 2 (444 B.C.) rather than with Artaxerxes' decree in Ezra 7 (457 B.C.).

2. See Froom, *Prophetic Faith,* 1:683-716.

3. *Ibid.,* 2:277 and 1:528. Sometimes Luther also applied the 1260 days to the Turk as being a kind of co-antichrist.

4. Froom, *Prophetic Faith,* 3:33-42, 125-134, 181-185. Parentheses indicate when each writer's contribution first appeared in print.

5. See Froom, *Prophetic Faith,* vols. 2 and 3. Also see C. Mervyn Maxwell, "An Exegetical and Historical Examination of the Beginning and Ending of the 1260 Days of Prophecy with Special Attention Given to A.D. 538 and 1798 as Initial and Terminal Dates" (M.A. thesis, Andrews University, 1951), appendix VI.

305

6. Froom, *Prophetic Faith,* 2:194-196.

7. *Ibid.,* 1:743-751.

8. *Ibid.,* 2:713-719. Petri ended the 2300 days 1847 years after the birth of Jesus, but he knew there was a question as to the precise year when Jesus was born.

9. *Ibid.,* pp. 719-722. His dates were 420 B.C. to A.D. 1880.

10. *Ibid.,* 3:404-408.

11. Ernest R. Sandeen, *The Roots of Fundamentalism: British and American Millenarianism, 1800-1930* (reprint, Grand Rapids, Mich.: Baker Book House, 1978), p. 22n.

12. Ellen G. White, *Testimonies for the Church,* 9 vols. (Mountain View, Calif.: Pacific Press Publishing Association, 1885-1909, 1948), 1:54.

13. William H. McNeill, *The Rise of the West* (Chicago: The University of Chicago Press, 1963), pp. 730-762.

14. *Ibid.,* p. 730.

15. Kenneth Scott Latourette, *A History of Christianity* (New York: Harper & Brothers, Publishers, 1953), p. 1061.

16. For an excellent discussion of modern nationalism and its relation to the French Revolution, see, e.g., Steward C. Easton, *The Western Heritage from the Earliest Times to the Present* (New York: Holt, Rinehart and Winston, 1961), ch. 17.

17. R. R. Palmer, *The Age of the Democratic Revolution,* 2 vols.; vol. 1, *The Challenge* (Princeton: Princeton University Press, 1959), pp. 13-20, esp. p. 7.

18. *Ibid.,* p. 19, citing the Polish revolutionary, Kollontay, in a book written after the failure of Thaddeus Kosciusko's uprising in the mid 1790s.

19. Douglas Johnson, *The French Revolution* (New York: G. P. Putnam's Sons, 1970), p. 74. Apparently Dr. Guillotine had in mind the device's speed and relative painlessness.

20. See M. A. Thiers, *The History of the French Revolution,* trans. from the last Paris ed., with notes (London: William P. Nimmo, 1877), pp. 447-453. Compare Durand de Maillane, *Histoire de la Convention nationale* (Paris, 1825), pp. 191-196, trans. in E. L. Higgins, *The French Revolution As Told by Contemporaries* (Boston: Houghton Mifflin Company, 1938), pp. 349, 350.

21. General Sir James Marshall-Cornwall, *Napoleon as Military Commander* (London: B. T. Batsford Ltd.; Princeton, N.J.: D. Van Nostrand Company, 1967), chs. 25, 26.

22. Samuel Eliot Morison, *The Oxford History of the American People* (New York: Oxford University Press, 1965), pp. 264, 265.

23. Easton, *Western Heritage,* pp. 505, 506.

24. Palmer, *Revolution,* pp. 11, 12.

25. *Ibid.* Palmer, however, separates himself from those who emphasize mainly the dependence of the Russian on the French Revolution.

26. V. H. H. Green, foreword, in John McManners, *The French Revolution and the Church,* ed. V. H. H. Green, Church History Outlines, no. 4 (London: S. P. C. K., 1969).

27. Williston Walker, rev. Cyril C. Richardson, Wilhelm Pauck, Robert T. Handy, *A History of the Christian Church* (New York: Charles Scribner's Sons, 1959), pp. 384, 385.

28. See, e.g., Philippe Erlanger, *St. Bartholomew's Night: The Massacre of Saint Bartholomew,* trans. from the French by Patrick O'Brian, Pantheon Books (New York: Random House, Inc., 1962), esp. pp. 123-133, 148, 166, 199. Erlanger argues that some Huguenots had unwisely engaged in various political activities and were not wholly blameless. Cf. *Blackwood's Magazine,* January 1836, pp. 21, 22. The Pope's joy is said to have cooled somewhat on receipt of later information; but he did not rescind his requests for either the medal or the frescoes, and these items are still on display in Rome.

29. John Bartlett, *Familiar Quotations,* 13th ed. (Boston: Little, Brown and Company, 1955), p. 115, which attributes the statement to either Henry IV or to his minister Sully in conversation with the king.

30. Walker, *History,* pp. 388, 389; Philip Schaff, *The Progress of Religious Freedom as Shown in the History of Toleration Acts,* reprinted from the papers of "The American Society of Church History," vol. 1 (New York: Charles Scribner's Sons, 1889) pp. 30-40.

31. See, e.g., Easton, *Heritage,* pp. 487, 488.

32. Graham Gargett, *Voltaire and Protestantism,* ed. Haydn Mason, Studies on Voltaire and the Eighteenth Century, no. 188 (Oxford: The Voltaire Foundation, 1980), pp. 457, 463, 464.

33. Thomas Paine, *The Age of Reason,* in Philip S. Foner, ed., *The Complete Writings of Thomas Paine,* 2 vols. (New York: The Citadel Press, 1969), 1:474.

34. McManners, *French Revolution,* pp. 98-105.

35. Thiers, *French Revolution,* pp. 372, 373.

36. McManners, *French Revolution,* p. 92.

37. *Ibid.,* pp. 86-97.

38. Thiers, *French Revolution,* p. 373.

39. Aimé Guillon, *Mémoires pour servir à l'histoire de la ville de Lyon pendant la Révolution,* 3 vols. (Paris, 1824), pp. 347, 348, in Higgins, ed., *French Revolution,* p. 330.

40. Thiers, *French Revolution,* p. 374.

41. George Rudé, *The Crowd in the French Revolution* (Oxford: Clarendon Press, 1959), p. 11.

42. Thiers, *French Revolution,* p. 374.

43. *Ibid.,* pp. 426, 427.

44. Green, foreword, in McManners, *French Revolution.* Emphasis supplied.

45. McManners, *French Revolution,* pp. 106-108.

46. Schaff, *Progress,* p. 44. Punctuation slightly adapted.

47. For a good brief overview see Skevington Wood, "Awakening," in *Eerdman's Handbook to the History of Christianity,* eds. Tim Dowley, et al., 1st American ed. (Grand Rapids, Mich.: Wm. B. Eerdman's Publishing Co., 1977), pp. 434-455.

48. Latourette, *History,* p. 1027, gives the British Methodist membership as 71,668 in 1790.

49. See, e.g., Edwin Scott Gaustad, *Historical Atlas of Religion in America* (New York: Harper & Row, Publishers, 1962), p. 81.

50. Latourette, *History,* p. 1034.

51. *Ibid.,* p. 1078. Punctuation slightly adapted.

52. Antonia Tripolitis, review of *Soviet Believers: The Religious Sector of the Population,* by William C. Fletcher, in *Church History* 52 (June 1983):252, 253, which gives 115,000,000 Christians (in a population of 273,000,000). Paul D. Steeves, review of *Soviet Evangelicals Since World War II,* by Walter Sawatsky, in *Journal of Church and State* 25 (Winter 1983):155-157, says "responsible estimates" put the ratio of Christians to the total population at somewhere between 20 and 45 percent.

53. Oral communication from a Chinese Christian who had been for many years imprisoned and set at hard labor for his faith, August 1983.

54. Article, "Bible Societies," *New Schaff-Herzog Encyclopedia of Religious Knowledge,* 2:88, 89.

55. United Bible Society statistics for "the early 1980s" apply to 1983. These figures and the others applying alone to the American Bible Society were obtained by phone from the American Bible Society, 1865 Broadway, New York, NY 10023.

56. Franklin H. Littell, *The Macmillan Atlas History of Christianity* (New York: Macmillan Publishing Co., 1976), p. 34.

57. *The English Hexapla* (London: Samuel Bagster and Sons, 1841).

58. Edgar J. Goodspeed, *Problems of New Testament Translation* (Chicago: University of Chicago Press, 1945), pp. 200, 201.

Revelation 11:19 to 14:20

The True Mother and Her Children

Introduction

"We raise our children in a Christian home. Why is it, then, that when they go to high school, they have such a terrible time fighting temptation?"

The question was asked in a Bible-study group a couple of weekends ago.

The conversation had come around to a typical experience of Christians in the secular world. The father who asked the question is a well-known professional in our town.

Revelation 11:19 to 14:20 helps provide an answer. It does so in the setting of a family.

Revelation 12 begins with a symbolic ideal mother projected onto the TV screen of the sky. Sun, moon, and stars add to her beauty. She is pregnant and eager for her baby to arrive. But even in a situation like this, Satan is present, shaped like a dragon, ready to grab the baby the minute it appears.

Miraculously, the baby is rescued and carried away to God's throne. The dragon then attacks the mother. And when the mother is miraculously protected, the dragon goes after her other children. Having lost mother and baby, he doesn't want the other children to get away.

Everyone knows the old-fashioned story about the plantation owner who often hunted ducks. "Sam," he said one day to his pious servant, "you're a wonderful Christian, but you're always telling me about the problems you have with the devil. I don't make any claim to being a Christian, yet the devil never gives *me* any trouble. How do you explain the difference?"

"Master," the servant responded humbly, "when you go hunting, which ducks do you send me after first? Do you send me to get the ones you've killed or the wounded ones that might still get away?"

The master got the point. Our present division of Revelation makes the same point. The children of the true mother have been brought up to "keep the commandments of God" and to cherish the "testimony of Jesus." Revelation 12:17, K.J.V. No wonder they are the special objects of Satan's attacks. They're alive! They might still get away from him! Sometimes it appears that the mother's efforts to bring them up are all in vain, for the enemy makes **"war"** with her children and seems to **"conquer them."** Revelation 13:7.

But the mother's efforts are emphatically not in vain. At the beginning of chapter 14 we're shown the happy ending. There they are, her victorious children, singing God's praise in glory with the Lamb on Mount Zion.

309

John's vision of the true mother and the dragon that attacked her child goes a long way to explain the problem of sin in the world.

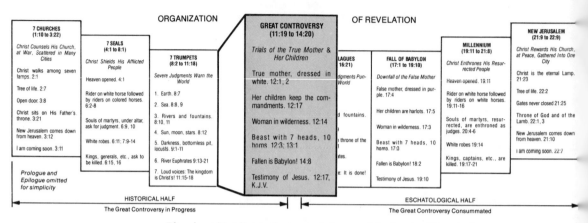

The chart highlights the central theme of the book of Revelation.

Revelation 14:1-5. The mother triumphs with them. Compare 19:7-9.

The great controversy between Christ and Satan. But Revelation 12-14 (as we'll call our present division, even though it really starts with the last verse of chapter 11) doesn't only explain our children's problems and reveal a happy future. These chapters also take us behind the scenes, unveiling the great controversy which has been going on between Christ and Satan for thousands of years—and which will soon be ended.

In the telling of the story of this great controversy, there is clear progression in the narrative overall. The story line, however, doesn't advance evenly from the beginning of chapter 12 to the end of chapter 14. Instead, there's a kind of living kaleidoscope or animated montage that carries us suddenly forward and backward in order to bring about the desired impression. Reading Revelation 12-14 is something like watching a movie of Abraham Lincoln that unexpectedly shows a shot of the White House (Lincoln's successful future) while doing Lincoln's boyhood in his log cabin, or that inserts a flash of his assassination into the middle of the Gettysburg Address.

THE GREAT CONTROVERSY: Trials of the True Mother and Her Children

1. Introductory sanctuary scene: The inner temple opened, the ark revealed. 11:19
2. First six great-controversy scenes. 12:1 to 13:18
3. Scenes of end-time assignment and assurance. 14:1-12
   a. Assurance: 144,000 on the sea of glass (fulfilled in heaven).
   b. Assignment: Three angels proclaiming messages (fulfilled on earth).
4. Consummation: Seventh scene, reaping earth's double harvest. 14:13-20

As we study chapters 12-14 we must be on the lookout for these abrupt transitions of thought.

Similarities to Daniel. As we proceed through this present division, we're going to be especially glad for our earlier study of Daniel. Already in Revelation we have been glad for Daniel. When studying "Thyatira" in Revelation 2:18-29, the angel with the little scroll in 10:1-7, and the 1260 days in 11:1-3, our acquaintance with similar material in Daniel helped us understand the new information.

The relationship between Daniel and Revelation is even more pronounced in chapters 12-14.

Organization charts. Please glance at the organization charts on the preceding page. When we examined the seven trumpets, we mentioned that they were paralleled in certain ways by the seven last plagues. Our present division (chapters 12-14) about the triumph of the true mother also has its parallel division (chapters 17 and 18), the downfall of the false mother. We'll observe numerous similarities and contrasts as we come to them.

Just before the seventh seal and just before the seventh trumpet we found interludes that we called scenes of end-time assignment and assurance.

We find a similar two-scene interlude in our present division, containing a scene of assurance (about the 144,000) and a scene of assignment (the three angels giving their messages).

That in Revelation there are *seven* churches and seven seals and seven trumpets and seven plagues is obvious. That there are seven songs sung about the fall of the false mother (18:1 to 19:10) is fairly obvious. Did John also have in mind seven separate scenes in his account of the true mother and the great controversy? He doesn't say so; but assuming that he may have, we have printed chapters 11:19 to 14:20 so as to show seven scenes, interrupted by two end-time scenes and introduced with a sanctuary scene.

Please read the chapters as they're printed on the next three pages and see whether the suggested headings help.

REVELATION 11:19 TO 14:20

INTRODUCTORY SANCTUARY
SCENE:
THE INNER TEMPLE OPENED, THE
ARK REVEALED

REVELATION 11:19

19 Then God's temple in heaven was opened, and the ark of his covenant was seen within his temple; and there were flashes of lightning, voices, peals of thunder, an earthquake, and heavy hail.

FIRST SIX GREAT-CONTROVERSY
SCENES

REVELATION 12

The first scene: The woman, her male child, and the red dragon introduced. 1 And a great portent appeared in heaven, a woman clothed with the sun, with the moon under her feet, and on her head a crown of twelve stars; [2]she was with child and she cried out in her pangs of birth, in anguish for delivery. [3]And another portent appeared in heaven; behold, a great red dragon, with seven heads and ten horns, and seven diadems upon his heads. [4]His tail swept down a third of the stars of heaven, and cast them to the earth. And the dragon stood before the woman who was about to bear a child, that he might devour her child when she brought it forth; [5]she brought forth a male child, one who is to rule all the nations with a rod of iron, but her child was caught up to God and to his throne, [6]and the woman fled into the wilderness, where she has a place prepared by God, in which to be nourished for one thousand two hundred and sixty days.

The second scene: The dragon makes war with Michael and His angels. 7 Now war arose in heaven, Michael and his angels fighting against the dragon; and the dragon and his angels fought, [8]but they were defeated and there was no longer any place for them in heaven. [9]And the great dragon was thrown down, that ancient serpent, who is called the Devil and Satan, the deceiver of the whole world—he was thrown down to the earth, and his angels were thrown down with him. [10]And I heard a loud voice in heaven, saying, "Now the salvation and the power and the kingdom of our God and the authority of his Christ have come, for the accuser of our brethren has been thrown down, who accuses them day and night before our God. [11]And they have conquered him by the blood of the Lamb and by the word of their testimony, for they loved not their lives even unto death. [12]Rejoice then, O heaven and you that dwell therein! But woe to you, O earth and sea, for the devil has come down to you in great wrath, because he knows that his time is short!"

The third scene: The dragon opposes the woman. 13 And when the dragon saw that he had been thrown down to the earth, he pursued the woman who had borne the male child. [14]But the woman was given the two wings of the great eagle that she might fly from the serpent into the wilderness, to the place where she is to be nourished for a time, and times, and half a time. [15]The serpent poured water like a river out of his mouth after the woman, to sweep her away with the flood. [16]But the earth came to the help of the woman, and the earth opened its mouth and swallowed the river which the dragon had poured from his mouth. [17]Then the dragon was angry with the woman, and went off to make war on the rest of her offspring, on those who keep the commandments of God and bear testimony to Jesus. And he stood on the sand of the sea.

REVELATION 13

The fourth scene: The leopard-bodied sea beast introduced. 1 And I saw a beast rising out of the sea, with ten horns and seven heads, with ten diadems upon its horns and a blasphemous name upon its heads. [2]And the beast that I saw was like a leopard, its feet were like a bear's, and its mouth was like a lion's mouth. And to it the dragon gave his power and his throne and great authority. [3]One of its heads seemed to have a mortal wound, but its mortal wound was healed, and the whole earth followed the beast with wonder. [4]Men worshiped the dragon, for he had given his authority to the beast, and they worshiped the beast, saying, "Who is like the beast, and who can fight against it?"

The fifth scene: The leopard-bodied beast blasphemes and persecutes. 5 And the beast was given a mouth uttering haughty and blasphemous words, and it was allowed to exercise authority for forty-two months; [6]it opened its mouth to utter blasphemies against God, blaspheming his name and his dwelling, that is, those who dwell in heaven. [7]Also it was allowed to make war on the saints and to conquer them. And authority was given it over every tribe and people and tongue and nation, [8]and all who dwell on earth will worship it, every one whose name has not been written before the foundation of the world in the book of life of the Lamb that was slain. [9]If any one has an ear, let him hear:

[10]If any one is to be taken captive,
    to captivity he goes;
if any one slays with the sword,
    with the sword must he be slain.

Here is a call for the endurance and faith of the saints.

The sixth scene: The lamb-horned beast aids the leopard beast. 11 Then I saw another beast which rose out of the earth; it had two horns like a lamb and it spoke like a dragon. [12]It exercises all the authority of the first beast in its presence, and makes the earth and its inhabitants worship the first beast, whose mortal wound was healed. [13]It works great signs, even making fire come down from heaven to earth in the sight of men; [14]and by the signs which it is allowed to work in the presence of the beast, it deceives those who dwell on earth, bidding them make an image for the beast which was wounded by the sword and yet lived; [15]and it was allowed to give breath to the image of the beast so that the image of the beast should even speak, and to cause those who would not worship the image of the beast to be slain. [16]Also it causes all, both small and great, both rich and poor, both free and slave, to be marked on the right hand or the forehead, [17]so that no one can buy or sell unless he has the mark, that is, the name of the beast or the number of its name. [18]This calls for wisdom: let him who has understanding reckon the number of the beast, for it is a human number, its number is six hundred and sixty-six.

INTERLUDE: SCENES OF END-TIME ASSIGNMENT AND ASSURANCE

REVELATION 14

Assurance: The 144,000 will sing on Mount Zion. 1 Then I looked, and lo, on Mount Zion stood the Lamb, and with him a hundred and forty-four thousand who had his name and his Father's name written on their foreheads. [2]And I heard a voice from heaven like the sound of many waters and like the sound of loud thunder; the voice I heard was like the sound of harpers playing on their harps, [3]and they sing a new song before the throne and before the four living creatures and before the elders. No one could learn that song except the hundred and forty-four thousand who had been redeemed from the earth. [4]It is these who have not defiled themselves with women, for they are chaste; it is these who follow the Lamb wherever he goes; these have been redeemed from mankind as first fruits for God and the Lamb, [5]and in their mouth no lie was found, for they are spotless.

Assignment: Three angels proclaim their messages. 6 Then I saw another angel flying in midheaven, with an eternal gospel to proclaim to those who dwell on earth, to every nation and tribe and tongue and people; [7]and he said with a loud voice, "Fear God and give him glory, for the hour of his judgment has come; and worship him who made heaven and earth, the sea and the fountains of water."

8 Another angel, a second, followed, saying, "Fallen, fallen is Babylon the great, she

who made all nations drink the wine of her impure passion.''

9 And another angel, a third, followed them, saying with a loud voice, "If any one worships the beast and its image, and receives a mark on his forehead or on his hand, [10]he also shall drink the wine of God's wrath, poured unmixed into the cup of his anger, and he shall be tormented with fire and sulphur in the presence of the holy angels and in the presence of the Lamb. [11]And the smoke of their torment goes up for ever and ever; and they have no rest, day or night, these worshipers of the beast and its image, and whoever receives the mark of its name.''

12 Here is a call for the endurance of the saints, those who keep the commandments of God and the faith of Jesus.

13 And I heard a voice from heaven saying, "Write this: Blessed are the dead who die in the Lord henceforth.'' "Blessed indeed,'' says the Spirit, "that they may rest from their labors, for their deeds follow them!''

CONSUMMATION: REAPING EARTH'S DOUBLE HARVEST

The seventh scene: Harvesting the grain and grapes. 14 Then I looked, and lo, a white cloud, and seated on the cloud one like a son of man, with a golden crown on his head, and a sharp sickle in his hand. [15]And another angel came out of the temple, calling with a loud voice to him who sat upon the cloud, "Put in your sickle, and reap, for the hour to reap has come, for the harvest of the earth is fully ripe.'' [16]So he who sat upon the cloud swung his sickle on the earth, and the earth was reaped.

17 And another angel came out of the temple in heaven, and he too had a sharp sickle. [18]Then another angel came out from the altar, the angel who has power over fire, and he called with a loud voice to him who had the sharp sickle, "Put in your sickle, and gather the clusters of the vine of the earth, for its grapes are ripe.'' [19]So the angel swung his sickle on the earth and gathered the vintage of the earth, and threw it into the great wine press of the wrath of God; [20]and the wine press was trodden outside the city, and blood flowed from the wine press, as high as a horse's bridle, for one thousand six hundred stadia.

Eve didn't simply eat some fruit. She opened the way for Satan to continue his war against Christ's people on earth.

The Message of Revelation 11:19 to 14:20

I. The First Family Sets the Stage

The unfamiliar voice seemed to come right out of the tree. It asked, "Did God say, 'You shall not eat of any tree of the garden'?"

Eve, our first human mother, peered into the branches to see who was talking to her—and found a talking snake! Recovering from her surprise, she spoke back to it.

"We may eat of the fruit of the trees of the garden," she replied, "but God said, 'You shall not eat of the fruit of the tree which is in the midst of the garden, neither shall you touch it, lest you die.' "

To Eve's complete astonishment, the serpent contradicted God directly and blatantly. "You will not die," it said. Genesis 3:1-4.

In the next several sections of our study together we're going to be looking carefully at the seven great-controversy scenes dealing with the trials of the true mother and her children. Before we do so, however, it will be very helpful if we first review what the Bible says about Satan's attack on our first human mother and on *her* children.

When the snake—which of course represented Satan—engaged Eve in conversation, it hung from the branches of the very tree whose fruit God had forbidden our first human parents to eat. Eve argued with the reptile momentarily.

Then impulsively she picked some of the forbidden fruit, ate it, and carried some more to her husband Adam and persuaded him to eat it.

Until then, our first parents had been innocent and naked. Now they felt ashamed and uncomfortable in each other's company. The mood had changed.

They wanted to get some clothes on. Fig leaves had to do.

"The eyes of both were opened, and they knew that they were naked; and they sewed fig leaves together and made themselves aprons." Genesis 3:7.

In the evening, God came to visit them. They hid in the bushes. God gently asked them to explain. Adam blamed Eve, and Eve blamed the snake.

Very sadly, God let them know that someday they would indeed have to die, just as He had warned them. Right away, He said, they would have to leave their beautiful garden home. Adam would have to work much harder in the future to get food out of the ground, and Eve would have a lot of pain when her babies came.

But God consoled them. He made clothes for them to replace their drying fig leaves. The clothes were "garments of skins," Genesis 3:21 says, fur coats. In the death of the furry animals that provided these coats we can see a symbol of the death of Jesus, who would one day die to provide us all with robes of His righteousness.

315

The first promise of salvation. God did something else to console our first parents. He gave the serpent a stinging rebuke that put everything that had happened in a wonderful new light.

> I will put enmity between you and the woman,
>   and between your seed and her seed;
> he shall bruise your head,
>   and you shall bruise his heel.
> Genesis 3:15.

When God spoke these mystic words of Genesis 3:15, He meant them to convey a lot more than a simple prediction that from then on people and snakes would fight each other, with people usually winning by hitting the snakes on the head! The voice that had spoken in the snake that day had been Satan's voice. God's promise implied hostility between the woman and Satan, a hatred that God would encourage. It also implied hostility between the seed of the woman and the seed of the snake.

The word *seed* means both "child" and "children." Like its synonym, *offspring*—and like *sheep* and *deer*—it is one of those unusual words that can function as either singular or plural. The underlying Hebrew word, *zera*, also has this characteristic. Its meaning is plural, for example, in Genesis 22:17 but singular in 4:25.

Reference to the serpent's seed meant that Satan would have "children," people who would act and talk like himself. Jesus in John 8:44 referred to people in His day who acted like "your father the devil." But the woman was to have children too, and God promised to assist and encourage every one of them who wanted to resist the children of the evil one.

Jesus as the special Seed of the woman. But though *seed* is plural in the second clause of God's promise in Genesis 3:15, it is singular in the third and fourth clauses, where it is referred to as "he" and "his." The promise of Genesis 3:15 is a sublime prophecy that someday a certain Son, a particular male Child, would arrive and, though terribly bruised in the contest, would conquer the devil at last.

Thus, in a very special sense, this promise of Genesis 3:15 was fulfilled in the life and death of Jesus Christ. Hebrews 2:14 expresses the matter this way, "Since therefore the children [human beings] share in flesh and blood, he [Jesus] himself likewise partook of the same [human] nature, that through death he might destroy him who has the power of death, that is, the devil." Jesus, the Son of God, became a man, born of a woman like any other child, and submitted Himself temporarily to death (He let Satan bruise His heel), so that thereby He could destroy Satan permanently (He would bruise Satan's head).

Just how Christ's death assures us of the ultimate death of Satan we'll discuss in the third section of this chapter, beginning on page 331.

For now, let us paraphrase God's beautiful promise in Genesis 3:15 this way:

I will see to it that the woman hates Satan
   and that her children will resist Satan's children.
One of her sons will hit Satan fatally on the head,
   but Satan will badly bruise Him.

The promise and Eve's own family. When God left Adam and Eve on the evening after they had sinned and He had given them this promise, they must have clung to each other for hours, weeping in the darkness. Again and again their minds must have probed the words of the promise, seeking a fuller understanding of its meaning.

Some time later, Eve gave birth to her first seed, her first child, a baby boy. She called him Cain and no doubt hoped and hoped that he was the "Seed" who would bruise the serpent's head.

As things turned out, however, Eve had other children; and as they grew up, Cain bruised the head of one of *them*. Cain murdered his brother Abel.

"Now Abel was a keeper of sheep, and Cain a tiller of the ground. In the course of time Cain brought to the Lord an offering of the fruit of the ground, and Abel brought of the firstlings of his flock and of their fat portions. And the Lord had regard for Abel and his offering, but for Cain and his offering he had no regard. So Cain was very angry, and . . . rose up against his brother Abel, and killed him. Then the Lord said to Cain, 'Where is Abel your brother?' " Genesis 4:2-9.

Both Cain and Abel had burned a sacrifice in worship to God. Abel was a shep-

Persecution began when Cain saw that God rejected him for worshiping in his own way while accepting his brother, who worshiped as God asked.

herd. He burned one of his lambs. Cain, who preferred to raise fruit and vegetables, burned some of his produce. Cain soon realized that his sacrifice didn't please God. The artist for Today's English Version shows the smoke of Abel's sacrifice being drawn straight up to heaven while the smoke of Cain's sacrifice drifts along the ground. In some such way, Cain learned God's disapproval of his own sacrifice.

"By faith," says Hebrews 11:4, "Abel offered to God a more acceptable sacrifice than Cain, through which he received approval as righteous, God bearing witness by accepting his gifts."

Abel's lamb prefigured the death of the woman's ultimate Seed. His lamb's death represented Christ's death as the Lamb of God, when the serpent would bruise Him. It showed that Abel had faith in the promise of Genesis 3:15. On the other hand, Cain's garden produce showed little spiritual insight into the meaning of Christ's sacrifice or the promise of the coming Seed or the kind of price that the Lamb of God would have to pay. Cain didn't ignore worship. He just wanted to worship in his own way rather than enter deeply into God's thoughts in God's way.

The first family typifies the great controversy. In this tragic family scene we find a model of the great-controversy scenes we are about to examine in Revelation 12-14. The first human family represents the entire human family, and especially the church family. The talking snake reveals Satan's determination to seduce and, if possible, destroy the human race. Eve's sin and her husband's represent how easily husbands and wives can spoil happiness by choosing their own way rather than God's.

In the quarrel between the two young men we can see the era of persecution, when during the 1260 years of Daniel 7:25 and Revelation 12:6 western Christian leaders tortured and executed other Christians.

"It was a strange contradiction," observes a distinguished commentator, "that the first murder came with an act of worship. It was while he was approaching God that Cain knew how much he hated his brother. He felt frustrated because he felt somehow that God's truth ranked Abel higher than himself; and if he knew within himself that this was what he deserved, he struck out all the more blindly and bitterly against the superiority that shamed him."[1]

God's words, "Where is Abel your brother?" (Genesis 4:9), foreshadowed the final judgment, announced by the first angel of Revelation 14, the judgment that commenced in 1844. See pages 349-356. One of the major questions God asks in this first phase of the final judgment is, "How have you treated your brother?" See also Matthew 6:14, 15; 1 John 4:20, 21.

And, as we have seen, the male seed of the woman represents especially Jesus Christ. Bruised by the serpent at the cross, Jesus will one day give Satan the ultimate death blow.

We are ready now to proceed with the seven scenes in the great controversy as portrayed in Revelation 12-14.

II. The Great Controversy Between Christ and Satan

1. The woman, her child, and the dragon introduced. Revelation 12:1-5

"A great portent appeared in heaven, a woman clothed with the sun." "She was with child." "And the dragon stood before the woman . . . , that he might devour her child, . . . but her child was caught up to God and to his throne." Revelation 12:1, 2, 4, 5.

The "woman," the "child," and the "dragon" of Revelation 12 remind us at once about Eve, her promised seed, and the lying serpent. They also remind us of every Christian parent whose children are tempted by Satan. In Genesis 3:15 God promised to help children become hostile to the serpent. The message of Revelation 12-14 provides insights to guide families in raising their children and in making decisions.

Additionally, from another standpoint, the woman of Revelation 12 represents God's people as a whole, all of them as a group. Commentators are virtually agreed on this "corporate" or collective understanding.

In the Old Testament, the people of Israel collectively are several times spoken of as a woman. Sometimes Israel as a whole is compared to an unfaithful wife, whose divine Husband, God, is going to forgive and restore her. See, for example, Hosea 2:19, 20; Isaiah 54:1-8. At other times Israel is compared to a beautiful young woman whom God has outfitted in gorgeous new clothes and chosen to take as His bride. See Ezekiel 16:8-14.

In the New Testament the Christian church as a whole is also spoken of as a bride. See 2 Corinthians 11:2; Ephesians 5:21-23. We should not suppose, however, that there are two brides, an Old Testament bride and a New Testament one. Actually there is only one bride. God has one people, not two. His bride was once a local, single-ethnic group; now it has become a worldwide, all-ethnic group. In God's renewed Israel there is neither "Jew nor Greek . . . neither male nor female." Galatians 3:28; see also GC 1:231-236.

The woman of Revelation 12, like the beautiful young woman of Ezekiel 16 (and like Eve in her God-given fur coat), is outfitted in luxurious apparel. She is "clothed with the sun, with the moon under her feet, and on her head a crown of twelve stars."

Light is the garment of God Himself. See Psalm 104:2. Jesus is the "sun of righteousness." Malachi 4:2. God's people are the "sons of light." Luke 16:8; 1 Thessalonians 5:5-8. Sun, moon, and stars are outstanding symbols of light. Their relationship to the woman of Revelation 12 shows that she is virtuous and good, a faithful wife and a true mother, gloriously garbed in bright righteousness. See Revelation 19:8. As a symbol of the church, she stands in marked contrast to the troubled churches of Pergamum and Thyatira. We may conclude that she represents the church of God at its very best, the ideal true church.

If this is so, and it is, then it follows that her "male child," Jesus Christ, was born to the ideal church. He was given to God's faithful people as a whole.

319

When the prophet Isaiah once had a baby boy, he regarded the child as a symbol of the coming Messiah or Christ. Inspired by the Holy Spirit, Isaiah composed a precious lullaby,

> To *us* a child is born,
>   to *us* a son is given.
>
> Isaiah 9:6; compare 7:14; 8:1-3.

To all of us who believe in this divine Baby, has He been born. And what is His name? "His name will be called 'Wonderful Counselor, Mighty God, Everlasting Father, Prince of Peace.' " Isaiah 9:6. Four names, just like William Arthur Philip Louis, Great Britain's royal son. But what special names Jesus has!

The woman of Revelation 12 was pregnant when John saw her, and was **"in anguish for delivery."** She was very eager for her baby to come. Loyal Christians around the world today are eager for Christ to come the second time. Loyal Israelites in Old Testament days were eager for Him to arrive the first time. Each loyal little girl, we are told, hoped that when she got married, she would become the Messiah's mother. Long centuries passed, and it seemed as though He would never come. But He did. "When the time had fully come, God sent forth his Son, born of woman." Galatians 4:4. He will surely come the second time too.

When we're at our wits' end wondering what to do in raising our families, let us not forget this Child who was born "to us"—and who in a special sense comes to us every day. See page 160. His names are "Wonderful Counselor" and "Everlasting Father." He has had experience helping families for thousands of years. He actually lived in a family once as a human son. He knows by observation and experience how to overcome suffering and temptation. See Hebrews 2:18; 12:3.

The red dragon attacks the Child. And who was it who inflicted suffering and temptation on this wonderful Child Jesus? **"Another portent appeared in heaven,"** says Revelation 12:3, 4; **"behold, a great red dragon,"** who **"stood before the woman . . . that he might devour her child when she brought it forth."** In 12:9 we find that the dragon is the same **"ancient serpent, . . . the Devil and Satan,"** who once sought to destroy Eve.

We're dealing with symbols! In the vision the dragon is seen in heaven—yet Jesus, as we all know, was born on earth. So whom on earth does the dragon symbol stand for? Everyone who has heard the Christmas story knows it was King Herod who sent soldiers to Bethlehem to destroy all the baby boys there, hoping to kill Jesus among them. Herod's soldiers missed the infant Jesus because in a dream God had warned His parents to escape. King Herod was a puppet of the Romans. Everyone knows, too, about Pontius Pilate—another Roman administrator—who nailed Jesus to the cross. It was *Rome* that tried to destroy Jesus. The great red dragon is Satan—and Rome acting on behalf of Satan.

Triumphantly, after Satan and Rome killed our Saviour, Jesus rose from the dead and **"was caught up to God and to his throne"** (verse 5), where He "always

320

lives" as our High Priest "to make intercession" for us (Hebrews 7:25, 26). Compare Hebrews 8:1, 2.

Frustrated in his attempt to kill the Son, the great red dragon now turned his hatred against the Son's mother. But the woman escaped into the **"wilderness,"** to a **"place prepared by God, in which to be nourished for one thousand two hundred and sixty days."** Revelation 12:6. We have heard of the 1260 days before, in Daniel 7:25 and Revelation 11:2, 3. They represent the 1260 years during which Roman Christianity oppressed God's more loyal Christians.

Reference to the **"wilderness"** in verse 6 reminds us of Israel's Old Testament escape from Egypt. After being held in Egyptian slavery for over a century, the Israelites, led by Moses, crossed miraculously through the Red Sea. The water dried up overnight to let them through. Then they camped like nomads for forty years in the Sinai desert. During these years they were nourished physically by manna (Exodus 16) and spiritually by the Ten Commandments (Exodus 20) and the teachings of Moses.

In this first scene of the great-controversy series we have been introduced to the woman (the ideal true church), to her male child (Jesus), and to the great red dragon (actually Satan but here a symbol of the Roman Empire—and also a symbol of the Roman Church insofar as it persecuted Christ's true followers during the 1260 years).

2. The dragon wars with Michael. Revelation 12:7-12

War seems like hell, but warfare actually started in heaven. It began as a conflict between **"the dragon and his angels"** on one side and **"Michael and his angels"** on the other. Michael we identified in GC 1:272-275 as Jesus Christ. (The name "Michael" means, "Who is like God?" Michael is an "Angel" only in the sense of being God's supreme Messenger.) The war that started in heaven was the great controversy between Christ and Satan that is still going on.

The Revised Standard Version's translation, *"Now* **war arose in heaven"** (verse 7), should not mislead us into supposing that the heavenly hostilities commenced at the end of the 1260 years of verse 6, or even at the moment when Jesus was caught up to God's throne in verse 5. In the underlying Greek there is no word for **"now."** The Greek can be translated simply, "And there was war in heaven," without any indication as to precisely when it began. See the New American Standard Bible and the New International Version. The Old Testament shows that the war began a long time ago.

When we first learned about the living creatures who sit on thrones surrounding God's throne, we found that the prophet Ezekiel (who lived around 600 B.C.) indicated that one of the living creatures (Satan, of course) had *already* been expelled from heaven. See Ezekiel 28:12-17 and page 154. But we'll examine the time for the onset of the great controversy in our next section, beginning on page 331.

Heaven's shout of victory. The main point in Revelation 12 is not the time when

321

the warfare began but the fact that the dragon was defeated. The dragon was **"thrown down."** The passage says repeatedly that he was thrown down. **"The great dragon was thrown down. . . . He was thrown down. . . , and his angels were thrown down with him."**

At the report of the dragon's defeat, a great shout went up in heaven.

> **Now the salvation and the power and the kingdom of our God**
> **and the authority of his Christ have come,**
> **for the accuser of our brethren has been thrown down,**
> **who accuses them day and night before our God.**
>
> **And they have conquered him by the blood of the Lamb**
> **and by the word of their testimony,**
> **for they loved not their lives even unto death.**
>
> **Rejoice then, O heaven and you that dwell therein!**
> **But woe to you, O earth and sea,**
> **for the devil has come down to you in great wrath,**
> **because he knows that his time is short!**
> Revelation 12:10-12.

This grand hurrah is located at the very center of Revelation, give or take a verse or two. (You might get your family together and prove this for yourselves!) Isn't the center of the book the right location for it? The accuser of our brethren is thrown down. Christ's authority is established. And even though Satan goes on accusing our brethren **"day and night,"** our brethren—our fellow Christians—are able to overcome him. By what means? By virtue of the blood of the Lamb, the word of their testimony, and their willingness to die rather than disappoint their Saviour. **"They loved not their lives even unto death."**

I once read of a young Christian in the South Sea Islands in the second world war who *for Christ's sake* refused to betray the location of some Allied soldiers. He refused, even though the invaders pulled out his fingernails one at a time. If we can instill faith and courage like this in our young people, they will overcome the dragon, no matter how their friends entice them and their enemies mock them. Christ won't let them down.

We saw in Revelation 4:8 that the four living creatures praise God "day and night." Evidently when Satan was one of them, he did the same. But now Satan accuses people day and night, endlessly looking for weaknesses to complain about. He even accuses **"our brethren,"** the people who are nearest to Jesus. Perhaps you know someone who has made a similar behavioral change after turning away from God.

The devil knows that his time is **"short,"** verse 12 says. But the devil has been tormenting and tempting people for thousands of years. How can his time be short?

"Short" is a relative term. It means very different things when it describes a short man and when it describes a short distance between two cities or between two heavenly galaxies! Satan was originally offered the privilege of living for eternity. By contrast, the few thousand years now granted him on earth are short indeed.

And that's the point. His time to tempt is not forever. It will end. We should remember this when trials seem never to end. In Christ, we too are offered endless life. Our longest trial in this life on earth is short compared with eternity.

This second scene, then, tells about the existence of the great controversy between Christ and Satan, Satan's decisive defeat, the "short" period that is left Satan to deceive people in, and the way "our brethren" overcome.

3. The dragon wars with the woman and with her "remnant" children. Revelation 12:13-17

The great controversy scenes flash back and forth. We were told in the introductory first scene that the great red dragon would persecute the woman for 1260 years. Now the 1260 years appear again in greater detail. In this scene they are designated **"a time, and times, and half a time."** See below. During these long painful years **"the serpent poured water like a river out of his mouth after the woman, to sweep her away with the flood. But the earth . . . opened its mouth and swallowed the river."**

Because waters in Daniel and Revelation sometimes symbolize "peoples and multitudes and nations and tongues" (as in Revelation 17:15), some commentators see in the **"water"** from the dragon's mouth a symbol of the armies that at times were commissioned by Christian Rome for the purpose of persecution. In this interpretation, the **"earth"** that opened its **"mouth"** and **"swallowed"** the water is seen to represent relatively uninhabited areas to which persecuted Christians fled for safety. (**"Earth"** is the opposite of **"sea."** See page 341.) It is well known that many Christians found relief from persecution by fleeing to the high mountain valleys of the Alps and to the sparsely populated British colonies in North America.

Another interpretation of the serpent's water focuses on the serpent's **"mouth"** as the source out of which the water flows. This view recalls the serpent's deceitful words spoken to Eve in Genesis 3 and sees the water as a stream of deceptive words, a flood of false doctrines, a cataract of lies. In this interpretation, the **"mouth"** of the **"earth"** that swallows the water includes archaeology and geology. Archaeology provides evidence from the earth that helps establish the historical accuracy of the Bible. Geology provides evidence, such as the absence of key fossils, the presence of disconformities, and the intense complexity of even the simplest life forms, that helps expose the bankruptcy of evolutionism.

Viewed as a whole, the symbolic language itself may be regarded as adapted from the story of the great Flood in Genesis 6-9. If God had not protected Noah and his family, the waters of the great Flood would have swept away the woman's seed (in this sense, Eve's descendants, the human race) and would thus have prevented the ultimate arrival of Jesus as the special Seed. But God did protect a human family and thus preserved the entire human family. When the Flood had lasted long enough, its waters were absorbed by "the face of the ground." Genesis 8:13.

In Revelation 12:14 God preserves the woman (now the true church) from being swept away by providing her not with Noah's ark but with **"the two wings of the great eagle."** Once again the language is adapted from the Old Testament. When the Israelites escaped from Egyptian slavery, Moses said that God had carried them on "eagles' wings." Exodus 19:4. God had borne them, he explained, on His "everlasting arms." Deuteronomy 33:27. God's powerful loving arms preserved Noah's family from the great Flood, protected Israel during the Exodus, and guarded the true church during the 1260 years. They protect us—and, I think, hug us—still.

The dragon turns against the "remnant." Frantic with frustration for failing even in 1260 years to destroy the true church, Satan in the end time directs his bitter attack against the **"rest of her offspring"**—or rather, the "remnant of her seed," K.J.V.—which still survives, as Noah and his family survived the great Flood. By destroying this little "remnant of her seed" he hopes even yet to annihilate the true church.

Satan's demonic desperation helps explain why it is that when we raise our children in Christian homes and send them into the world, they have "such a terrible time fighting temptation." See page 309.

And how can we identify the courageous end-time remnant, this gallant band of the woman's noble seed? Verse 17 says they **"keep the commandments of God and bear testimony to Jesus."** Or, as the King James Version has it more nearly in harmony with the underlying Greek, they "keep the commandments of God, and have the testimony of Jesus." See *Your Questions Answered*, pages 403-405.

There is much more to the "remnant" concept than meets the eye. See *Your Questions Answered*, pages 406, 407. For now, we observe that Revelation 12:17, R.S.V. closes by saying that the dragon **"stood on the sand of the sea."**

4. The leopard-bodied sea beast introduced. Revelation 13:1-4

The reason that the dragon **"stood on the sand of the sea"** (Revelation 12:17) appears to be that sand marks the place where earth and sea meet. Of the two beasts that are yet to appear in the seven great-controversy scenes, the first one rises out of the **"sea"** (13:1) and the second one out of the **"earth"** (13:11).

Right away the beast from the sea appeared to John to resemble the great red dragon. Like the dragon it had **"ten horns and seven heads."** But there was a difference. Whereas the dragon had royal crowns, **"diadems,"** on its seven heads, this new beast had diadems on its ten horns.

As the many-headed monster lunged up out of the waves and more of its hulk came into view, John experienced further surprises. He saw that overall the new

The lepoard-bodied beast with ten horns combined many features of beasts Daniel saw. But the new beast John saw, with two horns, was it a bison?

beast looked **"like a leopard."** Its feet, however, looked **"like a bear's,"** and its mouth was **"like a lion's mouth."** Leopard, bear, lion. We have run across this list before. In a vision six centuries earlier, Daniel saw a lion, a bear, a leopard—and a fourth, indescribable animal—emerge out of the sea. Altogether, they had seven heads and ten horns. (The leopard had four heads, the other three had one each, and the fourth beast had ten horns.) See Daniel 7 and GC 1:107-111.

Daniel's lion, bear, and leopard symbolized successively the Babylonian, Persian, and Greek Empires. His fourth beast symbolized Rome—and among its ten horns he saw an eleventh horn sprout up which was at first a "little horn" but which developed into a stout, blasphemous persecuting power. In the fifth great-controversy scene, which we'll be discussing next, we'll see that the behavior of the leopard-bodied beast was the same as the behavior of the little horn.

But before we proceed to that fifth scene, let's make sure we understand that the fourth scene we're looking at now outlines the leopard beast's career in an introductory way, much as the first scene in Revelation 12 outlined the dragon's and the woman's careers from the birth of Christ through the 1260 years.

This fourth scene introduces us to the leopard beast's career by informing us that (1) at the beginning of its career it emerged from the sea, and (2) the **"dragon gave"** to it **"his power and his throne and great authority."** Afterward, as John watched, he saw (3) that one of its heads suffered what to all appearance was a

325

"mortal wound." Amazingly, however, (4) it recovered from its mortal wound and as a result (5) all the world worshiped the leopard-bodied beast and its red-dragon sponsor and asked incredulously, **"Who is like the beast, and who can fight against it?"**

We'll understand this introductory survey as we proceed to look into the details offered in scenes five and six.

5. The leopard-bodied beast wars with the saints. Revelation 13:5-10

Reading over the fifth scene quickly, we find information that is useful for identifying and understanding the leopard-bodied beast. Verse 10, for example, refers to **"captivity"** and to being slain **"with the sword."** Skipping ahead into the sixth scene (Revelation 13:11-18) we read in verse 14 that the mortal wound referred to in verse 3 in the fifth scene was inflicted by a **"sword."** So linking verses 3, 10, and 14 together, we see that the blow that was intended to be fatal was (a) inflicted by a sword—by a military power of some sort—and that it (b) involved a captivity.

In this fifth scene that we're looking at now we notice the term **"forty-two months."** We met it first in Revelation 11:2, where we learned that, of course, it is the same as the 1260 days. See page 270. It is also the same as the **"time, and times, and half a time"** during which the dragon harassed the woman in our third scene above. Revelation 12:14.

As a matter of fact, the 1260 days are mentioned seven times in Daniel and Revelation. There are not (as some have supposed) several 1260-day periods. There is only one. It is mentioned seven times because it is so very important. See the box below.

The leopard-bodied beast **"opened its mouth to utter blasphemies against God,**

THE SEVEN REFERENCES TO THE 1260 DAYS

1. Daniel 7:25,   a time, two times, and half a time
2. Daniel 12:7,   a time, two times, and half a time
3. Revelation 11:2,   forty-two months
4. Revelation 11:3,   one thousand two hundred and sixty days
5. Revelation 12:6,   one thousand two hundred and sixty days
6. Revelation 12:14,   a time, and times, and half a time
7. Revelation 13:5,   forty-two months

One time	equals one year	equals	12 months	equals (12 ×30) 360 days.
Two times	equals two years	equals	24 months	equals (24 ×30) 720 days.
Half a time	equals		6 months	equals (6 ×30) 180 days.
A time, two times, and half a time		equals	42 months	equals (42 ×30) 1260 days.

---

blaspheming his name and his dwelling, that is, those who dwell in heaven. Also it was allowed to make war on the saints and to conquer them."

This summary is almost identical to what we learned about the little horn in Daniel 7. Wrote Daniel, "As I looked, this horn made war with the saints, and prevailed over them." Daniel sought an explanation, and a nearby angel responded that "he shall speak words against the Most High, and shall wear out the saints of the Most High, and shall think to change the times and the law; and they shall be given into his hand for a time, two times, and half a time." Daniel 7:21, 25. Daniel 8:11-14 adds that Rome was to oppose Christ's ministry in His sanctuary (His dwelling place) in heaven.

A chart confirms the comparison.

THE LITTLE HORN Daniel 7 and 8	THE LEOPARD-BODIED BEAST Revelation 13
Speaks great words against God	Utters blasphemies against God
Thinks to change time and law	
Tramples on the sanctuary and the host	Blasphemes God's name, His dwelling, and those who dwell in heaven
Wears out the saints for a time, two times, and half a time	Makes war with the saints for forty-two months

The Catholic church is avowedly Roman. Its official name today, as it has been throughout most of its long history, is The Holy Catholic and Apostolic Church of Rome. In GC 1:128 we heard Professor John L. McKenzie of the University of Notre Dame explain that "Roman Catholics believe that their Romanism is a reflection of the authentic Christianity of their church."[2]

But how did the Catholic church come to possess its unique Romanness?

The dragon gave its power and throne to the church. We read in the introductory fourth scene that the dragon (in this case, the Roman Empire) gave to the leopard-bodied beast (the Roman Church) **"his power and his throne and great authority."** Verse 2.

A throne is a symbol of authority. But because this passage already contains the words **"power"** and **"authority,"** we expect **"throne"** here to convey a more literal meaning. Basically, a throne is a place where an important person sits. Other words for throne are the Greek *cathedra*, and the Latin *sedes* which shows up in English as *see*. In the Catholic church, the *building* in which a bishop's throne (or *cathedra*) is located is called his "cathedral." The *city* in which his throne is located is called his "see." The ultimate see in Catholicism is the Holy See, the city where the Pope's throne is located. This city is *Rome*.*

*Specifically, since the 1929 Treaty of the Lateran with Italy, the Holy See has been Vatican City, a 108.7-acre tract on Vatican Hill, lying wholly within the city of Rome.

And how did the dragon, the Roman Empire, give its power, its authority, and the *place* of its rulership (its **"throne,"** or see, or city) to the Roman Church?

The empire was named for the city of Rome. A proverb claimed that all roads led to Rome. Rome was by far the West's largest city. Revered as the Eternal City, it pulsed with tremendous power and mystery.

Much of this formidable secular prestige was inherited by the Roman pope. Just being the pope of *Rome* gave him enormous influence. In addition, Emperor Constantine contributed hugely to the pope's prestige when in 330 he left Italy and founded Constantinople (now Istanbul) as the empire's new capital. Constantinople was some 1300 kilometers or about 800 miles away to the east, more than a month's marching time for an army. In the often quoted expression of Henry Edward Manning, the exuberant nineteenth-century British cardinal, the abandonment of Rome was the "liberation" of the pontiffs. With the passage of time, Cardinal Manning went on, "the Pontiffs found themselves alone; the sole fountains of order, peace, law, and safety"[3] in western Europe.

Several other emperors besides Constantine also conceded or offered power to the papacy. Step by step, the Roman Empire (the dragon) did indeed give its power, throne, and great authority to the Catholic Church (the leopard-bodied beast). A climax came in 538, when the armies of the Empire drove the Arian Ostrogoths out of Rome, an event described in some detail in GC 1:129, 145-147. By 538, therefore, the 1260 years could begin.

The deadly wound. In 1798, 1260 years later, the pope was taken into captivity and the Catholic Church was dealt a mortal blow. It happened just as Revelation had foretold, with remarkable accuracy.

The papacy had experienced other military defeats and even captivities during its long 1260 years, but this one was unique in two highly significant ways. It came as the climax of several centuries of decline in the influence of Catholicism on the minds of Europeans, and it was not merely a military coup but was a stroke deliberately intended to terminate the papacy forever.

During the French Revolution and under orders from the revolutionary French government, General Alexander Berthier issued a proclamation in Rome on February 15, 1798, informing Pope Pius VI and the people of Rome that the pope should *no longer "exercise any function."*[4]

Richard Duppa, a British writer who was in Rome at the time, says that the pope was arrested in the Sistine Chapel while he was celebrating the twenty-third anniversary of his coronation. Citizen Haller, the French commissary-general, and Cervoni, who commanded the French troops in Rome under General Berthier, "gratified themselves in a peculiar triumph over this unfortunate potentate. During that ceremony they both entered the chapel, and Haller announced to the sovereign Pontiff on his throne that his reign was at an end. The poor old man seemed shocked at the abruptness of this unexpected notice, but soon recovered himself with becoming fortitude." The pope's Swiss guards were dismissed, and Republican soldiers were installed in their place.[5]

In spite of the pope's advanced age and frail health (he was in his 80s), he was hustled off by French soldiers to a string of different addresses in Italy and southern France. He died in prison in the fortress city of Valence on August 29, 1799. For a while his body was left lying around unburied. In the words of George Trevor,

> The Papacy was extinct: not a vestige of its existence remained; and among all the Roman Catholic powers not a finger was stirred in its defense. The Eternal City had no longer prince or pontiff; its bishop was a dying captive in foreign lands; and the decree was already announced that no successor would be allowed in his place.[6]

About a century later, Joseph Rickaby, a Jesuit priest, observed that when, in August 1799 Pope Pius VI passed away as a French prisoner, "half Europe thought . . . that with the Pope the Papacy was dead."[7]

I had occasion once to examine the memoirs of Don Manuel de Godoy, prime minister of Catholic Spain at the time of the pope's captivity. I found no reference to the event. Even this important Catholic statesman didn't care enough about the pope to comment on his troubles.[8]

When, in 1798, General Berthier took the pope prisoner, it was widely believed that the Catholic Church was dead—forever.

The mortal wound healed. But, Revelation 13:3, 4 says, the **"mortal wound was healed, and the whole earth followed the beast with wonder. Men worshiped . . . the beast, saying, 'Who is like the beast, and who can fight against it?' "** We'll understand this part of the prophecy better after we look at the sixth scene.

6. The lamb-horned earth beast compels the world to worship the leopard-bodied beast. Revelation 13:11-18

"The whole earth followed the beast with wonder." Men asked, **"Who can fight against it?"** Revelation 13:3, 4. This prophecy hasn't been fulfilled yet. Even during the Middle Ages, when the Roman Church enjoyed enormous prestige, enemy armies, Christian as well as Moslem, dared to attack it. But there is a universalness in what John describes in Revelation 13:8 that we cannot overlook. **"All who dwell on earth will worship it, *every one* whose name has not been written . . . in the book of life."**

This sixth scene provides the key to the fulfillment of the prophecy, for another wild animal appears, this one rising like a plant out of the earth. Looking at it, John noticed it had only two horns, not ten like the other animals; and they were soft and short, like a lamb's. In Revelation, a lamb usually signifies Christ!

When John saw the Christlike (that is, the lamblike) horns, did he for a moment hope that this new animal would defend the saints and rescue them from the leopard-bodied beast? If he did, he was doomed to disappointment; for the lamb-horned beast soon **"spoke like a dragon."** Verse 11. Despite its friendly appearance, it talked just like Satan—just like the old serpent from the Garden of Eden and the old Roman Empire and the medieval church (looked at from its worst side).

The new beast was a wolf in sheep's clothing. In the Sermon on the Mount Jesus warned His followers to "beware of *false prophets*, who come to you in sheep's clothing but inwardly are ravenous wolves." Matthew 7:15. Three times, in Revelation 16:13; 19:20; and 20:10, the lamb-horned beast is called the "false prophet."

Far from delivering the saints from the leopard-bodied beast, the lamb-horned false prophet in John's vision used its power to cause almost the entire population of the world to **"make an image"** to the leopard-bodied beast and to receive the **"mark"** of that beast in **"forehead"** or **"hand."** John saw some exceptional persons refusing to worship it. These were the **"rest"** of the woman's **"offspring,"** the "remnant of her seed" (K.J.V.), the loyal band who **"keep the commandments of God."** Revelation 12:17. *Their* names were "written in the Lamb's book of life." Revelation 21:27. Threatened with a devastating boycott, forbidden to **"buy or sell,"** they retained their noble integrity and avoided the mark of the beast at the risk of their lives.

Only two sides remained: the loyal "remnant," who kept God's commandments, and all the rest of the world, who had the mark of the beast. We must look into this matter more carefully, beginning on page 377.

Summary so far. In Revelation 12 and 13 we have thus far reviewed several things we first learned when studying Daniel—things especially about the four empires and the 1260 days (or years) of the Roman Church.

We have also learned new things. Whereas Daniel 7:26, 27 told us that after the 1260 days the judgment would sit and take away the power of the Roman Church, Revelation 13 provides the startling *additional* information that before the completion of the judgment the church's deadly wound is to be temporarily healed and everyone whose name is not registered in the book of life will worship it.

Revelation 13 has also shown us that a false prophet, a wolf in sheep's clothing, a lamb-horned but dragon-voiced beast, will act as a special instrument in the end time, persuading the world to worship the beast and to receive its deadly mark.

III. Why Doesn't God Destroy the Devil?

Before we look at the grave question about the mark of the beast and proceed to chapter 14 with its three angels' messages, we owe it to ourselves to try to answer the agonizing question, "Why doesn't God destroy the devil?" Satan, who appears in prophecy as the dragon which manipulated Rome into destroying Christ and persecuting loyal Christians, is the same devil who has been giving the world serious trouble ever since the human race began. Yet on the very day when Satan deceived our first parents, God promised to send a Seed (Jesus) who would "bruise" the serpent's head. See Genesis 3:15.

In fact, Hebrews 2:14, 15 in the New Testament makes it plain that one of Christ's major goals in dying on the cross nearly 2000 years ago was to bring about the destruction of the devil. The passage says that Jesus took our human nature and died for us so that "through death" (that is, by means of His own death on the cross) "he might destroy him who has the power of death, that is, the devil, and deliver all those who through fear of death were subject to life-long bondage."

"If eventually, why not now?" Eve must have asked the anguished question repeatedly, especially after her eldest son Cain killed her other son Abel. Millions of people have been asking the question ever since, whenever they have endured pain and when loved ones have suffered and died. If God is going to destroy the devil someday, why didn't He do it long ago? Why doesn't He do it now?

Revelation 12 helps provide the answer. The great-controversy story in Revelation 12 helps provide the answer. It does so by pointing to such things as the number of persons involved, the evil nature of Satan and the arguments he raises, the loving nature of God, and the cosmic proportions of the whole conflict.

As for the number of persons involved and the conflict's cosmic proportions, Revelation 12:7 says that the dragon, or Satan, has *"angels."* Verse 4 says poetically that **"his tail swept down a third of the** *stars.***"** His stars are his angels. The one-third fraction may be literal or, like the one-third and one-fourth fractions in the seven trumpets, it may not represent a mathematical third of the angels. See page 238.

331

God's remaining loyal angels number "myriads of myriads and thousands of thousands." Revelation 5:11; compare Daniel 7:10. Satan's fraction may well represent a very large number of individuals.

How Satan deceived the angels. We'll return to this large number of individuals in a moment. First we want to know, if we can, just how Satan was able to deceive so many of the angels, intelligent beings that they are.

At one time Satan's name was Lucifer, which means Lightbearer, Day Star, and Son of the Dawn. See Isaiah 14:12, K.J.V. He was one of the glorious "living creatures" stationed beside God's throne. See page 154. He was "blameless," the very "signet of perfection." Ezekiel 28:15, 12. God made Lucifer perfect. Lucifer turned himself into the devil.

Not content to be seated beside God's throne with the other living creatures, Lucifer became ambitious to be seated right on God's throne. That is, he wanted to exercise the same authority as God, or at least the same authority as Michael, the fully divine Son of God. "I will set my throne on high," he said, "I will make myself like the Most High." See Isaiah 14:12-20. But no created being can equal the Creator!

Evidently when God opposed Lucifer's notorious and unreasonable ambition, Lucifer rallied popular support among the angels, persuading a **"third"** of them to follow him. This brings us to the kind of arguments he used.

Lucifer deceives Eve. The arguments that Satan used in heaven can most probably be inferred from the deceitful but persuasive conversation he held with Eve in the Garden of Eden *after* he was expelled from heaven.

Out of the dozens, perhaps hundreds, of fruit trees in the Garden of Eden, God forbade our first parents the use of only one. This slender restriction provided them with an opportunity to develop character and to demonstrate their loyalty. To make the arrangement perfectly clear, God stated plainly, "In the day that you eat of it you shall die." Genesis 2:17.

Speaking through the serpent, Satan blatantly contradicted God by telling Eve, "You will not die." Then he went on to insinuate that God had forbidden the tree because He didn't really love Eve. "God knows," the serpent said, "that when you eat of it your eyes will be opened, and you will be like God, knowing good and evil." Genesis 3:4, 5.

Analyze these arguments. Notice Satan's use of the Big Lie, the super falsehood that convinces by its very daring. The serpent's Big Lie, "You will not die," implied that *God* was a liar! It also implied that God's warning was meaningless. Eve would suffer no harm from disobeying. She *need not* obey God.

The accusation that God didn't want Eve to become "like God, knowing good and evil" implied that God didn't love Eve and that He selfishly kept good things away from her. Satan thus insinuated that for her own good and happiness, Eve ought to eat the forbidden fruit. She *ought not* to obey God.

In denying God's authority and in portraying Him as selfish and a liar, Satan grossly misrepresented God's character. Actually, he attributed to God his own evil character. But he gave the impression that he selflessly sought no advantage for himself, that he was concerned only for Eve and her happiness. No purveyor of patent medicine ever seemed more intent on benefiting his victim.

Lucifer deceives the angels. In some sophisticated form or another, Lucifer must have expressed these same basic arguments to the angels. Cunningly he persuaded them that God doesn't really love the beings He has created. God's laws, Lucifer intimated, are arbitrary, needlessly depriving His created beings of their rights and pleasures. For their own good and happiness, the angels *ought not* to obey God. Furthermore, God's warnings are meaningless; in all eternity no one had ever yet died, and no one, Lucifer implied, ever would. No harm could come from disobeying. The angels *need not* obey God.

Ardently desiring to raise his own political leverage, Lucifer appeared instead to seek only the welfare of the angels. He assured them that created beings (such as himself) know better what is for their own good than the Creator does. God dwells in ineffable glory and infinite comfort. What does He know about His creatures' real needs or about sacrificing Himself to meet these needs? If placed on the throne instead of Michael* the Son, Lucifer insisted, *he*, Lucifer, would do very much better than the Son at looking out for the angels' interests.

Knowing how patiently and graciously God has dealt with us human beings for thousands of years, we can reliably conceive how lovingly and caringly He labored to win back the rebellious angels. No doubt Lucifer himself didn't at first understand his own mutinous attitude. Inexperienced with sin, he could scarcely have foreseen sin's consequences. God earnestly warned him of his danger and patiently answered his questions. What God said later to rebellious Israel He must also have said to rebellious Lucifer, "As I live, says the Lord God, I have no pleasure in the death of the wicked, but that the wicked turn from his way and live; turn back, turn back from your evil ways; for why will you die?" Ezekiel 33:11.

But the time arrived when God could do nothing more to help His rebellious angels. The havoc Lucifer was wreaking in heaven had to stop. **"War arose in heaven, Michael and his angels fighting against the dragon; and the dragon and his angels fought."** Michael and His angels won the battle, and after that **"there was no longer any place"** for the dragon and his angels in heaven. **"The great dragon . . . and his angels were thrown down."** Revelation 12:7-9.

At Lucifer's defeat a shout of victory went up. See page 322.

The accuser of our brethren has been thrown down.

Rejoice then, O heaven and you that dwell therein!
Revelation 12:10, 12.

* We remind ourselves again that when calling Jesus by the name of "Michael the archangel," the Bible no more makes Him a mere angel than it makes Him an animal when it calls Him a "lamb." For the meaning of Michael the archangel see GC 1:272-275.

333

But a warning was also sounded, **"Woe to you, O earth and sea, for the devil has come down to you in great wrath, because he knows that his time is short!"** Verse 12. Driven out of heaven, Lucifer (now Satan or the devil) led his large army of angels to our planet and, as we have seen, quickly succeeded in deceiving Eve.

Ever since, Satan has succeeded all too easily in deceiving the rest of us and in mercilessly harassing us.

God's apparent dilemma. If God intended eventually to destroy the devil and his evil angels, why didn't He do so at the beginning of the great controversy instead of waiting for so many thousands of tear-stained, blood-drenched years of rebellion to pass by? We return to our original question.

Well, suppose that He had. What would have been the reaction among the large number of loyal angels? What happens in school when the teacher slaps a student hard in front of the class? Don't many of the other students jump to the conclusion that the teacher is unfair?

Large numbers of angels stood clear and firm in their loyalty to God and to His Son. But a sizable fraction, a **"third"**—presumably many millions—of heaven's keenly intelligent and highly motivated angels believed Satan's deceptions. So must there not have been a good many other angels who, though not electing to follow Satan, *wondered if perhaps* what he said was true?

If God had destroyed Satan and his committed angels right away, these unsettled angels would have been left with the matter unresolved. Doubts about God's justice and fairness would have lingered in their minds. Such doubts could have burst into another great controversy on some later day.

Right here we should remind ourselves of God's basic principle of freedom. "If you be unwilling to serve the Lord, *choose* this day whom you will serve." Joshua 24:15. "Let him who *desires* take the water of life without price." Revelation 22:17. "If the Son makes you free, you will be *free indeed*." John 8:36.

Satan and Rome coerce. God and His Son set free. God desires our love too much to destroy it by demanding it. Patiently He woos us, repeatedly offering insights into His kindness as He attempts to persuade us. He invites us to respond only if we choose to.

Speaking in human terms, God in His relation to Satan was in a true dilemma. If He destroyed Satan too soon, some angels would accuse Him of denying their freedom, of coercing their loyalty, of saying, "Obey Me or I'll kill you." But if God didn't destroy Satan, His patience would be misrepresented as weakness. Faced with this dilemma, our loving Father chose the more merciful path. He let Satan live on, even though He knew that as Satan harassed them, many people and angels would shout aloud, "Why doesn't God destroy the devil?"

Could God have started over? There is a related question which may at first seem absurd but which deserves to be asked. In order to avoid all misunderstanding *and* to prevent even the least unnecessary suffering, why didn't God simply destroy everyone in the universe all at once? Painlessly, in a nanosecond, employing perhaps some kind of cosmic neutron bomb, God surely could have eliminated every intelligent being from every one of His countless galaxies. No one (except the members of the Trinity Itself) would have remained alive. Then God could have started all over with a wholly new population, none the wiser for what had gone on.

None the wiser!

Apart from the obvious comment that God's love made such an expedient completely unthinkable, we perceive that God wanted the universe to become very much the wiser about Satan and sin (and also about Himself and His love) through *examination of evidence*. As the universe observed the results of Satan's rebellion, everyone everywhere would discern the consequences of sin. Even the still-wondering ones would find their questions fully answered. Given sufficient time, their loving loyalty would be forever secured.

Increasing complexity of the situation. Very quickly after the great controversy began, however, developments on earth made the situation dramatically more complex than it was already.

Adam and Eve did not die as soon as they ate the forbidden fruit. They *began* to die right away. But God graciously granted them a lease of time to learn more about Himself and about sin, time enough to rethink the situation, examine the evidence, repent, and come back to Him. The Lord "is forbearing toward you, not wishing that any should perish, but that all should reach repentance." 2 Peter 3:9. But in giving us more time, God left Himself open once again to misrepresentation. "Because sentence against an evil deed is not executed speedily, the heart of the sons of men is [all too often] fully set to do evil." Ecclesiastes 8:11.

"God is love," Satan reminds us. "He is so merciful that He will not allow you to suffer permanent harm," he says. As early members of the human family lived on, it seemed that God really *need not* be obeyed.

Human weakness as well as divine kindness contributed to the deepening complexity of the situation. People who attempted to obey God and overcome their sinful ways found themselves repeatedly failing. This led to yet another question, *Can* God be obeyed?

So here are the questions raised in the great controversy: (1) Is God unfair, selfishly imposing rules that deprive us of innocent joy, so that for our own good and happiness He *should not* be obeyed? (2) Is He so merciful and patient that He *need not* be obeyed? and (3) Does He demand more than we can possibly achieve, so that He *cannot* be obeyed?

These questions have not been raised by everyone alike. Depending on our temperaments, we tend to stress one or another of them.

Heaven answers the questions. In the councils of heaven, Father and Son determined to answer the questions in the only way that such questions could effectively be answered. One of them, the Son of God, would become a created being! He would live in the sin-blotched portion of the universe, born as the promised Seed of the woman. Genesis 3:15. See pages 316, 317. *On our level*, living with a

335

human nature weakened by thousands of years of sin, He would attempt to show that created beings are indeed able to obey God's laws, provided they keep in close touch with God. And He would love human beings even while they went about killing Him. In these ways the Son of God would attempt to provide convincing evidence that God really does love us—and that His laws of love *can* be obeyed by human beings.

Because the decision that Christ would die for us was made in heaven by the time our first parents sinned, 1 Peter 1:19, 20 speaks of Jesus as the "lamb" "destined [to die] before the foundation of the world." Revelation 13:8, when translated strictly in harmony with the underlying Greek, calls Jesus "the Lamb that was slain from the creation of the world." See the New International Version and the King James Version.*

When God first told the angels the amazing news about what Jesus planned to do, did any of them eagerly offer to take Christ's place? I am sure they must have. The thought that their beloved and divine Leader would suffer so much must have pained them deeply.

But if any of the angels did offer to take His place, Jesus had to turn them down. The suffering and death of an angel would have revealed an *angel's* love for God's created beings. It could not have fully answered the question about *God's* love for us. Only a member of the Trinity could do such a thing.

And so Jesus came! He "emptied himself, taking the form of a servant, being born in the likeness of men. And being found in human form he humbled himself and became obedient unto death, even death on a cross." Philippians 2:7, 8.

Born into a poor family and reared in a village with an unsavory reputation (see John 1:46), Jesus grew up to be gossiped about, accused, persecuted, tortured, and ultimately crucified. Yet He manifested consistent kindness to everyone under every circumstance. And He brought great joy, telling people things about God that changed their lives—and striding into village bazaars, touching all the loathsome lepers and dirty paralytics and bleeding ulcerated arms and legs, and leaving behind Him not one diseased person.

He even washed dirty feet. Walking sandalfoot on dusty roads—as Jesus did every day—can leave a person's feet soiled and uncomfortable. A custom arose in ancient times of having a servant wash guests' feet before a meal. How much better it must have made them feel. How dark the water must have turned.

Jesus' feet got as dirty as anyone else's. In the upper room prior to the Last Supper, one of the disciples should have washed His feet. On other evenings, presumably, the disciples had taken turns. But this time none of them moved. Apparently they had their hearts set on the top jobs in the new government they

---

* Henry Alford, *New Testament for English Readers*, 4:1885, says the words "slain from the foundation of the world" "may belong to 'is written' or to 'is slain.' The former connection is taken by many. But the other ['is slain'] is far more obvious; and had it not been for the apparent difficulty of the sense thus conveyed, the going so far back [in the Greek sentence] to 'is written' for a connexion would never have been thought of. The difficulty of the saying is but apparent: I Pet i.19,20 says more fully the same thing."

assumed Jesus was about to set up. At so critical a moment, each must have thought it would never do to get stereotyped as a footwasher.

So Jesus washed *their* feet. See John 13.

The disciples seem to have savored the spirituality of Christ's kindness, but they didn't fully comprehend it. See John 13:7. When Jesus was finished, Philip, one of the disciples, asked Him, "Lord, show us the Father, and we shall be satisfied." John 14:8.

Jesus replied patiently, "Have I been with you so long, and yet you do not know me, Philip? *He who has seen me has seen the Father.* . . . Do you not believe that I am in the Father and the Father in me?" Verses 9, 10. Philip had seen Jesus. He had seen Him preach and heal. He had watched Him hold children in His arms and tell their parents stories about lost coins and runaway sons. Only moments before, he had seen Jesus wash the disciples' dirty feet and had felt His hands wash his own. It just hadn't occurred to him that *God*, who in heaven sits surrounded by "living creatures" and myriads of angels, would on earth touch ulcers and hold children and tell stories and wash dirty feet.

Jesus came to undo the damage caused by Satan's misrepresentation of God. He came to provide trustworthy evidence, to show us what God is really like.

He came down to our level to show us.

Jesus washed the disciples' feet partly to show that God too is willing to wash dirty feet.

A few weekends ago I heard Kennard Wilson preach in his First Baptist church. During his morning message he mentioned that in a previous pastorate of his, several children, attracted by the love of Jesus, "adopted" grandparents at a local rest home. Making pastoral calls at the rest home one day, Ken Wilson said, he found an elderly inmate bowed far forward in her chair, her head pressed down on her hands deep in her lap, a picture of abject despair. But beside her, chattering sweetly to cheer the grandmother up, was her little adoptive granddaughter, with her chair drawn up close, her lithe young body bowed forward, her pretty little face resting on her hands deep in her lap, right next to the grandmother's face.

Watching Christ the Son of God come down to our level, the loyal angels became completely convinced that God is love. They were persuaded that so kind and self-sacrificing a God wouldn't even think of imposing rules and regulations that would mar anyone's happiness. They concluded that His laws are for our good and most certainly *should* be obeyed.

The angels also saw that God's laws *can* be obeyed, even by members of a race weakened through thousands of years of sin. Jesus was "made like his brethren in every respect" and "in every respect has been tempted as we are" (Hebrews 2:17; 4:15); yet He could state unequivocally at the end of His earthly career, "I have kept my Father's commandments" (John 15:10).

And God's mercy does not remove the *need* to obey. The onlooking angels saw sin unmasked, exposed for what it really is, producing its dreadful, ugly, abominable consequences. Sins of pride, jealousy, bitterness, and false ambition turned Lucifer the Morning Star, the glorious living creature, into a venomous monster, a dragon that pounced relentlessly on the kind and gracious Jesus. At the cross, God's way and Satan's way, God's laws and Satan's lies, faced each other eyeball to eyeball. The great controversy reached its climax. Satan's cruelty to Jesus destroyed forever his credibility with the onlooking universe. Humility and self-sacrifice gave Jesus the unqualified victory.

At the very thought of Christ's self-sacrifice, John heard the four living creatures and the twenty-four elders sing aloud, "Worthy art thou . . . , for thou wast slain and by thy blood didst ransom men for God." He heard the loyal angels sing, "Worthy is the Lamb who was slain, to receive power and wealth and wisdom and might and honor and glory and blessing!" He heard all the loving universe sing, "To him who sits upon the throne and to the Lamb be blessing and honor and glory and might for ever and ever!" Revelation 5:8-13.

Why the controversy continues. If then Christ's life and death convinced all the loyal angels of God's goodness and Satan's wickedness, could not God then and there have destroyed Satan without danger of upsetting any of them? Bruising the serpent, destroying Satan, was one of the reasons Jesus came and died. As we read earlier, "He himself likewise partook of" human "nature, that through [His own] death he might [gain the opportunity to] destroy him who has the power of death, that is, the devil." Hebrews 2:14. And if the main questions about God's law and His character were answered by Christ's life and death, why did the great controversy need to go on? If God won the war, why isn't it over?[9] Why didn't Heaven destroy the devil as soon as Jesus died on the cross?

The principal reason seems to be the dull stubbornness of human beings. Millions, billions of us, still prefer to believe what the serpent says about God instead of what the Bible says. Many of us are on Satan's side in the great controversy.

If God destroyed the devil today, He would have little logical reason not to destroy most human beings as well.

But the Lord is "forbearing" toward us, "not wishing that any should perish, but that all should reach repentance." 2 Peter 3:9. God continues to give *us* time, as He once gave Eve time, to reconsider the situation, examine the evidence, repent, and put our faith in Him.

Our responsibility to represent God. Vast numbers of earth's rebels haven't even heard the evidence yet. This is why those of us who do know it are commissioned to take the gospel to everyone in all the world. See pages 44-46. Not until everyone living at the time has had a chance to hear the evidence and freely make a decision on the basis of it will our merciful heavenly Father bring the great controversy to a close.

Laying aside atheists and animists and demon worshipers and other non-Christians who have never heard the evidence, how about those of us who consider ourselves Christians? How do we represent the heavenly Father to other people?

When you, dear father, scold your child and slap her angrily and then slouch in front of the TV instead of helping with her homework, what concept of the heavenly Father do you portray? Is not God extending the time of the great controversy to give you and your family—and all the rest of us and all our families—time enough to learn how to represent Him aright *at home*?

Some Christian ministers misrepresent God's character and His laws at church. Unwittingly echoing the words of the serpent, many a hard-working pastor these days implies that we do not *need* to keep one or another of God's commandments. We don't need to keep the one about adultery if our marriage isn't working, he implies. Nor do we need the commandment about always telling the truth if a white lie will help; or the one about keeping holy God's seventh-day Sabbath. Some pastors say that in the dispensation of grace we *ought* not to obey all the commandments. Some suggest that because the Sabbath commandment requires holiness ("Remember the sabbath day, to keep it holy." Exodus 20:8), we *cannot* keep it.

Pastors who teach such things need our prayers.

Only two sides at the end of time. The great controversy is drawing to its close. Most of the universe has already taken sides. Soon everyone on planet Earth will have taken sides also, and only two parties will remain among the human race.

One of these parties will be composed of people who have chosen to believe Satan's falsehoods. In spite of all the loving evidence provided to the contrary, they will continue to insist that God needlessly restricts our happiness. His laws,

339

they will say, should not, need not, or cannot be obeyed. This group will have the mark of the beast.

The other party will have the seal of God. This group will be made up of persons who have weighed the evidence carefully and who value deeply the God who was willing to make great sacrifices for our happiness. Utterly rejecting Satan's position, they take Christ's hand by faith and commit themselves wholeheartedly, at any personal cost, to believing, practicing, and teaching the truth about God's character and His laws.

"Here is a call for the endurance of the saints, those who keep the commandments of God and the faith of Jesus." Revelation 14:12.

IV. The United States in Prophecy

"Then I saw another beast which rose out of the earth; it had two horns like a lamb and it spoke like a dragon. It exercises all the authority of the first beast in its presence, and makes the earth and its inhabitants worship the first beast, whose mortal wound was healed." Revelation 13:11, 12.

First we had the great red dragon, then the leopard-bodied sea beast; now we have the lamb-horned earth beast. God has placed them on our prophetic TV screens for a reason, and He has promised us a blessing (see Revelation 1:3) as we attempt to understand them.

Attempts made in the Middle Ages to understand the lamb-horned beast were doomed to failure. It was scarcely possible for people to understand it until the leopard beast received its mortal wound. Prophecy is best interpreted after it's fulfilled. "I have told you before it takes place, so that *when it does take place,* you may believe," said Jesus at the Last Supper, during a conversation about future events. John 14:29.

The mortal wound came to be correctly understood during the French Revolution, when it was in process of being inflicted. The French Revolution occurred in the years following 1789. The pope was taken prisoner in 1798. We discussed these matters on pages 277-292.

Inasmuch as the lamb-horned beast was to cause people to worship the first beast **"whose mortal wound was healed,"** we know that the prophecy about the lamb-horned beast focuses on events after the wound was inflicted, that is, after 1798.

The lamb-horned beast has only two horns, not ten horns like the great red dragon and the leopard-bodied beast. Evidently it has only one head. (It isn't said to have four or seven heads like those other symbolic animals.) Its horns are lamb-like. Nothing about it resembles any part of the great red dragon or the leopard-bodied, lion-headed, bear-footed sea beast. We conclude that the lamb-horned animal is a unique beast, a distinct symbol of a new entity whose existence is essentially different from the others in the sequence of animal empires we have dealt with so far.

Out of the earth. The lamb-horned beast rose out of the earth. The four beasts of

Daniel 7 rose out of the sea, out of a stormy sea. The leopard-bodied beast, which was composed of Daniel's four beasts, also rose out of the sea. The false mother (the harlot) of Revelation 17:3, 15 sat on a beast that stood in the sea. But the lamb-horned beast rose out of the *earth*. The difference must be important.

"The waters that you saw, where the harlot is seated, are peoples and multi-tudes and nations and tongues." Revelation 17:15. When in closely related proph-ecies **"earth"** is contrasted with **"sea"** and **"sea"** represents vast populations, we perceive that **"earth"** represents an area with a very limited population.

This new animal's horns were *lamblike*. Twenty-nine times in Revelation **"lamb"** refers to Jesus Christ. Horns are used repeatedly in Daniel and Revela-tion as symbols of governmental power. So the earth beast, when John first saw it, was using its governmental power in a gentle, almost Christlike manner.

But it **"spoke like a dragon."** The dragon is a symbol for Satan and for earthly governments that carry out Satan's deceptive and oppressive plans. In chapters 12-14 the dragon represents Rome, in its pagan phase at first and later in its Chris-tian phase. So different from "Rome" in its appearance (lamb-horned, not dragonlike), so different in the area where it arose (the earth rather than the sea), and so different in the time of its emergence (around 1798, not in the Middle Ages or in ancient times), the lamb-horned beast nonetheless ends up deceiving and oppressing, just like the Roman powers. How disappointing.

"It works great signs [or miracles], **even making fire come down from heaven to earth in the sight of men."** We'll return to these ominous words in connection with Armageddon. See pages 434-446. **"Also it causes all, both small and great, both rich and poor, both free and slave, to be marked on the right hand or the forehead, so that no one can buy or sell unless he has the mark, that is, the name of the beast or the number of its name."** Revelation 13:13, 16, 17.

A nation which can cause **"all"** people to do something, God's followers alone excepted, has to be a powerful nation, a world leader.

What is the lamb-horned earth beast? Are we ready to attempt an identification of this gentle, lamb-horned symbol that John saw rising out of the earth, out of a relatively uninhabited area, the New World, around the time of the French Revo-lution, when the Old World leopard-bodied sea beast was receiving its mortal wound? What nation alone fits all these specifications and is also a preeminent world leader?

The United States of America. Of course.

July 4, 1776, is the date we take for America's birth, when, as Abraham Lincoln once said, this country's fathers brought forth upon this continent a nation "con-ceived in liberty." On July 4, 1776, the Declaration of Independence was signed. "We hold these truths to be self-evident," it said, "that all men are created equal; that they are endowed by their Creator with certain unalienable rights; among which are life, liberty, and the pursuit of happiness." Beautiful, gentle, almost Christlike words.

"Congress shall make no law respecting an establishment of religion, or pro-

hibiting the free exercise thereof," says the First Amendment, adopted with the rest of the Bill of Rights in 1791. The grandest achievement of the American Constitution was the creation of a nation with a friendly separation of church and state. The world had never seen such a thing before. Every other nation since ancient times had taxed the people to support a state religion, and most had oppressed religious dissidents. The French Revolution, a little later than the American, experimented with a hostile separation of church and state. Marxist countries have exceeded France's temporary example.

But America, with its friendly separation of church and state, salaried no clergy and taxed no congregation. She permitted denominations to proliferate and supported none of them. Her Congress said, "In God we trust," but elected not to define whether He is the God of Christians—or of Hindus.

So, yes, the United States fits the prophecy with astonishing precision. Certainly at its rise it revealed lamblike qualities and emerged in a relatively calm unpopulated area, **"the earth,"** in contrast to the Old World's seething and crowded **"sea."** American Indians roamed the shores and plains where the new settlers arrived, but not very many of them. An informed estimate places their number at a million or so in the more than three million square miles which later became the United States.[10]

The "toughest battle . . . ever fought on New England soil" between settlers and Indians involved only 3000 Indians and lasted no longer than three hours.[11]

An editor in Ireland in 1850 wrote about the "American Empire," "emerging" "amid the silence of the earth."[12]

Lamblike horns but dragonlike voice. So far so good. America did arise in a relatively peaceful fashion, in a relatively unpopulated place, and about the time of the deadly wound; comparatively speaking, it manifested gentle lamblike behavior and it has grown to become a top world power.

But the prophecy says that the lamb-horned beast was to speak **"like a dragon"** and, specifically, that it was to erect an **"image of the beast"** which had received the mortal wound, give it **"breath,"** and compel everyone on earth except God's true followers to **"worship"** it. **"By the signs which it is allowed to work in the presence of the beast, it deceives those who dwell on earth, bidding them make an image for the beast which was wounded by the sword and yet lived; and it was allowed to give breath to the image of the beast so that the image of the beast should even speak, and to cause those who would not worship the image of the beast to be slain."** Revelation 13:14, 15.

An image is something very much like something else. A boy who closely resembles his daddy is called "the spittin' image of his father." A statue worshiped by idolaters is a likeness, an image, of the god being worshiped. In Revelation 13:14-17 the **"image of the beast"** is a replica or copy of the beast. The Old World leopard-bodied beast was a persecuting union of church and state, a religious system wedded to national governments and empowered by them to oppress dissidents and heretics. The image of that beast will likewise be a persecuting union

343

When the flood of religious persecution in Europe was rising to unprecedented heights, the New World provided refuge.

of church and state, a religious system wedded to national government and empowered by it to oppress dissidents and heretics.

But is it possible? In view of America's wonderful Constitution and marvelous record of lamblike liberty, we are compelled to wonder if it is really possible that this country will ever engage in Old World persecution of a religious minority.

Bible prophecy, not the past, is the key to the future. Nonetheless, it may help us grasp the prophecy better if for a few moments we look at a few unhappy developments in America's past.

Sad to say, America (as we know too well) has already engaged in harassment of *racial* minorities—and she has even used her matchless Bill of Rights as an instrument of such oppression. In the famous 1857 Dred Scott decision, for example, the United States Supreme Court solemnly sanctioned slavery and formally affirmed that under the Constitution no Negro could be a citizen of the United States. The Court interpreted the Fifth Amendment, which protects "life, liberty, or property," so as to make it protect a slave-holder's ownership of a Negro as his personal *property*, regardless of the slave's right to enjoy his own personal *liberty*. [13]

In 1908 the Supreme Court, in the name of the Constitution, endorsed the right of an American state to shut down a *private Christian college* for no other reason than that it welcomed Negro faculty and students. [14]

In these two cases the Supreme Court limited the liberty of a racial minority in harmony with fads of popular opinion. The Red Scare after the first world war and the anti-Semitism and McCarthyism of the years before and after the second world war remind us that American popular opinion can be bitter.

The Supreme Court has denied certain rights also because of the need to balance the Bill of Rights with the Preamble. The Preamble begins with the famous phrase, "We the People of the United States," and goes on to list the lofty reasons why the Constitution was created in the first place: "To form a more perfect Union, establish Justice, insure domestic Tranquility, provide for the common defence, promote the general Welfare, and secure the Blessings of Liberty to ourselves and our Posterity."

In the 1880s, when Mormons quoted the First Amendment to justify polygamy as a feature of their religion, the Supreme Court opposed them on the basis that the Preamble requires "domestic Tranquility" and the "general Welfare."

It is unthinkable that people should be allowed to commit murder or arson in the name of their religion, for such activities clearly violate the freedom of other individuals. The government has an obligation to prevent, if possible, a Jonestown massacre.

But many thinking Americans deeply regret the action of the Supreme Court during World War II when, in the name of "a more perfect [national] Union" and the "common defence," it compelled elementary school children to salute the American flag, even if, as Jehovah's Witnesses, they believed it was idolatry to do so.

344

Also during the second world war, 70,000 Japanese Americans, born in the United States and loyal to her flag, were suddenly placed in concentration camps or "relocation centers" under orders issued by an army general at the request of the President and with the approval of Congress. I clearly remember the Monday morning when my Japanese classmates didn't come to school.

Justifying this legal injustice, the Supreme Court insisted in the name of "common defense" that a few Americans of Japanese ancestry were traitors, a war was in process at the time, and "war is an aggregation of hardships."[15]

Commenting on America's treatment of these 70,000 loyal citizens of Japanese ancestry, two widely read Constitutional authorities have since given us this solemn warning:

> In future wars, no person belonging to a racial, religious, cultural, or political minority can be assured that community prejudice and bigotry will not express itself in a program of suppression justified as "military necessity," with resulting destruction of his basic rights as a member of a free society.[16]

This warning that in time of military crisis "no person belonging to a . . . *religious . . .* minority" can be assured that *"community prejudice"* will not use the situation to justify destruction of his basic rights helps uncomfortably to make our understanding of Revelation 13 believable. We'll come back to it in a moment.

That loyal Japanese were hustled into "relocation centers" during World War II shows that in times of public stress basic rights may be ignored even in America.

The prophecy we are studying predicts a time when the United States will destroy certain minority religious rights as part of the process of erecting an **"image"** of Old World Roman Christianity. It indicates that America will do this after the **"mortal wound"** of the old Roman Christianity has been healed.

When the status of Roman Catholicism today is compared with what it was in the 1800s, there can be no doubt that the deadly wound is by now nearly healed.

Changing world attitudes toward Roman Christianity. In 1798 Napoleon intended there would never be another pope. In 1801, however, he signed a church-state treaty or "concordat" with a new pope! As prophecy had foreseen, the mortal blow would only wound, not kill, the Catholic Church. On the other hand, in 1870 the newly emerging nation of Italy deepened the church's woes for a while by taking away the Papal States, a considerable portion of the Italian peninsula, which the church had owned for centuries. Pope Pius IX in a huff, and all the popes after him till 1929, confined themselves in an ancient residence, the Castel Gandolfo, portraying a picture of the once-grand papacy suffering under house arrest.

But in 1929 Benito Mussolini signed a concordat granting the pope full authority over the State of Vatican City, 108.7 acres in Rome which include St. Peter's Cathedral. See page 327. Once again the pope was a monarch as well as a priest. The deadly wound was being healed.

Genial, open-hearted Pope John XXIII (1958-1963) and the procedural reforms voted at his Vatican Council II further restored Catholic influence in the world. In the 1980s Pope John Paul II may be the most respected man alive, the "number one Jesus man," as a New Guinean hailed him in pidgin in 1984.

Changing attitudes in America. The remarkable healing of the deadly wound has been clearly reflected in American popular opinion. In the 1800s strong tides of American hostility flowed against the Roman Church. In the 1840s an anti-Catholic political party known as the American Party and as the Know-Nothing Party won almost all the seats in the Massachusetts legislature and large votes in New York and Pennsylvania at a time when a far higher percentage of Americans than today lived on the Eastern seaboard.

When Colonel Stephen W. Kearny in 1846 dared to invite some priests to accompany the Catholic soldiers in his Army of the West as it marched out of Kansas City to take California away from Mexico, he was barraged with vitriolic criticism from Washington.[17]

When Pope Pius IX in 1852 sent a block of marble to be included in the Washington Monument, then being erected, mass protests were conducted. So intense was American outrage that the masons didn't dare hoist the big stone into place. Two years afterward feelings were still running so high that a group of irate Americans found where the stone lay in a storage shed, threw a chain around it, and dragged it into the Potomac.[18]

American anti-Catholicism was still very much alive a century later, even after Mussolini's 1929 concordat, which we spoke about a moment ago, had revealed

346

Anti-Catholic feelings ran so high in 1854 that one night the marble block the Vatican had sent for the Washington Monument was thrown into the Potomac River.

that the wound was being healed in Europe. When President Harry Truman on October 20, 1951, asked the Senate to approve his nomination of an Ambassador to the State of Vatican City, America was plunged into a vortex of protest and agony. "Hardly a Protestant church group in the country failed to express its opposition formally and often acrimoniously," and the President withdrew his proposal.[19]

But in March 1984, only thirty-three years later, President Ronald Reagan's nomination of William A. Wilson as ambassador to Vatican City was quickly approved by the Senate, 81-13. Only a few voices were heard worrying about church and state.[20]

Insofar as this change represents a reduction of bigotry, we rejoice. We are concerned, however, that it also represents a denial of history and, more seriously, a tendency away from the separation of church and state toward the union of the two, which has always in the past brought so much injustice and misery. If so, it can only lead to a new form of bigotry.

Increasingly, special interest groups in America want the government to enforce their special interests. Even Protestant Fundamentalists who used to insist on a strict separation of church and state now often stand with the Moral Majority in demanding government-sponsored moral regulations.

And Congress is only too eager to interfere with religion. In February 1981, 280

347

delegates representing almost all the organized religions in the country met in Washington to complain that the government was interfering in church activities far more than ever in the nation's history.[21]

What does the future hold? With such radical changes taking place, what does the future hold? Having watched Daniel's empires follow one another, Jesus fulfill the seventy weeks, the little horn rise and think to change times and law, and the 1260 days come to an end, there is something of which we can be perfectly sure: Bible predictions come true. The prophecy about the United States will be fulfilled.

America will flex her awesome political power to impose a pattern of religion which will directly oppose the Ten Commandments. She will lead the world to follow her example. As tensions escalate, perhaps as the plagues begin to fall, she will actually enact legislation imposing the death penalty on noncompliers.

But inasmuch as America is going to set up an **"image"** of the beast, we can assume she will consider herself well intentioned, as did the **"beast"** she is copying.

The Roman Church has always been helpful in many ways, and we have often assumed together that even when persecuting she intended to do God a service. She didn't obscure Christ's priestly ministry or change the commandments as a pretext for harassing heretics! She did what she thought was best and opposed conscientious minorities when they disagreed.

We may look for some global disaster, a super-power conventional war, perhaps, in which America is quickly outpaced; a financial collapse, thirdworld nations reneging on their loans and huge Western banks failing; genetic changes in pests resulting in cataclysmic crop failures. The Bible doesn't state the precise premise.

Pious American politicians, in response to the disaster, call for a return to the faith of the Founding Fathers and to a Puritan work ethic—both plausible, but a hazard to individual convictions about God's holy day.

In view of the national emergency—and of the Preamble's "general Welfare" and "common defence"—personal differences are suppressed. As panic spreads, the conscientious are accused as if they were scapegoats.

What did our Constitutional authorities say a few pages ago, commenting on the treatment of Japanese Americans? "In future wars" (they might have mentioned any national emergencies) "no person belonging to a . . . religious . . . minority can be assured that community prejudice and bigotry will not express itself in a program of suppression."

Congress and the President probably won't enact the initial legislation in order to upset the minority that keeps the commandments of God, any more than Nebuchadnezzar erected his golden image in order to throw Daniel's three friends into the furnace. Nebuchadnezzar even gave the men a chance to change their minds.

But when the men said bravely, "We will not serve your gods or worship the golden image which you have set up," the king's anger got the better of him. See Daniel 3:18 and GC 1:49-56.

The easiest thing to do when the image of the beast is set up will be to go along with the crowd. People who have believed the serpent's lies, that God's laws either should not, ought not, or cannot be obeyed (see pages 238, 243), will find compliance easy. They will be easily taken in by Satan's signs and wonders. See 2 Thessalonians 2:9-12. They will bow down to the image—and receive the mark of the beast.

But the people who cherish the **"faith of Jesus"** and have learned to conquer as Christ conquered (Revelation 3:21), will choose at the risk of their lives to honor God. They will consider loyalty to their Creator and Redeemer the most important consideration possible.

These courageous ones will soon find themselves singing on the sea of glass. See Revelation 15:2-4.

V. First Angel's Message: The Hour of Judgment

The encouraging scene of Christ's courageous ones singing on the sea of glass is found in the interlude near the end of the great-controversy scenes.

When we were studying the seven seals, we found an interlude between the sixth and seventh seals. It was composed of what we called scenes of assignment and assurance, designed to guide and encourage us as we face the formidable challenge of the end time. We heard four angels being ordered to hold the winds of strife until the 144,000 are sealed on their foreheads.

Between the sixth and seventh trumpets we found another interlude. It dealt with the new understanding of Daniel's time prophecies in the era of the French Revolution.

And now in Revelation 14:1-13, between the painful episode with the lamb-horned beast (13:11-18) and the dramatic second coming of the Son of man on the clouds (14:14-20), we find still another interlude designed to provide end-time encouragement and enlightenment. Three angels preach earth's ultimate messages of hope and doom (14:6-12); and the 144,000 appear again (14:1-5), this time on Mount Zion prophetically covered with victory and glory as they will be when the climactic conflict finally closes.

The 144,000 on Mount Zion. **"Mount Zion"** served in Old Testament times as a ceremonial name for Jerusalem and its temple. See, for example, Psalm 48:1, 2; Obadiah 17. In Revelation, Mount Zion serves as a name for New Jerusalem and God's throne. The 144,000 who stand there in Revelation 14:1-5 are men and women, boys and girls, who have stood unwavering in their loyalty to God.

No **"lie"** is on their lips. See Revelation 14:5. Undefiled with **"women"** (verse 4), they are untainted by intimacy with the false mother Babylon or with her harlot daughters. They have conquered every temptation to worship the beast and its image. Compare chapter 13:17 with 15:2. They are **"spotless."** Revelation 14:5.

The 144,000 on Mount Zion fulfill the prophecy of Zephaniah 3:12-15 about God's end-time people gathered on His "holy mountain":

> They shall seek refuge in the name of the Lord,
>   those who are left in Israel;
> they shall do no wrong
>   and utter no lies,
> nor shall there be found in their mouth
>   a deceitful tongue. . . .
>
> Sing aloud, O daughter of Zion;
>   shout, O Israel! . . .
> The King of Israel, the Lord, is in your midst;
>   you shall fear evil no more.

These marvelous people were willing to remain loyal to the Lamb at any cost to themselves. They **"loved not their lives even unto death."** Revelation 12:11. But they didn't rely on their own strength! They have endured by faith, believing that "the King of Israel, the Lord" was in their "midst." Now they receive eternal life and the right to accompany the Lamb on His tours through the universe. See Revelation 14:4.

The three angels' messages. Refreshed by this glimpse of future gladness, we are next informed of stern work remaining for us to do. A symbolic angel appears, highlighted against the sky like the true mother in Revelation 12:1. Like her, the angel appears to be located in heaven but is a symbol of a group of people on earth. See pages 90, 319.

Flying **"in midheaven"** this **"angel"** comes with the **"eternal gospel,"** completing Christ's long-ago commission to His followers to preach the gospel to everyone in the world. See Matthew 24:14.

There is urgency in his voice. **"Fear God and give him glory,"** he shouts loudly, **"for the hour of his judgment has come; and worship him who made heaven and earth, the sea and the fountains of water."** Revelation 14:7.

A second angel announces the downfall of the false mother. **"Fallen, fallen is Babylon the great,"** he says. Verse 8.

A third angel also appears. His message is the most dread warning in all Scripture. It tells about the punishment in store for everyone who, unlike the 144,000, **"worships the beast and its image, and receives a mark on his forehead or on his hand."**

But the third angel's message ends with hope, calling attention to **"the endurance of the saints, those who keep the commandments of God and the faith of Jesus."** (Verse 12 belongs to verses 9-11, as most modern versions group them.)

Then a heavenly voice, like a vesper bell, pronounces a benediction. It is the second of Revelation's seven beatitudes. See page 70. **"Blessed are the dead,"** it

351

'n the 1830s and '40s three angels began to proclaim a message specially prepared by God 'or the times we are living in.

says, **"who die in the Lord henceforth." "Blessed indeed,"** comments the Holy Spirit—here is the third beatitude—**"that they may rest from their labors, for their deeds follow them!"** Revelation 14:13.

The judgment and the gospel. The first angel, the one who says, **"The hour of his judgment has come,"** preaches the **"eternal gospel."** The judgment begins while humanity still has time to accept the gospel.

Gospel comes from Old English *godspel,* meaning "good news." In the New Testament, *gospel* translates *euangelion* (from which we get *evangel*), which also means "good news." An evangelist is a person who spends his career preaching the good news about Jesus.

The judgment itself is part of the good news. In Daniel 7 we found the saints repeatedly promised deliverance in connection with the judgment. In our study of the fifth seal in Revelation 6 we heard souls "under the altar," who were persecuted during the great tribulation of the 1260 years, pleading for the judgment to vindicate them. For them, the first angel's message that the long-awaited judgment has arrived at last is very good news.

"Give God glory," the angel says. Praise the Lord! The arrival of judgment hour is good news for all Christians who are abused, cajoled, mocked, fined, fired, or pressured in any way on account of their loyalty to God.

In our study of Daniel 9 we saw that God calls the first phase of the final judgment the "Day of Atonement." One of His purposes in the judgment hour is to remove everything that separates His dear people from one another and from Himself. His goal during this first phase of the judgment is to bring His people into the unity, the one-ness, the at-one-ment, that Jesus prayed for on His way to the Cross. See John 17 and GC 1:242-244. A judgment like this is certainly good news!

When studying Daniel 8 and 9 we looked at evidence that the first phase of the final judgment (the end-time Day of Atonement) was to begin at the end of the 2300 year-days of Daniel 8:14. We found that the 2300 year-days began in 457 B.C., when the 70 weeks of Daniel 9:24-27 began. Thus they were to end, and the heavenly judgment was to begin, in 1844. See GC 1:247-249.

We have seen how the sealed portion of Daniel's "little scroll" was opened, right on time, during the world-changing era of the French Revolution in the 1790s. See pages 276-279. The 1260 days having then been fulfilled, the attention of many Bible students turned to the 2300 days.

Judgment mistakenly limited to the second coming. It will be most helpful as we go along to remember that from very early times many Christians have limited the final judgment to the second coming. The so-called Apostles' Creed does so, as do various popular hymns, and as have numerous theologians and preachers. There *is* a judgment at the second coming, the separation of the "sheep" from the "goats." See Matthew 25:31-46. But the Bible presents four phases of the final judgment, of which the judgment at the second coming is only one:

   1. *Judgment before the second coming:* The Son of man comes to the

Ancient of Days (Daniel 7:9-14, 26, 27), cleanses the sanctuary (Daniel 8:14), and investigates the books (Daniel 7:10) to disclose who is qualified to be retained in the book of life. See Daniel 12:1, 2.

2. *Judgment at the second coming:* The Son of man, seated in glory, separates the sheep from the goats. Matthew 25:31-46.

3. *Judgment during the millennium:* During the 1000 years the saints sit on thrones, and judgment is committed to them as they examine the records of the unsaved and of the fallen angels. Revelation 20:4; 1 Corinthians 6:2, 3.

4. *Judgment at the end of the millennium:* At the close of the 1000 years sentence is executed, and the unsaved and death itself are thrown into the lake of fire. Revelation 20:12-15.

(You may wish to review our discussion of this important topic on GC 1:237-247.)

The judgment that was to begin at the end of the 2300 days is described in Daniel 7. It is the first phase of the final judgment, when the Son of man comes not to the earth but to the Ancient of Days.

Because Christians for so long have identified the final judgment exclusively with the second coming, when Bible students discovered the first angel's message and the end of the 2300 days, they assumed that the 2300 days revealed the date of both the judgment and the second coming. They were wrong about the second coming; they were wonderfully right, however, when they said that the judgment hour was at hand. For it was! Prophecy had foretold that the judgment (though not the second coming) would arrive in the 1840s.

The first angel fulfilled: the great second-advent awakening. In Europe, America, and in many other places around the world, the first angel's message began to be fulfilled in what is often called the great second-advent awakening. The term "second advent" refers to the movement's emphasis on Christ's second coming or second *advent*. We promised ourselves on page 279 that we would take a further look at this impressive interdenominational, intercontinental movement. It deserves our attention.[22]

Manuel de Lacunza (1731-1801) was one of the first in modern times to arouse interest in the second coming of Christ. A Spanish Jesuit assigned to serve in Chile, Lacunza returned to Spain when the Jesuit Order (the Society of Jesus) was banished from Chile in 1767. He died under mysterious circumstances in central Italy.

At some point in his difficult life, Lacunza's heart was warmed by the candle of Bible prophecy. He wrote an extensive manuscript in Spanish; but fearing that the Inquisition would burn it if its author became known, he substituted for his own name on the title page the Jewish name Juan Josafat Ben-Ezra. He also substituted "Messiah" for "Christ," as a Jewish Christian writer might have done, titling the book, *The Coming of Messiah in Glory and Majesty.*

Cherished hand-written copies in Spanish, and translations in Italian and

353

Latin, were soon circulating surreptitiously in southern Europe and South America, stimulating considerable interest in the second coming. Years after Lacunza's death the Inquisition did condemn his book, and in 1824 Pope Leo XII personally prohibited the publication of it "in any language whatsoever."

Edward Irving (1792-1834), who preached to high society in London and once addressed 12,000 people outdoors in Scotland, responded to the Catholic censorship by translating Lacunza's book into English. A British ambassador carried two hundred copies to Chile, the land where Lacunza once had served. Lacunza clubs still exist in Chile, dedicated to his memory.

Lacunza as a Jesuit priest followed in the footsteps of Francisco Ribera (1537-1591), the Jesuit priest who reformulated futurism in direct opposition to Protestant historicism.[23]

Nevertheless, Lacunza made a positive contribution by stirring up interest in the judgment, the second advent, and premillennialism.[24]

A fuller contribution to the fulfillment of the first angel's message was made by another European who, like Lacunza, was also a Catholic, at least for a while, and who, unlike Lacunza, was a real Jew. Joseph Wolff (1795-1862) as a boy was attracted to Catholic Christianity by the fulfillment of the Old Testament prophecies about Christ's first advent. While studying in Rome to become a Catholic missionary, he was led by second-advent prophecies to become a Protestant.

Wolff calculated that the 2300 days would end in 1847. Master of six languages and able to converse freely in eight others, this amazing Christian Jewish "missionary to the world" carried the judgment-hour message through many adventures to lands as far east as India. By invitation in 1837 he also preached at a worship service for the two houses of the United States Congress.[25]

Henry Drummond (1786-1860), British banker, member of Parliament, and Fellow of the Royal Society, contributed much time and wealth to the second-advent awakening and served as host to five prophetic conferences (1826-1830) which met in his splendid mansion at Albury Park.[26]

William Cuninghame (1776-1849), a Scottish layman who attended Drummond's prophetic conferences, wrote 21 books on the prophecies.[27] Other prominent participants in the Albury conferences included Joseph Wolff and Edward Irving, whom we have already met. Irving's interest in second-advent prophecy was stimulated by Lacunza's book, which he translated in 1826, the year of the first prophetic conference.

With two other second-advent preachers, James Frére and Lewis Way, Irving founded the Society for the Investigation of Prophecy, whose goal was to study "the speedy coming of our Lord." During one of his Scottish tours he converted the three Bonar brothers to the advent hope. Horatius Bonar served twenty-five years as editor of *The Quarterly Journal of Prophecy*. His fine hymn, beginning, "I heard the voice of Jesus say, 'Come unto Me and rest,' " is still widely loved.

But tragedy struck Irving's career. One Sunday in 1831 his sermon was interrupted by someone's talking in tongues. Later there were unusual experiments with faith healing. Many in the congregation were offended. Because Irving was a gentle pastor, he hoped the controversial manifestations were a latter-day outpouring of the Holy Spirit. But he was voted out of his pulpit and tried for heresy. He died brokenhearted in his early 40s. But he was buried, after a very large funeral, in the prestigious Glasgow Cathedral.[28]

We'll have occasion to visit Irving's congregation again on pages 517, 518.

In Germany, Johann Richter emphasized the second advent in his six-volume *Family Bible Commentary*. Leonard Kelber taught it to his schoolchildren in Bavaria. Johann Lutz, Catholic pastor, transformed his village from both poverty and sin by preaching on the second coming.[29]

In Geneva, Switzerland, Francois S. R. L. Gaussen (1790-1863), a close friend of Merle d'Aubigné, the famous church historian, became widely known for the work he did among families. Driven from his pulpit in the state church because he talked so much about the second coming, he got a job teaching in the Evangelical Society's School of Theology. A special method of his was to teach the book of Daniel to Sunday School children. When the children happily reported at home what they were learning, their parents came to hear Gaussen too.[30]

Children preach in Sweden. Children took an even more active part in the first angel's message in Sweden, where only official clergy were allowed to preach, and they were not interested in the second coming. In one of the most remarkable

When, in 1842 and 1843 the official clergy ignored the first angel's message in Sweden, it was preached by teenagers and children, some as young as six.

developments in the fulfillment of the first angel's message, during 1842 and 1843 youth and even little children preached the judgment hour.

Ole Boqvist and Erik Walbom, teenagers, were imprisoned and cruelly beaten under a stream of ice-cold water. Children as young as six gave sermons to groups sometimes as large as several thousand, urging people to repent because of the soon arrival of the judgment. Some of the children appeared to be in a vision or trancelike state while preaching. When not preaching they talked and acted like normal boys and girls.

A government physician, Dr. S. E. Sköldberg, submitted an official report based on numerous observations of the child preachers. The health department for a time forbade children to cross county lines in order to quarantine what it called the "preaching sickness"!

When the children were asked to explain what they were doing, they quoted two Bible texts in particular: Joel 2:28, 29, "It shall come to pass afterward, that I will pour out my spirit . . . [and] your sons and your daughters shall prophesy," and Revelation 14:7, **"The hour of his judgment has come."**[31]

Many other persons could be named who in the 1800s carried the first angel's message: Edward Bickersteth, British attorney and foreign missionary; Alexander Keith, minister of the Scottish Free Church; George Müller, founder of the famous Bristol Orphanage; H. Heintzpeter, keeper of the Royal Museum at The Hague; Daniel Wilson, Anglican bishop in India; Thomas Playford in Australia; and on and on. It is reported that in the 1840s as many as 700 Anglican ministers in Great Britain, besides numerous ministers of other denominations, preached **"the hour of his judgment has come."**[32] Thomas B. Macaulay, the famous historian and member of Parliament, recorded in 1844 that the number who believed in an imminent return of Christ included men "distinguished by rank, wealth, and ability. . . . Noblemen," he added, "and members of parliament have written in defence of it."[33]

Impressive as the early fulfillment of the first angel's message was in Europe and other areas around the world, it commanded even greater attention in North America, as we shall see in the following section.

VI. The Second-Advent Awakening in North America

The great second-advent awakening flourished vigorously in the United States, from which country it was exported to Christian believers and mission stations around the world. It was most closely associated with William Miller, the Baptist lay preacher.[34]

But for years Miller tried *not* to preach the first angel's message.

William Miller (1782-1849) was a farmer in an age when nearly all Americans lived on farms and George Washington and Thomas Jefferson retired to farms from the presidency. Miller was considered a good farmer. He was also a natural leader, being elected frequently to county offices such as justice of the peace and deputy sheriff. In the War of 1812 he served as lieutenant and captain.

Baptist William Miller aroused America to prepare for Christ's coming.

Miller was a family man, the eldest of sixteen children and the father of eight. He was converted in 1816 by a sermon on the duties of parents to their children which emphasized the need for fathers to lead out in daily family worship and give an example of personal spirituality.[35] In his later years he rejoiced that his children were all Christians.[36]

Not tall, slightly corpulent, round faced with bright, kindly eyes, Miller was blessed with a good memory, a pleasant manner, and an aptitude for reading history books and the Bible. His principal rule for interpreting the Bible was to let it explain itself, without the help of man-made commentaries.

In his first major study of the Bible (1816-1818) Miller began at Genesis 1 and proceded no faster than he could understand. When he found a difficult passage, he used Cruden's famous concordance to help him find other passages in the Bible that could explain it. A concordance is an index to all the words in the Bible. Years later he told how he did it:

> Whenever I found any thing obscure, my practice was to compare it with all collateral passages; and by the help of CRUDEN, I examined all the texts of Scripture in which were found any of the prominent words contained in any obscure portion. Then by letting every word have its proper bearing on the subject of the text, if my view of it harmonized with every collateral passage in the Bible, it ceased to be a difficulty. In this way I pursued the study of the Bible, in my first perusal of it, for about two years, and was fully satisfied that it is its own interpreter.[37]

When he came to the prophecies of Daniel and Revelation, he used history books to trace out their fulfillment, disciplining himself to find as nearly as he could the precise events in history that answered to the predictions.[38]

Using these principles, Miller by himself arrived at many of the same conclusions about the book of Daniel that we came to in the first volume of *God Cares*. Comparing what he found in Daniel with what he found in other parts of the Bible and in history books, he identified the 1260 days as years. He concluded, as we have, that they ran from the time of the Emperor Justinian in the 530s to the era of the French Revolution in the 1790s.

He discovered that like the 1260 days, the 2300 days of Daniel 8:14 are also years and that they began when the 70 weeks began in 457 B.C. and would end "around the year 1843." He noticed that the 2300 days were to end with the judgment, and he assumed—with nearly all other Christians—that the judgment would occur at the second coming of Christ. Assuming then that the end of the 2300 days was also the end of the world, he concluded (in 1818) that "in about twenty-five years," that is, around 1843, "all the affairs of our present state would be wound up."[39]

The soon coming of Christ was good news to Miller. He had already found in Jesus his "Saviour and Friend." The thought of seeing Him in a few years overjoyed him. He thought it would overjoy other people too.

But what if he were mistaken? Although Miller felt a burning obligation to take what he had learned and "tell it to the world," he hesitated to do so for thirteen years. For five years he sincerely feared he might be wrong. "I therefore feared to present it," he explained years later, "lest by some possibility I should be in error, and be the means of misleading any[one]."[40]

One day, for example, he noticed that in the Olivet Discourse Jesus said, "That day and hour no one knows, not even the angels of heaven, nor the Son, but the Father only." Matthew 24:36. Did this verse mean that his conclusions were all wrong? No, he decided after much reflection. Jesus was talking only about the day and hour of His return, not about the approximate year; and in the same discourse (Matthew 24:33) He said we could know when His return was "near, at the very gates."[41]

Besides, the statement is in the present tense. It is impossible that the Son Himself will *never* know when He's coming back!

When five years of continuing Bible study removed his doubts, Miller hesitated another eight years because of a deep fear of preaching.

His fear of preaching did not, however, keep him from talking with people privately and writing letters. His one-to-one conversations over an open Bible led many local people to appreciate the first angel's message.

In 1831, after he had hesitated for 13 years, Miller's conviction that he ought to preach seemed almost overpowering. On a Saturday morning in August he promised God that he would go out and preach—but only on condition that someone actually invite him to do so, something that no one had ever done.

358

To his horror, within half an hour a nephew who lived some sixteen miles away arrived on horseback with an invitation from his Baptist church. Very angry with himself and God, Miller stormed out of the house to pray in a nearby maple grove. There, after an hour of anguish, he at last consented.

William Miller really didn't want to preach about the 2300 days!

To his complete surprise, his first short series of meetings was effective. In thirteen families all but two persons accepted Christ as their Saviour.[42] Given the size of families in those days, the number of new Christians may have been fifty or more.

Soon Miller had more invitations from Baptist, Methodist, Congregational, Presbyterian, and Christian Connection* pastors than he could handle. His quiet but impressive Bible messages packed churches and led to revivals and many conversions.

Timothy Cole, the Christian Connection pastor in Lowell, Massachusetts, invited Miller on the recommendation of other pastors, without knowing what he looked like. At the railway station he was dismayed to see an old farmer get off the train. Too embarrassed even to introduce Miller to his congregation that evening, Pastor Cole took a seat among the people instead.

But as the sermon got underway, with Miller raising questions about the second coming and finding the answers in the Bible, the pastor changed his mind. Seeing that Miller "opened the Scriptures in a manner that did honor to the occasion, like a workman who needeth not to be ashamed" (see 2 Timothy 2:15), Cole after fifteen minutes proudly walked up to the platform and sat down behind Miller. Each night the congregation increased. When the series was over there were forty baptisms. In all, sixty joined the church.[43]

Ministers rally to Miller's message. Miller's local Baptist church gave him an official license to preach, and seventy or eighty ministers of various denominations[44] credentialed him unofficially to lecture on the prophecies.

Such endorsement was distinctly encouraging; nonetheless, for about eight years Miller labored alone as an itinerant lecturer and revivalist. December 1839 brought a welcome change when Joshua V. Himes (1805-1895), a minister in the Christian Connection, enlisted in his cause. Himes, the vigorous young pastor of the Chardon Street Chapel in Boston, was already well known in the city for his crusades against slavery, alcoholism, and war. For Miller he launched a periodical, *Signs of the Times*, the first of several Miller papers that he started. He also published well over forty second-advent books in five years.

Even before Himes volunteered his capable support, Miller had begun receiving significant assistance from Josiah Litch (1809-1886), a widely respected Methodist writer. Within a few weeks of first reading a copy of Miller's lectures, Litch wrote a 200-page book on second-advent prophecies.

Charles Fitch (1805-1844), a well-loved Congregational minister who at one

---

* The sizable denomination known as the Christian Connection, vigorous and popular in the first half of the 1800s, later blended into other denominations.

time had been an executive assistant to the famous evangelist Charles G. Finney, resigned his popular Boston pastorate in order to travel with the second-advent message.

Besides these outstanding leaders there were many more. We think especially of Joseph Bates, temperance advocate and former sea captain, and of James White, like Himes a minister of the Christian Connection, who in six wintry weeks influenced a thousand people to accept Christ.

But no one knows how many helpers there were. Contemporary estimates ran from 700 to 2000. Of 174 *known* ministers who preached Miller's message, about half were Methodist, a fourth were Baptist, and the rest included Congregationalists, Christians, Presbyterians, Episcopalians, Lutherans, Dutch Reformed, Quakers, and representatives of several other denominations.[45]

It is impressive that a considerable company of able, thinking men from all the major Protestant denominations supported Miller, not a few of whom had received far more education than he. The second-advent awakening in North America was a Christ-centered reformation that was warmly accepted by many, both laymen and leaders, in the respected churches of the day—and by thousands of infidels, Deists, and indifferent souls in the restless world outside the churches.

Ever wider grew the interest until Miller, Himes, and the other leaders were circulating almost incessantly around New York and New England, as far west as Illinois, up north into eastern Canada, and as far south as Maryland. Their opposition to slavery made them unwelcome in the deep South, and America hadn't yet annexed the far West.

Robert Winter took the word to England. The mails carried it to every post office in the United States and to every known English-speaking mission station around the world.[46]

Crowds come to camp meetings. The crowds desiring to hear the advent message grew too large for churches and rented halls. In May 1842 a "general conference" of Miller's leaders voted to hold three camp meetings that summer. So great was the public interest that more than thirty were held! There were more than fifty the following year, and still more the next, making at least 130 camp meetings, with a combined attendance in excess of half a million.

The poet John Greenleaf Whittier dropped in on the first camp meeting and years later still remembered the eloquent preachers burdened with the symbolic language of the Bible, the canvas paintings of Nebuchadnezzar's image and the beasts of Revelation—and the dim woodland arches, the white circle of tents, the smoke from the campfires rising like incense, and the sea of upturned, earnest faces.[47]

The camp meetings were often organized by local volunteer committees. Men, women, and children flocked in from every direction, crowding steamboats, overflowing railroad cars, and stuffing stagecoaches. Pedestrians trudged in from every side road, as one and all, the pious and the curious, made their way to the important meetings at the second-advent campground. Significantly, almost every believer carried a Bible.[48]

The overwhelming success of the camp meetings led the Millerites to contribute means for a big tent, and within four weeks they had one, the largest tent in America at the time, constructed by E. C. Williams, an advent believer. It required a permanent team of four to pitch and strike it. Its centerpole was 55 feet, its diameter 120 feet, and there was room inside for 4000 people. Several thousand more sometimes stood outside.[49]

Newspapers were astonished at the speed with which the tent was dismantled, transported by wagon, steamboat, or train, and raised near another town. When it was pitched, people wagered that it wouldn't fill. When meetings began, they were stunned to see it jammed. Railroads scheduled special trains to accommodate the crowds.

Estimates of the number of people who publicly identified themselves with the second-advent message in the thirteen years of Miller's movement (1831-1844) range from Miller's characteristically modest 50,000 to a scholarly estimate of around 135,000.[50] The figures are impressive, especially when it is remembered that John Wesley, the founder of Methodism, secured the loyalty of 70,000 in Britian in fifty years of ministry. See page 294.

The message makes Christians. More significant than the number of believers

The Millerites purchased a huge tent, and eager listeners filled it many times.

was the quality of the conversions. The quaint language of a writer who experienced the advent message reveals its power:

> There seemed to be an irresistible power attending its proclamation. . . . It produced everywhere the most deep searching of heart and humiliation of soul before the God of high heaven. It caused a weaning of affections from the things of this world—a healing of controversies and animosities—a confession of wrongs—a breaking down before God, and penitent, brokenhearted supplications to him for pardon and acceptance. It caused self-abasement and prostration of soul, such as we never before witnessed. As God, by Joel commanded, when the great day of God should be at hand, it produced a rending of hearts and not of garments, and a turning unto the Lord, with fasting and weeping and mourning.[51]

Young people attracted. In the previous section we found that in Sweden the first angel's message was preached exclusively by children and young people. In the United States also it held a special attraction for children and youth.

A teenage girl recalled many years afterward that every day she and her believing friends felt it was "their first duty to secure the evidence of their acceptance with God. Their hearts were closely united, and they prayed much with and for one another."[52] She remembered too that when the Millerites learned of some misunderstanding that separated any of them, they settled the difficulty between them at once. We can picture two or three men walking off behind a barn or into a grove of trees and returning a little later with moist cheeks and shining eyes, true friends again.[53] They wanted no ill will to separate them, not with Jesus coming again so soon.

A ten-year-old boy was especially moved by the congregational singing at the advent meetings. Anyone who heard it, he wrote in his fifties, "will not be likely to forget it. It seemed to have a peculiarly solemn and penetrating power, a heavenly sweetness which charmed the listener and softened the heart. Many went to the meetings to hear it."[54]

Some people attended the advent meetings to mock and make fun of the believers' interpretation of the Bible, but, this boy-grown-older remembered, "the power of the Spirit of God was present in their meetings, so that many who came with idle curiosity or as scoffers, were brought to give themselves to God, and humble themselves by confessing their sins with the deepest penitence . . . and then to rejoice with all their souls as the Lord poured his blessing upon them."[55]

The great disappointment. Miller himself did not presume to know the precise date for the end of the 2300 days. His earliest calculation, based on the best evidence he could find for the beginning of the 2300 days and the 70 weeks, was 457 B.C. He concluded that Christ would return "about the year 1843." Later calculations by his associates showed that the 2300 days couldn't correctly be expected to end until the spring of 1844; and in the summer of 1844 the date was refined to the Day of Atonement that year, October 22. See *Your Questions Answered,* pages 402, 403.

It was already August by then. Christ's coming was less than three months away. What joy! No more winters on this cold old earth. No more milking of cows morning and night. No more deaths of children from diphtheria and of young mothers from consumption. Families reunited! Angels, Bible heroes, the "golden home city," and Jesus Himself! Less than three months away. What joy indeed!

The midnight cry rang out, "Behold, the bridegroom cometh." Matthew 25:6, K.J.V.

Believers hastened to have abundant "oil" for their lamps and to persuade others to have it too. Preparing for winter seemed a denial of the faith. Why cut hay, pick apples, or dig potatoes if they would all burn in the presence of the Lord? Let the unharvested harvest testify to the times and lead others to heed the midnight cry.

As the last days of time ran out, Adventist businessmen closed their stores; mechanics locked their shops; employees gave up their jobs. At the camp meetings, hundreds confessed their faults and flocked forward for prayer. Large sums were donated so the poor could settle their debts and so the advent papers could be published—until the editors said they could use no more, and would-be donors turned away in grief.

As the great day drew near, Advent printers refused further contributions.

Anticipation. Publication. Preparation. Consecration. The climax at the close.

On October 19 the presses stopped running. The great tent had already been rolled up for the last time. The speakers had returned to their homes to be with their families. Joshua V. Himes hurried over to Miller's home.

Outside the movement, the world waited in suspense. Thousands who had never joined searched their hearts for fear it might be true.

October 22 dawned bright and clear over most of New England and the state of New York. Miller's people collected in companies large and small, in meetings solemn with prayer and joyous with praise. They watched all day, for they knew not what hour their Lord might come.

They waited all day, past noon, through the afternoon, pausing to milk their cows as the evening shadows grew long. The hours of night ticked slowly past. Finally in their disconsolate homes, their clocks tolled twelve at midnight. October 22 ended, and Jesus didn't come.

In spite of Miller's clear Bible evidence, in spite of his undeniable call to preach it, in spite of the wonderful change the message produced in its believers, Jesus didn't come.

Charles Fitch, whom we referred to a few pages ago, died from overwork and exposure on the Monday eight days before October 22. The paper reported that his widow and fatherless children were full of smiles, knowing they would see their husband and father in a few days.

We can hear the children ask on the twenty-third, "Mother, why didn't Daddy come?" Similar questions were asked in thousands of homes, for the death of children and young parents was common in those times. No wonder October 22 has gone down in history as the day of the great disappointment.

But Miller's faith remained strong that Christ would return soon. "I have fixed my mind upon another time," he said. "And that is *To-day, To-day,* and TO-DAY, until he comes, and I see HIM for whom my soul yearns."[56]

Miller passed to his well-earned rest in 1849. But the advent movement didn't die with him! Separated from the mistaken assumption that the judgment is the same as the second coming, and linked to the second and third angels' messages, proclamation of the first angel's message about the arrival of God's judgment hour is today more widespread and dynamic than Miller ever dreamed it could be. We'll become aware of this development near the end of section VIII. See page 377.

VII. Second Angel's Message: Babylon's Fall

The simple observation that Jesus didn't return in 1844 has persuaded many people that Miller was deluded and wrong. It is more to the point to say that although Miller was wrong on some points, he was the most nearly right person in the world.

Miller was right to preach about the second coming, a theme referred to scores of times (some say hundreds of times) in the New Testament. He was right to preach premillennialism, the visible personal return of Christ at the beginning of the thousand years. (In *premillennialism* the *pre-* means "before." See pages 515-520.)

Most ministers and writers of Miller's day, if they touched on the second advent at all, were postmillennialists. (The *post-* means "after.") They said that Christ won't appear visibly until after the end of an indefinite thousand years of peace and prosperity. Meanwhile, they said—don't be confused—that Jesus would very soon have an invisible and spiritual "second coming" to bring in this thousand years of peace.

Some of Miller's opponents actually agreed with Miller on the 2300 days. One of the most notable of these opponents was George Bush (1796-1859), Professor of Hebrew and Oriental literature in the University of the City of New York. But for them, what would begin in the 1840s was this thousand years of peace and prosperity prior to the visible second coming.

Such thinking was congenial to the optimism—the "era of good feeling"—which prevailed in America at the time. It also fitted well with the soaring hopes of the numerous reform associations and foreign missionary societies of the day. *Homo Americanus* would in their day pave the way to the ideal world.

The existence of American democracy and American Christianity, many Christians said, was convincing evidence that "the Son of God appears to be coming in his glory, conquering and to conquer the kingdoms of the earth." In fact, as Edward Beecher said in 1835, the churches of America were "aroused as never before" to the belief that "a glorious advent of the kingdom of God" was near at hand. What they had in mind by this "glorious advent of the kingdom of God" was not His visible return but a spiritual coming to convert the world and remove "all corruptions . . . and all abuses"—slavery, tyranny, warfare, poverty, drunkenness, and so on—from the social system.[57]

Miller the premillennialist. Against such a background, William Miller was the outstanding spokesman for premillennialism, the scriptural concept that Jesus must return literally before we can hope to have an era of true goodness. He read in 2 Timothy 3:1-5, 13 that people in the "last days" will be "inhuman, implacable, slanderers, profligate, fierce, haters of good, treacherous"; and that far from getting better and better, "evil men and impostors will go on from bad to worse, deceivers and deceived."

So Miller taught that only the personal appearance of Christ in power and glory can terminate evil and institute permanent peace.

The great second-advent movement was preeminently the premillennial movement of its day. *For this reason* it was ultimately derided and blamed. Miller's premillennialism and his message that the final judgment could be dated in 1844 were rejected, not because they were wrong—for they weren't wrong—but because they were unpopular. They didn't fit the contemporary optimism about the future of America and the conversion of the world.[58]

On the other hand, the American Civil War soon gave Miller's postmillennial enemies reason to believe they were dead wrong. Mourned the editors of the Baptist *Christian Review* in 1861, the year the Civil War began, "Our visions have been suddenly, rudely despoiled."[59]

Other failures should also have convinced theologians of the bankruptcy of postmillennialism. To take a couple of well-known examples: To most people "Oneida Community" means silverware, but once it was the name of an ambitious "perfect" community, intended to provide a model for an entire perfect planet. In the Oneida Community, men and women were matched—and rematched—by carefully developed theories. Far from solving the world's ills, the Oneida Community itself soon dissolved. Brook Farm, another model for the whole world, enlisted the support of intellectuals such as Nathaniel Hawthorne, Orestes Brownson, and Ralph Waldo Emmerson. It broke up in embarrassment when the barn burned down.[60]

Today there is a resurgence of premillennialism. But much of it centers on J. N. Darby's rapture doctrine and denies the first angel's message, that the hour of God's judgment has already begun. It also denies the third angel's message, as we shall see in due course. See pages 515-520.

This is unfortunate, for Miller was certainly right to preach from the Bible the first angel's message about the arrival of judgment hour at the end of the 2300 days in 1844.

William Miller was God's man for God's hour. He bore a true message about the arrival of the final judgment, a message about a grand new work which Jesus Christ was beginning in the heavenly sanctuary. Surely every Christian should have been thrilled to examine what he had to say about Jesus Christ.

How Miller might have been helped. Ministers and theologians, instead of criticizing Miller, as in the final analysis many of them did, might instead have prayed and studied with him. Using their superior education, they might have shown him from the Bible where he was wrong.

Daniel 7:9-14, 22 shows the Ancient of Days moving at judgment hour to a new location in heaven and the Son of man following Him there on the clouds of heaven, thereby calling the universe's attention to the grand new work They were inaugurating. Miller, so sure about the judgment that will take place at the second advent, happened not to notice that for the judgment scene in Daniel 7 the Son doesn't come to the earth. Daniel 7:13 says, "With the clouds of heaven there came one like a son of man, and he came *to the Ancient of Days*" and received His kingdom. Miller's opponents, to be helpful, might have called his attention to precisely what the passage says.

Christ's parable of the ten young women says that as the Bridegroom comes to the wedding there is a cry at midnight, "Behold, the bridegroom cometh." Matthew 25:6, K.J.V. The girls who are "ready" go in with Him to the wedding. In time the door is shut, and those who are then too late knock on the door in vain. Miller believed that the coming of the Bridegroom to the marriage was the same as Christ's coming to the judgment to receive His kingdom in Daniel 7. He believed it was time for him to preach the midnight cry, "Behold, the bridegroom cometh."

Thus far in his interpretation of the parable Miller was right. He was wrong only in supposing that the marriage of Christ to His kingdom takes place *on earth* and at the second coming.

Miller's ministerial enemies, if they had wanted to be helpful, should have shown him (a) that in Luke 19:11, 12 Jesus taught that He would receive His kingdom in "a far country," that is, in heaven, where Daniel 7 also portrays Him as receiving it. They might also have shown him (b) that in the parable of the waiting servants, Luke 12:35-37, Jesus said we must wait until He will "return from the wedding" (K.J.V.; see *Your Questions Answered*, pages 407-410) and that *then* He will have us "sit at table." That is to say, the wedding is first consummated by Christ's receiving His kingdom in heaven, and only after the wedding is over will the second coming take place.

Miller's opponents might have taught him these things—provided they had known them themselves. But on these crucial points they were as mistaken as he was. They too linked the marriage and the final judgment too closely to the second coming. Miller was ahead of the theologians because his mistakes were no worse than theirs, but his insights into Bible prophecy, though imperfect, were far superior to theirs.

At Christ's first coming, the religious leaders of the day might have learned a lot about Jesus by listening to Anna and Simeon, dear old folk who daily prayed in the temple (Luke 2:25-38); or by listening to Mary, the village girl from Nazareth; or to John the Baptist, the lay preacher at the Jordan.

At the arrival of judgment hour, the religious leaders of the day might have learned a great deal about Jesus by listening to William Miller, the Baptist lay preacher.

The second angel's message. As the attitude of most ministers and theologians hardened against the first angel's message in the summer and autumn of 1843, Miller's associates began to notice in a new way the second angel's message of Revelation 14:8, **"Another angel, a second, followed"** the first one, **"saying, 'Fallen, fallen is Babylon the great, she who made all nations drink the wine of her impure passion.' "**

Protestants since Luther's day had correctly seen Babylon as a symbol of the Roman church, a Christian body whose leaders at worst rejected elements of Bible truth and persecuted Christians who chose to believe them. By the second half of 1843 many Protestant churches in North America were ridiculing and rejecting the significant Bible truth Miller and his associates were preaching. Not content merely to disagree disagreeably, they also read out of membership many thousands of their loyal church folk who chose to believe it.

Miller's associates studied the second angel's message in the light of Revelation 17:5 and noticed that Babylon, herself a "harlot," is the "mother of harlots." Daughter harlots carry their mother's name. Miller's helpers felt compelled to

367

draw the conclusion that Babylon's daughters are Protestant churches which, like the Roman church, reject Bible truth and harass those who accept it.

Their conclusion was a solemn one, and it still deserves attention. Most of Miller's message was Bible truth, centered in Jesus Christ. It was blessed with marvelous power to change for the better thousands and thousands of people who accepted it. It was itself a fulfillment of prophecy, of the first angel's message. But most American churches finally rejected it.

Their leaders still reject it—or perhaps neglect it. Surely their rejection or indifference is becoming increasingly serious as evidence continues to mount that the 2300 days did lead to the date for the beginning of the final judgment.

When we come to Revelation 18:4 we'll hear Jesus make His final appeal to His dear followers who are still members of the "Babylon" churches. "Come out of her"—that is, Come out of Babylon—He says, "lest you take part in her sins, lest you share in her plagues."

VIII. Third Angel's Message: God's Commandment Keepers

"There's money waiting for you at the post office. Why don't you walk down and ask for your mail?"

These unspoken words, or others like them, impressed themselves on Joseph Bates (1792-1872) as he sat in his two-story home in Fairhaven, Massachusetts, in the fall of 1847. He had built the house several years earlier when he retired from being a sea captain. He had sold out his interest in his ship for $11,000.

Some of his fortune he had spent to start a silk-worm factory, considered a good bet in those days, though in his case it didn't work out. There's still a Mulberry Street in Fairhaven named for trees planted there to feed silkworms. Bates's interest turned to "temperance," and his industry languished. After helping many people quit the alcohol habit he committed himself to the great message William Miller was preaching. The second advent of Christ, he reasoned, would be the ultimate solution to alcoholism and to all other earthly woes.

The great disappointment of October 1844 hit him hard. He was well respected in his community. On October 23 he was so embarrassed to be seen in town he wished the ground would open up. But he soon regained his balance. As he renewed his study of the Bible he found himself entering the most fascinating period of his life—though not the most financially rewarding!

He was soon publishing several little books on Bible topics, which he handed out in return for whatever, if anything, people gave him. In the autumn of 1847, when he sat down to work on a 116-page book called *A Vindication of the Sabbath*, his cash flow was reduced to a single English coin, a York shilling. (Not till the western silver mines were worked after the Civil War did America produce her own silver coins in abundance.)

When under such dire circumstances Bates seemed to hear a voice telling him to pick up a donation at the post office, he was delighted.

But we're getting beyond ourselves.

The morning after. As we said a moment ago, on the morning after the great disappointment Joseph Bates wished the ground would open up and hide him from his friends.

He was not alone in his embarrassment and disappointment. Many thousands of other Christians from the various Protestant denominations felt the same way. They had joyfully "eaten" the "little scroll" of Daniel's prophecies and found them "sweet as honey." Now they understood what John had foretold, "When I had eaten it my stomach was made bitter." Revelation 10:10; see page 278.

But God cares! Light to explain the disappointment began to shine very soon.

Hiram Edson (1806-1882), who had been a steward in the Methodist church in the years leading up to 1844, still remembered many years later how when Christ hadn't come by midnight on the expected day, he and his family had "wept, and wept, till the day dawn." After a season of prayer, he felt better about things, believing as Christians always do in dark times that God would make it plain someday. He and a friend started walking to the homes of other friends to cheer them on. As they crossed a field certain Bible passages flashed into his mind, making things plain a lot sooner than he had expected.

Other disappointed believers also found the explanation in the Bible. Among these were three editors of Miller's papers: Enoch Jacobs, out west in Cincinnati; and on the eastern seaboard, Joseph Turner, in Portland, Maine, and Apollos Hale, in Boston. Turner and Hale may have studied together. Jacobs and Edson made their discoveries independently.

The two principal passages which Edson and the three editors reunderstood were ones we were talking about in the previous section. In Daniel 7 they noticed that at judgment hour Jesus was to go on the clouds of heaven to the Ancient of Days, not to the earth. In Luke 12:35-37, K.J.V., they noticed that when Jesus comes at the second advent He will be returning *from* the "wedding." Thus the "marriage" to His kingdom which is foreshadowed in the judgment scene of Daniel 7 is not the same as the second coming but is an event which precedes the second coming.

Very quickly in the papers which Jacobs, Turner, and Hale edited this new picture emerged explaining in Bible terms what had really happened in October 1844.[61]

"And ye yourselves like unto men that wait for their Lord, when he will *return from the wedding*." They read and reread the passage in the King James Version. (See *Your Questions Answered*, pages 407-410.) "Verily I say unto you, that he shall gird himself, and make them to sit down to meat, and will come forth and serve them." Luke 12:36, 37.

This is no ordinary parable. Ordinary parables take ordinary events and give them spiritual interpretations. But no lord in ancient times rewarded his obedient servants by dressing like a butler and serving them a meal! Jesus made this plain in another of his stories (an ordinary parable), in which He remarked that instead of serving his servant when the servant comes in tired and hungry from the field,

369

an employer will make the servant go on working and say, "Prepare supper for me, and gird yourself and serve me, till I eat and drink; and afterward you shall eat and drink." Luke 17:7, 8.

No, Christ's words about the lord who returns from the wedding and then girds himself and feeds his servants is a sublime promise, a sublime end-time prophecy.

"I am among you as one who serves," says Jesus. Luke 22:27.

God cares.

This parable-promise points to the marriage supper of the Lamb that Revelation l9:9 talks about. It will come true when His church (that is, His Kingdom, the true Mother, the Holy City, the Lamb's bride) has at last "made herself *ready*." It will happen when the bride is clothed in fine linen, clean and white, the fine linen being the righteous deeds of the saints. Revelation 19:7, 8.

Miller's followers go their ways. Sad to say, many of Miller's advent believers didn't pay attention to the Bible passages that explained their disappointment. Thousands instead decided they'd been altogether wrong. They either gave up all faith or returned to their former churches and looked for Jesus to return at the end rather than at the beginning of the thousand years.

Thousands of other advent believers concluded that they'd made a mistake in the way they calculated the 2300 days. They set several new dates for Christ to come. They exist today as a body of about 30,000 members known as Advent Christians.

Others, however, realized that their understanding of the 2300 days was unimpeachable. It was too firmly linked to the seventy weeks and the events of Christ's first coming ever to be proved in error. And they were right. Their position was very similar to what we found as we examined Daniel 8 and 9 in *God Cares*, volume 1. For a summary see GC 1:247, 248.

Believers in this third group, with their minds committed to extensive Bible study, paid increasing attention to Christ's high priestly ministry. The Miller movement had focused almost entirely on Jesus Christ—on Christ at the second coming, Christ the judge, Christ our only Saviour. Now the all-absorbing question was, "What is Christ doing *now*?"

They found the same answer in Leviticus 16 and 23 and Daniel 8:14 that we found there. See, for example, GC 1:183-188.

Jesus takes away sin. The believers in this third group became increasingly attracted to two Bible statements relating to Christ's high priestly ministry in the most holy place. The first is in Leviticus 16:30, "From all your sins you shall be clean before the Lord." The work of the high priest on the Day of Atonement/Day of Judgment was primarily to cleanse the people from their sins. This concept fitted perfectly with the words we looked at a moment ago about the bride's making herself ready and being clothed with the righteous deeds of the saints.

The other text was Revelation 11:19, the introductory sanctuary scene for Revelation 11:19 to 14:20, the division we're studying now. This verse says, "Then

370

God's temple in heaven was opened, and the ark of his covenant was seen." The believers reflected on Christ's 1844 high priestly journey on the clouds to heaven's equivalent of the most holy place. The most holy place in the Old Testament sanctuary was the location of the ark of the covenant, with the Ten Commandments written on stone tablets inside it.

"Sin is lawlessness." 1 John 3:4. If Jesus is today doing a special work to cleanse His people from their sins, they reasoned, He is doing a special work of renewing our interest in His law!

Then they looked at Revelation 12:17, K.J.V., and noticed that God's end-time people, the true "remnant" of the woman's seed, keep the commandments of God.

The third angel's message. They also noticed in a wholly new way that the first two angels are followed by a third one, and that this third angel warns against the mark of the beast and also describes God's end-time "saints" just as Revelation 12:17 does, as *keeping the commandments of God.*

In our next section we'll look at the mark of the beast. For now we're concentrating on this other aspect of the third angel's message, **"Here is a call for the endurance of the saints, those who keep the commandments of God and the faith of Jesus."** Revelation 14:12.

About the time when Bates and the others were coming to a new understanding of Christ's high priestly ministry, some Seventh Day Baptists told Bates about the Sabbath. They said it should be observed not on the first day of the week, as most devout Christians observed it, but on the seventh day, the day the Ten Commandments have it.

Wide-eyed with amazement, Joseph Bates reread the fourth commandment. Bates, like Miller and most other advent leaders, was a devout Sunday keeper. As a sea captain he had required Sunday rest and worship of his sailing crews. But never had the commandment seemed to read this way before: "Remember the sabbath day, to keep it holy. . . . The *seventh* day [Saturday] is a sabbath to the Lord your God." Exodus 20:8-10.

Being a man of decision Bates firmly made up his mind and soon became the leader of a very small but growing group of Sabbath-keeping Adventists. He wrote a forty-eight-page Bible study called, *The Seventh Day Sabbath, a Perpetual Sign.* It came out in August 1846.

James and Ellen White were married that same month. They were friends of his and also admirers of William Miller. Ellen (1827-1915), born Ellen Harmon, was a former Methodist; James (1821-1881), like Bates, was a former leader in the Christian Connection. James and Ellen carefully examined Bates's Bible verses and soon joined him in observing the seventh-day Sabbath.

Sacrificing for the Sabbath. A little over a year later, Bates sat down to write a further work on the Sabbath, the one he was working on at the beginning of this section, when his original $11,000 had been reduced to a York shilling. He believed that the Sabbath was so important that if he acted on his faith and wrote about the Sabbath so other people could learn about it, God would take care of his financial needs. He told only God his needs.

His wife, Prudence, wasn't aware of his extreme poverty. She interrupted him with the information that she needed a few pounds of flour to finish her baking. He promptly went to a nearby grocery, spent his lonely York shilling to purchase the amount she requested, and brought it home.

Poor Prudence was nonplussed. She was used to her captain husband's laying in provisions by the barrel. When he explained that he'd spent their last silver coin, she chided him for his imprudence and went away to weep.

But a little later, as Bates continued to write, the impression came that there was money at the post office. Sure enough, a letter was waiting for him—but with five cents postage due, and he didn't have a penny.

The postmaster told him to take the letter anyway and bring the few pennies another day. Bates, a true Yankee, refused, but said for the postmaster to open the letter, and if there was money in it, to take out the five cents and give him the change.

The postmaster found $10.00 inside, equivalent to half a month's wages. Bates never did learn who sent it; but he gratefully accepted his $9.95 change, stopped by the grocery to order a barrel of flour and a lot of other eatables, and called at the stationer's for writing paper and some pens. When the groceries were deliv-

Joseph Bates was right! There was money in the envelope!

ered, Prudence graciously apologized. Presumably she felt better about her husband's "imprudence."

Meanwhile, James White and his wife Ellen were making their own faith-filled sacrifices to spread the joyous word about the seventh-day Sabbath. To earn expenses to travel to one interested group, James White helped mow a field of hay in blistering weather at 87.5 cents an acre.

Over the years James White made many tough sacrifices to help spread the word about the Sabbath. His final sacrifice was his early death (at sixty) from malaria and overwork. (Malaria was common in America in the nineteenth century.) Jesus had said, "If you love me, you will keep my commandments." John 14:15. James White, Ellen, and Joseph Bates surely loved Jesus. If He wanted them to keep the Sabbath, they would keep it at any personal cost.

One of James White's most perplexing trials was the accusation that he got his beliefs from his wife! He knew better. Evidence that the 2300 days ended in 1844 came through William Miller (and several others) from the Bible. Evidence that the judgment *began* in 1844 was seen by Enoch Jacobs, Joseph Turner, and Apollos Hale in the Bible. Awareness of the seventh-day Sabbath came through Joseph Bates and the Seventh Day Baptists from the Bible!

By 1863 Bates and the Whites were leaders of some 3500 fellow believers, mostly former members of the various denominations, who were thrilled to learn about the three angels' messages and who wanted to express their love for Jesus by keeping His Father's commandments. They had not thought to organize a new denomination, but numbers and distance and ownership of a printing press made organization unavoidable. On May 21, 1863, they launched the Seventh-day Adventist church.

What is a Seventh-day Adventist? A Seventh-day Adventist is a person who believes (1) that the final judgment began in 1844 and that *therefore* we can know that the second advent of Christ is near.

A Seventh-day Adventist also believes (2) that because in 1844 Jesus moved into the most holy place, where the Ten Commandments are located, and because God's end-time "remnant" "saints" keep God's commandments, and because, as we said a moment ago, Jesus in a special sense is purifying His people from sin—and "sin is lawlessness"—everyone who loves Jesus and is looking for Christ's return should be keeping the Sabbath holy on the seventh day of the week.

As early Seventh-day Adventists continued their Bible study, they came upon additional Bible evidence pointing to commandment keeping and observance of the Sabbath. For instance, they noticed (a) that under the new covenant, which Christ ratified with His own blood, the Holy Spirit comes and writes God's law on our hearts.

"I will put my law within them, and I will write it upon their hearts," says God in Jeremiah 31:33. "I will put my spirit within you, and cause you to walk in my statutes and be careful to observe my ordinances." Ezekiel 36:27. See GC 1:170, 171, 226-229.

BIBLE DISCUSSION OUTLINE ABOUT THE SABBATH
You may enjoy rereading pages 82-85

HOW, WHY, WHEN, AND BY WHOM WAS THE SABBATH MADE?

1. Genesis 2:1-3. Who made the Sabbath?

2. John 1:1-3. Who joined with God in making the Sabbath?

3. Mark 2:27. For whom was the Sabbath intended?

4. Exodus 20:8-11; Ezekiel 31:17. What is the relationship between Sabbath and creation?

5. Exodus 31:13; Ezekiel 20:12, 20. What great personal truth about God do we discover as we keep the Sabbath?

HOW SHOULD THE SABBATH BE KEPT?

6. Exodus 20:8-11. Is the Sabbath more than an ordinary holiday?
   What about the members of the family? What about one's employees?

7. Exodus 16:22, 23. What is one way to get ready for the Sabbath?
   Note: The command "Remember the Sabbath" means that we not only keep the day when it comes but that we plan ahead so that when the day comes it can be free of jobs like mending and repairing and heavy kitchen duties. Children can help with the preparation.

8. Isaiah 58:13, 14. So far as possible, how should everyone in the family feel about the Sabbath each week?

9. Luke 23:54. What was Friday called in Christ's time?

10. Mark 1:32; compare Leviticus 23:32. When does the Sabbath begin and end?

   Note: Sabbath keeping families find sundown an attractive moment for family worship.

11. Leviticus 23:3. What about religious meetings (or convocations)?

12. Jeremiah 17:19-27. What did the prophet Jeremiah say about the Sabbath in the days of Daniel and Nebuchadnezzar?
    Note: Compare Nehemiah 13:15-22 (about 150 years later, after the return from Babylon).

JESUS AND THE SABBATH

13. Genesis 2:1-3; John 1:1-3. Where was Jesus when the Sabbath was made?
    Note: See Questions 1 and 2, above.

14. Luke 4:16. What was Christ's "custom" Sabbath by Sabbath?
    Note: See Question 11, above.

15. Matthew 12:12. Because religious leaders with minute regulations made Sabbath a nightmare for the ill (who were allowed no special care unless life was actually in danger), what did Jesus teach?

16. Mark 1:21-31; 3:1-5; Luke 13:10-17; 14:1-4; John 5:1-15; 9:1-7. What is the meaning for us today of Christ's seven Sabbath miracles?
    Note: In a career as short as Christ's every act was meaningful. Through these Sabbath miracles He comes to us each Sabbath saying, "Do *you* want to be healed?" (John 5), "Shouldn't *you* be free?" (Luke 13), "If you can't 'see' something, I'll give you light" (John 9).

    As Sabbath comes on we may accustom ourselves to seeing Jesus draw near and speak courage to us as He did to the man thirty-eight years paralyzed, "If you want to be strong, stand up. Do the thing you've been putting off. Step out by faith, and I'll give you victory" (John 5).

17. Matthew 5:17, 18. How did Jesus feel about the law and the prophets (including evidently what the prophets said about the law in Questions 7, 10, and 12 above)?

18. Matthew 24:20. What did Jesus say about the continued existence of the Sabbath decades after His death on the cross?

    Note: See page 43.

They also became aware (b) that in the great controversy between Christ and Satan, Satan is persuasively employing a battery of lies against God's law. "You *need not* keep them," "For your own good you *shouldn't* keep them," and "You *cannot* keep them," he says in all sorts of subtle ways. The dragon, the old serpent and Satan, is still much alive. The early Adventists didn't want to be deceived by him.

They thought a lot too about Jesus' death. Not only did the cross ratify the covenant promises; it also showed (c) that God has no way of changing His law.

Jesus in Gethsemane, a vigorous man of 33, was not eager to die. Three times in deepest anguish He implored His Father—"if thou art willing"—to remove the "cup" He was about to drink. Matthew 26:36-44; Luke 22:44. If there had been any way to save us other than having Jesus die, God would surely have found that other way. If He could have said, "My laws aren't all that perfect anyway; I'll change them to suit my human friends so they won't be guilty anymore," He would have done it. Then Jesus wouldn't have needed to die.

Setting His laws aside would have been a far easier way for God to forgive sinners than to have His Son die.

But the commandment is "holy and just and good." Romans 7:12. Changing it would have made it unholy, unjust, and bad. God's law is love. How could He have changed it?

The death of Jesus ratified the new covenant and demonstrated definitively and dramatically that the law cannot be changed. The cross confirmed the commandments. Christ's sacrifice helped establish the seventh-day Sabbath.

All these thoughts went through the minds of Seventh-day Adventists and persuaded them to keep the Sabbath in spite of personal cost and inconvenience.

Health, education, and missions. Seventh-day Adventists also came to see that if God's moral laws are important, His health laws must also be important. People who want to keep God's commandments will surely want to live in harmony with His physical laws. Hence began that freedom from tobacco, alcohol, and meat and that emphasis on exercise, fresh air, and practical faith that have become such well-known characteristics of American Seventh-day Adventists. It's been good for them! Numerous studies in recent years have shown that American Seventh-day Adventists suffer far fewer heart attacks, very much less cancer of certain types, and live an average six years longer than persons who follow the average American life-style.[62]

In the Old Testament, Daniel too found that healthful living was good for him! Daniel 1:8-16; see GC 1:17.

Under the prodding of Ellen White, Seventh-day Adventists in 1866 started their first health institution. They now operate about 155 hospitals and nearly 250 smaller health-care institutions. People who feel good find it easier to be good and do good. So health is an important part of the Seventh-day Adventist life-style. They believe God cares how we feel.

God also cares about children; so teaching them how to develop characters capable of coping with the final crisis has also become part of the Seventh-day Adventist way of life. In 1874 they opened their first college. They now operate the largest Protestant educational system worldwide.

A whole world deserves to know about the judgment and the commandments and the laws of health and Christ's high priestly ministry and His soon return to take us to supper. So in 1874 Seventh-day Adventists sent out their first overseas missionary. Actually they sent out a family of missionaries, a widowed father, J. N. Andrews, and his teenage Mary and Charles, who gave him quality help. Today there are 4,000,000 Seventh-day Adventists in 185 or so countries, not omitting China and the Soviet Union, and their numbers are increasing at a million every few years.

They believe that the advent movement is *a fulfillment of the three angels of Revelation 14:6-12* and that it is developing the "remnant" "saints" who keep God's commandments. They invite everyone everywhere to join the movement with them.

They remain grateful to Joseph Bates and all the others in the middle 1800s who sacrificed for Christ's sake to get the movement going.

IX. Mark of the Beast and Seal of God

"What's the funny mark on that man's face, Daddy?"

"It's not a funny mark, Son. It's very serious."

"I know; but what is it?"

"It's a stigma, or what you might call a charagma."

"But I still don't know what it is."

Roman slaves were often branded with marks burned on their foreheads.

"Well, it's three letters of the alphabet, F U G. It means that the man is a slave who ran away and was caught. To punish him his master labeled him a fugitive so everyone can know what a bad man he is."

"Will he always have the mark on him, Daddy?"

"Yes, Son, as long as he lives."

"Oh, I feel so sad for him."

Marks and seals in Bible times. As a boy, the apostle John quite possibly engaged in such a conversation with his father. As an old man he was well acquainted with the custom of tattooing or burning identification marks on people and animals. Western ranchers today brand their cattle. Farmers did the same in John's day. They also disgraced unruly slaves by branding them with their crimes.

The government often branded convicts. At some point in Roman history the military branded recruits, usually with a tattooed abbreviation of the name of the reigning emperor.

"The slave was marked on the forehead," says the *Theological Dictionary of the New Testament,* and "the soldier was usually marked on the hand."[63]

On the forehead or on the hand. This is interesting. Revelation 13:16, 17 says, **"It [the lamb-horned beast] causes all, both small and great, both rich and poor, both free and slave, to be marked on the right hand or the forehead, so that no one can buy or sell unless he has the mark, that is, the name of the beast or the number of its name."**

A brief word study. The ordinary Greek word for the kind of body mark we're talking about was *stigma.* Other words were *semeion* or "sign," *sphragis* or "seal," and *charagma* (KAH-rug-ma), meaning "mark." *Charagma* is the word John used for the "mark" of the beast; *sphragis* is his word for the "seal" of God. But apparently all the terms were more or less interchangeable.[64]

Marks and attitudes. An unruly slave detested his *stigma.* Think of our English words *stigma* and *stigmatize.*

But soldiers were proud of their tattoos. And being marked as the worshiper of a god was a high privilege.

"In Ethiopia," we learn, "children were dedicated to [the god] Apollo by a mark on the knee-cap. . . . The Syrians consecrated themselves to the gods Hadad and Atargatis by signs branded on the wrist or neck." Worshipers of other gods had marks on other parts of their bodies. The early historian Herodotus says that a runaway slave who got the mark of Hercules at a certain temple in Egypt became the slave of the god, and even his former owner wasn't allowed to lay hands on him.[65]

So a mark could be the sign of a god's servant and a guarantee of the god's protection. This too is interesting. God's "servants" who receive His "name" and "seal" in their foreheads are protected from the seven last plagues. In the vision of Ezekiel 9:1-8 everyone in Jerusalem was to die during Nebuchadnezzar's invasion except the sincere and earnest people who received God's protecting mark on their foreheads.

What is the mark of the beast? So we want to know about the mark of the beast. What is it and how can we avoid it?

As for what it is there are many answers. One is simply not to worry. It was something Nero put on Christians. No one has ever proved that Nero put marks on Christians; but, this answer says, he *was* the beast John had in mind.

Another answer is that the actual number 666 will be branded on people by the ruler of a future Roman empire.

So who is right?

Who or what is the beast? To identify the mark we must first identify the beast. It shouldn't be hard. The beast in question is the leopard-bodied sea beast whose "mortal wound was healed." Revelation 13:3, 11-17. On page 327 we compared this beast with Daniel's little horns:

THE LITTLE HORN Daniel 7 and 8	THE LEOPARD-BODIED BEAST Revelation 13
Speaks great words against God Thinks to change time and law	Utters blasphemies against God
Tramples on the sanctuary and the host	Blasphemes God's name, His dwelling, and those who dwell in heaven
Wears out the saints for a time, two times, and half a time	Makes war with the saints for forty-two months

As we decided before, the similarity reveals that the "beast" is the church of Rome.

So what, according to Daniel and Revelation, are the characteristic features or marks of the church of Rome, viewed from its less favorable side? (1) Blaspheming God and changing His law, (2) undermining the ministry of the heavenly sanctuary, and (3) oppressing God's saints.

In Revelation 12-14 the people who receive the mark of the beast stand in *contrast* to the saints who **"keep the commandments of God."**

The Catholic Church doesn't teach people to commit adultery or commit murder. The commandment which it claims to have changed is the fourth commandment, the one about the Sabbath. (You may wish to reread GC 1:134-143.)

It has made non-observance of Sunday a mortal sin. In the early Middle Ages priests "discovered" letters from heaven to frighten people into observing Sunday rather than the Sabbath. In 1054 Pope Leo IX excommunicated the entire Eastern Orthodox Church partly because the Orthodox celebrated the Sabbath. Of all the major branches of Christendom the Catholic Church became the one most opposed to the seventh-day Sabbath.

"The pope can modify divine law," said Petrus de Ancharano.

"The Sabbath, the most glorious day in the law, has been changed into the

379

Lord's day . . . by the authority of the church," declared the archbishop of Reggio at the crucial Council of Trent.

"We observe Sunday instead of Saturday because the Catholic Church transferred the solemnity from Saturday to Sunday," says *The Convert's Catechism*.

God didn't change His law even to excuse Jesus from Gethsemane and crucifixion. See page 376. But a body of Christian leaders felt free to change it, and to harass, persecute, and excommunicate millions of Christians who chose to obey it. The charge is serious indeed.

The mark of the beast in the **"forehead"** represents mental assent to the church's belief and behavior. The mark in the **"hand"** represents activity carried on in harmony with such beliefs. A person's "forehead" may not approve what his or her "hand" does, but actions speak louder than words.

God's two signs. Another way to understand the mark of the beast is to look at God's special signs.

There were two special signs which God asked His people to accept in Old Testament times. One was ritual circumcision. First performed around 2000 B.C. on Abraham, the father of the Jewish race, it was routinely performed on Jewish baby boys when they were a week old. It was an ethnic distinction. According to the apostle Paul it ceased to have saving significance when the Jewish people as a group ceased to be uniquely God's chosen people. See GC 1:231-236.

Today, "in Christ . . . there is neither Jew nor Greek, there is neither slave nor free, there is neither male nor female; for you are all one in Christ Jesus." Galatians 3:26-28.

After the cross, ritual circumcision counted for little one way or the other. The commandments, however, still mattered! Paul said in 1 Corinthians 7:19, "Neither circumcision counts for anything [any more] nor uncircumcision, but keeping the commandments of God."

Other translations make the meaning even clearer. "Circumcision is nothing and uncircumcision is nothing. Keeping God's commands is what counts." N.I.V. "Circumcision is nothing, and uncircumcision is nothing, but what matters is the keeping of the commandments of God." N.A.S.B.

Paul's message about the commandments was the same as John's. God's people are expected to keep them.

This brings us to the other sign, the one which God still uses to identify His followers. Given to the first human parents, it is offered to everyone without racial distinction.

Because it was offered to the entire human race, it was offered to the Jewish race along with all the others. So we find God saying to the Israelites at Mount Sinai, "You shall keep my sabbaths, for this is a *sign* between me and you throughout your generations, that you may know that *I the Lord, sanctify you*." "It is a *sign* for ever between me and the people of Israel that in six days *the Lord made heaven and earth,* and on the seventh day he rested, and was refreshed." Exodus 31:13, 17.

The Sabbath is a sign showing that God made us and that He sanctifies or re-makes us.

The setting for the statement was impressive. God had led the Israelites triumphantly out of Egypt. They were camping awhile at the foot of Mount Sinai. With a light-and-sound display that would make a top rock concert seem like a kindergarten murmur, God called attention to the Ten Commandments. There were "thunders and lightnings, and a thick cloud upon the mountain, and a very loud trumpet blast. . . . And the whole mountain quaked greatly." Exodus 19:16-18. Later, when Moses' helpers finished building the golden portable sanctuary or tabernacle, God had Moses place a copy of the Ten Commandments, carved in stone, in the "ark of the covenant" (or "ark of testament") in the sanctuary's innermost room, the most holy place. See Exodus 32:15, 16; 25:16, 21; Numbers 10:33; GC 1:165, 166.

We're on familiar ground! In the sanctuary scene (Revelation 11:19) which introduces the great-controversy division (11:19 to14:20) that we're studying now, the heavenly temple opened up so John could see deep inside it. He saw heaven's **"ark of his covenant."** As he looked, there were **"flashes of lightning, voices, peals of thunder, an earthquake, and heavy hail."**

God was taking John back to Mount Sinai!

God is calling us too back to Mount Sinai, back to the sanctuary, back to Jesus our High Priest, to the Ten Commandments and the Sabbath.

For the Sabbath wasn't made at Mount Sinai exclusively for the Jews. It was made at creation, at the very birth of our world. See Genesis 2:1-3. It was made by the Creator of the universe, *our* Creator. It was made "for man," Jesus said (Mark 2:27), for mankind, for humanity as a whole.

The Sabbath as a "sign" has been offered to all of us, to all of us who want to know our Creator, Redeemer, and Sanctifier as our very own.

The prophets and the Sabbath. People who give only casual thought to the matter assume that the Jews have kept the Sabbath more or less loyally all through their history. On the contrary, in ancient times they frequently abandoned it. The prophets Jeremiah and Ezekiel, contemporaries of Daniel, called earnestly for a Sabbath revival.

Jeremiah promised that if the Jews would keep the Sabbath again, God would protect them from the impending Babylonian invasion. "If you listen to me, says the Lord," Jeremiah wrote, "and bring in no burden by the gates of this city on the sabbath day, but keep the sabbath day holy and do no work on it, then there shall enter by the gates of this city kings who sit on the throne of David, . . . and this city shall be inhabited for ever." Jeremiah 17:24, 25.

In spite of God's heartfelt appeal, Jeremiah had to say, "Yet they did not listen or incline their ear, but stiffened their neck, that they might not hear and receive instruction." Verse 23. How very sad. And we know the tragic sequel. See GC 1:19-21.

Ezekiel, working also for a revival of Sabbath observance, recalled the prom-

THE TWO SIDES AT THE END OF TIME

PEOPLE OF GOD	FOLLOWERS OF SATAN
You may wish to add other items	

INSIGNIA

Receive SEAL OF GOD in forehead 7:1-3	Receive MARK OF BEAST in forehead or hand 13:16; 14:11

CHARACTER

Obey commandments of God. 12:17 Obey commandments of God. 14:12	
Worship the Creator. 14:7	Worship the beast and its image. 13:12; 14:9; 16:2; 19:20
No lie in their mouths. 14:5	Accept the lies of the false prophet. 19:20
Undefiled with women. 14:4	Cowardly, faithless, polluted, murderers, fornicators, sorcerers, idolaters, liars. 21:8
Spotless. 14:5	
Keep the faith of Jesus. 14:12 Have endurance. 13:10; 14:12	
Conquer beast, image, number. 15:2	Make an image of the beast. 13:14
Are fully ripe grain. 14:15	Are ripe grapes. 14:18

PRIVILEGES AND PUNISHMENTS

Names in the book of life. *Dan. 12:1	Names not in book of life. 17:8
Unable to buy or sell. 13:17 BUT redeemed (=bought). 14:3 Have testimony of Jesus. 12:17, KJV	Able to buy and sell. 13:17
Servants of God. 7:3 Saints. 14:12 God's "remnant." 12:17, KJV Belong to the 144,000. 7:4-8; 14:1-5	
Escape the plagues. 18:4	Suffer the plagues. 14:9-11; 16:2
Guests at the Lamb's wedding supper. 19:9	Fed to birds at God's supper. 19:17-21
Receive the eternal kingdom. *Dan. 7:27	Suffer permanent punishment 14:9-11

EXPERIENCE

Come out of Babylon. 18:4	
Celebrate fall of Babylon. 19:1-8	Mourn the fall of Babylon. 18:9-19
Praise God for judgments. 15:3, 4	Curse God for judgments. 16:9, 10, 11, 21
Sing in the Lamb's presence. 14:3	Suffer torment in the Lamb's presence. 14:9-11

*All other references are to Revelation

ises God gave at Mount Sinai some seven centuries earlier. "I gave them my sabbaths, as a *sign* between me and them, that they might know that *I the Lord sanctify them.*" Ezekiel 20:12.

"Hallow my sabbaths that they may be a *sign* between me and you, that you may know that *I the Lord am your God.*" Verse 20.

Sorrowfully, Ezekiel, like Jeremiah, had to add, "But the children [of Israel, the Israelites] rebelled against me; they did not walk in my statutes, and were not careful to observe my ordinances, by whose observance man shall live; they profaned my sabbaths." Verse 21.

The Sabbath is for everyone. Isaiah the prophet knew that the Sabbath wasn't only for the Jews. "The *foreigners* who join themselves to the Lord," he wrote, "to minister to him, to love the name of the Lord, and to be his servants, *every one* who keeps the sabbath, and does not profane it, and holds fast my covenant— these I will bring to my holy mountain, and make them joyful in my house of prayer." Isaiah 56:6, 7.

Look at Isaiah's language! It talks about God's "servants," "joyful" on God's "mountain." It sounds like the 144,000 servants of God, singing on Mount Zion! Isaiah's promise is made about "foreigners," non-Jews who keep the Sabbath.

The seal of God. God's end-time people keep the commandments and accept God's "seal." So what is the seal of God? It's the same as His sign!

In ancient times people signed their documents in the same way they sealed them. They stamped them with a signet ring or seal. See page 210. So "to sign" and "to seal" were the same thing. God's "sign" in our foreheads is the same as His "seal."

Nowadays we sign a document by writing our signature on it. Our signature or sign is our name. When we sign in some official capacity, we have a typist identify ourselves more fully, indicating our official capacity as part of our signature.

A bank manager has his secretary type, "Johnson Doe, Manager, First Federal of Bigtown." God conceivably could have a secretary type, "Lord God, Creator, Heaven and Earth." And this is just about the way God did sign His name in the Sabbath commandment!

"Remember the sabbath day, to keep it holy. . . . The seventh day is a sabbath to the *Lord your God*; . . . for in six days the *Lord made heaven and earth,* the sea, and all that is in them, and rested the seventh day; therefore the Lord blessed the sabbath day and hallowed it." Exodus 20:8-11.

How could God sign a document more significantly? How could He offer the Sabbath to us more authoritatively?

He doesn't force us to keep the Sabbath. Billions of people who neglect it or make light of it can testify to this. But He does come to us, make His request, and sign or seal it, "Lord God, Creator, Heaven and Earth."

God's name, the Lamb's name. The 144,000, who have God's seal in their foreheads, are also described as having God's name and the Lamb's name there too. Revelation 14:1-5.

Ancient worshipers had their god's literal name tattooed on their bodies. The "name" that Revelation talks about is much more than a tattoo! Names in Bible days represented a person's character. See pages 104-106. When God told Moses His "name" He listed His character qualities, "merciful and gracious, slow to anger, and abounding in steadfast love and faithfulness," and so on. Exodus 34:5, 6.

Fully matured Sabbath keepers have God's name in their foreheads in the sense that they have allowed God's Spirit to change their characters until they resemble God's character.

God is love. His law is love. When people obey Him fully, they love.

God is holy. His law is holy. When people obey Him fully, the Holy Spirit lives out in their lives the purity and honesty and unselfishness that mark the character of God Himself.

So how is God's name the same as His seal? We are sinners. If we are ever going to keep an entire Sabbath day holy, we need a distinct and deep-seated change in our most basic patterns. Jesus told Nicodemus that even a good man like him needed to be born again. See John 3:5. We can never keep a whole Sabbath holy unless something happens in us every day. We must be in such fellowship with Christ that we live purity, honesty, compassion, helpfulness all week.

God's people at the very end of time *will* be **"spotless,"** free from lies, true and honest, chaste, pure, kind. They will keep God's commandments even when faced with starvation and execution.

But how? They conquer the dragon **"by the word of their testimony,"** and they love not their lives **"even unto death."** Revelation 12:11.

But this is by no means all. How often our willpower lets us down! The overcomers have the **"blood of the Lamb."** In fact, they have the Lamb. They have Michael the great Prince. See Daniel 12:1. In some marvelous and mysterious manner He has come knocking and has been welcomed into their hearts. He has brought with Him all the gold, eye salve, and white raiment they can use. See Revelation 3:15-22.

Wonderful thought! He has brought Himself. And Colossians 2:9 says, "In him the whole fulness of deity dwells bodily." So when in His own special way He enters us in response to our faith, He brings His Godhead with Him! And then *we* are "filled with all the fulness of God"! Ephesians 3:17-19.

"You shall keep my sabbaths, for this is a *sign* between me and you . . . , that you may know that *I, the Lord, sanctify you.*" Exodus 31:13.

So this is how the 144,000, the "saints," God's "remnant," young and old, escape the mark of the beast and are able to keep all the commandments of God and stand complete in holiness and purity as God's fully ripened grain!

What difference does it make? Yet many still hold back. "What's the big deal?" they ask. "We're Christians and go to church, pretty often anyway. What difference does the day make?"

The serpent sweetly smiles, "God is Love. You *need not* keep the Sabbath."

"The requirement is unreasonable. For your own sake, you *shouldn't* keep it."
"It requires holiness, and you're a sinner. You *cannot* keep it."

The serpent is glad to have us go on worshiping God—providing we do so in our own way. He persuaded Eve to eat the forbidden fruit so she could become like God, not unlike Him. "You will be like God," he promised. Genesis 3:5. The serpent was pleased to have Eve honor God in her own way.

Cain worshiped God in his own way, with garden produce instead of a lamb. The Medieval Church worshiped God in its own way. Moslems by the millions worship God in their own way.

Cain and the Roman Church in time grew angry with people who worshiped God in His chosen way. Behaving angrily seems to be characteristic of many of us when we insist on worshiping God in our own way.

Mark of the beast now or later? But do all Christians who neglect the Sabbath have the mark of the beast now?

A mature student recently enrolled at the seminary where I teach. Till lately he served as an officer in a bank. Before he left the bank he visited the other officers to explain that he was leaving to enter the ministry. He also told them of his new conviction that His Lord and Saviour wanted him to keep the Sabbath. He was pleasantly surprised at their response. His co-workers congratulated him. And those who encouraged him most to follow his new convictions were Roman Catholics. I don't believe these Catholics have the mark of the beast!

The mark is imposed on people after the image of the beast is erected, after the mortal wound is healed. It is one of the final developments of the end time.

The seal of God (true Sabbath holiness) represents the character of the fully ripened grain of Revelation 14:15. The mark of the beast (deliberate hostile approval of the "beast's" rules and behavior as epitomized in coercive Sunday observance) represents the character of the ripened grapes of Revelation 14:17-20.

The mark is to be imposed globally under American church-state influence. Accompanied by demonic miracles it escalates into legislation that invokes the death penalty. Revelation 13:11-18. See pages 348, 349.

Because the mark pertains to events so very late in earth's history, we know that it relates to a situation after the gospel has been preached in all the world. See Matthew 24:14. Individuals will receive the mark only when they have had a chance to hear the evidence. The mark is a sign of rebellion, a kind of F U G stamped on a person who deliberately and knowingly runs away from God.

"Whoever *knows* what is right to do and fails to do it, for him it is sin." James 4:17.

The basic issue. So what shall we do? Shall we rebel and be "stiff-necked," like the people Jeremiah and Ezekiel had to deal with?

Or, less defiantly, shall we try not to know anything further about the matter? Shall we perhaps close this book thoughtfully and say, "Maybe sometime later"?

What *is* the basic issue? Surely it isn't merely one day against another.

Isn't the issue one of worship? According to the three angels' messages, people

385

in the end time either worship God, "who made heaven and earth," or they worship the beast. Which do we worship? (On the meaning of "worship," see section XI below.)

To put the matter another way, the basic issue is one of faith and affection. Do we genuinely *believe* that the Bible is true, that God is our Creator and Redeemer? Do we have the **"faith of Jesus"**? And do we so love God that we genuinely desire to do what He asks?

Do we genuinely want to *know* what He wants? Or are we afraid to learn, for fear we won't want to do it?

But when we do truly love and appreciate Him, we want to know what He wants of us, and we want to do it. Don't we?

Jesus thought so. "If you love me," He said, "you will keep my commandments." John 14:15.

> My Jesus, I love Thee, I know Thou art mine;
> For Thee all the follies of sin I resign;
> My gracious Redeemer, my Saviour art Thou;
> If ever I loved Thee, my Jesus, 'tis now.[66]

X. The Final Crisis and Your Family

Passengers from a sinking ship can live in the icy Atlantic, I understand, only about six minutes.

An American company in 1915 wanted to send a young expert to Britain on the *Lusitania*. The company changed its mind when Germany threatened to sink the ship. The young man insisted on going anyway. He said he was a strong swimmer and that lately he'd been sitting daily in a tub of ice water. At first he could endure only a few minutes, but he'd worked up to where he could take two hours easily.

He sailed with the *Lusitania*, but he didn't go down with her. He was rescued after five hours, still in excellent condition.[67]

Are there young people in your family? If there are, they face with you the final crisis. What fitness should they be training for if they're going to survive and come through with the Lord?

Here's a list of character qualities and other attributes to think about. You may wish to modify it here and there. I got most of it from an insightful book by Dr. Beatrice Neall.[68]

Characteristics for God's young "saints." On the basis of what we have studied so far, young people who want to be survivors should now be developing these characteristics:

1. power to make choices, to do the right thing at any cost, to love "not their lives even unto death" (see Revelation 12:11);

2. strength to resist peer pressure even when the whole world follows the beast (see Revelation 13:3):

386

3. ability to distinguish true from false even when the antichrist's deceptions are so persuasive they almost deceive the elect (see Matthew 24:24);

4. patience and endurance (see Matthew 24:13; Revelation 14:12);

5. strong loyalty to God and His people (in Revelation God's people are usually spoken of as a group; they hold together);

6. a conviction about values that puts service and eternal life ahead of buying and selling (see Revelation 13:17) and doing one's own thing here and now;

7. experience in worshiping God (see Revelation 14:6, 7);

8. the habit of buoyant faith (see Revelation 14:12; Daniel 6:10); and

9. the ability to express faith in words—for the people of God, including the young ones evidently, are to be channels of truth to others (Revelation 22:17), and they are to overcome Satan through the **"word of their testimony"** (Revelation 12:11).

The opposition: secular humanism. Dr. Neall, who is a Christian educator and a mother, is concerned because in all too many American public schools, young people are being taught a package known as "secular humanism," which cleverly undermines these character qualities.[69]

Secular humanism encourages young people to believe that we evolved from amino acids in a primordial ocean, and that there is no personal God, no life beyond the one we have now, and no moral absolutes. The best, then, that young people can do is to set their own values, live as comfortably as possible, look out for themselves, and make all the money and have all the fun they can. They must feel free to ignore standards held by parents, church, or the Bible.

Secular humanism is based on pagan concepts taught in ancient Greece and Rome. Thus, the lamb-horned beast, through many of its public schools, is teaching young people the lies of the dragon.

The young person who is trained in secular humanism (we'll call him George from a Greek word associated with the earth[70]) represents a completely different world view from the world view represented by Christine, a young Christian. George sees himself as a biological organism struggling for survival. Christine values herself as the crowning work of a personal God.

George is encouraged to accumulate things—money, clothes, cars, furniture, houses, boats. Christine is challenged to "win souls," to persuade people to love God.

George sees himself as a pawn of circumstances without ultimate responsibility for his behavior. Christine views herself as endowed by God with full accountability and the power of choice.

George is expected to make moral decisions on the basis of his personal judgment; Christine, on the basis of God's revealed will.

George is urged to seek meaning in self-fulfillment; Christine, in self-sacrifice.

The news media reveal that George—and his girl friend Georgine—are in serious trouble. Vandalism, violence, rape, illegitimate births (268,000 babies were born to unmarried teenagers in 1981), rampant V.D., teenage drinking, lying, and cheating, have apparently all been intensified by the situation ethics and the denial of moral absolutes which are so integral a part of secular humanism.

And secular humanism isn't the only threat to our children's character development.

The additional impact of television. Marie Winn, like Dr. Neall, is also a concerned mother. She has produced a well-researched and widely acclaimed study[71] on the effects of excessive television watching.

Marie Winn points out that by the time they're twelve, many children have stared into a TV screen for 10,000 hours in a half-darkened room, looking, looking, looking but often not comprehending, rarely evaluating what they see, not playing, not interacting with parents (except when parents come to take them away), not asleep and yet not really awake. The title of her book is *The Plug-in Drug*.

A *New York Times* book reviewer comments inside the front cover, "We all know the child on a television high, equipped with thumb and blanket—the glazed eye, the noncommunicative state, the total stupor that can't be broken into. . . . We had better pay attention" to Marie Winn's concerns.

High among Marie Winn's concerns is the permanently unbalancing effect TV watching has on brain and personality when very young children engage in it every day for hours. Watching TV without thinking much—like listening idly to background music, staring into a fire, or watching bubbles drift past on a stream— develops the right side of the brain at the expense of the left.

God gave us both sides of our brains—and we need the right side well developed, if only to enjoy the beauty of His creation. But it is in the left side of our brains that we evaluate situations, think logically, make decisions, and form sentences to express ourselves with.

Even "Sesame Street" was found by a team of independent researchers to have *retarded* children's normal mental development![72]

Children do learn from television. As they grow older there is little else, it seems, that some of them like to talk about. Among the things they learn are unreality and the quick fix. "Children today are often *less* mature in their ability to endure small frustrations," Marie Winn's research reveals, "or to realize that something takes a longer time to do, that it isn't *instant*. They're less tolerant of letting themselves become absorbed in something that seems a little hard at first, or in something that is not immediately interesting."[73]

Secular humanism and mindless TV-watching appear to be preparing an end-time generation with diminished ability to think logically, distinguish between right and wrong, express faith, endure hardship, serve sacrificially, resist peer pressure, and worship the Creator.

If we who are parents are content to leave our children glued to the tube for hours on end, we're not using all that time to learn who they really are and what their inner needs are. We're not interacting with them as we might, guiding and training them for the crisis ahead.

388

We haven't talked about rock music and drugs. It is said that more than half of the avowed Christians in America abuse drugs. What about the theology of movies? Did you know that the "Force" in *Star Wars* is based on the *mana* of animism and the *karma* of popular Hinduism? When children even in fun say, "May the Force be with you," they are invoking the demonic influence of paganism.[74]

Sabbathkeeping as a way to help our families. Revelation presents a Creator and a Lamb in the business of preparing us for whatever is ahead. Heaven *will* have a people ready for the final test, and each of us can belong to it by His grace.

One of God's finest plans for helping us to help our children train for the final conflict is the Sabbath commandment. "In it you shall not do any work," it says, "you, or your son, or your daughter, your manservant, or your maidservant." Exodus 20:10. The Sabbath commandment is a family commandment.

Adult Sabbath keepers do not work on the Sabbath, and they close down their businesses if they have any, so they and their employees can be free. If not working involves financial loss, children see that the Sabbath and the Lord of the Sabbath (Mark 2:27) are important to you, and they are influenced by your example not to "imitate evil but imitate good." 3 John 11. Further, by not going to their jobs, parents gain time for their families.

All the commandments involve love (Matthew 22:36-40), and the Sabbath is conspicuously a day for joy (Isaiah 58:13, 14). Unless the Sabbath is kept happily, it isn't kept. Family Sabbaths can be truly happy when loving adults take the day to spend it pleasantly helping their children learn more about God.

God showed intense interest in children when in Deuteronomy 6:6-8 He asked parents to teach their children "diligently," talking about His teachings in relation to all the big and little events that make up every day, getting up and going to bed, eating, walking, working. "And you shall bind them [God's teachings] as a *sign* upon your *hand*," He said, "and they shall be as frontlets between your eyes [that is, on your *foreheads*]."

A sign, on hand and forehead! It sounds like the seal of God. And so it is! The sealing angel of Revelation 7:1-3, like other symbolic angels in the book, symbolizes the ministers and teachers—and parents—who teach God's ways to others. See page 90. When parents and grandparents teach God's truth to their children, they cooperate with the angel in sealing their children so they can stand among the 144,000 and sing on the sea of glass.

Conscientious parents discipline and guide their children every day. They keep in touch daily with what they're learning in school so they can help them evaluate it in family discussions. The Sabbath provides a *special* occasion for sealing God's truth in the minds of our family members. With every television set turned off, family leadership has a unique opportunity to reverse the influence of secular humanism and the downward drag of contemporary culture.

What to do on the Sabbath. The Sabbath begins at sunset on Friday and ends at sunset on Saturday. See Leviticus 23:32; Mark 1:32. When the sun goes down early, as it does in winter in temperate zones, many Sabbath-keeping families

389

enjoy their Friday evening meal by candlelight. Many develop a family tradition of reserving a favorite food for the occasion too. For conversation, everyone can tell how God answered a prayer or in what way someone was kind to them or review some other happy event from the previous week.

The actual moment of the Sabbath's arrival deserves observance and a celebration. Hymns and other spiritual songs can be sung or played, something can be read from the Bible or other good book, and everyone can kneel for prayer. It's often best if the different family members take turns (even if there are only two of you) or if everyone reads or prays around the circle.

Among my earliest memories are such family sundown worships. Mother read short items suitable to our ages. We sang together (there were five of us children) while the oldest sister played on the piano. Several of us prayed, the youngest prayers being often the most interesting. Father prayed, and we recited the Lord's Prayer together.

Helping to vacuum and get the house in order Friday afternoon, celebrating family worship to welcome in the Sabbath, and enjoying the special supper all meant a lot to me. Coming home from school on the bus when I was ten, I wondered how families got along who didn't know about the Sabbath.

Sabbath-keeping parents take their children to church school (they call it "Sabbath School") on Saturday morning and to the worship service. There they learn to worship God with the rest of the local members, through public prayer and hymns and rededication. To help the littlest ones be "good," they can have a soft toy or "quiet book" that's reserved only for church.

For the noon meal on Sabbath I like hearing everyone retell the stories and interesting ideas they've heard in the different age-divisions of Sabbath School. We review the pastor's sermon. Sometimes we play Bible guessing games.

"I'm thinking of someone in the Bible whose name begins with J (or B, or M, or whatever)," says a child. Everyone else takes turns guessing the name of a Bible person until someone gets the right one. Then it's his turn to think up a new name.

Children more advanced in Bible study make the game more complicated by responding not simply with, "Was it Joseph?" or "Was it Judas?" but with, "Was it the boy who was sold into Egypt?" "Was it the man who betrayed Christ?" Or they play "twenty questions" about things specifically mentioned in the Bible.

When little children aren't eating or drinking—or watching TV—they're playing. They will play on Sabbath; but we'll lead them to play Sabbath games. It is of great importance that they learn as early as possible that Sabbath is a special day.

They can reenact the stories they hear in Sabbath School or do charades of Bible stories or use their blocks to build churches and mission stations. They can also listen to religious cassettes or be read to out of good books. Thousands of children on four continents enjoy *Your Story Hour* cassettes. Several million sets of Arthur Maxwell's *The Bible Story* and *Uncle Arthur's Bedtime Stories* have been read to children in over twenty languages by parents and grandparents and bigger brothers and sisters.[75]

391

A well-spent Sabbath is a happy time for all members of the family.

As they get older and play less, children can, let us say, make homemade cards to send to bereaved people listed in obituary notices or get together with other families and sing around a piano or guitar or read appropriate books—or be read to.

But the Sabbath shouldn't all be spent indoors. It's a day for walking in the park or, perhaps, if the children are small, a trip to the zoo—not, however, for ordinary play or joking or picnicking, but to learn about God the Creator who in six days made the interesting things in heaven and earth. Thus parents use the Sabbath as a precious opportunity to combat the fallacy of evolution.

On another Sabbath parents may take their families to visit people who are confined to their homes. Thus they teach them to serve others.

Sabbath and "final-crisis" fitness. It takes time for a garden to grow and for cakes to bake. It takes time for young Christians to mature. Sabbath provides a heaven-sent opportunity to find some of that needed time.

When parents teach their children to refrain from ordinary pleasures and toys on the Sabbath, they help them make decisions on the highest level, because God loves them and wants them to keep the day specially for Him. If their playmates, friends, or teachers urge them to engage in inappropriate activity, children learn, with parental encouragement, to resist peer pressure and choose God's will for their own.

When they discuss what they've learned in church and review God's blessing in their lives, they get experience in expressing their beliefs in words.

If the day seems a little long, as it may when in summer the sun sets late, they grasp something of the concept of "patient endurance."

Sabbath provides time to talk forgivingly about family troubles and to apologize for hasty words of irritation. It's a time too to talk about the troublous time ahead—and the marvelous deliverance God has planned. Help your family members picture themselves rising in glory to meet the Lord in the air and spending eternity with Him.

Sabbath provides time for longer family worships than may be possible on other days. There's plenty of time for stories about God's love and forgiveness. For stories too about the cross. The children can know that Jesus died for them as well as for their parents and that Jesus can give *them* all the help they need to resist temptation. "Little children, . . . he who is in you is greater than he who is in the world." 1 John 4:4.

Help them identify with Daniel, whom God delivered when he was thrown to the lions for his decision to stand true. Daniel 6; GC 1:95-103. Help them identify with Daniel's friends, who refused to worship the image that King Nebuchadnezzar set up. The Son of God walked with them in the fire. Daniel 3; GC 1:49-56. When the lamb-horned beast sets up the image to the leopard beast, God will be right there again to stand beside the young people who refuse to bow down.

The secret of victory is faith (1 John 5:4), and faith grows as we study God's Word (Romans 10:17).

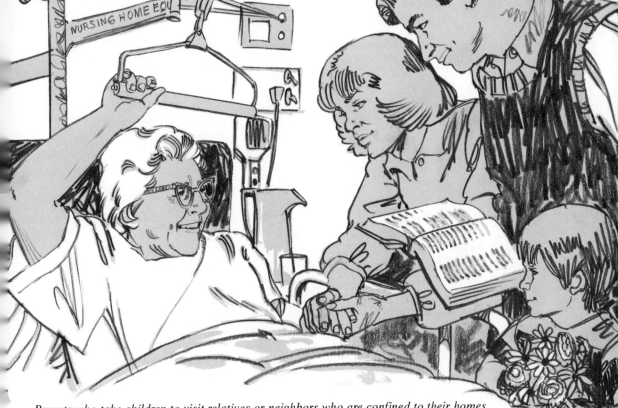

Parents who take children to visit relatives or neighbors who are confined to their homes on Sabbath afternoon are teaching them to be compassionate and caring.

Remind your family of the stories Jesus told in the Olivet Discourse. Those four parables were designed particularly to help us prepare for the last days. See pages 36-42. Help your children choose not to be like the steward who got high on alcohol and abused people. Help them choose instead to be like the servants who improved their talents and like the kind people who shared what they had with the underprivileged. Help them see themselves in the five sensible girls who made sure they had enough oil in their lamps so they could "shine for Jesus" when things didn't go as planned.

Plenty of help available. Parents have at their disposal all the help they need. God has promised in the New Covenant to send His Holy Spirit to write His laws on heart and mind. Read Jeremiah 31:33-35; Ezekiel 36:27. The gift of the Holy Spirit is not only for adults. Peter said on the Day of Pentecost, "The promise is to you *and to your children* and to . . . every one whom the Lord our God calls." Acts 2:39.

God has promised to put "enmity" between the serpent's seed and the woman's. His promise looks to the crucifixion of Jesus, but it has a closer application. It was made originally to a mother about her sons and daughters.

Satan, like a hunter, concentrates on the children who might get away. See page 309. The serpent intensifies his subtle lies, persuading young people in all kinds of ways that they *don't need to* or *shouldn't* or really *cannot* obey God. See pages

332, 333. Through music, drugs, and secular humanism he labors day and night to prevent them from preparing for the final crisis. We who are parents and grandparents must be in earnest. "Toil" and "energy" must be expended as well as time if we want to help young Christians mature. See Colossians 1:28, 29.

Satan and the beast coerce. God pleads. After all we do for our children, the final choice is theirs. God guarantees them this privilege. They may choose to be lost. Judas so chose in the very presence of Christ.

But as we (a) pray, (b) study, and (c) counsel with other Christians, God gives us ideas of things to do and say. God also impresses other Christians to influence our children. He "opens and closes doors," changing situations to make being bad harder and being good easier.

God has a thousand ways to answer our prayers, to put enmity between our children and the serpent, to remind them of His goodness, power, and promises.

Jesus is deeply committed to the salvation of our youth. He is the Lamb who died to save children and keep families together. See page 208.

He is actively engaged in helping parents help their children ripen as God's grain and stand true to Him during the crisis at the end of time. He cares.

XI. How Much Is He Worth?

A young man stepped into a florist shop to get his girl a corsage for the high-school banquet. His eyes roamed between the daisies and the orchids in the dis-

Daisies or orchids: what is she worth? How much is Jesus worth?

play case. He weighed his affections against his poverty. He was hoping to have some money left for his bike.

The florist helped him decide. "Well, Son," he asked after a while, "how much is she worth to you?"

As the lad walked out with an orchid, he could only wonder what had happened.

How much is God worth? How much is God worth to you? The question is relevant, because, as we have seen in the three angels' messages (Revelation 14:6-12), the final issue in the countdown of the great controversy is one of worship, whether we worship God and the Lamb or worship the beast. And "worship" is our response to what we think someone is *worth*.

In chapters 4 and 5 we looked through an open door at what we called Cosmic Control, God's throne in the heavenly sanctuary. See pages 147-149. What did we hear? We heard songs, marvelous songs, happy songs. Living creatures and elders sang, "*Worthy* art thou, our Lord and God, to receive glory and honor and power, for thou didst create all things, and by thy will they existed and were created." Revelation 4:11.

Angels by the thousand million joined the elders and living creatures and sang another song, "*Worthy* is the Lamb who was slain, to receive power and wealth and wisdom and might and honor and glory and blessing!" Revelation 5:12.

Worship is joyful praise. So *how* are we to worship God and the Lamb? First, by joyfully praising Them, giving Them thanks for whom They are and what They've done—for what They're worth.

God knows that when we praise Him for what He's worth, wonderful things happen to us. "The joy of the Lord is your strength." Nehemiah 8:10.

In the last days of time we'll need all the strength we can find to resist the pressures of the dragon, the beast, the false prophet, and the beast worshipers. Remembering joyfully that God made us and Jesus died for us will give us the faith we'll need to go through anything.

"In the world you have tribulation; but *be of good cheer*, I have overcome the world." John 16:33.

Faced with the lions of Babylon, what did Daniel do? Three times a day he "prayed and *gave thanks* before his God, as he had done previously." Daniel 6:10. See GC 1:101-103. When we're faced with the end-time beast of Babylon, we too can be assured that God will send His angel to protect us if we too worship God with praise.

Praising God, joyfully giving thanks, is a custom, a way of life, a habit, if you please, that we ought to be observing now. Daniel didn't learn to praise all at once; he'd done it "previously." Now, today, every day, when confronted with life's ordinary tribulations we ought to be in training for the last days.

When the bills are too high, the boss too demanding, our spouse or parents seemingly unbearable, should we not remember that the God who made everything is still alive and that Jesus, who lives for us (Hebrews 7:25), once died for us? Shouldn't we enjoy the privilege of remembering that God cares about us (1 Peter 5:7)? Shouldn't we enjoy the happiness of applying Heaven's power and love to this very moment and need?

This is worship, responding with joyful praise to what we know about God and the Lamb. And it's good for us to do it; for the "joy of the Lord is your strength."

So worship is joyful praise. It's also something else.

A Christian missionary, walking beside the Ganges one morning years ago, passed a Hindu mother sitting crosslegged near the river bank, cradling a baby girl in her arms, and rocking back and forth. A handsome little boy played nearby.

As the missionary drew close, he noticed that the woman was in distress. Her baby was dying. Hinduism teaches that we live many lifetimes on earth, one lifetime after another. The woman feared that some sin, committed either in her own previous existence or in that of the child's, had angered the gods and brought on the disease.

The missionary tried to comfort her, but she didn't know the Christian's God and couldn't understand.

Toward evening the missionary returned along the same path, the mother of the morning momentarily forgotten. He was startled to see her in the same place, in the same posture, still holding the baby girl and rocking back and forth. She was more weary now—and there was another difference. The little boy was gone.

In his mind he guessed what had taken place. Unwilling to believe it, he greeted her and asked about her son.

"I offered him to the Ganges as a sacrifice to my gods," she replied without looking up.

So it was true! The missionary gasped and in his horror blurted out, "But mother, your baby girl is about to die, and girls don't count for much in India. If you felt you had to sacrifice a child, why didn't you give *her* to the Ganges instead?"

For a moment the anguished woman fixed her eyes on the Christian. "Sir," she said scornfully, "my gods are worthy of my best."

Surely the Christian God is worthy of *our* best.

Surely the Lamb is worth everything to us. Far from expecting us to offer our children in human sacrifice, He sacrificed Himself in their behalf! He left heaven, grew up misunderstood, suffered anguish in Gethsemane and excruciating pain on Calvary. For us.

To know Him is to love Him. To love Him is to devote our all to Him.

Worship is loving obedience. Said Jesus, "If you love me, you will keep my commandments." John 14:15. When we love someone with all our hearts, we want to please him or her, make any sacrifice requested, do anything we're asked.

Jesus asks us to keep His commandments. The God-worshipers in Revelation keep the commandments.

What do the commandments say to us?

THE TEN COMMANDMENTS

I

You shall have no other gods before me.

II

You shall not make for yourself a graven image, or any likeness of anything that is in heaven above, or that is in the earth beneath, or that is in the water under the earth; you shall not bow down to them or serve them; for I the Lord your God am a jealous God, visiting the iniquity of the fathers upon the children to the third and the fourth generation of those who hate me, but showing steadfast love to thousands of those who love me and keep my commandments.

III

You shall not take the name of the Lord your God in vain; for the Lord will not hold him guiltless who takes his name in vain.

IV

Remember the sabbath day, to keep it holy. Six days you shall labor, and do all your work; but the seventh day is a sabbath to the Lord your God; in it you shall not do any work, you, or your son, or your daughter, your manservant, or your maidservant, or your cattle, or the sojourner who is within your gates; for in six days the Lord made heaven and earth, the sea, and all that is in them, and rested the seventh day; therefore the Lord blessed the sabbath day and hallowed it.

V

Honor your father and your mother, that your days may be long in the land which the Lord your God gives you.

VI

You shall not kill.

VII

You shall not commit adultery.

VIII

You shall not steal.

IX

You shall not bear false witness against your neighbor.

X

You shall not covet your neighbor's house; you shall not covet your neighbor's wife, or his manservant, or his maidservant, or his ox, or his ass, or anything that is your neighbor's.

Exodus 20:3-17.

"You shall love the Lord your God with all your heart, and with all your soul, and with all your mind. This is the great and first commandment. And a second is like it, You shall love your neighbor as yourself. On these two commandments depend all the law and the prophets." Matthew 22:37-40.

"If you love, you will keep my commandments." John 14:15.

They say to "love your neighbor as yourself." Matthew 22:39. Not to "bear false witness." Exodus 20:16. Not to lie to people or gossip about them. Not to mislead them in any way that will do them harm. To remember that God created everyone and that Jesus died for everyone, and so we ought to treat everyone honestly.

Not to "commit adultery." Exodus 20:14. Not to engage in sexual activity with anyone outside of marriage—or even to think about it. See Matthew 5:28. To remember that God made our spouses and died for them and wants us to be true to them and care for them genuinely.

Not to "covet." Exodus 20:17. In an age of crass materialism not to be greedy but to make sure we always have something over to share with the less fortunate; for God created and Jesus died for people who live in slums just as much as for the wealthiest of us.

The commandments also say to "love the Lord your God with all your heart." Matthew 22:37. Not to "take the name of the Lord your God in vain." Exodus 20:7. Not to use His loving name in an angry mood or in a light and joking mood. How unfitting it is when we're irritated to demand that the God of love "damn" someone!

But not to take God's name in vain also means not to claim to be one of His followers without acting like one. In the Middle East, some people who claim to be Christians kill Moslems almost as a way of life. In western Europe, some Catholics and Protestants terrorize one another. In America some white Christians try to keep black Christians out of their churches, and some black Christians hate them for it. If you love Me, don't take My name in vain.

"If you love me, you will keep my commandments." "Remember the sabbath day, to keep it holy." Exodus 20:8. Sabbath is the day every week when we remember in a special way that God is the creator of heaven and earth and of everything and everyone in them.

This is what the heavenly choirs praise God for. "Worthy art thou, our Lord and God, . . . for thou didst create all things." Revelation 4:11. This is what the first angel's message urges us to do: **"Worship him who** *made heaven and earth, the sea and the fountains of water."* Revelation 14:7. The first angel, who has himself sung the song a million times in the heavenly choirs, invites us to join in the happy song with the other angels, and the elders, and the living creatures.

The words of the first angel's invitation come right out of the Sabbath commandment, adapted a bit, like most of Revelation's quotations of the Old Testament. "Remember the sabbath day, to keep it holy . . . ; for in six days the Lord *made heaven and earth, the sea, and all that is in them*, and rested the seventh day; therefore the Lord blessed the sabbath day and hallowed it." Exodus 20:8-11.

The seventh day.

The little horn, God told Daniel, would think to change "the times and the law." Daniel 7:25. And it did.

God's Sabbath "according to the commandment" is the seventh day. See Luke 23:56 and pages 83, 84. It is a day for joy (Isaiah 58:13, 14) and for remembering God's creative power. It is a day, too, for remembering that Jesus lay in the tomb on a Sabbath, resting after giving His life for us and saying as He died, "It is finished." John 19:30.

The seventh-day Sabbath is a day of joyful remembrance of God's creative love and of Christ's redeeming love. It is a day for singing with the angels of Revelation 4 and 5. It is a day to renew our strength for the week ahead and for the time of trouble that lies ahead.

"If you love me, you will keep my commandments."

The great issue in the countdown of the great controversy is worship. Will we worship the beast, or will we worship God and the Lamb? Worship is our response to what we think someone is worth.

Isn't our God worth our very best?

But how much *is* He worth to you?

Further Interesting Reading

In Arthur S. Maxwell, *The Bible Story,* volume 10:
  "Last Message of Love," page 192.
In *Bible Readings for the Home:*
  "The Judgment-Hour Message," page 195.
In Arthur S. Maxwell, *Your Bible and You:*
  "Supreme Lawgiver," page 93.
  "Which Is God's Day?" page 369.
In Ellen G. White, *The Triumph of God's Love:*
  "New Light in the New World," page 271.
  "Why Were Sin and Suffering Permitted?" page 429.
  "Man's Worst Enemy" page 441.
  "The Impending Conflict," page 508.

Page numbers for each book refer to the large, fully illustrated edition.

Your Questions Answered

If you wish, you may skip around in this section for now or proceed at once to the next chapter, page 421.

1. Why didn't God show Miller his mistake? Some people wonder why God didn't intervene to prevent the great disappointment of October 1844 by showing William Miller ahead of time where he was wrong. There are at least two answers to this question.

a. God did show Miller where he was wrong! When the explanation of what really happened at the end of the 2300 days was finally discovered, it was discovered in the Bible—where it had been all along. Miller and his associates hadn't noticed it, but God wasn't at fault.

b. It is helpful to ask a counter question. Why didn't Jesus intervene to prevent the great disappointment His followers felt at the crucifixion? On Palm Sunday, five days before the crucifixion, even the disciples had joined Christ's triumphal entry as the happy crowd shouted again and again, "Blessed is the King who comes," "Blessed is . . . the King of Israel." Luke 19:38; John 12:13. The cheering people fully believed that Jesus was about to declare Himself king, conquer the Romans, and make Jerusalem the capital of the world.

How wrong they all were—and how disappointed when Jesus died! We still catch the sob in the voice of Cleopas one week after the triumphal entry, "We had hoped that he was the one to redeem Israel." Luke 24:21.

Jesus knew the crowd would be disappointed. So why did He allow the triumphal entry? Why didn't He stop the procession, show the people they were wrong, and send them home?

Far from doing that, Jesus actually sponsored the whole affair. He personally asked His disciples to get Him a donkey so He could fulfill the prophecy of Zechariah 9:9 about the king's riding into Jerusalem on an ass. See Matthew 21:1-11. And when the religious leaders advised Him to quiet the crowd, He refused. See Luke 19:39, 40.

So Jesus not only permitted but was responsible for the triumphal entry, an event which raised high the peoples' hopes that He would do something He had no intention of doing and which resulted in their great disappointment a few days later.

But look at the matter another way. Was Jesus Israel's King? Indeed! He was King of the universe. Was He the one who would redeem Israel? He came to redeem the whole world. The people used the right words, but they gave them the wrong meaning. The fault lay with them, not with Jesus.

Jesus knew they misunderstood, so why didn't He correct them? He tried to! Three times in advance He had told His disciples that He would be killed; they refused to believe Him! See Mark 8:31-33; 9:30-32; 10:32-34.

Further, the truth that the Messiah would be killed was predicted in the Old Testament, and had been written there for hundreds of years.

After Cleopas sighed, "We had hoped that he was the one to redeem Israel," the resurrected Jesus quoted to him and his companion passages in the Old Testament. "Beginning with Moses and all the prophets, he interpreted to them in all the scriptures the things concerning himself." Luke 24:27.

No doubt Jesus quoted Genesis 3:15 about the Seed that would be bruised. And Daniel 9:24-27, where Messiah was going to be "cut off." And Isaiah 53, about the Lamb led to the slaughter. Cleopas and his friend doubtless knew the verses well, perhaps by heart. But as Jesus showed them that the Bible had long before predicted that "the Christ should *suffer*" before He entered His glory, their hearts burned with excitement and relief. Luke 24:26, 32.

If Jesus knew His people would misunderstand and be disappointed, why didn't He just avoid the triumphal entry altogether? Because He knew He was about to do something in Jerusalem (in fulfillment of the 70-week prophecy) that was absolutely essential to the plan of salvation, and it was necessary that people know about it—so they could believe it and be saved.

Similarly, as the 2300 days drew to a close Jesus was about to begin another gracious work, absolutely essential to salvation. So His Spirit stirred up the great second-advent awakening in many countries around the world, to attract people's attention—so they could believe and be saved.

It is of more than passing interest that Miller's movement was ultimately opposed by the religious leaders of his day, just as was the triumphal entry. And the explanation of Miller's disappointment came not to seminary professors or mighty theologians. It came to ordinary folk as they studied their Bibles—and even to a couple of them, Hiram Edson and his friend, as, like Cleopas and his friend, they walked through the country!

But the important thing is that the answers in each case came out of the Bible. They had been there all along, only people hadn't been ready yet fully to understand.

2. Did William Miller's followers wear ascension robes and go insane? Strange stories still appear in print claiming that William Miller's joyous message frightened people into insanity and that a good many of his followers foolishly prepared muslin gowns ("ascension robes") to go to heaven in. Individuals are said to have climbed trees or onto rooftops or even up church steeples in order to be as close to heaven as possible on the great day; but all too often they tripped over their ascension robes and broke their necks.

It seems surprising that people who were frightened enough about the second coming to go insane would *also* climb trees in order to get as close as possible to the second coming. Nonetheless, Clara Endicott Sears made a collection of such stories and others that made merry with the Millerites. Her 1924 *Days of Delusion*[76] remains the principal source for modern writers.

401

Miller's messages did attract large numbers of people, who represented many social classes. It is statistically probable that there were some unbalanced individuals in his crowds. The gospel is supposed to attract needy people. Jesus said, "Those who are well have no need of a physician, but those who are sick." Matthew 9:12. Everett Dick demonstrated in his 1930 doctoral dissertation[77] both the overall sanity of the Miller movement and the fact that a few of Miller's followers did spend some time in mental institutions, then called "insane asylums."

Francis D. Nichol in his book *The Midnight Cry*[78] has proved, however, that no factual historical basis can be found for the vast majority of Mrs. Sears' stories, that some of the "Millerites" who spent time in insane asylums had been there before they heard of Miller (they had a previous record of instability), and that the criteria used at the time for determining insanity were hardly scientific. His research has been widely influential among professional American church historians[79] if not among writers for popular magazines.

As for ascension robes—well, don't many ministers put on robes to preach in? Don't choir members put on robes to sing in? Don't high school seniors robe up for their graduations? Brides wear gowns for their weddings. Most people at least wear their "Sunday best" when they go to church. We may assume that many of Miller's believers put on *their* Sunday best on the day they expected Christ to appear. *If* also they had made special robes for the occasion, they could scarcely have been regarded as crazy except by their enemies.

The factual evidence, however, is that they did not make ascension robes. Professor Whitney R. Cross, of West Virginia University, as well as Nichol, has examined the evidence and like Nichol has concluded that the scurrilous stories are unfounded. "Nor," Dr. Cross concludes, "does any scrap of genuine evidence substantiate the myth of the ascension robes." He also comments about Miller's followers, "No more moral and righteous people would seem ever to have inhabited this earth."[80]

Nichol searched for ascension robe stories in no fewer than ninety-one newspapers! He found no accounts based on fact. They were all based on rumor, "It is said," "We have heard," and so on. Indeed, he found no reports at all about ascension robes for the date October 22, 1844, when the believers actually looked for Christ to come![81]

As long ago as April 1868, James White, who was active in both the second-advent and Seventh-day Adventist movements, offered a generous reward to anyone who could produce a bona fide ascension-robe story.[82] He was never called on to hand over the cash.

3. How did Miller's associates arrive at the specific date October 22, 1844, as the time for Christ's return? October 22, 1844, at first blush seems an odd date on which to fulfill a grand prophecy. How did Miller's associates arrive at it?

First, as we have seen, they discovered that the cleansing of the sanctuary in Daniel 8:14 refers to the final judgment and that the 2300 days of that verse date the judgment to the year 1844. In these points they were correct.

Second, they noticed that the typological festivals of the Old Testament are divided into spring festivals (Passover, Wave-Sheaf, and Pentecost) and autumn festivals (Blowing of Trumpets, Day of Atonement, and Feast of Tabernacles). See Leviticus 23.

They noticed (as had many before them) that Jesus fulfilled the Passover type by dying on the very day of the Passover, at the very time of day when the Passover lamb was supposed to be sacrificed. He fulfilled the Wave-Sheaf ceremony by rising (as the first fruits of the dead, 1 Corinthians 15:20) on the very morning when the priest waved the sheaf of first-ripe barley.

And He fulfilled Pentecost by sending the Holy Spirit on the very day of Pentecost.

They further noticed that the Day of Atonement was a day of judgment. Leviticus 23:29, 30. (The Jews to this day consider the Day of Atonement a type of the final judgment.) See GC 1:185-187.

They reasoned (as had Isaac Newton the scientist long before them) that just as Jesus fulfilled the spring festival types in connection with His first coming and on the very day of those types, so in connection with His second coming He could be expected to fulfill the autumn festival types on the very day of the types. According to their understanding of the reckoning of a very strict Jewish sect, the Karaites, the Day of Atonement in 1844 was to fall on October 22. So this is how the date October 22, 1844, was arrived at.

In confirmation of their general line of reasoning they also observed that the 2300 days didn't really start until some time after Nehemiah reached Jerusalem in the late summer or early fall of 457 B.C. Thus the 2300 year-days couldn't be expected to end before the late summer or early fall of 1844. See also our discussion on GC 1:208, 209, 238-240.

4. Should Revelation 12:17 read, "Bear witness to" or "Have the testimony of"?

Should Revelation 12:17 read, "bear witness to Jesus" as the Revised Standard Version has it, or "have the testimony of Jesus" with the King James Version?

The question, which may not seem important at first glance, appears increasingly significant the more it is investigated. As we shall see, the different modern versions tend to reveal what their translators believed about spiritual gifts. Is the spiritual gift of prophecy manifested when any ordinary Christian talks about Jesus (the "liberal" position), or does it involve a direct, miraculous revelation from God to specially selected individual prophets (the view of "conservative" Christians)?

The conservative versions are close to the King James Version. The New International Version and the New American Standard Bible, for example, have "hold to the testimony of Jesus." Their translators apparently believed

403

that a prophet receives a revelation from Jesus, which other Christians then cherish or "hold" onto.

Less conservative versions tend to agree with the Revised Standard Version. The New English Bible has "maintain their testimony to Jesus," and the Jerusalem Bible has "bear witness to Jesus." Here the translators seem to have believed that everyone who talks about Jesus has the gift of prophecy.

To decide for ourselves which is best we need to consider several things.

a. The underlying Greek is *echonton ten marturian Iesou*. Translated literally it is simply, "having the testimony of Jesus," the way it is in the King James Version. So what linguistic basis do translators have for giving it any other way?

Iesou is the name of Jesus in what linguists call the genitive case, which is similar to our English "of" case. In English we use "of" in different ways. "The tail of a dog" uses "of" in a possessive sense, but "a pile of wood" or "a word of welcome" uses "of" to describe something. In Greek, too, the "of" case can be understood in different ways. *Iesou* can be translated to imply possession ("of Jesus," "belonging to Jesus"), source ("from Jesus"), goal or object ("to Jesus"), and description ("about Jesus").

b. In order to decide which is the best way to translate the phrase we're talking about, we need also to look at the four other places where it is used in Revelation. In doing so, we find that the Revised Standard Version isn't consistent. In 20:4 it gives "testimony *to* Jesus" (using the goal or object sense) as it does in 12:17; but in the other three verses, 1:2; 1:9; 19:10, it gives "testimony *of* Jesus" (using the possessive or perhaps the source sense). So in 1:2; 1:9; and 19:10 the Revised Standard Version gives the translation which the King James Version and the conservative modern versions give to 12:17.

c. We want to pay attention to 19:10. In this verse, the "testimony of Jesus" is defined. The angel tells John, "The testimony of Jesus is the spirit of prophecy." The most normal and straightforward understanding of the angel's statement is that when the Holy Spirit selects a person to receive the spiritual gift of prophecy, to serve as God's prophet or spokesperson, the message which the Holy Spirit gives to the prophet is a message from Jesus. The "testimony of Jesus is the spirit of prophecy."

First Peter 1:11 confirms this understanding. It refers to the "spirit of Christ" which inspired the Old Testament prophets. The messages of the Old Testament prophets came from the spirit of Jesus.

d. We need to look again at *echonton*, the word that means literally, "having" or "holding." (To pronounce it, rhyme the first syllable with *neck*.) The Revised Standard Version does a very strange thing when it translates this verb as "bearing witness." The Greeks had a very different word, *marturein*, which they used when they wanted to say "bear witness." John uses this other word in Revelation 1:2, where he says that he "bore witness" (R.S.V.) to what he saw in the vision. *Echonton* (or some other form of the verb *echo*) occurs with *testimony* in John 5:36 and 1 John 5:10. In each case the Revised Standard Version correctly translates it as "have" and "has," and *not* as "bear witness," the way it does, inconsistently, in Revelation 12:17.

e. Please reread, if you will, pages 78, 79. There we noticed that the "testimony of Jesus" is something for which John was punished, along with the "Word of God." Inasmuch as the "Word *of* God" in John's day was the divinely inspired revelation from God recorded in the Old Testament, it seems inescapable that the "testimony *of* Jesus" was the newly developing body of sacred literature, the New Testament, which the Holy Spirit was still inspiring Christ's apostles to write in John's day. It wasn't finished yet. John was about to be inspired with a direct revelation that would provide still another book to be added to the ongoing body of literature known as "the testimony of Jesus."

f. Translating the underlying Greek as directly as possible, God's end-time people are described in Revelation 12:17 as (1) keeping the commandments of God and as (2) "having the testimony of Jesus" (which is "the spirit of prophecy," 19:10). We conclude that God wanted us to know that His end-time "saints" would be outstanding in these two special ways.

Paul spoke of the church waiting for the second advent as "not lacking in any spiritual gift." 1 Corinthians 1:7. We are led to believe that Revelation 12:17 looked forward to the emergence in the end time of a group of Christians who would be notable for keeping the commandments and also for possession (having) a renewal of the spirit of prophecy through a person or persons in whom the gift of prophecy would reappear as in Bible times.

Much more could be said and has been said on this subject. Within our limitations here we draw the conclusion that those translations are correct which leave Revelation 12:17 closest to the underlying Greek, "having the testimony of Jesus," and that the meaning is that the commandment-keeping movement of the last days was to enjoy a revival of the spirit of prophecy.

5. Has the spirit of prophecy been manifested in our day? In the light of our discussion in the previous answer, we should expect to find a revival of the spirit of prophecy in the end time among a group of people who believe in keeping the commandments of God. We have seen in our overall discussion that keeping the commandments involves choosing to enter into the blessing of the seventh-day Sabbath.

Seventh-day Adventists make up the principal end-time group that believes in keeping the seventh day as the Sabbath. By them, the writings of Ellen G. White have been regarded as divinely inspired. Her life production of some 100,000 manuscript pages seems to meet the Bible tests for a true prophet and to carry its own evidence of coming from a divine source. It seems to be a "testimony of Jesus."

The Ellen G. White writings have spoken with spiritual effectiveness to people of many cultures and languages. *Steps to Christ* has been translated into

405

117 different languages, making Ellen G. White apparently "the fourth most translated author in the history of literature, its most translated woman writer, and the most translated American author of either sex."[83]

At her death in 1915 the New York City *Independent* said of her, "She showed no spiritual pride and she sought no filthy lucre. She lived the life and did the work of a worthy prophetess." In the 1950s William Foxwell Albright, the renowned archaeologist (he wrote over 800 articles and was awarded twenty-five honorary doctorates), investigated Ellen White and pronounced her an authentic prophet. Her philosophy of education, as expressed in her book *Education*, has been published with resounding praise by the government of Japan. Her instructions for better health—so strange when she wrote them, so normal today—have been praised by various experts.[84]

But a person gifted with the spirit of prophecy is not to be evaluated by recommendations. Faithfulness to the Bible is the acid test. God, "who never lies" (Titus 1:2), would never tell an end-time spokesperson anything contradictory to what He told the Bible prophets.

The best way for you to find out whether Ellen White wrote in the power of God is to read her writings! For a sampler, I recommend *Steps to Christ*. For a more substantial introduction, read *The Desire of Ages*, her impressive life of Jesus, and *The Great Controversy Between Christ and Satan*, both of which are available from the publishers of this book.

Many people have found them eminently worthwhile.

6. Should Revelation 12:17 read "rest" or "remnant"? The Revised Standard Version, along with the New American Standard Bible, the New English Bible, and the New International Version, reads that the dragon made war with the **"rest of her offspring."** The King James Version says that the dragon made war with the "remnant of her seed." Which is right—and does it matter?

The word *remnant* is a term used several times in the Old Testament and also by Paul in Romans 9-11. It is rich in theological significance. On the other hand, *"rest"* is just an ordinary word. The underlying Greek term in Revelation 12:17 belongs to the same family of words used for *remnant* by Paul and frequently (though not always) used for it in the Greek translation of the Old Testament (the LXX or Septuagint).

The significance of the remnant idea is brought out clearly in, for example, Kittel's *Theological Dictionary*, and very deeply in Professor Gerhard Hasel's *The Remnant*.[85]

In the ancient Middle East, tribes and even whole nations frequently faced extinction from famine or aggressive enemies. They found comfort in hoping that a "remnant" would survive any catastrophe, for the remnant would carry the potential of restoring and renewing the tribe or nation.

In the Bible, Noah and his family survived the Flood and thus prevented the entire human race from being annihilated. The remnant preserved and restored the human race. The exiles who returned from Babylon restored the fortunes of the Jewish race.

A remnant was made up of individual survivors, but it was thought of also in terms of a corporate entity, a body of survivors. Like a seed, a remnant carried the characteristics of the tribe or nation and would one day restore the tribe or nation to its original status or lead it to an even better one.

In the Bible, it is God who preserves the remnant of His people. See, for example, Genesis 45:7; Isaiah 10:20, 21; 37:31, 32.

The prophets Amos, Isaiah, Micah, Jeremiah, Obadiah, and Zephaniah speak of a remnant who survive overwhelming last-day disasters. Though "lame" and "outcast" to begin with (Micah 4:7; Zephaniah 3:19), they are forgiven all their sins (Jeremiah 50:20) and found to be without iniquity (Jeremiah 50:20; Isaiah 4:2-5) and free from all lies (Zephaniah 3:13). They stand on Mount Zion (Micah 4:7; Isaiah 4:2-5; Obadiah 17; Joel 2:32) in the presence of God, with the sound of singing (Zephaniah 3:14-17).

When we come back to Revelation, we find in 14:1-5 that the 144,000 are sinless and without lies—and that they stand with God on Mount Zion singing! Quite obviously, the 144,000 are the end-time "remnant" foretold by the Old Testament prophets.

These 144,000, who are victorious over the beast (Revelation 15:2-5), are the same as the "saints" in 14:12 who instead of worshiping the beast keep God's commandments; and these "saints" are the same as the people who keep God's commandments in 12:17.

Thus the commandment-keeping people in 12:17 are the "remnant," and the King James Version did right when it so designated them.

What difference does it make? (1) Use of the word *remnant* to identify the commandment keepers in Revelation 12:17 helps us associate the end-time saints with the grand predictions of the Old Testament prophets. (2) It helps us perceive the true significance of the commandment keepers as the group, the seed, that is specially identified as preserving and restoring God's true church. (3) It reaffirms the promise of the group's ultimate holiness, "lame" and "outcast" though it may appear for a while.

Not least by any means, (4) use of the word *remnant* in 12:17 reminds us that in the Bible the preservation and sanctification of the remnant is an act of God's transcending grace. Thus the principal actor in 12:17 is not really the dragon who makes war but the Lord Himself who behind the scenes is fulfilling His loving promises.

The very word *remnant* reminds us that God cares. It reminds us that in the end time God Himself is restoring His true church, His one fold (John 10:16), and inviting all who will to join it.

7. Should Luke 12:36 read "wedding" or "marriage feast"? In Luke 12:36 Jesus tells us to be as ready for His second coming as servants ought to be ready for the return of their master from a "wedding" (K.J.V.) or from a "marriage feast" (R.S.V.). Most modern translations agree with the Revised Standard Version.

There is no real problem within the passage itself, but a problem is involved when the passage is compared with other related second-coming prophecies.

Jesus in the Gospels and again in Revelation, when talking about last-day events made use of language about weddings and also about a great feast.

a. In the parable of the ten young women in the Olivet Discourse (Matthew 25:1-13) He likened Himself to the bridegroom and told His followers to be ready to go in with Him to the "marriage feast."

b. In the parable of the "marriage feast" (Matthew 22:1-14) He spoke of many invitations being sent out and pictured the king as offering all the guests a special wedding gown and then passing through the banquet hall to make sure everyone had the gown on. When he found a man who had refused to wear one, he had him removed.

c. In Revelation 19:9 a blessing is pronounced on everyone who is invited to the "marriage supper" of the Lamb, and we learn (in verses 7, 8) that the bride is now ready, clothed in "fine linen," "bright and pure," the "righteous deeds of the saints." (Earlier, in 7:14, Revelation says that the saints make their robes white by washing them in the blood of the Lamb. Thus it's the Lamb's blood that makes the linen of the bride so white, bright, and pure.)

d. And now we have the present passage, Luke 12:35-37, which presents Jesus as coming to earth *after* the "marriage feast" is all over! If this isn't confusing enough, read the passage again and find that after the Master's return from the marriage feast He will have His servants "sit at table"—no doubt with Abraham and all the Gentiles from east and west—while He graciously serves them.

Before we analyze these passages and attempt a solution, let's remember that in Daniel 7 Jesus is portrayed as coming to the judgment scene in heaven (in 1844) *there* to receive His kingdom; and in Luke 19:11, 12 Jesus specifically warned His followers that He was not going to receive His kingdom in Jerusalem but was to receive it in a "far country," *after which* He would return to the earth. Inasmuch as the Lamb's bride is the New Jerusalem, the capital and symbol of His kingdom, we can know that receiving His kingdom and marrying His bride are the same thing—and that it is done in heaven before the second coming.

In 2 Corinthians 11:2 Paul speaks of himself as having "betrothed" (engaged) the church to Christ as a "pure bride." In Ephesians 5:25-27 Paul speaks of Jesus as having died to assure the success of a process that would make His church-bride completely pure, "holy and without blemish."

The pattern of the pictures. So let us put all these pictures together:

1. In 1844 Jesus came to the Ancient of Days to receive His kingdom (Daniel 7:9-14); that is, He then came as the Bridegroom to marry His bride (Matthew 25:1-13). Those Christians who have enjoyed a true relationship with Him

408

(who have had oil in their lamps) have followed Him in faith and trust as He has been engaged in the wedding ceremonies.

2. Since 1844 the judgment has been going on (Daniel 7) in which the King has been examining everyone who throughout human history has claimed to be His follower. These people *as a whole* have made up His church, His betrothed bride. But *as individuals* not all have been true and faithful. Many have taken His name in vain. They have disregarded His commandments. Many have even persecuted fellow believers who wanted to obey God. These untrue, unkind followers are found in the preadvent judgment not to have on the white-linen wedding garment. Matthew 22:1-14. They are removed from the book of life. Then the church is purged and pure and faithful. The bride is clean and white. Revelation 19:7-9; Ephesians 5:25-27.

3. The bride at last being *ready* for Him, Jesus marries her; that is, He receives His kingdom. Daniel 7:14; Luke 19:11, 12. The door to the wedding is shut, and any who at so late a date want to get in are found to be unprepared and unworthy. Matthew 25:1-14; compare Revelation 22:11.

4. Immediately after the marriage, Jesus returns to the earth (Luke 12:35-37) to gather His waiting servants.

5. Thereupon He causes His faithful servants to sit down and eat (Luke 12:35-37) by taking them to the marriage supper of the Lamb (Revelation 19:9).

This sequence of events makes good sense. But a little confusion is introduced to our western minds when Luke 12:35-37 is so translated that it implies that Jesus comes back after the conclusion of the very "marriage supper" which He is going to have us eat! This confusion is introduced by the Revised Standard Version and several other modern versions.

The Greeks didn't have a word for it. The confusion can be eliminated when we understand the linguistic explanation of it. The Greek language, in which the New Testament was originally written, used words for "marriage" (*gamos* and *gamoi*) which included *both* the wedding ceremony itself and the wedding feast.

In modern western weddings we make a clear distinction between the wedding ceremony and the wedding reception, and both are usually brief.

In Bible times repeating the covenant vow (see Malachi 2:14) seems to have taken very little time, while the feast was a major community event that might go on all night or even all week. Eating together in the company of a large company of guests was essential. Thus a marriage actually connoted in most people's minds a big feast!

This use of the word was all right for most purposes. But it did leave the Greeks handicapped when they wanted, for whatever reason, to speak of what we think of as the wedding ceremony alone. *Gamos* and *gamoi* had to make do most of the time for both the vow and the feast.

However, if the Greeks didn't have a common term for the vow as distinct from the feast, they did have a term for the feast alone when that was what they wanted to emphasize. And it is *this* term which is used in Revelation 19:9 to describe what the saints are being invited to, the "marriage supper" of the Lamb.

So now the difficulty is taken care of. The master will return from the *gamoi*, that is from the "marriage" but *not* from what we would call the reception or "marriage feast." He will have married His kingdom, His church, His bride, insofar as the covenant vow is concerned.

But in order for the marriage to be in every sense finalized, there will be a big feast, the "marriage supper" of the Lamb. It will follow immediately. The Master will welcome his servants to "sit at table"—with Abraham and the redeemed Gentiles—back up in heaven, the Bridegroom's home, where the covenant vow was spoken.

Incidentally, we mustn't confuse the bride with the wedding guests. The bride is the church as a whole; church members as individuals are the guests. The bride is New Jerusalem, the symbol of Christ's entire human kingdom. See Revelation 21:9, 10. Individual members of it are not the city itself but the residents who have homes there. See John 14:1-3.

8. What does Revelation 14:11 mean when it says smoke ascends "for ever and ever"? Revelation 14:10, 11 says that people who receive the mark of the beast will be **"tormented with fire and sulphur,"** and that the **"smoke of their torment goes up for ever and ever; and they have no rest, day or night."**

The picture of **"smoke"** ascending up **"for ever and ever"** is, like so much of Revelation, adapted from the Old Testament. It comes from Isaiah 34:8-10, which says that in the day of God's vengeance the land of Edom will be turned into pitch and her soil into brimstone (or sulphur). "Night and day it shall not be quenched; its smoke shall go up for ever [in Hebrew: for ever and ever, as in the K.J.V.]."

Now notice that the Isaiah passage goes on, in verses 11-17, to talk about the birds and wild animals that were going to inhabit the land of Edom! Birds and wild animals can't live on smoke and sulphur! And chapter 35 follows without a break, promising a complete renovation!

So this passage that Revelation borrows from—the dramatic language about pitch, brimstone (or sulphur), a fire that burns night and day, and smoke that goes up for ever and ever—describes a very temporary situation!

How can this be? Doesn't "for ever" mean everlasting?

We mustn't forget idioms and metaphors, those colorful expressions that can't be translated literally. What would an ancient Greek or Hebrew have done with our idioms, "right on the money," "the cutting edge," "left of center," and "the rat race"?

Exodus 21:6, K.J.V., says that under certain circumstances a slave was to serve his master "for ever." This represents a literal translation of the Hebrew but is clearly impossible. The Revised Standard Version and some other mod-

410

The Dead Sea area. Smoke is not still rising from Sodom and Gomorrah.

ern versions quite properly have the slave serving his master "for life." In this instance, "for ever" is a Hebrew idiom meaning, "as long as the person lives."

When the Bible says that God lives for ever and ever, the meaning is eternal, for God is immortal and cannot die. See 1 Timothy 1:17; 6:16. But when it says that the smoke of the wicked goes up for ever and ever, the meaning is only as long as the sinners live—which won't be very long, considering the heat.

The Bible sometimes speaks of "eternal fire." In 2 Peter 2:6 and Jude 7 Sodom and Gomorrah, cities which were burned to "ashes" in the time of Abraham (about 2000 B.C.), are presented as "an example" of "eternal fire." Archaeologists can't locate their ruins. I've been to the Dead Sea myself and haven't noticed any smoke rising. The "eternal fire" was eternal in its effects. The cities were destroyed permanently.

As for the related expression "unquenchable fire" in Matthew 3:12, the term should be understood as it stands. An unquenchable fire is simply one that can't be forced to stop burning before it's through. We hear of multi-alarm fires that firemen can't put out. They're "unquenchable," but ultimately they burn themselves out. An atom bomb represents unquenchable fire.

Malachi 4:1-3 says, "For behold, the day comes, burning like an oven, when all the arrogant and all evildoers will be stubble; the day that comes shall burn them up, says the Lord of hosts, so that it will leave them neither root nor branch. . . . They will be ashes under the soles of your feet, on the day when I act, says the Lord of hosts."

The prophets understood the idioms and metaphors of their own language. They didn't think sinners would burn "for millions of years," the way we understand "for ever." Nor did Jesus think they would. His brilliant story about

411

the rich man and Lazarus (Luke 16:19-31) should be seen as a parody of a popular but ghastly superstition. How much cooling of the tongue could be accomplished in the heat of hell by a fingertip of water?

God cares! He loves people. He hates sin, not because He's cruel but because He's Love, and love is the opposite of selfishness. He will remove stubborn sinners at the end in order to remove stubborn selfishness, but He'll be a Lover still. He simply couldn't watch His creatures writhe in flames for "ever and ever," the way we use the term. Thank God we know it's an ancient idiom that doesn't mean what it seems.

9. What is the meaning of 666? "This calls for wisdom: let him who has understanding reckon the number of the beast, for it is a human number, its number is six hundred and sixty-six." Revelation 13:18. The Phillips translation has, "Understanding is needed here." Monsignor Knox reads, "Here is room for discernment."

Evidently wisdom is needed. Deciphering 666 has proved a puzzle.

Modern languages have at their disposal both numbers and letters. Greek, Hebrew, and Latin, languages of New Testament times, had only letters, some of which did double duty as numbers. In Greek, "A," the first letter of the alphabet, was used for 1. In Latin, capital I served for 1, it being made with a single penstroke. And so on.

Most people have assumed that 666 is to be understood by calculating the numeric value of the letters in somebody's name. The New English Bible even has, the *"numerical value of its letters"* is 666, which isn't quite fair, since the underlying Greek says simply, **"its number is,"** as the Revised Standard Version does.

Some people have made light of the number 666, showing that it can be applied to all sorts of famous people's names. But this is foolish, for it is not the name of any random individual; it is the number of the beast.

Commentators who think that the beast was Nero say that the letters NERON, in Hebrew, add up to 666. But it seems a bit arbitrary to call Nero "Neron," which wasn't his name, and to evaluate him in Hebrew, which he didn't speak. Besides, we have seen that the beast isn't Nero. See pages 379, 380.

If, as we have seen, the leopard-bodied beast is a symbol for Roman Christianity at its worst, then the number 666 applies in some way to it. The number is the number of a man, our text says; and in Daniel 7 the Roman church is characterized as a horn with "eyes like the eyes of a man, and a mouth speaking great things." Second Thessalonians 2:3 speaks of the "man of lawlessness."

Latin is the official language of the Catholic Church. The pope, in Catholic theology, stands for the whole church. One of the pope's titles is said to be *Vicarius Filii Dei*, "Vicar of the Son of God." In response to a reader's question, the Catholic journal *Our Sunday Visitor* for April 18, 1915, replied, "The letters

413

Could Sunday worship be mandated in America? Many people urge Constitutional amendments to require school prayer and to regulate abortion. Why not Sunday observance also?

inscribed in the Pope's mitre [his priestly crown] are these, *Vicarius Filii Dei,* which is the Latin for Vicar of the Son of God. Catholics hold that the Church, which is a visible society, must have a visible head."

The numeric value of this title, using the numeric values of Latin letters, is easy to calculate (as the *Visitor* acknowledged).

V	5	F	0	D	500
I	1	I	1	E	0
C	100	L	50	I	1
A	0	I	1		
R	0	I	1		
I	1				
U	5				
S	0				

Total, 666

Here may be the true meaning of 666. But inasmuch as (a) there is some uncertainty about the official status of this title, and (b) the Bible doesn't actually state that 666 is to be calculated on the basis of the numeric value of the letters in a name, let us look for other possibilities.

In Revelation 17 the beast is linked with the harlot of "Babylon." The number 6 and multiples of it such as 12, 36, 60, and 600 were significant to ancient Babylon. Sixty was the number of Anu and Marduk, her supreme gods at different times. See GC 1:49, 50. A popular amulet worn by Babylonian priests contained this mysterious configuration of numbers in a square:

1	32	34	3	35	6
30	8	27	28	11	7
20	24	15	16	13	23
19	17	21	22	18	14
10	26	12	9	29	25
31	4	2	33	5	36

With your pocket calculator, add up each line, horizontally and vertically, and see what you get. Then add up all 6 horizontal lines and all 6 vertical ones, and see what you get.

This amulet shows that 666 was of considerable interest to ancient Babylonian religion. Here's something else. The fertility god Ningiszida of ancient Babylon, a god whose worship was supposed to encourage intercourse and enhance reproduction, was represented by two serpents wrapped six times around each other.[86]

Now let's try still another approach, asking the Lord for **"understanding"** and **"wisdom."**

414

The most prominent number in Revelation is seven. There are seven churches, seven trumpets, and so on. Seven is also the number of God's sabbath, the seventh day of the week, the day which God has chosen to remind us of **"him who made heaven and earth, the sea and the fountains of water."** Revelation 14:7. God's end-time saints worship the Creator and keep His commandments. They are to be seventh-day people.

So seven is a number that honors God.

The number 666 is a **"human"** number (R.S.V.). The underlying Greek can be translated fairly as "the number of a man" or as "the number of man [mankind]." The sixth day, Friday, is the day when man was created. Does 666 then, with its triple sixes, point to man focused inward on himself, on his own ways of doing things, on his own creativity—like the Babylonian king Nebuchadnezzar, boasting of his own activity in defiance or neglect of the true Source of all creativity? See Daniel 4:30 and GC 1:59-61.

In contrast, the crowning day of creation is the seventh day, when God delights in His work (Exodus 31:17) and invites man to enter into His joy (Isaiah 58:13, 14)—when God rests (Genesis 2:2) and man enters into His rest (Hebrews 4:10).

Professor Neall, whom we met on page 386, has discussed this interesting concept:

> Six is legitimate when it leads to seven; it represents man on the first evening of his existence entering into the celebration of God's creative power. The glory of the creature is right if it leads to the glory of God. Six hundred sixty-six, however, represents the refusal of man to proceed to seven, to give glory to God as Creator and Redeemer. It represents man's fixation with himself, man seeking glory in himself and his own creations. It speaks of the fullness of creation and all creative powers without God— the practice of the absence of God. It demonstrates that unregenerate man is persistently evil. The beasts of Rev 13 represent man exercising his sovereignty apart from God, man conformed to the image of the beast rather than to the image of God. Man apart from god becomes bestial, demonic. . . .
>
> The mark of the beast, then, is a rejection of the sovereignty of God— the Sabbath principle which is designed to encourage man to seek his dignity not in himself or in nature, but in communion with God and participation in God's rest. It is the Sabbath which distinguishes between the creature and the Creator, which reveals who deserves worship and who does not. It is the Sabbath which demonstrates God's sovereignty and man's dependence. Six hundred sixty-six by contrast is the symbol of the worship of the creature rather than the Creator.[87]

Viewed in the light of this interpretation, *coercive* Sunday observance, *defi-*

415

antly linked with a determination to worship God *in our own way* in spite of Christ's end-time ministry on our behalf in the heavenly sanctuary and of the Ten Commandments which are located beside Him, constitutes the mark of the beast.

References

1. Walter Russell Bowie, Exposition of Genesis, *The Interpreter's Bible,* 12 vols. (New York: Abingdon Press, 1952-1957), 1:518.

2. John L. McKenzie, S.J., *The Roman Catholic Church,* ed. E. O. James, History of Religion Series (New York: Holt, Rinehart and Winston, 1969), p. xii. McKenzie's frank acknowledgment of his church's Romanism stands in contrast to other attempts by some American Catholics to mute this Romanness. See, e.g., the widely distributed *The Faith of Millions*, rev. ed. (Huntington, Ind: Our Sunday Visitor, Inc., 1963, 1974), by John O'Brien who, like McKenzie, is also of the University of Notre Dame.

3. Henry Edward Manning, *The Temporal Power of the Vicar of Jesus Christ*, 2d ed. with preface (London: Burns & Lambert, 1862), pp. xxvii, xxix.

4. John Adolphus, *The History of France*, vol. 2 (London: George Kearsley, 1803), p. 365.

5. Richard Duppa, *A Brief Account of the Subversion of the Papal Government. 1798*, 2d ed. (London: G. G. and J. Robinson, 1799), pp. 46, 47.

6. George Trevor, *Rome: From the Fall of the Western Empire* (London: The Religious Tract Society, 1868), p. 440.

7. Joseph Rickaby, "The Modern Papacy," in *Lectures on the History of Religions*, vol. 3, lecture 24, p. 1 (London: Catholic Truth Society, 1910).

8. Manuel de Godoy, *Príncipe de la Paz (1767-1851): Memoirs of Don Manuel de Godoy, Prince of the Peace,* ed. J. B. d'Esménard, 2 vols. (London: Richard Bentley, 1836).

9. I am indebted for this question to Dick Winn and the title of his book: *If God Won the War, Why Isn't It Over?* (Mountain View, Calif.: Pacific Press Publishing Assn., 1982).

10. See, e.g., Samuel Eliot Morison, *The Oxford History of the American People* (New York: Oxford University Press, 1965), p. 15, and Merwyn S. Garbarino, "Indian, American," *World Book Encyclopedia* (1973), 10:127, 138n.

11. Morison, *American People*, p. 110, referring to the Great Swamp Fight of November 19, 1675, with the Narragansetts.

12. *The Dublin Nation*, quoted in J. N. Andrews, *The Three Messages of Revelation XIV, 6-12,* 5th ed., rev. (Battle Creek, Mich.: Review and Herald Publishing Co., 1892), pp. 85, 86.

13. Alfred H. Kelly & Winfred A. Harbison, *The American Constitution: Its Origins and Development*, rev. ed. (New York: W. W. Norton & Company, Inc., 1948, 1955), pp. 384-391.

14. See, e.g., *ibid.*, p. 492. The case is known as *Berea College v. Kentucky*.

15. The court case is *Korematsu v. United States* (1944). See e.g., Carl Brent Swisher, *Historic Decisions of the Supreme Court,* an Anvil original (Princeton, N.J.: D. Van Nostrand Co., 1958), p. 162.

16. Kelly and Harbison, *American Constitution*, p. 861.

17. Margaret L. Coit and the editors of Time-Life Books, *The Sweep Westward*, in Henry F. Graff, ed., The Life History of the United States, vol. 4 (New York: Time-Life Books, 1963), p. 109.

18. Anson Phelps Stokes, *Church and State in the United States*, 3 vols. (New York: Harper & Brothers, 1950), 1:833.

19. Leo Pfeffer, *Church State and Freedom*, rev. ed. (Boston: Beacon Press, 1953, 1967), p. 302.

20. In another switch of attitudes, the "Third Dudleian Lecture" at Harvard University, originally endowed (in the 1750s) to sound a *warning* every four years against the "Romish Church," was in 1979 assigned to Pope John Paul II! The pontiff appreciated the invitation but had to decline. See George Huntston Williams, "The Ecumenical Intentions of Pope John Paul II," *Harvard Theological Review* 75(1982): 142.

21. See Dean M. Kelly, "Uncle Sam, Church Inspector," *Liberty*, May-June 1984, pp. 3-5.

22. This section is based primarily on LeRoy Edwin Froom, *The Prophetic Faith of Our Fathers*, 4 vols. (Washington, D.C.: Review and Herald Publishing Assn., 1946-1954) and R. W. Schwarz, *Light Bearers to the Remnant* (Mountain View, Calif.: Pacific Press Publishing Assn., 1979), pp. 24-30.

23. Froom, *Prophetic Faith*, 2:507-510.

24. *Ibid.*, 3:303-324.

25. *Ibid.*, 3:461-481.

26. *Ibid.*, 3:434-439, 449-456.

27. *Ibid.*, 3:364-376.

28. *Ibid.*, 3:514-526. For a recent book on Irving, not always fair to his views, see Arnold Dallimore, *Forerunner of the Charismatic Movement: The Life of Edward Irving* (Chicago: Moody Press, 1983).

29. Froom, *Prophetic Faith*, 3:701-703, 299; M. Ellsworth Olsen, *A History of the Origin and Progress of Seventh-day Adventists* (Washington, D.C.: Review and Herald Publishing Assn., 1925), pp. 99-101.

30. Froom, *Prophetic Faith*, 3:687-700.

31. *Ibid.*, 3:671-686.

32. Mourant Brock, *Glorification* (American Millennial Association reprint, 1845), in Froom, *Prophetic Faith*, 3:705, 706.

33. Thomas B. Macaulay, *Critical and Miscellaneous Essays* (Philadephia: Cary and Hart, 1844), vol. 5, p. 324, in Froom, *Prophetic Faith*, 3:268.

34. The best modern biography of William Miller is Francis D. Nichol, *The Midnight Cry* (Washington, D.C.: Review and Herald Publishing Assn., 1944). The earliest older biography is Sylvester Bliss, *Memoirs of William Miller* (Boston: Joshua V. Himes, 1853). Other older ones were prepared by Isaac Wellcome and James White. Miller's life and career are described in popular form in the early chapters of C. Mervyn Maxwell, *Tell It to the World*, 2d rev. ed. (Mountain View, Calif.: Pacific Press Publishing Assn., 1976, 1977, 1982).

35. Bliss, *Memoirs*, pp. 64-66. For the book from which Miller frequently read sermons, Bliss mistakenly names the author as Proudfoot instead of Alexander Proudfit.

36. William Miller, Feb. 4, 1843, to *Signs of the Times*, in Bliss, *Memoirs*, pp. 180, 181.

37. William Miller, *Apology and Defence* (Boston: J. V. Himes, 1845), p. 6.

38. Miller held himself to 14 "Rules of Interpretation." Rule 11 required him to use "good sense"; Rule 14, to have faith; and Rule 13, to make sure that a proposed fulfillment matches the prediction in every detail—or to search in history for another event that does so match it. See Isaac C. Wellcome, *History of the Second Advent Message and Mission, Doctrine and People* (Yarmouth, Maine: The Author, 1874), pp. 45, 46.

39. Miller, *Apology*, p. 12.

40. *Ibid.*, pp. 13, 17.

41. *Ibid.*, pp. 13, 14.

42. *Ibid.*, p. 19.

43. The story is partly retold and partly quoted from Bliss, *Memoirs*, in Nichol, *Midnight Cry*, pp. 66-68.

417

44. Nichol, *Midnight Cry*, p. 53, and Miller, *Apology*, pp. 19, 20.

45. Everett N. Dick, "William Miller and the Advent Crisis, 1831-1844" (doctoral dissertation, University of Wisconsin, 1930), pp. 267-269.

46. See *The Midnight Cry*, August 24, 1843, p. 1, and *Signs of the Times,* March 8, 1843, p. 4, and November 15, 1943, p. 109.

47. John Greenleaf Whittier, *Prose Works*, 1:425, 426, in Nichol, *Midnight Cry*, p. 110.

48. See Joseph Bates, *Second Advent Way Marks and High Heaps* (New Bedford, Mass.: Press of Benjamin Lindsey, 1847), pp. 11, 12.

49. See Froom, *Prophetic Faith,* 4:655-662. There are, however, some difficulties in his account. The tent appears to have been reduced rather than increased in size, to make it more manageable. See David Tallmadge Arther, "Joshua V. Himes and the Cause of Adventism, 1839-1845" (M.A. thesis, The University of Chicago, 1961), p. 108.

50. Miller, *Apology*, p. 22 for the lower figure. For the higher figure, see Dick, "Advent Crisis," pp. 263, 264.

51. Editorial, *The Midnight Cry*, Oct. 31, 1844, pp. 110, 111.

52. Ellen G. White, *The Great Controversy Between Christ and Satan*, rev. ed. (Mountain View, Calif.: Pacific Press Publishing Assn., 1911), p. 403.

53. See Ellen G. White, "Notes of Travel" in *Historical Sketches of the Foreign Missions of the Seventh-day Adventists* (Basle: Imprimerie Polyglotte, 1886), p. 213.

54. George I. Butler, "Advent Experience," No. 2, *Review and Herald*, February 17, 1885, p. 105.

55. *Ibid.*

56. William Miller, Letter, *The Midnight Cry*, Dec. 5, 1844.

57. See Timothy Smith, *Revivalism and Social Reform in Mid-Nineteenth-Century America* (New York: Abingdon Press, 1957), pp. 225, 226.

58. See *ibid.,* p. 228.

59. "The National Crisis," *The Christian Review* 26 (1861):492 in Smith, *Revivalism*, pp. 230, 231.

60. For these examples and several others, in a brief overview, see Lawrence Maxwell, "Christ Coming Soon," *Signs of the Times,* January 1971, pp. 18-25.

61. See especially *The Advent Mirror*, January 1845, edited by Joseph Turner and Apollos Hale. Enoch Jacob's views appeared in his *Western Midnight Cry* (soon renamed *The Day-Star*) for November 29 and December 30, 1844.

62. See, e.g., Lewis R. Walton and Herbert E. Douglass, *How to Survive the '80s* (Mountain View, Calif.: Pacific Press Publishing Assn., 1982), esp. chapter 2.

63. Otto Betz, *"Stigma,"* Gerhard Kittel and Gerhard Friedrich, *Theological Dictionary of the New Testament,* tr. and ed., Geoffrey W. Bromiley, 9 vols. (Grand Rapids, Mich.: Wm. B. Eerdmans Publishing Company, 1964-1974), 7:659. For several references to marks on slaves see Thomas Wiedemann, *Greek and Roman Slavery* (Baltimore: The Johns Hopkins University Press, 1981), esp. pp. 193, 194.

64. Betz, *"Stigma,"* p. 658. Compare Karl Heinrich Rengstorf, *"Semeion, Semaino, Semeioo, Asemos, Episemos, Eusemos, Sussemon,"* Kittel and Friedrich, *Theological Dictionary,* 7:204.

65. Betz, *"Stigma,"* pp. 660. Herodotus, *Persian Wars,* 2.113; Modern Library.

66. William Ralf Featherstone, *The Church Hymnal* (Washington, D.C.: Review and Herald Publishing Assn., 1941), no. 276.

67. The employer was Lord Joseph Duveen, American head of the art firm that bore his name. See Herbert Douglass, *The End* (Mountain View, Calif.: Pacific Press Publishing Assn., 1979), p. 152, and *Christianity Today*, February 2, 1979.

68. For the next several pages I am indebted for some good ideas to Beatrice S. Neall, *The Concept of Character in the Apocalypse With Implications for Character Education*

(Washington: University Press of America, Inc., 1983), esp. pp. 166, 167, 205, 200 in this order.

69. For an argument that old-fashioned values are still taught in some public schools see Thomas E. Robinson, " 'Where There Is No Vision': Are Public High Schools Teaching Values?" *Liberty*, May-June, 1984, p. 17.

70. Dr. Neall's name for "George" is Émile, from Rousseau.

71. Marie Winn, *The Plug-in Drug* (New York: Bantam Books, 1977, 1978). The next few paragraphs draw heavily from pp. 37-40, 47, 48, 100, 108, 121, 171.

72. Winn, *Plug-in Drug*, pp.37-40. Children were found to have benefitted from "Sesame Street" only in widely publicized families which on the quiet had been carefully prepared in advance.

73. *Ibid.*, p. 171.

74. Conversation with Russell Staples, 1984; research paper by Stanley Maxwell, 1983.

75. The cassettes are available from Your Story Hour, Box 366, Medina, Ohio 44258. The Arthur S. Maxwell sets are available from the publishers of this book.

76. Clara Endicott Sears, *Days of Delusion* (Boston: Houghton, Mifflin Company, 1924).

77. Everett N. Dick, "Advent Crisis."

78. Nichol, *Midnight Cry*, chaps. 23-27.

79. For a survey of the changes which Nichol's evidence produced in books that touched on the Miller experience, see especially Jerome L. Clark, *1844*, 3 vols. (Nashville: Southern Publishing Assn., 1968), 1:50-83.

80. Whitney R. Cross, *The Burned-over District: The Social and Intellectual History of Enthusiastic Religion in Western New York, 1800-1850* (Ithaca, N.Y.: Cornell University Press, 1950), p. 306.

81. Nichol, *Midnight Cry*, chap. 25, esp. p. 389n.

82. James White, "Clerical Slander," *Advent Review and Sabbath Herald*, April 14, 1868, p. 281.

83. Roger W. Coon, *A Gift of Light* (Washington, D.C.: Review and Herald Publishing Assn., 1983), p. 21.

84. See, for example, *ibid.*, pp. 52-60.

85. Volkmar Herntrich and Gottlob Schrenk, *"Leimma, Hupoleimma, Kataleipo (Kata-, Peri-, Dialeimma),"* Kettel and Friedrich, *Theological Dictionary*, 4:194-214. Gerhard F. Hasel, *The Remnant: The History and Theology of the Remnant Idea from Genesis to Isaiah*, Andrews University Monographs, Studies in Religion, vol. 5., 3d ed. (Berrien Springs, Mich.: Andrews University Press, 1980).

86. Several of the above ideas were borrowed from Edwin R. Thiele, *Outline Studies in Revelation* (Angwin, Calif.: The Author, n.d.), pp. 216-218. Each line on the amulet adds up to 111. The 6 horizontal lines add up to 666, as do the 6 vertical ones.

87. Neall, *Character in the Apocalypse*, pp. 153-155, giving credit for some of her ideas to Herman Hoeksema and Hans LaRondelle.

The Seven Last Plagues

Introduction

Among all the warning symbols in Revelation, which ones trouble *you* most? Many people, no doubt, feel worried about the mark of the beast and the seven last plagues. We examined the mark on pages 377-386. Now it's time to look into the plagues.

"I saw another portent in heaven, great and wonderful, seven angels with seven plagues, which are the last, for with them the wrath of God is ended." Revelation 15:1.

In place of **"with them the wrath of God is *ended*,"** the New English Bible has, "with them the wrath of God is *consummated*." The key word in the underlying Greek is translated as "made perfect" in Hebrews 11:40. The point is that the seven last plagues represent the peak or upper limit of punishment. And they are poured out "unmixed" (Revelation 14:10), that is, undiluted with the mercy of God which always before has limited the suffering. There is going to be another outpouring of punishment at the end of the thousand years. See Revelation 20:11-15.

The two halves of Revelation. With the chapters that tell about the seven plagues we enter the second half of Revelation (chapters 15-22), the half that deals exclusively with the end time.

As we have seen in our study so far, each of the four divisions in the *first* half of the book provides a survey of events from John's day to the end time. Each division in its own way warns about the 1260-year apostasy.

The earliest of the seven churches are faithful or nearly so, but Thyatira, the main church of the 1260 years, is in deep apostasy.

The first of the four horsemen rides a white horse, but the other three horsemen represent war, famine, and pestilence; and as they ride past we hear the groans of martyrs persecuted during the 1260 years.

The seven trumpets startle us with the apostasy of Jews, Christians, and Moslems alike, and focus on the two witnesses who prophesy in sackcloth during the 1260 years.

The great-controversy scenes review the birth of Jesus to a pure and noble mother; but soon we are shown the mother fleeing into the wilderness for 1260 years and her end-time "remnant" being harrassed by the dragon and the lamb-horned beast.

A steady shift of emphasis causes the trumpets and great-controversy scenes to deal more heavily with end-time events than the seven churches and seven seals do. But the four divisions in the *second* half of Revelation, dealing with the plagues, the fall of Babylon, the millennium, and New Jerusalem, focus entirely on last-day events.

421

The seven last plagues will fall on all who worship the beast or receive its mark. Families who remain faithful to God will be shielded from them.

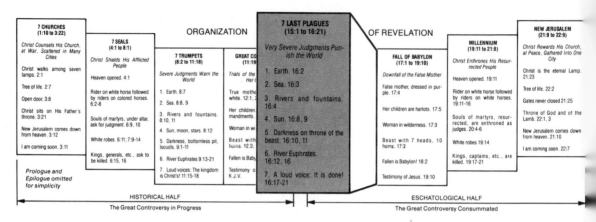

The seven last plagues begin the second half of Revelation. Prophecies from here on focus on events to take place soon, in the end time.

Inasmuch as we are all now living in the last days (see pages 274-280), it is understandable that we be concerned about the second half of Revelation and especially about the seven plagues. They are due to fall soon.

Introductory sanctuary scene. Like each of the four divisions in the first half of Revelation, the seven-plague division also begins with an introductory sanctuary scene. But there are important differences this time. Before looking at them, let's remind ourselves of things we know already.

The seven churches start with Jesus as High Priest among the lampstands; the seven seals open with Jesus as the Lamb close beside the throne; the seven trumpets begin with an angel offering incense at the golden altar; and the great-controversy scenes commence with a view of the ark containing the Ten Commandments in the inner part of the heavenly temple. Each introductory scene is related in a special way to the message that follows in its division.

As we enter the first division of Revelation's second half, the intro-

ductory sanctuary scene differs from the others in significant ways: (1) It is the *last one* we're going to find; (2) in it the temple opens to release the seven plague angels and then *closes up*; and (3) the scene is *accompanied* by a view of the redeemed singing on the sea of glass.

Two preparatory scenes. It is appropriate that the second half of Revelation begin with *two* scenes. This is the half of the book in which we read about final punishment and final rewards. Here the stubbornly rebellious receive the plagues and are sentenced to the sea of fire. Here the unflinchingly loyal are installed on thrones and forever settled in New Jerusalem homes.

As we enter these chapters that describe the most glorious and the most disastrous episodes in the story of man's relationship with God, the dual preparatory scenes *encourage* us with the joy of those who choose to be loyal to God and *warn* us that God in His goodness will not forever allow sinners to go on being mean. As this second half of Revelation begins, God's

422

sanctuary in heaven, where Jesus has so long interceded for sinners, is closed so no one can enter it. See pages 446-450.

Helpful literary arrangement. In each introductory section in our book we have become accustomed to having two outline charts, one of Revelation's overall chiasm and the other, an outline of the division being discussed.

This time we're going to develop a third chart, uncovering the arrangement of Revelation's second half. Once again, acquaintance with literary structure is going to help us considerably in understanding the message.

The four divisions of chapters 15-22 can be laid out this way:

A   Description: The plagues. 15:1 to 16:21

B   Narration: Circumstances related to the plagues. 17:1 to 19:10

B′   Narration: Circumstances related to the Holy City. 19:11 to 21:8

A′   Description: The Holy City. 21:9 to 22:9

Experienced as we are with literary structures, we see at once that we've run into another helpful chiasm. Being old hands at such matters, we'll not be suprised to discover a *further* literary structure woven into it.[1]

Look at Revelation 17:1-3 and 21:9, 10 as they are arranged on the next two pages. These are the passages that mark the beginning of the divisions **B′** and **A′** in our little chart above. Notice how similar they are.

The similarities here are intentional. We've learned that literary devices in Daniel and Revelation are not accidents or coincidences! They help us to know how the book was originally organized in John's mind and how the different parts fit together. They help us understand John's message.

SEVEN LAST PLAGUES: Very Severe Judgments Punish the World. 15:1 to 16:21

1. Dual preparatory scenes. 15:1-8
   a. The redeemed on the sea of glass sing the song of Moses and the Lamb
   b. Introductory sanctuary scene: Seven angels receive the seven plagues

2. First six plagues. 16:1-14, 16

3. Scenes of end-time assignment and assurance. 16:15
   a. Assurance (from heaven): I am coming!
   b. Assignment (on earth): Stay awake and keep your garments!

4. Consummation: The seventh plague. 16:17-21

Revelation 17:1, 2	Revelation 21:9, 10
Then one of the seven angels who had the seven bowls came and said to me,	Then came one of the seven angels who had the seven bowls full of the seven last plagues, and spoke to me, saying,
"Come, I will show you the judgment of the great harlot who is seated upon many waters. . . ."	"Come, I will show you the Bride, the wife of the Lamb."
And he carried me away in the Spirit into a wilderness, and I saw a woman sitting on a scarlet beast.	And in the Spirit he carried me away to a great, high mountain, and showed me the holy city Jerusalem coming down out of heaven from God.

Now compare the verses that *end* each of these divisions:

Revelation 19:9, 10	Revelation 22:6-9
And the angel said to me, "Write this: Blessed are those who are invited to the marriage supper of the Lamb."	And he said to me, "These words are trustworthy and true. . . ." Blessed is he who keeps the words of the prophecy of this book.
And he said to me, "These are true words of God."	I John am he who heard and saw these things. And when I heard and saw them,
Then I fell down at his feet to worship him, but he said to me, "You must not do that!	I fell down to worship at the feet of the angel who showed them to me; but he said to me, "You must not do that!
I am a fellow servant with you and your brethren who hold the testimony of Jesus. Worship God." For the testimony of Jesus is the spirit of prophecy.	I am a fellow servant with you and your brethren the prophets, and with those who keep the words of this book. Worship God."

We can now redo our little chiasm on the previous page, adding information to reveal the synonymous parallel that exists within it. This gives us the "Second Half of Revelation" chart on the next page.

We're now better prepared to appreciate the right-hand half of the sequence-of-events chart that we introduced on page 62. Maybe you'd like to take a few moments to look at it again right now. We have been studying the prophecies represented by the vertical arrows. Now our study shifts to prophecies connected with the horizontal arrows.

This introduction has served to prepare us for the entire second half of Revelation, chapters 15 through 22. We begin with chapters 15 and 16.

THE SECOND HALF OF REVELATION: A DUAL FOCUS ON THE ULTIMATE PUNISHMENT OF THE REBELLIOUS AND ON THE ULTIMATE REWARD OF THE RIGHTEOUS IN THE END TIME

1. *Focus on punishment*
   A The plagues 15:1-16:21

   B Circumstances related to the plagues: Fall of Babylon, the false mother 17:1-19:10

   A plague angel shows John the great harlot. 17:1-19:8
   Afterward John attempts to worship the angel. 19:9, 10

2. *Focus on reward*
   B′ Circumstances related to the holy city: The millennium 19:11- 21:8

   A′ The holy city: Descent of New Jerusalem, the Lamb's bride 21:9-22:21

   A plague angel shows John the Lamb's bride. 21:9-22:7
   Afterward John attempts to worship the angel. 22:8, 9

REVELATION 15

1 Then I saw another portent in heaven, great and wonderful, seven angels with seven plagues, which are the last, for with them the wrath of God is ended.

TWO INTRODUCTORY SCENES

Victory scene: The song of Moses and the Lamb. 2 And I saw what appeared to be a sea of glass mingled with fire, and those who had conquered the beast and its image and the number of its name, standing beside the sea of glass with harps of God in their hands. ³And they sing the song of Moses, the servant of God, and the song of the Lamb, saying,

"Great and wonderful are thy deeds,
O Lord God the Almighty!
Just and true are thy ways,
O King of the ages!
⁴Who shall not fear and glorify thy
name, O Lord?
For thou alone art holy.
All nations shall come and worship
thee,
for thy judgments have been
revealed."

Sanctuary scene: Seven angels receive plague bowls; the sanctuary opens—and closes. 5 After this I looked, and the temple of the tent of witness in heaven was opened, ⁶and out of the temple came the seven angels with the seven plagues, robed in pure bright linen, and their breasts girded with golden girdles. ⁷And one of the four living creatures gave the seven angels seven golden bowls full of the wrath of God who lives for ever and ever; ⁸and the temple was filled with smoke from the glory of God and from his power, and no one could enter the temple until the seven plagues of the seven angels were ended.

THE SEVEN LAST PLAGUES

REVELATION 16

The executive order. 1 Then I heard a loud voice from the temple telling the seven angels, "Go and pour out on the earth the seven bowls of the wrath of God."

The first three plagues. 2 So the first angel went and poured his bowl on the earth, and foul and evil sores came upon the men who bore the mark of the beast and worshiped its image.

3 The second angel poured his bowl into the sea, and It became like the blood of a dead man, and every living thing died that was in the sea.

4 The third angel poured his bowl into the rivers and the fountains of water, and they became blood.

Heavenly voices praise God's justice. 5 And I heard the angel of water say,

"Just art thou in these thy
judgments,
thou who art and wast, O Holy One.
⁶For men have shed the blood of
saints and prophets,
and thou hast given them blood to
drink.
It is their due!"
⁷And I heard the altar cry,
"Yea, Lord God the Almighty,
true and just are thy judgments!"

The fourth and fifth plagues. 8 The fourth angel poured his bowl on the sun, and it was allowed to scorch men with fire; ⁹men were scorched by the fierce heat, and they cursed the name of God who had power over these plagues, and they did not repent and give him glory.

10 The fifth angel poured his bowl on the throne of the beast, and its kingdom was in darkness; men gnawed their tongues in anguish ¹¹and cursed the God of heaven for their pain and sores, and did not repent of their deeds.

The sixth plague—preparation for Armageddon—and a parenthetical word of assignment and assurance. 12 The sixth angel poured his bowl on the great river Euphrates, and its water was dried up, to prepare the way for the kings from the east. ¹³And I saw, issuing from the mouth of the dragon and from the mouth of the beast and from the mouth of the false prophet, three foul spirits like frogs; [14]for they are demonic spirits, performing signs, who go abroad to the kings of the whole world, to assemble them for battle on the great day of God the Almighty. [15] ("Lo, I am coming like a thief! Blessed is he who is awake, keeping his garments that he may not go naked and be seen exposed!") [16]And they assembled them at the place which is called in Hebrew Armageddon.

The seventh plague. [17] The seventh angel poured his bowl into the air, and a loud voice came out of the temple, from the throne, saying, "It is done!" [18]And there were flashes of lightning, voices, peals of thunder, and a great earthquake such as had never been since men were on the earth, so great was that earthquake. [19]The great city was split into three parts, and the cities of the nations fell, and God remembered great Babylon, to make her drain the cup of the fury of his wrath. [20]And every island fled away, and no mountains were to be found; [21]and great hailstones, heavy as a hundredweight, dropped on men from heaven, till men cursed God for the plague of the hail, so fearful was that plague.

The Message of Revelation 15, 16

I. The Seven Last Plagues

The plagues and heavenly voices. A heavenly voice starts the first plague. Other heavenly voices follow the third plague, interrupt the sixth one, and bring on the seventh.

To begin with, **"a loud voice from the temple"** tells the seven plague angels, **"Go and pour out on the earth the seven bowls of the wrath of God."** Revelation 16:1. The voice comes from the temple. It may be the voice of one of the four living creatures. We heard living creatures in chapter 4 praising God and in chapter 6 inviting us to "Come" at the opening of each of the first four seals.

Or the heavenly voice may be the voice of the Lamb. In Revelation 6:15-17 the evildoers ask mountains to hide them from "the wrath of the Lamb."

Or it may be the voice of God Himself. We think of God and Jesus as being incomprehensibly kind and gracious; and that's what They are. But we reminded ourselves on pages 229, 230 and will review again on page 468, that in order to protect the innocent, love must finally punish the evil. It deeply upsets God to see His followers suffer. God does care.

And the angels care. As they have watched the age-long controversy, Satan and his followers versus Christ and His followers, they have been outraged by the crimes committed by the cruel against the good. They have longed for the day when God will terminate the trials of the true-hearted.

This longing for justice and fair play explains the song of the **"angel of water"** in Revelation 16:5, 6. He has poured his bowl into the **"rivers and the fountains of water"** and watched them turn to **"blood."** With appreciation for the fitness of such a punishment, he sings with joy,

> **Just art thou in these thy judgments,**
> **thou who art and wast, O Holy One.**
> **For men have shed the blood of saints and prophets,**
> **and thou hast given them blood to drink.**
> **It is their due!**

As John watched these things in his vision, he sensed that even the altar wanted to say something. We remember that in Revelation 6:9-11 the martyrs are portrayed as being "under the altar." The altar has witnessed sufferings enough, the frightful persecution during the great tribulation of the 1260 years and many another persecution besides. Now it too shares the satisfaction of the angel of water and sings in verse 7,

> **Yea, Lord God the Almighty,**
> **true and just *are* thy judgments!**

428

Christ is coming! The next heavenly voice is unquestionably Christ's. It says, **"Lo, I am coming like a thief!"** Verse 15. See also Revelation 3:3. To come **"like a thief"** means to come at an unexpected moment. It cannot mean to come silently or invisibly, as some Bible readers have wondered. Thieves sometimes make a lot of noise, hammering their way through walls and blowing up vaults. And they are quite visible when they demand money in a bank holdup.

Christ's announcement is an encouragement. He hasn't forgotten His people. They are still His; and He *is* coming for them. It is also an earnest warning. **"Blessed is he who is awake, keeping his garments that he may not go naked and be seen exposed!"**

Clothing in Revelation represents character, especially the righteous character of the people of God, which they receive by faith from Jesus Christ. See Revelation 3:18; 7:14; 19:8. Final victory and joy will come to those believers who keep on believing and obeying till He comes. Said Jesus in the Olivet Discourse, "He who endures to the end will be saved." Matthew 24:13.

"The seventh angel poured his bowl into the air, and a loud voice came out of the temple, from the throne, saying, 'It is done!' And there were flashes of lightning, voices, peals of thunder, and a great earthquake such as had never been since men were on the earth, so great was that earthquake." Revelation 16:17, 18. On the cross, as Jesus closed His life of humiliation and suffering, He cried out triumphantly, "It is finished." Now as the humiliation and suffering of His people draw to a close, He cries out with enormous satisfaction and relief, **"It is done!"**

All nature in heaven and earth seems to respond with kindred joy. **"Voices"** of angels, rumblings of **"thunder,"** and the groaning of the world's greatest **"earthquake"** second the cry.

The plagues and the trumpets. We have noticed more than once that there are striking similarities between the seven plagues and the seven trumpets. The first four in each case are directed against the earth, sea, rivers and springs, and heavenly bodies. The fifth in each case is associated with darkness, the sixth with the river Euphrates, and the seventh with a loud voice or loud voices. See pages 58, 262. The suggestion has been made that the plagues are the same as the trumpets.

On closer examination, however, the differences outweigh the similarities. For example, though it is true that both the first trumpet and the first plague affect the earth, the first *trumpet* causes "a third of the earth," "a third of the trees" and "all green grass" to be burned up; but the first *plague* causes **"foul and evil sores"** to break out on **"the men who bore the mark of the beast and worshiped its image."** Compare Revelation 8:7 with 16:2.

The third trumpet and the third plague both affect rivers and springs, but the third *trumpet* only makes the water "bitter," whereas the third *plague* turns it into **"blood."** Compare 8:10, 11 with 16:4. Even more striking, whereas the fourth trumpet causes sun, moon, and stars to be dimmed, the fourth plague does the opposite. It causes the sun to **"scorch men with fire; men were scorched by the fierce heat."** Compare 8:12 with 16:8, 9.

429

Some similarities exist in every case, but notable differences show that trumpets and plagues are not the same. Something else is notable. The trumpets were fulfilled in truly serious disasters. If the fulfillment of the plagues will be far worse, what awesome troubles lie ahead?

The plagues and the Exodus. In addition to comparing the plagues with the trumpets, it is helpful to compare them with the plagues God sent on Egypt at the time of the Exodus. See Exodus 7:20 to 12:30.

No one suggests that the end-time plagues are the same as the Exodus plagues. Just the same, there are interesting similarities. See the chart on the next page.

How many aspects of the Exodus plagues resemble aspects of the final plagues? A river, blood, frogs, boils, hailstones, and ominous darkness. During the actual Exodus that followed the Exodus plagues, the Red Sea dried up for a night to let the Israelites walk across. When Egyptian charioteers tried to dash through and kill the Israelites, God made the Red Sea close in on them. In the morning the Israelites sang with joy:

> The Lord is a man of war;
> the Lord is his name.
> > Exodus 15:3.

In other words, there was a kind of **"battle . . . of God the Almighty"** in connection with the Exodus plagues, even as there will be one (usually called Armageddon) in connection with the end-time plagues.

So there are similarities. One of the most dreadful similarities is the sheer terror of the Egyptian plagues. Those plagues were real enough, and bad enough. What will the final plagues be like?

Are the plagues literal or symbolic? The language of Revelation is usually symbolic, often impressionistic. The language describing the plagues may well be nonliteral. But it loses little of its force if taken as it reads. **"Foul and evil sores,"** **"blood of a dead man,"** **"men gnawed their tongues in anguish,"** **"great hailstones, heavy as a hundredweight"** are serious enough taken literally. The **"darkness"** **"on the throne of the beast"** and the **"foul spirits like frogs"** that come out of the mouths of **"dragon,"** **"beast,"** and **"false prophet"** require some interpretation, but they are scarcely mysterious at this stage in our study of Revelation.

"Their bodies are covered with sores, the stench of death in seas and rivers fills their nostrils with the odor of corruption, their bodies are scorched with fire, and then suddenly they are precipitated into the utmost darkness."[2]

The picture is ominous if the words are taken as they stand.

It is equally alarming if, on the other hand the language is taken as figurative. We may, for instance, think of the bloody waters as foreboding convulsive global carnage, the world bathed with butchery, awash in a maelstrom of malice.

The sores when regarded as figurative remind us (as radio speaker Donald Grey Barnhouse has observed), that "medically speaking, a sore is the outward

THE EXODUS PLAGUES Exodus 7-12	THE SEVEN LAST PLAGUES Revelation 16
"Bring out the people of Israel from the land of Egypt." Exodus 6:26	"Come out of her [Babylon], my people, . . . lest you share in her plagues." Revelation 18:4
1. River Nile: Blood 2. River Nile: Frogs 3. Earth: Gnats 4. Flies 5. Cattle: Fatal disease 6. Ashes: Boils 7. Heaven: Hailstones 8. Egypt: Locusts 9. Heaven: Palpable darkness 10: Firstborn: Death Red Sea dried up, God battles Egypt	1. Earth: Sores (boils) 2. Sea: Blood 3. Rivers: Blood 4. Sun: Scorching heat 5. Beast's throne: Painful darkness 6. River Euphrates: Dried up, God battles nations. 7. Air: Hailstones, etc.

sign of some inner corruption, and it would, therefore, be entirely fitting that the corruption of the hearts of these rebels should be manifest before all men." "Here, under the first bowl of wrath, . . . all will be outwardly what they are inwardly."[3] Such an interpretation adds possible meaning to Christ's counsel in Revelation 16:15, **"Blessed is he who is awake, keeping his garments that he may not go naked and be seen exposed!"** Having refused to "wear" Christ's goodness, the rebellious in earth's worst crisis find themselves without spiritual resources. In particular, the spiritual leaders who encouraged them to break God's commandments are revealed as corrupt and bankrupt.

On pages 439-441 in our next section we'll see if perhaps some of the plagues are literal and others symbolic.

Who receive the plagues? In any case, the plagues fall on the beast and on things and people connected with it. And the punishments fit the crime. Sin in mind and muscle (forehead and hand) is met with loathsome sores. People who have shed rivers of blood are faced with rivers of blood. Religious leaders who preferred tradition rather than the clear light of the Bible discover that the so-called light of tradition has blinded them to the true light and left their hearts wastelands. Excruciating darkness (the pain resulting from extremely low temperatures?) reenforces the same point, especially for those leaders who allied themselves with the Roman traditions that have come from the throne of the beast.

431

Old Testament law required persons convicted of notorious idolatry, adultery, blasphemy, or stubborn rebellion to be stoned to death. The stoning was done by the entire community, indicating everyone's abhorrence of the great crime. See Deuteronomy 13:2-11; 21:18-21; 22:23, 24; Leviticus 24:16. Under the seventh plague the people who have worshiped the beast, blasphemed God, and refused to repent are hailstoned to death while heavenly voices approve.

To put the matter simply, the plagues fall on people in the end time who, knowing better, stubbornly persist in the blasphemy of refusing to obey God, the idolatry of following their own judgment, and the murder of approving the persecution of the "remnant" "saints" who cherish God's Sabbath and the loving, honest way of life it represents.

Daniel and his three friends gave an example of faithful loyalty to God even when faced with death in a furnace or in a lions' den.

Jesus gave an example of faithful loyalty to God even when faced with the cross. In the Olivet Discourse He urged us to prepare for the second coming, keep oil in our lamps, help the underprivileged, and improve our talents in the service of others. See pages 36-42.

Revelation repeatedly calls for character development. It warns us to "conquer" (see Revelation 2, 3) our weaknesses and temptations, wash our robes in the blood of the Lamb (7:14), refuse the beast and its image (15:2), and receive the seal of God (7:1-8).

In our own time, in the end time which we occupy today, knowledge of all these matters and of the fulfillment of prophecy is widespread. The book of Daniel is now open, as Daniel 12 and Revelation 10 predicted. The first angel's message about the arrival of the judgment hour is already widespread and will soon have been proclaimed to every "nation and tribe and tongue and people." Revelation 14:6.

Two thousand years of history have shown that the Christian church at its worst has tampered with the Ten Commandments, obscured Christ's ministry in the heavenly sanctuary, and harrassed God's true believers.

Supremely, Christ's death on the cross has shown that God would rather suffer death in support of His Ten Commandments than change any of them in any particular.

The sin that brings on the plagues is the sin of *rejecting all this enlightenment*. It is the sin of turning one's back on truth and mocking, harrassing, even persecuting those who put their faith in Jesus and choose to cherish His loving requirements.

God's people will not be entirely free from suffering during the falling of the plagues. They have been invited to the wedding supper and will be longing for Christ's return from the heavenly marriage to escort them to it. But for now they will still be living on earth. See Luke 12:35-37 and *Your Questions Answered*, pages 407-410.

In His famous prayer on the way to the cross, Jesus said, "I do not pray that thou shouldst take them out of the world, but that thou shouldst keep them from the evil one." John 17:15. You may want to reread our discussion about Revelation 3:10 on pages 111-113.

Hebrews 13:5, reminds us that He has said, "I will never fail you nor forsake you."

Encourage your young people. Christian young people think about the final tribulation in opposite ways. Some don't take it any more seriously than a TV drama that isn't true. Others have nightmares about it.

It's right to have a healthy fear of something as dreadful as the seven last plagues. Most people will suffer indescribably. But God loves children and young people. God's promises are for youth as much as for anyone else.

Little children can remember, "The angel of the Lord encamps around those who fear him, and delivers them." Psalm 34:7.

Daniel 12:1 says that when the time of trouble comes, "Michael, the great prince" will be in "charge of your people." "At that time your people shall be *delivered*." If ever God has cared for His people, He will then!

The promises of Psalm 91 are for *everyone* who sincerely trusts.

> Because you have made the Lord your refuge,
>   the Most High your habitation,
> no evil shall befall you,
>   no scourge come near your tent.
> For he will give his angels charge of you
>   to guard you in all your ways.
>   Psalm 91:9-11.

In the plague of darkness, as in all the last plagues, God's wings will be the refuge of His people, as He promised in Psalm 91.

The Valley of Jezreel today. Does the Bible say it is Armageddon?

II. The Battle of Armageddon

"We have had our last chance. If we do not devise some greater and more equitable system [for settling international problems] Armageddon will be at our door."[4]

General Douglas MacArthur was standing on the battleship *Missouri* after the Japanese surrender, September 2, 1945. On August 6, less than a month before, at 8:15 on a sunny Monday morning, a B-29 nicknamed *Enola Gay* after the pilot's mother had dropped the first atomic bomb and changed the course of history. MacArthur felt burdened to warn the world that another war with similar weapons would inevitably escalate into Armageddon.

Stark words written by Winston Churchill after the horrors of even the first world war assumed apalling new significance after that first atomic bomb fell. "Death," he said, "stands at attention, obedient, expectant, ready to serve, ready to shear away the peoples *en masse*; ready, if called on, to pulverise, without hope of repair, what is left of civilisation. He awaits only the word of command. He awaits it from a frail, bewildered being, long his victim, now—for one occasion only—his Master."[5]

In the decades that have elapsed since the second world war, human beings have fought at least 125 wars of various sorts, including America's longest war, the one in Viet Nam![6] Even so, "Death" still stands waiting at attention, and the Armageddon MacArthur had in mind hasn't yet arrived.

434

Four different interpretations. To tell the truth, there are many different ideas as to what Armageddon is all about. In popular articles and books it often appears as (1) the ultimate global war, ending in total annihilation. Attractive Christian publications, drawing on additional data from the seven trumpets and Daniel 11, speak of Armageddon (2) as being either a specific location near Mount Carmel, a few miles inland from the Mediterranean, or the Middle East in general, the home of Arab oil and Dead Sea minerals. They foresee it as the focus of a last-day convergence of vast armies—Russians pressing down from the north, Africans driving up from the south, Europeans and Americans swarming in from the west, and 200,000,000 Chinese marching over from the east.[7] See the map on page 438.

Still another important interpretation views the battle of Armageddon as (3) "the final struggle between the powers of evil and the Kingdom of God."[8]

With so many interpretations available, we remind ourselves that *Armageddon* is a Bible word, occurring only in the account of the sixth plague, and that the right way to begin an interpretation is to let the Bible as far as possible explain itself. So let us see if we can decide what John himself had in mind.

The sixth plague. **"The sixth angel poured his bowl on the great river Euphrates, and its water was dried up, to prepare the way for the kings from the east. And I saw, issuing from the mouth of the dragon and from the mouth of the beast and from the mouth of the false prophet, three foul spirits like frogs; for they are demonic spirits, performing signs, who go abroad to the kings of the whole world, to assemble them for battle on the great day of God the Almighty. ('Lo, I am coming like a thief! Blessed is he who is awake, keeping his garments that he may not go naked and be seen exposed!') And they assembled them at the place which is called in Hebrew Armageddon."** Revelation 16:12-16.

Where–or what–is Armageddon? We need to admit that the passage we have just read poses difficulties. To begin with, no place called Armageddon is known to have existed in Bible times.

A small but important fortress town called Megiddo is known to have existed since very early times. It occupied a rise of ground south of a valley usually called the plain (or valley) of Esdraelon but which in Zechariah 12:11 is called the plain of Megiddo. This plain is fairly fertile though somewhat swampy, triangular in shape, about 18 to 20 miles on a side,[9] and approximately 300 square kilometers, or something under 200 square miles in total area—perhaps two-thirds the size of Lake Tahoe, or somewhat smaller than Chicago. It served for some pretty important battles long ago, but rather obviously it doesn't offer much room for the modern armies of **"the kings of the whole world."** No one seriously supposes that 200,000,000 Chinese soldiers could be effectively deployed there.

Even so, the plain of Megiddo isn't Armageddon.

Difficulties with Armageddon. Not only is there no known geographical site called Armageddon, but there is trouble also with the word itself. John spoke of the **"place which is called *in Hebrew* Armageddon."** Necessarily, however, he gave us the Greek form of the word, for he was writing Revelation in Greek.

435

Scholars who are authorities in both languages usually suggest that the Hebrew word John had in mind was *Har-megiddo,* meaning the "Mountain of Megiddo." The suggestion presents immediate problems, partly because no mountain of that name is known to have existed and partly because a mountain is obviously unsuited to massive military maneuvers. Further, although Hebrew names often mean something as Hebrew words, *Megiddo* doesn't seem to have any clear meaning,[10] raising the question as to whether there is a mistake.

Perhaps the spelling "Armageddon" is incorrect. The Greek manuscripts of Revelation offer a variety of spellings, some of which suggest that the Hebrew name John really had in mind was *har-mo'edth.* In Isaiah 14, *har-mo'edth* is the word for the mountain where God has His throne. In verse 13, the demon prince of Babylon aspires to seat himself on *har-mo'edth* and take over the government of the universe.

Yet another possibility is *har-migdo,* "his fruitful mountain," or Mount Zion. The *Interpreter's Dictionary*[11] recommends this as the "most likely" meaning, inasmuch as Revelation 9:13 to 11:14; 14:14-20 and 16:12-16 take much of their imagery from the Old Testament book of Joel, where "it is from Mount Zion that the power of God in his warfare against the forces of evil is to proceed."[12] See Joel 3:16. Remember that the 144,000—who are the "saints" and the "remnant"— stand on Mount Zion. The dragon makes war with this group.

Let us not take lightly the difficulties which the word *Armageddon* invokes. Familiarity with the word and our well-established habit of assuming that we know what it means shouldn't be allowed to mislead us. Suppose instead of Mount Megiddo we read "Mount Omaha"? Right away we'd know we had a puzzle on our hands. Omaha is located in the Great Plains, and there isn't any peak called Mount Omaha.[13]

Suppose we read, "And they [the froglike demons] assembled them [the kings of the whole world] at the place which is called in America, Capitol Hill." We might then infer that we were not reading about an actual military engagement at all. We would conclude that we were dealing with metaphors about a world-wide political struggle to take control of the United States government.

Or again, suppose we read that all the enemies of the United States were to meet at Waterloo or at Valley Forge? *Then* we'd take the language to hint at a great victory for the Stars and Stripes.

Careful attention to words is vital to one's understanding of a passage!

Another Bible name for the place. A further difficulty with the word *Armageddon,* in addition to the fact that we aren't quite sure it's the right word, and if it is, we don't know of any such geographical location, is the additional fact that it isn't the only name given in the Bible for the site of earth's end-time battle. Joel 3:12 calls the location of this battle the "valley of Jehoshaphat." We had occasion to refer to this prophecy when talking about Joel's locusts on pages 233-235. As you read the passage, look for words like *nations, war, harvest,* and *day of the Lord.*

436

Proclaim this among the nations:
Prepare war,
  stir up the mighty men.
Let all the men of war draw near,
  let them come up.
Beat your plowshares into swords,
  and your pruning hooks into spears;
  let the weak say, "I am a warrior."

Hasten and come,
  all you nations round about,
  gather yourselves there.
Bring down thy warriors, O Lord.
Let the nations bestir themselves,
  and come up to the valley of Jehoshaphat;
for there I will sit to judge
  all the nations round about.

Put in the sickle,
  for the harvest is ripe.
Go in, tread,
  for the wine press is full.
The vats overflow,
  for their wickedness is great.

Multitudes, multitudes,
  in the valley of decision!
For the day of the Lord is near
  in the valley of decision.
The sun and the moon are darkened,
  and the stars withdraw their shining.

And the Lord roars from Zion,
  and utters his voice from Jerusalem,
  and the heavens and the earth shake.
But the Lord is a refuge to his people,
  a stronghold to the people of Israel.
               Joel 3:9-16.

Joel's references here to a sickle, ripe harvests, a gathering of all the nations, the time of the judgment, a great earthquake, and the Lord's roaring out of Zion convince us that he is talking about the same end-time battle which John describes under the sixth and seventh plagues in Revelation 16. But Joel locates the

437

battle not in Armageddon but in some place that he calls the "valley of Jehoshaphat."

The valley of Jehoshaphat. King Jehoshaphat was one of the finest kings who ever ruled the Jews in Old Testament times. One of the most impressive stories in the Bible comes from his reign. See 2 Chronicles 20.

A coalition of foreign tribes invaded Judea and camped in one of its valleys. At headquarters in Jerusalem, Jehoshaphat offered a marvelous prayer of faith and encouraged the people to trust God. A prophet, assuring him that God would provide the victory, said, "The battle is not yours but God's. . . . You will not need to fight in this battle; take your position, stand still, and see the victory of the Lord on your behalf." 2 Chronicles 20:15-17.

Next morning, instead of putting his best warriors at the head of his army, the good king instructed his temple choir to take the lead, praising the Lord as they walked. And when the choir members reached the watchtower on a ridge overlooking the valley where the hostile coalition was camped, they joyously discovered that the enemy tribes had fallen into a quarrel and wiped one another out. You can see the singers waving their arms and shouting to the soldiers to come and see!

This victory that God won for Jehoshaphat was won in a valley. Perhaps this is the valley that came to be known as the valley of Jehoshaphat. But even if so, we're no better off geographically than with Armageddon, for no one knows precisely where the place is.

But the valley of Jehoshaphat has given us an idea. Look at Judges chapters 4 and 5 when you have time. There you'll find another story of a miraculous deliverance of the Israelite people from their enemies, this time under the leadership of Deborah and Barak. Notice especially Judges 4:15 and 5:20-23. Judges 5:21

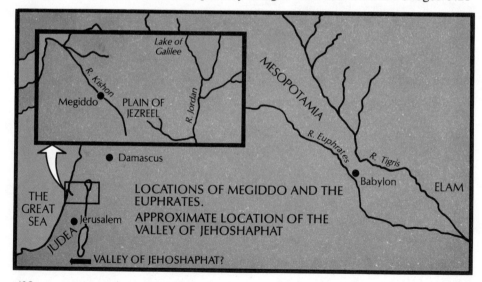

LOCATIONS OF MEGIDDO AND THE EUPHRATES.
APPROXIMATE LOCATION OF THE VALLEY OF JEHOSHAPHAT

says the battle took place along the swampy banks of the river Kishon—the river that flows north through the *plain of Megiddo*!

And this experience reminds us of another miraculous deliverance that took place in a little valley right next to the plain of Megiddo. Gideon with only 300 men—and the Lord's special intervention—in a night battle put to rout an army of Midianites that had swarmed over the land like locusts. See Judges 6, 7.

Armageddon as a symbol. Is it possible then that we should regard Armageddon not as a specific place (there being no such place!) but as being instead a symbolic *reminder* that in earth's final rebellion against truth and right, the God of truth and right will utterly *destroy His enemies* and totally *protect and preserve His people?*

Incidentally, it isn't necessary for us to assume that all seven plagues must be literal or all seven symbolic. The first four *seals,* with their four famous horsemen, are obviously symbolic, but the sixth seal, with its signs of the end and its account of the second coming, is just as obviously literal. So if the language of the first four plagues is taken as literal, we are still free to consider the language of any or all of the remaining plagues as symbolic.

Indeed, the voices, lightning, great earthquake, hailstones, and removal of islands and mountains under the seventh plague all seem to be literal. Only the splitting of the **"great city"** may need symbolic interpretation as a precursor of the complete breakup of society in earth's final panic.

The drying up of Euphrates. So now let's take a closer look at the passage about the sixth plague, Revelation 16:12-16. Looking at it again, the first thing we notice is that the sixth plague is concerned primarily not with Armageddon but with the river Euphrates! **"The sixth angel poured his bowl on the great river Euphrates, and its water was dried up, to prepare the way for the kings from the east."** Revelation 16:12.

In fact, verses 12-16 list three very different activities: (a) God's angel dries up Euphrates in preparation for the kings from the east, (b) Satan's demons gather the nations to "Armageddon," and (c) Jesus Christ comforts and cautions His people.

If commentators would spend more time on the drying up of the Euphrates, the meaning of "Armageddon" might take care of itself.

A good many commentators take for granted that the actual river will be dried up, thereby removing a barrier to the maneuvering of large armies, notably the armies of China, perhaps 200,000,000 strong.

The Euphrates is a major river, more than 2235 miles long, that flows through Turkey, Syria, and Iraq and irrigates large agricultural areas, especially in Iraq. A drought sufficiently serious to dry it up would be a major disaster for the people living in the area.

We seriously wonder, nonetheless, how much its drying up in the ordinary sense would contribute to the passage of modern armies.

In any case, before the Chinese (let us say) reached the banks of the Euphrates they would have had to face such truly formidable barriers as the Himalaya mountains and the deserts and mountains of Iran. Having surmounted these, it seems unlikely they would find the Euphrates much of an obstacle even if it were running full. Where the Euphrates flows through Syria, the area most likely for a crossing, it is much less than a mile in width. Ancient armies managed to cross it, using handmade boats and pontoon bridges. On D-Day, June 6, 1944, the Allies successfully crossed the English Channel in places where the Channel is 100 miles wide, and in stormy weather at that.

A symbolic interpretation. So let's try a symbolic interpretation of the drying up of the Euphrates, just as we have tried a symbolic meaning for Armageddon.

There is general agreement that under the seventh plague the **"great city"** which is **"split into three parts"** is Babylon. And everyone agrees that in Revelation the term **"Babylon"** doesn't refer to the literal city of that name but is a symbol which has something to do with Rome.

Now in Daniel's day, the real river Euphrates flowed right through the real city of Babylon. On the night when Cyrus's forces, led by Darius the Mede, attacked the city, the water level of the river was much lower than usual. The attack came at a season when the river was normally low, and some ancient historians say that the enemy troops had dug a diversion canal to lower the water still further. This lowering of the water enabled the invaders to wade into the city along the river bed, the route that offered the greatest opportunity for success. See GC 1:75-78.

In June 1944, ships bearing millions of troops easily crossed the English Channel. No modern army would need the Euphrates (inset) to literally dry up.

UPI / BETTMANN (D-DAY)   DR. G. R. FATTIC, JR. (RIVER EUPHRATES)

One of King Cyrus's earliest acts after his conquest of Babylon was to release the Jewish captives from their exile and permit them to return home to Judea. See GC 1:207. Because of Cyrus's generosity, the prophet Isaiah spoke of him almost as if he were Jesus Christ. He quoted God as calling Cyrus His "shepherd" and His "anointed," the person He had chosen to "subdue nations." In the same context Isaiah also quoted God as saying, "I will dry up your rivers." See Isaiah 44:27 to 45:1.

King Cyrus was ruler of Persia, a nation lying to the east of Babylon. Thus Cyrus was a king from the east. At the second coming, Jesus will first appear in the east. It seems, then, that *the events surrounding the fall of ancient Babylon were a symbolic model for the world-gripping events of Armageddon.*

In Daniel's day the Euphrates provided Babylon with trade, communication, and life-giving water for drinking and irrigation. When flowing full, it also contributed to the city's defenses. The Euphrates was vital to Babylon's support.

What does the Bible say will provide vital support to the end-time Babylon, support which will suddenly be removed?

Euphrates in the last days. We remind ourselves that in Revelation 17:15, where the great city Babylon is likened to a harlot, "the waters that you saw, where the harlot is seated, are peoples and multitudes and nations and tongues." So the **"river Euphrates"** in this prophecy is a symbol of the world's population, organized under human governments.*

Next, we remember that in Revelation 13, after the beast gets over its mortal wound, it enjoys unprecedented prominence. The lamb-horned beast causes all the population of the world to construct an image of it. Revelation 13:11-17 goes on to delineate a hostile, coercive drama in which God's followers are threatened with death if they refuse to adopt the state-manipulated religion.

When on pages 471-478 we examine Revelation 17:12-14, we're going to find a similar scenario portrayed in different words. There "ten horns" in the end time "give over their power and authority to the beast; they will *make war*" (on whom?) "*on the Lamb.*" The way earthly governments make war on the Lamb is by opposing His truth and persecuting His people. So Revelation 17:12-14 is the same as Revelation 13:11-17. Both describe the triumph of Babylon as all the nations coercively support its false religion in opposition to Jesus Christ. Modern Babylon trusts in her "Euphrates" (the support of the world's populations) as naively as ancient Babylon did in hers (the literal river).

But a *revulsion* sets in. Revelation 17:16 says that the horns (the nations of the whole world) will turn against the harlot (the great city Babylon); "they will make her desolate and naked, and devour her flesh and burn her up with fire."

Now notice verse 17, "For God has put it into their hearts [the hearts of the

---

*On page 251 we interpreted the river Euphrates of the sixth trumpet as a general geographic reference, in harmony with a similar use of the term in Isaiah 8:7. We have established that the seven plagues are not the same as the seven trumpets. The first six trumpets, located in the historical half of Revelation, apply to more-or-less localized areas or communities. The sixth and seventh plagues, in the end-time half of Revelation, affect the whole world.

nations] to carry out his purpose." We are at once reminded that the drying up of the river Euphrates in the sixth plague proceeds from God. An angel of God dries up the Euphrates. At the moment when millions and millions of people around the world suddenly see through the hypocrisy of their spiritual leaders and loath the clergy in whom they have reposed their confidence, God claims to have had a part in bringing about their new insight. His angel pours out the new enlightenment. The resulting sense of disillusionment is an overwhelming "plague" indeed.

It results in the "drying up" of the "Euphrates," that is, in the withdrawal of popular support from the end-time false religious system known as "Babylon."

Will there be a world war? Nothing we have read so far denies the probablity of dreadful fighting among the nations in the last days. In fact, prophecies *other* than the one about Armageddon indicate there will be. Human beings seem to be always fighting, and it is unimaginable that the time of trouble such as never was will not be marked with fierce military combat. Churchill's "Death" still "stands at attention" and will then most probably be horrifically employed. See page 434.

The seventh trumpet (Revelation 11:15-18) speaks of the time when "the nations raged," God's "wrath" came, and the time arrived for destroying "the destroyers of the earth." The reference to God's wrath dates the prophecy to the falling of the plagues, in which God's wrath is "perfected." (See page 421.) The raging of the nations, who are angry with one another much of the time anyway, must imply a particularly vicious malevolence. The phrase, "destroyers of the earth," suggests atomic warfare.

But this international fighting has little if anything to do directly with the symbolic drying up of Euphrates or with symbolic Armageddon, which have to do with a hostile situation of a different sort. At **"Armageddon"** the kings of earth are assembled by demons to fight not so much against each other as against the Lamb.

Egypt and Babylon, slavery and exile. A few moments ago we spoke about the release of God's Old Testament people from Babylon. And on page 431 we compared the end-time plagues with the Exodus plagues. John's vision of the plagues links Egypt (where the Jews were held as slaves) with Babylon (where they were held as exiles).[14] His vision also links the Jews' glorious release from Egyptian slavery with their happy return from Babylonian exile. God fought against the Egyptian army at the Red Sea. He supported King Cyrus in his attack on Babylon, which involved drying up the Euphrates. In each instance God worked miraculously to release His people from bondage.

On the plain of Megiddo in Deborah's day God worked miraculously to deliver His people from an army of occupation. In the time of King Jehoshaphat, God intervened to deliver them from an invasion. And in the valley of Jehoshaphat, the valley of decision, in Joel's end-time vision, God arrives accompanied by His angels to reap earth's harvest at judgment hour.

Viewed in all this light, the battle of Armageddon will not be World War III.

442

Nor will it be a military engagement on a cramped battlefield near the Mediterranean coast, fought in the hope of winning oil and Dead Sea minerals. And *neither will it be a battle confined in any special sense to the Middle East*. Remember: Neither "valley of Jehoshaphat," nor "river Euphrates," nor "Babylon," nor "Armageddon" itself offers us any localized geographical significance.

The battle of Armageddon will be a worldwide conflict pitting rebellious man and evil spirits against the Creator and His loyal followers. The outcome will be the eternal deliverance of God's people when the Lamb and the One "who is seated on the throne" (see Revelation 6:16, 17) arrive on the scene as the **"kings from the east."**

Preparation for **"the kings from the east."** Now, how does the drying up of the river Euphrates as we have perceived it above **"prepare the way for the kings from the east"?**

Jesus will not return to harvest the earth's grain and grapes until both the grain and grapes are fully ripe. See Revelation 14:14-20. In Christ's parable about the wheat and the weeds (or tares, K.J.V.) both wheat and weeds were to grow together till the harvest. Only when both are ripe can the harvesters be certain of the difference. See Matthew 13:24-30.

In the great controversy between Christ and Satan that we talked about on pages 319-331, we saw that God has allowed earth's history to continue this long so that everyone on earth and in the rest of the universe can see clearly the differences which result from following Him and from following Satan.

Under the seven last plagues the characters of people on the two sides are plainly manifested. Rebels against God become confirmed in their rebellion, refusing to repent, continuing to blaspheme, and eager, if possible, to take the lives of God's followers. God's people remain faithful in their obedience, preferring, if necessary, to lay down their lives rather than dishonor God.

Once the two camps are unequivocally differentiated, once the wheat and tares, the grain and grapes, are fully ripe, there is no reason for further delay. There will be nothing more that God can do to save the wicked and nothing more that He needs to do for the righteous—except deliver them.

Thus the *moment of truth* which is represented by the drying up of the Euphrates prepares the way for Christ's return, at the head of the armies of heaven. See Revelation 19:11-16.

Satan's demonic trinity. Revelation 16:13-16 says that the nations are gathered to Armageddon by three froglike demons who come out of the mouths of the three symbolic monsters of Revelation 12 and 13, the **"dragon,"** the **"beast,"** and the **"false prophet"** (the lamb-horned beast).

We are intrigued that dragon, beast, and false prophet constitute three entities, just as there are three members in the Holy Trinity.

Revelation speaks of the throne of God—and of the throne of the beast.

Jesus at Calvary received a mortal wound and was resurrected. The leopard beast receives a mortal wound and is healed.

443

Christ's name, Michael, means, "Who is like God?" As people worship the beast they ask, "Who is like the beast?"

The lamb-horned beast is called the false prophet, a counterpart of the Holy Spirit, the avenue of true prophecy. In John 16 the Holy Spirit leads us into all truth and into the worship of God, but the false prophet teaches lies and persuades people to worship the beast.

Satan's trinity even pretends to create an image of the beast, as God created man in His own image. God breathed into man the breath of life. A member of Satan's trinity breathes life into the image of the beast.

God sends three angels preaching the final messages at judgment hour. His angels call on every nation, tribe, tongue, and people to believe the gospel and worship the God who created heaven and earth. Satan sends out three demons with messages from the mouth of the dragon, beast, and false prophet to assemble the nations for their great battle against the Lamb.

God offers to stamp us with the seal of God. Satan offers the mark of the beast.

God's "remnant" in the end time keep the commandments, have Christ's testimony, cling to their faith in Jesus, and are privileged to sing on the sea of glass.

Satan too has a "remnant" (see Revelation 19:21, K.J.V.). They have chosen to believe his lies, that God's law *need not*—or *should not,* or *cannot*—be obeyed. They are consigned to the lake of fire.

Satan's demonic parousia. The three demonic spirits go out **"performing signs."** Revelation 16:14. In Revelation 13 also we read about "great signs, even making fire come down from heaven" worked by the false prophet (the lamb-horned beast).

The apostle Paul warned that before Christ's coming the "lawless one" would come with "pretended signs and wonders, and with all wicked deception." 2 Thessalonians 2:9, 10.

When Jesus was on earth He too worked signs and wonders. His motive was to help us believe in Him, and believing have eternal life. See John 20:30, 31.

The demonic spirits work miracles to persuade us to worship the beast and gather us to Armageddon to make war.

Beyond making fire come down from heaven, we don't know what other miracles the demons will perform. We do know their purpose is to lie. They will pose as Jesus Christ, evidently. "False Christs and false prophets will arise and show great signs and wonders, so as to lead astray, if possible, even the elect," warned Jesus in the Olivet Discourse. Matthew 24:24. See pages 19-24.

Satan's biggest lie in the Garden of Eden was, "You will not die." Genesis 3:4. He used it to prove that Eve didn't need to obey God. Christ's greatest miracle was to resurrect Lazarus. Will one of the demons appear to resurrect the dead to "prove" that he is Christ? Will he appear to talk to the dead, to prove, as the serpent taught, that people don't really die?

If so, belief in spiritualism is poor preparation for Satan's final delusions. So too is acceptance of any other concept of the natural immortality of the soul.

If we allow ourselves to be deceived now, how easily we will be deceived by false resurrections later on.

Even this isn't all. Paul speaks in 2 Thessalonians 2:8-10 of the "coming" of the lawless one with satanic activity. He says that Christ will destroy him by *His* "coming." The underlying Greek word for *coming* in each instance is *parousia*.

Many Christians apply this Greek word, *parousia*, to an invisible coming of Jesus seven years before His visible coming. In the Olivet Discourse Jesus earnestly warned His followers not to be deceived by misleading accounts of His *parousia*. Carefully, carefully He emphasized that His *parousia* is to be as visible as the lightning that flashes from the east across the sky. See Matthew 24:27.

The unique "sign of the Son of man" is His visible appearance "on the clouds of heaven with power and great glory." Matthew 24:30.

Paul, in 1 Thessalonians 4:16, 17, described Christ's *parousia* as with clouds and trumpet blast and the Archangel's voice. "Behold, he is coming with the clouds," says Revelation 1:7, "and every eye will see him."

We have been warned! Satan's end-time deceptions persuade "those who are to perish, because they refused to love the truth and so be saved." God permits Satan to unveil his most insidious delusions, "to make them believe what is false, so that all may be condemned who did not believe the truth but had pleasure in unrighteousness." 2 Thessalonians 2:10, 11.

Thus the two sides in the battle of Armageddon are clearly drawn.

Was MacArthur right? If General Douglas MacArthur, standing on the *Missouri* on September 2, 1945, conceived Armageddon as nothing more than an

After signing the peace treaty with Japan, September 1945, General MacArthur warned that Armageddon lay at the world's door. Was he right?

immense military engagement, we must say that he wasn't well informed. But perhaps we'll agree that in the next two sentences of his speech he revealed considerable insight. To solve humanity's ills he called for a substantial "improvement of human character," an improvement commensurate with humanity's advances in science, art, and literature over the past 2000 years; and he urged that the solution to human ills "must be of the spirit if we are to save the flesh."

Maybe the general was more right than we realized.

III. The Temple Filled With Smoke

When we were boys at home, my twin brother and I loved to read.

We both still remember Mother's reminders, repeatedly requesting us to interrupt our reading (now that we'd been at it quite a while) and get started on whatever job it was we knew we were supposed to be doing. We truly meant to obey her, and we planned to do so—just as soon, that is, as we reached the end of the page. Which all too often became the end of the chapter, or even the end of the book.

Mother was patient, but only to a point. After a good many quiet appeals she would announce, with only a trace of impatience, "Very well then, I'll do the job myself. If you're not going to help, you don't have to."

The finality of her words, the intimation that we had drained our cup of mercy, produced the slamming of books and an apologetic and somewhat bleary-eyed march into the kitchen or bathroom or garden or wherever else the job was that needed to be cared for.

On a far more serious level, there will evidently come a final moment for the whole world when God in His own way will announce, "If you don't want to obey Me, you don't have to."

An extremely solemn development. Revelation touches on this extremely solemn development a number of times. Revelation 22:11 is a clear example. A voice from heaven declares in the most final possible terms,

> Let the evildoer still do evil,
> and the filthy still be filthy,
>   and the righteous still do right,
>   and the holy still be holy.

At first reading, this extraordinary anouncement seems incomprehensible. We can understand that God would want the holy to go on being holy, but how can we explain His telling wrongdoers to go on doing wrong?

A little reflection reveals that the form of speech involved here isn't uncommon after all. Most of us use it and hear other people use it fairly often. There's even a Latin name for it, "*idem per idem*."[15]

For example, after we've tried in vain to find a reason for some childish foolishness, don't we shrug our shoulders and end the discussion by smiling, "Boys will be boys"? Spanish-speaking people stop worrying and sigh, "*Qué será, será* (whatever will be, will be)." Distraught parents sometimes cut off discussion with their children by shouting, "You'll do what you're told, and that's that!"

In the Bible, Queen Esther announced her unshakable decision to be brave by saying, "If I perish, I perish." Esther 4:16. God announced His unswerving determination to be kind when He announced, "I . . . will show mercy on whom I will show mercy." Exodus 33:19. When Moses wanted to know His name, God replied without revealing very much, "I am who I am." Exodus 3:14.

So what we have in Revelation 22:11 is another "and that's that" kind of statement. It terminates persuasion and announces an irrevocable decision. God's mind is forever made up. "Let the good be good," He says, "and let the evil be evil." Enough is enough, and that's that.

The temple filled with smoke. The fearful moment of this final decision is portrayed in the sanctuary scene which introduces the seven plagues. John saw the heavenly temple open up to release the seven angels, and as they filed out with their lethal potions, the temple closed behind them. **"The temple was filled with smoke from the glory of God and from his power, and no one could enter the temple until the seven plagues of the seven angels were ended."** Revelation 15:8.

The language here, as in so much of Revelation, is adapted from the Old Testament. At the dedication of the first temple King Solomon mounted a small bronze platform, knelt down, spread his arms, and offered a truly magnificent prayer. When he finished, "the glory of the Lord filled the temple. And the priests could not enter the house of the Lord, because the glory of the Lord filled the Lord's house." 2 Chronicles 7:2; see also 2 Chronicles 6:13; 1 Kings 8:54. That long-ago infilling of glory marked the *commencement* of priestly ministry in Solomon's temple. The end-time glory foreseen in Revelation 15 will soon mark the *termination* of priestly ministry in the heavenly sanctuary. Today we can still "with confidence draw near to the throne of grace" (Hebrews 4:16), but then **"no one"** will be able to enter.

Theologians call the moment when the sanctuary shuts "the close of probation," that is, the termination of opportunity for people to be tested (or "proved" or "probed") to see which side they have chosen to be on. For thousands of years God has agonized, watching human beings as they have taunted and tortured other human beings. He has permitted "probationary" time to continue so that everyone—including the taunters and the torturers—could have plenty of time to repent.

But enough is enough. When the gospel has indeed been preached to *everyone* in all the world (See Matthew 24:14; Revelation 14:6, 7) and every individual has had *adequate opportunity* to decide where he or she wants to stand in relation to God and His loving commandments, "probation" for everyone closes, and the temple of God is **"filled with smoke from the glory of God and from his power,"** and **"no one"** can enter it **"until the seven plagues of the seven angels"** are ended.

The importance of character. The one qualification essential for eternal life is

447

character, born and bred by the Holy Spirit, marked by faith and love. See John 3:5; Galatians 5:22-24; Revelation 21:27. Sincerity is fundamental. We are to love God with all our hearts, souls, and minds, and our neighbors as ourselves. See Matthew 22:34-40. Repentance and confession that are prompted merely by fear (such as the terrible fear of the falling of the plagues) are not sincere. When the crisis passes, people return to what they were.

Probation closes before the plagues fall because repentance after they fall won't mean anything. The pre-advent phase of the judgment will have ended, and our gracious Saviour will already have sealed every sincere heart, retained it in the book of life, and sealed it for deliverance. He who reads our hearts will also know who are too heedless and loveless to feel at home in the Holy City.

No one but themselves to blame. More than a century before the onset of the great Flood God announced through Noah, "My spirit shall not abide in man for ever." God did not arbitrarily reject the generation then living. "The Lord saw that the wickedness of man was great in the earth, and that every imagination of the thoughts of his heart was only evil continually." Even so, He mercifully promised, "His days shall be a hundred and twenty years." See Genesis 6:1-8.

For 120 years Noah, God's "herald of righteousness" (2 Peter 2:5), pleaded with his long-lived contemporaries to change their wicked ways. Only after repeated refusals did God at last take Noah's family alone into the ark. "And the Lord shut him in." Genesis 7:16.

For seven days after the door of the ark was closed, the weather continued calm. Can you hear the crowds mocking Noah and his family, locked inside the ark with all their animals? When after seven days the rain came, the people's feelings abruptly changed. See Genesis 7:10.

And there was no one but themselves to blame.

Jesus, our Lord and Saviour, finally announced to the Jewish people of His day, "Your house is forsaken and desolate." Matthew 23:38; see GC 1:231. Jesus didn't want to reject their house (or temple); He came from heaven to glorify it by His presence. It was they who chose to reject Him. "He came to his own home, and his own people received him not." John 1:11.

When Christ announced that the Jerusalem temple was left desolate, no lightning fell from heaven. The rituals continued as before. Priests and Levites daily, weekly, yearly performed their appointed round of sacrifices and sprinklings and circumcisions, inspections, purifications, and blessings. The choirs sang, the people came and went, the sun rose, the sun set, and only the most spiritual perceived that what Jesus had said was ominously true, their house was forsaken and desolate. After almost forty years the Roman armies came, and then everyone knew.

And there was no one but themselves to blame.

The prophet Hosea once sadly remarked, "Ephraim is joined to idols, let him alone." Hosea 4:17.

The five young women in the Olivet Discourse, who didn't care enough to prepare extra oil, arrived at the wedding in a rush but found the door had been shut. See Matthew 25:1-13; pages 37-39.

Jesus talked about the sin against the Holy Spirit that cannot be forgiven. See Matthew 12:32. The Holy Spirit convinces us of our sins and persuades us to repent and change. See John 16:8. If we persistently refuse, God honors our response. "My spirit shall not abide in man for ever." He removes His Spirit from us so that we are no longer bothered by our sins. "Ephraim is joined to idols, let him alone."

Let the righteous still do right. But Revelation 22:11 tells us that when the moment comes in the end time to say, "Let the evildoer still do evil," God will add the resplendent, ringing words,

> [let] the righteous still do right,
> and the holy still be holy.

Though millions in the last days receive the mark of the beast indicating they have chosen the character of Satan, millions of others receive the seal of God. Accepting God's light, responding to the Holy Spirit, repenting of their sins, redirecting their lives, they become so settled in the truth of God that they cannot be moved away from it. Neither the **"dragon,"** the **"beast,"** nor the **"false prophet,"** by persuasion, deception, allurement, or threat can move them from their fixed determination to do what's right—the loving, honest, truthful, upright thing—though the heavens fall.

When God's Spirit *departed* from the old temple, leaving it desolate, It *came* in Pentecostal power to the group of praying, trusting Christians who chose with all their hearts to believe and obey Jesus. See Acts 2.

So it will be again. When God's Spirit departs from the churches and church members of spiritual Babylon, it will come with Pentecostal power to the praying, trusting Christians, young and old, who choose with all their hearts to believe and obey their Lord. See Joel 2:28-32; Acts 3:19.

These Spirit receivers will be overcomers and conquerors. They will wear the seal of God. His "name" (or character) will appear "in their foreheads." Their clear eyes and confident smiles will reveal the integrity and faith that burns within. They win the victory over the beast and his image. When Jesus comes they will be caught up to meet Him in the air. They will sit with Him on His throne.

How desirable it is that we place ourselves among their group!

Repentance too late—or today. We reviewed a moment ago how God removes His Spirit from people who find themselves persistently annoyed by Him. To a large degree, they cease to feel conviction about their sins. But even without the Holy Spirit to convict us, in a crisis like the plagues, memory alone will suffice to recall a person's guilt. If you or I at that time have any sins on our conscience, any unsurrendered selfishness, any clung-to disobedience, we will be overcome

449

by our own sense of guilt. If we, who have known so much about God, falter under persecution, we can be sure that Satan's angels and the people with the mark of the beast will exult at our embarrassment. We'll **"walk naked,"** our inner weakness exposed as truly as that of the beast worshipers. See page 431.

But evidently it will be too late then to have our sins forgiven, for Michael will have stood up (see Daniel 12:1), and the heavenly sanctuary, filled with glory, will be closed. Christ's intercession for sin will have ceased.

How important that we commit ourselves wholly to God and to His loving laws *now* while mercy lingers. Now is the time to confess our sins, make things right with people we have wronged, and believe that the Lamb who died to redeem us has forgiven us wholeheartedly. Now is the time to accept the New Covenant promises and let the Holy Spirit impress God's gracious ways on our hearts and minds. Now is the time to enter into the peaceful, joyous life-style of true Sabbath "holiness."

Now is the day of salvation. Now is the time to come fully to God while there's still nothing between us and Him but that great big door, opened as wide as the sky. See pages 133-135. "Behold, now is the acceptable time; behold, now is the day of salvation." 2 Corinthians 6:2.

> Today, when you hear his voice,
> do not harden your hearts.
> Hebrews 4:7

Reader of this book, however old or young you are, if you hear the dear Spirit of God speaking to you, reminding you again to make a decision you've repeatedly put off, please don't wait till you finish reading this book. Don't wait even till you finish reading this chapter. Bow your head before you end this page and say with simple sincerity of heart,

"Lord Jesus, I want to be Your loyal follower.

"In the crisis of the end time, I truly desire to be found on Your side.

"I confess myself a sinner deeply in need of Your forgiveness.

"By Your grace and power, I commit myself to obey Your commandments and live a life of holiness and love."

Further Interesting Reading

In *Bible Readings for the Home:*
   "The Seven Last Plagues," page 224.
In Ellen G. White, *The Triumph of God's Love:*
   "Who Are the Angels?" page 447.
   "The Time of Trouble," page 537.

Page numbers for each book refer to the large, fully illustrated edition.

References

1. I am indebted at this point to Charles H. Giblin, "Structural and Thematic Correlations in the Theology of Revelation 16-22," *Biblica* 55 (1974):487-504.

2. Donald Grey Barnhouse, *Revelation* (Grand Rapids, Mich.: Zondervan Publishing House, 1971), p. 299.

3. *Ibid.,* pp. 289, 290. Barnhouse, however, prefers a literal interpretation.

4. Douglas MacArthur, *A Soldier Speaks: Public Papers and Speeches of General of the Army Douglas MacArthur*, ed. Major Vorin E. Whan, Jr., USA (New York: Frederick A. Praeger, Publishers, 1965), p. 151.

5. Winston S. Churchill, *The Aftermath* (1929), quoted in Winston S. Churchill and the Editors of *Life*, *The Second World War*, 2 vols. (New York: Time Incorporated, 1959), 2:587.

6. See Lance Morrow, "The Metaphysics of War," *Time*, May 17, 1982, p. 88.

7. See, for example, Hal Lindsey with C. C. Carlson, *The Late Great Planet Earth* (Grand Rapids, Mich.: Zondervan Publishing House, 1970).

8. See, for example, George Eldon Ladd, *A Commentary on the Revelation of John* (Grand Rapids, Mich.: William B. Eerdmans Publishing Co., 1972), p. 216.

9. Denis Baly, *The Geography of the Bible: A Study in Historical Geography* (New York: Harper & Brothers Publishers, 1957), pp. 148-154.

10. As an exception, the famous *Gesenius' Hebrew and Chaldee Lexicon* (reprinted, Grand Rapids, Mich.: William B. Eerdmans Publishing Co., 1949), p. 447, hesitatingly suggests that "perhaps" it means "place of crowds."

11. See, for example, *The Interpreter's Dictionary of the Bible*, art. "Armageddon."

12. *Ibid.*

13. My colleague William Shea thinks that the Mount of Megiddo is Mount Carmel and as such provides a type or forerunner of Armageddon. King Ahab (like the demon spirits) gathered his entire nation (the world) to Mount Carmel (Armageddon) for a contest between God and Baal (the Lamb and the beast) to see who should be worshiped. God sent fire from heaven and won the contest (compare the "kings from the east"). The false prophets of Baal (like the beast, dragon, and false prophet) were slain. William H. Shea, "The Location and Significance of Armageddon in Rev 16:16," *Andrews University Seminary Studies,* 18 (Autumn 1980): 157-162.

14. My colleague Hans LaRondelle first called my attention to this linking of Babylon and Egypt to the seven last plagues.

15. See Jack R. Lundbom, "God's Use of the *Idem per Idem* to Terminate Debate," *Harvard Theological Review,* 71 (July-October 1978):193-201. Lundbom attributes the term *idem per idem* to the well-known Old Testament scholar, S. R. Driver.

Revelation 17:1 to 19:10

The Fall of Babylon

Introduction

Revelation 17, 18, and the first ten verses of chapter 19 (that is, Revelation 17:1 to 19:10) make up the division we have called "The Fall of Babylon."

To help remember how this division fits into the overall outline of Revelation, please take a moment to glance at the organizational charts on the next page.

As you can see from our main chart, our present division (17:1 to 19:10) has links to the previous division, the one about the great controversy and the trials of the true mother (11:19 to 14:20). But our present division also stands in striking relationship with the final division of the book (21:9 to 22:9), the one about the Lamb's bride, the holy city New Jerusalem.

We have already noticed how the two divisions about the harlot city and the holy city begin and end alike. See pages 423-425. In each case, a plague angel begins the division by inviting John to come and see something—either Babylon (the great city, the harlot) or New Jerusalem (the holy city, the Lamb's bride). In each case, when the angel has shown John what he has to show him, John is momentarily overwhelmed and gratefully attempts to worship the angel. The angel, of course, reminds John that he *is* an angel and that we should worship only God.

Each angel tells John about the cities themselves and about their relationships with "kings" and "nations." There is, however, a noteworthy contrast. Babylon, says the first angel, has become full of demons and impurity and sits on waters that represent the sea of humanity. Kings and nations drink her wine, commit immorality with her, reign with her, then hate and make war with her, and finally weep while she burns.

On the other hand, nothing impure or unclean enters New Jerusalem. The river of life flows from her. Kings and nations drink her living water, eat the fruit of her tree of life, and bring in through her open gates their glory and honor.

We observed on page 56 that great literary artists devise creative patterns but don't become slaves to them. So we're not surprised that even though these Babylon and New Jerusalem divisions are in many ways similar in their literary arrangement, there is at least one particular in which their organization is very different. There are seven "songs" about the fall of Babylon that have no parallel in the division about New Jerusalem. These seven songs have their own special literary arrangement, which we'll look at when we come to them.

We're impatient to get on to the glorious scenes at the end of the book. But the messages about Babylon are

453

John saw the great city, Babylon, burning in a vast fire. But first he heard an angel call God's people to come out and be safe.

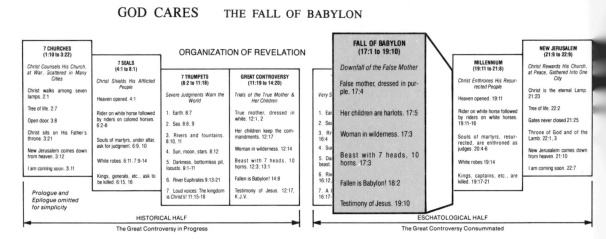

ORGANIZATION OF REVELATION

7 CHURCHES
(1:10 to 3:22)

Christ Counsels His Church, at War, Scattered in Many Cities

Christ walks among seven lamps. 2:1

Tree of life. 2:7

Open door. 3:8

Christ sits on His Father's throne. 3:21

New Jerusalem comes down from heaven. 3:12

I am coming soon. 3.11

Prologue and Epilogue omitted for simplicity

7 SEALS
(4:1 to 8:1)

Christ Shields His Afflicted People

Heaven opened. 4:1

Rider on white horse followed by riders on colored horses. 6:2-8

Souls of martyrs, under altar, ask for judgment. 6:9, 10

White robes. 6:11; 7:9-14

Kings, generals, etc., ask to be killed. 6:15, 16

7 TRUMPETS
(8:2 to 11:18)

Severe Judgments Warn the World

1. Earth. 8:7
2. Sea. 8:8, 9
3. Rivers and fountains. 8:10, 11
4. Sun, moon, stars. 8:12
5. Darkness, bottomless pit. locusts. 9:1-11
6. River Euphrates 9:13-21
7. Loud voices: The kingdom is Christ's! 11:15-18

GREAT CONTROVERSY
(11:19 to 14:20)

Trials of the True Mother & Her Children

True mother, dressed in white. 12:1, 2

Her children keep the commandments. 12:17

Woman in wilderness. 12:14

Beast with 7 heads, 10 horns. 12:3; 13:1

Fallen is Babylon! 14:8

Testimony of Jesus. 12:17, K.J.V.

FALL OF BABYLON
(17:1 to 19:10)

Downfall of the False Mother

False mother, dressed in purple. 17:4

Her children are harlots. 17:5

Woman in wilderness. 17:3

Beast with 7 heads, 10 horns. 17:3

Fallen is Babylon! 18:2

Testimony of Jesus. 19:10

Very S[...]

1. Ear[...]
2. Se[...]
3. Ri 16:4
4. Su[...]
5. Dar beast.
6. Riv 16:12
7. A l 16:17-

MILLENNIUM
(19:11 to 21:8)

Christ Enthrones His Resurrected People

Heaven opened. 19:11

Rider on white horse followed by riders on white horses. 19:11-16

Souls of martyrs, resurrected, are enthroned as judges. 20:4-6

White robes 19:14

Kings, captains, etc., are killed. 19:17-21

NEW JERUSALEM
(21:9 to 22:9)

Christ Rewards His Church, at Peace, Gathered Into One City

Christ is the eternal Lamp. 21:23

Tree of life. 22:2

Gates never closed 21:25

Throne of God and of the Lamb. 22:1, 3

New Jerusalem comes down from heaven. 21:10

I am coming soon. 22:7

HISTORICAL HALF   ESCHATOLOGICAL HALF

The Great Controversy in Progress   The Great Controversy Consummated

Punishments fall in rapid succession upon the unrepentant. No sooner are the plagues poured out than calamity strikes their city, Babylon.

as much a "revelation of Jesus Christ" (Revelation 1:1) as any other portion of the book. There are important things that we and our families need to know about the fall of the false mother, the fall of the great city Babylon.

THE SECOND HALF OF REVELATION: A DUAL FOCUS ON THE ULTIMATE PUNISHMENT OF THE REBELLIOUS AND ON THE ULTIMATE REWARD OF THE RIGHTEOUS IN THE END TIME

1. *Focus on punishment*

  A The plagues 15:1-16:21

  B Circumstances related to the plagues: Fall of Babylon, the false mother 17:1-19:10

      A plague angel shows John the great harlot.   17:1-19:8
      Afterward John attempts to worship the angel.   19:9, 10

2. *Focus on reward*

  B′ Circumstances related to the holy city: The millennium 19:11- 21:8

  A′ The holy city: Descent of New Jerusalem, the Lamb's bride 21:9-22:21

      A plague angel shows John the Lamb's bride.   21:9-22:7
      Afterward John attempts to worship the angel.   22:8, 9

THE FALL OF BABYLON, THE FALSE MOTHER

REVELATION 17

The Judgment of the Great Harlot

A plague angel invites John to view the judgment of the great harlot. 1 Then one of the seven angels who had the seven bowls came and said to me, "Come, I will show you the judgment of the great harlot who is seated upon many waters, ²with whom the kings of the earth have committed fornication, and with the wine of whose fornication the dwellers on earth have become drunk."

The appearance of the great harlot. 3 And he carried me away in the Spirit into a wilderness, and I saw a woman sitting on a scarlet beast which was full of blasphemous names, and it had seven heads and ten horns. ⁴The woman was arrayed in purple and scarlet, and bedecked with gold and jewels and pearls, holding in her hand a golden cup full of abominations and the impurities of her fornication; ⁵and on her forehead was written a name of mystery: "Babylon the great, mother of harlots and of earth's abominations." ⁶And I saw the woman, drunk with the blood of the saints and the blood of the martyrs of Jesus.

The harlot and her relationship with kings and nations. When I saw her I marveled greatly. ⁷But the angel said to me, "Why marvel? I will tell you the mystery of the woman, and of the beast with seven heads and ten horns that carries her. ⁸The beast that you saw was, and is not, and is to ascend from the bottomless pit and go to perdition; and the dwellers on earth whose names have not been written in the book of life from the foundation of the world, will marvel to behold the beast, because it was and is not and is to come. ⁹This calls for a mind with wisdom: the seven heads are seven mountains on which the woman is seated; ¹⁰they are also seven kings, five of whom have fallen, one is, the other has not yet come, and when he comes he must re-

main only a little while. ¹¹As for the beast that was and is not, it is an eighth but it belongs to the seven, and it goes to perdition. ¹²And the ten horns that you saw are ten kings who have not yet received royal power, but they are to receive authority as kings for one hour, together with the beast. ¹³These are of one mind and give over their power and authority to the beast; ¹⁴they will make war on the Lamb, and the Lamb will conquer them, for he is Lord of lords and King of kings, and those with him are called and chosen and faithful."

15 And he said to me, "The waters that you saw, where the harlot is seated, are peoples and multitudes and nations and tongues. ¹⁶And the ten horns that you saw, they and the beast will hate the harlot; they will make her desolate and naked, and devour her flesh and burn her up with fire, ¹⁷for God has put it into their hearts to carry out his purpose by being of one mind and giving over their royal power to the beast, until the words of God shall be fulfilled. ¹⁸And the woman that you saw is the great city which has dominion over the kings of the earth."

SEVEN SONGS ABOUT BABYLON'S PUNISHMENT

REVELATION 18

Two Heavenly Songs Warn About the Plagues

An angel calls with a mighty voice. 1 After this I saw another angel coming down from heaven, having great authority; and the earth was made bright with his splendor.

God's people summoned out of Babylon.
2 And he called out with a mighty voice,
    "Fallen, fallen is Babylon the great!
    It has become a dwelling place of
        demons,
    a haunt of every foul spirit,
    a haunt of every foul and hateful
        bird;
³for all nations have drunk the wine
    of her impure passion,

and the kings of the earth have
    committed fornication with her,
and the merchants of the earth have
    grown rich with the wealth of
    her wantonness."
[4] Then I heard another voice from heaven
saying,
    "Come out of her, my people,
    lest you take part in her sins,
    lest you share in her plagues;
    [5] for her sins are heaped high as
        heaven,
    and God has remembered her
        iniquities.
    [6] Render to her as she herself has
        rendered,
    and repay her double for her deeds;
    mix a double draught for her in the
        cup she mixed.
    [7] As she glorified herself and played
        the wanton,
    so give her a like measure of torment
        and mourning.
    Since in her heart she says, 'A queen
        I sit,
    I am no widow, mourning I shall
        never see,'
    [8] so shall her plagues come in a single
        day,
    pestilence and mourning and
        famine,
    and she shall be burned with fire;
    for mighty is the Lord God who
        judges her."

Three Earthly Songs Bewail the Plagues

The kings say, "Alas! Alas!" **9** And the
kings of the earth, who committed fornication and were wanton with her, will weep
and wail over her when they see the smoke
of her burning; [10] they will stand far off, in
fear of her torment, and say,
    "Alas! alas! thou great city,
    thou mighty city, Babylon!
    In one hour has thy judgment
        come."
The merchants say, "Alas! Alas!" **11** And
the merchants of the earth weep and mourn
for her, since no one buys their cargo any

more, [12] cargo of gold, silver, jewels and
pearls, fine linen, purple, silk and scarlet,
all kinds of scented wood, all articles of
ivory, all articles of costly wood, bronze,
iron and marble, [13] cinnamon, spice, incense, myrrh, frankincense, wine, oil, fine
flour and wheat, cattle and sheep, horses
and chariots, and slaves, that is, human
souls.
    [14] "The fruit for which thy soul longed
        has gone from thee,
    and all thy dainties and thy splendor
        are lost to thee, never to be
        found again!"
[15] The merchants of these wares, who gained
wealth from her, will stand far off, in fear of
her torment, weeping and mourning aloud,
    [16] "Alas, alas, for the great city
    that was clothed in fine linen, in
        purple and scarlet,
    bedecked with gold, with jewels, and
        with pearls!
    [17] In one hour all this wealth has been
        laid waste."
The seafarers say, "Alas! Alas!" And all
shipmasters and seafaring men, sailors and
all whose trade is on the sea, stood far off
[18] and cried out as they saw the smoke of her
burning,
    "What city was like the great city?"
[19] And they threw dust on their heads,
    as they wept and mourned, crying out,
    "Alas, alas, for the great city
    where all who had ships at sea
        grew rich by her wealth!
    In one hour she has been laid waste.
[20] Rejoice over her, O heaven,
    O saints and apostles and prophets,
    for God has given judgment for you
        against her!"

Two More Heavenly Songs Speak About the Plagues

A mighty angel hurls a millstone. **21** Then
a mighty angel took up a stone like a great
millstone and threw it into the sea, saying,
    "So shall Babylon the great city be
        thrown down with violence,
    and shall be found no more;

²²and the sound of harpers and
  minstrels, of flute players and
  trumpeters,
 shall be heard in thee no more;
and a craftsman of any craft
 shall be found in thee no more;
and the sound of the millstone
 shall be heard in thee no more;
²³and the light of a lamp
 shall shine in thee no more;
and the voice of bridegroom and
  bride
 shall be heard in thee no more;
for thy merchants were the great
  men of the earth,
 and all nations were deceived by
  thy sorcery.
²⁴And in her was found the blood of
  prophets and of saints,
 and of all who have been slain on
  earth.''

REVELATION 19

God's people rejoice in heaven. 1 After
this I heard what seemed to be the loud
voice of a great multitude in heaven, crying,
 ''Hallelujah! Salvation and glory and
  power belong to our God,
² for his judgments are true and just;
 he has judged the great harlot who
   corrupted the earth with her
   fornication,
 and he has avenged on her the blood
  of his servants.''
³ Once more they cried,

 ''Hallelujah! The smoke from her
  goes up for ever and ever.''
⁴ And the twenty-four elders and the four
living creatures fell down and worshiped
God who is seated on the throne, saying,
''Amen. Hallelujah!'' ⁵And from the throne
came a voice crying,
 ''Praise our God, all you his servants,
  you who fear him, small and great.''
⁶ Then I heard what seemed to be the voice
of a great multitude, like the sound of many
waters and like the sound of mighty
thunderpeals, crying,
 ''Hallelujah! For the Lord our God
  the Almighty reigns.
 ⁷ Let us rejoice and exult and give
  him the glory,
 for the marriage of the Lamb has
  come,
 and his Bride has made herself
  ready;
⁸ it was granted her to be clothed with
  fine linen, bright and pure''—
for the fine linen is the righteous deeds of
the saints.

*The angel pronounces a blessing, and
John attempts to worship him.* 9 And the angel said to me, ''Write this: Blessed are
those who are invited to the marriage supper of the Lamb.'' And he said to me,
''These are true words of God.'' ¹⁰Then I
fell down at his feet to worship him, but he
said to me, ''You must not do that! I am a
fellow servant with you and your brethren
who hold the testimony of Jesus. Worship
God.'' For the testimony of Jesus is the
spirit of prophecy.

The Message of Revelation 17:1 to 19:10

I. The Harlot and Her Daughters

The most urgent message of Revelation 17:1 to 19:10 (the division we're studying now) is for us and our families to come out of Babylon, if we're still there. We must come out so we can avoid the sins and plagues of Babylon and so we can sing with the Lamb around God's throne.

"Come out of her [Babylon], **my people,"** says Jesus in chapter 18:4. Because we know He loves us, we want to please Him. But how can we know whether we're actually in Babylon and need to come out?

We'll come to this important question as soon as possible. See page 461. But first there are some other things to look at in chapter 17, including a mysterious puzzle and a tremendous power struggle.

The mysterious puzzle deals with the beast's seven heads, **"five of whom have fallen, one is, the other has not yet come,"** and with the beast itself—the beast that **"was, and is not, and is to ascend from the bottomless pit."** Revelation 17:10, 8. We'll leave the solution till we get to *Your Questions Answered,* pages 471-478.

A tremendous power struggle. Revelation 17 has a dual climax, two cataclysmic conflicts of supernatural proportions. In one of these vast battles the **"beast"** and the **"ten kings"** (which are the **"ten horns"**) make war against the **"Lamb"**; in the other battle they turn on the **"great harlot"** who rides on the beast and destroy her. **"The ten horns that you saw, they and the beast will hate the harlot; they will make her desolate and naked,* and devour her flesh and burn her up with fire."** Revelation 17:16. See pages 441, 442.

The harlot and the beast. In Bible prophecy, a "woman" represents a community of God's people. See our discussion on page 319. The woman clothed with the sun (see Revelation 12:1, 2) symbolizes God's ideal true church. The harlot dressed in red holding a **"cup"** of blasphemy filled with the **"wine"** of martyr blood, represents a Christian church which has apostatized, persecuted, and committed **"fornication."** Revelation 17:2-6.

The symbolic concept of "fornication" comes from Ezekiel 16. There Israel, God's people in Old Testament times, was likened to a poor woman whom God made beautiful and then graciously married. But Israel faithlessly committed "immorality" with her idolatrous neighbor nations. She eagerly adopted their paganism, made mutual-aid treaties with them, and, like them, oppressed God's faithful followers.

The great harlot of Revelation 17 has **"committed fornication"** with the **"kings."** Verse 2. The great Christian church of the Middle Ages engaged in im-

---

* Forcing harlots to walk with their skirts over their heads was once a common punishment. See Jeremiah 13:22; Nahum 3:5.

moral relations with Christian governments in order to get power to persecute God's true followers. This immoral union of church and state resulted in large numbers of martyrs. It also resulted in a general lowering of Christian morality. Religious leaders often failed to rebuke the sins of government leaders for fear of losing their police power and financial support.

On pages 441, 442 we looked into the meaning of the battle of the beast against the harlot. We'll have still more to say about it on pages 492-494 and especially in *Your Questions Answered,* pages 471-478.

This final convulsive collusion of the ten kings is only part of the **"judgment"** against the claims of corrupted, apostate Christianity. In Daniel 7 the "little horn"—which is essentially the same as the harlot—is shown undergoing judgment in heaven. See GC 1:115-135. Revelation 17 predicts a grisly counterpart to the heavenly judgment. The nations that have eagerly conspired with the harlot as a way of controlling their citizens see her at last as the undesirable monstrosity that she really is. In spiteful contempt they expose and disgrace her in one of the two terrible battles predicted in Revelation 17.

The ten kings against the Lamb. The other terrible battle in chapter 17, the earlier of the two conflicts, takes place when the ten kings **"will make war on the Lamb"—"and the Lamb will conquer them, for he is Lord of lords and King of kings, and those with him are called and chosen and faithful."** Verses 13, 14.

Christ will appear as King of kings and Lord of lords at His second coming, at the beginning of the millennium. See Revelation 19:11-16. He will be accompanied by His Father, the One "who is seated on the throne." Revelation 6:16. Thus the second coming of Christ is the arrival of the "kings from the east" (Revelation 16:12); and the battle that takes place at that time is the battle of Armageddon. See pages 434-436.

They make war on the Lamb; but as G. B. Caird and others have observed, "the only way in which earthly kings can wage war on the Lamb is through his followers."[1]

"I am Jesus, whom you are persecuting," said Jesus to Paul back in Paul's bad days as a persecutor. By speaking this way to Paul, Jesus identified Himself with the Christian people whom Paul was hurting. See Acts 9:5. "As you did it to one of the least of these *my brethren,*" Jesus said to all of us in the Olivet Discourse, *"you did it to me."* Matthew 25:40.

Revelation 12:17 says that in the end time the dragon will go out to "make war" with "those who keep the commandments of God." Armageddon is not a battle of East against West but of error against truth, of the dragon's followers against those who keep the commandments of God and faithfully follow the Lamb.

The harlot as Babylon. When John saw the harlot of Revelation 17, he noticed that she was wearing her name on her forehead. It was faddish in John's day for harlots to wear their names on headbands.[2] Her own name for herself was **"Babylon the great, mother of harlots."** Verse 5.

We're already familiar with **"Babylon"** as the name of an ancient empire. The

459

word itself comes from *Babel,* as in "the tower of Babel." Several towers of Babel existed in the ancient Middle East, the ruins of some of which are still standing. (For pictures of one such tower, also known as the temple tower of Etemenanki, see GC 1:61, 62.) Typically each tower of Babel had at its summit a special shrine for pagan worship. *Babel* originally meant, "the gate of God." A tower of Babel was a notable place of worship—of man-made worship.

At the very first tower of Babel the builders were confounded one day when they broke out in an irksome gift of tongues. They suddenly found themselves taking to one another in different languages. Because they could no longer communicate intelligibly, "Babel" came to have a new and negative significance. It came to mean "confusion." See Genesis 11:1-9.

Harlot Babylon considers herself a gate of God, *the* gate of God. *Extra ecclesiam non salus est* was for centuries her official Latin doctrine, "Outside the church [of Rome] there is no salvation." But evidently in God's sight she was a place of confusion. Her teachings, a misleading mixture of truth and error, created a monumental muddle.

She taught that the day of judgment will occur at the second coming—but sinners are condemned to hell as soon as they die. She taught that God is love—but He makes sinners burn in anguish literally for ever and ever. She taught that the Bible is God's word—but when church councils differ from the Bible they are more clear and authoritative than the Bible. She taught that all of the Ten Commandments are morally binding—but in her catechisms she *removed* from the second commandment the prohibition against images and *changed* the Sabbath commandment so as to place Sunday as a holiday in the place of Sabbath as God's holy day. See also GC 1:178, 179.

The harlot as the mother of harlots. On her headband the harlot called herself **"Babylon the great, mother of harlots."** The Catholic Church has long styled herself the Mother Church. In a sense, she has been right in doing this, for she has given birth to many daughter churches. Sad to say, when viewed from their very worst aspects, the daughter churches have also shown a tendency to become "harlots."

Daughters are not born harlots. They become such by choosing to. Unmarried, they are known by their mother's name. The harlot daughters we're talking about are called "Babylon," like their mother.

Before we proceed let us remind ourselves once more that Daniel and Revelation tend to comment selectively on persecuted people and persecuting churches and nations. Thus they emphasize the worst side of churches and states, as a warning to believers.

Exceptionally, Revelation 2:19 refers to the very fine contributions made to society by the Catholic Church—and rightly so, for in the Middle Ages (not to speak about positive contributions today) the Catholic Church provided almost the only schools and hospitals in the West. She also helped keep alive a knowledge about God and His Son Jesus. See page 122.

But for our sakes, Daniel and Revelation long ago warned that there would be another, darker side to the picture. The Roman Church would be characterized by (1) opposition to God's commandments, (2) denial or obscuring of Christ's ministry in the heavenly sanctuary, and (3) persecution of God's most faithful followers. See page 327.

The Roman Church has revealed these three characteristics more or less almost since its inception. On the other hand, the major Protestant churches came to birth with a determination to do better than the "Mother Church."

Martin Luther, founder of the Lutheran Church, rediscovered three grand pillars of God's truth, "justification by faith," the "Bible alone" as ultimate authority, and the "priesthood of believers." John Calvin, of the Congregational and Presbyterian churches, learned anew that God, not a priest or the saints, decides whether we're going to be saved or lost. John Wesley, of the Methodist and Nazarene churches, rediscovered "free grace," that salvation is not granted only to a few persons who have been selected by God in advance (as St. Augustine taught), but is available freely to everyone who believes. Baptists rediscovered "believers' baptism," meaning that people are not expected to be made church members before they understand and believe what the church teaches.

As it came into existence, each major Protestant church glowed in the light of some newly restored aspect of God's wonderful truth. All Christians today can be immensely grateful for the magnificent discoveries made by the founders of these churches. We should also, of course, be grateful to the Catholic Church for the aspects of truth which it preserved in the Middle Ages.

Tragically, in the 1840s, at the height of America's great religious revival and of the great second-advent awakening, the leaders of most Protestant churches in America rejected the three angels' messages of Revelation 14:6-12. In doing so they (1) neglected or even opposed the Sabbath of God's Ten Commandments and (2) denied Christ's new ministry of judgment and atonement in the most holy place of the heavenly sanctuary. At times then and since they (3) have sometimes spoken very harshly—in books and papers and on radio and TV—against faithful Christian Sabbath observers. When Revelation 13 is fulfilled, these denominations and others like them can be expected to unite with the state to inflict cruel boycotts and capital punishment on Sabbath observers.

They will cause "all, both small and great, both rich and poor, both free and slave, to be marked on the right hand or the forehead, so that no one can buy or sell unless he has the mark, that is, the name of the beast or the number of its name." Revelation 13:16, 17. See pages 340-349.

Are you in Babylon? Many wonderful Christians worship God today in the Catholic Church and in Protestant denominations. They love God and deeply desire to serve Him. They do not realize that they are members of "Babylon." They haven't yet become concerned that their churches deliberately oppose one or more of the Ten Commandments and that their pastors ignore or obscure Christ's special new heavenly ministry.

This is why Jesus is sounding His warning today, in the end time. He wants His good-hearted people—men and women, boys and girls—in every apostate communion to wake up to the serious danger they're in, the danger of participating in Babylon's final sins and of suffering in her dreadful plagues. He wants them to *come out of Babylon* right away. He cares!

Come out of Babylon **"my people,"** He says (Revelation 18:4) and get ready to sing around God's throne.

II. Come Out of Babylon—and Sing!

Accepting Christ costs something. Jesus recognized this. He said that people "take up his cross" when they choose to follow Him. See Matthew 16:24.

Many people, especially young ones full of life and afraid of their peers, think only of the cost, their personal cross.

This is unfortunate! For Jesus also said, in Matthew 16:25, "Whoever loses his life for my sake will *find* it." Paul, who was beaten, stoned, and imprisoned for Christ, was able to say, "This slight momentary affliction is preparing for us an eternal weight of glory beyond all comparison." 2 Corinthians 4:17.

Revelation 18 shows that refusing to accept Christ's plan for our lives costs much more in the long run than following Him.

At the second coming there will be no middle ground for undecideds. There will be only two sides, the ripened grain and the ripened grapes (Revelation 14:14-20), those with the seal of God and those with the mark of the beast, those who praise Christ and those who hide from Him. See page 382.

The seven songs about Babylon. In the seven songs about Babylon (Revelation 18:1 to 19:10) the two sides are those who choose to stay in Babylon and those who choose to come out. Those who stay in, intone three mournful lamentations; those who come out sing hallelujahs around the throne.

When you first read them, the seven songs may not seem like songs. However, they were written as Hebrew *poetry*, like the psalms, which were meant to be sung. The final poem (Revelation 19:1-8) is unquestionably a song. It's the basis for Handel's "Hallelujah Chorus." Some of the others you may think of as suitable for a country-western singer, delivering a message accompanied by a guitar—in this case, an ancient portable harp. (For a picture of one, see GC 1:57.)

The seven songs are arranged in a chiasm. We might have expected it!

The middle three songs come from earthly voices—those of kings, merchants, and seafarers crying "Alas! Alas!" over the destruction of the great city. The first two songs and the last two are sung by heavenly voices, and the second one in each of these pairs calls attention to God's people. The songs can be arranged like this:

A   Mighty voice of an angel: **"Fallen is Babylon!"**
   B   Heavenly voice: **"Come out of her, my people."**
      C   Lament of the kings: **"Alas! alas!"**

462

  C' Lament of the merchants: **"Alas! alas!"**
  C" Lament of the seafarers: **"Alas! alas!"**
 A' Voice of a mighty angel: **"So shall Babylon . . . be thrown down."**
  B' Heavenly voice: God's people rejoicing at Babylon's fall.

Songs based on Old Testament language. As elsewhere in Revelation, the language is freely adapted from the Old Testament.

"Fallen is Babylon" (Revelation 18:2) is taken from Isaiah 21:9 and Jeremiah 51:8, which refer to the defeat of ancient Babylon. **"In her heart she says, 'A queen I sit, I am no widow, mourning I shall never see' "** (Revelation 18:7) is adapted from Isaiah 47:8: "You [Babylon]. . . say in your heart, 'I am, and there is no one besides me; I shall not sit as a widow or know the loss of children.' "

"The sound of harpers and minstrels, of flute players and trumpeters . . . shall be heard in thee no more" (Revelation 18:22) is similar to what Ezekiel 26:13 says about Tyre, another evil ancient city. **"Come out of her, my people, lest you . . . share in her plagues"** (Revelation 18:4) comes from Jeremiah 51:6, 45 in reference to ancient Babylon.

A good many other parallels from ancient messages can be cited. See GC 1:81, 82. But the message of the seven songs themselves is as current and relevant as any in the Bible. For all who have taken up their cross and followed Christ, the message of the seven songs is "timely, stirring, cheering, and true."[3] For those who haven't left Babylon yet, it is extremely urgent.

1. The song of the angel who brightens the whole world. The first of the seven songs comes from an angel with a **"mighty voice"** who has **"great authority"** and who makes the earth **"bright"** with his **"splendor."** He states emphatically, **"Fallen, fallen is Babylon the great! It has become a dwelling place of demons, a haunt of every foul spirit."** Revelation 18:1, 2.

Who is this angel, and what is his **"splendor"**?

We are familiar with *angel* meaning "messenger," often a human messenger. See page 90. The angels of the seven churches, the three angels of Revelation 14, even the sealing angel of chapter 7, represent *Christians entrusted with God's message.*

"Splendor" is translated from the Greek *doxa*, given as "glory" in the King James Version. When applied to humans, it refers to the *glory of God's character manifested in their lives.* When Moses asked God to reveal His *glory*, God pronounced His *name*, "The Lord, a God merciful and gracious," and so on. Exodus 34:6, 7; see pages 104-106. The most glorious thing about God is His *characteristic* habit of being gracious to people.

In the end time God puts His name—His character, His glory—in the foreheads of His people. So the first angel of Revelation 18 is a symbol of God's end-time people, men and women, old and young, whose lives, words, and genuine faith are a "glory" in their homes, neighborhoods, schools, and work places.

The Holy Spirit produces in Christ's followers the "fruit of the Spirit" (Galatians 5:22, 23), "love, joy, peace, patience, kindness, goodness, faithfulness," and so on, the very attributes of God's own character. And the New Covenant (Jeremiah 31:33, 34 and Ezekiel 36:27) promises that the Spirit will write God's law in our hearts and minds. His law of loving obedience to God and unselfish service to others. His law of true holiness, summed up and renewed in true Sabbath keeping. As the last moments of time tick past, God's Spirit *ripens* these fruits. It *seals* His gracious character in His people permanently. In this way God develops a people whose daily lives and sweetly winsome witness brighten the earth with His glory.

2. **"Come out of her, my people."** The second song in Revelation 18 is spoken by a heavenly voice but not by an angel's. It calls God's people, **"my people."** Revelation 18:4. This is the voice of the Lamb. It calls **"my people"** to come out of Babylon.

It may seem surprising that Christ has people in Babylon! Babylon has been described as a harlot and the haunt of demons. In the very song we're looking at, Babylon's sins are **"heaped high as heaven."** Verse 5.

Daniel and Revelation emphasize the negative aspects of a church or government in order to make a certain point. Babylon by this moment in Revelation represents all religions that claim to worship God but refuse against clear light to obey Him.

But within Babylon are many good-hearted individuals whose optimism and gentle ways have kept them from perceiving the full wickedness surrounding them. God does not condemn their breadth of spirit. By urging them to come out **"lest you take part in her sins"** (verse 4), He reveals that He does not yet hold them responsible for the sins of their communities, of which they have been largely unaware.

But the time has come for a change, for a clear-cut decision. Christ warns them, in the strongest terms, of the extreme danger of their situation. They must now call sin by its right name and *come out* of Babylon. Outside Babylon, they will find a "remnant" living clean, dedicated lives, keeping God's Sabbath, and looking out for ways to help their neighbors, revealing that with God's help His commandments can be obeyed. Revelation 12:17, K.J.V.; see *Your Questions Answered*, pages 406, 407.

God's people who are still members of ordinary religious bodies are called upon by Christ Himself to resign their current membership (courteously, we may assume) and courageously realign themselves with this other group, the remnant of the woman's seed, the "saints" who keep the commandments of God and have the faith of Jesus.

The choice is ours; but it is not one we can regard lightly. Our Saviour says, **"Come out."**

An extremely serious situation. **"Come out of her,"** He says, **"lest you take part in her sins, lest you share in her plagues; for her sins are heaped high as heaven."** Revelation 18:4, 5. The original Babylon was the tower of Babel, constructed of sun-baked bricks and intended to be taller than any possible worldwide flood. Babylon's sins in the end time, laid one above another like bricks, reach high as heaven, God says, **"So shall her plagues come in a single day, pestilence and mourning and famine, and she shall be burned with fire; for mighty is the Lord God who judges her."** Verse 8.

The previous song described Babylon as **"a dwelling place of demons, a haunt of every foul spirit."** Verse 2. Could a more serious indictment be leveled against a religious institution?

The sins of the end-time Babylon are her worst because they are committed against the clearest evidence. Guilt is deepest when we know best what is right. "That servant who knew his master's will, but did not make ready or act according to his will, shall receive a severe beating. But he who did not know, and did what deserved a beating, shall receive a light beating. Every one to whom much is given, of him will much be required." Luke 12:47, 48; see also John 9:41.

At the end of the end time, knowledge about (1) God's law of love and Sabbath holiness, (2) Christ's gracious Day of Judgment/Day of Atonement ministry in the heavenly sanctuary, and (3) the wickedness of oppressing those who trust the truth, will have spread to everyone alive. Rebelling then will be sin indeed.

Come out and be "at one." On this Day of Judgment/Day of Atonement (At-one-ment) a dual work of sorting out and cleaning up is going on. See GC 1:180-188. In heaven the pre-advent judgment is removing from the book of life those who through the ages have claimed to be God's but who haven't chosen to behave as if they were. On earth, the living are removing themselves from Babylon and choosing to live entirely for God. Christ is teaching us about the Sabbath to help us enter into entire commandment-keeping obedience.

When the dual process is done, every name in the book of life will represent a believer who trusts God implicitly and loves fellowman unselfishly. The judgment will have sorted out the hypocrites, while the atonement will have gathered the sincere into a unique fellowship.

Sad to say, most people in Babylon don't think the warning applies to them. They are comfortable with the serpent's lies, "You *need not,* or *should not,* or *cannot* obey God's laws." **"In her heart she** [Babylon] **says, 'A queen I sit, I am no widow, mourning I shall never see.' "** Revelation 18:7.

Breaking the Sabbath seems like eating the forbidden fruit in Eden, a matter of little consequence, even desirable. The underlying issue of loyalty to Creator and Redeemer is denied.

3, 4, 5. The three lamentations. On page 459 we saw that the end-time "kings of the whole world" support the beast in a final outburst of enthusiasm for persecuting God's true worshipers, then turn against the harlot in a bitter revulsion of feeling. Now, in chapter 18, we notice that as the kings, merchants, and seafarers cry out, **"Alas! alas! thou great city,"** they **"stand far off,"** putting a distance between themselves and her. Revelation 18:9.

They are lamenting, but they are not lamenting her sins or their own guilt as her

465

accomplices. The kings lament the suddenness of her judgment, **"in one hour has thy judgment come."** Revelation 18:9. The merchants and seafarers lament the destruction of such vast stores of merchandise, because they **"gained wealth from her"** and **"grew rich by her wealth."** Verses 15, 19. (In poetic material like this, the long warehouse inventory, adapted from Old Testament language, should be taken as a unit, signifying commercial advantages.) Not one king, merchant, or seafarer has anything to say about her crimes and demons or about the **"blood of prophets and of saints, and of all who have been slain on earth."** Verse 24.

Perhaps of greatest interest to us are the of the seafarers' bitter words in verse 20:

> **Rejoice over her, O heaven,**
> **O saints and apostles and prophets,**
> **for God has given judgment for you against her!**

The translation obscures the full meaning of the last line. A literal translation says, "God has judged her judgment against you." The meaning is that Babylon for centuries has falsely condemned God's saints, apostles, and prophets. She has excommunicated the saints and turned them over to the state for execution. She has borne false witness against the prophets and apostles, forbidding common people to read the Bible, and holding opinions of theologians and church councils as more authoritative than the Scriptures. She has judged and falsely condemned saints and apostles and prophets.

But in 1844 commenced the first, pre-advent, phase of the final judgment. Babylon—the "little horn" of Daniel 7, the "man of lawlessness" of 2 Thessalonians 2—and the true saints as well, all who in every age have claimed to worship God, have by the time of this announcement in John's vision been investigated. And where Babylon has been found to have wrongfully condemned the saints, apostles, and prophets, God has judged the judgment oppressive, condemned the condemnation, and ruled against the oppressor in favor of the oppressed. The sentence which the false witnesses imposed on God's people, God now imposes on the false witnesses.

The Old Testament established such a principle. Scholars refer to the "law of malicious witness" in Deuteronomy 19:16-19. When someone accused another person, both were to be brought to trial, and if the accuser was found to have made a false, malicious accusation, the judge was required to "do to him as he had meant to do to his brother." Professor G. B. Caird observes,

> Babylon has brought a malicious accusation against the martyrs, which has resulted in their death. But the case has been carried 'before the Lord,' to the court of final appeal, where judgments are true and just. There Babylon has been found guilty of perjury, and God has therefore required from her the life of her victims, exacting from her the penalty she exacted from them.[4]

6. The song of the mighty angel. As John watched, the visionary screen which had changed abruptly so many times since Revelation began, changed yet again. A **"mighty angel"** appeared. Revelation 18:21. Considering the power and glory of ordinary angels, what did this one look like? He had a **"millstone"** in his hand, a wheel-shaped rock far too heavy for an ordinary mortal. With a tremendous sweep of his arm he heaved it into the sea. As it fell with an enormous splash, he announced in no uncertain tones, **"So shall Babylon the great city be thrown down with violence, and shall be found no more."**

John's mind must have raced back to Daniel's day, when Seraiah stood in old Babylon on the bank of the Euphrates, read from a scroll the prophecy of Jeremiah 51 against the ancient city, rolled the scroll up, tied a rock to it, and hurled it into the river. See GC 1:82, 83. Similar, but what a difference between a rock and a millstone. Similar, but what a difference between ancient Babylon, a square mile or so in size, ruling a "world" located within the Middle East, and modern Babylon, representing all false religion in the world at the end time.

Similar, but what a contrast between the several thousand Jews Nebuchadnezzar exiled to Mesopotamia, and the **"blood of prophets and of saints, and of all who have been slain on earth."** Revelation 18:24.

Similar, but what a contrast between the night when the Euphrates dried up and Cyrus's forces entered the ancient city, slaying Belshazzar and liberating the Jews, and the time when wordwide support for Babylon dries up, the kings of the earth war against the religious leaders who have misled them, and Christ appears, leading the armies of heaven to destroy the kings, rich men, and merchants, and everyone else who has resisted Him, and rescues the millions of true saints who would rather lose their lives than break His law of goodness and peace.

7. The song of rejoicing in heaven. Another contrast. Far above the merchants, kings, and seafarers, far above the smoking ruins of Babylon, John heard what seemed to be the **"loud voice of a great multitude in heaven, crying,**

> **Hallelujah! Salvation and glory and**
> **power belong to our God,**
> **for his judgments are true and just;**
> **he has judged the great harlot who corrupted**
> **the earth with her fornication,**
> **and he has avenged on her the blood of his servants."**
> Revelation 19:1, 2.

As John lifted his face to see where the sound came from, the celestial choristers repeated the theme. **"Once more they cried,**

> **'Hallelujah! The smoke from her**
> **goes up for ever and ever.' "**
> Verse 3.

467

"Hallelujah" is Hebrew. It is pronounced, of course, as if the *j* were a *y*. It means "praise (*hallel*) you (*u*) Jehovah or Yahweh (*jah* or *yah*)." Sometimes it occurs in English spelled more nearly as the Greeks spelled it, "alleluia."

The saints were praising God because the great city was in flames. Their joy contrasted with the lamentations of the merchants, kings, and seafarers. We can understand their joy, but was it right? Was God pleased to have them act so happily when punishment was inflicted? The twenty-four elders and even the four living creatures thought it was all right! They **"fell down and worshiped God,"** saying, **"Amen. Hallelujah!"** Verse 4.

But how did God feel about such ebullience while great Babylon burned? If in his vision John also wondered how God felt, he didn't have to wait long to find out. **"From the throne came a voice crying,**

> **'Praise our God, all you his servants,**
> **you who fear him, small and great.' "**
> Verse 5.

It was as if a songleader asked a congregation to join with the choir on the chorus. The result was dramatic. **"Then I heard what seemed to be the voice of a great multitude, like the sound of many waters and like the sound of mighty thunderpeals,"** echoing again the heavenly hallelujah,

> **Hallelujah! For the Lord our God**
> **the Almighty reigns.**
> Verse 6.

So God is pleased to have us rejoice at the eradication of evil. God would much rather have sinners repent than be punished. He has "no pleasure in the death of the wicked." Ezekiel 33:11. He is "not wishing that any should perish, but that all should reach repentance." 2 Peter 3:9.

But if people persist in their sins—that is, if they continue defrauding their neighbors, oppressing the poor, and defiling the earth, God has no choice but to eliminate them when He eradicates sin. He is determined to guarantee the safety and joy of the innocent.

A voice came **"from the throne"** encouraging saints and angels to praise Him for eliminating the common enemy.

The marriage of the Bride. But there was more to sing about in John's vision than the burning of Babylon. The voice which summoned the paean of praise went on to say,

> **"Let us rejoice and exult and give**
> **him the glory,**
> **for the marriage of the Lamb has come,**

and his Bride has made herself ready;
it was granted her to be clothed with
    fine linen, bright and pure"—
for the fine linen is the righteous
    deeds of the saints.

                    Verses 7, 8.

As the cascading cadences faded at last, the friendly plague angel who had accompanied John all the while said with great feeling, **"Write this: Blessed are those who are invited to the marriage supper of the Lamb."** Verse 9.

Only 2500 people received invitations to the wedding of Prince Charles and Lady Diana. How many millions more would like to have been invited! But to the wedding supper that follows the marriage of the Lamb we are all invited. "The Spirit and the Bride say, 'Come.' " Revelation 22:17.

Babylon, used in Revelation as a symbol of false religion, was once a real city. The Lamb's Bride, New Jerusalem, also a real city, is used in Revelation to symbolize the entire company of humans who choose to trust and serve God in love, truth, and holiness. Her **"fine linen"** wedding gown symbolizes the **"righteous deeds of the saints."**

Christ "marries" New Jerusalem at the end of the investigative judgment, when He receives from the Ancient of Days "dominion and glory and kingdom."

Heaven's amazing Ruler will personally serve the redeemed at His own marriage supper!

See Daniel 7:14. The Day of Judgment/Day of Atonement (see page 465) has purified His church and left it clean, full of the righteousness that comes by faith, wholly sincere, and loyal to all His desires. **"The Bride has made herself ready."**

The kingdom is the "Bride" and the "holy city." New Jerusalem stands for Christ's human kingdom in the same way that London stands for Great Britain and Canberra for Australia. Individual believers, who have homes in the city, are called "guests" at the wedding. See *Your Questions Answered*, pages 407-410.

Promptly after the wedding is consummated in heaven, Jesus comes to earth to take His people to the wedding supper. Directing them to sit at table, He delightedly dons an apron and serves His servants! See Luke 12:35-37. Wonder, O heavens, be amazed, O earth! When Christ the Conqueror, the Son of man on the clouds of heaven, receives His kingdom from the Ancient of Days, He celebrates His conquest by showing *us* a good time!

What a moving sight this will be for the saints. What a humbling, joyous experience! **"Blessed"** indeed **"are those who are invited to the marriage supper of the Lamb"**!

John attempts to worship the angel. Heavenly choral splendors and ineffable wedding-supper prospects momentarily cost John his presence of mind. Dazed, he impulsively regarded his angel guide as an object of reverence. **"I fell down at his feet to worship him,"** he says. Revelation 19:10.

But the angel restrained him. **"You must not do that!"** he said quickly. **"I am a fellow servant with you and your brethren who hold the testimony of Jesus. Worship God. For the testimony of Jesus is the spirit of prophecy."** Revelation 19:10. (For comment on this verse, see *Your Questions Answered*, pages 403-406.)

The seven songs about Babylon are a source of courage. Be sure everyone in your family knows about them. They show that God cares enough to reverse the false judgments made against us. He cares enough to invite us to the wedding supper. He cares enough to warn us about Babylon's imminent fall. He cares enough to say, **"Come,"** a verb that requests motion toward the speaker. In asking us to leave Babylon, Jesus desires us to come close, to be "at-one" with Him.

Nevertheless, His call to break our ties with religious organizations where we and our family members feel comfortable may seem like taking up a cross. Yet is it not entirely for our good? The climax of history is close. Those who reject the call will soon lament their indecision. But those who obey, no matter what the seeming cost, will soon be singing with the Lamb around God's throne.

Come out of Babylon? Come out *and sing*.

Further Interesting Reading

In Ellen G. White, *The Triumph of God's Love:*
  "God's Final Message," page 527.

Page numbers refer to the large, fully illustrated edition.

Your Questions Answered

1. What are the "beast," the "harlot," the "seven heads," and the "ten horns"?
We observed on page 458 that Revelation 17 contains a perplexing puzzle. It talks about the **"beast"** that **"was, and is not, and is to ascend from the bottomless pit and go to perdition"; "it is eighth but it belongs to the seven." "The seven heads are seven mountains on which the woman is seated."** They are also **"seven kings, five of whom have fallen, one is, the other has not yet come."** Verses 8, 11, 9, 10.

As for the **"ten horns,"** they are **"ten kings who have not yet received royal power, but they are to receive authority as kings for one hour, together with the beast. These are of one mind and give over their power and authority to the beast; they will make war on the Lamb, and the Lamb will conquer them." "And the ten horns . . . and the beast will hate the harlot; they will make her desolate and naked, and devour her flesh and burn her up with fire."** Verses 12-14, 16.

A person is tempted to sigh, "Impossible!" Yet chapter 17 is as much a part of "the revelation of Jesus Christ" (Revelation 1:1) as is any other chapter in the book. There's a blessing to all who read it (Revelation 1:3). We should make an effort to understand.

Indeed we may find that the solution is simpler than we supposed.

A survey of interpretations. Many interpretations of this puzzle have been offered over the years. One interpretation of the **"seven heads"** starts with a list of seven Roman emperors as "heads" of the Roman state: Augustus, Tiberius, Claudius, Caligula, Nero, and so on. Another cites a string of successive Roman administrative styles: republic, consular, triumvir, decemvir, and more. Still another interpretation offers a succession of seven end-time popes, as heads of the Roman Church.

Now, in Jeremiah 51:24, 25 and Daniel 2:35, 44, 45, a "mountain" is a symbol of a kingdom or nation. See page 238. With this in mind, one of the simplest of the many interpretations of our puzzle looks at the seven heads as seven persecuting powers viewed *from the time when* John was writing Revelation.

In this scheme the five **"heads"** (or **"mountains"** or **"kings"**) which had **"fallen"** (before John's day) are listed as Egypt, Assyria, Babylon, Persia, and Greece. The head that **"is"** is seen as the Roman Empire, which was ruling in John's day. The head that **"has not yet come"** is taken to be the Roman Church, which in many ways resembles a nation and which in John's day had not yet risen to power. Egypt and especially Assyria were enemies of God's people in Old Testament times. We are familiar with the other governments.

As for the **"ten horns"** which are **"ten kings,"** they are perceived in this interpretation to be the nations of Europe, which in John's day were not yet in place. The **"hour"** they were to reign is the 1260 days. This interpretation has much to commend it.

There is another fairly simple interpretation, one which, however, views the

471

puzzle *from the end time* rather than from John's day. It sees the five **"fallen"** heads as Babylon, Persia, Greece, Roman Empire, and Christian Rome. The sixth head (in the end time) **"is"** Christian Rome in its wounded state, to be followed soon by the seventh head that **"has not yet come,"** Christian Rome in its revived condition. The **"hour"** when the ten kings reign with the beast is a brief period at the very end of time when with dictatorial intensity they aid the beast in reviving harsh persecution. For an overview, see charts on these pages.

THE FOUR BEASTS OF REVELATION 12, 13, AND 17

CHRISTIAN ROME DURING THE 1260 YEARS

SATAN AND PAGAN ROME

U.S.A. (FALSE PROPHET IN THE END TIME)

THE END-TIME FORM OF THE LEOPARD-BODIED BEAST

AFTER HOWARD LARKIN, JOE MANISCALCO, JIM PADGETT

THE SEVEN HEADS AND TEN HORNS

SEVEN HEADS	TEN HORNS
Five are fallen	
1. BABYLON	No crowns yet
2. PERSIA	No crowns yet
3. GREECE	No crowns yet
4. ROMAN EMPIRE	No crowns yet
5. CHRISTIAN ROME	Crowns: European monarchies
one is	
*6. CHRISTIAN ROME, WOUNDED	Again no crowns: Democracies
one is coming	
7. CHRISTIAN ROME, REVIVED	New power: Dictatorships
8. BEAST (Demonic sum of all Roman style persecuting governments.)	

*The time of the vision is the hour of judgment, the end-time, beginning in 1798/1844 at the end of the 1260 and 2300 year-days. See pages 274-280, 352, 353.

Three basic questions. There are three basic questions that we ought to ask when trying to understand our puzzle: (1) From what time frame are we to look at it? (2) Are we to use any persecuting powers that we haven't already met in our study of Daniel and Revelation? and (3) Is the language to be taken as it stands or in an accommodated sense? Let's look at the questions one at a time.

1. *The time frame.* In Revelation 21:9, 10 an angel invited John to watch the holy city come down from heaven. This invitation certainly carried John's mind forward to the end of the millennium. Similarly, at the beginning of Revelation 17 (the chapter we're now studying) an angel gave John an invitation to come and see the "**judgment**" of the great harlot. This invitation drew his mind forward to the beginning of the end time. See pages 422-425.

So shouldn't Revelation 17 be interpreted from the viewpoint of 1798/1844 and later, the era of the judgment and the end time? This is the time frame for the judgment scene in Daniel 7, the opening of the little scroll in Revelation 10, and the preaching of the first angel's message of Revelation 14:6, 7, "The hour of his judgment has come." We have often reminded ourselves that the second half of Revelation, in which our puzzle is located, is concerned almost exclusively with the end time.

473

2. *The empires.* It seems, too, that we should be reluctant to add empires (such as Egypt and Assyria) to the ones that are so prominent in Daniel and in the rest of Revelation. The prophecies of Daniel are our key to the interpretation of Revelation. Daniel gives us Babylon, Persia, Greece, Roman Empire, and the Roman Church, but says nothing about Egypt and Assyria.

The beast of Revelation 17 is the same as the leopard-bodied beast of chapter 13, both of which stand in water and have seven heads and ten horns. There *seem* to be four animal symbols in chapters 12, 13, and 17—the dragon, the lamb-horned beast, the leopard-bodied sea beast, and the scarlet-colored sea beast. However, Revelation 16:13 and 20:10 speak of them as only three, the "dragon" (or "devil"), the "false prophet" (which is the lamb-horned animal), and the "beast" (not the "beasts").

The dragon and the beast, both having seven heads and ten horns, represent one and the same spirit of church-state persecution. (Church-state persecution is a primary concern of Revelation.) Their seven heads call attention to the same sevenfold sequence of persecuting government. But whereas *(a)* the dragon calls special attention to *non-Christian persecution,* and *(b)* the beast calls attention to the old-fashioned *Catholic-style persecution, (c)* the lamb-horned beast calls attention to end-time *Protestantism* as it finally lapses into a dragonlike, beastlike spirit of persecution.

As for the two stages of the "beast" itself, its leopard-bodied stage (chapter 13) calls attention to persecution during the Middle Ages, and its scarlet-colored stage (chapter 17) calls attention first to its weakness at the beginning of the judgment hour and second to its dramatic but brief resurgence as an old-fashioned Catholic-style persecuting power immediately prior to the second coming.

3. *The language.* A third guideline for interpreting the heads and horns, the harlot, and the beast is that some of the language in chapter 17 is used in an accommodated sense. We read in verse 8 that the beast **"is not"**; yet even while we're listening to the angel tell us this, we're looing at the beast through John's eyes. We can see it standing in the water with the great harlot riding on its back!

In a similar way, the ten kings are said in verse 12 to have **"not yet received royal power."** But in verses 1 and 2 they have already as kings gone to bed with the harlot. **"I will show you . . . the great harlot,"** says the angel, **"with whom *the kings* of the earth have committed fornication."** So they once did have royal power. In chapter 13 we saw them wearing their crowns during the 1260 years. In a little while from now they're going to get **"authority as kings"** again (no doubt as totalitarian states) and rule with the beast for an **"hour"** (verse 12), during which they will **"make war on the Lamb"** (verse 14) and turn against the harlot (verse 16). See pages 441, 442.

So the beast **"is not"** in comparison with what it used to be and in comparison with what it will be; and the same is true for the kings. After a manner of speaking, in a certain sense, in comparison with their tremendous though temporary future reign as oppressive totalitarian states, the kings haven't yet begun to reign. They're something like John Paul Jones, skipper of the *Bonhomme Richard.* As every American schoolchild knows, when John Paul Jones was already well embroiled with the British frigate *Serapis* he shouted out, "I have not yet begun to fight." He had indeed begun to fight, but he said he hadn't, in view of the punches he still intended to land.

The beast an eighth but of the seven. What about the beast that is **"an eighth"** while it also **"belongs to the seven"**? Verse 11.

Let's not make the problem too hard. The beast isn't an eighth *head*! It's a beast, and the seven heads all belong to it!

When we add up seven numbers we get a total, which is an eighth number. But this eighth number belongs to the seven; it is sum and substance of the others.

When the beast's head received a "mortal wound," the beast as a whole was critically injured. And when the wound is healed, the beast as a whole is healed. Of course! See Revelation 13:3, 12, 14.

During the beast's serious illness its lamb-horned rival occupies front center. The beast appears to have been upstaged permanently; but it hasn't been. In fact, the lamb-horned animal soon offers the beast its services in order to help it stage its comeback. The beast recovers and rises to its greatest power yet, as symbolized by its seventh head. See pages 340-349.

Applying our three rules now, we see that of the **"seven heads"** the **"five"** that are **"fallen"** are entities familiar to us: (1) Babylon, (2) Persia, (3) Greece, (4) Roman Empire, and (5) Christian Rome. By the time of the vision (in the 1798/1844 **"judgment"** era), Christian Rome **"is"** enduring a critical illness resulting from a "mortal wound." So we are now living in the time of the sixth head—(6) Wounded Christian Rome—an unprecedented era of *separation of church and state.* The final head will be (7) Christian Rome Revived—and as it revives, the entire beast (**"an eighth"**) will realize its climactic self-actualization. The **"ten horns,"** which once represented the intolerant kingdoms of Europe and which are now more-or-less tolerant democracies, will momentarily become harshly intolerant totalitarian entities.

The beast and the harlot. We have said that the beast and the harlot John saw represented a separation of church and state. This observation is confirmed by the most significant difference between the leopard-bodied beast of chapter 13 and the scarlet-colored beast we're looking at in chapter 17. The beast in chapter 17 has the great harlot **"sitting"** on its back. Church (the harlot) and state (the beast) though related are now observed as distinct entities.

For centuries the medieval church and the European states were so interrelated and mutually supportive that they could be characterized by a single complex symbol, the leopard-bodied beast. Historians commonly regard the history of the Middle Ages as virtually church history.

During most of the 1260 years, kings and princes occasionally opposed a pope politically, but most of them loyally enforced the papacy's theological beliefs. As we have seen, however, around 1798 a wholly new concept emerged, church and state separated in a republican environment. Partly by means of this very concept, Catholicism received its apparently mortal wound (Revelation 13:3), and the United States began its climb to world prominence.

The angel has taken John into a **"wilderness."** We remember that the woman of chapter 12, the true church of God, endured a wilderness experience for 1260 years. While she was persecuted, God nourished her. But now the con-

Religious liberty did not come easily to America. Roger Williams was exiled in winter! Jefferson and others argued tirelessly for freedom.

fused church, the harlot of chapter 17, endures a wilderness experience in the end time while God judges her for having persecuted.

For a wilderness person, the harlot sports an extravagant getup. She is **"arrayed in purple and scarlet"** (in John's day the expensive dyes of royalty) **"and bedecked with gold and jewels and pearls."** But her finery and jewelry seem tawdry beside the true mother's sunshine gown and starry crown. See Revelation 12:1.

The harlot holds **"in her hand a golden cup full of abominations and the impurities of her fornication." "And I saw the woman,"** says John, **"drunk with the blood of the saints and the blood of the martyrs of Jesus."** Revelation 17:4, 6.

This particular language about her bloodshed and prostitution is adapted from an old prophecy (or "oracle") "concerning Nineveh." "Woe to the bloody city, all full of lies and booty . . . who betrays nations with her harlotries." Nahum 1:1; 3:1-4. We have become somewhat accustomed to hearing the Roman Church called Babylon. Nineveh was the capital of the Assyrian Empire, the most bloodthirsty of all ancient powers.

The harlot of the medieval Roman Church committed fornication by uniting with the state to compel people under the pain of death to accept her erroneous doctrines. Her persecutions were cruel. But when John sees her riding on the beast, her power to persecute is temporarily in eclipse. She is suffering under the separation of church and state.

But though the beast and the harlot are shown as separate entities, they are virtually identical in character. Morally there is little to choose between them. Both are colored **"scarlet."** Both demand unswerving loyalty and, given the opportunity, both persecute relentlessly. Their final bitter conflict is a "diamond cut diamond" episode of hateful internecine rivalry.

Satan's "at-one-ment." In the passage we're discussing (Revelation 17:13, 14) all the ten kings give their power to the beast. In the passage about the lamb-horned beast or false prophet (Revelation 13:11-17), the lamb-horned beast, a symbol of America, persuades everyone in the world to erect an image in worship of the beast. In the Armageddon passage (Revelation 16:13, 14) the dragon, the false prophet, and the beast (whose comeback the false prophet has vigorously promoted) send demons to assemble the "kings of the whole world."

In these three passages we have one and the same global development viewed from different perspectives, the response of the **"ten kings"** to American leadership. The entire world responds under America's influence to advance the cause of religious oppression.

When we first met the ten horns in Daniel 7 they stood for the nations of Europe. See GC 1:129. But in Revelation 17:12 they appear in the end time to represent the "kings of the whole world," as in Revelation 16:14. Once Roman Christianity, too, was confined to Europe. In our day it has been spread very widely.

477

Before the 1798 era—before the industrial revolution, before the American and French revolutions, before the worldwide distribution of Western ideas, and so on—the appropriate prophecies of Daniel and Revelation applied largely to Europe and the Middle East. But now the appropriate prophecies are universal in their application.

This is in harmony with the basic principle we looked at first in GC 1:36. Bible prophecy tends to select for mention those religious and political entities which exist where God's people live, because prophecy frequently concerns itself with the persecution of God's people and because God's people possess Scripture and can benefit from the inspired instruction. In the end time the gospel goes to all the world, God's people are found in every nation, and Bible prophecy speaks of all the world's nations.

What the lamb-horned beast persuades the whole world to do in Revelation 13 is knowingly to oppose God's commandments by, among other things, setting up an alternate day of worship and supporting it with economic penalties and capital punishment. People who resist find themselves unable to buy or sell, and many are sentenced to death. This is the situation symbolized also in Revelation 17 (our present chapter), when the beast musters the kings of the earth to make war with the Lamb.

The beast, now represented dynamically and demonically by its seventh head and all its horns, is a ghastly realization of the global village, the one-world idea, gone satanic. Here is the devil's counterfeit of Christ's atonement—human beings "at one" with God. Here is the entire human race, God's own saints excepted, standing as one, single-mindedly in sullen opposition against its Saviour.

No wonder the beast, who masterminds this malice, is described as coming out of the **"bottomless pit"** as it goes on its way to **"perdition."** Verse 8.

Of course the whole wicked plan fails completely. **"The Lamb will conquer them."** Verse 14. Deliverance of God's faithful followers is one of the major themes of Daniel and Revelation. God cares!

God's true people, young and old, have chosen to come out of every "harlot" community. They stand united in their loyalty to the Lamb. They survive every bitter attack launched against them and at the second coming are caught up into the clouds to meet their Lord. See 1 Thessalonians 4:16-18.

In utter frustration, realizing that they have been completely misled and in the process have lost their opportunity for eternal life, the world's masses turn against their religious leaders with vicious hostility. They **"burn"** the harlot **"with fire."**

But the beast and the false prophet are themselves "thrown alive into the lake of fire," and everyone still alive on earth (who has not been caught up into the clouds with Jesus Christ) is slain. See Revelation 19:20.

Then the thousand years of the millennium will begin. See Revelation 20.

References

1. G. B. Caird, *A Commentary on the Revelation of St. John the Divine*, ed. Henry Chadwick, Harper's New Testament Commentaries (New York: Harper & Row, Publishers, 1966), p. 220.

2. Carl Schneider, *"Metopon,"* Gerhard Kittell and Gerhard Friedrich, *Theological Dictionary of the New Testament,* tr. and ed. Geoffrey W. Bromiley, 9 vols. (Grand Rapids, Mich.: Wm. B. Eerdmans Publishing Company, 1964-1974), 4:637.

3. Edwin R. Thiele, *Outline Studies in Revelation* (Angwin, Calif.: the author, n.d.), p. 264.

4. Kenneth A. Strand, "Two Aspects of Babylon's Judgment Portrayed in Revelation 18," *Andrews University Seminary Studies* 20 (Spring 1982):53-60. Compare Caird, *Revelation,* pp. 229, 230.

Revelation 19:11 to 21:8

The Millennium

Introduction

Some of the future events predicted in Revelation you and your family may not live to see. But an event connected with the millennium every one of us will experience. We will all be present at the judgment scene which marks the millennium's close.

Every person who has ever lived will at that time gather around Jesus Christ. We'll gather either as His friends inside the Holy City looking out, or as His enemies, outside the city looking in. Where we will be then depends on our choices now.

The millennium has been a popular subject. Amillennialists, postmillennialists, and premillennialists have interpreted it in widely differing ways. See *Your Questions Answered*, pages 515-520. But surprisingly perhaps, considering the great interest it has aroused, the millennium is referred to in the Bible only in Revelation 20. As for the word *millennium* itself, it doesn't appear at all in the common English translations of the Bible. And it isn't present in the underlying Greek, where we find *chilia ete* (KILL-e-uh ET-e), "a thousand years," instead.

Millennium means "a thousand-year period." It is adapted from the ancient Latin translations of the Bible and is composed of two Latin words, *mille* and *ennium*. *Mille*, "a thou-

sand," shows up in *millimeter*, a thousandth of a meter, and in *millipede*, a tiny animal with a lot of legs. *Ennium* is used in *biennium*, a two-year period, and is related to *annus*, "a year," which occurs in *annual* and *anniversary*. You can remember to write *n* twice in *millennium* if you remember how to spell *annual* and *anniversary*.

Although the millennium is discussed in Revelation 20, the chapter breaks which begin and end this chapter don't mark the beginning and end of the millennium division. The end of the fall-of-Babylon division and the beginning of the New Jerusalem division, the divisions located on either side of the millennium division, indicate that our present division begins with chapter 19:11 and continues to 21:8. We have referred to this division as "Circumstances Related to the Holy City: The Millennium." See the chart on the next page.

In our overall chiastic diagram of Revelation (see the next page), the millennium division is paired with the division about the seven seals. There are many similar and contrasting parallels between the two divisions. Several of these parallels, which you may like to review, are listed in the chart. Besides them we can point to (a) the *sealing* of the 144,000 and the very different *sealing* of Satan, (b) the *four winds* and the *four quarters* of the earth, and (c) the redeemed who are

481

Confined to the ruined earth with his angels, Satan will have a thousand years to prove—if he can—that he's a better ruler than God.

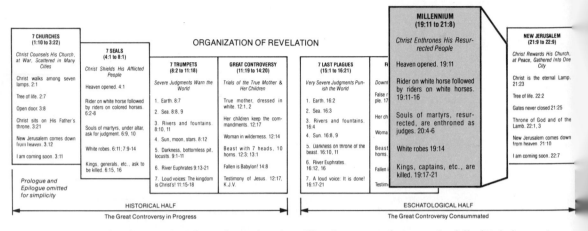

The organization chart shows that the millennium comes between the fall of Babylon and the establishment of the New Jerusalem in the new earth.

assembled at God's throne *singing* and the wicked who are assembled at God's throne being *sentenced to death*. No doubt you and your family can find additional parallels.

We are always on the lookout, of course, for a new chiasm. We aren't disappointed! The seven scenes in our present division may be arranged to look like this (next page):

THE SECOND HALF OF REVELATION: A DUAL FOCUS ON THE ULTIMATE PUNISHMENT OF THE REBELLIOUS AND ON THE ULTIMATE REWARD OF THE RIGHTEOUS IN THE END TIME

1. *Focus on punishment*
   A   The plagues   15:1-16:21

   B   Circumstances related to the plagues: Fall of Babylon, the false mother   17:1-19:10

   A plague angel shows John the great harlot.   17:1-19:8
   Afterward John attempts to worship the angel.   19:9, 10

2. *Focus on reward*
   B′   Circumstances related to the holy city: The millennium   19:11-21:8

   A′   The holy city: Descent of New Jerusalem, the Lamb's bride   21:9-22:21

   A plague angel shows John the Lamb's bride.   21:9-22:7
   Afterward John attempts to worship the angel.   22:8, 9

A Christ *descends from heaven* as *Conqueror*.

B His *enemies* are *slain*.

  C Satan is *bound* so he cannot *deceive the nations*.

    D The redeemed sit on judgment thrones a thousand years.

  C' Satan is *released* and *deceives the nations* again.

B' Christ's resurrected *enemies* are judged and *slain*.

A' The Holy City *descends from heaven*—and it and the renewed earth are given to Christ's fellow *conquerors*.

The millennium division can be outlined under three headings:

THE BEGINNING OF THE MILLENNIUM

1. Christ returns at His second coming, the righteous rise in the first resurrection.

2. All sinful humans and institutions are destroyed.

3. Satan is bound.

THE MILLENNIUM

4. The redeemed reign and judge with Christ a thousand years.

THE CLOSE OF THE MILLENNIUM

5. Satan is released, musters the wicked around the beloved city, and is destroyed.

6. The wicked rise in the second resurrection, followed by final judgment and the second death.

7. The Holy City descends, and the earth is renewed.

An exhortation about conquerors and cowards.

In this outline the first three scenes constitute a unit. The binding of Satan, which prevents him from deceiving the nations, is accomplished by the second coming, which destroys all sinful humans and removes the redeemed (John 14:1-3) to heaven. Satan is unable to deceive the nations during the thousand years, because during this period there are no nations left on earth to be deceived.

The last three scenes, like the first three, also form a unit, focusing on the descent of the Holy City and on the final destruction of sinners.

Several events in this division are mentioned out of chronological sequence. The first resurrection will take place at the second coming, described in the first scene, and obviously happens before the resurrected saints sit on thrones early in the fourth scene, but the first resurrection isn't expressly named until nearly the end of the fourth scene. Similarly, the release of Satan in the fifth scene is made possible by the second resurrection, which isn't described until the sixth scene; and Satan and the nations are able to surround the city in the fifth scene because the city has already descended to earth, a development which, however, is not described until scene seven.

Like the fall-of-Babylon and New Jerusalem divisions, the millennium division closes with a word of exhortation. The fall-of-Babylon division ended with a blessing on everyone who receives an invitation to the Lamb's wedding supper. The New Jerusalem division will end with a blessing on people who pay attention to the message of Revelation. The present division ends with a promise to conquerors and a warning to cowards.

CIRCUMSTANCES RELATED TO THE HOLY CITY: THE MILLENNIUM

REVELATION 19:11-21

The first scene: The second coming of Christ. 11 Then I saw heaven opened, and behold, a white horse! He who sat upon it is called Faithful and True, and in righteousness he judges and makes war. 12His eyes are like a flame of fire, and on his head are many diadems; and he has a name inscribed which no one knows but himself. 13He is clad in a robe dipped in blood, and the name by which he is called is The Word of God. 14And the armies of heaven, arrayed in fine linen, white and pure, followed him on white horses. 15From his mouth issues a sharp sword with which to smite the nations, and he will rule them with a rod of iron; he will tread the wine press of the fury of the wrath of God the Almighty. 16On his robe and on his thigh he has a name inscribed, King of kings and Lord of lords.

The second scene: The destruction of sinners. 17 Then I saw an angel standing in the sun, and with a loud voice he called to all the birds that fly in midheaven, "Come, gather for the great supper of God, 18to eat the flesh of kings, the flesh of captains, the flesh of mighty men, the flesh of horses and their riders, and the flesh of all men, both free and slave, both small and great." 19And I saw the beast and the kings of the earth with their armies gathered to make war against him who sits upon the horse and against his army. 20And the beast was captured, and with it the false prophet who in its presence had worked the signs by which he deceived those who had received the mark of the beast and those who worshiped its image. These two were thrown alive into the lake of fire that burns with sulphur. 21And the rest were slain by the sword of him who sits upon the horse, the sword that issues from his mouth; and all the birds were gorged with their flesh.

REVELATION 20

The third scene: The binding of Satan. 1 Then I saw an angel coming down from heaven, holding in his hand the key of the bottomless pit and a great chain. 2And he seized the dragon, that ancient serpent, who is the Devil and Satan, and bound him for a thousand years, 3and threw him into the pit, and shut it and sealed it over him, that he should deceive the nations no more, till the thousand years were ended. After that he must be loosed for a little while.

The fourth scene: The redeemed judge for a thousand years. 4 Then I saw thrones, and seated on them were those to whom judgment was committed. Also I saw the souls of those who had been beheaded for their testimony to Jesus and for the word of God, and who had not worshiped the beast or its image and had not received its mark on their foreheads or their hands. They came to life, and reigned with Christ a thousand years. 5The rest of the dead did not come to life until the thousand years were ended. This is the first resurrection. 6Blessed and holy is he who shares in the first resurrection! Over such the second death has no power, but they shall be priests of God and of Christ, and they shall reign with him a thousand years.

The fifth scene: Satan is released, musters the nations, and is burned. 7 And when the thousand years are ended, Satan will be loosed from his prison 8and will come out to deceive the nations which are at the four corners of the earth, that is, Gog and Magog, to gather them for battle; their number is like the sand of the sea. 9And they marched up over the broad earth and surrounded the camp of the saints and the beloved city; but fire came down from heaven and consumed them, 10and the devil who had deceived them was thrown into the lake of fire and sulphur where the beast and the false prophet were, and they will be tormented day and night for ever and ever.

484

The sixth scene: Sinners are resurrected, sentenced, and burned. 11 Then I saw a great white throne and him who sat upon it; from his presence earth and sky fled away, and no place was found for them. 12And I saw the dead, great and small, standing before the throne, and books were opened. Also another book was opened, which is the book of life. And the dead were judged by what was written in the books, by what they had done. 13And the sea gave up the dead in it, Death and Hades gave up the dead in them, and all were judged by what they had done. 14Then Death and Hades were thrown into the lake of fire. This is the second death, the lake of fire; 15and if any one's name was not found written in the book of life, he was thrown into the lake of fire.

REVELATION 21:1-8

The seventh scene: The holy city descends. And the earth is renewed. 1 Then I saw a new heaven and a new earth; for the first heaven and the first earth had passed away, and the sea was no more. 2And I saw the holy city, new Jerusalem, coming down out of heaven from God, prepared as a bride adorned for her husband; 3and I heard a loud voice from the throne saying, "Behold, the dwelling of God is with men. He will dwell with them, and they shall be his people, and God himself will be with them; 4he will wipe away every tear from their eyes, and death shall be no more, neither shall there be mourning nor crying nor pain any more, for the former things have passed away."

Exhortation. 5 And he who sat upon the throne said, "Behold, I make all things new." Also he said, "Write this, for these words are trustworthy and true." 6And he said to me, "It is done! I am the Alpha and the Omega, the beginning and the end. To the thirsty I will give from the fountain of the water of life without payment. 7He who conquers shall have this heritage, and I will be his God and he shall be my son. 8But as for the cowardly, the faithless, the polluted, as for murderers, fornicators, sorcerers, idolaters, and all liars, their lot shall be in the lake that burns with fire and sulphur, which is the second death."

The Message of Revelation 19:11 to 21:8

I. The Second Coming of Christ

Several times Revelation has brought us up to Christ's second coming, only to backtrack and lead us through the course of history.

Chapter 1 promised that Jesus would come "with the clouds" and "every eye" would see Him (verse 7), but what followed in chapters 2 and 3 was the Lord's correspondence with the seven churches. In the Philadelphian letter Jesus promised, "I am coming soon" (Revelation 3:11), but in chapters 4 to 7 we found ourselves learning about the seven seals, beginning from John's time in the first century.

Under the sixth seal (Revelation 6:12-17), signs of the second coming were fulfilled in the sun, moon, and stars. Sinners cried out for rocks and mountains to hide them from the "wrath of the Lamb." But in chapters 8 to 11 John again took us back to his own day, this time to tell the story of the seven trumpets.

After the three angels' end-time messages (Revelation 14:6-12), John showed us Jesus seated on a white cloud, ready for the second coming. We heard voices calling for the grain and grapes to be harvested (Verses 14-20)—but *then* John led us back a little way in time to learn about the seven plagues.

The second coming is a major, recurring theme in Revelation, no doubt about it. In Revelation 19 we have a fairly extensive treatment of it.

At the beginning of the seven-seals division, John looked through an open door (Revelation 4:1, 2) and saw God's throne inside the heavenly sanctuary. At the beginning of the great-controversy division he looked deep into the inner arena of the sanctuary and saw the ark of the Ten Commandments (Revelation 11:19). But now—in the nineteenth chapter—**"heaven"** itself is **"opened,"** and John sees Jesus as a celestial general seated astride an imposing **"white horse."** Majestically, gallantly, He gallops down the concourses of space at the head of a vast galactic cavalry, the **"armies of heaven."** Every soldier is arrayed in **"fine linen, white and pure"** and, like their Lord, is mounted on a snow-white steed. Revelation 19:11-16.

Christ's five names. American soldiers wear name tags on their uniforms. John notices that Jesus is wearing the name **"King of kings and Lord of lords"** and that He is known as **"The Word of God"** and **"Faithful"** and **"True."** He's called **"Faithful"** and **"True"** because this is what He is—completely dependable and utterly genuine, a covenant-keeping God, a Friend who would rather die than break a promise. See GC 1:234-238. He *is* a God who cares!

By linking the names **"Faithful"** and **"True"** with the designation **"eyes . . . like a flame of fire,"** John reminds us that our heavenly Warrior is the same attentive Pastor who has thoughtfully tended His "smoky churches and

487

At the second coming, the Lamb of God appears as "King of kings and Lord of lords," leading heaven's armies to rescue His people.

awkward Christians" for so many centuries, as foretold in chapters 1 to 3. In His letters to the seven churches, Jesus stood among the seven lampstands and introduced Himself to us as "faithful and true" (Revelation 3:14) and as having "eyes like a flame of fire" (Revelation 2:18). See page 97.

John says that Christ on horseback is called **"The Word of God."** Revelation 19:13. The name occurs in the New Testament only here and in John's Gospel (John 1:1) and in John's first epistle (1 John 1:1), which reminds us about who it was who wrote the book of Revelation. Jesus *is* God's "Word" (or God's "Speech"), for He expresses in ways we can at least partly understand the deep and loving thoughts that God the Father thinks about us.

Christ's royal title, **"King of kings and Lord of lords,"** is written, John tells us, **"on his robe and on his thigh."** Revelation 19:16. Swords in John's day were worn at the left thigh, as pistols today are worn on a person's hip. Christ's sword is no doubt the "sword of the Spirit," which is "the word of God." See Hebrews 4:12.

Christ's fifth name isn't told us. John saw it but couldn't read it. He says, in fact, that only Jesus knows what it is. See Revelation 19:12. There are mysteries of beauty in the character of our Saviour that in all eternity we'll never fully comprehend. How *can* He be so patiently forgiving? So eloquently kind?

Christ's blood-stained robe. Although Christ's horse is white, His robe is red. It has been **"dipped in blood."** Revelation 19:13. The language comes from Isaiah 63:1-6. So too does the phrase about His treading a **"winepress."** In Isaiah 63 God's robe is stained with His enemies' blood. The blood is portrayed as the scarlet juice of grapes crushed under God's feet in an old-fashioned winepress. But in Revelation 19 Jesus hasn't yet entered the winepress; so why is *His* robe red?

As usual, John has adapted rather than merely adopted Old Testament ideas. Christ's robe is stained with His *own* blood. At the cross, the serpent "bruised" Christ's "heel." Now at the second advent He arrives to start "bruising" Satan's "head." See Genesis 3:15 and pages 316, 317.

We saw on page 334 that God chose not to destroy Satan early in the great controversy in order to avoid unnecessary misunderstanding. If God had destroyed Satan quickly, many created beings might well have concluded that God was impatient and arbitrary, precisely as Satan had alleged.

But by allowing Satan to torture and kill Him, Jesus demonstrated His own infinite goodness and Satan's unparalleled badness. Now Jesus can eliminate oppressors and ultimately destroy the devil without being misunderstood. Jesus became a man and died on the cross so that "through death he might [obtain approval to] destroy him who has the power of death, that is, the devil, and deliver all those who through fear of death were subject to lifelong bondage." Hebrews 2:14, 15.

The blood on Jesus' robe certifies His right to destroy the destroyer of His people. It also certifies His right to claim and rescue His people. With His own "precious blood" He has "ransomed" them. 1 Peter 1:18, 19. They are *His*.

Jesus is still the Lamb that was slain. But at the second coming the wicked seek

488

to hide from the *"wrath* of the Lamb." Revelation 6:16. The wrath of the Lamb is divine outrage based on infinite, self-denying love for people who have been sorely oppressed.

Jesus is still the Shepherd who tirelessly leads and cares for His sheep. Compare John 10:11 and Isaiah 40:11. His symbolic **"rod of iron"** (Revelation 19:15) is a shepherd's rod, iron-tipped to protect His sheep by fending off wolves.

Jesus and His diadems. Jesus in John's vision wears **"many diadems,"** or kingly crowns. Revelation 19:12. The multiple diadems on the dragon (12:3) and on the beast (13:1) were a blasphemous parody of Christ's kingly authority. Satan is the "ruler of this world" (John 12:31) only because he snatched the kingdom from its rightful Lord.

Although Jesus (along with His Father) has always been King of the universe, in Revelation we haven't seen Him crowned before—except in chapter 14:14 where, as here, He is coming to gather the redeemed. When did He start wearing these diadems?

Daniel 7:13, 14 shows that at the close of the pre-advent phase of the final judgment, which began in 1844 and ends just before the second coming, Jesus, the Son of man, was to receive "dominion and glory and kingdom" from God the Father, the Ancient of Days. Christ's kingdom on this earth becomes truly His when, as a result of the judgment and of the preaching of the three angels' messages, His church comes to be composed entirely of individuals fully committed to His service. (In the final analysis, a kingdom belongs to a king only to the extent that its people choose to obey him.)

Immediately upon receiving His kingdom in its fullness, Jesus rushes off— jumps on His **"white horse"** and gallops away—to rescue from the earth His loyal but harassed citizens and share His kingship with them.

To put the matter another way, during the pre-advent phase of the judgment, Christ's church becomes "bright and pure" (Revelation 19:8), "without spot or wrinkle or any such thing" (see Ephesians 5:26, 27). By clothing herself in "fine linen" (the "righteous deeds of the saints"), she thus makes herself "ready." Revelation 19:7, 8. At once Jesus marries His church, symbolized as New Jerusalem. Immediately after the wedding (see Luke 12:35-37) He returns to His waiting servants on earth to invite them to attend the "marriage supper of the Lamb." Revelation 19:9; see also pages 407-410.

Armies of angels. The armies of heaven that follow Jesus at the second coming are composed of angels. In the Olivet Discourse Jesus said that at His second coming "all the angels" would accompany Him. See Matthew 25:31. The angels will perform the highly important function of gathering the redeemed and leading them into Christ's presence. "He will send out his angels with a loud trumpet call, and they will gather his elect." Matthew 24:31.

You can see them now in your mind's eye, filling the sky in every direction, excitedly escorting God's redeemed people from their homes and hiding places and from their graves to the cloud where Jesus is enthroned.

Some Bible readers have suggested that these armies are made up of saints who went to heaven when they died. But we have learned elsewhere in our study what the Bible says happens to people when they die. See pages 73-77; 214-220.

Symbolic and literal language. The first scene in the millennium division is the second coming of Christ. The language about horses, armies, and a sword, like so much of the language in Revelation, is symbolic, even impressionistic. Symbolic language in chapter 14:14-17 pictures Jesus with a *sickle* reaping His righteous *grain*. In the Olivet Discourse Jesus described His second coming symbolically in terms of separating *sheep and goats*. See Matthew 25:32.

John described the second coming in more nearly *literal* terms in Revelation 1:7, "Behold, he is coming with the clouds, and every eye will see him."

John had personally heard Jesus state that He would return on heavenly clouds, visible to all the world. To the high priest at His trial Jesus swore solemnly under oath, "Hereafter you will see the Son of man seated at the right hand of Power, and coming on the clouds of heaven." Matthew 26:64. John, standing in the high priest's palace that terrible Thursday night before the crucifixion, heard Jesus as He made this prophecy; and he included it in Revelation 1:7.

Paul too described the second coming in literal language in 1 Thessalonians 4:15-17. He wrote about it on the authority of "the word of the Lord." "The Lord himself," he said, "will descend from heaven with a cry of command, with the archangel's call, and with the sound of the trumpet of God. And the dead in Christ will rise first; then we who are alive, who are left, shall be caught up [we'll be "raptured," says the Latin version] together with them in the clouds to meet the Lord in the air."

In the New Testament, angels also taught that Jesus will be returning in this manner, visibly, openly, on the clouds. Shortly after Christ's death and resurrection, the disciples watched Jesus leave the earth and ascend into the sky. Jesus "was lifted up, and a cloud took him out of their sight." But standing at their side to reassure the disciples were two friendly angels. They looked like ordinary "men," but they were dressed in "white robes," like the white-robed heavenly soldiers who accompany Jesus in Revelation 19. "This Jesus, who was taken up from you into heaven," said the two angels to the disciples (John among them), "will come in the same way as you saw him go into heaven." Acts 1:9-11.

We should remember that Jesus not only traveled to heaven on clouds but that He also traveled on clouds to launch the pre-advent judgment portrayed in Daniel 7:9-14. Indeed, His Olivet Discourse language about the Son of man coming on the clouds of heaven at the second coming was adapted directly from Daniel 7.

Clouds are always composed of something. We speak, for instance, of clouds of dust, clouds of water droplets, clouds of locusts. The clouds Jesus travels on, we can believe, are clouds of angels. These angels compose His galactic cavalry during the second-coming scene in Revelation 19:11-16.

See how you like the hymn about Christ's three journeys on the clouds. Maybe you and your family would even like to sing it.

Christ, the Lord, all power possessing

Matt. 28:18-20; Dan. 7:9-14; Rev. 1:7
C. Mervyn Maxwell, 1984 (1925 -)

CWM RHONDDA 8.7.8.7.8.7.7.
John Hughes (1873 - 1932)

1. Christ, the Lord, all power pos-sess-ing, Part-ing, mount-ed heav-en's height,
2. Dan - iel views earth's judg-ment hour, An - gels gath-ering, o - pen books.
3. Rev - e - la-tion's word ful - fill-ing, Trum-pet, voic-es pierce the air.

Gra - cious hands out-stretched in bless-ing, Clouds re-ceived Him from their sight.
God, en-throned in flam - ing pow - er, For His Son's ar - riv - al looks.
Saint and sin - ner faint - ing, thrill-ing, Ev - ery eye be - holds Him there.

Christ as-cend - ed, Christ as - cend - ed, Christ as-cend-ed on the
Christ ap-proach - es, Christ ap-proach-es, Christ ap-proach-es on the
Christ is com - ing, Christ is com - ing, Christ is com-ing on the

clouds (on the clouds), Christ as - cend - ed on the clouds.
clouds (on the clouds), Christ ap-proach - es on the clouds.
clouds (on the clouds), Christ is com - ing on the clouds.

Words copyright 1984 by C. Mervyn Maxwell.

Alternate tune, UNSER HERRSCHER

Stanza 1 is based on Matthew 28:18-20; Luke 24:50, 51; Acts 1:9-11, K.J.V.
Stanza 2 is based on Daniel 7:9-14.
Stanza 3 is based on Matthew 24:30; 1 Thessalonians 4:15-18; Revelation 1:7.

II. The Great Supper of God

John's attention was diverted from the second-coming scene to the second scene in our present series—the great supper of God and the destruction of the enemies of good. Revelation 19:17-21.

John noticed an angel by himself **"standing in the sun."** Once before, he had seen a woman by herself, the true mother, "clothed with the sun." The dragon had attacked her and her baby Boy. Revelation 12:1-6.

The angel delivered a grisly invitation to **"all the birds that fly in midheaven."** Raising his voice he shouted, **"Come, gather for the great supper of God, to eat the flesh of kings, the flesh of captains, the flesh of mighty men, the flesh of horses and their riders, and the flesh of all men, both free and slave, both small and great."**

We read about a similar assortment of people once before, in Revelation 6:15, 16. We heard them crying for the rocks and mountains to hide them from the face of God and the wrath of the Lamb. Isaiah the prophet also saw such people, hiding in the "caverns of the rocks," throwing their gold and silver idols to moles and bats. Isaiah 2:20, 21. The prophet Haggai warned against the uselessness of earning wages only to "put them into a bag with holes." Haggai 1:6. Investments, credit cards, promotions, extravagant pleasures, prestige, will mean nothing at all to the frightened people who have not prepared themselves for the second coming of Christ.

The angel standing in the sun invited the birds that fly **"in midheaven"** to attend the **"great supper of God."** Like the vultures and other carrion eaters to whom this call was issued, the three angels of Revelation 14:6-12 had also once flown "in midheaven." They had borne a message about the judgment, the seventh-day Sabbath, the eternal gospel, and the faith of Jesus. How the victims of the supper angel wish they had paid attention to the messages of those other angels.

Like the vultures and the three angels, a symbolic eagle had once flown "in midheaven." Revelation 8:13. It had screeched out, "Woe, woe, woe," warning that the three final trumpets would be even worse than the first four trumpets had been. But John had been given few details about the special "woe" aspect of the seventh trumpet. He had been shown only that under the seventh trumpet the nations would rage, God's wrath would come, the dead would be judged, and the time would arrive for "destroying the destroyers of the earth." Revelation 11:14-18. By now in our study we know that the rage of the nations climaxes in Armageddon, that God's wrath includes the seven last plagues, and that destruction of the destroyers involves the lake of fire and the great supper of God.

Armageddon and its outcome. **"I saw the beast and the kings of the earth with their armies,"** John says, **"gathered to make war against him who sits upon the horse and against his army."** Revelation 19:19. This is the Battle of Armageddon, which we read about first in chapter 16:14, 16 and again in 17:13, 14.

Armageddon isn't a battle of the East against the West; it's an attack of Satan and the human race against the Lamb of God. It's fought in the only ways human beings can attack a heavenly Being, by opposing His truth and oppressing His people. It is organized through the lying propaganda of the froglike spirits who come out of the mouths of the beast, the dragon, and the false prophet. Their lying propaganda is accompanied by misleading miracles, signs, and wonders. Presumably it will include apparent resurrections of people from the dead. Evidently it will include an imitation "second coming," which is the *parousia* of the "man of lawlessness." See 2 Thessalonians 2:3 and pages 444-446.

Satan's message, as usual, will be that God's law *need not, cannot,* or *should not* be obeyed; but his message will be enforced by demonic coercive measures, ranging from severe economic harrassment to the death penalty. Those people who refuse to conform will find themselves unable to buy or sell. A little later they will be targeted for execution. See Revelation 13:11-17. The wicked process reaches its peak under the sixth plague (Armageddon, Revelation 16:12-16), when almost the whole world polarizes in hostility against the small minority who by God's grace keep His commandments and are sealed by His Spirit in mind and hand, thought and deed.

We're left in no doubt as to the outcome of Armageddon. Just in time, the "kings from the east" arrive, the Father and the Son, He who sits on the throne and the Lamb of God. Revelation 16:12. "The Lamb will conquer them, for he is Lord of lords and King of kings." Chapter 17:14. The white-horse Rider appears in His blood-stained robe, accompanied by the armies of heaven. To rescue His people He slays their foes, and an angel standing in the sun calls on the birds to feed on the enemies at the great supper of God.

Here is the supernatural Stone of Daniel 2:34, 35, 44, 45, smiting the great image on its feet and grinding the nations to dust so fine the winds of summer blow them away.

Christ's appearance as holy Warrior reminds us again of the Israelites' Exodus from Egypt. When God delivered His people by drowning their enemies in the Red Sea, the Israelites danced and chanted gratefully, "The Lord is a man of war." Exodus 15:3.

But truly, Jesus is the Prince of Peace. See Isaiah 9:6. He doesn't prefer war. Satan, not He, began the great controversy.

For thousands of years Jesus has been patient. He has limited Satan from expressing many of his worst hostilities, but in general He has allowed him to pursue his own pertinacious inclinations. How pained Jesus must have been all through the long, long centuries to see injustice, famine, warfare, and pestilence prevalent in the world. But He has had to let rebellion unveil its innate horrors, because we have needed to learn by observation how dreadfully bad sin is and to what awful kinds of things sin leads. See pages 331-340.

Now, in spite of thousands of years of God's mercy, in spite of Christ's loving life and death, in spite of the messages of the three angels in the end time, and in spite of the fact that only recently the whole earth has been illuminated with God's glory lived out in the character of God's loyal ones (pages 463, 464)—in spite of all these considerations, the vast majority of earth's inhabitants prefer Satan's insolence to God's commandments and join him in waging war against the Lamb, their Saviour. Like Eve in Eden (page 315), they choose to trust the words of the serpent—and of the beast and the false prophet—rather than the Word of God.

So **"the beast was captured, and with it the false prophet who in its presence had worked the signs by which he deceived those who had received the mark of the beast and those who worshiped its image. These two were thrown alive into the lake of fire that burns with sulphur. And the rest were slain by the sword of him who sits upon the horse, the sword that issues from his mouth; and all the birds were gorged with their flesh."** Revelation 19:20, 21.

No human sinner left alive. We must observe clearly that all unsaved human sinners are destroyed at the second coming. Not one is left alive. When the beast and the false prophet are cast into the lake of fire, *all the "rest"*—every remaining sinful human—is **"slain."**

Unrepentant and rebellious, they have failed to accept God's invitation to feast at the marriage supper of the Lamb. Now in a prophecy almost repellent in its realism,[1] their dead bodies become food for birds of prey at the great supper of God.

But Christ's famous nonhuman enemy, along with his demonic cohorts, remains alive, helpless and hopeless, throughout the thousand years.

Satan bound for a thousand years. In the third scene of our present series (Revelation 20:1-3), John saw an angel come down from heaven holding in his hands, **"the key of the bottomless pit and a great chain."** Fascinated, John watched as the angel **"seized the dragon, that ancient serpent, who is the Devil and Satan, and bound him for a thousand years, and threw him into the pit, and shut it and sealed it over him, that he should deceive the nations no more, till the thousand years were ended. After that,"** John learned in some mysterious manner, Satan **"must be loosed for a little while."**

These two events, the binding and releasing of Satan, mark the beginning and end of the thousand years. So does another pair of events that we'll look at in the next section, the first and second resurrections.

We found on page 250 that the term "bottomless pit" (*abussos* or *abyss* in Greek) appears in Revelation 9:1, 2 for the lifeless, sandy sweeps of the vast Arabian Desert. In Romans 10:7, *abyss* is the grave, something even more lifeless than the Arabian Desert. In the old Septuagint translation of Genesis 1:2, *abussos* is the Greek word underlying the English word *deep* (in the R.S.V.). It helps describe the surface of our planet before Creation week, when it was "without form and void."

Jeremiah 4:23-26 says that the earth is going to be "waste and void" again sometime. Looking ahead to that fearful future, Jeremiah wrote, "I looked, and lo, there was *no man*. . . . The fruitful land was a desert, and all its cities were laid in ruins before the Lord, before his fierce anger." The sky "had no light," he added, and the mountains "were quaking." Isaiah 24:1-3, too, speaks of a time when the "earth shall be utterly laid waste and utterly despoiled."

The idea has become popular that the millennium will be a golden age for planet Earth. According to these Bible prophecies, however, the thousand years will be "the world's millennial night."[2]

And what will Satan be doing all these darkened, dismal thousand years? Nothing at all, except bitterly regretting the loss of his place in heaven, futilely plotting his final desperate attempt to get it back, and, I expect, suppressing vicious infighting and countering countless accusations among his fallen-angel followers. Having taught his angels to rebel against God, he can hardly count on them to be loyal to himself or to one another.

Divorced parents who teach their children to hate the other parent run the risk of being hated themselves in the long run.

I read once of a criminal in the Middle Ages who for punishment was locked in a barrel along with poisonous spiders and snakes. I thought of Satan chained among his demon hordes during the thousand years.

The Bible says that Satan will not be deceiving the nations during all this long period. And why not? Because there won't be anyone left alive on earth to listen to him. His chain is a symbol of his circumstances. We all use the expression "my hands are tied."

The wicked will *all* have been slain at the second coming, and the righteous will all have been caught up to "the *clouds*" to "meet the Lord *in the air.*" 1 Thessalonians 4:17. They will have been carried away ("raptured") in triumph to that beautiful home city which Jesus, in John 14:1-3, said He was going to prepare for us all.

The righteous are taken to heaven. At the last supper before His crucifixion, Jesus dropped some hints about His upcoming departure from the earth which made His disciples extremely apprehensive. They asked Him what He meant by what He said, and He reassured them. He promised solemnly that if He went away He would come back to get them, and meanwhile He would be preparing a special place to take them to.

Christ's words as translated in the King James Version are very famous and dearly loved, "Let not your heart be troubled: ye believe in God, believe also in me. In my Father's house are many mansions: if it were not so, I would have told you. I go to prepare a place for you. And if I go and prepare a place for you, I will come again, and receive you unto myself; that where I am, there ye may be also."

The statement shows that the place Jesus was promising to prepare for His people was not located here on earth! It was far away. It was in His "Father's house."

And when Jesus said He would come back and "receive you unto myself; that where I am, there ye may be also," didn't He make it plain that He plans to take us away to that prepared place?

If He had intended to tell the disciples that on His return He was planning to live with us here, wouldn't He have said something like, "I am coming back again so that where *you* are I can be also"? But this is the opposite of what He said!

There will indeed be a time when Christ will bring His prepared place down to earth, but that time isn't the second coming. It's at the end of the thousand years.

When Jesus gathers His people and leaves planet Earth at the beginning of the thousand years, there will be only one kind of human left alive—the loving, loyal, dedicated, forgiving, sincerely beautiful kind. And everyone like this will be safe and happy with Jesus, speeding on that joyous song-filled voyage through the starry sky to the Father's house.

Then who and what will be left on earth? Satan and his anguished fallen angels. Darkness closing in, and the deepening chill of millennial night. The earth's surface, broken by earthquake and charred by fire. Twisted girders and crumbled concrete, where factories and airports and vast populous cities once stood. And among the only sounds: the sigh of the wind, the moaning of evil spirits, the flapping of wings, and the tearing of flesh as the birds of prey gorge themselves at the great supper of God.

May everyone who reads this book be among the happy crowd accompanying Jesus Christ on His triumphal journey home.

As the redeemed on the cloud start heavenward with Christ and the angels, birds of prey swoop down to tear at the dead bodies of the wicked.

III. Judgment and the First Resurrection

We come to the fourth scene in the millennium division, Revelation 20:4-6. **"Then I saw thrones,"** John says, **"and seated on them were those to whom judgment was committed."**

Long before, Daniel too had viewed a judgment scene involving many thrones. See Daniel 7:9-14. But the pre-advent phase of the final judgment which Daniel described will have been completed before John's millennial judgment scene begins.

Two groups who judge. Whom does John see carrying on this millennial judgment? He singles out two groups for special mention, (a) **"The souls* of those who had been beheaded for their testimony to Jesus and for the word of God,"** and (b) those **"who had not worshiped the beast or its image and had not received its mark on their foreheads or their hands."** He adds, **"They came to life, and reigned with Christ a thousand years."** The underlying Greek and some English translations do not have **"they came to life"** but simply that "they lived."

The people in John's second group were alive at the second coming, valiantly resisting the dragon's lies and threats, courageously refusing to worship the beast or its image, sincerely celebrating the seventh-day Sabbath.

I trust that I and my family—and you and your family—will all belong to this second, happy group.

John's first group, the beheaded martyrs who have been resurrected, seems unduly limited. It includes only martyrs, not all the other believers who have died through the years; and of the martyrs, it names only the relatively few who were beheaded. Many martyrs were burned or drowned or tortured to death. Even the apostle Peter apparently was martyred by crucifixion,[3] not by losing his head; yet Jesus included Peter along with His other disciples when He promised that in the future kingdom they would "sit on thrones judging." Luke 22:28-30. Paul told the believers in Corinth that one day *they* would "judge the world." 1 Corinthians 6:2.

Revelation is a book of symbols! The beheaded martyrs stand symbolically for all of the martyrs. And if John focuses on the martyrs rather than on the millions of other believers who sleep in Christ and who will one day live and reign and judge with Him, we remember that Revelation as a whole is concerned primarily with persecuted Christians and with the nations and religious bodies which persecute them.

Elsewhere the Bible lets us know that all believers (not just the martyrs) will come to life at the second coming. For instance, 1 Corinthians 15:22, 23 says, "As in Adam all die, so also in Christ shall all be made alive. But each in his own order: Christ the first fruits, then *at his coming those who belong to Christ*."

"This is the will of my Father," said Jesus in John 6:40, "that *every one* who sees the Son and believes in him should have eternal life; and I will raise him up

---

* For the Bible meaning of "souls" see pages 214-220.

497

at the last day." Even Revelation 20:6 says, **"Blessed and holy is he who shares in the first resurrection!"** All the blessed and holy people who are dead come to life at the second coming.

By exception, a few persons who are neither blessed nor holy also come back to life at that time. Daniel 12:1, 2 says that at the end of the world, when Michael stands up, "many of those who sleep in the dust of the earth shall awake, some to everlasting life, and *some to shame* and everlasting contempt."

The ones who are resurrected to shame and contempt are referred to in Revelation 1:7 as "every one who pierced him." They come to life just long enough to share the fulfillment of the oath Christ made to the high priest at His trial that the high priest would see the Son of man coming on the clouds. These people, who shared in crucifying Christ, would probably prefer not to be resurrected.

Daniel says that "many" who sleep will "awake" at this time, because there are many others who will not awaken. Says Revelation 20:5, **"The rest of the dead did not come to life until the thousand years were ended."** These are the people who at the close of the thousand years will be resurrected only to be judged, convicted, punished, and die again.

"This is the first resurrection," says John, summarizing what we have read so far. Revelation 20:5. At the beginning of Revelation, John had heard Jesus declare, "I died, and behold I am alive for evermore, and I have the keys of Death and Hades." Chapter 1:18. Jesus will use those keys to glorious effect at His second coming, raising His loving followers to eternal youth and reuniting families and friendships long separated by death. What marvelous happiness, what joyful tears, what squeals of delight! One of the major messages of Revelation is the glory of the first resurrection.

"Blessed and holy is he who shares in the first resurrection! Over such the second death has no power, but they shall be priests of God and of Christ, and they shall reign with him a thousand years." Revelation 20:6.

By mentioning a first resurrection John implies a second.

The millennium begins with the resurrection of the righteous and ends with the resurrection of the wicked. Those who are raised at the beginning are raised to everlasting life. Those who are raised at the end live only a short time before dying again forever.

Significance of the millennial judgment. It would be difficult to over emphasize the significance of the judgment which the redeemed carry on during the thousand years. This judgment does not, however, decide who among the dead are to be saved or lost. That decision has already been made. Everyone who is dead during the millennium is irretrievably lost.

Evidently, then, the redeemed are going to audit books, reexamining the evidence on which God has made His decisions. "Do you not know that the saints will judge the world?" 1 Corinthians 6:2, 3 asks. "Do you not know that we are to judge angels?"

Many people who are saved will miss their loved ones. Imagine your own feelings if you find yourself there with the Lord but without one or more members of your immediate family. Mothers will wait with bated breath, hoping that God will tell them their son or daughter really is among the millions who are saved and will be showing up soon in the crowd. Husbands will grieve for absent wives, children for parents and grandparents. Tears will not all be wiped away till the thousand years have closed. See Revelation 21:4.

Among our greatest surprises upon arriving at the heavenly city will be discovering people there whom we thought would never make it. Other people won't be there we were certain would be. Many people may be surprised if *we* arrive there.

Many happy people will be surprised to find *themselves* there! When Jesus thanks them for feeding and clothing Him in the person of the hungry and economically deprived, they will protest in astonishment, "Lord, whenever did we see You hungry or in rags?" See Matthew 25:34-40.

Confidence in God's leadership. God wants us to have complete confidence in His leadership. This is why He has already spent several thousand years patiently dealing with His creatures in heaven and on the earth. Another thousand years? Why not?—if it will serve to answer everybody's questions about how God has dealt with us.

At the end of the thousand years, individuals we have known will be committed to annihilating flames. God is deeply concerned that before this happens we will have had time to understand completely why such a fate is required.

During the thousand years the righteous will serve as **"priests."** One of a priest's privileges, by definition, is to talk with God on behalf of others. It appears that during the thousand years God will actually invite His people to dialogue with Him about the nature and fate of their loved ones.

It's the kind of thing God did for Abraham before He committed Sodom and Gomorrah to annihilating flames. You might like to review the gripping account in Genesis 18.

In Genesis 18 God, traveling on foot and looking like an ordinary human, paid Abraham a surprise social call. Hospitable as always, Abraham had his unrecognized Guest rest a bit and enjoy something good to eat. After the meal, Abraham accompanied Him a little distance on His journey. At an elevated spot (as we may assume) overlooking the doomed cities in the Jordan Valley, they stood together and talked awhile—and God told Abraham what He was about to do.

Abraham was shocked. But understanding at last who his Guest really was, the dear old man immediately began interceding for the two wicked cities. He knew many businessmen and their families there. Bad as they were, surely the cities as a whole were not so bad that they had to be destroyed.

Sensing God's own concern, Abraham boldly reminded Him of His fairness. "Shall not the Judge of all the earth do right?" he asked. Then humbly and earnestly he requested God not to destroy the cities if in Sodom there were as few as fifty righteous people among the total population.

499

To Abraham's great encouragement, God quickly accepted his terms. But on second thought Abraham feared there might not be as many as fifty righteous. He lowered his figure to forty-five, and then successively to forty, thirty, twenty, and ten. And each time God graciously agreed.

When next morning the cities were destroyed, Abraham was heartbroken—but he understood. He knew without doubt that God was too loving and fair, that He cared about people too much to have destroyed the cities without sufficient reason. And Abraham also came to realize that the cities were far more evil than he had supposed. They didn't contain even ten upright persons.

Later Abraham learned that the three or four good folk who did live in Sodom were rescued by God before the holocaust.

The righteous who are alive when Jesus comes, and the millions of others who are raised in the first resurrection, will serve as judges and priests during the thousand years. Functioning in their dual capacity they will fill a crucial role in the great-controversy process. They will confirm to their eternal satisfaction how earnestly and patiently God cared for lost sinners. They will perceive how heedlessly and stubbornly sinners spurned and rejected His love. They will discover that even seemingly mild sinners secretly cherished ugly selfishness rather than accept the value system of their Lord and Saviour.

IV. The Second Resurrection and the Lake of Fire

"And when the thousand years are ended, Satan will be loosed from his prison and will come out to deceive the nations which are at the four corners of the earth, that is, Gog and Magog, to gather them for battle; their number is like the sand of the sea. And they marched up over the broad earth and surrounded the camp of the saints and the beloved city; but fire came down from heaven and consumed them, and the devil who had deceived them was thrown into the lake of fire and sulphur where the beast and the false prophet were, and they will be tormented day and night for ever and ever." Revelation 20:7-10.

Don't let it worry you that the Bible talks about the **"four corners"** of the earth. We who live in the age of science talk about a "square meal." Language abounds in metaphors.

The symbolic terms **"Gog"** and **"Magog"** are adapted from the names of ancient Israel's northern enemies in Ezekiel 38:2. Here they stand for all of God's enemies—northern, southern, eastern, and western—all of the unsaved nations of all the world's generations.

Under Satan as their grand marshal, the unsaved nations stream in from the four directions of the compass and lay siege to the **"beloved city."**

Revelation focuses on two cities, the great city, which is the harlot, the false mother, and Babylon; and the holy city, which is the Lamb's bride, the true mother, and New Jerusalem. In Revelation 17, you remember, the kings of the earth turned against the harlot city, to "devour her flesh," "burn her up with fire," and "hate" her. Verse 16. Babylon was the hated city.

By contrast, the **"beloved city"** is New Jerusalem, the Lamb's bride. It is a symbol of the Christian Church, which Christ *"loved"* and "gave himself up for." Ephesians 5:25.

The second resurrection. We have seen that Revelation sometimes provides summary introductory scenes and fills in the details in later scenes. The scenes which introduce the true mother (chapter 12:1-6) and the leopard-bodied beast (chapter 13:1-4) are examples of this procedure. See pages 319-331. In Revelation 20, as we read about Satan and the nations attacking the beloved city, we wonder where the wicked nations can have come from, they all being dead. We wonder how they could gather around New Jerusalem, the city being up in heaven.

We get our answers in the more detailed scenes which follow. In the sixth scene we learn that at the end of the thousand years the wicked dead are all raised to life in the second resurrection. In scene seven we learn that New Jerusalem comes floating down from heaven.

Arranging the events in true chronological sequence, we see that New Jerusalem descends and the lost are raised to life immediately at the end of the millennium. After this, the lost gather around the city and are destroyed.

The unsaved dead are raised to life by the voice of Jesus, who presumably comes down to earth along with New Jerusalem and all its happy, loving inhabitants. In John 5:28, 29 Jesus made plain that *"all* who are in the tombs will hear his voice." Those who have "done good," He went on, will rise "to the resurrection of life"; but "those who have done evil" will, on hearing His voice, rise "to the resurrection of judgment." The two groups hear His voice a thousand years apart.

Surrounded by the vast numbers of sinful people who come to life in the second resurrection, all eager to be deceived again, Satan is effectively released from his symbolic pit and chain. At once he sets about persuading the nations that they can successfully attack New Jerusalem, just as the end-time nations once attacked and overcame the great city Babylon. Revelation 17:16.

How can they be so foolish? We wonder how Satan and his followers can be so foolish!

But isn't all sin foolish? The wise thing in every situation is to follow God's leadership and accept His will. Whenever, even in the little things of life, we choose our own way in defiance of God's way, we are being foolish. The more wicked we become, the more foolishly we behave. Having resisted God for thousands of years, Satan commits this final folly, the closing chapter in his relentless but fatuous attempt to sieze God's throne and reign on it in place of Jesus Christ.

His followers having likewise accustomed themselves to irrational thinking, they are deluded by Satan's deceptive predictions and line up behind him. Perhaps, in their desperation, they conclude they have no other chance, no other hope. Perhaps Satan's miraculous signs and wonders convince them that he has supernatural powers that more than match the Lord's.

We may assume that the propaganda of the "three frogs" is called into play. In a sense, this terminal conflict is a second episode in the battle of Armageddon, the ultimate battlefield of the great controversy between Christ and Satan, the agelong war of the dragon against the Lamb.

Can you see them now, marching in from every direction, converging on the immense and glorious holy city? In their ranks is every sinner who ever lived, except for the repentant, forgiven, transformed ones who are already safe with Christ. The giants who lived before the Flood are there, and some who came later, such as Goliath and his clan, towering over everyone else. Alexander the Great is there and his Hellenistic hosts. So too are Genghis Khan, Attila the Hun, Napoleon, and Hitler, and all the other emperors and generals like them, men of unquestionable military talent, some of whom in their first life fought many a war and never lost a significant battle.

Millions, no, multiplied billions of men and women follow them, rank on rank. Satan and his demons lead the way and consolidate the flanks. With such an army, Satan's propaganda machine insists, the city must fall. Or perhaps it says that at the sight of such an immense army God will even yet change His law rather than destroy the lives of so many of His intelligent created beings, every one a person for whom Christ died.

In Satan's last battle, against the Holy City, the resurrected wicked will be led by commanders like Napoleon, Genghis Khan, Hitler, Attila.

The immense hostile throng takes its position under the transparent golden walls of the beloved city, alert for the signal to attack. The dust settles. A hush prevails. Suddenly, God again assumes the initiative, and we enter the sixth scene of the millennium division.

Judgment at the great white throne. Says John, **"I saw a great white throne and him who sat upon it; from his presence earth and sky fled away, and no place was found for them. And I saw the dead, great and small, standing before the throne, and books were opened. Also another book was opened, which is the book of life. And the dead were judged by what was written in the books, by what they had done. And the sea gave up the dead in it, Death and Hades gave up the dead in them, and all were judged by what they had done. Then Death and Hades were thrown into the lake of fire. . . . And if any one's name was not found written in the book of life, he was thrown into the lake of fire."** Revelation 20:11-15.

Here in the sixth scene of the millennium division is the fourth and closing phase of the final jugment. In the first phase of the judgment, Father and Son moved to a new place in the heavenly sanctuary, the dealings of the oppressive little horn were reviewed, the saints were exonerated, and the beast was condemned to the lake of fire. Daniel 7:9-14. See GC 1:115-119. In the second phase, Jesus at His second coming separated the "sheep" from the "goats," taking the sheep to heaven and consigning the goats to death. Matthew 25:31-46. See pages 41, 42. In the third phase of judgment, the redeemed during the thousand years at God's invitation evaluated His dealings with sinners and dialogued with Him on their behalf. See pages 498-500. Now in the fourth and ultimate phase of the final judgment, every human who has ever lived gathers around God's great white throne.

What a moment this will be! "All who have ever lived on this earth will be there. All the kings and their subjects; all the conquerors and the peoples they have subjugated; all the tyrants and the people they have persecuted; all the popes and the priests; all the preachers and their congregations; all the rich and the poor; all the cruel and the kind; all the mean and the generous; all—yes, all the people of all nations, all languages, all colors, and all climes."[4] Some will be safe and comfortable inside the city. Most will be lost and terrified, outside.

Every knee will bow. Now is to be fulfilled the prediction of Philippians 2:10, 11 that "at the name of Jesus every knee should bow, in heaven and on earth and under the earth, and every tongue confess that Jesus Christ is Lord, to the glory of God the Father."

But how can all these people bow their knees to Christ and call Him "Lord" when large numbers standing at the throne lived their lives before Jesus Christ was born, or passed their lifetimes in non-Christian lands? They do not know who Jesus is. Many others standing at the throne are angry to be found outside the city, believing themselves quite as good as anyone who has been admitted.

God is still concerned that everyone perceive His fairness. He wants the lost especially to acknowledge that He wanted to save them and that it was their own

503

day-by-day decisions that made them what they have become. Evidently, then, He will at this moment provide some means whereby everyone can know about Jesus—and can see himself or herself as being truly unfit for the society of the good, gentle, unselfish people.

We can assume that God will stage a breathtaking panoramic dramatization of the great controversy from beginning to end. In imagination even now we can see it being played in the sky above the city. There it is, God's happy, peaceful heaven before sin began there. Lucifer's own joy before he cherished jealousy and turned himself into the devil. The tragic war in heaven. Satan and his rebellious angels being "thrown down." Revelation 12:8.

The drama shifts to earth. God creates our first human parents happy, holy, and healthy—and Satan uses a serpent to spoil their joy and ours. The drama continues, reaching the birth of Jesus and reviewing His unselfish life and cruel death. "Every one who pierced him" remembers the events of His death only too clearly. The gospel went out into the world, and often those who believed it were harrassed and destroyed.

Throughout the drama, everyone recalls the part he played personally in his neighborhood, in his home, in the secrets of his own heart. All persons of all generations "gaze fixedly upon that great white throne, so awful in its sublime majesty, as upon their ears there falls anew a recounting of God's wondrous plan of salvation, of love unstinted, unmeasured and immeasurable, poured out for a race that was lost."[5]

The evidence of God's unlimited selflessness and of their own heedless selfishness is overwhelmingly convincing. Everyone who refused to admit the evidence years ago while mercy lingered admits it now when doing so is useless and too late. Even Satan is constrained by the evidence to acknowledge Christ as King of kings and himself as a miserable troublemaker. "At the name of Jesus *every knee*" will bend, "in heaven and on earth."

The great controversy is drawing to its close. The goodness and fairness of God, the superiority and suitability of His sense of values and His recommended lifestyle stand fully vindicated by the evidence. In the light of plain facts, the whole universe, both loyal and rebellious, unanimously declares that God's ways are just and true.

Remember, you and every member of your family will be there. If you are inside the city, how happy and satisfied you will be. You will reach out and touch your loved ones again and again to realize anew that they are there, to thrill in the assurance that they will be with you forever and ever.

Your eyes will roam over the guilty, grieving, panic-stricken ranks outside and then turn to linger on the radiant form of Jesus. You will love Him as you have never loved Him before. Over and over you will murmur, "Thank You, thank You, Jesus, for all You've done to rescue me from a life of sin."

But what if any of us are outside the city? How we'll long to live our lives again. With what anguish will we recall the moment when we read this page and wish we could change the decision we are making now. How we will regret the mistakes we made, the silly sins we held onto, the nonsense we cherished that God's law cannot, need not, or should not be obeyed.

God help us all decide here and now to be inside the city—and to do everything we can in the meantime to have our loved ones inside with us.

The lake of fire. **"If any one's name was not found written in the book of life, he was thrown into the lake of fire."** Revelation 20:15. The lake of fire burned briefly at the beginning of the thousand years, destroying the beast and the false prophet. Chapter 19:20. Now at the end of the thousand years it flames up again to receive Satan and all the sinners of earth who have come back to life in the second resurrection.

John was well acquainted with rivers in Palestine that ran seasonally and were dry the rest of the year. People who live in arid climates today are similarly acquainted with rivers—and lakes—that fill up in the rainy season but otherwise are perfectly dry. The lake of fire seems to be similarly seasonal. It exists as a **"lake"** only when freshly kindled. Jesus sets it aflame at His second coming. Fire from heaven relights it briefly at the end of the thousand years.

As for the term **"for ever and ever,"** let us thank God it is an idiom for *annihilation* and doesn't mean what it seems to! See pages 410-413. Unrepentant sinners will be **"consumed."** Revelation 20:9.

No doubt most sinners will disappear in an instant. God has no pleasure in the death of the wicked! See Ezekiel 33:11; page 468. Some who have been conspicuous for their stubborn selfishness will suffer only a little less briefly.

"That servant who knew his master's will, but did not make ready or act according to his will, shall receive a severe beating. But he who did not know, and did what deserved a beating, shall receive a light beating. Every one to whom much is given, of him will much be required." Luke 12:47, 48. The punishment will be proportional and adequate—and quickly completed. Satan will doubtless burn the longest, but soon even his sufferings will come to an end.

Death itself will be destroyed! Don't forget it. "Death and Hades [the grave] were thrown into the lake of fire." Revelation 20:14. "The last enemy to be destroyed is death." 1 Corinthians 15:26.

The lake of fire is the ending place for all of Christ's enemies—and for every spirit of enmity against what is right and good—for all eternity.

Here is the time for the fullest application of the principle expressed in Nahum 1:9, "Affliction shall not rise up the second time" (K.J.V.). "Distress will not rise up twice" (N.A.S.B.). "Trouble will not come a second time" (N.I.V.).

"How do you imagine Yahweh?" asks the Jerusalem Bible in its translation of this verse. "He it is who utterly destroys: *oppression will not lift its head a second time.*"

Thank God for a promise such as this!

When the final lingering flame flickers out in the lake of fire, all sinful hostility of every kind imaginable will flicker out with it and will never exist again.

505

V. New Earth and Everlasting Joy

"Then I saw a new heaven and a new earth; for the first heaven and the first earth had passed away, and the sea was no more. And I saw the holy city, new Jerusalem, coming down out of heaven from God, prepared as a bride adorned for her husband." Revelation 21:1, 2.

Here in the seventh scene we read for the first time about the descent of the Holy City from the skies, something we inferred from the massing of the nations around the beloved city (Revelation 20:9) in the fifth scene. See pages 500, 501. Perhaps the descent of the city is mentioned *here* because it will float in the air while the earth burns in the lake of fire, and will again settle down to earth as the planet cools.

"And I heard a loud voice from the throne saying, 'Behold, the dwelling of God is with men. He will dwell with them, and they shall be his people, and God himself will be with them; he will wipe away every tear from their eyes, and death shall be no more, neither shall there be mourning nor crying nor pain any more, for the former things have passed away.' And he who sat upon the throne said, 'Behold, I make all things new.' " Revelation 21:3-5.

The seventh scene in the millennium division presents the climax toward which all the book has been moving. It is also one of the most appealing passages in literature.

What a tender, affectionate picture of God it presents, fondly placing His arm around us, wiping our eyes as our parents did when we were little, and putting an entirely new aspect on things. Truly God cares!

The theme of a joyful new earth is a frequent one in the Bible. " 'What God has prepared for those who love him,' God has revealed to us through the Spirit." 1 Corinthians 2:9, 10. And if it has been "revealed" to us, then it belongs "to us and to our children." Deuteronomy 29:29.

"According to his promise," says 2 Peter 3:13, "we wait for new heavens and a new earth in which righteousness dwells." Isaiah sang the same theme around 700 B.C., quoting God as He promised,

> I create new heavens
>   and a new earth;
> and the former things shall not be remembered
>   or come into mind. . . .
>
> I create Jerusalem a rejoicing,
>   and her people a joy.
> I will rejoice in Jerusalem,
>   and be glad in my people;
> no more shall be heard in it the
>   sound of weeping

John wrote: "I saw the holy city, New Jerusalem, coming down out of heaven from God, prepared as a bride adorned for her husband.'

and the cry of distress.
Isaiah 65:17-19.

So what—or rather Who—is the spring of all this bubbling happiness? God Himself! God wipes away the tears. God removes all cause for mourning. God creates His people a joy. God Himself rejoices. **"Behold, the dwelling of God is with men."** Revelation 21:3.

We have all known people who made us feel better just by being close. In the second world war, King George of England found that by visiting the sites of bombing raids he could cheer the victims immeasurably. But he could scarcely visit all the places. Newspapers quoted one plucky soul whose home had just been gutted. "If only the King would come," she said, "we'd all feel better."

Being close to the King of kings, God's loyal people will feel a good deal better than they do now! "In thy presence," said David in Psalm 16:11, "there is fulness of joy."

Not merely fullness of joy, the verse says, but fullness of joy for eternity. "In thy right hand are pleasures for evermore." Everlasting happiness.

How long is everlasting? How do *you* visualize eternity? Help your children express their understanding of it.

Years ago when our family lived in California, we enjoyed camping in Yosemite Valley. Dramatic Half Dome towered 4,000 feet above us at the head of nearly vertical granite cliffs. Someone invited us to think of a flock of birds soaring over Half Dome once every thousand years, one of the birds accidently brushing the monolith each time with a feathered wingtip. "When Half Dome has been worn away," our friend smiled cheerily, "eternity will have just begun."

Perhaps you would rather think of eternity in terms of light years and the silent cycles of the stars. In any case,

> When we've been there 10,000 years,
>   Bright shining as the sun,
> We've no less days to sing God's praise
>   Than when we first begun.[6]

All things new. **"I make all things new,"** God promises. Revelation 21:5. And those of us who are with Him, safe inside New Jerusalem as it settles back to earth after the lake of fire has gone out, will watch Him make it new. When He created our earth in the first place, "he spoke, and it came to be; he commanded, and it stood forth." Psalm 33:9. What a thrill to hear Him call again for waterfalls and waterfowl, for animals and trees, and watch the things take form before our eyes!

He will make new heavens and a new earth. By **"new heavens"** we can probably understand the rejuvenation of our solar system and of the nighttime appearance of the starry sky.

The old "sea" was "no more," John says, gone for good, evaporated off in the thunderous firestorm that made earth and sky flee away from the great white throne. See Revelation 21:1; 20:11. "The heavens will pass away with a loud noise, and the elements will be dissolved with fire, and the earth and the works that are upon it will be burned up." 2 Peter 3:10.

At present, water covers 75 percent of our planet's surface. (Some astronomers have suggested calling our home globe Ocean instead of Earth.[7]) So far as we understand, some such immense quantity of water is vital to the maintenance of animals and plants. The other planets in our solar system don't have oceans and are devoid of the animals and plants we know.

But wouldn't our planet's surface be a great deal more attractive if its vital blanket of ocean were torn into little patches; that is to say, if it were divided into countless lovely lakes, small and large—many with sailboats on them catching the breeze?

Perhaps this is what God has in mind for His sparkling new seas. For certain, He has something in mind for our dry old deserts! Deserts now blight a third of the 25 percent of our planet's surface that isn't ocean. But one day, "The wilderness and the dry land shall be glad, the desert shall rejoice and blossom." Isaiah 35:1. And if the desert will laugh and flower, what about forests, orchards, meadows, and river valleys?

New but still recognizable. God has promised to make all things new. But evidently things won't be so entirely new that we won't recognize anything or anybody. A new car is still a car, even if the color, horsepower, and brandname are changed. A metal baseball bat is recognizable beside an old wooden one.

Isaiah 65:21 says we'll "build houses and inhabit them" and set out plants and "eat their fruit." Evidently there'll be houses and plants and fruit; but the houses will be of new design and new materials. Plants and fruit will represent new varieties, textures, and taste.

Lions, Isaiah 65:25 tells us, will "eat straw like the ox." So lions will be recognizable even though changed beyond a doubt. We don't at present know many vegetarian lions!

People will be new, with new bodies, new memories, new vigor, new freedom from the old inner bent to evil. "The eyes of the blind shall be opened, and the ears of the deaf unstopped; then shall the lame man leap like a hart, and the tongue of the dumb sing for joy." Isaiah 35:5, 6.

But though God's people will be "new," they won't be so new that we won't recognize one another. After His resurrection from the dead, Mary recognized Jesus by the way He said her name; Thomas identified Him by the scars in His hands and side; Cleopas and his friend, by the familiar way He offered thanks before a meal. See John 20:11-16, 26-29; Luke 24:30, 31.

Of course, by the time the earth is recreated at the end of the millennium, the redeemed will have had a thousand years to get accustomed to one another's new appearance.

Bodies with ability. Our new bodies won't be vaporous "souls," as timid folk have sometimes supposed. In His resurrected body Jesus could still eat regular food; and He invited His disciples to handle Him and confirm that He was made of sturdy stuff, of "flesh and bones." Luke 24:39. God's redeemed will not be puffs of mist. They will build houses, set out plants, and eat fruit. They will "long enjoy the work of their hands." Isaiah 65:22.

Sabbath in the new earth. Sabbath keeping is another "new" yet by no means unfamiliar custom that will be regularly observed on the earth made new. "For as the new heavens and the new earth which I will make shall remain before me, says the Lord; so shall your descendants and your name remain. From new moon to new moon, and *from sabbath to sabbath*, all flesh shall come to worship before me, says the Lord." Isaiah 66:22, 23.

The weekly Sabbath was one of God's finest birthday presents to the newly created human race. See Genesis 2:1-3. We are reassured to learn that it won't be taken away from us, in spite of the terrible way we have behaved.

What wonderful Sabbath gatherings we can anticipate! In the congregation, millions of redeemed brothers and sisters in Christ—an astounding sight for any of us and a special surprise for people who in their former lives—as in John's day—knew only little house churches! See Philemon 2 and Colossians 4:15. For class teachers, Peter and Paul taking their turns along with Enoch and Elijah. For musical selections, there'll be the best in human choirs and angel choirs and even the living creatures quartet!

Satan, in his jealous huff, has insinuated for thousands of years that God's law—especially His law about the Sabbath—*needn't* be obeyed, or *couldn't* be, or *shouldn't*. How happy the people will be who refused to believe him and trusted God instead.

One family's imaginings. In our family once in a while we happily speculate on the amazing new things that God just *may* be planning for us all.

"Death shall be no more." Revelation 21:4. Will flower petals rather than falling to the ground be absorbed into the developing fruit? Will new earth apples produce protective enzymes to keep themselves from going bad?

Will our bodies shine? Philippians 3:21 says that God plans to give us "glorious" bodies resembling Christ's glorified body. Fireflies shine because a complex of chemicals in their bodies is switched on like a light when their nerve systems stimulate the release of the chemical pyrophosphate. If our blood were redesigned to carry the right complex of chemicals, and if glands lying under our skin produced the necessary pyrophosphate, we too might glow! If the pyrophosphate were produced only under emotional stimulation, we would glow when we were happy or hungry or in love.

What about travel? God is going to enable us to fly through interstellar space, between earth and heaven, at each end of the millennium. What other travel plans does He have for us? If the speed of light is too slow for reaching outer galaxies, will He have us dart there at the speed of thought?[8]

510

Will you join me this afternoon on the backside of the moon? Will you sled with me tomorrow on the ice fields of Haley's comet? For a breather, we could sit and feel the comet's "dirty iceberg"[9] composition disintegrating on its sunny side and watch it streaming away a light year's distance or so.

Or how about a game of catch on an asteroid for half an hour, tossing its boulders into orbit—and ducking before we get hit by them on the back of our heads?

What thoughts do you enjoy? Maybe our family's imaginings mean little to you. Very well, do some dreaming of your own! How will you and the members of your family feel to be completely fit and strong, as coordinated as Olympic athletes, as free from pain as children, and know that you'll remain this healthy and serene for eternity?

How will you feel knowing that you can study into anything that interests you and that no length of time, however extensive, required to get to the bottom of things will be of any consequence? (Does antimatter really exist, as some scientists say?)

How will you feel to talk with Moses, Adam, and Enoch? What questions will you pose to the apostle Paul? What questions about Revelation would you like to ask the apostle John? How will it be to have Gabriel preach a sermon—or conduct a lab course in celestial navigation?

"Neither shall there be . . . pain any more." Revelation 21:4. What does this

One of heaven's many joys will be planting vines and reaping abundant crops.

mean? No more broken bones—and no more broken homes either or broken promises? Will we open our hearts to people, maintaining truly lifelong friendships, without fear of betrayal or of any painful misunderstanding, ever?

How will you feel to live in a place—a whole nation, a whole world—without a fire department, because there won't be any fires? Without a hospital, because there won't be any ill health? Without police or soldiers, because there'll be neither crime nor war?

How will it be never to need the words *cancer, accident, hunger,* or *fear, drug abuse, bankruptcy, terrorist,* or *bomb?*

The Lord's prayer will at last be gloriously fulfilled, "Thy will be done, on earth as it is in heaven." Matthew 6:10. Daniel 2:35 will be at last completely realized. "The stone that struck the image became a great mountain and filled the whole earth."

"They shall not hurt or destroy in all my holy mountain," Isaiah 65:25 promises, and the reason is given in Revelation 21:8, **"the cowardly, the faithless, the polluted, as for murderers, fornicators, sorcerers, idolaters, and all liars, their lot shall be in the lake that burns with fire and sulphur, which is the second death."**

New earth and new covenant. It's nice to know that murderers and sorcerers and liars won't be able to break into the earth made new; but there's a somber side to this information. The new earth is not for everyone, not even for everyone who would like to be there. The new earth is for people whose desire to be there is so strong they make important changes in their lives ahead of time and let God qualify them for citizenship. **"He who conquers shall have this heritage."** Revelation 21:7. In the letters to the churches we read seven times about the importance of conquering. See pages 115-120.

Evidently *we* had better not be **"cowardly"** or **"faithless"** or **"fornicators."** We'd better stop being **"polluted"** in any sense of the word. We'd better give up telling lies. **"All liars"** will end up, not in the new earth but in the lake of fire. So will the **"faithless"** people who promise something and fail to go through with it. And the **"cowardly"** people who are ashamed to admit that they're Christians, afraid in public to stand up for what is right—they too will be missing there.

The unforgiving will be left out, people who hold a grudge, who can't seem to get over their desire to get even with someone. "If you forgive men their trespasses, your heavenly Father also will forgive you; but if you do not forgive men their trespasses, neither will your Father forgive your trespasses." Matthew 6:14. Inasmuch as "all these things are thus to be dissolved," 2 Peter 3:11 exclaims, "what sort of persons ought you to be in lives of holiness and godliness!"

Such sort of holy, godly persons as we need to be we can never be on our own. We give in to weakness all too easily; we repeatedly do the cheap, mean thing. We cannot be fit for the earth made new until we are ourselves made new. "Truly, truly, I say to you," said Jesus, "unless one is born anew, he cannot see the kingdom of God." John 3:3.

But God, who deeply desires us to enjoy His gorgeous new earth, has provided

512

the new covenant whereby we can each be made anew. And Jesus died to activate the new covenant, showing how very dear indeed we are in His eyes. See GC 1:234-238. In the new covenant God promises that if we'll cooperate with Him He will (1) completely forgive all our sins, (2) send His Holy Spirit to write His loving law in our hearts and minds, and (3) become our God and draw each one of us into membership among His people. Jeremiah 31:31-33; Ezekiel 36:26.

Revelation 21:3 is quoting the new covenant when it says, **"Behold, the dwelling of God is with men. He will dwell with them, and *they shall be his people,* and God himself will be with them."**

"Also he said, *'Write this,* for these words are trustworthy and true.' And he said to me, 'It is done! I am the Alpha and the Omega, the beginning and the end. To the thirsty I will give from the fountain of the water of life without payment.' " Revelation 21:5, 6.

"The beginning and the end." God made the earth "very good" at the beginning of human history. Genesis 1:31. It was soon severely scarred by sin; but at the end of sin He'll make the whole earth new again, and it will be very good indeed!

"The beginning and the end." "I am sure that he who began a good work in you will bring it to completion at the day of Jesus Christ." Philippians 1:6.

"The beginning and the end." All who by faith drink the spiritual water of life offered to us free (see Isaiah 55:1) on this present earth, who drink it until they are justified and sanctified and glorified, will drink it literally and be filled with immortal life in the earth made new.

Further Interesting Reading

In Arthur S. Maxwell, *The Bible Story,* volume 8:
    "Signs of His Coming," page 160.
    "How Jesus Will Return," page 170.
In *The Bible Story,* volume 10:
    "When Jesus Comes," page 196.
    "Good Wins at Last," page 210.
In *Bible Readings for the Home:*
    "Christ's Second Coming," page 246.
    "Manner of Christ's Coming," page 250.
    "The Resurrection of the Just," page 255.
    "The Millennium," page 260.
In Arthur S. Maxwell, *Your Bible and You:*
    "History's Glorious Climax," page 457.
In Ellen G. White, *The Triumph of God's Love:*
    "God's People Delivered," page 555.
    "The Earth in Ruins," page 571.

Page numbers for each book refer to the large, fully illustrated edition.

513

Your Questions Answered

If you wish, you may skip around in this section for now or proceed at once to the next chapter, page 523.

1. Does Paul say Christ will bring the redeemed from heaven with Him at the second coming? A popular interpretation of 1 Thessalonians 4:14 is that at the second coming Jesus will bring with Him the "disembodied souls" of the righteous so they can be reunited with their bodies at the resurrection.

This interpretation of the passage would be correct (a) if it were really what the passage says and (b) if when Christians die their "disembodied souls" really went to heaven.

As for (a), the verse doesn't *say* Jesus will bring disembodied souls with Him. It says, "For since we believe that Jesus died and rose again, even so, through Jesus, God will bring with him *those who have fallen asleep.*" The message is that just as God resurrected Jesus and brought Him out of the grave, so "through Jesus" as His divine Agent God will resurrect Christians who have "fallen asleep" and *"bring"* them, too, *out of the grave*.

How God will do this through Christ is described in the following verses, especially verses 16 and 17, "The Lord himself will descend from heaven with a cry of command, with the archangel's call, and with the sound of the trumpet of God. And the *dead in Christ will rise* first; then we who are alive, who are left, shall be caught up together with them in the clouds to meet the Lord in the air." God will bring the dead out of their graves when Jesus calls them to come back to life.

As for (b) and the question about what happens to us when we die or "fall asleep," see again our discussion on pages 73-77, 214-220.

2. Is the millennium really a thousand years long? Because Revelation is a book of many symbols, there is a possibility that the thousand years of chapter 20 is symbolic rather than literal. If so, acquaintance with the message of the book as a whole suggests that the fulfillment will require less rather than more than a thousand years. Our study has indicated two purposes for the millennium: the punishment of Satan and his fellow rebels on earth and an examination (judgment) by the redeemed in heaven. The nature of God's mercy suggests that, if anything, He would prefer to keep Satan in chains a shorter rather than a longer period. The nature of God's wisdom suggests that the redeemed saints won't need a full thousand years to satisfy themselves, as they audit the records, that the Judge of all the earth has, in fact, done right. The nature of God's love suggests that He will give His redeemed people all the time they need to get their questions answered.

The thousand years should not be seen as 365,000 years on the basis of a day for a year. This principle applies principally to the 2300 *days* of Daniel 8:14 (which speaks of 2300 evenings and mornings, where the phrase evenings and mornings means days), and to the 1260 *days* (which are referred to seven times in Daniel and Revelation, twice expressly as 1260 days). The prophecy of Revelation 20, however, doesn't talk about a "thousand days" and certainly not about "365,000 days." It speaks instead about a unique prophetic entity, a "thousand years." Nor does Psalm 90:4 apply here, with its observation that a thousand years in God's sight is like a day. This statement applies to all thousand-year periods, not just the millennium, and says how all of them appear to God, not what they really are. The approximately 2,000 years which have passed since the cross may seem like only a couple of days to our eternal and infinite God, but to say that, in fact, only two days have passed since the cross would be meaningless.

In the absence of compelling guidelines as to how or why we ought to interpret the thousand years of Revelation 20, it is best for us to use the Bible's own term for the period. When the millennium actually arrives, God will likely inform us unequivocally as to whether the period is literal or not.

3. What are the main interpretations of the millennium? We noticed on page 481 that there are three main interpretations of the millennium: premillennialism, postmillennialism, and amillennialism. Some subdivisions of premillennialism are important enough for us to glance at also.[10]

Premillennialism. There is general agreement that most Christian writers during the first three or four centuries can be described as premillennialist.[11] In *premillennialism* the *pre-* means "before," and these Christians believed that Jesus was going to come literally, soon, and *before* the millennium.

As long as the Roman Empire was dominated by pagan rulers, and especially when it was hostile to the church, most Christians believed that only the personal intervention of Jesus Christ at His second coming could bring about a state of affairs under which His followers could sit on thrones and judge the world as promised in Revelation 20:4. Hence most Christians were premillennialists.

Amillennialism. In 313 Emperor Constantine issued a decree giving the church religious freedom. In 325 he presided at the most crucial moments of the pivotal Council of Nicaea. In 336 he was baptized. In 380 and 381 Emperor Theodosius the Great required Roman citizens to be Trinitarian Christians! By the early 400s, the army was expected to consist only of Christian soldiers. Many bishops enjoyed greatly enhanced prestige and influence.

In such a setting, first Tichonius, a Donatist "heretic," and then the great St. Augustine (354-430) taught that the millennium had already begun.[12] The church's bishops, Augustine observed, were already sitting and judging on their episcopal thrones in fulfillment (so he said) of Revelation 20:4; thus there was no need to wait for a future millennium. In *amillennialism* the *a-*

515

means "no" and refers to the belief that there is no future millennium, only the one we're living in now.

As a part of his total position, Augustine also taught that the "antichrist" was a future individual who would persecute for three and a half years at the end of the millennium, just before the literal second coming of Christ.

Because of Augustine's great influence in other matters, his amillennialist views held the field during the Middle Ages, though premillennialist groups sprang up from time to time.

Millennialism in the Reformation. Most Protestant writers early in the Reformation era (that is, in the 1500s) were still amillennialist—but not exactly of the Augustinian type. They believed they were living nearly at the *end* of the millennium and that the the literal second coming was close at hand. They were also convinced that "antichrist" had already appeared in the form of Christian Rome and that his 1260 days, which were 1260 years on the year-day principle, were running out.[13] The year-day principle and the belief that the "antichrist" was fulfilled in the Roman Church, viewed from its darker side, were hallmarks of the Protestant Reformation.

By the early 1600s Luther's grand emphasis on Bible study resulted in a revival of premillennialism. Johann Alsted (1588-1638), a well-known Reformed theologian, began to teach premillennialism again in Germany. In Britain Joseph Mede (1586-1638), an influential theologian at Cambridge University, quite independently of Alsted came reluctantly to the conclusion that amillennialism was wrong, after years of patient thought and Bible study.[14]

Partly as a result of Mede's influence, Britain in the 1600s experienced a great new interest in the second advent of Christ, many writers on the subject looking for it to take place at the beginning of a future millennium.

Accompanying this resurgence of premillennialism in Britain was continued confidence in the Reformation understanding of the year-day principle and of the fulfillment of Daniel and Revelation in the history of the Roman church.[15] It should be added that in the 1600s Britain witnessed a significant new interest in Christ's ministry in the heavenly sanctuary; and besides this, Britain also experienced a sharp new conviction that the fourth commandment, the one about the Sabbath, was morally binding on Christians.[16] Indeed, as early as the 1570s a deep impression was felt by many that "England needed an improved Sabbath observance." The belief gained ground that Sabbath observance was essential to the realization of the millennial New Jerusalem.[17]

Postmillennialism. But about a century after the revival of premillennialism came an outburst of postmillennialism. What Augustine had been to amillennialism, Daniel Whitby (1638-1726) was to postmillennialism.[18] Whitby, a clergyman in the Church of England, like Augustine, gathered up, systematized, and popularized ideas that had earlier occurred to other minds.

In *postmillennialism*, the *post-* means "after." Whitby insisted that Christ's literal second coming would occur after the millennium. In this he agreed

516

with Augustine. He also made use of Augustine's idea that the antichrist would appear for three and a half years at the end of the millennium, a view which by now sharply distanced him from the Protestant Reformation.

But Whitby also urged, this time in harmony with the premillennialists, that the beginning of the millennium was still future, something Augustine had denied. To round out his view he taught that the first resurrection would be fulfilled in the conversion of the Jews (who would thus "come to life" spiritually), and that after their own conversion the Jews would help convert the Gentiles and thus help bring in a thousand years of Christ's reign over human affairs.

Many British Christians felt comfortable with Whitby's views. They naturally liked the idea that soon the world would become a happier place. They began to focus increasing attention on the Jews and their conversion to Christianity.

American Christians, in contrast to their British counterparts, tended to remain premillennialist during the 1700s; but with the American Revolution and the enthusiastic rise of the new United States they became convinced that God was about to use America to usher in a new age for the whole world. Thus around 1800 many Americans switched and became postmillennialists.

At the same time, the termination of the 1260 days in the French Revolution increased peoples' interest in the year-day principle. Restudy of the year-day principle, in turn, led some postmillennialists and many premillennialists in Britain and America (and to some extent in other countries as well) to hope that the millennium would begin at the end of the 2300 year-days, that is, some time in the middle 1800s. See our discussion on pages 274-278, 349-356.

The widespread hope that Christ was coming in the middle 1800s has been called the great second-advent awakening. In the United States the principal protagonists of premillennialism in the face of a great tide of postmillennialism were, as we have seen, the Baptist lay preacher William Miller and his numerous associates. In Britain the principal premillennialists in the 1820s included Henry Drummond, a wealthy banker and member of Parliament, William Cunninghame, George Faber, and for a while Edward Irving.

But before we go on, let us notice that amillennialism, premillennialism, and postmillennialism are all alive today, and that though they all use the word *millennium*, they mean rather different things by it. Amillennialists, who believe we're living in the millennium now, say that the millennial life-style is the one we're experiencing now. Postmillennialists say that life during the thousand years will be in many ways similar to what we know now but enhanced by economic prosperity and continuous world peace. Only premillennialists say that, as a result of Christ's visible second coming, the millennium will represent a radically different age.

Adventism and premillennialism. Now let's get back to where we were a few moments ago. We were saying that the great second-advent awakening occurred at a time (the 1820s to 1840s) when postmillennialism was enjoying con-

517

siderable influence among British and American Protestants—and that at this time (especially in the 1830s and 1840s) William Miller and his associates were the most prominent proponents of premillennialism in the United States.

In the British Isles at about this same time (the 1830s and 1840s) John Nelson Darby (1800-1882) began to emerge as one of premillennialism's most outstanding advocates. As a young Anglican minister serving in Ireland, Darby attended the Powerscourt prophetic conferences in Dublin, which were modeled on the earlier Albury Park prophetic conferences conducted by Henry Drummond in south England. Later he settled for a while in Plymouth, on the south coast of England.

Though always a premillennialist, in the process of his career Darby championed a controversial form of millennialism as unique in its own way as Augustine's and Daniel Whitby's were in theirs.

We mentioned on page 353 that Manuel de Lacunza, the Chilean missionary whose writings did much to stimulate the new interest in Christ's second advent, was a Jesuit. As a Jesuit, Lacunza held to a concept of prophecy that was strongly influenced by his Jesuit predecessor, Francisco Ribera, who had rejuvenated what is often known as "futurism." Ribera—and also his brilliant disciple, Cardinal Roberto Bellarmine—consciously opposed the Reformation doctrine that the little horn of Daniel and the abomination of 2 Thessalonians and the beast of Revelation were symbols of the worst in Roman Christianity. Instead, Ribero and Bellarmine said, these symbols were yet to be fulfilled in the future, in a brief three and a half years by a personal antichrist who had not yet appeared. This brand of futurism was "devised by Jesuit scholars," observed British writers of the time, "specifically to counter the Protestant understanding of history."[19]

Edward Irving translated Lacunza's work, *The Coming of Messiah in Glory and Majesty*, from Spanish into English. In the process, perhaps unwittingly, he popularized Ribera's and Bellarmine's anti-Protestant interpretations along with the second-advent hope.

Through Lacunza, evidently, Darby adopted Ribera's futurism. In harmony with Whitby's postmillennialism, Darby also taught that the beginning of the millennium would be marked by the conversion of Jews who would proceed at once to convert large numbers of Gentiles. As his own special contribution—though there remains a controversial question as to exactly who originated the new idea[20]—Darby taught that Christ's second advent will occur in two stages, the first a pre-tribulation "secret rapture" of the church, and only the second stage, seven years later, being visible, when Jesus will come to rescue the recently converted Jews and their numerous Gentile adherents.

Darby became an almost incessant traveler, visiting many different countries to spread his beliefs. He made several trips to the United States. By his death in 1882 he could count nearly one hundred small study groups in America dedicated to his ideas, in addition to others in other countries.

Not that everyone who liked Darby's futurist premillennialism accepted his entire system. Many conservative evangelical Protestants through the years who have lined up with his futurism have insisted that God has only one special people, His church, and not two special people, His church *and* the Jews, as Darby insisted. "In Christ Jesus," they have quoted from Galatians 3:26-28, "there is neither Jew nor Greek . . . ; for you are all one." Many have also insisted that the Bible nowhere teaches a pre-tribulation secret rapture but says instead that at His coming, "every eye will see him." Revelation 1:7.[21]

Thus the advent awakening in Britain resulted in various forms of *futurist* premillennialism. On the other hand, the advent awakening in North America resulted in an updated form of *historicist* premillennialism. This American historicist premillennialism continued to proclaim a single second coming at the beginning of the thousand years. Using the tools of modern scholarship it found increasing evidence in favor of the Reformers' year-day principle and warned that the Protestant Reformers were right in the way they identified the little horn and the man of lawlessness. This form of premillennialism also honored the English Reformation by augmenting its regard for the fourth commandment and for Christ's ministry in the heavenly sanctuary. It taught from the Bible that at the end of the 2300 year-days Jesus commenced a heavenly ministry as vital in its own way as His death on the cross. And it called dynamic attention to the privileges of the seventh-day Sabbath of the fourth commandment. In the process it circled the world and won millions of adherents.

Premillennialism in demand. Between Darby's death in 1882 and the Great Depression of the 1930s a form of postmillennialism sometimes called the social gospel gripped the more liberal and modernist theologians and ministers in the United States. Poor immigrants were suffering severely in America's large industrial cities. To meet their needs, countless sermons and books called for social activism and social legislation that would turn America into the kingdom of God, create "alabaster cities" "undimmed by human tears,"[22] and in effect make the second coming of Christ unnecessary.

But a great many Americans, especially in small towns, hungered for books and sermons that glowed with the "blessed hope" of the second coming.

Different forms of premillennialism were available to meet their need. Each form was an outgrowth of the great second-advent awakening, and each maintained a thrilling emphasis on the second coming. One of the views, *historicist* in its interpretation of prophecy, taught that the fulfillment of Daniel and Revelation in the history of God's dealings with His church is rich with lessons and encouragement for men and women today. It called attention to the judgment that Jesus began in the heavenly sanctuary at the close of the 2300 days. And it invited people to keep all the Ten Commandments, rejoicing that under the New Covenant God's Holy Spirit is able and eager to seal us into joyous, loving obedience to all God's requirements, including the privileges of the Sabbath commandment.

Futurist premillennialism, however, particularly of Darby's preferred variety called attention less to the heavenly sanctuary than to the rebuilding of a Jewish temple in the Middle East, where the old sacrifices and circumcision would be renewed. The seventh-day Sabbath would be observed by converted Jews, no doubt, but for church members to keep it would be wrong if not impossible.

Many Americans, now hungry for a premillennial second coming, have chosen the type that leaves out the Sabbath. From the standpoint of the message in *God Cares*, this seems very sad. By confining Sabbath observance to the Jews, these premillennial Christians are, in effect, saying that even with the help of the Holy Spirit, church people today *cannot, need not,* or *should not* keep the fourth commandment. They say that church people need not keep the seventh-day Sabbath because it is only for Jews; they should not keep it, for to do so would be a form of legalism; and in view of "original sin," they cannot keep the day holy anyway.

In focusing attention on the Middle East and a future Jewish temple, these futurist premillennialists are in danger of neglecting the special contemporary work of Jesus in the heavenly sanctuary. Thus they come very close to repeating the mistakes of the medieval Christian church. See pages 326, 327. Perhaps they are innocently tripped into this position by Darby's doctrine that prophecy says nothing about the medieval church.

One of the many purposes of *God Cares* is to let people who love Christ's appearing know that there is more than one premillennial option available.

References

1. Charles R. Erdman, *The Revelation of John* (Philadelphia: The Westminster Press, 1966), p. 152.

2. Uriah Smith, *The Prophecies of Daniel and the Revelation*, rev. ed. (Mountain View, Calif.: Pacific Press Publishing Assn., 1944), p. 739.

3. Tertullian, *On Prescription Against Heresies*, 36; ANF 3:260, says that Peter endured a passion like his Lord's. Compare John 21:18, 19.

4. Arthur S. Maxwell, *Great Prophecies for Our Time* (Mountain View, Calif.: Pacific Press Publishing Assn., 1943), pp. 290-292.

5. *Ibid.*

6. This stanza, commonly sung as part of John Newton's "Amazing Grace," is not included in his *Olney Hymns* (London: W. Oliver, 1779), the source of "Amazing Grace." Wayne Hooper, letter to the author, November 19, 1984, says, "Our best information indicates it was written by John P. Reese."

7. Ron Miller and William K. Hartmann, *The Grand Tour: A Traveler's Guide to the Solar System* (New York: Workman Publishing, 1981), p. 43.

8. See Arthur Whitefield Spalding, *Christ's Last Legion* (Washington: Review and Herald Publishing Assn., 1949), pp. 752, 753.

9. Miller and Hartmann, *Grand Tour*, p. 177.

10. Two books that discuss aspects of various millennial views are Millard J. Erickson, *Contemporary Options in Eschatology: A Study of the Millennium* (Grand Rapids,

Mich.: Baker Book House, 1977) and Robert G. Clouse, ed., *The Meaning of the Millennium: Four Views*, with contributions by George Eldon Ladd, Herman A. Hoyt, Loraine Boettner, and Anthony A. Hoekema (Downers Grove, Ill.: InterVarsity Press, 1977).

11. See, for example, Clouse, ed., *Millennium*, p. 9.

12. See LeRoy Edwin Froom, *The Prophetic Faith of Our Fathers*, 4 vols. (Washington, D.C.: Review and Herald Publishing Assn., 1946-1954) 1:465-489. Augustine's views are preserved in his *City of God*, bk. 20, esp. chs. 6-9; NPNF, 2d ser., 2:425-431.

13. B. W. Ball, *The English Connection* (Cambridge, England: James Clarke, 1981), pp. 202, 214, 215.

14. *Ibid.*, p. 214, 216; compare Froom, *Prophetic Faith*, 2:610, 611, 542-549.

15. Ball, *English Connection*, p. 202. See also Bryan W. Ball, *A Great Expectation: Eschatological Thought in English Protestantism to 1660*, Heiko A. Oberman, ed., Studies in the History of Christian Thought, vol. 12 (Leiden: E. J. Brill, 1975).

16. Ball, *English Connection*, pp. 102-119; 138-158; Winton U. Solberg, *Redeem the Time* (Cambridge: Harvard University Press, 1977), pp. 27-80.

17. Solberg, *Redeem the Time*, pp. 54, 58. By "Sabbath" most English Sabbath observers meant Sunday; but their theology and practice emphasized the fourth commandment as moral and binding and prepared the way for seventh-day Sabbath observance.

18. Daniel Whitby announced his postmillennialism in his *A Paraphrase and Commentary on the New Testament*, 2 vol., 2d ed. (London, 1706), 2:715-742.

19. Ball, *English Connection*, p. 205.

20. See Ernest R. Sandeen, *The Roots of Fundamentalism,* reprint (Grand Rapids, Mich.: Baker Book House, 1978), pp. 64, 90; and Dave MacPherson, *The Incredible Cover-up* (Plainfield, N.J.: Logos International, 1975).

21. For a comparison of the two forms of futurist premillennialism, see, for example, two popular works, W. Graham Scroggie, *The Great Unveiling* (Grand Rapids, Mich.: Zondervan Publishing House, 1979), which favors the secret rapture, and George Eldon Ladd, *The Last Things* (Grand Rapids, Mich.: William B. Eerdmans Publishing Co., 1978), which strongly opposes it. Sandeen, *Roots of Fundamentalism*, pp. 208-232, presents a history of the controversy in an early stage of it.

22. Katharine Lee Bates, "America the Beautiful," 1904, *The Church Hymnal,* (Washington, D.C.: Review and Herald Publishing Assn., 1941), no. 503.

Revelation 21:9 to 22:21

The Lamb's Bride

Introduction

We are drawing close to the end of Revelation. We are now ready for the New Jerusalem division and the final conclusion. Congratulations for staying by! We are also getting near to the end of our helpful overall chiasm, which has served us so very well.

Introduction and conclusion (prologue and epilogue). Revelation's introduction, or prologue (chapter 1:1-8), told us that Jesus sent His "angel" to reveal what must "soon take place." Just before the conclusion, or epilogue (chapter 22:10-21), we are reminded that **"the Lord, the God of the spirits of the prophets, has sent his angel to show his servants what must soon take place."** Revelation 1:1; 22:6.

Revelation began with a blessing on the one who "reads" the book "aloud" and on those who "hear" it read. It ends with a blessing on everyone who **"keeps the words of the prophecy of this book."** Chapter 1:3; 22:7.

At the beginning John was told to write down what he would see and send it "to the seven churches." At the end Jesus reminds him that the message of the book is **"for the churches."** Revelation 1:11; 22:16. It is for us and for our families.

The seven churches discussed in the first division of the book were scattered in seven cities. Seeing them embattled by temptation and persecu-tion, Jesus encouraged them with promises to the "conquerors." In the New Jerusalem division we find the church at peace, free from all its one-time enemies, settled happily in the Holy City. The promised rewards are being fulfilled.

As you follow along, you will notice that we are commencing our New Jerusalem division with Revelation 21:9 and ending it at 22:9. We're doing this in view of what we talked about on pages 422-425. On those pages we found that the fall-of-Babylon division (chapter 17:1 to 19:10) presents a striking contrast to the New Jerusalem division (chapter 21:9 to 22:9) and that the two divisions begin and end in similar ways.

Each division *begins* with John's being taken by a plague angel to see something. Each *ends* with John's falling at the feet of the angel and being reminded to worship God instead.

New Jerusalem, real or symbolic? Thoughtful readers have asked whether perhaps New Jerusalem is symbolic rather than an actual city. They point to its possibly cubic proportions, its transparency, and especially to its relationship to the great city Babylon. Babylon, they point out, represents the totality of people who have persecuted and who have chosen to worship God in their own way. By comparison, they say, New Jerusalem is a symbol of the fellowship of sincere

523

GOD CARES THE LAMB'S BRIDE

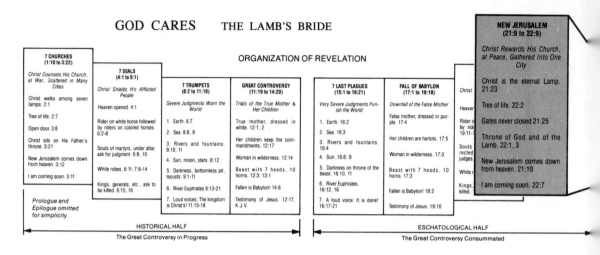

From seven churches to New Jerusalem, God has known every development before it occurred.

Christians who have endured persecution and have chosen to obey God at any cost.

These Bible readers cite Ephesians 2:20, where the apostles are spoken of as the foundation of the church. In Revelation the names of the apostles are written on the foundations of the Holy City. New Jerusalem, they conclude, is the church of God, purified, glorified, and immortalized. It is not, they say, an actual city.

Undoubtedly New Jerusalem is a symbol of the church. It is the symbol of Christ's "kingdom," which He "marries" at the consummation of the pre-advent judgment. See *Your Questions Answered*, pages 407-410.

But a thing can be a symbol and still be real. In the news, "the White House" and "Washington" often stand for the United States. Though they are symbols without a doubt, there is also a real White House, and isn't Washington a real city?

In Bible times "Babylon" was a symbol, but Babylon was also a real city. In fact, "Babylon" would have had little if any symbolic value in the

book of Revelation if it hadn't been an actual city in the time of Daniel. The fallen mother church is called "Babylon" because she resembles the oppressive actual city of the same name. Likewise, the Lamb's bride or church is called "New Jerusalem" because she resembles the glory and purity of an actual city of that name.

In Old Testament times God asked Abraham to leave his house in the civilized city of Ur and spend the rest of his life as a nomad, living in tents. He encouraged Abraham to do this by promising him a home someday in a permanent city. Abraham took God seriously and "looked forward to the city which has foundations, whose builder and maker is God." Hebrews 11:10. Compare Genesis 12:1-9. God took His own promise seriously: "God is not ashamed to be called their God, for he has prepared for them a city." Hebrews 11:16.

When Christ's disciples pointed to the sacrifices they had made, Jesus encouraged them with promises of real rewards. "Every one who has left houses or brothers or sisters or father

524

or mother or children or lands, for my name's sake, will receive a hundred-fold, and inherit eternal life." Matthew 19:29.

And, of course, in the upper room just before the cross, Christ spoke of real rewards in words that are unforgettable: "Let not your heart be troubled," He said. "In my Father's house are many mansions: if it were not so, I would have told you. I go to prepare a place for you. And if I go and prepare a place for you, I will come again, and receive you unto myself; that where I am, there ye may be also." John 14:1-3, K.J.V.

New Jerusalem is a real city, to which Jesus went home to "prepare" in some way for us.

Revelation an open book. In the epilogue, Jesus said to John, **"Do not seal up the words of the prophecy of this book, for the time is near."** Revelation 22:10. The long-time prophecies in the book of Daniel were sealed until the end time. See Daniel 12:4. But as we saw on pages 274-278, these long-time prophecies were unsealed when the end time commenced around 1798 and 1844. Christ's command, **"Do not seal up"** this book of Revelation, is located next to His assertions in verses 12 and 20, **"I am coming soon."** It seems, therefore, that Revelation was to be open and understandable, especially in the last days. And as we have seen, it is in our day that Revelation has been most clearly understood.

Like Daniel, the book of Revelation contains the 1260-day prophecy and

---

THE SECOND HALF OF REVELATION: A DUAL FOCUS ON THE ULTIMATE PUNISHMENT OF THE REBELLIOUS AND ON THE ULTIMATE REWARD OF THE RIGHTEOUS IN THE END TIME

1. *Focus on punishment*

   A   The plagues   15:1-16:21

   B   Circumstances related to the plagues: Fall of Babylon, the false mother   17:1-19:10

   A plague angel shows John the great harlot.   17:1-19:8
   Afterward John attempts to worship the angel.   19:9, 10

2. *Focus on reward*

   B′   Circumstances related to the holy city: The millennium   19:11- 21:8

   A′   The holy city: Descent of New Jerusalem, the Lamb's bride   21:9-22:21

   A plague angel shows John the Lamb's bride.   21:9-22:7
   Afterward John attempts to worship the angel.   22:8, 9

525

references to the final judgment based on the 2300-day prophecy. These prophecies were sealed in the book of Daniel and didn't require further sealing in Revelation. On the other hand, there is much in Revelation that in John's day was to take place **"soon." "The time is near,"** Jesus explained to John. Notably, the letters to the seven churches required immediate comprehension if the local congregations were to benefit from them.

Revelation isn't open in the sense that it can all be easily understood at first reading! There are things in it we're not certain we understand even yet. But the book is filled with practical counsels, encouraging promises, and thrilling prophecies that Jesus intended should begin to help His people right away. So he told John not to seal the book.

"Let the evildoer still do evil, and the filthy still be evil, and the righteous still do right, and the holy still be holy." "Behold, I am coming soon, bringing my recompense, to repay every one for what he has done." Revelation 22:11, 12. For a discussion of these verses see pages 446, 447.

The book is not to be tampered with. **"I warn every one who hears the words of the prophecy of this book: if any one adds to them, God will add to him the plagues described in this book, and if any one takes away from the words of the book of this prophecy, God will take away his share in the tree of life and in the holy city."** Revelation 22:18, 19.

Once again we are reminded of Revelation's serious purpose. Superficiality is to play no part in our relationship with Christ and His message. Even in our interpretation of the book of Revelation we must be on guard lest we depart so far from the true meaning that we virtually write our own prophecy. What does *Christ* say? and What does *He* mean? must be our earnest questions.

By contrast, how different is this recent opinion of a prominent professor of New Testament. Said he, "The Scripture is the church's book. It was written by the church [and] for the church." "There's no reason . . . that I can see why the church can't add to its Scripture—delete from its Scripture. I think the church can do with its Scripture what it wants to."[1] How sad!

They shall reign for ever and ever. Don't overlook Revelation 22:5, **"They shall reign for ever and ever."**

At the end of explaining Nebuchadnezzar's dream about the great image, Daniel was inspired to tell the king, "The God of heaven will set up a kingdom which shall never be destroyed." Daniel 2:44. In the great vision of Daniel 7, the Son of man approached the Ancient of Days at judgment hour, and "to him was given dominion and glory and kingdom"—which He immediately shared with His people. "The kingdom and the dominion and the greatness of the kingdoms under the whole heaven shall be given to the people of the saints of the Most High." Daniel 7:13, 14, 27.

In Revelation 3:21 Jesus promises, "He who conquers, I will grant him to sit with me on my throne, as I myself conquered and sat down with my Father on his throne."

A recurring, unifying theme of both Daniel and Revelation is this promise of our becoming kings and reigning with God and Christ. A king is rich, powerful, and free. When the redeemed receive eternal life and a home in New Jerusalem, they will be richer than any mortal king. Authorized to share in God's own decision making, they'll be powerful without a doubt. And, free not only from persecution and temptation but even from every vice, resentment, and regret, the redeemed will be truly free. "If the Son makes you free, you will be free indeed." John 8:36. **"They shall reign for ever and ever."**

John attempts to worship the angel. What John says about such matters and about New Jerusalem itself are things well beyond our comprehension. As the vision of them faded from his view, the old man stood spellbound, wondering whether he could believe what in the Spirit he had seen and heard. The angel reassured him. At the same time he reminded him of his obligation to put it all down in a book and send it to the churches.

"These words are trustworthy and true," the angel said. **"And the Lord, the God of the spirits of the prophets, has sent his angel to show his servants what must soon take place."** Quoting the Lord God, the angel continued, **" 'And behold, I am coming soon.' Blessed is he who keeps the words of the prophecy of this book."** Revelation 22:6, 7.

John was overwhelmed and not a little confused. Was this glorious person beside him only an angel quoting the Lord God, or was He the Lord Himself?

He tells us, **"When I heard and saw"** these things, **"I fell down to worship at the feet of the angel who showed them to me"**! His experience reminds us of the truly radiant appearance that angels can assume. John had mistakenly attempted to worship an angel once before, at the triumphant climax of the vision about the fall of Babylon.

Now, as then, the angel interrupted him quickly. **"You must not do that!"** he explained to the grateful old man. **"I am a fellow servant with you and your brethren the prophets, and with those who keep the words of this book. Worship God."** Revelation 22:8, 9.

John was deeply moved by the splendor of what his eyes had seen and his ears heard. Alone again on Patmos, how could he ever feel lonely again? Christ was alive; he knew it without a doubt. And Christ was indeed preparing a place for John as He had promised He would in the upper room of long before, on the night before His dreadful trial and crucifixion.

Like John, everyone who loves Jesus enjoys thinking about New Jerusalem. It's time we read what John wrote about it.

NEW JERUSALEM AND THE CONCLUSION

REVELATION 21:9-27

A plague angel invites John to see the holy city. 9 Then came one of the seven angels who had the seven bowls full of the seven last plagues, and spoke to me, saying, "Come, I will show you the Bride, the wife of the Lamb."

The appearance of the city. 10 And in the Spirit he carried me away to a great, high mountain, and showed me the holy city Jerusalem coming down out of heaven from God, [11]having the glory of God, its radiance like a most rare jewel, like a jasper, clear as crystal. [12]It had a great, high wall, with twelve gates, and at the gates twelve angels, and on the gates the names of the twelve tribes of the sons of Israel were inscribed; [13]on the east three gates, on the north three gates, on the south three gates, and on the west three gates. [14]And the wall of the city had twelve foundations, and on them the twelve names of the twelve apostles of the Lamb.

15 And he who talked to me had a measuring rod of gold to measure the city and its gates and walls. [16]The city lies foursquare, its length the same as its breadth; and he measured the city with his rod, twelve thousand stadia; its length and breadth and height are equal. [17]He also measured its wall, a hundred and forty-four cubits by a man's measure, that is, an angel's. [18]The wall was built of jasper, while the city was pure gold, clear as glass. [19]The foundations of the wall of the city were adorned with every jewel; the first was jasper, the second sapphire, the third agate, the fourth emerald, [20]the fifth onyx, the sixth carnelian, the seventh chrysolite, the eighth beryl, the ninth topaz, the tenth chrysoprase, the eleventh jacinth, the twelfth amethyst. [21]And the twelve gates were twelve pearls, each of the gates made of a single pearl, and the street of the city was pure gold, transparent as glass.

The city and its relationship with kings and nations. 22 And I saw no temple in the city, for its temple is the Lord God the Almighty and the Lamb. [23]And the city has no need of sun or moon to shine upon it, for the glory of God is its light, and its lamp is the Lamb. [24]By its light shall the nations walk; and the kings of the earth shall bring their glory into it, [25]and its gates shall never be shut by day—and there shall be no night there; [26]they shall bring into it the glory and the honor of the nations. [27]But nothing unclean shall enter it, nor any one who practices abomination or falsehood, but only those who are written in the Lamb's book of life.

REVELATION 22

1 Then he showed me the river of the water of life, bright as crystal, flowing from the throne of God and of the Lamb [2]through the middle of the street of the city; also, on either side of the river, the tree of life with its twelve kinds of fruit, yielding its fruit each month; and the leaves of the tree were for the healing of the nations. [3]There shall no more be anything accursed, but the throne of God and of the Lamb shall be in it, and his servants shall worship him; [4]they shall see his face, and his name shall be on their foreheads. [5]And night shall be no more; they need no light of lamp or sun, for the Lord God will be their light, and they shall reign for ever and ever.

The angel pronounces a blessing, and John attempts to worship him. 6 And he said to me, "These words are trustworthy and true. And the Lord, the God of the spirits of the prophets, has sent his angel to show his servants what must soon take place. [7]And behold, I am coming soon."

Blessed is he who keeps the words of the prophecy of this book.

8 I John am he who heard and saw these things. And when I heard and saw them, I fell down to worship at the feet of the angel who showed them to me; [9]but he said to me, "You must not do that! I am a fellow servant with you and your brethren the prophets, and with those who keep the words of this book. Worship God."

528

The conclusion (or epilogue). 10 And he said to me, "Do not seal up the words of the prophecy of this book, for the time is near. [11]Let the evildoer still do evil, and the filthy still be filthy, and the righteous still do right, and the holy still be holy."

12 "Behold, I am coming soon, bringing my recompense, to repay every one for what he has done. [13]I am the Alpha and the Omega, the first and the last, the beginning and the end."

14 Blessed are those who wash their robes, that they may have the right to the tree of life and that they may enter the city by the gates. [15]Outside are the dogs and sorcerers and fornicators and murderers and idolaters, and every one who loves and practices falsehood.

16 "I Jesus have sent my angel to you with this testimony for the churches. I am the root and the offspring of David, the bright morning star."

17 The Spirit and the Bride say, "Come." And let him who hears say, "Come." And let him who is thirsty come, let him who desires take the water of life without price.

18 I warn every one who hears the words of the prophecy of this book: if any one adds to them, God will add to him the plagues described in this book, [19]and if any one takes away from the words of the book of this prophecy, God will take away his share in the tree of life and in the holy city, which are described in this book.

20 He who testifies to these things says, "Surely I am coming soon." Amen. Come, Lord Jesus!

21 The grace of the Lord Jesus be with all the saints. Amen.

529

The Message of Revelation 21:9 to 22:21

I. The Bride, the Lamb's Wife

"Come," said one of the plague angels to John, **"I will show you the Bride, the wife of the Lamb."** Revelation 21:9.

In Revelation 17 a plague angel—perhaps the very same plague angel—had invited John to see a very different woman. That time she was the great city, Babylon, who had been immoral with kings. This time John sees a pure and beautiful woman, worthy of the Lamb Himself.

This holy woman, too, is a city, but she is a glorious, radiant, effulgent city, prosperous, clean, and safe.

"In the Spirit he carried me away to a great, high mountain, and showed me the holy city Jerusalem coming down out of heaven from God." Revelation 21:10.

John had watched the city's descent only a few moments earlier. See chapter 21:2. So why was he being shown it again?

We're used to instant replays on TV. Evidently God wanted John to notice things he hadn't seen the first time.

What a sight meets his gaze as he and the angel reach the mountain peak! In the clear, fresh air above them, floating majestically, almost unbelievably, is an entire city, a far larger city than till now John had thought could possibly exist. It's a beautiful city. It shines with **"the glory of God, its radiance like a most rare jewel, like a jasper, clear as crystal."** Revelation 21:11.

The Holy City settles imposingly onto the ground far below; and as John continues to pay rapt attention, his friendly angel points out some of the city's more conspicuous features.

A city foursquare. To convince John that the city really is as big as it looks, the angel miraculously measures it for him with a special golden rod. Revelation 21:15, 16. He shows John that the city is **"foursquare"** and extends for nearly 1400 miles, or **"twelve thousand stadia"** according to the Roman way of measuring. Presumably, the 1400 miles represent its circumference. If so, the city is about 350 miles on a side, roughly the size of New Mexico.

One of the mysteries about the city is that John says its **"length and breadth and height are equal."** Verse 16. Some commentators see a reference to the cubic most holy place in the Old Testament temple. See 1 Kings 6:20. Others picture a very tall city center, marking the location of God's throne. Still others interpret **"equal"** as "in proportion."

When the angel measures the wall he shows it to be 144 cubits (Revelation 21:17), though whether this is a reference to its height or to its thickness John doesn't say. A cubit, as we learned on GC 1:50, 165, is equivalent to half of a man's arm length, usually about 45 centimeters, or 18 inches. On such a basis, the wall is approximately 65 meters, or about 216 feet. In the present instance John explains that it is **"a *man's* measure, that is, an *angel's*,"** so the size in our terms may be quite different. (The angel Gabriel appeared to Daniel once in the "appearance of a man." See Daniel 10:18; 9:21. And the Greek word for **"man"** applied to John's angel is *anthropos*, which can be translated simply, "person.")

A city of twelves. As John's manlike angel calls attention to one feature after another, John notices that the city has twelve gates (Revelation 21:12, 13), three gates on each of its four sides. Each gate is named for one of the twelve Israelite tribes, Judah, Reuben, Gad, and so on. For a list of the tribes, see Revelation 7:5-8.

The doors that hang at the gates are huge opalescent pearls. An angel has been detailed to stand watch beside each one.

The city reposes on twelve superb foundations, each one named for one of Christ's twelve apostles, Peter, James, Andrew, and the rest. For a list of their names see Acts 1:12-26. Enraptured, John, a Roman exile, persecuted for his faith, sees his own name on one of the foundations!

Twelve gates, twelve tribes, twelve foundations, twelve apostles. So many twelves! With a moment's effort—provided you include twelve thousand, and count a hundred and forty-four as twelve times twelve—you can discover twelve twelves.*

All through Revelation we have found sevens. Sometimes we have found a seven expressed as four plus three: four seals with horsemen and three seals without horsemen, for instance; three woe trumpets and four other trumpets. Only in chapters 7 and 12 have we found twelves before. In chapter 12 we saw twelve stars sparkling in the pregnant mother's crown. In chapter 7 we saw 12,000 of God's servants being sealed in each of the twelve tribes, making a total of 144,000 special end-time saints. There is a direct connection between these end-time saints and the twelve gates of New Jerusalem, for each gate is named for one of the tribes.

But although New Jerusalem's twelves mark a break with all the sevens, the break is by no means complete. If seven is three plus four, twelve is three times four.

The twelve tribal gates link New Jerusalem to the Jewish church before the Cross. The foundations named for the twelve apostles point to the close link between Christ's Old Testament church and His new Israel, the church of the Christian era. See Ephesians 2:20.

The twelve foundations are presumably laid side by side; otherwise the lower ones would be invisible. They attract John's special attention because of their color and composition. Each one is made out of a different jewel! See Revelation 21:19, 20. Here is another link with the Old Testament. The Old Testament high priest was outfitted with a costly breastpiece bearing precious stones engraved

---

*Twelve gates, pearls, angels, tribes, foundations, names, apostles, jewels, kinds of fruit, plus 12,000 stadia, and 144 as 12 x 12.

Jewels in the breastpiece of the high priest
Exodus 28:15-21

topaz

emerald

sapphire

jacinth (zircon)

agate

amethyst

beryl

onyx (black)

jasper

sardius

carbuncle (garnet)

diamond

Jewels in the foundations of New Jerusalem
Revelation 21:19, 20

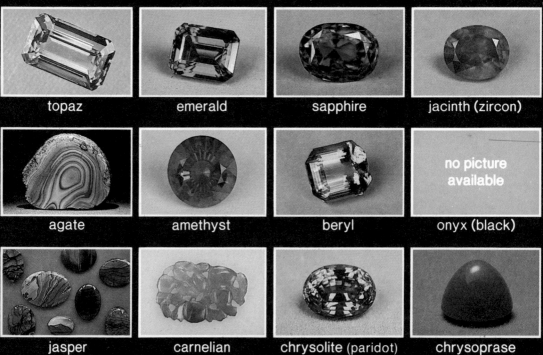

topaz

emerald

sapphire

jacinth (zircon)

agate

amethyst

beryl

onyx (black)

jasper

carnelian

chrysolite (paridot)

chrysoprase

with the names of the twelve tribes. See Exodus 28:15-21. The stones in the breastpiece were laid in a square, three stones in each of four rows. Many of the stones in the breastpiece and in the city foundations are the same. Unfortunately, experts tell us they cannot be certain of the modern identification or color of some of the jewels.[2]

A transparent, walled city. As for the wall of the city, John says it is made of transparent jasper. The main street is paved with transparent gold. In fact, the city as a whole looks like transparent gold. Revelation 21:11, 18, 21.

On one of my bookshelves I have a pair of jasper bookends cut and polished for me by a friend who found the rock in the Mohave Desert many years ago. The jasper is a mixture of various shades of brown. It is attractive. It is also completely opaque.

But John says that New Jerusalem is made of transparent jasper, and even of transparent gold. Any gold I know is as opaque as my jasper. Quite evidently John is using ordinary language to describe things very much out of the ordinary. But then, haven't we all talked about a golden sky at sunset? We know the sky isn't solid gold!

Military insecurity has made city walls a necessity throughout most of human history. But why does a new earth city need a wall? The Bible doesn't say; but personally, I like walls. I think we all like our homes to have walls! I especially like gardens to have walls, mossy stone walls, ivy-covered brick walls, rotting old wooden walls, serpentine walls. Walls impart a sense of mystery, hiding part of the whole so we don't see everything at once. Walls, even glass walls, also impart a sense of belonging, like friendly arms embracing us. I like walls—provided they have doors in them that I can go through whenever I want to. I like to walk past a walled country estate and look in through its open gates. I like even better to walk to a walled public park and go in through its open gates.

The walls of New Jerusalem are friendly walls, strong like a strong friend's arms. And they're provided with open gates, gates that stay open all day and know no night. **"Its gates shall never be shut by day—and there shall be no night there."** Revelation 21:25. They are gates that let people enter. **"The Spirit and the *Bride*** [that is, the *city*] **say, 'Come.' "** Revelation 22:17. No one is kept out for racial reasons, certainly. Though the gates are named for Jewish tribes, the **"nations"** (usually translated "Gentiles," see page 45) enter through them freely. See Revelation 21:24 and 22:2.

A city with no physical temple. Still standing on the mountain peak, John gazes where his angel points, making still further observations. Says John approvingly, **"I saw no temple in the city."** Revelation 21:22.

For more than a thousand years, not counting the Babylonian captivity of Daniel's day and a short time thereafter, the Old Testament temple was the pride and glory of old Jerusalem. But John sees no temple in New Jerusalem. He explains, **"For its temple is the Lord God the Almighty and the Lamb."** Revelation 21:22.

The tabernacle and temple that symbolized God's dwelling place among His

Many stones in New Jerusalem's foundations were also in the High Priest's breastpiece. Not all have been identified, but aren't these beautiful!

chosen people in ancient times had curtains that veiled God's glory. While allowing God to come fairly close to His people, the veils actually separated Him from them. His love made the temple a reality; their sins made the veils a necessity. "You cannot see my face; for man shall not see me and live," said God back in those sad old days. Exodus 33:20.

But John, in vision, is standing on a mountain in the good new days of God's eternity, and sin doesn't exist anymore. **"There shall no more be anything accursed,"** nor any one **"who practices abomination or falsehood."** Revelation 22:3; 21:27. The happy people who throng God's throne carry His **"name"** written **"on their foreheads."** Chapter 22:4. Their characters have come to resemble His own. "He who is left in Zion and remains in Jerusalem will be called holy." Isaiah 4:3. There is no longer any need for separating veils; so there is no longer any need for a temple to hang such veils in! God's loving, obedient people **"shall see his face."** Revelation 22:4.

The heavenly sanctuary or temple has been a prominent feature of the book of Revelation. We have had numerous occasions to refer to it. Christ portrayed Himself as standing by the lamps when dictating His letters to the seven churches. He was introduced as the Lamb before the throne in the holy place. From the altar of incense fell the warning judgments of the seven trumpets. When the temple's inner arena was opened in the end time, "the ark of his covenant" was seen, heralding the end-time commandment keeping of the 144,000. From the same inner court came the seven last plagues. And then the temple was filled with the glory of God so no one could enter it.

But as John and the angel gaze over the city in Revelation 21, the heavenly sanctuary as we have known it has completed its role as the site of Christ's intercession, judging, and Day of Atonement. "Michael, the great prince" has arisen (see Daniel 12:1), the people found in His book have been delivered and resurrected, and no longer is there any need for the ordinary heavenly sanctuary or temple to exist. John says, **"I saw no temple in the city."**

A city of abundance. There's no need, either, for power stations any more. Nor is there occasion for debates about fossil, fission, and fusion generators to manufacture electricity. There is no need even for the sun as a source of energy! **"They need no light of lamp or sun, for the Lord God will be their light." "The glory of God is its light, and its lamp is the Lamb."** Revelation 22:5; 21:23.

No one will ever run out of food or water—no, nor of life itself. The angel shows John **"the river of the water of life, bright as crystal, flowing from the throne of God and of the Lamb."** And **"on either side of the river"** John sees the **"tree of life with its twelve kinds of fruit, yielding its fruit each month."** Revelation 22:1-3. Anyone who has seen a banyan tree can visualize a single tree with many trunks. The fruit of the tree of life evidently contains enzymes and vitamins that prevent the aging process. Even its leaves have **"healing"** powers, preventing every kind of disease. There is neither pain nor death in the earth made new. See chapter 21:4.

534

The city where God makes His home with us. Long ago Jesus lived with human beings for something over thirty years. He was called "Emmanuel," a name that means "God with us." See Matthew 1:23. Now God the Father and God the Son, and apparently the Holy Spirit too (see Revelation 22:17), make the Holy City not only our home but also Theirs, permanently, forever. **"The throne of God and of the Lamb shall be in it, and his servants shall worship him; they shall see his face, and his name shall be on their foreheads."** Revelation 22:3, 4.

How very gracious of God to arrange such a thing, especially after all the anguished grief we've caused. The only adequate explanation is that God likes us and actually wants to live near us. God really cares!

And how we'll love God and enjoy living next to Him!

Have you ever thought about what it will be like to live near God and be able to look into His face—into His powerful, intelligent, yet dear and friendly face? Get your family to talk about God's face. Encourage them to describe it in their own words.

Have you thought what it will be like not only to look into His face but also to listen to Him sing?

When God has us all together with Him at last, He will rejoice over us (see Isaiah 62:5) "as the bridegroom rejoices over the bride." Zephaniah 3:17, 18 promises that He will "exult" over us "with loud singing as on a day of festival."

In Revelation 4 and 5 we listened to angels and elders and living creatures praise God for saving human beings. We heard music more marvelous than anyone has sung on earth. No doubt the angels and elders and living creatures will sing again, just as beautifully, when God gets us at last into His presence. But when God Himself rejoices over us, do you suppose His voice will be any less glorious than theirs? Won't the Creator outperform all His created beings singing in chorus together? What a song we'll hear when God rejoices over us!

And think about the eye contact! God will sing like a bridegroom to his bride. I believe that while God sings, with all His infinite love and tender thoughtfulness, He will manage somehow to look into the eyes of each and every one of us, as if to say, "It's because *you* are here that I feel so glad."

When we are privileged to see God seated on His throne with the living creatures and twenty-four elders surrounding Him and have heard the glorious singing and all, will we see little children climbing into His lap the way in Bible times they climbed into the lap of Jesus? Will young people feel free to walk up to God and ask Him questions? I like to think so.

I'm looking forward to seeing Jesus, aren't you? We've read about Him, heard sermons about Him, pictured Him healing sick people, praying in Gethsemane, serving as our High Priest, coming for us on the clouds. But "face to face with Christ my Saviour, face to face, what will it be?"[3]

Jesus, the very thought of Thee,
    With sweetness fills my breast;

> But sweeter far Thy face to see,
> And in Thy presence rest.[4]

New Jerusalem isn't just a beautiful city. It's the place where, life without end, for ever and ever, God and Christ and the redeemed are going to make their home together.

II. Come! Come! Come!

"The Spirit and the Bride say, 'Come.' And let him who hears say, 'Come.' And let him who is thirsty come, let him who desires take the water of life without price." Revelation 22:17.

"He who testifies to these things says, 'Surely I am coming soon.' Amen. Come, Lord Jesus!" Revelation 22:20.

The book of Revelation closes with arms outstretched. Arms of invitation, prayer, and love.

The Holy Spirit, the sparkling waters flowing along the golden boulevard, and the whole eternal city in all its radiant loveliness hold their arms out, welcoming us, urging us to come. And we who believe are urged to pass the invitation on, holding out our arms, welcoming other people, urging them to come.

And if we love Jesus the way John did, we'll be on our knees with our hearts uplifted praying, "Lord Jesus, don't You wait much longer. Please come soon."

"The Spirit and the Bride say, 'Come.' And let him who hears say, 'Come.' " Christian evangelists, pastors—and neighbors—who believe what Revelation teaches say, "Come." Christian wives and husbands, children, brothers, and sisters sweetly invite one another to come to Christ, drink of the water of life, and find eternal life.

"I am the Alpha and the Omega, the first and the last, the beginning and the end." Verse 13. What Jesus begins, He is able to complete. "I am sure," said the apostle Paul in Philippians 1:6, "that he who began a good work in you will bring it to completion." He is the "pioneer and perfecter of our faith." Hebrews 12:2. If we choose to go with Him, He makes us "more than conquerors through him who loved us." Romans 8:37.

Outside or inside? But if, when He calls and calls again, if when the Spirit and the Bride say, **"Come,"** we choose not to accept the invitation, what then?

"Outside are the dogs and sorcerers and fornicators and murderers and idolaters, and every one who loves and practices falsehood." Revelation 22:15.

God cares! Heaven has only a few more sentences before the book comes to its end, yet once more it reminds us of the importance of character choices. New Jerusalem and the new earth are not for everyone. God is not playing church. He is in earnest. People who choose to be unfaithful to their marriage vows and people who can't be trusted to tell the truth, as well as murderers, idol worshipers, sorcerers, and **"dogs"** (impure evil doers, see Philippians 3:2) will be left out, consumed away in the lake of fire.

536

But how **"blessed are those who wash their robes, that they may have the right to the tree of life and that they may enter the city by the gates."** Revelation 22:14. These happy people find themselves among the **"nations"** who will walk in and out of those glorious open gates where the angels stand to greet them as they pass; and they'll know they have a *right* to pass through. They won't have earned the right. None of us can earn eternal life. Christ purchased the right for us at Calvary, confirmed it during the first phase of the final judgment, and from the Ancient of Days has received kingdom and dominion and shared it at once with His saints. See Daniel 7:13, 14, 27.

Instead of **"wash their robes"** the famous King James Version has "do his commandments." Some Greek manuscripts have one phrase, some the other. The words in Greek are much more similar than they are in English: *plunontes tas stolas auton* [wash their robes] and *poiountes tas entolas autou* [do his commandments]. Either translation will do. Revelation 7:14 points to the need to wash; Revelation 14:12 shows we must obey.

"I Jesus have sent my angel to you with this testimony for the churches." Revelation 22:16. Once again we have evidence that the "testimony of Jesus" (chapter 12:17; 1:2, 9) is the message He gives to us, not the witness we bear about Him. See *Your Questions Answered*, pages 403-406.

"He who testifies to these things says, 'Surely I am coming soon.' " Revelation 22:20. When studying the letters to the seven churches we found warnings that Jesus would "come" to Ephesus, Pergamum, and Sardis with specific punishments. These were not references to the second coming. The only reference to the second coming as occurring "soon" was made in the letter to the Philadelphians, a congregation which represented the whole church near the end of time.

The introduction (or prologue) to Revelation (chapter 1:1-7) says, "Behold, he is coming with the clouds," but says nothing about His coming soon. But in the conclusion (or epilogue) we find, **"Surely I am coming soon"**—and we find it, as we have just observed, in an end-time setting.

Living in the end time. We are living in the end time now. We're in the time of Laodicea, the final stage of the church. See Revelation 3:14-22. We're under the sixth seal, between the falling of the stars and the rolling back of the sky. Chapter 6:12-17. We're between the sixth and seventh trumpets, waiting for the nations to express their final anger and for Christ to take His great power and begin to reign. See chapter 11:14-18. We're in the time of the lamb-horned beast, waiting for the leopard-beast's mortal wound to heal, its image to be erected, and its mark to be affixed. Chapter 13:3, 11-17.

The first angel is announcing that the final judgment is already under way. He is calling everyone to worship God the Creator on the Sabbath of His choice. Revelation 14:6, 7. The second angel is preaching that Babylon is fallen. Chapter 14:8. The third angel is earnestly warning against the mark of the beast. He is at the same time pointing to the patient endurance of those who keep the commandments of God and have the faith of Jesus. Chapter 14:9-12.

537

All over the world, in response to the world-wide proclamation of the gospel in its judgment-hour setting, individuals, families, communities, are "coming out" from all other forms of religion, seeking to keep the commandments of God through faith in Jesus and forming an end-time special people, "the remnant" of the woman's seed. Chapter 14:12; 12:17, K.J.V.

Meanwhile, as the three angels proclaim their heaven-sent message, Satan's three froglike demons are going abroad from the mouths of the dragon, the beast, and the false prophet, deceiving everyone they can and drawing them to the battle of the great day of God Almighty. Revelation 16:13-16. In every charming, persuasive, seductive manner they're telling us we *don't need to,* or *shouldn't,* or *cannot* obey God's law.

We live in the Valley of Decision at the hour of decision. Eternal life and eternal death are the stakes. Which side will you be on?

Which side will your neighbor or friend be on?

Which side will the members of your family be on?

Jesus, the Passover Lamb, died to save children as well as adults, to keep families together. "The things that are revealed belong to us and to our children." Deuteronomy 29:29.

I personally hope to see your whole family say, "Come." If you wish, you may write to me in care of the publishers of this book, and I will regularly remember you and your loved ones in my prayers.

Will you say, "Come?" Will you find ways to *entice* the members of your family to love Jesus? Will you be such a pleasant, helpful Christian that your family members will want to be in the Holy City with you?

Revelation study groups. As we closed the first volume of *God Cares* we talked about conducting study groups in our homes. Reports of numerous such study groups have come to my attention. Would you like to lead a Revelation study group? Almost anyone can do it, because the members of the group read and share, so that no one has to be the last word or the scholar.

Revelation 1:3 promises a blessing for anyone who "reads aloud the words of the prophecy" and for "those who hear." You would be more than repaid for your time and effort! So would everyone who came.

"The Spirit and the Bride say, 'Come.' And let him who hears say, 'Come.' " You could say, "Come" to a family member or to a neighbor or two or to a friend. Two of you would be enough for a start. Ten would probably be too many.

Ask the people (or person) to come to your home at some suitable time. Have everyone read a portion of this book, along with the appropriate Revelation passage. Then let them discuss the meaning of what they have read. Take time near the end or at the beginning to have everyone pray aloud who is willing to, remembering one another and your loved ones and the work of God in other places.

"I Jesus have sent my angel to you with this testimony for the churches."

"He who testifies to these things says, 'Surely I am coming soon.' "

"Amen. Come, Lord Jesus!"

538

Jesus invites us, "Come unto Me." He offers forgiveness, healing, rest. Let's go to Him now, while we can—and live with Him forever.

Further Interesting Reading

In Arthur S. Maxwell, *The Bible Story,* volume 10:
"All Things New," page 205.
In *Bible Readings for the Home:*
"The Home of the Saved," page 545.
"The Conflict Ended," page 552.
"The Game of Life," page 554.
In Arthur S. Maxwell, *Your Bible and You:*
"Your Eternal Home," page 465.
In Ellen G. White, *The Triumph of God's Love:*
"The Controversy Ended," page 581.

Page numbers for each book refer to the large, fully illustrated edition.

References

1. Burton Throckmorton, Jr., professor of New Testament at the Bangor (Maine) Theological Seminary, and member of the inclusive-language lectionary committee of the National Council of the Churches of Christ in the U.S.A., as quoted in *Christianity Today*, December 16, 1983, p. 40.

2. See for example R. C. H. Lenski, *The Interpretation of St. John's Revelation* (Minneapolis: Augsburg Publishing House, 1943, 1963), p. 640.

3. Frank A. Beck, "Face to Face With Christ My Saviour," *The Church Hymnal* (Washington, D.C.: Review and Herald Publishing Assn., 1941), no. 545.

4. Bernard of Clairvaux, tr. Edward Caswall, "Jesus, the Very Thought of Thee," *ibid.,* no. 158.

Acknowledgements

My colleague Kenneth A. Strand, editor of *Andrews University Seminary Studies,* helped immeasurably with his insights into the chiastic structure of Revelation; he also read a large portion of the manuscript. Many other colleagues, too, assisted generously. Andrews University administrators arranged sabbaticals and about two years of leave during the six years of research and writing. At the Pacific Press, Herbert Douglass and his team encouraged me graciously and treated the manuscript like a treasured friend. Lawrence Maxwell, my twin, served skillfully as editor. Artists John Steel and James Converse absorbed tremendous deadline pressures. My wife Pauline was unfalteringly supportive. May God bless them all. May He also richly bless all the readers of this book—and their families.

Selected Bibliography

Ancient Authors

Ambrose. *Letters.* Translation in The Nicene and Post-Nicene Fathers, 2d ser., vol. 10.

Barnabas. *Epistle.* Translation in The Ante-Nicene Fathers, vol. 1.

Chrysostom, John. *Discourses Against Judaizing Christians.* Translation in Fathers of the Church, vol. 68.

Clement of Alexandria. *Who Is the Rich Man That Shall Be Saved?* Translation in The Ante-Nicene Fathers, vol. 2.

Herodotus. *The Persian Wars.* Translation in The Modern Library.

Hippolytus. *Christ and Antichrist.* Translation in The Ante-Nicene Fathers, vol. 5.

Ignatius. *To the Magnesians.* In *The Apostolic Fathers.* Text and translation in The Loeb Classical Library.

Irenaeus. *Against Heresies.* Translation in The Ante-Nicene Fathers, vol. 1.

Josephus: With an English Translation. 9 vols. Text and translation in The Loeb Classical Library.

Julius Africanus. *Chronography.* Translation in The Ante-Nicene Fathers, vol. 6.

Justin. *Dialogue with the Jew Trypho.* Translation in The Ante-Nicene Fathers, vol. 1.

_____ . *First Apology.* Translation in The Ante-Nicene Fathers, vol. 1.

The Koran. Translation in Everyman's Library.

The Koran. Translation in The Penguin Classics. 3d rev. ed.

The Martyrdom of Polycarp. In *The Apostolic Fathers.* Text and translation in the The Loeb Classical Library.

Procopius. *History of the Wars.* Text and translation in The Loeb Classical Library.

Tacitus. *Annals.* Translation in The Penguin Classics.

Tertullian. *First Apology.* Translation in The Ante-Nicene Fathers, vol. 3.

_____ . *The Prescription Against Heretics.* Translation in The Ante-Nicene Fathers, vol. 3.

General

Ahlstrom, Sydney. *A Religious History of the American People.* New Haven, Conn.: Yale University Press, 1972.

Alford, Henry. *The New Testament for English Readers*. 4 vols. Reprint. Grand Rapids, Mich.: Baker Book House, 1983.

Anderson, Roy Allan. *Unfolding the Revelation*. Rev. ed. Mountain View, Calif.: Pacific Press Publishing Assn., 1953, 1961, 1974.

Arthur, David Tallmadge. "Joshua V. Himes and the Cause of Adventism, 1839-1845." Unpublished master's thesis, University of Chicago, 1961.

Aulard, A. *Christianity and the French Revolution*. Translated by Lady Frazer. Boston: Little, Brown, and Company, 1927.

Ball, Bryan W. *The English Connection: The Puritan Roots of Seventh-day Adventist Belief*. Cambridge, England: James Clarke, 1981.

_____. *A Great Expectation: Eschatological Thought in English Protestantism to 1660*. Studies in the History of Christian Thought. Edited by Heiko A. Oberman. Vol. 12. Leiden: E. J. Brill, 1975.

_____. Review of Emmerson, Richard Kenneth. *Antichrist in the Middle Ages: A Study of Medieval Apocalypticism, Art, and Literature*. Seattle: University of Washington Press, 1981. *Andrews University Seminary Studies*, 22 (1984): 363-368.

Baly, Denis. *The Geography of the Bible: A Study in Historical Geography*. New York: Harper & Brothers, Publishers, 1957.

Barnes, Albert. *Notes, Explanatory and Practical, on the Book of Revelation*. New York: Harper & Brothers, Publishers, 1858.

Barnhouse, Donald Grey. *Revelation*. Grand Rapids, Mich.: Zondervan Publishing House, 1971.

Bartlett, John. *Familiar Quotations*. 13th ed. Boston: Little, Brown and Company, 1955.

Bates, Joseph. *Second Advent Way Marks and High Heaps*. New Bedford, Mass.: Press of Benjamin Lindsey, 1847.

Bauer, Chrysostomus, O.S.B. *John Chrysostom and His Time*. Translated by M. Gonzaga. 2 vols. Vol. 1, Westminster, Md.: The Newman Press, 1959; vol. 2, London: Sals and Co. (Publishers), 1959, 1960.

Beckwith, Rogert T. and Wilfrid Stott. *This is the Day: The Biblical Doctrine of the Christian Sunday in its Jewish and Early Church Setting*. London: Marshall, Morgan & Scott, 1978.

Bible Readings for the Home. Rev. ed. Mountain View, Calif.: Pacific Press Publishing Assn., 1963, 1967.

Bickersteth, Edward. *Practical Guide to the Prophecies*. London: Seeleys, 1852.

Blass, F. and A. Debrunner. *A Greek Grammar of the New Testament and Other Early Christian Literature*. Translated by Robert W. Funk. Chicago: The University of Chicago Press, 1961.

Bliss, Sylvester. *Memoirs of William Miller*. Boston: Joshua V. Himes, 1853.

Bokenkotter, Thomas S. *A Concise History of the Catholic Church*. Garden City, N.Y.: Doubleday & Company, Inc., 1977.

Bownde, Nicolas. *The Doctrine of the Sabbath, Plainely Layde Forth*. London, 1595.

Bruce, F. F. *The Books and the Parchments*. 3d ed., rev. London: Pickering & Inglis Ltd., 1950, 1953, 1963.

Bunch, Taylor G. *The Seven Epistles of Christ*. Washington, D.C.: Review and Herald Publishing Assn., 1947.

Burton, Maurice and Robert Burton. *The International Wildlife Encyclopedia*. 20 vols. New York: Marshall Cavendish Corporation, 1969-1970.

Caird, G. B. *A Commentary on the Revelation of St. John the Divine*. Harper's New Testament Commentaries. Edited by Henry Chadwick. New York: Harper & Row, Publishers, 1966.

Cary, M. *A History of Rome Down to the Reign of Constantine*. 2d ed. London: Macmillan & Co. Ltd., 1954.

Case, Shirley Jackson. *The Revelation of John: A Historical Interpretation*. Chicago: The University of Chicago Press, 1910.

Chadwick, Owen. *The Popes and European Revolution.* Oxford: Clarendon Press, 1981.

————. *The Reformation.* The Pelican History of the Church. Vol. 3. Grand Rapids, Mich.: Wm. B. Eerdmans Publishing Co., 1964.

Charles, R. H. *A Critical and Exegetical Commentary on the Revelation of St. John.* 2 vols. Edinburgh: T. & T. Clark, 1920.

Churchill, Winston S. and the editors of *Life. The Second World War.* 2 vols. New York: Time Incorporated, 1959.

Clouse, Robert G., ed. *The Meaning of the Millennium: Four Views.* Downers Grove, Ill.: InterVarsity Press, 1977.

Committee on Diet, Nutrition, and Cancer, Assembly of Life Sciences, National Research Council. *Diet, Nutrition, and Cancer.* Washington, D.C.: National Academy Press, 1982.

Cooper, Douglas. *Living God's Joy.* Mountain View, Calif.: Pacific Press Publishing Assn., 1979.

Crook, John. *Law and Life of Rome.* Ithaca, N.Y.: Cornell University Press, 1967.

Cross, Frank L., ed. *Oxford Dictionary of the Christian Church.* London: Oxford University Press, 1957.

Cross, Whitney R. *The Burned-over District: The Social and Intellectual History of Enthusiastic Religion in Western New York, 1800-1850.* Ithaca, N.Y.: Cornell University Press, 1950.

Cumming, John. *Apocalyptic Sketches; or Lectures on the Book of Revelation.* London: Hall, Virture, and Co., 1851.

Dallimore, Arnold. *Forerunner of the Charismatic Movement: The Life of Edward Irving.* Chicago: Moody Press, 1983.

Darnell, Robert. Letter to the Author. March 22, 1982.

Davidson, Richard M. *Typology in Scripture: A Study of Hermeneutical Tupos Structures.* Andrews University Seminary Doctoral Dissertation Series. Vol.

2. Berrien Springs, Mich.: Andrews University Press, 1981.

Dawson, Christopher. *The Gods of Revolution.* New York: New York University Press, 1972.

Dick, Everett N. "William Miller and the Advent Crisis, 1831-1844." Doctoral dissertation, University of Wisconsin, 1930.

Dobson, James C. *Straight Talk to Men and Their Wives.* Waco, Tex.: Word Books, Publisher, 1980.

Dolan, John P. *Catholicism: An Historical Survey.* Barron's Compact Studies of World Religions. Woodbury, N.Y.: Barron's Educational Series, 1968.

Douglass, Frederick. *Life and Times of Frederick Douglass: Written by Himself.* Rev. ed. Boston: De Wolfe, Fiske & Co., 1895.

Douglass, Herbert E. *The End: Unique Voice of Adventists About the Return of Jesus.* Mountain View, Calif.: Pacific Press Publishing Assn., 1979.

Duckworth, G. E. *Structural Patterns and Proportions in Vergil's Aeneid.* Ann Arbor: University of Michigan Press, 1962.

Duppa, Richard. *A Brief Account of the Subversion of the Papal Government. 1799.* 2d ed. London: G. G. and J. Robinson, 1799.

Easton, Stewart C. *The Western Heritage from the Earliest Times to the Present.* New York: Holt, Rinehart, and Winston, 1961.

The Encyclopaedia Britannica.

The English Hexapla. London: Samuel Bagster and Sons, [1841?].

Erdman, Charles R. *The Revelation of John: An Exposition.* Philadelphia: The Westminster Press, 1936.

Erickson, Millard J. *Contemporary Options in Eschatology: A Study of the Millennium.* Grand Rapids, Mich.: Baker Book House, 1977.

Erlanger, Philippe. *St. Bartholomew's Night: The Massacre of Saint Bartholomew.* Translated from the French by Patrick O'Brien. Pantheon Books. New York: Random House, 1962.

Fiorenza, Elisabeth Schüssler. "Composition and Structure of the Book of Revelation." *The Catholic Biblical Quarterly,* 39 (1977): 344-366.

_____ . The Eschatology and Composition of the Apocalypse." *Catholic Biblical Quarterly,* 30 (1968): 537-569.

Ford, Desmond. "The Abomination of Desolation in Biblical Eschatology." Ph.D. dissertation, University of Manchester, 1972.

Foxe, John. *Book of Martyrs.* New York: Charles K. Moore, 1842.

Froom, LeRoy Edwin. *The Prophetic Faith of Our Fathers.* 4 vols. Washington, D.C.: Review and Herald Publishing Assn., 1946-1954.

Gargett, Graham. *Voltaire and Protestantism.* Studies on Voltaire and the Eighteenth Century. Edited by Haydn Mason. No. 188. Oxford: The Voltaire Foundation, 1980.

Gesenius, William. *Hebrew and Chaldee Lexicon.* Translated by Samuel Prideaux Tregelles. 3d ed. Grand Rapids, Mich.: Wm. B. Eerdmans Publishing Company, 1949.

Gibbon, Edward. *The Decline and Fall of the Roman Empire.* 3 vols. The Modern Library of the World's Best Books. New York: The Modern Library, n.d.

Giblin, Charles H. "Structural and Thematic Correlations in the Theology of Revelation 16-22," *Biblica,* 55 (1974): 487-504.

Godoy, Manuel de. *Príncipe de la Paz (1767-1851): Memoirs of Don Manuel de Godoy, Prince of the Peace.* Edited by J. B. d'Esménard. 2 vols. London: Richard Bentley, 1836.

Gold, Thomas and Steven Soter. "The Deep-Earth-Gas Hypothesis," *Scientific American,* June 1980, pp. 154-161.

Goodspeed, Edgar J. *Problems of New Testament Translation.* Chicago: University of Chicago Press, 1945.

Gordon, C. D. *The Age of Attila: Fifth-Century Byzantium and the Barbarians.* Ann Arbor, Mich.: The University of Michigan Press, 1960.

Green, V. H. H., ed. *Church History Out-lines.* No. 4: *The French Revolution and the Church,* by John McManners. London: S.P.C.K., 1969.

Grosvenor, Melville Bell and Gilbert M. Grosvenor, eds. *National Geographic Atlas of the World.* 4th ed. Washington, D.C.: National Geographic Society, 1975.

Guy, Fritz. "Confidence in Salvation: The Meaning of the Sanctuary." *Spectrum,* 11 (1980): 47.

_____ . " 'The Lord's Day' in Magnesians." *Andrews University Seminary Studies,* 2 (1964): 1-17.

Hales, E. E. Y. *Revolution and Papacy, 1769-1846.* Garden City, N. Y.: Hanover House, 1960.

Harrington, Wilfrid J., O.P. *Understanding the Apocalypse.* Washington, D.C.: Corpus Books, 1969.

Hasel, Gerhard F. *The Remnant: The History and Theology of the Remnant Idea from Genesis to Isaiah.* Andrews University Monographs, Studies in Religion. Vol. 5. 3d ed. Berrien Springs, Mich.: Andrews University Press, 1980.

Haskell, Stephen N. *The Story of the Seer of Patmos.* Nashville: Southern Publishing Assn., 1905.

Heyd, Uriel. "The Later Ottoman Empire in Rumelia and Anatolia." In *The Cambridge History of Islam.* Edited by P. M. Holt, Ann K. S. Lambton, and Bernard Lewis. 2 vols. Cambridge, England: Cambridge University Press, 1970.

Higgins, E. L. *The French Revolution as Told by Contemporaries.* Edited by William L. Langer. Boston: Houghton Mifflin Company, 1938.

Hoge, Dean R. and David A. Roozen, eds. *Understanding Church Growth and Decline, 1950-1978.* New York: The Pilgrim Press, 1979.

Holt, P. M., Ann K. S. Lambton, and Bernard Lewis. *The Cambridge History of Islam.* 2 vols. Cambridge: The University Press, 1970.

Inalcik, Halil. "The Heyday and Decline of the Ottoman Empire." In *The Cam-*

545

bridge History of Islam. Edited by P. M. Holt, Ann K. S. Lambton, and Bernard Lewis. 2 vols. Cambridge, England: Cambridge University Press, 1970.

The Interpreter's Bible. Edited by George Arthur Buttrick, et al. New York: Abingdon Press, 1952-1957. 12 vols.

The Interpreter's Dictionary of the Bible. Edited by George Arthur Buttrick. 4 vols. New York: Abingdon Press, 1962.

Japas, Salim. Cristo en el Sanctuario. Mountain View, Calif.: Pacific Press Publishing Assn., 1980.

Jeremias, Joachim. Jerusalem in the Time of Jesus. Translated by F. H. and C. H. Cave from Jerusalem zur Zeit Jesu, 3d ed., 1967. Rev. ed. London: SCM Press Ltd., 1969.

Johnson, Douglas. The French Revolution. The Putnam Pictorial Sources Series. New York: G. P. Putnam's Sons, 1970.

Johnsson, William G. "Defilement and Purgation in the Book of Hebrews." Ph.D. dissertation, Vanderbilt University, 1973.

_____ . "The Heavenly Cultus in the Book of Hebrews—Figurative or Real?" In The Sanctuary and the Atonement: Biblical, Historical, and Theological Studies. Edited by Arnold V. Wallenkampf and W. Richard Lesher. Washington, D.C.: General Conference of Seventh-day Adventists, 1981.

_____ . "Killing for God's Sake." Liberty, May-June, 1983.

Jones, A. H. M. The Later Roman Empire, 284-602: A Social Economic and Administrative Survey. 2 vols. Norman, Okla.: University of Oklahoma Press, 1964.

Kelly, Alfred H. and Winfred A. Harbison. The American Constitution: Its Origins and Development. Rev. ed. New York: W. W. Norton & Company, Inc., 1948, 1955.

Kendrick, T. D. The Lisbon Earthquake. Authorized American ed. Philadelphia: J. B. Lippincott Company, [1955].

Kepler, Thomas S. The Book of Revelation: A Commentary for Laymen. New York: Oxford University Press, 1957.

Kiddle, Martin, assisted by M. K. Ross. The Revelation of St. John. The Moffatt New Testament Commentary. Edited by James Moffatt. London: Hodder and Stoughton Ltd., 1940.

Kittel, Gerhard and Gerhard Friedrich, eds. Theological Dictionary of the New Testament. 9 vols. Translated and edited by Geoffrey W. Bromiley. Grand Rapids, Mich.: Wm. B. Eerdmans Publishing Company, 1964-1974.

Koch, H. W. Medieval Warfare. A Bison Book. London: Dorset Press, 1982.

Ladd, George Eldon. A Commentary on the Revelation of John. Grand Rapids, Mich.: Wm. B. Eerdmans Publishing Company, 1972.

_____ . The Last Things: An Eschatology for Laymen. Grand Rapids, Mich.: Wm. B. Eerdmans Publishing Co., 1978.

Lampe, G. W. H. A Patristic Greek Lexicon. Oxford: Clarendon Press, 1961.

LaRondelle, Hans K. The Israel of God in Prophecy. Andrews University Monographs, Studies in Religion. Vol. 13. Berrien Springs, Mich.: Andrews University Press, 1983.

Leage, Richard William. Roman Private Law. Edited by C. H. Ziegler. London: Macmillan and Co., 1946.

Lecky, William Edward Hartpole. History of the Rise and Influence of the Spirit of Rationalism in Europe. Authorized ed. 2 vols in 1. London: Longmans, Green, and Co., 1865, 1910.

Leggitt, Deryl Herbert. "An Investigation into the Dark Day of May 19, 1780: Its Causes, Extent, and Duration." M.A. thesis, Seventh-day Adventist Theological Seminary, 1951.

Lenski, R. C. H. The Interpretation of St. John's Revelation. Minneapolis: Augsburg Publishing House, 1943, 1963.

Lewis, Bernard. Islam: From the Prophet Muhammad to the Capture of Constantinople. Vol. 1. Documentary History of Western Civilization. London: The Macmillan Press Ltd., 1974.

_____ . *Islam in History: Ideas, Men and Events in the Middle East.* LaSalle, Ill.: Open Court Publishing Co., 1973.

Lewis, C. S. *A Grief Observed.* Afterword by Chad Walsh. A Bantam Book. New York: Bantam Books, Inc., 1961, 1976.

Lewis, Richard B. "Ignatius and the 'Lord's Day.' " *Andrews University Seminary Studies,* 6 (1968): 46-59.

Liddell, Henry George and Robert Scott. *A Greek-English Lexicon.* Revised by Henry Stuart Jones and Roderick McKenzie. 2 vols. Oxford: Clarendon Press, 1940; reprinted 1951.

Lindsay, Thomas M. *A History of the Reformation.* 2 vols. 2d ed. Edinburgh: T. & T. Clark, 1907.

Lindsey, Hal, with C. C. Carlson. *The Late Great Planet Earth.* Grand Rapids, Mich.: Zondervan Publishing House, 1970.

_____ . *The Rapture: Truth or Consequences.* Toronto: Bantam Books, 1983.

Littell, Franklin H. *The Macmillan Atlas History of Christianity.* New York: Macmillan Publishing Co., 1976.

Lowrie, Samuel T. *An Explanation of the Epistle to the Hebrews.* New York: Robert Carter & Brothers, 1884.

Lund, Nils Wilhelm. *Chiasmus in the New Testament: A Study in Formgeschichte.* Chapel Hill: University of North Carolina Press, 1942.

Luther, Martin. *Luther's Works, American Edition.* Edited by Jaroslav Pelikan and Helmut T. Lehman. 55 vols. St. Louis, Mo.: Concordia Publishing House, 1955- .

MacArthur, Douglas. *A Soldier Speaks: Public Papers and Speeches of General of the Army Douglas MacArthur.* Edited by Vorin E. Wham, Jr., USA. New York: Frederick A. Praeger, Publishers, 1965.

McConkey, James H. *The Book of Revelation.* Pittsburgh: Silver Publishing Society, 1921.

McFayden, Donald. "The Occasion of the Domitianic Persecution." *The American Journal of Theology,* 24 (January, 1920): 46-66.

McKenzie, John L., S. J. *The Roman Catholic Church.* History of Religion Series. Edited by E. O. James. New York: Holt, Rinehart and Winston, 1959.

McManners, John. *The French Revolution and the Church.* Church History Outlines. Edited by V. H. H. Green. London: S. P. C. K., 1969.

McNeill, William H. *The Rise of the West: A History of the Human Community.* Chicago: The University of Chicago Press, 1963.

MacPherson, Dave. *The Incredible Cover-Up: The True Story on the Pre-Trib Rapture.* Plainfield, N. J.: Logos International, 1975.

Maillane, Durand de. *Histoire de la Convention nationale.* In *The French Revolution as Told by Contemporaries.* Edited by E. L. Higgins. Boston: Houghton Mifflin Company, 1938.

Manning, Henry Edward, D.D. *The Temporal Power of the Vicar of Jesus Christ.* 2d ed., with preface. London: Burns & Lambert, 1862.

Marshall-Cornwall, General Sir James. *Napoleon as Military Commander.* London: B. T. Batsford, and Princeton, N. J.: D. Van Nostrand Co., 1967.

Maxwell, A. Graham. *Can God Be Trusted?* Nashville: Southern Publishing Assn., 1977.

Maxwell, Arthur S. *The Bible Story.* 10 vols. Washington, D.C.: Review and Herald Publishing Assn., 1953-1957.

_____ . *Great Prophecies for Our Time.* Mountain View, Calif.: Pacific Press Publishing Assn., 1943.

_____ . *Your Bible and You.* Washington, D.C.: Review and Herald Publishing Assn., 1959.

Maxwell, C. Mervyn. "An Exegetical and Historical Examination of the Beginning and Ending of the 1260 Days of Prophecy." M.A. thesis, Andrews University, 1951.

_____ . *Tell It to the World.* 2d rev. ed.

Mountain View, Calif.: Pacific Press Publishing Assn., 1976, 1977, 1982.

Maxwell, Lawrence. "Christ Coming Soon." *Signs of the Times,* January 1971, pp. 18-25.

Maxwell, Spencer G. *I Loved Africa.* [Guildford, Surrey, England]: The author, 1975.

Meier, John P. "Nations or Gentiles in Matthew 28:19." *The Catholic Biblical Quarterly,* 39 (1977): 94-102.

Michaelson, Victor. *The Mystery of the Beast and His 7 Heads: A Comprehensive Exposition of Past, Present, and Future History.* Box 5141, North Branch, NJ 08876: The author [1984].

Miller, Ron and William K. Hartmann. *The Grand Tour: A Traveler's Guide to the Solar System.* New York: Workman Publishing, 1981.

Miller, William. *Apology and Defence.* Boston: J. V. Himes, 1845.

Millman, Peter Mackenzie. Art. "Meteor." *Encyclopaedia Britannica,* 15th ed., 1979.

Mole, Robert Lee. "An Inquiry into the Time Elements of the Fifth and Sixth Trumpets of Revelation Nine." B.D. thesis, Seventh-day Adventist Theological Seminary, 1957.

Morison, Samuel Eliot. *The Oxford History of the American People.* New York: Oxford University Press, 1965.

Morris, Canon Leon. *The Revelation of St. John.* The Tyndale New Testament Commentaries. Edited by R. V. G. Tasker. Grand Rapids, Mich.: Wm. B. Eerdmans Publishing Company, 1969.

Muirhead, James, et al. *Historical Introduction to the Private Law of Rome.* 3d ed. London: A. & C. Black, 1916.

Musurillo, Herbert, ed. and trans. *The Acts of the Christian Martyrs.* Oxford: Clarendon Press, 1972.

Myres, John L. *Herodotus: Father of History.* Oxford: Clarendon Press, 1953.

Neall, Beatrice S. *The Concept of Character in the Apocalypse with Implications for Character Education.* Washington, D.C.: University Press of America, 1983.

The New Schaff-Herzog Encyclopedia of Religious Knowledge. 1960 reprint.

Newton, Isaac. *Observations Upon the Prophecies of Daniel and the Apocalypse of St. John.* London, 1733.

Newton, John. *Olney Hymns.* 3 vols. London, 1779.

Nichol, Francis D. *The Midnight Cry.* Washington, D.C.: Review and Herald Publishing Assn., 1944.

Nichols, James Hastings. *Democracy and the Churches.* Philadelphia: The Westminster Press, 1951

Nogueres, Henri. *The Massacre of Saint Bartholomew.* Translated by Claire Eliane Engel. New York: The Macmillan Co., 1962.

Odom, R. L. "The Sabbath in the Great Schism of A.D. 1054." *Andrews University Seminary Studies,* 1 (1963): 74-80

Olsen, M. Ellsworth. *A History of the Origin and Progress of Seventh-day Adventists.* Washington, D.C.: Review and Herald Publishing Assn., 1925.

Oster, Kenneth, *Islam Reconsidered.* An Exposition-University Book. Hicksville, N.Y.: Exposition Press, 1979.

Ozment, Steven. *The Age of Reform 1250-1550: An Intellectual and Religious History of Late Medieval and Reformation Europe.* New Haven, Conn.: Yale University Press, 1980.

Paine, Thomas. *The Age of Reason.* In *The Complete Writings of Thomas Paine.* Edited by Philip S. Foner. 2 vols. New York: Citadel Press, 1969.

Palmer, R. R. *The Age of the Democratic Revolution.* 2 vols. Vol. 1: *The Challenge.* Princeton: Princeton University Press, 1959.

————, ed. *Rand McNally Atlas of World History.* Chicago: Rand McNally & Company, 1957.

Papalia, Diane E. and Sally Wendkos Olds. *Human Development.* New York: McGraw-Hill Book Company, 1978.

Parry, V. J. "Warfare." In *The Cambridge History of Islam.* Edited by P. M. Holt, Ann K. S. Lambton, and Bernard Lewis. 2 vols. Cambridge, England: Cambridge University Press, 1970.

Pfeffer, Leo. *Church State and Freedom.* Rev. ed. Boston: Beacon Press, 1953, 1967.

Postgate, Raymond. *Story of a Year: 1798.* New York: Harcourt, Brace and World, Inc., 1969.

Previté-Orton, C. W. *The Shorter Cambridge Medieval History.* 2 vols. Cambridge, England: The University Press, 1953.

Price, Ira Maurice. *The Ancestry of Our English Bible.* 3d rev. ed. Revised by William A. Irwin and Allen P. Wikgren. New York: Harper & Row, Publishers, 1906, 1934, 1949, 1956.

Proudfit, Alexander. *Practical Godliness.* Salem, Mass., 1813.

Qualben, Lars P. *A History of the Christian Church.* Rev. and enl. ed. New York: Thomas Nelson and Sons, 1933, 1958.

Rickaby, Joseph. "The Modern Papacy." *Lectures on the History of Religions.* Vol. 3, lec. 24. London: Catholic Truth Society, 1910.

Robertson, Archibald Thomas. *Word Pictures in the New Testament.* 6 vols. New York: Harper & Brothers, Publishers, 1930-33.

Robinson, Thomas E. " 'Where There Is No Vision': Are Public High Schools Teaching Values?" *Liberty,* May-June, 1984, p. 17.

Rudé, George. *The Crowd in the French Revolution.* Oxford: Clarendon Press, 1959, 1960.

Rush, Alfred C., C.SS.R. *Death and Burial in Christian Antiquity.* The Catholic University of America Studies in Christian Antiquity. Edited by Johannes Quasten, S.T.D. No. 1. Washington, D.C.: The Catholic University of America Press, 1941.

Sandeen, Ernest R. *The Roots of Fundamentalism: British and American Millenarianism, 1800-1930.* Reprint. Grand Rapids, Mich.: Baker Book House, 1978.

Schaff, Philip. *The Progress of Religious Freedom as Shown in the History of Toleration Acts.* Reprinted from the Papers of the American Society of Church History, vol. 1. New York: Charles Scribner's Sons, 1889.

Schroeder, H. J., O.P., trans. *Canons and Decrees of the Council of Trent.* St. Louis: B. Herder Book Co., 1941.

Schwarz, R. W. *Light Bearers to the Remnant.* Mountain View, Calif.: Pacific Press Publishing Assn., 1979.

Scroggie, W. Graham. *The Great Unveiling.* Grand Rapids, Mich.: Zondervan Publishing House, 1979.

Shea, William. "The Chiastic Structure of the Song of Songs." *Zeitschrift für die Alttestamentliche Wissenschaft,* 92 (1980): 378-396.

_____ . "The Location and Significance of Armageddon in Rev 16:16." *Andrews University Seminary Studies,* 18 (Autumn 1980): 157-162.

_____ . *Selected Studies on Prophetic Interpretation.* Daniel and Revelation Committee Series. Vol. 1. Washington, D.C.: General Conference of Seventh-day Adventists, 1982.

_____ . "The Structure of the Genesis Flood Narrative and Its Implications." *Origins,* 6 (1979): 8-29.

Smith, Timothy. *Revivalism and Social Reform in Mid-Nineteenth-Century America.* New York: Abingdon Press, 1957.

Smith, Uriah. *The Prophecies of Daniel and the Revelation.* Rev. ed. Mountain View, Calif.: Pacific Press Publishing Assn., 1944.

_____ . *The Sanctuary and the Twenty-three Hundred Days of Daniel VIII, 14.* Battle Creek, Mich.: Steam Press of the Seventh-day Adventist Publishing Assn., 1877.

Solberg, Winton U. *Redeem the Time.* Cambridge: Harvard University Press, 1977.

Spalding, Arthur Whitefield. *Christ's Last Legion.* Washington, D.C.: Review and Herald Publishing Assn., 1949.

Spicer, W. A. *Beacon Lights of Prophecy.* Washington, D.C.: Review and Herald Publishing Assn., 1935.

Stirling, William. *The Cloister Life of the*

Emperor Charles the Fifth. 2d London ed. Boston: Crosby, Nichols & Company, 1853.

Strand, Kenneth A. *Interpreting the Book of Revelation*. 2d ed., rev. and enl. from *The Open Gates of Heaven*, 1970, 1972. Worthington, Ohio.: Ann Arbor Publishers, 1976, 1979.

————— . "Two Aspects of Babylon's Judgment Portrayed in Revelation 18." *Andrews University Seminary Studies*, 20 (Spring 1982): 53-60.

————— . "The Two Witnesses of Rev. 11:3-12." *Andrews University Seminary Studies*, 19 (Summer 1981): 127-135.

Sweet, William Warren. *The Story of Religion in America*. Rev. and enl. ed. New York: Harper & Brothers, Publishers, 1930, 1939, 1950.

Thatcher, Oliver J. and Edgar Holmes McNeal, eds. *A Source Book for Medieval History*. New York: Charles Scribner's Sons, 1905, 1933.

Theron, Daniel J. *Evidence of Tradition*. Grand Rapids, Mich.: Baker Book House, 1958.

Thiele, Edwin Richard. *The Mysterious Numbers of the Hebrew Kings: A Reconstruction of the Chronology of the Kingdoms of Israel and Judah*. Rev. ed. Chicago: The University of Chicago Press, 1965.

————— . *Outline Studies in Revelation*. Angwin, Calif.: The Author, n.d.

Thiers, M. A. *The History of the French Revolution*. Translated from the last Paris ed., with notes. London: William P. Nimmo, 1877.

Thompson, James Westfall and Edgar Nathaniel Johnson. *An Introduction to Medieval Europe, 300-1500*. New York: W. W. Norton & Co., Inc., Publishers, 1937.

Trevor, George. *Rome: From the Fall of the Western Empire*. London: The Religious Tract Society, 1868.

Tyler, Royall. *The Emperor Charles the Fifth*. Fair Lawn, N.J.: Essential Books, Inc., 1956.

Unreached Peoples Directory. Monrovia, Calif.: Missions Advance Research and Communication Center, 1974.

Vaglieri, Laura Veccia. "The Patriarchal and Umayyad Caliphates." In *The Cambridge History of Islam*. Edited by M. Holt, Ann K. S. Lambton, and Bernard Lewis. 2 vols. Cambridge, England: Cambridge University Press, 1970.

Vanderwaal, C. *Hal Lindsey and Biblical Prophecy*. St. Catharines, Ontario: Paideia Press, 1978.

Verhoeven, F. R. J. *Islam: Its Origin and Spread in Words, Maps and Pictures*. London: Routledge & Kegan Paul, 1962.

Vincent, Marvin. *Word Studies in the New Testament*. Reprint of the 1887 ed. 4 vols. Grand Rapids, Mich.: Wm. B. Eerdmans Publishing Co., 1946, 1957.

Wagner, C. Peter and Edward R. Dayton, eds. *Unreached Peoples '79*. Elgin, Ill.: David C. Cook Publishing Co., 1978.

Walker, Williston. *A History of the Christian Church*. Revised by Cyril C. Richardson, Wilhelm Pauck, and Robert T. Handy. New York: Charles Scribner's Sons, 1959.

Walton, Lewis R. and Herbert E. Douglass. *How to Survive the '80s*. Mountain View, Calif.: Pacific Press Publishing Assn., 1982.

Walvoord, John F. *The Blessed Hope and the Tribulation: A Biblical and Historical Study of Posttribulationism*. Grand Rapids, Mich.: Zondervan Publishing House, 1976.

Watson, Alan. *The Law of the Ancient Romans*. Dallas: Southern Methodist University Press, 1970.

Watson, Fletcher G. *Between the Planets*. Rev. ed. Cambridge: Harvard University Press, 1956.

Weber, Timothy P. *Living in the Shadow of the Second Coming: American Premillennialism, 1875-1925*. New York: Oxford University Press, 1979.

Wellcome, Isaac C. *History of the Second Advent Message and Mission, Doctrine and People*. Yarmouth, Me.: The Author, 1874.

Were, Louis F. *The Woman and the*

Beast in the Book of Revelation: Studies in Revelation 12-20. Reprint of the 1952 ed., Berrien Springs, Mich.: First Impressions, 1983.

Wesley, John. *Works.* 14 vols. Reprinted from the 3d. (1872) ed. Grand Rapids, Mich.: Baker Book House, 1979.

Whitby, Daniel. *A Paraphrase and Commentary on the New Testament.* 2 vols. 2d ed. London, 1706.

White, Ellen G. *Child Guidance.* Nashville: Southern Publishing Assn., 1954.

_____ . *The Desire of Ages.* Mountain View, Calif.: Pacific Press Publishing Assn., 1898, 1940.

_____ . *The Triumph of God's Love.* Mountain View, Calif.: Pacific Press Publishing Assn., 1950.

White, John. *Parents in Pain: A Book of Comfort and Counsel.* Downers Grove, Ill.: InterVarsity Press, 1979.

Wiedemann, Thomas. *Greek and Roman Slavery.* Baltimore: The Johns Hopkins University Press, 1981.

Williams, George Huntston. "The Ecumenical Intentions of Pope John Paul II." *Harvard Theological Review,* 75 (1982): 142-176.

Williamson, Ronald. *Philo and the Epistle to the Hebrews. Arbeiten zur Literatur und Geschichte des Hellenistischen Judentums.* Edited by K. H. Rengstorf, et al. Leiden: E. J. Brill, 1970.

Winn, Marie. *The Plug-in Drug.* New York: Bantam Books, 1977, 1978.

Wood, A. Skevington. "Awakening," "John and Charles Wesley," and "The Methodists." In *Eerdman's Handbook to the History of Christianity.* Edited by Tim Dowley, et al. 1st American ed. Grand Rapids, Mich.: Wm. B. Eerdman's Publishing Co., 1977.

Woolsey, Raymond. *The Power and the Glory: God's Hand in Your Future.* Washington, D.C.: Review and Herald Publishing Assn., 1978.

The World Book Encyclopedia. 1973 ed.

Zurcher, J. R. *Christ of the Revelation.* Translated by E. E. White. Nashville: Southern Publishing Assn., 1980.

551

Topical Index

561

Scriptural Index

Genesis 1:2, pp. 250, 494; **1:24, 27, 30,** p. 216; **1:31,** p. 513; **2:1-3,** pp. 84, 376, 377, 381, 510; **2:2,** p. 415; **2:7,** p. 215; **2:8, 9,** p. 100; **2:9, 16, 17,** p. 217; **2:17,** p. 332; **2:19,** p. 216; **ch. 3,** p. 323; **3:1-4, 7, 21,** p. 315; **3:4,** p. 444; **3:4, 5,** p. 332; **3:5,** p. 385; **3:15,** pp. 316-319, 331, 335, 401, 488; **3:24,** p. 217; **4:2-9,** p. 317; **4:9,** p. 318; **4:10,** p. 218; **4:25,** p. 316; **ch. 6-9,** p. 323; **6:1-8,** p. 448; **7:10, 16,** p. 448; **8:13,** p. 324; **ch. 9,** p. 157; **11:1-9,** p. 460; **12:1-9,** p. 524; **15:1,** p. 175; **ch. 18,** p. 499; **19:24,** p. 236; **19:4-8,** p. 303; **22:17,** p. 316; **28:12,** p. 155; **32:28,** p. 105; **43:33,** p. 79; **45:7,** p. 407; **48:16,** p. 228; **ch. 49,** p. 213; **49:9,** p. 157.

Exodus 3:1-6, p. 228; **3:2-5,** p. 171; **3:14,** pp. 158, 447; **5:2,** p. 303; **6:26,** p. 431; **ch. 7-12,** pp. 300, 431; **7:20-12:30,** p. 430; **ch. 11, 12,** p. vi; **ch. 12,** p. 208; **15:3,** pp. 430, 493; **ch. 16,** p. 321; **16:22, 23,** p. 376; **19:4,** p. 324; **19:6,** pp. 79, 80, 208; **19:9,** pp. 158, 159; **ch. 20,** p. 321; **20:3-17,** p. 397; **20:7-11, 14, 16, 17,** p. 398; **20:8,** p. 339; **20:8-10,** p. 371; **20:8-11,** pp. 274, 376, 383; **20:10,** pp. 83, 389; **20:24,** pp. 159, 161; **21:6,** p. 410; **ch. 25-30,** pp. 162, 165; **25:16, 21,** p. 381; **25:40,** p. 170; **28:15-21,** pp. 532, 533; **29:42, 43,** p. 172; **31:13,** pp. 376, 380, 384; **31:17,** p. 380, 415; **32:15, 16,** p. 381; **33:9,** p. 171; **33:9, 10,** p. 172; **33:19,** p. 447; **33:20,** p. 534; **34:5, 6,** p. 384; **34:6, 7,** p. 463.

Leviticus 16, pp. 171, 370; **16:30,** p. 370; **ch. 23,** pp. 370, 403; **23:3,** p. 377; **23:29, 30,** p. 403; **23:32,** pp. 376, 389; **24:1-4,** p. 97; **24:16,** p. 432; **ch. 26,** pp. 180, 183; **26:2-12,** pp. 180, 182; **26:14-33,** p. 182.

Numbers 4:7, p. 163; **10:33,** p. 381; **25:1-9,** p. 103; **31:16,** p. 103.

Deuteronomy 6:6-8, p. 389; **13:2-11,** p. 432; **19:16-19,** p. 466; **21:17,** p. 79; **21:18-21,** p. 432; **22:23, 24,** p. 432; **28:15, 52, 53, 68,** p. 26; **29:29,** pp. vi, 36, 80, 161, 256, 506, 538; **33:27,** p. 324.

Joshua 24:15, p. 334.

Judges 4, 5, p. 438; **4:15,** p. 438; **5:20-23,** pp. 438, 439; **ch. 6, 7,** p. 439.

1 Kings 6:20, p. 530; **8:54,** p. 447; **ch. 16-21,** p. 106; **ch. 17,** p. 300; **19:5,** pp. 155, 156; **19:18,** p. 107.

2 Kings 1, p. 300; **19:35,** p. 156; **23:13,** p. 29.

1 Chronicles 24, p. 153.

2 Chronicles 6:13, p. 447; **7:2,** p. 447; **20:15-17,** p. 438.

GOD CARES

9, pp. 240, 333; **12:7-12,** pp. 321-323; **12:8,** p. 504; **12:9,** p. 320; **12:10-12,** p. 322; **12:10, 12,** p. 333; **12:11,** pp. 351, 384, 386, 387; **12:12,** p. 334; **12:13-16,** p. 59; **12:13-17,** pp. 323, 324; **12:14,** pp. 59, 324, 326; **12:17,** pp. 59, 78, 309, 324, 330, 371, 382, 403-407, 459, 464, 537, 538.

Revelation 13, pp. 312, 313, 327, 331, 345, 379, 415, 441, 443, 444, 461, 472-475, 478; **13:1,** pp. 59, 68, 324, 489; **13:1-4,** pp. 324-326, 501; **13:2,** p. 327; **13:3,** pp. 326, 379, 386, 475, 476, 537; **13:3, 4,** p. 330; **13:5-8,** p. 59; **13:5-10,** pp. 326-330; **13:7,** p. 309; **13:8,** pp. 330, 336; **13:10,** pp. 326, 382; **13:11,** p. 324; **13:11, 12,** p. 340; **13:11-17,** pp. 379, 441, 477, 493, 537; **13:11-18,** pp. 326, 330, 331, 340-349, 385; **13:12,** pp. 382, 475; **13:13,** p. 341; **13:14,** pp. 326, 382, 475; **13:14-17,** p. 343; **13:16, 17,** pp. 341, 378, 382, 461; **13:17,** pp. 349, 382, 387; **13:18,** pp. 413-416.

Revelation 14, pp. 55, 109, 278, 279, 309, 313, 314, 318, 331, 463; **14:1,** p. 190; **14:1-5,** pp. 310, 349, 382, 383, 407; **14:1-12,** p. 310; **14:1-13,** p. 349; **14:4,** p. 351; **14:5,** p. 214; **14:6,** p. 432; **14:6, 7,** pp. 263, 304, 349-356, 387, 447, 473, 537; **14:6-12,** pp. 349, 374, 395, 461, 487, 492; **14:7,** pp. 297, 356, 382, 398, 415; **14:7-12,** p. 351; **14:8,** pp. 59, 364-368, 537; **14:9-11,** pp. 368-375; **14:9-12,** pp. 382, 537; **14:10,** pp. 410, 421; **14:11,** pp. 410-413; **14:12,** pp. 340, 371, 382, 387, 407, 537, 538; **14:13,** pp. 70, 352; **14:13-20,** pp. 310, 443; **14:14,** pp. 182, 489; **14:14-17,** p. 490; **14:14-20,** pp. 59, 349, 436, 462, 487; **14:15,** pp. 382, 385; **14:17,** p. 164; **14:17-20,** p. 385; **14:18,** pp. 228, 382.

Revelation 15, pp. 426, 447; **ch. 15, 16,** pp. 262, 421-451; **ch. 15-22,** pp. 165, 421, 423, 425; **15:1,** p. 421; **15:1-8,** p. 423; **15:1-16:21,** pp. 58, 68, 423, 425, 454, 482, 525; **15:2,** pp. 152, 432; **15:2-4,** pp. 349, 382; **15:2-5,** p. 407; **15:5,** pp. 164, 168; **15:5-8,** p. 262; **15:8,** pp. 168, 446-450.

Revelation 16, pp. 68, 260, 271, 426, 427, 431, 438; **16:1,** p. 428; **16:1-21,** p. 423; **16:2,** pp. 382, 429; **16:2-4,** p. 58; **16:4,** p. 429; **16:5-7,** p. 428; **16:8, 9,** p. 429; **16:8-11,** p. 58; **16:9,** p. 44; **16:9-11,** pp. 382, 428; **16:12,** pp. 58, 459; **16:12-16,** pp. 435, 436, 439, 493; **16:13,** pp. 330, 474, 477; **16:13-16,** pp. 443, 538; **16:14,** pp. 444, 477, 492; **16:15,** pp. 70, 429, 431; **16:16,** pp. 58, 477, 492; **16:17, 18,** p. 429; **16:17-21,** p. 58; **16:21,** p. 382.

Revelation 17, pp. 311, 349, 414, 455, 458, 459, 471-478, 530; **17:1,** p. 238; **17:1, 2,** pp. 424, 474; **17:1-3,** p. 423; **17:1-19:10,** pp. 59, 423, 425, 453-479, 482, 523, 525; **17:2,** p. 458; **17:2-6,** p. 458; **17:3,** p. 341; **17:3-5,** p. 59; **17:4,** p. 477; **17:5,** pp. 367, 459; **17:6,** p. 477; **17:7-14,** pp. 471-478; **17:8,** pp. 382, 458, 474, 478; **17:8-14,** p. 471; **17:9,** p.68; **17:10,** pp. 68, 458; **17:11,** p. 475; **17:12,** p. 474; **17:12-14,** p. 477; **17:12-17,** p. 441; **17:13, 14,** pp. 459, 492; **17:14,** pp. 474, 478, 493; **17:15,** pp. 238, 323, 341, 441; **17:16,** pp. 441, 458, 471, 474, 500, 501; **17:17,** p. 441.